RESEARCH INSTITUTIONS AND LEARNED SOCIETIES

The Greenwood Encyclopedia of American Institutions

Each work in the *Encyclopedia* is designed to provide concise histories of major voluntary groups and nonprofit organizations that have played significant roles in American civic, cultural, political, and economic life from the colonial era to the present.

1. *Labor Unions*
Gary M Fink, Editor-in-Chief

2. *Social Service Organizations*
Peter Romanofsky, Editor-in-Chief

3. *Fraternal Organizations*
Alvin J. Schmidt

4. *Political Parties and Civic Action Groups*
Edward L. Schapsmeier and Frederick H. Schapsmeier

5. *Research Institutions and Learned Societies*
Joseph C. Kiger, Editor-in-Chief

The Greenwood Encyclopedia of American Institutions

Research Institutions and Learned Societies

editor-in-chief
JOSEPH C. KIGER

GREENWOOD PRESS
Westport, Connecticut • London, England

Library of Congress Cataloging in Publication Data
Main entry under title:

Research institutions and learned societies.

   (The Greenwood encyclopedia of American institutions,
ISSN 0271-9509 ; no. 5)
   Includes index.
   1.   Learned institutions and societies—United States—
Dictionaries.   2.   Research institutes—United States—
Dictionaries.   3.   Research libraries—United States—
Dictionaries.   I.   Kiger, Joseph Charles.   II.   Series.
AS25.R47   061'.3   81-6651
ISBN 0-313-22061-1   AACR2

Library of Congress Catalog Card Number: 81-6651
ISBN: 0-313-22061-1
ISSN: 0271-9509

First published in 1982

Greenwood Press
A division of Congressional Information Service, Inc.
88 Post Road West, Westport, Connecticut 06881

Printed in the United States of America

10 9 8 7 6 5 4 3 2 1

TO JEAN

CONTENTS

M

N

CONTRIBUTORS

William T. Alderson, Director, Museum Studies and Art Conservation, University of Delaware, Newark, Delaware

Carl B. Amthor, Vice-President for Administrative Affairs, Associated Universities, Inc., Washington, D.C.

Ray A. Billington, Senior Research Associate, Huntington Library, Art Gallery, Botanical Gardens, San Marino, California

Henry V. Bohm, President, Argonne Universities Association, Argonne, Illinois

William S. Budington, Executive Director, The John Crerar Library, Chicago, Illinois

Daniel Callahan, Director, Hastings Center, Institute of Society, Ethics and the Life Sciences, Hastings-on-Hudson, New York

Leslie Caine Campbell, Professor of History and Associate Dean, School of Arts and Sciences, Auburn University, Auburn, Alabama

Giles Constable, Director, Dumbarton Oaks Research Library and Collection, Washington, D.C.

Vicky Cullen, Publications and Information Manager, Woods Hole Oceanographic Institution, Woods Hole, Massachusetts

W. D. Cummings, Executive Director, Universities Space Research Association, Columbia, Maryland

Phyllis Dain, Professor of Library Service, School of Library Services, Columbia University, New York, New York

Margaret P. O'Neill Davis, Director, Office of Public Information, The Wistar Institute of Anatomy and Biology, Philadelphia, Pennsylvania

William Diebold, Jr., Senior Research Fellow, Council on Foreign Relations, Inc., New York, New York.

Robert B. Downs, Dean Emeritus, Library School, University of Illinois, Urbana, Illinois.

Frank K. Edmondson, Professor of Astronomy, Indiana University, Bloomington, Indiana

Ralph T. Fisher, Jr., Professor of History and Director, Russian and East European Center, University of Illinois, Urbana, Illinois

E. McLung Fleming, Research Associate, Henry Francis du Pont Winterthur Museum, Wilmington, Delaware.

Philip J. Gambaccini, Senior Staff, Institute of Public Administration, New York, New York

Patsy A. Gerstner, Chief Curator, Howard Dittrick Museum of Historical Medicine, Cleveland, Ohio

Weldon B. Gibson, Executive Vice-President, SRI International, Menlo Park, California

Henry L. Giclas, Astronomer, Lowell Observatory, Flagstaff, Arizona

Thomas D. Gillies, Director, Linda Hall Library, Kansas City, Missouri

Larry D. Givens, Associate Professor of History, University of Mississippi, University, Mississippi

Margaret J. Gorove, Associate Professor of Art and Chairman, Department of Art, University of Mississippi, University, Mississippi

Jack Harmon, Director of Public Relations, Southwest Research Institute, San Antonio, Texas

John B. Hench, Research and Publication Officer, American Antiquarian Society, Worcester, Massachusetts

Robert Hessen, Deputy Archivist, Hoover Institution on War, Revolution and Peace, Stanford, California

Curtis M. Hinsley, Jr., Professor of History, Colgate University, Hamilton, New York

Hudson Hoagland, President Emeritus, Worcester Foundation for Experimental Biology, Shrewsbury, Massachusetts

James R. Hunkler, Coordinator, Corporate Communications, Battelle Memorial Institute, Columbus, Ohio

Sidney Hyman, Author, Chicago, Illinois

Philip L. Johnson, Executive Director, Oak Ridge Associated Universities, Oak Ridge, Tennessee

Charles N. Kimball, President Emeritus, Midwest Research Institute, Kansas City, Missouri

William J. Lanouette, Staff Correspondent, *National Journal*, Washington, D.C.

C. X. Larrabee, Public Information Director, Research Triangle Institute, Research Triangle Park, North Carolina

Shelley Lotter, Public Information Specialist, Department of Public Affairs, Memorial Sloan-Kettering Cancer Center, New York, New York

Anne Camille Maher, Graduate Student, Boston College, Boston, Massachusetts

James C. Matheson, Vice-President, Universities Research Association, Inc., Washington, D.C.

James E. McCormack, Director, The New York Academy of Medicine, New York, New York

Raymond L. Muncy, Professor of History and Chairman, Department of History and Social Science, Harding University, Searcy, Arkansas

Michael V. Namorato, Associate Professor of History, University of Mississippi, University, Mississippi

Matthew H. Nitecki, Curator, Fossil Invertebrates, Field Museum of Natural History, Chicago, Illinois

Paula C. Norton, Manager, Public Relations, IIT Research Institute, Chicago, Illinois

Elizabeth K. Patterson, Member, Institute for Cancer Research, Fox Chase Cancer Center, Philadelphia, Pennsylvania

Patricia Piety, Foundation Editor, Charles F. Kettering Foundation, Dayton, Ohio

Franklin H. Portugal, Author, Washington, D.C.

Kent A. Price, Associate Director of Public Affairs, Resources for the Future, Inc., Washington, D.C.

John F. Priest, Professor of Religion and Chairman, Department of Religion, Florida State University, Tallahassee, Florida

Theodore K. Rabb, Professor of History, Princeton University, Princeton, New Jersey

Frank P. Radovsky, Assistant Director, Bernice P. Bishop Museum, Honolulu, Hawaii

Norman F. Ramsey, Higgins Professor of Physics, Harvard University, Cambridge, Massachusetts, and President, Universities Research Association, Inc., Washington, D.C.

Susan Robbins, Head, Publications and Information Office, Population Council, New York, New York

James I. Robertson, Jr., C. P. Miles Professor of History, Virginia Polytechnic Institute and State University, Blacksburg, Virginia

Ernest E. Schneider, Staff Member, Hudson Institute, Croton-on-Hudson, New York

Bruce Sinclair, Director, Institute for the History and Philosophy of Science and Technology, University of Toronto, Toronto, Canada

Bruce L. R. Smith, Senior Staff, Advanced Study Program, Brookings Institution, Washington, D.C.

John Sobotka, Archivist, Eastland Collection, University of Mississippi, University, Mississippi

James A. Steed, Assistant Archivist, Smithsonian Institution, Washington, D.C.

Robert Steyer, Public Affairs Associate, Office of Public Affairs, American Museum of Natural History, New York, New York

James H. Strickland, Manager of Public Relations, Southern Research Institute, Birmingham, Alabama

Roger D. Tate, Jr., Department of History and Political Science, Somerset Community College, Somerset, Kentucky

Jackson Taylor, Jr., Associate Professor of History, University of Mississippi, University, Mississippi

Lawrence W. Towner, President and Librarian, The Newberry Library, Chicago, Illinois

Louis L. Tucker, Director, Massachusetts Historical Society, Boston, Massachusetts

Joseph F. Wall, Professor of History, Grinnell College, Grinnell, Iowa

John H. Williams, Public Information Officer, East-West Center, Honolulu, Hawaii

Conrad E. Wright, Executive Assistant to the Director, Institute of Early American History and Culture, Williamsburg, Virginia

Louis B. Wright, Staff, National Geographic Society, Washington, D.C.

PREFACE

Our modern research institutions and learned societies may be defined as nongovernmental, not-for-profit organizations aiding the promotion or performance of basic research and the advancement of knowledge in one or more of the broad areas of knowledge, such as the humanities, physical/biological sciences, and social sciences. This definition would include those organizations collecting, discussing, analyzing, and disseminating the results of such activities. It would exclude those set up in the main for business purposes or educational, instructional, and scholarship purposes and research organizations that are integral units of a college or university. It would also exclude those designed primarily for the professional advancement of or applied research in such areas as law, librarianship, medicine, education, and religion. Professional organizations, such as the American Library Association, will be included in another volume in the Greenwood Encyclopedia of American Institutions, *Professional Organizations.*

This *Research Institutions and Learned Societies* volume of the encyclopedia contains historical sketches of 164 organizations. With the exception of the International Council of Scientific Unions* (ISCU), International Council for Philosophy and Humanistic Studies* (CIPHS), and International Social Science Council* (ISSC), which are located abroad, all have been set up and were or are located in the United States. These organizations have had a significant influence on our development, yet most Americans, even those relatively well informed, are unaware of or little informed about them. For example, how many persons, even knowledgeable ones, know what the Battelle Memorial Institute* (BMI) is and does? To illustrate the matter another way, how many can differentiate

---

*An asterisk (*) after a title indicates that there is a brief history of the organization in this work. Initials in lieu of names have been used therein only when no ambiguities are involved and where such usage was and is commonly accepted within and without the organization.

between the history and function of the American Philosophical Society* (APS) and the American Philosophical Association* (APA)?

Organizations similar to our research institutions and learned societies can be traced back to the beginnings of Western civilization in the eastern Mediterranean. Their modern counterparts emerged in Europe with the scientific revolution of the sixteenth and seventeenth centuries. Impressed and influenced by the scientific advances made by such bodies, particularly the Royal Society of London, founded 1660, our first organizations of this type, the Library Company of Philadelphia and the APS, were established in Philadelphia in 1731 and 1743. Since that time, particularly after the Civil War, thousands of these organizations have been set up, bearing a bewildering variety of titles: institution, institute, society, academy, association, council, center, corporation, foundation, organization, library, laboratory, museum, observatory, and board. They are now found in every state in the Union, operating at the local, state, regional, national, and international levels. They range from those with founding dates in the eighteenth century to those founded yesterday; those with miniscule operating budgets to those with millions of dollars; those with staff numbering one or two persons to those with thousands; those of a nonmembership category to those with thousands of members; those concentrating their efforts on one discipline within one area of knowledge to those spanning all knowledge; and those with none or a few publications annually to those issuing a large number of titles each year.

In selecting the relatively few research institutions and learned societies for inclusion in this work, the one all-inclusive and prevailing determinant was that each be of national or international scope and significance in its interests and operation. Our approximately eighty nationally significant learned societies and the coordinating councils of which they are officially members or have close ties with presented few selection problems. This is so because our national learned societies are broadly based and are usually individual membership organizations, which generally evolved from a felt need for such a society by a significant number, nationally and internationally, of those interested in and working in one or more disciplinary areas in the humanities, physical/biological sciences, or social sciences. Furthermore, our coordinating councils have invariably extended membership to or formed close ties only with learned societies of this same type and, therefore, of national scope and significance. In the humanities and social sciences, for example, a thorough screening process precedes election to membership in the American Council of Learned Societies* (ACLS), and national membership of the proposed society is a primary requisite for admission. The councils, in turn, are *ipso facto* performing research and coordinating operations of a disciplinary-spanning and coordinating nature at the national and international level, (see Joseph C. Kiger, "Learned Societies," *Dictionary of American History* [1976], and "Disciplines" and

"Learned Societies in the United States," *Encyclopedia of Education* [1971]). In short a winnowing process is at work here that, for all practical purposes, eliminates the need for a selection process in this learned society grouping.

Selection of our outstanding national research institutions presented more problems. Both learned societies and research institutions by definition perform largely the same functions. There are, however, several important structural differences. In contrast to our learned societies, many if not most of our research institutions were set up *de nouveau* to study or conduct research for specific or general purposes. They generally rely on a relatively small number of hired staff or appointed fellows to carry on their activities. Thus national membership as a selection criterion for inclusion in this volume was usually not present. Also, although most have had working relationships over the years with our learned societies and councils, they generally have had no official connection with the councils and thus lack what might be called the accrediting function performed for the learned societies by the coordinating councils. Consequently, in selecting the approximately sixty-five outstanding national research institutions for inclusion herein, age and historical significance together with size and budget were the principal criteria. An attempt was made, however, to include institutions representative of all areas of knowledge and, to a lesser extent, various sources of funding, for example, endowment, industry, government, and foundation. With a few exceptions, where their historical significance warranted inclusion, only extant institutions are included and described. A list of all of these organizations, arranged according to these three major groupings, learned society, coordinating council, and research institution, appears in appendix 1.

Foundations—nongovernmental, nonprofit organizations established to maintain or aid social, charitable, religious, educational, or artistic activities through grants—will be included in another volume of this encyclopedia, *Foundations*. In selecting research institutions for this volume, it was sometimes difficult to differentiate between research institutions and foundations, particularly "operating foundations," which make few or no grants to other institutions or individuals but rather carry on their own programs with their own staff. Although such operating foundations may carry out activities similar to those of research institutions, organizations that have traditionally been classified as foundations, such as the Russell Sage Foundation, which during much of its history operated with its own staff, are included in the *Foundations* volume.

At the same time some research institutions and learned societies were included that did not fit exactly the definitions set out above. For example, the Smithsonian Institution* is included because it is a semigovernmental organization and because of its long, wide-ranging, and trail-blazing research efforts. A few organizations with ostensibly local or regional title and scope were admitted because of their age and the fact that they provide resources or operate programs of national significance. Examples in this category are the Academy of Natural Sciences of Philadelphia,* the Massachusetts Historical Society,* and the American Association for State and Local History* (AASLH). For somewhat similar reasons, plus the fact that some research institutions connected with universities have historically maintained a high degree of independence (see Harold Orlans, *The Non-profit Research Institute* [1972], a few organizations such as Harvard University's Peabody Museum of Archaeology and Ethnology* have also been included. Also, several groups of universities associated together in the operation of research laboratories and other activities, such as Universities Research Association, Inc.,* (URA), and Oak Ridge Associated Universities* (ORAU), have been included.

As in the case of previously published companion volumes in this encyclopedia, the historical sketches of the research institutions, councils, and learned societies that follow vary significantly in length and extent of information and in amount of interpretation provided. This relative plenitude or paucity depends to a large degree on the quantity and quality of the records and accounts on which they are based. There are no archives or centers that have systematically gathered historical material on all organizations of this type. It should be noted, however, that the ACLS did conduct an unpublished survey of its member societies in the 1930s and 1940s, which provides a great deal of information about the founding and history of these societies up to that time and which is filed at the ACLS. In addition, the ACLS in the 1950s, in association with Broadcast Music Incorporated, prepared brief historical accounts of various humanistic learned societies, which bore the overall title *World of the Mind.* These two sources, where referred to in the individual brief histories presented in this work, are cited, respectively, as Survey and *World of the Mind.*

An increasing number of these organizations, however, are making systematic efforts to amass, process, and make available such material in their own archives. (Unless otherwise noted in their brief history, the archives and records of individual organizations are located at their headquarters office or building.) Examples are such institutions as the National Academy of Sciences* (NAS), American Council on Education* (ACE), Brookings Institution,* The Franklin Institute,* American Society for Microbiology* (ASM), and American Chemical Society* (ACS). The last has always had a deep sense of history as reflected in the fact that it has made each twenty-five-year period since its founding in 1876 the occasion for the publication of a book-length history of the ACS. Thus, many organizations have kept complete and accessible records, and their officials have been able in some cases to provide published histories, accounts, and reminiscences about them. Primary reliance for such material about many, however, had to be placed on intermittent articles and fragmentary accounts about them appearing in their publications or in other journals. In a few cases historical information was primarily to be had via conversations or correspondence with persons connected with the founding and operation of a society or institution. Basic statistical information on members, meetings, publications, awards, finances, and so on, to the extent available, has been provided for each organization. Also bibliographical references to the sources utilized, which also provide further information about the organization chronicled, are made at the conclusion of each sketch.

I wish to express my deep appreciation to the sixty-eight contributors who have provided brief histories for this volume. Their names follow their entries and are also provided, along with their affiliations, in the contributors section. Unsigned entries have been prepared by the editor.

The officials and other personnel connected with the organizations studied herein have been universally helpful and cooperative in providing information and answering many questions about their history and operation. With few exceptions, they have critically reviewed the brief histories of their respective organizations. Special mention is due to Robert M. Lumiansky, president, American Council of Learned Societies, and Philip Handler, then president, National Academy of Sciences, for their cooperation and aid in bringing this work to completion. Such aid included travel grants from each of their institutions, which made it possible to visit research centers for historical information and material not otherwise available.

I am grateful to officials of the University of Mississippi, including the University Committee on Faculty Research, who were generous in providing funds for research and other forms of aid toward completion of this volume.

The officials of Greenwood Press, particularly James T. Sabin, vice-president, Arthur H. Stickney, former editor, Research and Professional Books, and Cynthia Harris, editor, Reference Books, were always interested in and tactfully responsive to numerous questions that arose regarding format and style. They and their associates were constantly on the alert for errors and mistakes; nonetheless, neither they nor the contributors are responsible for any that may appear herein.

My wife Jean, who has lived with me and learned societies, councils, and research institutions for over thirty years, has been my constant and unfailing aider and abettor, and it is to her that this volume is dedicated.

Joseph C. Kiger

_A_ ———————————————————————

ACADEMY OF NATURAL SCIENCES OF PHILADELPHIA. This academy was organized and held its first meeting on January 25, 1812, when a group of seven Philadelphians met at Mercer's Cake Shop to discuss their mutual interests in natural history. Although by 1812 Philadelphia could boast of a distinguished history in the development of scientific societies, no such group had emerged before then specifically to serve interests in natural history. The seven who formed the academy were John Speakman, an apothecary; Jacob Gilliams, a dentist; Gerard Troost, a physician and chemist; John Shinn, Jr., a chemist; Nicholas S. Parmentier, a distiller; Camillus Macmahon Mann, a physician; and Thomas Say, a naturalist. Their goal was to create an organization for the discussion of mutually interesting topics in natural history and a center for the diffusion of ideas concerning it. They intended it to be a place for the pursuit of the subject by all who were interested, a goal that has never been forgotten. A permanent collection of books and specimens was considered essential as a basis for study and research.

Dozens of others who shared the founders' interests soon joined them, and although the first years of the academy were financially difficult, it survived with members' dues and fees from occasional public lectures given by members. This small income paid the rent for a meeting room and bought an occasional book or specimen for the permanent collection. In 1817 the academy was incorporated, the first issue of the _Journal of the Academy of Natural Sciences of Philadelphia_ was published, and William Maclure was elected president of the organization. Maclure, a successful businessman and philanthropist, was rarely present for meetings, but with his help the financial condition improved rapidly. His financing helped with the general activities of the academy as well as with the publication of the _Journal_. Maclure served as president until his death in 1840, by which time the academy was in reasonably stable financial condition, and with the opening of a museum, in 1828, it became an institution for the general public as well as for members. From its beginning, the collection of specimens and books was available for use by members, but it was Maclure who urged public access to the collection. The museum was intended to be a place for both the education of the public in the various areas of natural history and the enjoyment of these subjects. As such it was an affirmation of the founders' wish that the academy be for everyone to enjoy and learn about natural history, and it is the oldest continuously operating natural history museum in the United States today.

The early members of the academy were dedicated to the scholarly pursuit of natural history, and most of the leading naturalists in the United States were either members or carried on voluminous correspondence with members. Many members were in frequent contact with foreign naturalists, thereby helping Americans enter the mainstream of activities in these areas. Until about the middle of the nineteenth century, scientific pursuits were easily incorporated in the general knowledge. As the sciences became more complex, however, those who actively pursued a given science became specialized scholars. Reflecting this change, greater stress was placed on purely scientific activities after 1840, including the publication of the *Proceedings of the Academy*, which began in 1841 and provided a place of publication for the scholarly papers written by academy members. The *Journal*, published intermittently after 1817 as funds permitted, resumed publication with a second series in 1847 that continued until 1912. Several departments and divisions emerged within the academy after midcentury. Among the earliest were a Biological Department in 1858, a Conchology Section in 1866, an Entomological Section in 1876, and a Mineralogical Section in 1877. A strong commitment to basic and applied research developed in these years and continues today.

By the late 1860s over two hundred thousand specimens were housed in the academy, and over twenty thousand volumes were in its library. There was great concern for the needs of this collection, including the need for more space and greater protection from visitors, who by then numbered as many as one hundred thousand persons a year. According to the curators, their passage through the museum stirred up dust, which covered the specimens and caused damage to the exhibit cases as well. The preceding years of growth had necessitated a series of moves by the academy from an original room rented on the second floor of a house on Second Street near Race Street, to a house on Second Street north of Arch Street, to a hall built for it on the north side of Arch Street near Second Street in 1815, and to still larger quarters at the southeast corner of Twelfth and Sansom streets in 1826. In 1840 a move was made to a building at the northwest corner of Broad and Sansom streets, to which additions were made twice before 1868. New land was acquired in 1868 at the corner of Nineteenth and Race streets to meet the urgent needs for expansion, and a new facility was opened in 1876 in time for the Centennial Celebration.

Scientific studies continued, with volunteer curators in charge of the collections. Noted scholars in the various fields of natural history actively used the collections. In 1860 the children of August E. Jessup established a fund to aid young men (in 1893 young women were made eligible as well) who wished to study natural history. Although there was technically no restriction on how and where the young recipients of this money studied, it was hoped that they would study at the academy and offer their services to it. Many followed this plan and proved of valuable help with the collection.

Although the academy diverted many of its energies after 1840 to the development of a sound scientific commitment, it should be repeated that the early intent that it be for all those who had any interest in natural history was never forgotten. In fact, many members continuously urged that it not forget this original goal. Thus, when the numbers of visitors began to have the previously noted effect on the collection in the 1860s and some members wanted to charge an admission fee of ten cents per person to discourage visitors, the proposal was firmly rejected as contrary to the purpose of the academy. Also, when the new building was opened in 1876, new bylaws were adopted giving emphasis to the academy's position in fostering the "popular taste" for natural science and encouraging interest by those who were not themselves full-time scientists. To encourage systematic popular instruction, the appointment of professors and assistants was suggested, but a lack of sufficient funds led to a long delay in the first appointment of a professor and the eventual abandonment of this plan. Nevertheless, the academy was able to provide lectures for the general public, and its museum continued to expand.

The building at Nineteenth and Race streets was enlarged in 1891 with an amphitheater for public lectures. Another annex was completed in 1894, and still more space was added to the building in 1908, creating more room for the collection, research, and the museum. The academy occupies this same building today, although many additions and changes have altered the size and appearance of the complex. A program of expansion, begun in 1977, led to the restoration and modernization of the original buildings, the addition of a 426-seat auditorium, and an eight-level research building.

The attention given to research and scientific activities in the nineteenth century plus a persistent dedication to keeping the academy as a place of public interest, particularly through the museum, had successfully created a large, multi-purpose institution as the twentieth century began. Throughout the twentieth century the academy has continued to pursue both its professional and its public goals. Scientific work has been represented in many ways in addition to the basic research conducted at the academy. It has sponsored and/or participated in many expeditions, to such places as Africa, Alaska, Mexico, and northern Greenland. Scientific publications are issued regularly. These include monographs and special publications as well as the *Proceedings*. The academy is deeply involved in systematic, evolutionary, and ecological research today, and the new research building has some of the most advanced facilities in the world for these studies. The academy's library, which grew steadily in the nineteenth century, has become a major source in systematics, or modern taxonomy. Because the organization is one of the oldest scientific institutions in the United States, the library collection and the archives provide an invaluable resource for the study of the history of all areas of the natural sciences. To meet the needs of the public, the museum has steadily changed its approach to exhibits and has sought consistently to make them timely, informative, and interesting. Also, the academy has conducted a series of lectures, various classes, nature camps, nature walks, live animal demonstrations, and special participatory programs for young people. A popular magazine called *Frontiers* was started in 1937 and has been an important addition to public programs.

The current program of expansion and revitalization concentrates upon plans to renovate the library. Thus, the academy has successfully combined its founders' goals and has emerged as one of the nation's most important centers for the study and enjoyment of all those subjects included under natural history.

For further information, see Samuel G. Morton, "History of the Academy of Natural Sciences of Philadelphia," *American Quarterly Register* 13 (1840-1841); Edward J. Nolan, *A Short History of the Academy of Natural Sciences of Philadelphia* (1909); Albert Linton Morris, *The Academy of Natural Sciences of Philadelphia. 150 Years of Distinguished Service* (1962); and Patsy A. Gerstner, "The Academy of Natural Sciences of Philadelphia, 1812-1850," in Alexandra Oleson and Sanborn C. Brown, eds., *The Pursuit of Knowledge in the Early American Republic* (1976).

PATSY A. GERSTNER

ALABAMA RESEARCH INSTITUTE. See Southern Research Institute.

AMERICAN ACADEMY AND INSTITUTE OF ARTS AND LETTERS. The Academy-Institute seeks to foster, assist, and sustain an interest in literature, music, and the fine arts in American society. Composed of recognized leaders in these areas, the Academy-Institute singles out and encourages individual artists and their work through varied ways, including the presentation of awards and prizes to both members and nonmembers.

The honor of election to this historic institution is considered the highest formal recognition of artistic merit in this country. The reputation of the Academy-Institute stems in part from the illustrious names of some of the founding figures of the institute, for example, Henry Adams, John Burroughs, William Dean Howells, William and Henry James, John LaFarge, Edward McDowell, Mark Twain, Theodore Roosevelt, and Woodrow Wilson, and later members such as Julia Ward Howe (admitted in 1907, forty-seven years after she wrote the "Battle Hymn of the Republic," and remaining the institute's only female choice for nineteen years), Winslow

Homer, Pearl S. Buck, Willa Cather, William Faulkner, Robert Frost, Edward Hopper, John Marin, Edna St. Vincent Millay, Ben Shahn, John Steinbeck, Igor Stravinsky, Thomas Wolfe, Frank Lloyd Wright, John Cage, Robert Motherwell, and Duke Ellington, to name only a few.

The present title of the organization came about in 1976 with the merger of the National Institute of Arts and Letters and the American Academy of Arts and Letters. The institute traces its history back to 1898, when it was established as an offspring of the American Social Science Association.* It was the first organization devoted entirely to literature and the arts, and its initial membership of 150 American painters, sculptors, architects, composers, and writers was soon enlarged to 250, where it has remained. In 1904 at the insistence of some institute members, who felt that the large size lessened its prestige, a smaller group on the model of the Institut de France was founded. This inner body of 50 persons chosen for special distinction from the membership of the institute was named the American Academy of Arts and Letters. The problem of selecting the academy was delicately handled by Robert Underwood Johnson, who devised a system whereby 7 members were chosen by the institute, these then chose 8 others, then the 15 chose 5 more, and so on until the full complement of 50 was reached.

The institute was incorporated by an Act of Congress in 1913, and the academy was similarly incorporated in 1916. All of the privileges granted by these charters were retained when the two groups merged to form the American Academy and Institute of Arts and Letters.

Today, as during the many years of their separate but related existence, the Academy-Institute has its headquarters in Manhattan, elegantly housed due to the generosity of Archer Milton Huntington. Mr. Huntington, who was elected to the institute in 1911 and to the academy in 1919, provided the land and endowments totaling nearly three million dollars. He financed the erection of a Palladian-style administration building, designed in 1923 by William M. Kindall of McKim, Mead, and White (all academicians), and the northerly building, also of Italian Renaissance inspiration, designed by another academician, Cass Gilbert. This latter building houses the art gallery and entrance to the auditorium, which is under the terrace that links the two buildings located on the west side of Broadway between 155th and 156th streets.

The endowments have allowed the Academy-Institute to maintain upkeep of its property as well as to continue the programs of awards and prizes, exhibitions of art and manuscripts, readings and performances of new work, and purchase of works of art and their distribution to museums.

The Academy-Institute is governed by an eleven-member board of directors, which appoints the working committees, one of whose most important functions is selecting the recipients for the various awards and prizes. The highlight of each year is the annual May meeting when the creative artists in different fields of endeavor gather at the complex on Audubon Terrace.

Seventeen Academy-Institute awards and various special awards are given annually to nonmembers to encourage their work, which is then included in the annual spring exhibitions of art, manuscripts, and books. There are awards of merit, gold medals, and other awarded certificates of achievement. With one exception, the Richard Rodgers Production Award, no application may be submitted for any of the awards, fellowships, or scholarships.

The May meeting is also the occasion for announcing the names of the new honorary members, foreign citizens distinguished in the arts. A small sample of deceased honorary members includes names such as Alvar Aalto, Charlie Chaplin, T. S. Eliot, Aldous Huxley, Albert Schweitzer, George Bernard Shaw, and Arnold Toynbee.

The new regular members of the institute are also announced at this annual meeting, as are those institute members who will move into the limited academy slots. Until 1936, when it abandoned dues altogether, the institute levied an annual charge of five dollars, a sum which caused some to resign and others, such as Thomas Eakins, to decline election. During the late 1930s there was a move by some academy members to free themselves from having to elect their membership from that of the institute. The more conservative members of the academy, led by the benefactor Mr. Huntington, did not approve of some of the institute's new members, especially writers such as Carl Sandburg, John Steinbeck, Ezra Pound, William Faulkner, and John Dos Passos. For nearly eighteen months a battle raged over this issue, resulting in the decision that the academy would continue to limit its membership to those already elected to the institute.

A unique feature of the academy is the fact that each member inherits a chair at the time of election to that body; the number of each chair is assigned according to the order of each original member's election. Since 1923 these chairs have been a concrete reality, and each has a plaque listing the names and dates of tenure of the occupants. For example, chair number 12 descended to Arthur Miller via John Quincy Adams Ward, Abbott Lawrence Lowell, Frederick Law Olmsted, Jr., and Reinhold Niebuhr; and Georgia O'Keeffe's name is on chair number 26, previously held by John Burroughs, Charles Dana Gibson, Douglas Southall Freeman, and E. E. Cummings.

Today the luster of the past continues with new glow as the American Academy and Institute of Arts and Letters encourages a full range of artistic styles. It occupies a unique place in the history of American culture.

For further information, see the following articles: Malcolm Cowley, "Sir: I Have the Honor," *Southern Review* (Winter, 1972); and Geoffrey T. Hellman, "Profiles: Some Splendid and Admirable People," *New Yorker* (February 23, 1976). See also a 1980 informational brochure published by the Academy-Institute.

MARGARET J. GOROVE

AMERICAN ACADEMY OF ARTS AND LETTERS. See American Academy and Institute of Arts and Letters.

AMERICAN ACADEMY OF ARTS AND SCIENCES. John Adams of Massachusetts was the moving spirit behind the creation of the second learned society in the United States, the American Academy of Arts and Sciences. Conversations with academicians in France and concern for Boston's scholarly reputation in the light of Philadelphia's American Philosophical Society* (APS) led to the incorporation of the academy in 1780. Governor James Bowdoin of Massachusetts was its first president. He was succeeded in 1791 by John Adams. In the 1820s John Quincy Adams was president of the United States and the American Academy simultaneously, and members of the Adams family have continued to be interested in and connected with its operation. Other early members included such eminent men as George Washington, Benjamin Franklin, Thomas Jefferson, Alexander Hamilton, and James Madison. One of the first research activities of the academy, undertaken in conjunction with Harvard College, was to dispatch a committee to Maine to observe the solar eclipse of October 27, 1780. Undertaken with special permission from blockading British naval forces, the expedition was hampered by bad weather and finally missed observing the total eclipse because of miscalculations in latitude. This mistake did result, however, in the discovery of a solar astronomical phenomenon now known as "Bailey's Beads."

Meetings of the American Academy were held originally in October, January, March, and May. Beginning in 1846, monthly meetings have been held during the period October through May. The meeting in May is an "annual" meeting devoted to the transaction of much of the business of the academy and attracting the largest attendance. Early meetings were apparently convened at the residences of members, Harvard College, or other public buildings. During most of the nineteenth century, the academy was domiciled with the Boston Athenaeum. Although members often expressed sentiment for a permanent meeting building, it was not until 1904 that a building was purchased at 28 Newbury Street, Boston. In 1911 additional space at 26 Newbury Street was provided through the generosity of Alexander Agassiz, president of the academy from 1894 to 1903. In addition to providing administrative and meeting rooms, these quarters were used to house the academy library, which then included a special collection of the serial records of other learned societies. From 1957 to 1980, the American Academy was located at Brandegee House in Brookline, Massachusetts; in the fall of 1980, it moved to Norton's Woods, Cambridge, into a house built for it through a gift of Mr. and Mrs. Edwin H. Land. Mr. Land, chairman of the board of the Polaroid Corporation, was president of the academy from 1951 to 1954. Parenthetically it should be noted that the academy sold the bulk of its library in 1946 to the Linda Hall Library*

(LHL), Kansas City, Missouri. With the academy holdings, totaling some sixty-two thousand items, as the base of its collection, the LHL has become a noted scientific and technological library.

Beginning with the establishment in 1796 of the Rumford Fund by Benjamin Thompson, Count Rumford, the income from a number of such bequests, including those of Francis Amory and Caryl P. Haskins, has been at the disposal of the American Academy. The proceeds of the Rumford Fund and the Amory Fund are disbursed as prizes for outstanding achievement in the physics of heat and light and in reproductive biology, respectively, whereas the Haskins gift supports the Emerson-Thoreau Prize in Literature. Other prizes awarded include a Social Science Prize and a Humanities Prize. The academy's other endowment, including the Permanent Science Fund, is relatively small and, although used earlier for these purposes, does not now permit it to support research and publication in scientific fields.

The American Academy first began publication with its *Memoirs*, of which four volumes were published between 1780 and 1821. Nineteen more were issued between 1833 and 1957. During the early years the *Memoirs* usually contained short communications to the secretary describing the results of scientific experiments or extraordinary monographs, running between one hundred and three hundred or more pages, on some limited phase of scientific activity and usually contributed by academy fellows. In 1848 the *Proceedings* were added, and by 1873 eight volumes had appeared containing condensed accounts of the academy meetings held during that period. Beginning in 1873, records of meetings, reports of officers, and biographical notices of deceased members, together with papers read at meetings, were published annually.

In 1955 the academy superseded volume 86 of the *Proceedings* with a new journal called *Daedalus*. By that time professional, specialized journals filled the role formerly filled by the *Proceedings*, and there was an apparent need for a new type of journal in the face of this specialization. Since its inception, each issue of *Daedalus* has focused on a single topic that affects the intellectual community and society at large. Among topics recently considered have been the future of American higher education and the oil crisis.

In addition to *Daedalus*, the American Academy currently publishes a *Bulletin*, which appears monthly during the academic year and describes various ongoing activities of the society, and an annual *Records*, which lists its membership, reports of committees, and other items of an official and administrative nature.

Concomitant to this restructuring of the academy publishing program was an increase in the size and scope of the projects and studies conducted under its auspices. Diverse in content and approach, they range through the sponsoring and holding of conferences and deliberations resulting in the establishment of the International Center of Insect Physiology and Ecology in Nairobi, the convening of a symposium on chemical and biological warfare, to broad-scale studies of human values and the environment and the growth and institutionalization of knowledge in America.

The original incorporation act designated sixty-two residents of Boston as fellows and charter members of the American Academy of Arts and Sciences. Early limitations on membership as to number and residence were gradually modified so as to make it a national organization. By 1911 the limitation on resident members, those within a fifty-mile radius of Boston, had been raised to four hundred and that on nonresident members to two hundred. Since that time membership regulations have been further amended so that today there is no limitation and the academy has a membership of about twenty-three hundred fellows, including a small number of foreign honorary members, less than one-third of whom now live within easy traveling distance of Boston.

The astronomer, Maria Mitchell, who was elected a fellow in 1848, was the first woman member. Since that time over one hundred women have been elected to membership. Election to membership in the academy has always remained honorific with a rigorous nominating and electing procedure.

In the post-World War II decades, with the broadening of its scope of activities and the increase in percentage of membership living outside the Boston area, members located away from the East Coast of the United States urged the establishment of regional centers of the academy. In 1970, this movement culminated in the establishment of the Western center of the American Academy, which is now located at the Center for Advanced Study in the Behavioral Sciences* at Stanford, California. Still under development is a similar Midwest center for the Mississippi Valley, which presently maintains a peripatetic existence. Both centers offer their constituencies a program of activities consisting of general meetings, discussion groups, and cooperative research projects.

The American Academy of Arts and Sciences elects the customary institutional officers; it conducts its business from offices, headed by an executive officer, located in Boston, Massachusetts.

For further information, see the publications of the academy discussed above and an informational *Blue Book*, last published by the academy in 1977. See also Survey, American Academy of Arts and Sciences; and Harlow Shapley, "The American Academy of Arts and Sciences," *World of the Mind* (1958).

AMERICAN ACADEMY OF RELIGION. This academy is a learned and professional society of college and university professors and others engaged in teaching and research in the study of religion as an academic discipline. Its primary purpose, as a learned society, is to stimulate scholarship, foster research, and promote learning in the complex of disciplines that constitute religion as a field of academic inquiry. Its secondary purpose, as a professional society, is to keep its membership informed of developing programs and newly available materials in the field and of opportunities for study grants and research funds and to provide information about academic positions at every level. This duality of purpose is reflected in the content of the programs of the national and regional meetings and the nature of the publications sponsored by the academy. This duality is perhaps most succinctly expressed by the fact that it was a founding member of the Council on the Study of Religion (1969), an organization designed to coordinate the activities of diverse societies engaged in the study and teaching of religion, and is a constituent member of the American Council of Learned Societies* (ACLS).

The academy began as the result of an informal meeting of four members of the Society of Biblical Literature and Exegesis* (SBL) in December, 1908: Ismar J. Peritz, Irving F. Wood, Raymond Knox, and Olive Dutcher (later Mrs. Lawrence Doggett). They were concerned to form an organization that would promote scholarly teaching in the Biblical field as the SBL promoted scholarly research.

They agreed to invite a number of persons who shared that concern to meet the following year. Attendants at that meeting formed an organization that is the lineal and legal ancestor of the present American Academy of Religion. Its first president was Charles Foster Kent of Yale University, who held the position until his death in 1925. Since that time a new president has been elected annually. Membership of the organization increased slowly but steadily. In 1934 there were 345 members, in 1949 there were 760, and in 1959 the membership had reached 1,180. The decades of the 1960s and 1970s witnessed tremendous expansion in departments of religion in American universities and colleges, in both the public and private sectors. This expansion was reflected in the growth in membership in the academy, which in 1980 numbered approximately 4,500.

Rapid growth was only one aspect of the change in the study of religion in American education. New fields of study and a wide diversity of methodologies were introduced into the curricula of departments of religion. The academy reflected and in part stimulated those changes. Insight into its changing nature and scope is patent in its changes of name. The original "Association of Biblical Instructors in American Colleges and Secondary Schools" changed in December, 1922, to "National Association of Biblical Instructors," and in December, 1963, to the present "American Academy of Religion." Initially, the primary concern was to develop significant curricula and to set adequate standards for Biblical instruction, for Biblical study constituted the core, usually the entirety, of religious studies at the preprofessional or pregraduate level. As the field of religious studies expanded, the constituency of the organization's membership was not reflected accurately in a name that emphasized Biblical instruction. The field today embraces a complex of subfields ranging from pedagogy and methodology to the utilization of aesthetics and the social and behavioral sciences as applied to religious phenomena from the origins of *homo sapiens* to the headlines of tomorrow's newspaper. Only an academy of diversely trained scholars can appropriately encompass that spectrum, and that diversity is implicit in the present name of the organization.

This transition is also reflected in the name changes of the organization's journal. Founded in 1933 as the *Journal of the National Association of Biblical Instructors*, it became in 1937 the *Journal of Bible and Religion*, and in 1967 the present *Journal of the American Academy of Religion.*

Consistent with the purpose of the organization outlined above, its present activities fall into three major categories: national and regional meetings; a diverse publications program; and consistent efforts to evaluate, review, and enhance the professional dimensions of the academic study of religion. Further, in cooperation with like-minded societies, through the Council on the Study of Religion (CSR) and the ACLS, it seeks to interpret to the broader public the nature of the study of religion as an integral segment of human culture.

The academy normally holds its annual meeting jointly with the SBL, and the total attendance at this meeting for the past several years has averaged three thousand. The broad scope of the study of religion is fully reflected in the program units of the annual meeting. Program interests are reflected in permanent sections, working groups constituted for a specific period of time, consultations organized on an ad hoc basis, and small seminars.

Recognizing that interested members cannot always attend a national meeting, early on the organization encouraged meetings at the regional level. Presently nine regions have formal organizations and meet on an annual basis at a time other than that of the national meeting.

Publications have been a vital concern of the organization from the beginning. In the early years stress was laid on preparing materials that would enhance instruction at the secondary and lower college levels. One of the founders, Peritz, had from the outset dreamed of a national journal, and that dream was realized in 1933. The journal, now the *JAAR*, remains the center of the academy's publication program. That center, however, has been enormously expanded. In 1970 a monograph series was initiated, and since that time a number of other series were begun designed to make readily and inexpensively available the best of current research and to provide teaching aids for instruction in colleges and universities. To further these aims the academy joined with the SBL in 1975 to found Scholars Press, an organization which has marked a significant breakthrough in scholarly publishing both in religion and cognate fields.

Although in recent years the academy has focused more on its role as a learned society, it has not neglected the professional dimension. In cooperation with other organizations, through the coordinating efforts of the CSR, it maintains an international placement service, which benefits institutions seeking qualified personnel and young scholars seeking initial employment and matches needs and skills of others in the profession.

Further, on the professional level, the academy consistently pursues activities to improve the quality of instruction in the field of religion, to enhance the standards of the profession, and to interpret the role of the study of religion in the broader fields of academe and beyond.

The academy is financed primarily through members' dues and institutional subscriptions to its journal. Income from other publications is normally utilized in a revolving fund to further additional publications. From time to time the academy receives and disburses funds from foundations for special projects.

For further information, the following articles contain historical reminiscences presented at the meetings celebrating the twenty-fifth, fortieth, and fiftieth anniversaries of the founding of the organization. Eliza H. Kendrick and Ismar J. Peritz, "Twenty-Five Years of the National Association of Biblical Instructors," *Journal of the National Association of Biblical Instructors* (1935); Elmer W. K. Mould, "The National Association of Biblical Instructors," *Journal of Bible and Religion* (January, 1950); and, all appearing in the April, 1960, issue of the *Journal of Bible and Religion*, Olive D. Doggett, "Golden Memories of a Charter Member"; Dwight M. Beck, "Reminiscences"; Carl E. Purinton, "Journal of Bible and Religion: The Formative Years." There is no formal history of the academy. The rationale for the change of name to the American Academy of Religion is set forth by Clyde A. Holbrook, "Why an Academy of Religion"; and Robert Smith, "Report of the NABI Self-Study Committee," both in *Journal of Bible and Religion* (April, 1964). In 1978 the academy authorized the establishment of an archival center to be located in the office of the executive director.

JOHN F. PRIEST

AMERICAN ANTHROPOLOGICAL ASSOCIATION (AAA). Before 1902 contact among U.S. anthropologists was maintained by Section H (Anthropology) of the American Association for the Advancement of Science* (AAAS), by the publication of an independent quarterly journal, *American Anthropologist*, and by the existence of local organizations such as the Anthropological Society of Washington, D.C. The advance in the extent and importance of anthropology and the inadequacies of existing means for promoting and strengthening it spurred the creation of a national anthropological association. Thus, in 1901 and 1902, various members of the local societies in Washington and New York and Section H (Anthropology) of the AAAS, particularly W. J. McGee and Franz Boas, met for the purpose of creating such an association. Ultimately, in May, 1902, the American Anthropological Association was incorporated: "to advance the science of anthropology in all its branches and to further the professional interest of American anthropologists."

Although the national AAA was a partial outgrowth of the Anthropological Society of Washington, D.C., and the American Ethnological Society of New York, these two local organizations and the Philadelphia Anthropological Society retained their separate identities and are still active. Also, a Central States Branch of the AAA was organized in 1923. The members of these local societies and the branch pay separate dues to these organizations in addition to those of the AAA.

Since its beginnings the AAA has engaged in such activities as investigations of the teachings of anthropology in the United States, examination of the status of anthropology in governmental agencies, and efforts to prevent vandalism in various ruins of anthropological significance. It has passed resolutions on such diverse matters as the U.S. treatment of the American Indian and evolution.

Following the founding of the AAA the *American Anthropologist* became its official publication, and it now appears quarterly. It contains articles on anthropology and allied subjects, reports of field work, book reviews, and comments. From 1905 to the 1960s the association intermittently published the *Memoirs*, which included essays of the same type to be found in the *Anthropologist* but too long for inclusion there. A *News Bulletin* of the association was established in 1947, and, following several changes in title, is now published as the *Newsletter*. The latter prints information of general interest to the profession but not scholarly or research reports.

The annual meetings of the AAA are held in the fall. Earlier they were often convened with those of the AAAS or such societies as the American Folklore Society* (AFS) or the Linguistic Society of America* (LSA). These meetings, held in cities in all sections of United States, have followed the usual societal pattern of the presentation of reports and papers and the conduct of AAA business.

There are several classes of membership in the association: members, open to any applicant; fellows, possessing the requisite professional qualifications and approved by the executive board; foreign fellows, professional anthropologists in other countries; liaison fellows, persons active in other fields but interested in anthropology; and institutional subscribers, such as libraries. From the original 175 members of 1903, the AAA has had a steady growth; climbing to 1,000 by 1929, and now standing at about 10,000.

The AAA elects the customary institutional officers; its staff, headed by an executive secretary, carries on its work from offices located in Washington, D.C.

For further information, see the publications of the AAA discussed above, particularly George W. Stocking, Jr., "Franz Boas and the Founding of the American Anthropological Association," *American Anthropologist* (February, 1960). See also Franz Boas, "The American Ethnological Society," *Science* (January, 1943); Fred Eggan, "The American Anthropological Association," *AAAS Bulletin* (May, 1943); and

D. B. Stout, "American Anthropological Association," *Dictionary of Folklore, Mythology, and Legend* (1949).

For information on the publications of the AAA, see Frederic de Laguna, *Selected Papers from the American Anthropologist, 1888-1920* (1960).

AMERICAN ANTIQUARIAN SOCIETY. The first of learned societies created in the nineteenth century, this society is different from the American Philosophical Society* (APS) and the American Academy of Arts and Sciences* in that its interests and activity have been confined to one particular aspect of the humanities. It is similar to the two older societies in that its membership is elective. It can lay claim to being the third oldest historical society in the United States and the first to be national rather than local or regional in its title and interest.

The American Antiquarian Society was founded by a Massachusetts printer, Isaiah Thomas. Born in poverty and lacking formal schooling, Thomas became a successful businessman and during the Revolutionary War published one of the leading newspapers supporting the colonial cause. After the war he continued to accumulate wealth and turned his attention to the acquisition of documents and other materials relating to the early history of the American colonies. The culmination of these efforts was the incorporation, in 1812, of the society, which was empowered to collect and preserve the materials for a study of American history and antiquities. Thomas was elected the first president of the society; since then, many distinguished Americans have been members or served as officers of the society, including twelve presidents of the United States.

In its early days the society devoted itself to the encouragement of historical study and the collection of objects of American antiquarian interest for its museum, but its chief interest lay in the books and manuscripts from which its library gradually came into being. The founder, author of a *History of Printing in America*, had a considerable collection of American printed matter, which he had agreed to turn over to the society as soon as it had a safe and convenient repository. By the time that condition was fulfilled in 1820, this nucleus of a library had grown, largely through the generosity of Mr. Thomas, to about six thousand volumes. By its continued increase, the library soon overshadowed the museum, and the other objects the society had been acquiring were placed with other organizations. Since then the library has been the primary object of the society's efforts.

The society's library houses Americana of the period through 1876; the collections are large and broad within that chronological span. By 1854 its 6,000 volumes had increased to some 23,000. In the next three decades it more than tripled to approximately 80,000. Twenty-five years later it passed the 100,000 mark; by 1937 it had nearly 500,000 titles, and now its approximately 650,000 entries form one of the most imposing collections pertaining to America in the country, ranking with the New York Public Library* and the Library of Congress. It has attempted to "collect everything printed in this country before 1820," including books and newspapers. So well has it succeeded that approximately two-thirds of the extant titles that come under this description are found on its shelves.

The library is particularly strong in its collection of early American children's books, social history, local histories and genealogies, biographies, bibliographies, American religious works, and political pamphlets and broadsides. The manuscript collection numbers something over one million pieces. Even larger, and also of great value is the society collection of American newspapers, the number of issues held being estimated at two million. This collection was built upon the acquisitions of its founder, Isaiah Thomas, for the preparation of his *History of Printing in America.*

The main activities of the society center around the library; so the semiannual meetings are relatively simple affairs. At the April meeting, usually held in Boston, a report of the society's governing council is presented, new members are elected, and scholarly papers are presented. The program of the annual meeting in October, invariably held at Worcester, is similar save that the treasurer and the librarian also present reports and officers are elected for the following year.

The society sponsors two fellowship competitions. Three are short-term fellowships, in which six to nine scholars are selected for societal residency of one to three months. This competition is funded from various grants and the society's endowment. The other, funded by a National Endowment for the Humanities grant, is a competition for at least two scholars who are to be in residence at the society for up to a full year.

Two series of publications carry the society seal, the *Transactions* and the *Proceedings.* The former, published from 1820 to 1911, contains manuscript and documentary materials for early American history. Since the latter date this material has been incorporated in the American Antiquarian Society *Proceedings,* which have appeared since the founding of the Society and contain reports, bylaws, obituaries, papers read at meetings, other scholarly articles, and lists of officers, members, and staff. Other publications have appeared from time to time, such as indexes and bibliographies, facsimile reprints, books of essays, handbooks of information, and catalogs of the library. Currently the society is engaged with Readex Microprint Corporation in reprinting in microprint from nearly every book, pamphlet, and broadside printed in America from 1639 to 1820. It is also undertaking other major bibliographical research projects. The North American Imprints Program (NAIP) will result in the creation of highly detailed cataloguing records in machine-readable (computer) form of all North American imprints dated through 1800. The Catalogue of American Engravings Project will provide scholarly access to all works of that genre executed before 1821. In addition, the society sponsors several educational and public programs, including courses, seminars, colloquia, lectures, concerts, and exhibits.

The society membership has always been honorary and is conferred by election at a meeting upon persons eminent in the field of the society's activities. Rules adopted in 1831 limited the number of members to 140, which has since been raised to 400. During the nineteenth century fees were charged, but in 1925 all fees and dues were abolished. Although the founder often expressed the wish that the society "comport with the name it bears" by embracing all of the Americas within its membership, practical reasons dictated that approximately half of all members have been chosen from the Northeast. Nowadays members are elected from all parts of the country. The names of most of the leading historians of the past and present century have appeared on society rolls, although a substantial portion of the membership has always been composed of persons whose interests in historical studies were those of writers, collectors, and society benefactors, rather than teachers.

The society elects the customary institutional officers; it conducts its business from the library, under the direction of a director and librarian, located in Worcester, Massachusetts.

For further information, see the various reports of the director of the society published in the *Proceedings*. See also Nathaniel Paine, *An Account of the American Antiquarian Society* (1876); Clarence S. Brigham, *American Antiquarian Society Handbook of Information* (1909); Agnes Edwards, "The Library of the American Antiquarian Society," *Massachusetts Magazine* (January, 1916); Marcus A. McCorison: *A Society's Chief Joys* (1969) and "The Nature of Humanistic Societies in Early America," *The Pursuit of Knowledge in the Early Republic* (1976). See also Survey, American Antiquarian Society; Clifford K. Shipton: "The American Antiquarian Society," *William and Mary Quarterly* (April, 1945) and "The American Antiquarian Society, *World of the Mind* (1959); and James E. Mooney, "The American Antiquarian Society," *ACLS Newsletter* (December, 1968).

AMERICAN ASSOCIATION FOR STATE AND LOCAL HISTORY (AASLH).

The American Association for State and Local History was created in 1940 by a group of historical society directors and staff members who wanted an organization through which they could improve the effectiveness of their institutions. The idea was not new: half a century earlier a similar group had established the Mississippi Valley Historical Association, only to see it shift quickly into a national organization of academic American historians and eventually change its name to the Organization of American Historians* (OAH). Subsequently the society directors gravitated to the American Historical Association* (AHA), which in 1904 established a Conference of State and Local Historical Societies that met annually at the AHA meeting. A steady increase in numbers and enthusiasm led the conference, with the blessings of its parent organization, to a meeting in December, 1940, at the New-York Historical Society,* at which the conference was disbanded and the new association begun.

Christopher Crittenden, director of the North Carolina Department of Archives and History and chairman of the conference, became the association's first president. In his opening message to the membership, Crittenden noted the existence of more than a thousand historical organizations in the United States and Canada. He noted, too, that there were many individuals interested in local history, both in academic institutions and in many kinds of professional and volunteer endeavor. The association, he declared, would help both. It pledged itself to cooperation with patriotic and civic organizations, the National Park Service, and the Works Progress Administration (WPA) Historical Records Survey; it would compile lists of local historians and genealogists, encourage the writing of good state and local histories, and promote the establishment of adequate courses on these subjects; and finally, it planned to serve as a clearinghouse for "information on how to organize a historical society, how to mark historic spots, how to conduct historical tours, how to stage historical celebrations and pageants, how to preserve historic buildings, how to prepare and broadcast historical radio programs and other similar topics."

It is not surprising that at almost every governing council meeting of the AASLH during the early years there were discussions of the feasibility of establishing a full-time paid directorate. In the meantime the committed professionals who had established the organization were working hard for its success, in addition to carrying on their regular jobs. President Crittenden became acting editor for a series of monographic studies on the work of historical societies; Vice-President Edward P. Alexander wrote as the first of this series *What Should Our Historical Society Do?*, a discussion of programs that historical societies ought to undertake. Council member S. K. Stevens undertook the compilation of a directory handbook to historical societies but reported some difficulty in getting a return of his questionnaires.

Through the war years the association continued its growth by means of such volunteer effort. A bimonthly newsletter, *State and Local History News*, was begun in 1941. Additional monographs were published, including several dealing with wartime history in state and local contexts. Busy professionals continued to give unsparingly of their time to advance the association's programs, and association and editorial offices moved about the country to meet the convenience of these volunteer workers.

The major turning point in the association's development came in 1949. With a rash confidence that is astounding even in retrospect and with deep conviction that history should be presented to an intelligent lay audience in attractive and readable form, the association launched a popular magazine of history, which it called *American Heritage*. Profusely illustrated with both black-and-white and color illustrations, it was a revolutionary and highly successful departure from the staid and somber historical publications of the day. Circulation climbed steadily over the next five years to just under twenty thousand copies per quarterly issue, and with this growth an association of professional historians found itself in a business operation of mushrooming complexity. The biggest burden of all rested on Earle W. Newton and S. K. Stevens, editor and business manager, respectively. Both held full-time jobs, Stevens with the Pennsylvania Historical Commission and Newton at the Vermont Historical Society and later at Old Sturbridge Village. Foundation funds helped defray costs of color plates and author fees, but it was the promotional ingenuity of Newton and Stevens, coupled with their editorial and business skills, that kept the magazine going.

The success of *American Heritage* attracted the attention of other publishers. In 1954 the New York firm of Thorndike, Jensen and Parton made an offer to take over publication of the magazine. The organization that had possessed the courage to undertake the experiment had the wisdom to see that the magazine would be more likely to realize its goals through the efforts of professional publishers than by continued dependence on the limited resources of the association. The transaction was approved. American Heritage Publishing Company was organized to publish the magazine and since then has become a major world publisher. The association, which continues to be an active sponsor of the magazine, has been able to undertake many important programs over the past quarter-century because it has shared in the magazine's financial success.

With the increase in association income after 1954, Dr. Clement M. Silvestro was employed as assistant to the president, on a half-time basis. Offices were established in the State Historical Society of Wisconsin, whose director, Clifford L. Lord, was then association president. Silvestro divided his time between the association and the society until October of that year, when the job was made full-time through consolidation with the editorship of *History News*.

Silvestro served as director until 1964, when he left to join the staff of the Chicago Historical Society. In his seven years as director, he doubled the membership, strengthened the publications program, increased representation of the association at state and regional conferences of historical societies, completed the first truly comprehensive survey of historical society activity, and established the association in a position of real leadership for the profession.

William T. Alderson, Tennessee state librarian and archivist, succeeded Silvestro and established a new headquarters for the association in Nashville, Tennessee. In the ensuing fourteen years under his direction the AASLH underwent an enormous expansion from an annual budget of $65,000 and a staff of four to an annual budget of $1.3 million and a staff of thirty-five. This expansion reflected not only an again doubled membership but the development of federal grant-supported programs to provide increased services to the profession. The association pioneered in the establishment of training seminars and workshops held throughout all of the United States, including Alaska and Hawaii, and in independent study courses for historical society and agency professionals. It created major series of audio and audiovisual materials for staff instruction. In its largest single project, undertaken in partnership with the W. W. Norton Company, the association published histories of each of the fifty states and the District of Columbia as part of the commemoration of the nation's bicentennial.

The most significant accomplishment of those years was, however, the emergence of the AASLH as the major publisher of technical and professional literature of the historical society and museum professions. Building from the modest newsletter of earlier years, the association converted *History News* into a monthly magazine with widely acclaimed technical leaflet inserts on an endless list of do-it-yourself projects and topics. Similarly, the earlier series of "bulletins" gave way to a greatly expanded paperback and hardcover book publishing program producing half a dozen or more new titles each year on topics ranging from oral history to the care of museum collections, from planning bicentennial observances to furnishing historic houses, from the collection of old photographs to the interpretation and publication of local history.

Alderson left the association to become director of museum studies at the University of Delaware in 1978. He was succeeded by Gerald W. George, who had joined the AASLH staff in 1973 as editor of the bicentennial state history series. Under George's leadership the association has greatly expanded *History News*, inaugurated a new series of seminars on the study and interpretation of local history, and continued its vigorous programs of professional training and publication.

In forty years the association has been a major force in the growth of local history from a neglected and often scorned province of the antiquarians to an important area of scholarly research. Through its highly competitive awards program, annual national and regional meetings, and training programs it has contributed importantly to the raising of standards for historical agency work by both volunteers and paid staff. Its pioneering development of *American Heritage* led a continuing movement to expand the audience for history and encourage greater awareness of our past, a movement of which the widely acclaimed bicentennial state histories are an important part. And its vigorous publications program on the techniques and practices of historical agencies and museums has enabled the smallest and most remote historical institutions to execute correctly the many tasks of preserving the cultural heritage of the United States and Canada.

For further information, see Walter Muir Whitehill, *Independent Historical Societies* (1962); and William T. Alderson, "The American Association for State and Local History," *Western Historical Quarterly* (April, 1970). There is little published material dealing with the history of the association. *History News*, published by the AASLH and referred to above, is a good source for most of the association's history.

WILLIAM T. ALDERSON

AMERICAN ASSOCIATION FOR THE ADVANCEMENT OF SCIENCE (AAAS). Several converging and overlapping events led to the founding of the AAAS. Various unsuccessful attempts had been made to set up national scientific institutions in the nation's capital, particularly the National Institute for the Promotion of Science. Tied in with the creation of the latter, a dispute arose as to the exact disposition to be made of the bequest in the 1830s of an Englishman, James Smithson, "to the United States of America, to found at Washington, under the name of the Smithsonian Institution, an Establishment for the increase and diffusion of knowledge among men." Finally, there was the movement for a broadening of the area of operation of an existing society, the Association of American Geologists and Naturalists, in emulation of the British Association for the Advancement of Science, founded in York, England, in 1831.

After Washington became the national capital in 1800-1801, a number of attempts were made to establish a national learned society or institution there. A United States Military Philosophical Society held a meeting there in 1808. The Metropolitan Society was organized there between 1810 and 1816, and, in the latter year, this became the Columbian Institute for the Promotion of Arts and Sciences. Daniel Webster, John C. Calhoun, Henry Clay, John Quincy Adams, and many other prominent figures of the day participated in its activities. By 1840 the Columbian Institute, under the leadership of Joel R. Poinsett of South Carolina, had metamorphosed into the National Institute for the Promotion of Science, which was projected as a national organization and included eight sections or branches devoted to various areas of learning. The National Institute was incorporated by an act of Congress in 1842, and in the process the organization changed from an "institution" to an "institute." It had secured the introduction of congressional bills to place the Smithson bequest under its control and management and was able to get congressional appropriations in 1841 and 1842 for several projects. At this time its resident membership grew to over two hundred, with more than one thousand corresponding members.

Despite this auspicious beginning, inept management of the several projects under its control and developing political and scientific opposition to its drive for the control of the Smithson bequest boded ill. The political opposition to the National Institute, led by Senators Benjamin Tappan of Ohio and Rufus Choate of Massachusetts, was based on its antidemocratic nature. The developing scientific opposition, centering in a group of New England leaders of the already established Association of American Geologists and Naturalists, rested on their belief that the National Institute, although it included most of the recognized scientists of the day on its rolls, was controlled by politicians and scientific amateurs.

Nevertheless, in April, 1844, the National Institute held a scientific congress in the capital that was attended by many political leaders, including President John Tyler and former president John Quincy Adams. Of the forty-three scientific papers presented there, over a score were authored by outstanding men of science in the United States. Significantly, however, the Association of American Geologists and Naturalists, which had been invited to the congress, proceeded instead with a separate meeting or congresss of its own in May, 1844.

Ultimately, in 1846, an act of Congress was passed calling for the creation of a separately endowed and controlled Smithsonian Institution.* The same act specified a board of managers, and one named to this board was Alexander Dallas Bache. A great-grandson of Benjamin Franklin, possessed of enviable ties to the political, social, and scientific leaders of the day, and head of the U.S. Coast Survey from 1843 to 1867, Bache was largely responsible for having his friend, Joseph Henry, named the first head of the new and now independent Smithsonian Institution. Thus, the National Institute, although it legally lingered on through the 1850s, died aborning and was swept into oblivion with the onset of the Civil War.

The National Institute's all-inclusive nature and the very favorable publicity attendant on its congress of 1844 was not lost on the Association of American Geologists and Naturalists and, particularly, its leaders, but they nevertheless distrusted it. The association recognized the benefits to be derived from such an all-inclusive scientific association—were they to lead it. Accordingly, as early as 1845, it was announced at an association meeting that "a constant effort has been made to counteract the impression that the objects of the Association are exclusively geological or directed to those cognate subjects only which have a direct bearing upon that subject." In an 1847 Boston meeting, the decision was made to enlarge the membership and scope of the association by becoming an American Association for the "Promotion" of Science. Three Bostonians, Henry D. Rogers, Benjamin Peirce, and Louis Agassiz, the latter newly arrived from Europe, were selected to draft the constitution for the new association. Thus, at a Philadelphia meeting on September 20, 1848, the by this time American Association for the "Advancement" of Science came into being with a constitution clearly borrowed by Rogers, albeit with minor differences, from that of the British Association for the Advancement of Science.

Since its founding the AAAS has held meetings in all parts of the country, although tending to concentrate on the larger cities on the East Coast. It has engaged in scientific publication, the *Proceedings* being published from the beginning until 1948. Selected symposium volumes based on symposia held at annual meetings have been published since 1934. The weekly *Science* and the *Scientific Monthly* became official AAAS journals in 1900 and 1915, respectively. They were both published continuously until 1958, when the *Monthly* was merged with *Science*. The *AAAS Bulletin*, a monthly publication with articles of historical and general interest, was published from March, 1942, through December, 1946. Resurrected in January, 1961, as a mostly quarterly news media for the AAAS, it was terminated in 1974.

Also, a quarterly *Science Education News* was established in the early 1960s, and an annual *Directory* or *Handbook* has been published since 1959. *Science 80*, a popular magazine covering all fields of science, was launched in 1979; it is issued ten times a year.

The AAAS has offered membership to all persons interested in any aspect of science. In this regard it is quite similar to other learned societies and institutes. It differs from them, however, in its all-inclusive disciplinary character. Its relationship to the learned societies has been historically conditioned, too, by the AAAS's being the spawning ground of societies and not vice versa.

Originally membership in the AAAS and the programs at the annual meeting were divided into rather fluid sections. The constitution of 1874, however, provided for two definite sections: Mathematics, Physics, and Chemistry (A); and Natural History (B). This set a precedent, and as science became more specialized and membership increased the number of sections did likewise. There were twelve by 1895; and at present twenty-one: Mathematics (A), Physics (B), Chemistry (C), Astronomy (D), Geology and Geography (E), Biological Sciences (G), Anthropology (H), Psychology (J), Social and Economic Sciences (K), History and Philosophy of Science (L), Engineering (M), Medical Sciences (N), Agriculture (O), Industrial Science (P), Education (Q), Dentistry (R), Pharmaceutical Sciences (S), Information, Computing, and Communication (T), Statistics (U), Atmospheric and Hydrospheric Sciences (W), General (X).

The sections have been a centripetal as well as centrifugal force within the AAAS. Created to supply a demand by members for more specialized grouping, there have been numerous examples of members branching out and organizing such independent societies as the Geological Society of America* (GSA), Botanical Society of America* (BSA), American Physical Society* (APS), American Anthropological Association* (AAA), and History of Science Society* (HSS).

It thus became apparent as early as the 1890s that the AAAS would have to set some policy regarding the sections and their offspring. A committee to consider the problem was created in 1895, and as a result of its and other deliberations the learned societies were given "affiliated" or "associated" status within the AAAS by the terms of the constitution of 1899 and, in 1901, extended representation on the legislative council. The AAAS, therefore, originated as an individual membership society, and it was not until the development of a great number of learned societies after the Civil War that the question of its relationship to them arose. By deliberate action of the AAAS at the turn of the century such societies were invited and did become affiliated with it. Although they have always had some influence within the AAAS, because of its tremendous number of individual members with greatly varying interests and the vast number of sections and committees set up within the AAAS's structure, this influence has been diffused.

Furthermore, the constitution that went into effect in 1973 considerably lessened that influence by reducing societal representation on the council. The AAAS, more so than any other coordinating organization, is in the delicate position of balancing the sometimes conflicting objectives and desires of groups of individual members and the learned societies.

In addition to the members associated with it through the almost three hundred affiliated societies and regional and state academies, the AAAS's own membership has grown from an original 461 to 1,004 in 1854; 1,030 in 1879, after a drop as a result of the Civil War; 2,000 in 1883; 4,000 in 1903; 11,000 in 1920; 62,000 in 1960; and approximately 130,000 today. Although five different types of membership are provided for—annual, life, fifty-year, emeritus, and student—the main distinction in membership, since 1874, has been between that of ordinary members and some fifteen thousand fellows.

Together with a council of eighty-five members, the organizational structure of the AAAS includes a thirteen-person board of directors, which acts as its legal representative and performs the functions of an executive or governing committee.

Besides the affiliated societies and academies, the AAAS has provided for the creation of autonomous divisions that receive some financial support from it. In 1915 the Pacific Division was set up; in 1920 the Southwestern and Rocky Mountain Division; and in 1951 the Alaska Division. These divisions are very active; they hold their own meetings, elect their own officers, and utilize the AAAS's journals to make announcements. They have undoubtedly been another significant factor in making it one great union of scientists and learned societies.

In the 1960s and '70s, the AAAS devoted much of its energies to problems that involved all of science and the relationship of science to government and society as a whole. Ancillary to this effort was a recognition of the need to increase public awareness of science and its potential for good and evil for humanity.

This policy was reflected in the 1960s in programs for improving science education. For example, a Commission on Science Education, funded by the National Science Foundation and operating from 1962 through 1974, developed a new science curriculum for the elementary grades. In 1958 a Committee on Science in the Promotion of Human Welfare was set up in response to a call for the AAAS to adopt a more active political and social role. In the 1960s and 1970s it sponsored studies and investigations on the impact of and relationship to science of such areas as the environment and secrecy. A Committee on Scientific Freedom and Responsibility, with much the same activities and goals, was established in 1970 and discharged in 1974. One with the same name was established in 1976 and is an ongoing operation. More recently, an Office of Opportunities in Science provides a variety of aids for minorities, women, and the handicapped seeking careers in science. Also, an Office of Public Sector Programs coordinates the activities of fellows stationed in the U.S. Congress. This office, too, has sponsored colloquia on research and development provisions in the federal budget and summer internships for scientists with mass media groups and conducts a number of regional seminars annually dealing with such topics as energy, population, and the environment.

AAAS action on the energy issue exemplifies its current interest and involvement with problems of an intertwined scientific-social-public nature. The AAAS played a leading role in providing information on the energy shortage before it even became a national issue. In addition to regional AAAS seminars, *Science* published several issues on the topic. When President Carter presented a national energy program, the AAAS made a critical analysis of it. Thus, the AAAS has become much more concerned and active with projects concerning science and its effects on society and relatively less with the technical aspects of the various disciplines comprising its membership.

The AAAS, which maintains its headquarters in Washington, D.C., holds annual winter meetings. Principal officers include a retiring president, a president, a president-elect, a treasurer, eight other directors, and an executive officer. These thirteen constitute a board of directors responsible for the conduct of AAAS affairs. In 1980 the AAAS reported an individual membership of 130,000 persons.

For further information, see the weekly *Science* and an annual *AAAS Handbook* published by the AAAS. There is no definitive history of the AAAS. For the founding and early years, see Sally Gregory Kohlstedt, *The Formation of the American Scientific Community—The American Association for the Advancement of Science 1848-1860* (1976). See also Herman L. Fairchild, "The History of the American Association for the Advancement of Science," *Science* (April, 1924); and Forest R. Moulton, "The American Association for the Advancement of Science—A Brief Historical Sketch," *Science* (September, 1948).

AMERICAN ASSOCIATION FOR THE ADVANCEMENT OF SLAVIC STUDIES (AAASS). The "Triple A Double S" is an interdisciplinary professional association designed to advance scholarly study, publication, and teaching as they pertain to the Soviet Union and Eastern Europe. Any interested person may join. It is governed by a board made up of directors elected at large as well as directors representing national professional associations in various disciplines, regional associations, and member institutions. The association sponsors the *Slavic Review* and other publications, arranges national conventions in cooperation with various regional associations, maintains an active network of committees, and assists in any way it can to serve the needs of the Slavic and Eastern European field.

Although the AAASS dates only from 1960 as a membership organization, it is the direct descendant of earlier groups. As an instrument for planning and coordination, it stemmed from the Joint Committee on Slavic Studies (JCSS), set up in 1938 under the American Council of Learned Societies* (ACLS) and then converted in 1948 to a joint committee of the ACLS and the Social Science Research Council* (SSRC). In its role as the publisher of an interdisciplinary scholarly journal, the AAASS traces its ancestry to the London-based *Slavonic and East European Review*. When, in 1941 war interrupted that journal, the JCSS sponsored in the United States the *American Slavic and East European Review (ASEER)*. After the war, when the British journal resumed publication, the American journal kept going as well. In 1948, when the *ASEER* was being edited at and subsidized by Columbia University, a corporation was established called the American Association for the Advancement of Slavic Studies, to serve merely as a legal umbrella for the journal. However, because the *ASEER* was interdisciplinary and covered the whole Eastern European and Russian area, its several hundred subscribers provided the natural basis for a membership organization whenever the time was ripe.

An important forerunner of the AAASS as an interdiscplinary membership organization was the Washington (D.C.) Unclassified Forum, which brought together scholars who were working for the government during World War II. It operated continuously from 1945 onward and was based after 1948 at the Brookings Institution.* Interdisciplinary contacts were also fostered by the various universities that developed Russian and Slavic area programs after the war, especially Columbia and Harvard in the East and, in the West, the University of California at Berkeley and the University of Washington. Among other antecedents one may cite the American Association for Teachers of Slavic and East European Languages (AATSEEL) and the Slavic subsection of the Modern Language Association of America* (MLA), both of which were national in membership although limited in their disciplinary scope.

By the late 1950s, with increased funds from Ford and other foundations and sizable grants from the federal government under the National Defense Education Act, interdisciplinary centers were starting up at many universities. The various professional organizations in such disciplines as history, political science, and economics were setting up subgroups of persons specializing in Russia and Eastern Europe, like that begun earlier in the MLA. Plans for a national professional organization were laid by a JCSS subcommittee, which began its work in May, 1957, and made its proposals in October, 1959. Representatives of the JCSS and the AAASS met in March, 1960, and agreed that the AAASS would be transformed into a membership organization. The letter inviting people to join the new organization was dated June 1, 1960.

In its development since then, the association has striven not to supplant existing groups but rather to help these and other groups cooperate across geographical, institutional, and disciplinary boundaries. The association had its headquarters and produced its *Newsletter* from 1960 to mid-1969 in Champaign-Urbana, at the University of Illinois; from mid-1969 to the end of 1979 the headquarters was in Columbus, at the Ohio State University; and in 1980-1981 at the University of Illinois at Chicago Circle. It moved to Stanford University in January, 1982. The sponsoring university in each case subsidized the association to a significant degree with personnel, space, and miscellaneous expenses.

The growth in membership of the association is recorded in the *Newsletter* and also in the *Directory of Members*, four editions of which were published at Illinois in the 1960s and two at Ohio State in the 1970s (the most recent being in 1974). After a rapid rise to about 1,280 by the end of 1962, the membership grew by roughly 10 percent per year up to about 2,300 in 1969. Since then it has stayed generally in the 2,300-2,600 range.

Despite its small size, the AAASS has sponsored extremely valuable scholarly publications. This has been possible only thanks to generous institutional support which supplemented the income from dues and subscriptions. The association's own journal, the *Slavic Review*, has demanded sizable subsidies in personnel and facilities, especially from the institutions that offered it a home. Before 1960 the *ASEER* had been supported for more than a decade by Columbia. At the end of 1960 it was moved to the University of Washington. There under its new editorship it was expanded and renamed the *Slavic Review*, with the subtitle *American Quarterly of Soviet and East European Studies*. Except for a second sojourn at Columbia, between 1965 and 1968, the *Review* stayed at Washington through 1975. Since then it has been at the Champaign-Urbana campus of the University of Illinois, where the term of the current editor runs until 1985.

The *Current Digest of the Soviet Press* (CDSP) was based from 1949 to 1969 in New York, where it was subsidized by Columbia and the ACLS. Since 1969 it has been sponsored by the AAASS and published in Columbus at the Ohio State University, with support from that institution.

The American Bibliography of Soviet and East European Studies began in the 1950s and up to 1969 (for volumes through 1966) was produced at and subsidized by Indiana University. The volumes for 1967 to 1972, inclusive, were produced under AAASS sponsorship at Ohio State. Since then the *Bibliography* has been prepared at the Library of Congress in cooperation with the AAASS.

Even with such help from the institutions named, the association needed more. During the 1960s supplementary assistance came in the form of yearly cash contributions from several universities, contributions which from 1964 to 1969 were channeled through the Slavic Publications Fund administered by the ACLS for the benefit of both the *Slavic Review* and the *CDSP*. During the 1970s such support was greatly expanded through the device of institutional membership, under which several dozen universities and other bodies gave up to two hundred dollars per year.

In its first decade the coordinating role of the association was relatively modest. It facilitated cooperation among subgroups in various disciplines, including economics, geography, history, language and literature, library science, political science, and sociology. It also encouraged the founding of regional associations, following the example of the Washington Unclassified Forum (which later became the Washington, D.C., Chapter of the AAASS) and the Far Western Slavic Conference (later renamed the Western Slavic Association), which met first in 1959. The Midwest Slavic Conference gathered first in 1962, as did the Southern Conference on Slavic Studies and the Bi-State (Kansas-Missouri) Slavic Conference (later renamed the Central Slavic Conference). In 1963 came the Southwestern AAASS, now called the Southwestern Association for Slavic Studies. The Northeastern Slavic Conference, now called the New England Slavic Association, began in 1967, whereas the Rocky Mountain Association for Slavic Studies began in 1968. (The other main regional association, the Mid-Atlantic Slavic Conference, started up only in the mid-1970s). These regional associations usually held meetings yearly, whereas the association held its first two national meetings in 1964 and 1967.

With the decade of the 1970s came a great increase in activities and responsibilities, made possible in large part by funds from the Ford Foundation. The AAASS assumed responsibility for the *CDSP*, which moved from New York to Columbus at almost the same time as the AAASS headquarters moved from Champaign-Urbana to Columbus. The secretaryship, which had simply been carried by a faculty member on top of other full-time university duties, became an executive secretaryship calling for a faculty member on 50 percent released time. The office staff was expanded. The national convention became an annual affair, the number of sessions multiplied greatly, and the number of participants at individual conventions tripled and quadrupled to well over one thousand. The *Newsletter*, which had appeared only twice yearly, soon was being published more often during the year, and it became a uniquely important channel of communication within the field, bringing together various disciplines, regional groupings, and types of organizations. In short order the association developed a network of committees to perform various services for the field. The impact of these committees has been extensive in such realms as bibliography and documentation, publications, and especially research and development, for which help came from the Ford Foundation, the U.S. Office of Education, the National Endowment for the Humanities, the International Communications Agency, and the Department of State. The association developed a broader publications program, including teaching materials that it was hoped would enable the association to become self-supporting. But the difficulties were many, and the number of members did not expand sufficiently to meet the need.

In the late 1970s and early 1980s, still with help from the Ford Foundation, the association has been passing through a difficult period of retrenchment. Its scholarly and professional services continue to be highly valued, however, and the loyalty of its core members and institutions remains strong.

The AAASS elects the customary institutional officers; it conducts its business from an office, headed by an executive secretary, presently located in Stanford, California.

For further information, see the publications of the AAASS discussed above, particularly the *AAASS Newsletter*. See also a 217-page manuscript history of the AAASS, from its origin to 1969, by Ralph T. Fisher, Jr.

RALPH T. FISHER, JR.

AMERICAN ASSOCIATION FOR THE ADVANCEMENT OF THE HUMANITIES (AAAH).†

A new initiative to strengthen and advance the humanities was the idea of James M. Banner, Jr., associate professor of history at Princeton University. The immediate stimulus was the crisis over the chairmanship of the National Endowment for the Humanities (NEH) in 1976 and 1977. President Gerald R. Ford's renomination of the endowment's chairman, Ronald S. Berman, had failed to win approval in Congress, and President Jimmy Carter's initial efforts to fill the post had been equally unsuccessful. What troubled Banner and others was that the politics of the appointment were obscured from public view and that individual humanists, whom the outcome would most affect, possessed few means to influence it. More important, the issues raised by the NEH controversy seemed symptomatic of other problems facing the humanities. According to the AAAH prospectus, these difficulties included

the uncertain levels of public and private support for humanistic scholarship and for the teaching and dissemination of humanistic knowledge; the erosion of the humanities and of the teaching of literacy in the schools; the lack of information available to humanists about the policies of public and private institutions which affect their work; and the absence of effective organization among humanists generally.

Banner conceived of founding an organization to confront these problems. In his view, individual humanists needed to be brought together behind common efforts. They needed a forum for communication and for unified undertakings that cut across disciplinary lines. And they needed an organization that would be responsive to, and representative of, the national community of professional and lay people who wished to advance the cause of the humanities.

Yet, unlike scientists, humanists had no general membership organiza-

---

†Reprinted, with changes, from Theodore K. Rabb, "American Association for the Advancement of the Humanities," *Humanities Report* 1, no. 1, by permission of the American Association for the Advancement of the Humanities.

tion. Existing scholarly and professional groups, like the American Council of Learned Societies* (ACLS), were composed of constituent institutions; and they had not tried to provide information on the humanities or to organize humanists effectively.

In the spring of 1976, Banner and his Princeton colleague, Professor of History Theodore K. Rabb, began to plan an organization in which humanists—regardless of field, institution, or type of work—would combine for purposes common to them all. As their ideas took shape, two existing groups influenced them. The first was Common Cause, on whose national governing board Banner served. This public affairs lobby had proved to be a highly effective national membership organization. The second was the American Association for the Advancement of Science* (AAAS), which provides a wide range of services to the scientific community.

After seeking the advice of other academic humanists, senior officials of the NEH, and officers of related organizations, such as the Smithsonian Institution,* Banner and Rabb prepared the AAAH planning document in November, 1977. The purposes of AAAH, it stated, would be "to promote the interests of the humanities in the United States and to foster greater public understanding of the importance of the humanities in American life." To achieve these goals, the AAAH would keep its membership informed about policies and actions of government agencies and educational and research institutions at all levels. It would promote, both among humanists and the wider public, a better awareness of achievements in the humanities. And it would foster cohesion and purpose among those devoted to the advancement of the humanities in general, beyond the individual disciplines.

In addition, they decided that the AAAH would undertake initially the following activities:

— publication of *Humanities Report* as a source of information and analysis;
— representation of the humanities before governmental agencies and other institutions, within the limits of laws governing the activities of charitable and educational tax-exempt organizations;
— sponsorship of conferences, research projects, and reports to explore major issues facing the humanities; and
— establishment of better links with the press and with appropriate groups in such fields as medicine, science, industry, and the law.

On October 11, 1977, the initial AAAH board of directors—composed of Banner, Rabb, and John W. Shumaker, professor of classics and dean of humanities and fine arts at the State University of New York at Albany— filed its papers of incorporation in the District of Columbia.

The board held its first meeting in New York City on November 10, 1977. During the following six months, the Exxon Education Foundation, the Ford Foundation, the Rockefeller Foundation, and the Dyson-Kissner Corporation of New York announced grants totaling $125,000 to underwrite the AAAH's development. As a result, it was able to inaugurate full-scale activities in January, 1979, by opening an office at 918 Sixteenth Street, N.W., in Washington, D.C., launching a membership drive, and beginning regular publication of *Humanities Report*.

By 1980, its board of directors had grown to fifteen members. In addition to Banner, Rabb, and Shumaker, they were Shirley S. Abrahamson, justice, Supreme Court of Wisconsin; Daniel Callahan, director, Institute of Society, Ethics and the Life Sciences, the Hastings Center,* Martha E. Church, president, Hood College; Louise George Clubb, professor of comparative literature, University of California at Berkeley; Douglas M. Knight, director and president, Questar Corporation; Leslie Koltai, chancellor, Los Angeles Community College District; Robert Kotlowitz, vice-president and director of programming, WNET/Thirteen in New York; Harry McPherson, attorney, Verner, Liipfert, Bernhard and McPherson; Edmund D. Pellegrino, president, The Catholic University of America; Patricia M. Spacks, professor of English, Yale University; Robert Wedgeworth, executive director, American Library Association; and Aubrey L. Williams, professor of English, University of Florida.

The first annual meeting of the organization was held in Washington, D.C., in March, 1980. Over 450 humanists—university and college professors, secondary school teachers, librarians, independent scholars, and cultural administrators—participated in the two days of meetings, which were designed to assess the condition of the humanities nationally and to begin shaping a unified public identity for humanists.

For further information, see the *Humanities Report*, published by the AAAH.

THEODORE K. RABB

AMERICAN ASSOCIATION OF ANATOMISTS (AAA). Anatomical research was not well developed in the United States prior to the twentieth century. Although there had always been a few competent anatomists at the older universities and hospitals, the spread of proprietary medical schools discouraged such research and left the teaching of anatomy primarily to practical surgeons. The movement for reform in this and other areas of medical education was dramatically accelerated in 1910 by the famous Abraham Flexner report on the condition of U.S. medical schools. The American Association of Anatomists (AAA) was an integral part of this reform because of the role it played in building up research and teaching in the anatomical aspects of medicine and medical education.

Called the Association of American Anatomists until 1908, the AAA was set up by a group of anatomists attending a meeting of the Congress of American Physicians and Surgeons held on September 17, 1888, at Georgetown University, Washington, D.C. The association and the congress were affiliated until 1906.

The founders of the organization were primarily surgeons and practical teachers with little experience in research, but they were interested in improving teaching as part of the reform movement. The association was strengthened, moreover, by a number of young men trained in Europe, who wanted to make anatomy a scientific discipline rather than primarily an aid to medical and surgical practice. Thus, they encouraged AAA members to conduct research in cytology, genetics, hematology, and other fields having a morphological basis. Those who led in this development occupied prominent positions in the early history of the AAA. Joseph Leidy, one of the outstanding scientists of his day and professor of anatomy at the University of Pennsylvania, was the first president of the association. Franklin P. Mall of Johns Hopkins University, who replaced long lectures and demonstrations on anatomy with guided dissections, Charles S. Minot of Harvard University, renowned for his work in embryology, and many others of equal eminence served as AAA presidents.

Such men took an active part in organizing the Wistar Institute of Anatomy and Biology* in Philadelphia, which during the first half of the twentieth century was a center of the new spirit in anatomy. Founded in the first decades of the nineteenth century by Professor Caspar Wistar of the University of Pennsylvania, the Wistar Institute was until the 1890s primarily a museum of anatomical specimens. At that time, Professor Wistar's grandnephew, General Isaac Jones Wistar, set up endowments, eventually totaling over three million dollars, which provided the means for an expanded range of activities, including the establishment of research laboratories. Significantly, of the ten members of an advisory board created by the Wistar Institute in 1905, eight were anatomists.

The Wistar Institute had played an important role in the publications of the AAA. The *American Journal of Anatomy* and the *Anatomical Record*, which began publication in 1901 and 1906, respectively, were founded by AAA members to provide information about anatomists and present their research findings. These journals were initially published under the auspices of the Anatomical Journal Trust, a holding organization with three anatomists acting as trustees. In 1908 the two journals were leased to the Wistar Institute and eventually conveyed to it outright. The trust was continued as a memorial to Professor Minot, however, and was not finally wound up until 1948, when its funds were turned over to the AAA. From 1908 until 1980, the Wistar Institute has been the primary media for the publication of American anatomical research. Control of scientific policy and choice of editors, however, always resided in the AAA. In 1980, the Wistar Institute sold eight of the ten journals it had been publishing to Alan R. Liss, Inc. Liss will also publish the other two, namely the anatomical journals, but with Wistar retaining title to them for a ten-year period, after which the titles revert to the AAA. This arrangement has relieved the AAA of the financial and routine editorial burdens associated with publication.

From its founding until 1919, the AAA usually held its annual meetings during the last week in December. At that time they were shifted to the spring of the year. The meetings have been held in all sections of the country and include the usual presentation of papers and demonstrations, transaction of business, including election of officers, and social intercourse among the members. Attendance at these meetings in the past ten years has averaged about seventeen hundred persons. AAA membership is open to persons working in anatomical or cognate sciences who possess the M.D. or Ph.D. or their equivalent and who have engaged in research and published on an anatomical subject. The policy of electing to membership persons distinguished in a cognate field has been followed from the beginning; such members include surgeons, pathologists, zoologists, physiologists, and anthropologists. Honorary members from abroad have been included from time to time. Because of its selective policy, growth has been slow but steady, and the association now numbers approximately twenty-eight hundred members.

The AAA elects the customary institutional officers; it conducts its business from a secretary-treasurer's office located in Richmond, Virginia.

For further information, see the publications of the AAA discussed above, particularly Nicholas A. Michels, "The American Association of Anatomists, A Tribute and Brief History," *Anatomical Record* (1955).

AMERICAN ASSOCIATION OF ECONOMIC ENTOMOLOGISTS. See Entomological Society of America.

AMERICAN ASSOCIATION OF IMMUNOLOGISTS (AAI). Dr. Martin J. Synnott conceived the idea in 1912 of founding a Society of Vaccine Therapists, whose membership would include those who had worked under Sir Almroth E. Wright, Saint Mary's Hospital, London. Others who had worked in equally famous European laboratories were also invited to join, and the name of the proposed organization was changed to the more inclusive "American Association of Immunologists." A meeting was held in May of 1913, in Washington, D.C., followed by one on June 19, 1913, in Minneapolis, which marked the creation of the AAI with about fifty charter members. At a meeting in Atlantic City on June 22 of the following year, the details of organization were completed. It was at this meeting, too, that mention was made of Dr. Arthur F. Coca's plans to set up a *Journal of Immunology* modeled after the German *Zeitschrift für Immunitätsforschung*. The AAI thereupon voted that Dr. A. P. Hitchins, chairman of its governing council, be authorized to represent it in negotiations with Dr. Coca regarding the proposed journal. The AAI members believed that AAI involvement in the publication was mandatory for the association's future development. Dr. Coca had been negotiating publication arrangements with the Williams and Wilkins Company of Baltimore, and a representative of that publishing firm, together with Dr. Hitchins and other AAI members, plus Dr. Coca, then president of the New York Society of Serology and Hematology, and several members of that society, were present at a conference held in New York City on October 7, 1915. Those present agreed that the two societies would sponsor an official publication to be named the *Journal of Immunology*. Parenthetically, the New York society was soon superseded by the AAI, and its members voted, in 1920, to dissolve and transfer its assets to the AAI.

Publication of the *Journal of Immunology* was begun in 1916, and it continued to be issued under that name down to 1944, when it became the *Journal of Immunology, Virus-Research, and Experimental Chemotherapy*. Although intended to be more indicative of the scope of the journal, the new name proved so unwieldy that it was eventually changed back to the original and present *Journal of Immunology*. Dr. Coca was appointed the initial managing editor and served in that capacity, under varying title, until 1948.

The *Journal* has undoubtedly been the major achievement of the AAI. It has provided a medium for scientists in serology, virology, epidemology, immunochemistry, and other immunological fields to publish their findings. The *Journal* has expanded significantly since its founding, particularly in the 1970s. In 1979, for example, it published 884 articles for a total of 5,650 pages.

Annual meetings have been another medium for communication among AAI members. They were held jointly with the New York Society for Serology and Hematology until 1918, and with the American Association of Pathologists and Bacteriologists* (AAPB) until 1939. The AAI has met jointly with the Federation of American Societies for Experimental Biology* (FASEB) since 1940, two years prior to becoming a member of FASEB in 1942.

Active membership in the AAI is open to scientists with a record of published research in some aspect of immunology. It is of interest to note that a bylaw of the 1927 AAI constitution, since revised, provided that the failure of a member to submit a research paper for presentation at the annual meeting at least once in three years would be tantamount to resignation. Its growth, therefore, has been selective and gradual, its membership presently numbering about three thousand.

The AAI elects the customary institutional officers, together with a council of five, and conducts its business from a secretary-treasurer's office located at FASEB headquarters in Bethesda, Maryland.

For further information, see the publications of the AAI discussed above, particularly Geoffrey Edsall, "What Is Immunology," *Journal of Immunology* (1951). See also an unpublished historical summary of the *Journal of Immunology* by A. F. Coca.

AMERICAN ASSOCIATION OF PATHOLOGISTS, INC. (AAP). This learned society resulted from the 1976 merger of two older organizations:

the American Association of Pathologists and Bacteriologists (AAPB), founded in 1901, and the American Society for Experimental Pathology (ASEP), founded in 1913. From their beginnings the interests of many of the members of the two societies overlapped, and they had often held meetings at the same time and place. Despite this and despite discussions of amalgamation from the 1930s onward, the two pursued their separate courses until 1976. A history of the AAP is, to this point therefore, the two relatively separate histories of the AAPB and ASEP presented below.

The older of the two predecessor societies, the AAPB, was founded in 1901. The association grew out of a desire on the part of a number of members of the Association of American Physicians for the formation of a society devoted to experimental science as represented by pathology and bacteriology. Although there was a significant cleavage in the association on the matter, opposition being based on the grounds that the proposed society would duplicate and weaken existing ones, Drs. William T. Councilman and Harold C. Ernst took the lead in seeking support from some forty colleagues for the proposed organization. Subsequently, an organizational meeting was held on April 30, 1900, in Washington, D.C. At this meeting, attended by some fifteen persons, a motion was passed calling for the drafting of a constitution creating a new society. At a follow-up meeting, held in New York City on January 26, 1901, the constitution calling for the creation of the AAPB was adopted; officers were elected, Dr. Councilman, president, and Dr. Ernst, secretary; and a governing council was named.

The first scheduled meeting of the new AAPB, held in Boston on April 5 and 6, 1901, resulted in discussions about an official journal. Secretary Ernst proposed and it was approved that the *Journal of the Boston Society of Medical Sciences*, of which he was editor, be changed to the *Journal of Medical Research* and be made the official AAPB publication. This *Journal*, with most of its financial support coming from the AAPB, remained its official publication until 1924, when it was superseded by the AAPB's monthly, the *American Journal of Pathology*. These journals contain papers and reports on pathology and bacteriology, and the proceedings of the annual meetings of the association, together with other news about it and its members.

The "Path and Bac," as it was familiarly called by its members, engaged in only a few joint operations with other societies, such as the Congress of Physicians and Surgeons, until its disbandment in 1942; it did not affiliate with other organizations and did not engage in any licensing or evaluation activities. Nevertheless, the AAPB endorsed certain measures that it thought would benefit the pathological and bacteriological sciences. In 1938, for instance, it recommended passage of a bill by Congress that would have provided adequate housing for the Army Medical Museum and Library, and in 1946 it sent a representative before a congressional committee to support appropriations for the Army Institute of Pathology.

The reluctance to engage in joint operations, however, never extended to AAPB annual meetings. They were often held in conjunction with other scientific societies, such as the American Association of Immunologists* (AAI), and, although the Path and Bac never became a member of the Federation of American Societies for Experimental Biology* (FASEB), meetings were usually scheduled immediately prior to or after those of the FASEB. In the early decades meetings were usually held where a medical school, rather than a hotel or resort, could be host. Later, they were held in larger cities with adequate facilities for an enlarged membership and expanded programs. Such meetings were held all over the United States and several times in Canada. Portions of these meetings were usually devoted to some particular debate-evoking topic, thus, appropriately, calling for a referee, designated later as moderator and chairman, at the meetings.

The AAPB established the unusual and highly personalized Gold-Headed Cane Award in 1919. It was patterned on a similar award made since the eighteenth century by the Royal College of Physicians in London. Initially, the gold-headed cane was awarded Dr. Ernst, in recognition of his long service as secretary, with the provision that upon his death or relinquishment the cane would revert to the AAPB for further award. Over twenty-five men, all distinguished scientists, have been the proud possessors of the cane, now being awarded annually.

In 1972, a new annual award was established: the Rous-Whipple Award for the most significant contribution for the year in biomedical research in pathology.

Membership in the AAPB rested upon nomination by two members accompanied by the presentation of evidence of creditable research in pathology or bacteriology and an indication of continuing productivity. Proposals to create honorary or other types of membership were consistently rejected. Although membership was open to foreigners, they were required to have spent a significant period of study in the United States and to meet all other requirements for membership. Partially as a consequence, the growth in membership was slow but steady, and by the time of the merger membership totaled only about thirteen hundred. The AAPB's roster at that time, however, included most of the outstanding pathologists and bacteriologists of the country.

The American Society for Experimental Pathology (ASEP), the other predecessor of the AAP, was organized at the turn of the century by a small group of scientists who recognized the growing importance of experimental procedures in the field of pathology. The initiative in the formation of a society to develop such aspects of pathology was taken by Drs. Richard M. Pearce and S. J. Meltzer. In 1913, shortly after the FASEB had been founded, these two, who believed that a society devoted to experimental pathology should be established for inclusion in the FASEB, wrote to seven of their colleagues urging it, and, following their initial approval, an additional sixteen pathologists of note were invited to become, with the original nine, charter members of the proposed society. Subsequently, in a meeting at the Hygienic Laboratory of the U.S. Public Health Service in May, 1913, ASEP was founded, and Dr. Pearce was elected its first president.

The ASEP constitution stated that its object was "to bring the productive investigators in pathology, working essentially by experimental methods, in closer affiliation with the workers in other fields of experimental medicine." It was agreed that membership should be restricted initially to forty persons, and it was not until 1924 that it was opened more widely to experimental pathologists. From that time on, membership increased to about three hundred in 1946, approximately seven hundred in 1963, and about fifteen hundred at the time of merger with the AAPB.

In 1913, ASEP applied for and was admitted to membership in FASEB, and it held annual meetings as a constituent member of the latter. Many of the papers presented there have been published in abstract form in the FASEB *Proceedings*. In 1956 the *A.M.A. [American Medical Association] Archives of Pathology* became the official journal of the ASEP. In the same year the society established the Parke-Davis Award, to be conferred annually for meritorious work in experimental pathology.

Sentiment, however, snowballed for the establishment of ASEP's own scientific journal; by 1967, a poll of members showed that 69 percent of the seven hundred members responding favored such a move. This development dovetailed with the often discussed (as early as the 1930s) merger with the AAPB and the concomitant probability of making its *American Journal of Pathology* the official organ of a united organization. Thus, at the April, 1969, annual meeting, the ASEP did indeed accept an offer to cosponsor the *Journal* with the AAPB, and this action was a material factor leading to the eventual outright merger of the two societies seven years later.

Under the terms of the merger, all of the members of either organization became members of the AAP, active, honorary, or emeritus, and the combined membership now totals about twenty-one hundred. Because the ASEP was already a member of the FASEB and both organizations wanted to retain it, for this and other legal reasons, the AAPB was legally affiliated with the ASEP in a new AAP. In any case, following the setting-up of the new organization, it was decided that some of the offices would be shared until 1980. As a result, for example, there were copresidents for the year 1976-1977. The various awards of the two predecessor organizations were also taken over in their entirety and have continued to be conferred by the AAP.

The AAP elects the customary institutional officers; it conducts its business from an office, headed by an executive officer, located in the FASEB buildings in Bethesda, Maryland.

For further information, see the following detailed and interpretative histories by Dr. Esmond R. Long, a noted pathologist as well as historian of science, *A History of Pathology* (1965), *History of the American Society*

some have been held in conjunction with the meetings of the American Association for the Advancement of Science* (AAAS). Attendance at the present time ranges from five hundred to seven hundred persons.

Accelerating developments in specialized subfields of astronomy have made it necessary to establish divisions of the American Astronomical Society. The divisions of Planetary Astronomy, High Energy Astrophysics, and Solar Astronomy were formed in 1969. The Division of Dynamical Astronomy followed in 1970, and the Historical Astronomy Division in 1980. The divisions provide a structure and organization for areas that encompass more than one discipline. They meet at least once a year, often in conjunction with meetings of the parent society. In addition, the divisions take turns providing invited speakers to summarize their field to the full meetings of the society.

The AAS maintains its national headquarters in Washington, D.C., and holds biannual meetings. Principal officers include the president, two past presidents, two vice-presidents, secretary, treasurer, an education officer, and an executive officer located at the national headquarters. A council is composed of the above officials plus nine other councillors. The present membership of the AAS is about four thousand.

For further information, see the monthly *Astronomical Journal* and the quarterly *Bulletin* published by the AAS. The origin and early history, together with a detailed discussion of the astronomical context in which the society was founded, is described in Richard E. Berendzen, "Origins of the American Astronomical Society," *Physics Today* (December, 1974). See also Dean B. McLaughlin, "The American Astronomical Society," *AAAS Bulletin* (October, 1943); Joel Stebbins, "The American Astronomical Society, 1897-1947," *Popular Astronomy* (October, 1947); and Dirk Brouwer, "One Hundred Years: 1849-1949," *Astronomical Journal* (December, 1949).

AMERICAN CHEMICAL SOCIETY (ACS). This learned society was founded in 1876. Prior to that year and coincidentally with a similar development abroad, two relatively short-lived local chemical societies had been formed in Philadelphia during the late eighteenth and early nineteenth centuries.

Discussion as to the desirability of forming a truly national chemical society took place at an 1874 meeting of seventy-seven chemists in Northumberland, Pennsylvania, to celebrate the centennial of Priestley's discovery of oxygen. Those present failed to act, however, because several participants doubted that there were or would be enough chemists in the United States to support a society devoted solely to chemists, and many thought that chemists would be better served by establishing stronger representation in the American Association for the Advancement of Science* (AAAS), in which that same year a subsection devoted solely to chemistry had been established. Parenthetically, by 1882 the membership of this subsection had grown to such dimensions that it was made a full section, one of three in existence at that time.

In the meantime, a group of New York chemists who had attended the Priestley celebration, rejecting the notion of a local society, in 1876 had founded a national ACS with 80 of its 133 organizing members living outside the New York City area. By the 1880s, however, dissatisfaction over difficulties encountered by non-New Yorkers in attending meetings and alleged dominance of societal affairs by New Yorkers resulted in a sharp drop in ACS membership. More important was the outright secession of Washington, D.C., members in 1884, and their creation of a Chemical Society of Washington. Also, a movement to found a rival and more definitely national society was started. These developments led to the adoption of a new ACS constitution in 1890, which provided for meetings to be held outside New York (the first was held that year in Newport, Rhode Island) and for the establishment of reasonably autonomous local sections. The reorganized society thus began operation in 1892 with sections in New York, Rhode Island, Cincinnati, and, in 1893, Washington D.C. The New York charter of the society was retained until 1937, when the U.S. Seventy-Fifth Congress gave it a national charter.

Over the years the ACS has stimulated interest in the field of chemistry by the creation or administration of more than thirty awards and medals in various areas of chemistry. More than eighty awards and annual lectures in chemistry have been established by ACS sections and divisions. In the 1920s prize essay contests in chemistry were held under ACS auspices, and the ACS bought and distributed chemistry books of interest to the general reader to various libraries. Thus, from its early days the society has had a substantial program in education. Particularly important in recent years has been its work in continuing education for chemists and chemical engineers, through its ACS short courses and related audio, film, and correspondence interaction courses. A related ACS program is the administration of more than $5.8 million each year in grants and fellowships for basic research, principally through income from the Petroleum Research Fund, a charitable scientific and educational trust set up in 1944.

World Wars I and II saw the ACS offering its services to the government in various consultative capacities. In large part due to the activities of the society, the Chemical Warfare Service was established as a unit of the U.S. Army, and in recognition the service adopted the society's colors, cobalt blue and gold, as its own.

National meetings of the society, held semiannually since 1890, usually take place in the spring and fall. They have been convened in various parts of the United States. Society business is transacted, members form contacts with one another, and scientific papers and demonstrations are presented at the meetings. Attendance has increased year by year, and registrations of ten thousand persons or more are not unusual.

Publication by the American Chemical Society has been a primary accomplishment. The foundation of its present-day huge publishing program was the *Journal of the American Chemical Society*. Under its present name and ownership this publication dates from 1879, when it succeeded the *Proceedings of the American Chemical Society*, which for a time had appeared as a section of a privately owned publication that failed in 1877. In a reorganization of 1892-1893, Dr. Edward Hart merged his own *Journal of Analytical and Applied Chemistry* with the *Journal of the American Chemical Society* and assumed the editorship of the merged *Journal*, a post he held until 1901. The 1893 volume was the first of the merged *Journal*, and it has been published continuously since that date. Since this original venture the society's list of publications has grown to seventeen journals, four magazines, a single-article announcement service, and two divisional publications. The ACS also has an extensive program of secondary publications, *Chemical Abstracts*, and the numerous related services that now make up what is called the Chemical Abstracts Service. The latter (its annual budget in 1980 was in excess of thirty-four million dollars) is generally agreed to be a disciplinary model and provides indispensable research materials for chemists throughout the world.

Since 1919, the ACS has been a leader in efforts to increase public understanding of science. The ACS News Service, established in that year, was the first such staff unit to be sponsored by a scientific society in the United States. Today, through its Office of Public Relations, which includes the news service, the ACS conducts a broad program of public information, including a radio series broadcast each week by some five hundred stations.

From 1896 to 1912, except in 1907, the ACS held joint summer meetings with the AAAS in addition to its own meetings, usually in December. The latter arrangement with the AAAS proved satisfactory until 1912, when the difficulty of finding suitable accommodations for the members of the two groups and dissatisfaction on the part of some society members with the time of meeting of the AAAS caused a discontinuance of the arrangement.

Membership in the society has expanded to about 110,000 persons, making it the largest U.S. learned society devoted to a single discipline. Membership, as either a member or an associate member, is open to all persons with an adequate background of education and experience in chemistry, chemical engineering, or a closely related field.

One of the principal reasons for the growth in membership of the American Chemical Society appears to be that the national organization has been able to provide its 178 local sections, located in every state and in the District of Columbia and Puerto Rico, with a feeling of unity and solidarity. Of equal importance is the ACS's success in bridging the chasm that traditionally divides pure and applied chemical scientists in other countries. This accomplishment has been attributed to the foresight of Dr. Marston T. Bogert, president of the ACS in 1907-1908, who foresaw that the society would disintegrate unless some method were devised whereby chemical specialists could gather in essentially autonomous units. Accordingly, he instituted the ACS divisional system, which provides for a great deal of autonomy for each division within the societal structure. During Dr. Bogert's presidency there were five divisions established within the ACS; by 1926 there were seventeen; today there are thirty-one.

The ACS elects the customary institutional officers. A staff, headed by an executive director, conducts its business from an impressive eight-story building in Washington, D.C.

For further information, there are thorough and extensive accounts of the ACS. It has been fortunate in that its leaders have always had a deep sense of and interest in ACS history. Each twenty-five years since its founding has seen the preparation of an official and detailed history. Beginning with a "Twenty-Fifth Anniversary Number," *Proceedings of the American Chemical Society* (1902); there followed Charles A. Browne, ed., "A Half-Century of Chemistry in America," *Journal of the American Chemical Society, Special Issue* (1926)); Charles A. Browne and Mary Elvira Weeks, *A History of the American Chemical Society, Seventy-Five Eventful Years* (1952); and Herman Skolnik and Kenneth M. Reese, *A Century of Chemistry* (1976). In the same year a centennial issue of *Chemical and Engineering News* (April, 1976), was published containing articles dealing with the historical development of chemistry in the United States over a hundred-year period. See also "The American Chemical Society," *AAAS Bulletin* (April, 1943); and *American Chemical Society in Brief*, a leaflet, undated, describing present-day activities of the ACS.

AMERICAN COMPARATIVE LITERATURE ASSOCIATION (ACLA). This learned society was organized in 1960 to strengthen and support the study and teaching of comparative literature in American colleges and universities. Since 1962 it has held triennial meetings at Columbia University (1962), Harvard University (1965), Indiana University (1968), Yale University (1971), University of Southern California (1974), University of Illinois (1977), and University of North Carolina, Chapel Hill (1980). The ACLA also holds annual meetings in conjunction with those of the Modern Language Association of America* (MLA), as well as special meetings.

The official publication of the ACLA is the ACLA *Newsletter*, and news and notices about its affairs are published therein. Three other publications having the active support of ACLA membership are *Comparative Literature, Comparative Literature Studies*, and the *Yearbook of Comparative and General Literature*. The ACLA also publishes directories and other special publications and helps to support the International Comparative Literature Association, in conjunction with which it has been engaged in several extensive international projects.

The ACLA has a membership of approximately seven hundred, the overwhelming majority being scholars in institutions of higher learning in the United States and abroad.

The ACLA elects the customary institutional officers; it conducts its business from an office, headed by a secretary-treasurer, located in Binghamton, New York.

For further information, see the publications of the ACLA discussed above. See also "New Constituent Society: American Comparative Literature Association," *ACLS Newsletter* (Winter, 1974).

AMERICAN COUNCIL OF LEARNED SOCIETIES (ACLS). The American Council of Learned Societies was organized shortly after World War I by twelve learned societies: American Philosophical Society* (APS), American Academy of Arts and Sciences,* American Antiquarian Society* (AAS), American Oriental Society,* American Philological Association* (APA), Archaeological Institute of America* (AIA), Modern Language Association of America* (MLA), American Historical Association* (AHA), American Economic Association* (AEA), American Philosophical Association* (APA), American Political Science Association* (APSA), and American Sociological Association* (ASA).

The initiative in calling the organizational meeting in Boston for September 19, 1919, rested with officials of the American Academy of Arts and Sciences and the AHA. The immediate purpose of the organization was to provide representation in the Union Académique Internationale (International Union of Academies [UAI]) in the absence of an official organization, similar to a European academy, to represent the United States abroad. It was this absence of such an organization and the many attendant difficulties facing any attempt to form one that resulted in the plan for creating a federative council from among existing organizations.

From its original list of twelve societies, the ACLS has periodically added others to its roster. By 1960 it was composed of thirty constituent societies, and by 1980 this number had reached forty-three. Membership, however, has always been highly selective, requiring a three-fourths vote of all ACLS members at an annual meeting. Although the ACLS has taken discrete initiative on some occasions, a requisite for application by nonmember organizations has always included extensive dossiers outlining the history, purpose, membership, publications, and financial condition, plus extensive discussions with ACLS officials. A 1977 six-point policy statement on criteria for admission states, as the first point:

1. A constituent society should have substantial humanist interests and should be concerned with a reasonably broad field of study. New societies should not be admitted if they are concerned with areas in which existing constituent societies are actively and productively interested, or if their individual members are predominantly included in the membership of one or more constituent members. A new society must demonstrate not only that it has a different intellectual focus or interdisciplinary concern but also that it represents an important and well populated field of study.

Additional points postulate that a prospective member should be national in membership, concerned with research, include a substantial proportion of scholars, and be able to demonstrate that it is stable and active.

The ACLS originally consisted of two delegates from each of the constituent societies, but in 1946-1947 a revision of the bylaws reduced the number of delegates from two to one. Also, a board of directors, consisting of twelve members, since 1957 enlarged to thirteen, was created as a part of the ACLS and voted broad powers to manage the funds and affairs of the ACLS. The board, which holds four meetings a year, has developed a continuity of policy based on the needs of the ACLS and the humanities as a whole rather than the sometimes differing interests of the individual societies. The delegates from the constituent member societies have always been named on the basis of criteria established by the societies. Members of the board of directors and its officers are elected by the delegates.

In addition to the representation described above, a conference of secretaries or executive officers of the constituent societies has regularly met at the time of the annual meeting of the ACLS, as well as holding a separate meeting in the fall. The secretaries consider the many problems of mutual concern to the societies, particularly those involved in the operation of respective executive offices, exchange ideas, and report the results of their deliberations to the ACLS for needed action.

In 1967 the council's bylaws were amended to make the annual dues of each constituent society dependent upon size and resources. Thus, in some cases, dues jumped from $300 to $2,000 annually, which led to a substantial overall increase of funding from this source. This change was part of the council's "Fiftieth Anniversary Campaign" (1919-1969), which had as its major goal the raising of $5 million toward endowment. By February, 1970, the goal had been reached. Approximately $2.5 million came from newly created "associates": universities, colleges, and research libraries. These associates, now numbering about one hundred, have continued to provide support to the ACLS of about $150,000 annually. The ACLS's current programs, however, are still chiefly supported by foundations and federal agencies, notably the Ford Foundation, Andrew W. Mellon Foundation, Carnegie Corporation of New York, and the National Endowment for the Humanities.

From its beginnings, the ACLS has continued to represent American humanists internationally by providing two delegates to the annual meetings of the UAI. Numerous collaborative ventures have been carried on under UAI auspices. Prior to the 1960s they were generally concerned with European classical antiquity and its projection into the Middle Ages. Since then, a number of projects have been launched that are non-European in scope and interest. In addition, the promotion of humanistic studies in the United States became one of the ACLS's major concerns at an early period. The outstanding results of this activity were the publication of the *Dictionary of American Biography* (DAB), the fifth supplement of which appeared in 1977; the *Linguistic Atlas of New England* (the published portion of the *Linguistic Atlas of the United States and Canada*); and various grants-in-aid and research programs in the humanities.

In the 1930s the ACLS laid the groundwork for the study of Eastern Europe, the Middle East, and the Far East that was to prove so valuable to the United States in World War II. When this national emergency arose, the ACLS was prepared to make a unique contribution by identifying the linguistic, intelligence, and other specialists necessary for the prosecution of war in areas totally unfamiliar to all but a very few Americans. In addition, the ACLS aided in devising procedures to train other persons as specialists in these areas in the shortest possible period of time.

Since the 1950s, the major fellowship and research programs conducted by the ACLS have been fellowships and grants-in-aid for the work of individual humanistic scholars; the operation of about ten joint committees with other learned organizations, particularly the Social Science Research Council* (SSRC), such as the Joint Committee for Scholarly Communication with the People's Republic of China; a Program of Travel Grants for Participation in International Congresses and Conferences Abroad; an American Studies Program, whose original aim was the promotion of the "record and study of American culture in the universities of Free Europe" and later expanded to other parts of the globe; the administration and funding, since 1968, of the International Research and Exchanges Board (IREX); and, since 1971, the administrative and fiscal responsibility for the Universities Service Center in Hong Kong.

In line with its earlier and continuing sponsorship of the *Dictionary of American Biography*, the ACLS has undertaken additional publication ventures. Work on a *Dictionary of Scientific Biography* was launched in 1965. This fifteen-volume work detailing the careers and accomplishments of scientists in all periods of history and all areas of the world was completed in 1978. The National Enquiry into the Production and Dissemination of Scholarly Knowledge, sponsored by the ACLS from 1976 to 1979, conducted an investigation of all aspects of the publication and dissemination of humanistic scholarship and in 1979 presented a report of its findings and recommendations entitled *Scholarly Communication: The Report of the National Enquiry* (1979).

Probably the greatest achievement of the ACLS in the 1960s and 1970s was the catalytic role it played in the founding of the National Endowment for the Humanities and its subsequent support of that federal agency. At the 1962 ACLS annual meeting, the following resolution was adopted:

Resolved, That this Council very strongly urges that the Federal Government, in the national interest and for the strengthening of our scholarly intellectual resources on the broadest possible front, extend its support of higher education and research to include all the humanities and social sciences on the same basis as mathematics, the natural sciences, and technology.

The ACLS's concern over this lack of federal aid for the humanities and social sciences had been growing for several years prior to 1962. Concern for our scientific prowess, in the wake of the 1958 Soviet launching of Sputnik, witnessed the creation of the National Aeronautics and Space Administration (NASA), increased funding for the National Science Foundation (NSF), and the passage of the National Defense Education Act (NDEA). Except for NDEA support for foreign languages, however, the massive sums appropriated left the humanities out in the cold. Writing in 1961, Dr. Robert M. Lumiansky, chairman of the board of directors of the ACLS from 1957 to 1974 and its current president, stated that this imbalance was perverting U.S. education and culture. The culmination of such thinking was the 1963 adoption by the ACLS of a resolution calling for the creation of a national commission that would have the mandate of making an in-depth investigation of the state of the humanities in the United States and, particularly, their relationship to the federal government. Eventually sponsored by the ACLS, the Council of Graduate Schools in the United States, and the United Chapters of Phi Beta Kappa, the twenty-member Commission on the Humanities was set up and, in 1964, issued its report. In summary, it concluded that the humanities in the United States needed a great deal of financial aid; the federal government should provide this aid in the national interest; and the creation of a National Humanities Foundation would be the most desirable institution to administer such aid. Within one year President Lyndon B. Johnson had signed a bill, in large measure a reflection of these recommendations, that brought into existence the National Foundation on the Arts and Humanities and its subsidiaries the National Endowment for the Arts and the National Endowment for the Humanities. One measure of the success of the latter is that the initial budget of $2 million became approximately $145 million by the early 1980s.

All ACLS activities have been carried on through the years by a relatively small executive staff with the help of an extensive system of committees. In recent years, as has been pointed out, there has been an increasing number of joint committees, particularly with the SSRC. Executive heads of the ACLS have included Waldo G. Leland, who assumed office in 1924 and became director emeritus in 1946, Richard K. Shryock, Cornelius Kruse, Charles E. Odegard, and Mortimer Graves. In 1957 Frederick Burkhardt was named president of the ACLS, and this change was accompanied by a shift of its headquarters from Washington, D.C., to its present location in New York City. On July 1, 1974, Dr. Robert M. Lumiansky succeeded Dr. Burkhardt and is the current president of the ACLS.

The ACLS has always had a close relationship with its member societies, having been the outgrowth of common action by a group of societies. Even though the 1946-1947 reorganization resulted in the creation of a governing board of directors that was one step removed from the elected representatives of the societies, these same representatives vote on who is elected to the board. Furthermore, from the first, the conference of secretaries of the societies met annually within the council's larger annual meeting. The conference recommends measures to the council which, although not mandatory for action by the latter body, are carefully considered and almost always acted upon. The dues paid by all societal members, particularly since the 1960s, are impressive; practically all ACLS publications have been of direct interest to one or more of its societal members; finally, it has been quite successful in aiding its member societies by interceding with the government, foundations, and other groups for financial aid for projects carried out by the individual societies rather than the ACLS.

The ACLS, which now maintains its headquarters at 800 Third Avenue, New York, New York 10022, holds annual meetings. Principal officers include a chairman, vice-chairman, secretary, treasurer, and an appointed president. The board of directors consists of the above officers plus eight other elected members.

For further information, see the quarterly *ACLS Newsletter* and the *Annual Report* published by the ACLS, particularly, "A Brief History of ACLS Activities," *ACLS Newsletter* (Spring, 1980). There is no definitive history of the ACLS. For a brief account of its founding, see Waldo G. Leland, "The International Union of Academies and the American Council of Learned Societies," *International Conciliation* (September, 1920).

AMERICAN COUNCIL ON EDUCATION (ACE). The American Council on Education is composed of institutions of higher learning, national and regional educational associations, and other organizations with educational interests. It was organized in 1918 by eleven national educational associations to coordinate the work of educational institutions and organizations during World War I. Membership has since been greatly expanded and presently includes about sixteen hundred members and affiliates in the following catagories:

Institutions: About 1,400 two- and four-year colleges, universities, and technical postsecondary schools that are nonprofit, legally authorized to grant degrees, and duly accredited.

Constituent organizations: About 60 national nonprofit associations and organizations in postsecondary education.

Associated organizations: About 110 local, state, regional, and other limited-constituency nonprofit organizations in postsecondary education; organizations that provide services to higher education but have no members as such; organizations primarily interested in elementary and secondary education; and such other nonprofit organizations as the ACE board of directors approves.

Affiliates: About 60 organizations and agencies concerned with higher education, including postsecondary institutions that are candidates for accreditation, secondary schools, libraries, education and fraternal societies, and foreign education associations.

The first three membership categories have ACE voting privileges; the affiliate category may send representatives to ACE meetings and participate in its activities in other ways but is not entitled to cast votes at annual meetings.

The ACE operates through its staff and a multitude of commissions, task forces, and five operating divisions, with memberships representing a broad cross section of the American academic community. Historically, some of these groups have been organized on an ad hoc basis for specific purposes and for relatively short periods of time. Others have had a long service. The ACE's American Youth Commission, for example, was in existence throughout most of the depression years of the 1930s, when its research and reports on the youth of that decade, particularly in regard to education, were widely acclaimed. The ACE's present-day Division of Governmental Relations has had, under varying titles, an even longer career, and it is primarily through such an entity that the ACE's unique role in governmental relations is carried out. Providing an explanation of this role, President Peltason in a 1978 memorandum to the ACE's board of directors urged:

We must strengthen and extend our influence on public policy primarily through our basic coordinating role among the associations. The Congress and the Executive Branch must be kept fully informed of the academy's views on the wide range of legislative and executive action significant to higher education. Because of increased federal regulatory activity, we must constantly monitor the government and provide it with information which will at once enhance the effectiveness of the regulations while preserving the essential qualities of our institutions.

In addition, interrelated federal and state policies and the growing involvement of state governments in college and university operations demand that we establish a capacity, working with other groups, to provide information to state policy makers as well as to our membership.

The ACE maintains a publication program which, over the years, has issued a wide range of specialized and general educational works. More recent books, for example, include *Sponsored Research Policy of Colleges and Universities* (1954), *College Law: A Guide for Administrators* (1963), and *American Universities and Colleges* (1973). Periodicals include the *Educational Record*, established in 1920, which presents articles on all phases of higher education, and *Higher Education and National Affairs*, a weekly which reports significant government, ACE, and other national activities to educational institutions and organizations.

The ACE's major concerns have always been the provision of a forum for the discussion and solution of broad educational problems; the maintenance of liaison among its members, particularly the institutional, and the federal government; and the conduct of studies and dissemination of findings bearing on these matters. During the Depression, however, there was some advocacy for the transformation of the ACE to a predominantly research institution similar to the Social Science Research Council* (SSRC). Although this did not take place, it should be noted that over the years the ACE has aided in the promotion of basic research and scholarship in the humanities and social sciences. Thus, the American Historical Association* (AHA) and the Modern Language Association of America* (MLA) have found the ACE a willing partner in some of their efforts. In 1928, for example, the ACE established a Committee on Modern Languages at the request of the MLA. Through the following decades, until its termination in 1955, this committee made a number of contributions to the solution of language problems. The ACE, moreover, has always maintained liaison with other research institutions, particularly our other national coordinating councils, the National Research Council, the American Council of Learned Societies* (ACLS), and the SSRC. The outstanding example of such cooperation among the four is the Conference Board of Associated Research Councils established by them in 1944. Membership of this board consists of two administrative officers from each of the four councils and a secretary. A major project of the board has been the activities of a Council for International Exchange of Scholars. From its organization as a then committee under board auspices in 1948 until 1975-1976, when it assumed a semi-independent status, the council cooperated with the Department of State and Board of Foreign Scholarships in an exchange of scholars program between the United States and foreign countries. This council program is now administered under ACE auspices.

The ACE has held annual meetings from its beginning. Until the 1960s they were held alternately in Washington, D.C., and Chicago. Since then they have been held in major cities all over the United States.

The governing body of the ACE is a board of directors composed of thirty-six members elected on a staggered basis and according to a specified formula from among its three categories of members. The principal officers elected or appointed by the board are a chairman, vice-chairman, secretary, treasurer, and president. The latter is the chief executive officer of the ACE. Samuel P. Capen (1919-1922), Charles R. Mann (1923-1934), George F. Zook (1934-1950), Arthur S. Adams (1951-1961), Logan Wilson (1961-1971), and Roger W. Heyns (1971-1977), have served as previous executive heads of the ACE. The present president, J. W. Peltason, has offices located in the ACE's National Center for Higher Education located at One Dupont Circle, Washington, D.C. 20036.

For further information, see *American Council on Education Today*, *Annual Reports* (1920 to date), and the *Educational Record*, published by the ACE. See also Charles G. Dobbins, *American Council on Education: Leadership and Chronology 1918-1968* (1968), and *American Council on Education: Programs and Services, 1958-1975* (1976).

AMERICAN DIALECT SOCIETY (ADS). The English Dialect Society, founded in 1873, was undoubtedly an inspiration for the establishment of a similar society in the United States. It was nearly two decades later, however, before an American Dialect Society was founded at Harvard University. Led by a group of language instructors located there, particularly Charles Hall Grandgent, Edward S. Sheldon, Francis J. Child, Lebaron R. Briggs, and George Lyman Kittredge, 28 persons were present at the organizational meeting at Harvard on March 30, 1889, wherein a constitution was adopted and officers elected. The first annual meeting was held at Sever Hall at Harvard on December 30, 1889, and there were 140 members enrolled by that time. From that time down to the present, the last week in December has been the annual meeting time for the society, in joint session with the Modern Language Association of America* (MLA). The relationship between the societies has always been close, many of the early presidents of the ADS eventually serving as president of the MLA.

A statement of purpose, issued in 1912 by then President Calvin Thomas, said that the society was organized to conduct studies of characteristics of spoken English and other nonaboriginal dialects in the United States and Canada.

The collection of materials on dialect by the ADS and its members, begun from the first, found a publication outlet in 1890 with the establishment of *Dialect Notes*. From that date until its demise in 1939, with the advent of World War II, six volumes were issued, each containing five to twenty parts, containing articles and news about the society and its members. A successor journal, *Publication of the American Dialect Society*, appeared in 1944.

Meanwhile, in 1925, *American Speech* had been founded. Although the founding editors were Louise Pound, Kemp Malone, and Arthur G. Kennedy, H. L. Mencken was referred to as the "pa" of the publication, and he is alleged to have been operating behind the scenes during the early years of the journal. By the 1970s, it had developed strong ties with the Columbia University languages faculty, was being published as a quarterly by the Columbia University Press, and had become a very important journal in the study of American English. The officers and members of the ADS had always been active in the affairs of *American Speech*, its stated purpose paralleled and overlapped that of the society, and it was certain to provide a sounder and broader base for publication than its *Publication*; so it was a happy concatenation of events that saw the ADS in 1973 assume sponsorship of *American Speech* as its official quarterly with the *Publication* becoming an occasional monograph series.

Membership of the ADS presently totals about two thousand. It elects the customary institutional officers; it conducts its business from an office, headed by an executive secretary, in Ontario, Canada N6A 3K7.

For further information, see the publications of the ADS discussed above, particularly, Louise Pound, "The American Dialect Society: A Historical Sketch," *Publication of the American Dialect Society* (April,

1952); and *"American Speech* and the American Dialect Society," *American Speech* (January, 1970); and *"American Speech* Looks Ahead," *American Speech* (April, 1970).

AMERICAN ECONOMIC ASSOCIATION (AEA). This learned society was organized in Saratoga, New York, in 1885, by a group of young economists and social scientists then attending a meeting of the American Social Science Association* and the American Historical Association* (AHA). One of the primary reasons for its founding was the same motive that had inspired the AHA a year earlier: the drive for professionalization by university scholars. The other was their desire to create a reform organization that would be more effective than the American Social Science Association in challenging the laissez-faire concept in the operation of the economy. The prime mover in its formation and the man who served as first secretary-treasurer was Richard T. Ely. The early leaders of the AEA and their immediate successors were instrumental in the initial adoption and continuation of the policies that were to ensure the effectiveness and growth of the organization: the AEA should not take a partisan attitude in the study of commercial and public policy; it should be national in scope; and it should be open to anyone having a *bona fide* interest in economics.

Since its founding the AEA has held annual meetings that have been open to all schools of economics. The meetings have usually consisted of topics devoted to the ramifications of a single topic or theme or those of a more general socioeconomic interest. If any recent change in the tone of the annual meetings is discernible, it is that the latter category appears to have gained ground against the former. Thus, although the format of meetings is still broad, from the late 1960s on, papers presented have increasingly dealt with such problems as pollution, race and sex discrimination, poverty, urban decay, and even heroin addiction. The filling of positions has always been a significant activity at annual meetings. Since 1911, the AEA has provided an employment placement service for members. Starting in the 1950s, this service was expanded through cooperation with the U.S. Employment Service and assistance in the maintenance of a National Registry for Economists.

Prior to 1911, the AEA published the papers and reports of its annual meetings in connection with the publication of monographs on specialized economic topics. At that time, the quarterly *American Economic Review*, which contains articles, book reviews, and noteworthy economic news, was established. Also, from that time forward, the papers and reports of meetings were published each year as *Papers and Proceedings* in a fifth number of the *Review*. In 1969 the AEA launched a second quarterly, the *Journal of Economic Literature*. Although it does contain survey articles and book reviews, the *Journal* is designed as a bibliographical and abstracting aid for economists and other social scientists. The AEA, since the early

1940s, has sponsored a number of publications put out by Richard D. Irwin, Inc. These include the AEA *Index of Economic Journals*, seventeen volumes covering the period 1886-1975; a reading series, republished articles on economics, thirteen volumes; and a contemporary economics series, eleven volumes. Also, the AEA has issued occasional monographs and translations of significant foreign economic works. A *Directory of Members*, containing biographical and statistical material about the AEA and its members, is published intermittently.

Prior to 1910, the vast majority of the members were in the academic profession. Increased interest in economics after that time on the part of the business community and professional and governmental personnel saw not only a large overall increase in membership but a particularly large increase among these groups. Thus, whereas overall individual membership increased from about fifteen hundred in 1910 to about eleven thousand in 1960, approximately nineteen thousand in 1970, and about twenty-one thousand today, a survey in 1970 revealed that 55 percent of the total individual membership by that time was employed by other than educational institutions.

The AEA has recognized and promoted outstanding achievement in the discipline in several ways. Since the late 1940s, two major awards have been presented: the Frances A. Walker and the John Bates Clark medals. The former is given every five years "to the living American economist who in the judgment of the awarding body has during his career made the greatest contribution to economics"; the latter is awarded biennially "to the American economist under the age of forty who is adjudged to have made a significant contribution to economic thought and knowledge." Distinguished foreign scholars have been recognized by election as honorary foreign members, up to a limit of twenty-five. In 1964, a new category of distinguished fellow was established. In addition to all past presidents and holders of the Walker Medal, the AEA now awards this title to a maximum of twelve economists of outstanding distinction from the United States and Canada, although only two fellows may be appointed in any one year.

The AEA has always been concerned with American education at all levels. During the mid-1950s there was a heightening of interest in the teaching of economics in undergraduate colleges and secondary schools. In 1955 a Committee on Economic Education was established, and it has remained one of the most active AEA committees. Projects in economic education that it has sponsored or encouraged include a television series, materials evaluation studies, high school competency tests, appraisal of the economic content of major high school texts, and the development and evaluation of new teaching methods, especially in elementary college courses. Much of the work in connection with the last project was done in the late 1960s in cooperation with the Joint Committee on Economic Education. Together, the AEA committee and the JCEE undertook pilot projects in course development, effectiveness studies, and the publication of a series of small supplementary monographs. One of their most ambitious efforts was the publication of the *Journal of Economic Education*, in which the AEA has assumed an advisory role. The *Journal* is specifically designed to make available information on teaching economics at the college level.

In 1972 the Committee on Economic Education noted the tightening job market for research-oriented Ph.D. holders and the accelerating concentration on teaching rather than research in community and junior colleges. Accordingly, it proposed renewed efforts to promote teacher training for doctoral programs and the development of closer ties by economists with these expanding colleges. In part because of such recommendations, a Visiting Economic Scholars Program was inaugurated in 1974 to promote visits by prominent economists to smaller colleges and, during 1974-1975, eight such visitations took place.

The seething economic and social conflicts of the late 1960s and 1970s were reflected perhaps more in the AEA than in other learned societies. At the annual business meeting in 1969, a group of "radical economists" presented a statement denouncing it and its leadership, maintaining that "the AEA plays directly destructive roles in our society. It serves to insure the perpetuation of professionalism, elitism, and petty irrelevance. It serves to inhibit the development of new ideas, ideas which are reflective of social reality." Although the action and statement were ruled out of order, the same meeting saw the passage of a vote to censure the U.S. State Department for refusing an alleged Mexican radical economist's entry into the United States. The year 1972 witnessed the AEA adopting a resolution opposing political discrimination against radical economists in government and universities. The movement climaxed in 1974 with the establishment of a Standing Committee on Political Discrimination, designed to investigate and report on instances of alleged political discrimination in employment practices and to recommend reasures against violators.

Meanwhile, although relatively not as heated, the issue of discrimination against minorities surfaced. One of the earliest indications of unrest was a statement presented by a Caucus of Black Economists at the 1969 annual meeting. The statement criticized the AEA for social and racial bias and failure to be professionally concerned with the problem of minorities, particularly discrimination in employment, and demanded more black representation and power in the AEA and the encouragement of minority activities in the discipline. As a result, a Committee on the Education and Training of Minority Group Economists was established, which successfully set up various fellowships and summer teaching programs for blacks. In 1974, a Standing Committee on the Status of Minority Groups in Economics was established to continue and expand such programs for blacks and other minorities.

The program of the 1971 annual meeting included a series of papers on the role of women in economic life. At the business meeting, the Woman's Caucus alleged sex discrimination in the profession and successfully urged the creation of a Committee on the Status of Women in the Economic Profession. The new committee undertook an examination of women in economics and recommended affirmative action programs in their behalf. Made a standing AEA committee in 1974, the CSWEP currently publishes a newsletter circulated to over eighteen hundred women economists and has conducted several workshops on the status of women. Further investigations of the future of women in economics have also been undertaken.

The AEA elects the customary institutional officers; it conducts its business from an office, headed by a secretary and a treasurer, located in Nashville, Tennessee.

For further information, see the publications of the AEA discussed above, particularly for its early history, Richard T. Ely, "The American Economic Association," *AEA Papers* (April, 1910) and "The Founding and Early History of the American Economic Association," *American Economic Review* (March, 1936). See also Richard T. Ely, *Ground Under Our Feet: An Autobiography* (1938).

For later histories of the AEA appearing in the *American Economic Journal*, see A. W. Coats, "The First Two Decades of the American Economic Association," (September, 1960) and "The American Economic Association 1904-1929," (June, 1964). See also A. W. Coats, "The American Economic Association's Publications: An Historical Perspective," *Journal of Economic Literature* (March, 1969); and Harold F. Williamson, "The American Economic Association," *ACLS Newsletter* (Fall, 1972).

See also Mary O. Furner, *Advocacy and Objectivity. A Crisis in the Professionalization of American Social Science, 1865-1905* (1975); and Thomas L. Haskell, *The Emergence of Professional Social Science: The American Social Science Association and the Nineteenth-Century Crisis of Authority* (1977).

AMERICAN ELECTROCHEMICAL SOCIETY. See Electrochemical Society, Inc.

AMERICAN ENTERPRISE ASSOCIATION. See American Enterprise Institute for Public Policy Research.

AMERICAN ENTERPRISE INSTITUTE FOR PUBLIC POLICY RESEARCH (AEI). Led by Lewis H. Brown, then chairman of the Johns-Manville Corporation, a group of businessmen founded the American Enterprise Association, predecessor of the American Enterprise Institute for Public Policy Research in 1943 to provide the Congress with scholarly information on the nation's economic problems in the postwar era. At its establishment and up until the early 1950s, the AEI's financial support was provided almost exclusively by U.S. business corporations. During this early period, the association employed law firms to analyze legislative issues on a pro-con basis. The objective was to ensure that both sides of proposed legislation were available to the Congress. At that time, AEI's impact on public policy formulation was practically nil. Although the institute still prepares legislative analyses, the overwhelming thrust now is idea formulation and long-range public policy research to offer policy makers problem-solving options.

In 1954, with an annual budget of eighty-five thousand dollars and only four full-time employees, the AEI almost went out of existence. At that time, however, the late William J. Baroody, Sr., left a post with the U.S. Chamber of Commerce to take over direction of the organization. He initially tried to have the name "American Enterprise Association" changed to "Institute for Public Policy Research," but a resultant compromise with his board of trustees saw the emergence of its present-day title. Not an idle whim on his part, the proposed name change reflected Baroody's belief that the AEI had to conduct the kind of research activities that would provide a solid underpinning for its pronouncements and publications. An important step in bringing this about was the gradual replacement by academic scholars of the overwhelming cadre of businessmen involved in such activities. By the 1970s this change had enhanced the AEI's stature, both inside and outside academia, although its reputation as a conservatively oriented organization has remained. This appears to be due in large part to the subjects selected for research by the AEI and the people chosen to conduct such research. Thus, although the AEI itself has never taken policy positions, the research scholars and fellows affiliated with it have usually fallen in the conservative orbit and are generally members of the Republican rather than the Democratic party; Milton Friedman, for example, has served on the AEI's Council of Academic Advisors and former President Gerald R. Ford is presently a distinguished fellow. On the other hand, some of its studies have resulted in publications that run contrary to the usual conservative position. A recent publication, for example, called for the demilitarization of the Indian Ocean area. Also, the AEI has had a number of prominent Democrats on its staff, including Ben Wattenberg, Austin Ranney, and Jeane Kirkpatrick. Moreover, William J. Baroody, Jr., who succeeded his father as president of the AEI in 1978, argues that such semantic labeling obscures a basic ideological alteration in the United States in which the distinction between liberal and conservative has been replaced by whether or not one believes that the private sector, churches, foundations, voluntary associations, and so forth should play a greater role in solving social problems rather than having the nation rely largely on a centralized national government.

In any case very tangible evidence of the success of this new approach can be seen in the change since the 1950s in the amount and source of funding of the AEI's activities. By 1960 its budget had grown to about $250,000 with 12 full-time staff; these figures surged to $2.5 million and 41, respectively, by 1972; and by 1980 the budget was almost $10 million and full-time staff numbered about 140. This phenomenal growth was accompanied by a significant shift in the source of AEI funding from corporate and individual supporters to the point that, in 1980, such funding accounted for only 20 percent of the total annual budget, with the other 80 percent derived from general, special purpose, and corporate foundations. It should be noted, in this connection, that the AEI has never solicited or accepted federal government contracts.

Despite this surge in resources at its disposal, AEI officials have sensed the need for a more stable base of support than annual appropriations from outside sources. Therefore, in 1978, a multimillion-dollar development drive was launched with the initial purpose of endowing specific AEI chairs and, possibly later, financing a move from the leased quarters it now occupies to a headquarters building of its own. With former President Gerald R. Ford as honorary chairman, contituing progress is being made toward the attainment of this dual objective.

The research program at AEI is presently carried on in ten broad study areas: economics, energy, foreign affairs, government regulations, health policy, legal policy, defense policy, political and social processes, social security and retirement, and tax policy. Within these broad areas, an AEI Program Priorities Committee develops specific projects for their accomplishment that uses AEI resident and visiting scholars together with outside consultants. A recently launched undertaking in the area of political and social processes, for example, was a study of the U.S. Congress as an institution and the impact of its processes, politics, and policies. In addition to staff members, the AEI has distinguished and senior fellows; about thirty resident, visiting, and research fellows and journalists; as well as some fourteen resident and visiting scholars. In addition, approximately seventy-five adjunct scholars perform research for the AEI, on a part-time basis, at U.S. and overseas colleges and universities.

The AEI also sponsors what it calls an outreach program for the American public through its sponsorship, or cosponsorship with other organizations, of conferences, seminars, telecasts, radio broadcasts, and so on devoted to specific current public policy issues. The highlight of the program is the annual year-end "public policy week," held by the AEI in Washington, D.C., in which prominent participants, by a variety of means, assess the year's activities touching on these issues.

Publications, which in a large measure cap all of these AEI activities, are a major component in its programs. From its 1940s beginnings, the AEI in fiscal 1980 issued 125 publications. This total was the result of a mix of 45 studies, 16 conferences and panel discussions, 15 legislative analyses, 26 journals, reviews, and newsletters, 8 special analyses and reports, and 15 reprints. Four periodicals are issued on a regular basis and include the bimonthly *AEI Economist: AEI Foreign Policy and Defense Review*, issued ten times a year; the bimonthly *Regulation: AEI Journal on Government and Society*; and the bimonthly *Public Opinion*.

The AEI elects the customary institutional officers; it conducts its activities from offices located at 1150 Seventeenth Street, N.W., Washington, D.C. 20036. The chief executive officer, almost from AEI's beginnings to 1978, had been William J. Baroody, Sr., a Lebanese immigrant to the United States. His son, William J. Baroody, Jr., became president upon his retirement.

For further information, see a 1978 booklet of information about the AEI and the following recent journalistic accounts: "The Conservative's Think Tank," *Business Week* (May 2, 1977); "The Other Think Tank," *Time* (September 19, 1977); "The 'Shadow Cabinets'—Changing Themselves as They Try to Change Policy," *National Journal* (February 25, 1978); "The Economic Wind's Blowing Toward the Right—For Now," New York *Times* (July 16, 1978); "Two Think Tanks with Growing Impact," *U.S. News and World Report* (September 25, 1978); and "The Reasonable Right," *Esquire* (February 13, 1979).

AMERICAN FOLKLORE SOCIETY (AFS). This society traces its origins to the developing mid-nineteenth-century European and American interest in the "lore"—stories, songs, superstitions, and so forth still held and in use by rural "folk." Coining the new word *folklore* to supersede what was then called popular antiquities,the folklorists maintained that it was just as meaningful and necessary to preserve the ballads, tales, and beliefs of nineteenth-century rural folk as it was the remains of earlier civilizations. Thus, European societies for this purpose were founded in the 1870s, and on January 4, 1888, in Cambridge, Massachusetts, an American Folklore Society was founded.

The encouragement of research, including the collection, preservation, and publication of original and unpublished folklore material, has always been one of the major activities of the AFS. From 1945 to the mid-1970s a Committee on Research in Folklore was set up, and during that period it made annual reports on folklore work then in progress by individual members of the AFS. Also, various status of studies reports for selected areas and groups, such as Afro-American folklore, Spanish American folklore, and Plains Indians, have been prepared by the Committee on Research. Much of the above material has appeared in the AFS's quarterly, *Journal of American Folklore*, which has been regularly published since its founding in 1889. In addition to such reports, the *Journal* contains articles on such diverse and varied subjects as ballads, child sacrifice, voodoo worship, songs of Indians, and black folk art. Annual reports of AFS officers also appeared in the *Journal* until the establishment, in 1972, of the quarterly *Newsletter*; since then such reports have been summarized therein. In 1894, when a decision to publish monographic material not suitable for the *Journal* was made, the first volume of the *Memoirs* appeared and have since been published at irregular intervals. The AFS also publishes a Bibliographical and Special Series, which was established in 1950. Also, in 1963, it launched a quarterly *Abstracts of Folklore Studies*. Initially covering European and American folklore journals, the *Abstracts* gradually widened its coverage to the world. *Abstracts* ceased to be published, however, in the mid-1970s, and the two separate book series were combined under one title, Publications of the American Folklore Society (New Series). Volume 1 appeared in 1980.

The AFS held its first annual meeting in Philadelphia in November, 1889, and they have since continued to be held late in the fall. Up until the 1960s, they were usually held jointly with the Modern Language Association of America* (MLA) or the American Anthropological Association* (AAA), whose interests lay in the same general areas. Since then, however, the AFS has met separately. These meetings have followed the usual societal pattern of reports, symposia, and the reading and discussion of folklore papers.

Soon after its founding the AFS encouraged the establishment of regional folklore societies, partly to stimulate the interest of members in folklore in general and partly to facilitate the study of diverse folklore elements in various regions. These branches include the Colorado Folklore Society, Mississippi Folklore Society, and Northeast Folklore Society. Information about the societies, including periodic directories for them, was published in the *Journal* until the inception of the *Newsletter* in 1972, where it now appears.

In the past few years the society has been developing sections to focus on members' special interests. These sections are self-constituted by petition and deal with such subjects as folklore and women, folklore archiving, and children's folklore.

Regular membership in the AFS is open to all persons interested in folklore. In addition to several other categories of membership—joint husband-wife, student, sustaining, institutional, life, honorary—in 1959 the AFS instituted a category of fellows, persons who have distinguished themselves by their work in folklore. From an original 250, the total membership of the AFS grew to about 1,500 in the 1960s, and now stands at about 3,000.

The AFS elects the customary institutional officers; it conducts its business from an executive secretary-treasurer's office located in Hershey, Pennsylvania.

For further information, see the publications of the AFS discussed above, particularly the following *Journal of American Folklore* articles by Wayland G. Hand, "North American Folklore Societies" (July-September, 1943); "American Folklore Society After Seventy Years: Survey and Prospect'' (January-March, 1960); and ''North American Folklore Societies, Supplement II'' (January-March, 1969). See also MacEdward Leach, ''American Folklore Society,'' *Standard Dictionary of Folklore, Mythology, and Legend* (1949); and Anna H. Gayton, ''The American Folklore Society,'' *World of the Mind* (1958).

AMERICAN GEOGRAPHICAL AND STATISTICAL SOCIETY. See American Geographical Society.

AMERICAN GEOGRAPHICAL SOCIETY (AGS). The American Geographical and Statistical Society, shortened in 1871 to the American Geographical Society, was founded in New York City on October 9, 1851. The approximately thirty founding members included such prominent New Yorkers as George Folsom, later U.S. chargé d'affaires to Belgium; Henry Grinnell, a shipping magnate and owner of the famous clipper ship the *Flying Cloud*; Charles A. Dana, later editor of the New York *Sun*; and Henry J. Raymond, founder of the *New York Times*. Grinnell was elected the society's first president, but as he was unable to accept the honor, George Bancroft, the dean of American historians, was chosen and so served from 1851 to 1854.

Reflecting the backgrounds and interests of its founders, the society was viewed as a means to provide New Yorkers in particular and Americans in general with information about the different parts of the world with which, in the 1850s, they were coming into closer and closer contact. Such information was to be in the form of published geographical material, maps, and statistical data. The need and demand for such organizations had been met several decades earlier in various countries in Europe.

The original bylaws of the AGS provided for three classes of membership: ordinary, corresponding (terminated in 1948), and honorary. In 1978 this was changed to provide the following options: fellows, which includes individuals and nonprofit organizations; and corporate associates. The original bylaws also provided for a governing executive committee, somewhat later referred to as the board of trustees, and ever since 1854 a council. The society membership during its early years never numbered more than a hundred, but it launched a number of activities at that time that have been continued down to the present day. Private and public lecture and discussion meetings were held and, in December, 1854, the first of continuing annual meetings of the council at which officials of the society are elected and other business is conducted. The only formal members of the AGS are the members of the council, and only they vote on societal matters. In 1852 the first publication of the society, a *Bulletin* modeled ''after the manner of the Geographical Society of Paris,'' was issued.

The Civil War and the rise of internal disagreements within the society at that time caused a hiatus in activities, but it was never serious enough to threaten the society's existence. The election of Charles P. Daly as president in 1864, an office that he held continuously to 1899, ushered in a period of calm, steady advance for the organization in membership, wealth, and range of activities. The AGS sponsored expeditions to various parts of the world, with particular emphasis on South America and Africa. By 1886 the society's library contained more than eighteen thousand volumes and three thousand maps, much of this material dealing with the geographical aspects of the westward movement in the United States. The AGS was the major influence in the 1884 authorization by the U.S. Congress of the convening of an International Meridian Conference in Washington, D.C. This conference led to the adoption of the Greenwich prime meridian and our standard time zones.

Early meetings of the society had been held in the offices of members, in rented rooms in buildings of the old New York University, or in Clinton Hall. The year 1867 saw a transfer to a more commodious suite of rooms in the newly constructed Cooper Institute building. Then, in 1876, it purchased a house of its own at 11 West 29th Street where it stayed until 1901, when the society constructed a larger one at 15 West 81st Street. The AGS, however, remained there only ten years before moving to a location on Audubon Terrace at Broadway and 156th Street.

This change stemmed from the interest in the society of a man who had become a fellow of the society in 1893 and had been elected its president in 1907, where he continued to serve until 1916. This individual was Archer M. Huntington, son and heir of Collis P. Huntington, the wealthy builder of the Southern Pacific Railroad. In addition to scholarly and artistic interests that had led him to provide financial assistance to several other research institutions and learned societies, such as the Hispanic Society of America,* American Numismatic Society,* and American Academy and Institute of Arts and Letters,* Archer M. Huntington became a leader and benefactor of the AGS. It was he who donated Audubon Terrace land to the society, then bought the society's building at Eighty-First Street—thus providing some of the cash for the initial costs of the much larger new building—and finally provided most of the money for the additional costs of construction of the Audubon Terrace headquarters.

Probably a matching or perhaps even greater contribution of Huntington to the AGS, however, was his determining role in the decision to hire Dr. Isaiah Bowman as the executive head of the society. From the time he began work as director-librarian of the AGS on July 1, 1915, until his resignation in 1935 to become president of Johns Hopkins University, Bowman, with his talent and leadership, ushered in what were undoubtedly some of the most stirring decades in the society's existence.

One of the first changes (1915) wrought by the new director was a change in title of the *Bulletin* to the *Geographical Review*, with an accompanying broadening of its scope and content and rejuvenation of its style. Carried forward as a quarterly from 1920 to the present, this periodical has been the linchpin in the AGS's publication program. Also, there was a concomitant increase in the AGS' production of books, maps, and atlases. The renowned "Millionth Map" of Hispanic America, for example, was begun in 1922 and brought to completion in 1945 at a cost of about half a million dollars.

Now almost forgotten was the impressive role played by Dr. Bowman and the AGS during World War I. The U.S. government made extensive use of the society's resources in our war effort and, perhaps more so, in President Woodrow Wilson's drive for a lasting peace. Thus the "Inquiry," as it came to be called, composed of some 150 geographers, historians, and other specialists engaged in amassing and interpreting data needed for this effort, was headquartered in the AGS building. Dr. Bowman played a major role in the recruitment and supervision of these specialists and later accompanied President Wilson and the American delegation to Paris in December, 1918, in the futile effort to achieve a lasting peace there.

During the 1920s the AGS was little troubled by financial worries. Huntington and other benefactors, publication sales, and dues from memberships, which had climbed to about six thousand in the late 1920s, covered expenses. The onset of the Great Depression, however, saw the end of what have been called the "halcyon" years; and, despite grants from the Rockefeller Foundation, retrenchments were carried forward from that time on down to Dr. Bowman's departure in 1935. His successors and executive heads of the AGS from that time to 1950, Raye R. Platt, secretary, 1935-1938, and John K. Wright, director, 1938-1949, despite World War II government contracts, were never able to place the organization on a sound financial footing. In all but four of the fifteen years from 1935 to 1950 the society ran an annual deficit, and by 1951 warnings were issued that it faced bankruptcy. Rather than retrenchment, however, the principal remedial measure adopted was the launching of a development program. Unfortunately, the desired results were not achieved. Thus, during the ensuing directorships of George H. T. Kimble, Charles H. Hitchcock, Shannon McClure, Burton W. Adkinson, Robert B. McVee, and Sarah K. Myers the AGS maintained its activities under this financial pressure. A new periodical *Focus*, issued ten times a year, was inaugurated in 1951; books, maps, and atlases were still published; the library and map collection were added to; and the AGS continued to sponsor lectures and symposia and to conduct research on a wide variety of geographical topics. Also, the society carried on the recognition of outstanding achievements in its area of interest through an ongoing awarding of various honorary fellowships and medals. The medals include, in the order of their first award: Cullum Geographical (1896); Charles P. Daly (1902); David Livingstone Centenary (1916); Samuel Finley Breese Morse (1928); George Davidson (1952); O. M. Miller Cartographic (1968); and Van Cleef Memorial (1970).

In the mid-1970s, however, it became clear that the society's resources were no longer sufficient to sustain all of these activities. The decision was then reached that, due to the high costs associated with their maintenance and upkeep, the AGS Library and Map Collection would be disposed of to some other institution. Successful negotiations for a transfer were concluded with the University of Wisconsin-Milwaukee, and for a time it appeared that the AGS might sell its New York headquarters building and relocate there also. Legal objections from New York State authorities, plus the increasing threat of bankruptcy caused by the resultant delay, finally led to a compromise whereby the AGS collections were finally moved in 1978 but the society headquarters remained in New York.

With the transfer of the AGS collections and the resultant cutback in activities and personnel, all accomplished without impairing the publication of *Geographical Review* and *Focus*, the Audubon Terrace headquarters building became far too large. The cost of operating the building, moreover, was escalating. A decision was reached to reopen the selling or leasing of the building to an appropriate institution. Ultimately, in the spring of 1980, the AGS Council voted unanimously to sell the building to Boricua College, a young New York City college designed to meet the educational needs of Puerto Rican and other Spanish-speaking people in the United States. One of the conditions of the sale was that the society would continue to occupy part of the building until June, 1981. The society has since moved to offices located at 25 W. 39th Street, New York, N.Y., 10018.

The present director, Dr. Sarah K. Myers, was the executive in large measure responsible for carrying the AGS through these crises. Grants of one hundred thousand dollars each from the National Geographic Society* and the Andrew W. Mellon Foundation in 1978, and one of forty thousand dollars from the Exxon Corporation in 1979, were powerful aids in her arriving at a balanced budget for the society. With these problems now behind them, the council has turned its attention to revitalizing the society. In September, 1980, they authorized Dr. Myers to develop a series of new AGS activities designed to contribute to the awareness and understanding of the geography of urban America, especially New York.

For further information, see the detailed history of the AGS from its beginning to 1951, by a former director, John K. Wright, *Geography in the Making—The American Geographical Society 1851-1951* (1952). See also the AGS publications discussed above, particularly the annual reports to the AGS council appearing in the *Geographical Review*; the *AGS Newsletter*; and occasional features in the *Geographical Review* entitled "The American Geographical Society," and "Presentations of the Society's Medals." In a somewhat broader vein, see John K. Wright, "The Field of the Geographical Society," in Griffith Taylor, ed., *Geography in the Twentieth Century* (1951).

AMERICAN GEOLOGICAL INSTITUTE (AGI). The catalyst in the creation of the AGI was a speech by Dr. Carey Croneis at the 1942 annual meeting of the American Association of Petroleum Geologists. Pointing out the low academic status occupied by geologists, Croneis attributed that condition to inept public relations and stressed this as a compelling reason for the creation of an American Geological Institute. A meeting to consider the matter was held at Fort Worth, Texas, on April 10, 1943. One hundred geologists in attendance there endorsed the concept of an AGI, and an organizational committee was named. The latter composed a statement of purpose and a draft constitution for the proposed organization, which was submitted to eleven existing geological and allied organizations. A year later representatives of nine of the eleven met in New York, and, although there was some sentiment advanced for a reorganization of the Geological Society of America* (GSA) to provide the services envisioned for an AGI, the decision was reached that a new council of societies would be better.

Matters drifted for a year, and then developments took a new course with the calling of a meeting by the National Research Council (NRC) and the GSA. In addition to representation there of the NRC and the GSA, those from the other ten geological organizations, plus Section E (Geology and Geography) of the American Association for the Advancement of Science* (AAAS) participated in this meeting. Two review committees were named, and further deliberations took place as a result of this meeting. Ultimately, on May 2, 1947, at an annual meeting of the Division of Geology and Geography of the NRC, President Detlev W. Bronk suggested to the geologists present that they might wish to create, under NRC auspices and sponsorship, an AGI similar to the American Institute of Biological Sciences* (AIBS), then being created under NRC auspices. Representatives of the interested societies eventually fell in line with this plan, and a constitution embodying it was subsequently ratified by them.

The founding meeting of the AGI was held in Washington, D.C., on November 15, 1948. It was June 1, 1949, however, before Dr. David M. Delo, the first executive director, assumed office, and then on a half-time basis; it was not until 1953 that it became a full-time position. The fledgling AGI was plagued with financial problems from the outset, and only in 1955 did dues to it from the member societies on something of a regular basis evolve. Even then such monies were made available subject to an annual review. Furthermore, throughout the 1950s and on into the first few years of the 1960s, the total cost of AGI operations exceeded these dues paid by the societies. The deficits were made up by members of a Committee of One Hundred and Committee of One Thousand, leaders in the geological field, who annually contributed ten to one hundred dollars each in support of the AGI.

Thus the institute drifted until September, 1957, when, after what was essentially a vote of no confidence by the executive committee of the American Association of Petroleum Geologists, it almost went under. Although this vote was shortly reversed, the narrow escape from extinction resulted in the creation of a high-level task force of geologists, representing the entire spectrum of the earth sciences, to study all aspects of the AGI's administration and operation. With Drs. Croneis and Beebe playing leading roles, this group in 1960 submitted recommendations resulting in the 1963 reorganization and resultant rejuvenation of the AGI. Two key changes were made. First, it became an organization completely independent of the NRC. Second, a restructuring forced the more active representation and participation in AGI affairs of the member societies. This structure was streamlined in 1972 by the creation of the present governing board consisting of one representative (who must be a society officer) from each of the member societies.

These reorganizations were a material factor in the vastly augmented program of activities carried on by a now stable AGI in the 1960s and 1970s. One of the more noteworthy, still being carried on today, is GeoRef, short for Geological Reference File Project, a computerized bibliographic data base. At the AGI, GeoRef editors process the world's annual geological literature, currently running at about one hundred thousand titles annually. About fifty thousand of them are entered each year into the GeoRef data base for utilization in publication and computer form by individual geologists. Also, the AGI collects and maintains numerical data about geoscientists—faculty, students, minorities, and so on—and provides information about the earth sciences to other groups, particularly governmental entities. Other major activities of the AGI include the publication of *GeoTimes*, the monthly news magazine for earth scientists and, since 1959, translations from Russian serials and books, which are published in another AGI publication, *International Geology Review*.

The AGI, which maintains its headquarters at 5205 Leesburg Pike, Falls Church, Virginia 22041, is presently composed of eighteen member societies and organizations. It does not hold inclusive, annual meetings; its policies and operations are formed and carried through by meetings of its governing board, held at least twice a year, plus recommendations of committees and the professional staff headed by an executive director. The board consists of one representative from each of the eighteen member societies, plus the nonvoting executive director; each society representative has a weighted vote based on the size of his or her society. The board elects the principal officers, a president, vice-president, and secretary-treasurer, and appoints the aforementioned executive director.

For further information, see the monthly *GeoTimes* published by the AGI, particularly a series therein (May, 1967-October, 1967) on the history of the AGI. See also *AGI in Profile* (1976), an account of its activities published by the AGI.

AMERICAN GEOLOGICAL SOCIETY. See Geological Society of America.

AMERICAN GEOPHYSICAL UNION (AGU). Soon after the establishment of the National Research Council (NRC) in 1916, the chairman of that organization, Dr. George E. Hale, together with Dr. Louis A. Bauer, a geophysicist associated with the NRC, came to the conclusion that the time was ripe for the establishment of an NRC committee or group in geophysics. They included in the latter such subjects as geodesy, geological physics, meteorology, terrestrial magnetism and electricity, seismology, and oceanography, and it was in order to bridge the gaps between these closely related subjects that they urged the new organization.

Initially the NRC view was that, rather than create a new entity, geophysics should be merged with an existing geography committee. Within a few months, however, geophysics received a separate status by being included in a new Division of Physics, Mathematics, Astronomy, and Geophysics. So matters rested until the conclusion of World War I, when an NRC reorganization brought up the question of naming representatives to it from the various divisions. Those segments of divisions, such as physics and mathematics, with national societies could easily dispose of the problem by referring it to them. The geophysicists, with one or two exceptions, simply did not have national societies that were very active in their major areas of concern. This problem plus a related international one, the creation of an American section of a proposed international geophysical union (see the International Council of Scientific Unions* [ICSU]), was met by the appointment of an NRC committee to consider the entire matter. On March 4, 1919, Dr. R. S. Woodward, its chairman, made a report which stated:

The earth is at once the subject and the object of many sciences. Of these the most important are Astronomy, Geodesy, Geology, Meteorology, Seismology, Terrestrial Magnetism, Terrestrial Electricity, Tides and Volcanology. . . . that progress in the future is most likely to result from active cultivation of the borderlands that now serve to distinguish, but only indefinitely, the several fields of geophysics, and that in order to promote research and discovery in geophysical science in general, steps be taken by the American Section of the International Geophysical Union toward the formation of a new society to be called the American Geophysical Society.

The formation of an American section soon followed the submission of Woodward's report, and this section was also designated as the Geophysics Committee of the Division of Physical Sciences within the NRC. Ultimately, too, the establishment of a geophysical society was referred to it. The members of this composite section-committee eventually recommended that it be set up as the American Geophysical Union and that this union be made a separate NRC committee. Following NRC approval, by 1921 the organizational structure had so evolved that the union played a dual role:

the executive committee of the AGU had become the Committee on Geophysics of the NRC; and the AGU, as a whole, became the American National Committee of the International Geodetic and Geophysical Union. This relationship prevailed until the reorganization of the National Academy of Sciences* (NAS) complex in the 1970s, when the AGU became a completely independent learned society. At the same time, a U.S. national committee for the international union was designed within the newly created Assembly of Mathematical and Physical Sciences of a restructured NRC. The original close ties and relationship, however, have continued, and the executive director of the AGU is currently serving his third four-year term as secretary of the U.S. national committee.

The AGU made an initial contribution to science by the leading role its members played in the first organizational meeting of the international union at Brussels in 1919. In the 1930s it sponsored a number of scientific research expeditions in cooperation with other institutions. In the 1950s, the AGU played a major role in the initiation of the highly publicized International Geophysical Year (IGY).

Since 1920, the union has published the *Transactions*, annually and usually in several parts until 1945, and as a bimonthly from 1945-1958. It contains the scientific papers, discussions, and reports presented at the AGU annual and regional meetings. Starting in 1959, the *Transactions* became a quarterly containing information of general interest to geophysicists but excluding purely scientific papers. At the same time the latter were transferred to the AGU's *Journal of Geophysical Research*. Other publications established since then include *Review of Geophysics and Space Physics* (1963), *Water Resources Research* (1965), and *Geophysical Research Letters, 1974*. Also, in 1969, *Radio Science*, formerly published by the U.S. Department of Commerce, was taken over by AGU. The AGU has also published maps and charts and special studies dealing with specific geophysical subjects and publishes several books each year, including a series on Antarctic research. It also has an extensive program of translations of Soviet and Chinese publications.

Annual meetings or assemblies of the AGU have been held every year since 1920. They are scheduled for the spring of the year, usually for a four- or five-day period, and they were always held in Washington, D.C., until 1978, when the meeting began alternating in and out of Washington, D.C., every other year. Starting in 1961, a second annual meeting has been held in the West; the first such meeting was held in December at the University of California, Los Angeles. One of the major events of the spring meeting since 1939 has been the awarding of the William Bowie Medal to a distinguished geophysicist. An increasing number of regional meetings have also been called, and, since 1919, the union has provided representatives at the now quadrennial meeting of the international union.

Membership in the AGU was originally restricted to sixty-five persons.

This limit was raised to seventy-five in 1922 and to one hundred in 1928; then in 1930 limitation as to membership was removed. From that time on membership has steadily increased to its present approximate thirteen thousand. In addition to regular membership, the AGU has associate and corporate membership.

The AGU elects the customary institutional officers; it conducts its business from an office, headed by an executive director in Washington, D.C.

For further information, see the publications of the AGU discussed above, particularly John A. Fleming, "Origin and Development of the American Geophysical Union." *Transactions, American Geophysical Union* (February, 1954). See also Louis A. Bauer, "The Organization and Aims of the American Geophysical Union," *Bulletin, National Research Council* (January, 1924).

AMERICAN HISTORICAL ASSOCIATION (AHA). This association was one of the organizations spun off from the American Social Science Association* as the result of dissatisfaction with its "amateur" makeup and operation on the part of the emerging "professional" historians, economists, and political scientists within its ranks. Although suggestions had been made in 1880 that history be made an association division, presumably strengthening its role therein, no action was taken on such proposals. By 1884 a substantial number of the professional academic historians in the United States had rejected this step and were calling for the creation of a separate AHA. Thus, of the "teachers and friends" of history who assembled at the 1884 annual meeting of the American Social Science Association in Saratoga, New York, only John Eaton, its president and U.S. commissioner of education, opposed the founding of an independent AHA. Those opposed to Eaton's viewpoint held that the American Social Science Association had overspecialized in such subjects as prison reform and social welfare, and was dominated by "amateur" nonacademic interests and that the historians wanted an association of their own that could aid in establishing high professional standards for historical training and research. Thereupon the AHA was organized.

Those who played a leading role in the formation of the new organization included President Daniel C. Gilman and Professor Herbert B. Adams of Johns Hopkins University, who became secretary of the AHA and remained so until his death in 1900, and Professors Charles Kendall Adams of the University of Michigan and Moses Coit Tyler of Cornell University.

The AHA grew rapidly; from an initial 41, the membership had risen to 287 by the time of the second annual meeting in 1885, and by 1890, there were 620 members.

In 1889, the association was incorporated in the District of Columbia by an act of Congress: "for the promotion of historical studies, the collection and preservation of historical manuscripts and for kindred purposes in the interest of American history and of history in America." The 1889 act also provided that the association should have its offices in Washington, D.C., that it should make reports regarding historical matters to the secretary of the Smithsonian Institution,* who should then transmit to Congress such reports as he or she saw fit. One of the lasting benefits to the AHA from this governmental connection was that its annual reports, which included historical material, were printed at government expense. Some early members did not like this arrangement, alleging the possibility of "censorship" by the Smithsonian. J. Franklin Jameson in 1909 acknowledged that the Smithsonian had ruled that essays dealing with the Christian religion could not be printed in the annual reports, but he held that "few members now doubt" that the governmental connection was a "wise step." From the governmental standpoint, the advantage of having a group of professional historians to look to for advice in connection with manuscripts, archives, and the like has been inestimable.

Although the teaching of history has been an AHA concern since its inception, in the past three decades it has been particularly so, from secondary school through the graduate level.

The 1955 establishment of a Service Center for the Teaching of History marked the beginning of a continuing effort to bridge the gap between history teachers, particularly those at the secondary school and college level, and professional historians. The center has produced teaching aids, pamphlets, and bibliographic materials as well as arranged for conferences and summer workshops on the effective teaching of history.

The AHA during the same period established committees on graduate education and Ph.D. programs that examined, drew conclusions, and made recommendations about graduate training in history. A conclusion was arrived at, for example, that the time interval between the beginning of doctoral work and the awarding of the degree was generally too long and recommended various measures to shorten it. Similarly, the Doctor of Arts degree in history was explored as an alternative to the Doctor of Philosophy, and tentative conclusions and recommendations concerning it were made.

The AHA has frequently been called upon to act in an advisory capacity to the government and has appointed special committees for that purpose, such as the Committee on Governmental Historical Documentary Publications and the Committee on a National Archives Buildings. Due largely to the efforts of the archives committee and J. Franklin Jameson, managing editor of the *American Historical Review* during the early 1900s, the National Archives were established.

The AHA currently confers various prizes, awards, and fellowships to encourage historical research and study. They are offered in European, American, and Asiatic history. Perhaps the two most prestigious are the

Albert J. Beveridge Award and the Harmsworth Professorship. The former is given annually for the best book in American history and carries a cash award of one thousand dollars. In the awarding of the Harmsworth Professorship, an AHA committee assists the electors of Oxford University in the annual selection of an American professor to lecture in U.S. history at that institution.

The AHA holds annual meetings during the week between Christmas and New Year's. Seven of the first eleven meetings were held in Washington, D.C., and there was some sentiment to continue that city as a permanent meeting place. In 1896, however, opponents forced a move to New York. Since that time an informal practice has been adopted whereby the AHA meets one year in an Eastern city, the next in a Western, and the third in Washington. Until the 1940s these meetings were often held in conjunction with the meetings of other organizations, such as the American Economic Association* (AEA) and the American Political Science Association* (APSA); since that time each of these societies has become too large for such joint meetings. Many sessions at the annual meetings, however, are now held jointly with historical groups of a regional or special nature, such as the American Catholic Historical Association and the Conference on Latin American History.

The late 1960s and early 1970s saw a number of tumultuous annual meetings characteristic of those of other learned societies during the Vietnam War era. Events at the 1968 Democratic National Convention in Chicago sparked a successful drive to change the scheduled annual meeting site from that city to New York City. At one point in the 1969 meeting, AHA President John K. Fairbank wrestled for control of the presiding officer's microphone with Professor Howard Zinn, one of a "radical caucus" calling for the end of the Vietnam War and alleged political and racial oppression in the United States. Although resolutions in this vein and others of a similar nature introduced at this and other annual meetings ultimately failed to pass, the agitation and debate they engendered were a significant factor in increasing AHA attention to the problems of minorities and women in the historical profession. By 1973 an assistant executive secretary had been appointed for the specific purpose of dealing with such problems.

The AHA has several official publications. The *Annual Report* is published as a public document by the Government Printing Office and is for sale by the Superintendent of Documents. It is distributed to AHA members, members of Congress, American libraries recognized as depositories of public documents, and a considerable number of foreign libraries. Another publication of the AHA is its journal, the *American Historical Review*, which is published five times a year. Founded in 1895, it contains articles, edited documents, some general historical news, and critical reviews of historical publications.

The *AHA Newsletter*, first published in 1962, contains news of general educational interest, staff appointments, awards, faculty openings, and minutes of the council and provides a forum for members to express their opinion on matters of concern to historians.

Membership in the AHA has always included those professionally engaged in historical work and those with a general interest in history. It is open to anyone paying dues. Between 1959 and 1970, the AHA, like other learned societies, experienced a tremendous growth, expanding from about eight thousand to more than twenty thousand members. However, 1970 appears to have been a watershed, and membership presently totals approximately fifteen thousand, about the same as its closely related organizations, the AEA and APSA.

A Pacific Coast branch of the AHA was organized in 1903 so that members living in the Far West might hold meetings and conduct activities of their own while retaining membership in the parent organization. Attempts to work out a similar arrangement with other sections of the country, however, did not materialize and led, undoubtedly, to the creation of a number of regional and state historical organizations.

The manifold AHA activities are conducted from an office, headed by an executive director, located in Washington, D.C. He acts for the elected governing council and through numerous committees, either permanent or ad hoc. These committees utilize the services, freely offered, of hundreds of AHA members. The most important standing committees at the present time, in addition to the administrative ones, are those on Research, Teaching, and the Profession; International Historical Activities; Women Historians; Affiliated Societies; Quantitative Research; the First Books Program; and various joint committees with the Organization of American Historians* (OAH), American Society for Legal History* (ASLH), and other learned societies.

The year 1973 saw a change in the number of AHA officers. Until that time it had elected annually a president and vice-president. In that year a constitutional change created three AHA divisions: research, teaching, and professional, each with its own vice-president.

For further information, see the publications of the AHA discussed above, particularly "Report of the Organization and Proceedings," *Papers, American Historical Association* (1885), and *Annual Report, American Historical Association* (1920). See also J. Franklin Jameson, "The American Historical Association, 1884-1909," *American Historical Review* (October, 1909) and "The American Historical Review, 1895-1920," *American Historical Review* (October, 1920); and Survey, AHA.

For recent interpretive accounts of the origin of the AHA, see Thomas L. Haskell, *The Emergence of Professional Social Science* (1977); and Laurence Veysey, "The Plural Organized World of the Humanities," *The Organization of Knowledge in Modern America, 1860-1920* (1979).

AMERICAN INSTITUTE OF BIOLOGICAL SCIENCES (AIBS). This institute developed from a similar impetus that had, at an earlier period, spurred the creation of the American Institute of Physics* (AIP) and caused the American Chemical Society* (ACS) to alter itself so as to take on a variety of additional activities, that is, the need for a central organization that could serve physicists, chemists, or, in this case, biologists, as a whole.

The drive for a strong, central voice for biologists grew out of informal meetings at the Marine Biological Laboratory* (MBL) in Woods Hole, Massachusetts, during the summers of 1938 and 1939. Leaders in these discussions were Drs. Robert Chambers, Newton Harvey, Elmer Beetler, and William Duryee. The intervention of World War II postponed formal actions until 1945. The National Research Council (NRC) of the National Academy of Sciences* (NAS) was reluctant to initiate action that might weaken its Division of Biology and Agriculture. Pressures from research biologists, nevertheless, induced the NRC to sponsor an open discussion of the matter at the December, 1946, meeting of the American Association for the Advancement of Science* (AAAS) in Boston. Papers on the need for a national organization were read by Drs. Robert F. Griggs, R. E. Cleland, and H. B. Tukey, and subsequently a follow-up meeting was called by the NRC to be held in Washington, D.C., on March 18, 1947. This meeting included fifteen biologists of note and constituted itself the advisory committee for an AIBS. An agreement was reached at this meeting to establish an organizing board composed of one member from each member society of the Division of Biology and Agriculture of the NRC, and a subcommittee was appointed to prepare a tentative constitution for the board. On April 11, 1947, this organizing board met and adopted a provisional constitution calling for setting up the AIBS within the framework of the NRC. It also recommended that the AIBS be launched upon ratification of the constitution by ten of the twenty-seven societies to be invited to become members and that control of the new organization be placed in a governing board composed of representatives of the prospective society members. By the end of 1947, twelve societies had accepted membership, and the AIBS came into being at a February 20, 1948, meeting at the NRC. An executive committee of the governing board was named, and this committee subsequently chose Dr. Clarence J. Hylander as the first executive secretary of the new organization.

Operating under the auspices of the NRC in the late 1940s and early 1950s, the AIBS could point to a number of accomplishments during these early years. In January, 1951, the first issue of the *AIBS Bulletin* was published. Launched initially as a bimonthly "news and views" publication, by 1963 it had gradually been transformed into a scientific journal of note. Recognition of the change was made in that year, when it became a monthly with the new title *Bio Science* and it has been so published down to the present. This early period saw two other significant accomplishments.

The AIBS was largely instrumental in the revision of the Selective Service laws following World War II whereby occupational deferments were provided for biologists in addition to other scientific groups. Also, the AIBS played a somewhat similar role in the 1950s in the formation and organization of the National Science Foundation. Thus, whereas earlier legislation virtually ignored the biological sciences, the final law embodying the NSF saw biology emerge, with medicine, as a strong division within the foundation. Consequently, when Dr. H. Bentley Glass called for an AIBS independent of the National Research Council in 1954, he could point to these and other accomplishments as proof that it was ready to stand alone. Subsequently, although the AIBS has continued to maintain close liaison with the NAS and the NRC, it became an independent organization in 1955.

The period from 1955 saw truly extraordinary growth in the AIBS budget and activities. This period overlapped the launching of Sputnik I by the Soviet Union. The resultant explosion in the availability of federal funds for scientific purposes paralleled the surge in AIBS expenditures. These were the years when the highly successful AIBS Films Series and the Biological Science Curriculum Study (BSCS) were funded and launched. These were the years when the AIBS began its advisory program for various governmental agencies. These were the years when the staff numbered in excess of one hundred, and, in addition to the main offices in Washington, D.C., suboffices were being maintained in Baltimore, Maryland, Kansas City, Missouri, and Boulder, Colorado. By 1962, the total annual budget had reached approximately two million dollars, but, ominously, all but a miniscule portion was attributable to grants and contracts from the federal government, particularly the National Science Foundation. Then, late in 1962, the AIBS suffered a severe crisis when the NSF froze its assets. The reasons advanced by the foundation were poor record keeping by the AIBS, deduction of too much overhead from NSF grants, and unauthorized diversion of funds from one project to another. In retrospect, it appears that there were grounds on both sides for complaint as to the way things had been handled up to and including the crisis. In any case, although an ensuing audit revealed no fraud, faulty financial management left the AIBS some four hundred thousand dollars in debt to the NSF. An agreement was eventually reached whereby the AIBS was to repay this money over a period of years. At the same time overall spending was curtailed, staff reduced, programs readjusted, and rigorous financial controls imposed. Also, a change was made providing for individual membership in the AIBS. This move was designed to place greater financial reliance in the future upon membership dues rather than overhead from grants and contracts. Thus, the AIBS today has about eighty-five hundred individual members in addition to forty-two adherent society members and eight industrial members.

After weathering the 1962 crisis, the AIBS resumed its stated role of "a federation of scientific societies dedicated to advancement of the biological,

medical, and agricultural sciences and their application to human welfare."
In addition to continued publication of *Bio Science* and the sponsorship of
an annual meeting for both individual members and adherent societies, a
major activity of the ensuing decades at the national and international levels
has been the Special Science Program established in the 1960s, which provided biologists with an opportunity to affect the biological programs of
government agencies. Thus, thousands of biologists, under AIBS auspices,
have served on advisory panels and committees and published reports on
numerous research projects.

In the 1970s, with the establishment of its Public Responsibilities Program, the AIBS created a Department of Government Relations to follow
activities and establish a national network of biologist representatives to
respond to requests for advice from congressional delegations and state
legislators. Through a monthly newsletter, *AIBS Forum*, this AIBS department makes reports to individual AIBS members and society member
officers on public policy issues affecting them and the biological sciences.

The AIBS elects the customary institutional officers; it conducts its
business from an office, headed by an executive director, located in
Arlington, Virginia.

For further information, see *The AIBS Story*, a twenty-seven-page short
history of the AIBS published by it in 1972. See also the publications of the
AIBS discussed above, particularly the following articles appearing in the
AIBS Bulletin: Clarence J. Hylander, "The American Institute of
Biological Sciences: A Historical Resume" (January and April, 1951);
James G. Dickson, "American Institute of Biological Sciences, A Progress
Report" (January, 1959); and Hiden T. Cox, "The AIBS After Ten Years"
(November, 1959). See also Robert W. Krauss, "AIBS at the Crossroads—
History and Future for U.S. Biology," *Bio Science* (April, 1974).

AMERICAN INSTITUTE OF NUTRITION (AIN). This institute traces its
origin to the increasing interest in the field of nutrition by various members
of the American Society of Biological Chemists* (ASBC) and their desire,
expressed as early as the 1920 ASBC annual meeting that a journal devoted
to nutrition be established. Thus, Dr. John R. Murlin, professor of
physiology at the University of Rochester, took the lead in the 1928 incorporation of the AIN for the specific purpose of founding a *Journal of
Nutrition*, ownership of which was originally vested in Dr. Murlin and four
other incorporators. Although the new *Journal* received a large number of
manuscripts and papers for publication, it ran deficits initially. In 1933,
therefore, the corporation turned to the Wistar Institute of Anatomy and
Biology* and negotiated an agreement whereby ownership of the *Journal*
was transferred to the institute. It was also agreed that the institute would
not only publish the *Journal* but also meet any resultant deficits. A condition of this arrangement, however, was that a learned society would sponsor

the *Journal* and that all members would be required to subscribe to it. The AIN was thereupon reorganized in 1934 as a membership society with 178 charter members and with subscription to the *Journal* as a requirement for membership. This arrangement with the Wistar Institute was maintained until January 1, 1968, when the AIN reacquired the *Journal of Nutrition* from the Wistar Institute but with its Wistar Press continuing as the printer of the *Journal*. Dr. Murlin continued as editor of the *Journal* until 1939. He was succeeded by Dr. George W. Cowgill, 1939-1959; Dr. Richard H. Barnes, 1959-1960; Dr. Frederick W. Hill, 1961-1979; and the present editor, Dr. James S. Dinning.

Until 1960, the monthly *Journal of Nutrition* was the only publication in the United States and Canada devoted solely to that field. With the organization at that time of a Division of Clinical Nutrition, now the American Society for Clinical Nutrition (ASCN), but still a division of the AIN, the latter began publication of another monthly, the *American Journal of Clinical Nutrition*.

Another major accomplishment of the AIN has been the annual meetings it has held since 1933. Until 1940, they were held at the site of the annual meetings of the Federation of American Societies for Experimental Biology* (FASEB) but one day earlier. Since AIN became affiliated with the FASEB in 1941, annual meetings have, of course, been held with the other FASEB member societies.

The AIN served as host and sponsored the Fifth International Congress on Nutrition held in the United States in September, 1960, which was attended by approximately twenty-three hundred nutritionists, of whom nearly six hundred were from sixty-seven countries other than Canada and the United States. In August, 1981, the AIN and its division, ASCN, hosted the Twelfth International Congress on Nutrition in San Diego, California. It should be noted in this connection, too, that the AIN nominates members for the U.S. National Committee of the International Union of Nutritional Sciences. Nationally, the AIN has consistently cooperated on nutritional problems and programs with governmental agencies, business firms, and other organizations and is one of six societies sponsoring the National Nutrition Consortium.

The AIN for many years sponsored several awards in the field of nutrition: Borden, Mead Johnson, Osborne, Mendal, and Conrad A. Elvejehm. Recently the Lederle and Bio Serv awards were added as well as the Foremost-McKesson Research Scholarships. As many as five fellows are selected annually in recognition of distinguished service to nutrition.

Membership standards have always been high in that prospective members must show concrete evidence of research accomplishment. This normally consists of three original research papers, following those credited to the Ph.D., in refereed scientific journals. It should be noted, too, that approximately 95 percent of the present members have either a Ph.D. or

M.D. degree or both. The AIN, nevertheless, has grown from the initial 178 members to over 2,000 today. It has the following categories of membership: active, which includes foreign members, who comprise about 5 percent of the total membership; associate; emeritus; and honorary, elected for the first time in 1960. The latter are distinguished individuals of any country who have contributed to the advance of the science of nutrition. After 1981 distinguished foreign scientists will be elected as fellows of the AIN.

The AIN elects the customary institutional officers; it conducts its business from an office, headed by an executive officer, located at FASEB headquarters in Bethesda, Maryland.

For further information, see a commemorative issue published by the AIN in 1978, entitled *A History of the American Institute of Nutrition 1928-1978*, which includes the proceedings of a symposium commemorating the fiftieth anniversary of the *Journal of Nutrition*. See also the following articles in the *Journal of Nutrition:* John R. Murlin, "Editorial—Transfer of the *Journal of Nutrition* to the Wistar Institute" (March, 1934); "Proceedings of the First Annual Meetings of the American Institute of Nutrition" (May, 1934); George R. Cowgill, "John R. Murlin—Honor Volume" (January, 1946); E. S. Nassett, "John Raymond Murlin—Investigator, Teacher, Colleague" (January, 1946); Harry J. Deuel, Jr., "Biography of Graham Lusk" (May, 1950).

AMERICAN INSTITUTE OF PHYSICS (AIP). The AIP was founded in 1931 as a means to preserve communication among physicists as a whole in the face of increasing expense of journal publication and the dispersal of physicists into an increasing number of special fields. Leaders in physics were aware that in other disciplines, such as chemistry, this problem had been solved by structuring the different special fields as divisions or sections within one central society. The American Physical Society's* (APS) Committee on Applied Physics, however, explored this plan and rejected it in favor of an "Institute of Physics," which would allow it and other existing individual societies to retain their autonomy. Acting upon a December, 1930, report of the committee calling for the establishment of such an institute and led by Drs. Karl T. Compton, George B. Pegram, and others, the APS, the Optical Society of America, and the Acoustical Society of America formed a joint committee that met at Columbia University on February 27, 1931. Pursuant to recommendations adopted at that meeting and with the offer of a grant for start-up purposes from the Chemical Foundation, these societies agreed to establish the AIP. A governing board, consisting of three members from each society, together with three from the Society of Rheology, which had been invited to join the AIP, held its first meeting on May 3, 1931, in Washington, D.C. Shortly thereafter, on January 27, 1932, the American Association of Physics Teachers was admitted as a founder society with the other four.

Retrospectively, Dr. Henry A. Barton, director of the AIP for its first twenty-six years, had this to say as to the reasons for its founding:

The American Institute of Physics began in October, 1931, a time of great difficulty for our science. This was the decade of the Great Depression, and a widespread "stop-science" movement blamed us for society's problems. It was also a time of divisiveness within physics. In 1899, one group, the American Physical Society, could encompass all physicists, but separatism had given rise to five societies. The leaders of that time, men such as Paul D. Foote, George B. Pegram, F. K. Richtmyer, and Karl T. Compton, conceived of the rather close federation, that is, AIP, to bring physicists together again, to improve the relations between physics and the rest of society and, not incidentally, to serve as the publisher of the increasingly important U.S. physics literature. [*Physics Today* (June, 1971)]

Except for a temporary, legalistic interval at the time of incorporation and a period from 1946 to 1958, the AIP has had no individual members of its own. Members of the individual societies are automatically members of the AIP. Four additional member societies have been added since its founding: American Crystallographic Association, American Astronomical Society* (AAS), American Association of Physicists in Medicine, and American Vacuum Society. In addition to these regular member societies, the AIP constitution provides for the following four other types of membership: associate member society, which in the past served as an interim step prior to admission to the AIP as a regular member society; affiliated society, some fifteen local, regional, or national organizations interested in physics; corporate associates, some one hundred major corporations and laboratories whose annual dues contribute toward the support of the AIP's programs; and sponsorship of a Society of Physics Students with about six thousand members in chapters at some 450 colleges and universities.

Publication of the journals of its member societies has, from the beginning, been a major activity of the AIP. Thus, the *Physical Review* and *Review of Modern Physics* as well as its *Bulletin* are published for the APS. The AIP publishes the *Journal of the Optical Society of America*; *Journal of the Acoustical Society of America*; *Journal of Vacuum Science and Technology*; and *American Journal of Physics* for the American Association of Physics Teachers; the *Astronomical Journal* for the AAS; and *Medical Physics* for the American Association of Physicists in Medicine. Ownership and editorial control of these publications have been retained by each of the societies, but the AIP handles routine publication matters. The AIP, in its own name, publishes and edits the *Review of Scientific Instruments, Journal of Applied Physics, Physics of Fluids, Journal of Mathematical Physics,* and *Physics Today*. The latter journal is a news and communication medium rather than a technical journal and has a circulation in excess of seventy thousand.

Since the 1950s, the AIP has engaged in an extensive translation program of Russian-language journals and occasionally books dealing with physics. The program, started with the assistance of grants from the National Science Foundation, is completely self-supporting. Negotiations for a similar Chinese journal program, to begin in the early 1980s, are currently underway. AIP sponsors the publication of other books from time to time and cooperates with the United Kingdom's Institute of Physics in its publication program. As a result the AIP today publishes approximately 90 percent of all journal articles published on physics research in the United States and about 25 percent of the world's physical literature.

The AIP carries on other programs designed to advance physics and to serve the public interest through physics. Its education program is concerned with strengthening education in physics at all levels and has included such projects as a visiting physicist program for high schools, colleges, and universities, course content improvement, design of physics buildings, construction of teaching apparatus, and preparation of career booklets. The public information program promotes a wider public understanding of physics. In addition to setting up press rooms and news conferences at member society meetings, the AIP has held seminars for science news writers to provide them with background information essential to an understanding of rapidly advancing fields of physics so that they may better interpret physics to the lay public. Other activities include manpower studies and operation of a free placement service for the use of employers and of physicists seeking jobs. The AIP holds an annual meeting of its corporate associates as well as occasional assemblies of society officers. Also it cooperates with other institutions in sponsoring conferences in interdisciplinary fields. The AIP administers and annually awards various prizes in recognition of distinguished achievements in physics and makes grants to support research projects by chapters of its Society of Physics Students. One of its more recent accomplishments was the establishment, early in the 1960s, of the Niels Bohr Library. Providing extensive manuscript and other archival resources for research in the history of physics, the library's holdings form the core of an ongoing program to study the development of contemporary physics and tell the story of its impact upon society.

From 1931 until 1957 Dr. Henry A. Barton was director of the AIP. His successors included Drs. Elmer Hutchinson, Ralph A. Sawyer, and Van Zandt Williams. The present director, Dr. H. William Koch was elected in 1967. From a membership in the five founding societies of an estimated thirty-five hundred, the number of physicists represented by the AIP grew to about twenty-five thousand in 1960 and more than fifty thousand today. These figures exclude the affiliated societies and corporate associates.

Initially housed in offices at the Chemical Foundation building, during World War II the AIP acquired and renovated a brownstone office building of its own at 57 East Fifty-fifth Street in New York City. Subsequent growth spurred the purchase and move into its present headquarters building at 335 East Forty-fifth Street, New York, New York 10017. Since that time the increase in the publication program has forced the acquisition of additional leased space in two other locations in New York City and one in Stony Brook, Long Island. In 1977 the decision was reached to acquire a building and site at Woodbury, Long Island, which would become the center for the AIP's publishing activities. Thus the staff of about 380 would be allocated between the Forty-fifth Street and Woodbury sites, with publishing personnel located primarily at the latter.

The AIP does not hold inclusive, annual meetings, its policies and operations being carried through by meetings of its governing board, generally held twice a year, plus recommendations of its committees and the professional staff. The board presently consists of twenty-eight members, twenty-three of whom are elected by the member societies according to a formula based upon the number of members within each society and two at-large members elected by the board. The board also elects the chairman, secretary, and director, who are ex officio members. The director serves as the principal executive officer of the AIP.

For further information, see *Annual Report* and *Purpose and Program* published by the AIP. There is no comprehensive history of the AIP. For brief accounts of it by its first director, see H. A. Barton, "The Story of the American Institute of Physics," *Physics Today* (June, 1956), and "Four Decades of AIP," *Physics Today* (June, 1971).

AMERICAN MATHEMATICAL SOCIETY (AMS). Prior to the founding of Johns Hopkins University in 1876, very little study, research, or writing in abstract mathematics was done in U.S. colleges and universities. In that year the English mathematician Professor J. J. Sylvester began teaching at Hopkins, and his students, plus those who had studied at German universities, provided a nucleus of such mathematicians, which resulted in this country in increased interest in the subject and in the founding of such mathematical journals as the *American Journal of Mathematics*, 1878, and the *Annals of Mathematics* in 1884. The *Journal* was established at Johns Hopkins University and has been published continuously by that university with the collaboration, since 1927, of the AMS. The *Annals* was established at the University of Virginia and published there until 1899. Subsequently Harvard University and later Princeton University took it over. Since 1933 the Institute for Advanced Study* (IAS) has engaged with Princeton in its publication.

It is against this background that, in 1888, six members of the Mathematics Department at Columbia University, led by a young mathematics instructor, Dr. Thomas S. Fiske, organized the New York Mathematical Society. By 1890 the members, who had increased to 22, decided that they wished to publish another journal that would be devoted to critical articles and reviews and provide news of mathematical interest. They also decided that they would seek a national membership base for the undertaking. Circular letters, therefore, were sent to mathematicians in other sections of the United States outlining the proposal and inviting them to join the society, with the result that membership jumped to 174 in 1891, and the first number of the monthly, later bimonthly, *Bulletin, American Mathematical Society*, appeared at that time. By 1894 membership had increased to such an extent, and on a nationwide basis, that the New York Mathematical Society, justifiably, became the American Mathematical Society.

In 1900 the AMS began publication of the bimonthly *Transactions* containing mathematical articles presented at its meetings; in 1940 *Mathematical Reviews*, which is international in its circulation and coverage; in 1950, the *Proceedings*; and in 1954 the *Notices*. The latter journal contains material of a business and news nature that formerly appeared in the *Bulletin*. The AMS has engaged in a translation program of foreign mathematical books and articles, particularly Russian, and has from time to time sponsored the publication of books, special surveys, memoirs, reviews, and similar material.

Reflecting its origin, the AMS has been primarily interested in pure research and scholarship in mathematics, with the teaching of mathematics a subsidiary interest. The reverse of this is true of another society, the Mathematical Association of America* (MAA). Through the years, the AMS has been the recipient of a number of different funds; and it has used the prizes and other awards made from these funds as an incentive to mathematical research. They include the Bocher Memorial Prize in Analysis; the Frank Nelson Cole Prize in Algebra, and the Frank Nelson Cole Prize in the Theory of Numbers; the Oswald Veblen Prize in Geometry; the George David Birkoff Prize in Applied Mathematics, the Norbert Weiner Prize in Applied Mathematics, and the LeRoy P. Steele Prizes. Each of these prizes is awarded for a significant mathematical research publication.

The primary achievement of the AMS, however, has been the usual learned society one of providing an information network for U.S. mathematicians. This has been accomplished by its publications and by the meetings held under its auspices, which include those held in January and August jointly with the MAA and other groups as well as sponsored ones, such as summer mathematical institutes, held in various sections of the country.

Ordinary membership is open to professionally qualified mathematicians. Contributing, institutional, and corporate membership is open to individuals and organizations interested in furthering the work of the AMS. The total present membership is approximately nineteen thousand.

The AMS elects the customary institutional officers; it maintains a business office, headed by an executive director, located in Providence, Rhode Island. An editorial office for *Mathematical Reviews* is located in Ann Arbor, Michigan.

For further information, see the publications of the AMS discussed above, particularly Thomas S. Fiske, "Mathematical Progress in America" *Bulletin, American Mathematical Society* (February, 1905); and Gordon L. Walker, "Publications of the American Mathematical Society," *Notices, American Mathematical Society* (April, 1960). For a now outdated history of the AMS, see Raymond C. Archibald, *A Semicentennial History of the American Mathematical Society, 1888-1938* (1938). See also R. G. D. Richardson, "American Mathematical Society," *Proceedings, Casualty Actuarial Society* (November, 1924); and J. R. Kline, "American Mathematical Society," *AAAS Bulletin* (May, 1943).

AMERICAN METEOROLOGICAL SOCIETY (AMS). The organization of the AMS in 1919 can be traced to a concern about the future of meteorological science following the ebb of interest in it, particularly by the U.S. government, after World War I. Professor Charles F. Brooks of Harvard University, noting the sharp reductions in the 1919 governmental appropriation for the *Monthly Weather Review*, took the lead in urging that an organization be set up to counteract this development. Following discussion and correspondence with academic colleagues, government workers, and others, it was he who announced in the summer of 1919 that an organizational meeting for an AMS would be held in Saint Louis on December 29 of that year. At this meeting a constitution and bylaws, modeled after those of the American Physical Society* (APS), were adopted; immediate membership of the new society was arranged within the American Association for the Advancement of Science* (AAAS); officers were elected, Professor Robert Decourcy Ward of Harvard University being named the first president; and by January, 1920, the AMS numbered 586 members.

The monthly *Bulletin* of the AMS, under the editorship of Professor Brooks from 1920 to 1936, has been published continuously and contains meteorological papers, reviews, notes, and correspondence. The increasing demands for worldwide knowledge of weather conditions during World War II resulted in 1944 in the establishment of the bimonthly *Journal of Meteorology*, to be devoted to technical articles at the professional level. In 1962, the *Journal of Meteorology* was superseded by the *Journal of the Atmospheric Sciences*, and a new *Journal of Applied Meteorology* was inaugurated. The *Journal of Physical Oceanography* was established in 1971. The AMS has also sponsored the publication of *Weatherwise* from 1948 until 1976; since 1978, the AMS has been affiliated with the Helen Dwight Reid Educational Foundation in its publication of *Weatherwise*. The AMS has also published *Meteorological and Geoastrophysical Abstracts* since 1950, and the *Monthly Weather Review* since 1974 (formerly published by the National Oceanic and Atmospheric Administration). During the 1950s and 1960s it sponsored the translation and publication of foreign-language articles and journals dealing with meteorology. In addition, the AMS has published various other works, the best-known being the *Compendium of Meteorology* (1951), containing over one hundred articles on all phases of meteorology; the serial, *Meteorological Monographs*, now containing thirty-nine issues in seventeen volumes; and the *Glossary of Meteorology*, now in its third printing.

The AMS has set up various awards to spur research and writing in meteorology. These include, among others, the Meisinger, Carl-Gustaf Rossby, Charles Franklin Brooks, and Father James B. Macelwane awards; they cover all facets and levels of meteorological work. The AMS presently sponsors a guidance service, employment service, and professional directory in its efforts to aid meteorologists and to make a career in the field more attractive.

Annual meetings, in December or January, have been held in various cities in the United States and Canada and are devoted to scientific presentations, discussions, official business, and social activities. The AMS also sponsors or cosponsors annually twenty to thirty national and international meetings and conferences on a variety of subjects in atmospheric sciences and related fields. In addition, members have organized some eighty local chapters throughout the world. These chapters serve as hosts to conferences and provide an additional means of communication about meteorological subjects. They are presently located in forty-six states and several foreign countries.

Membership in the AMS's formative years was about equally divided between meteorologists and those with a subsidiary interest in meteorology. Between the two world wars the membership grew from its original 600 to 2,883 at the end of 1945. From the latter date to the present it has grown to almost 10,000. Nine percent of this total membership resides outside the United States, and about 3 percent are women.

There are now five grades of membership: corporation, open to organizations interested in the advancement of meteorological knowledge; member (formerly called professional), open to persons possessing requisite educational qualifications or experience; associate member, persons actively interested in meteorology; students, collegians enrolled at least half time in institutions of higher learning; and fellow, elected by the council in recognition of their significant contributions to science. Fellow and member grades comprise about 7,300 persons, corporation members number over 120, students about 1,100, and associate members comprise the remainder.

In all of its activities, the AMS has been aided by the work of its governing council and executive committee, its various commissions, now numbering five, their constituent boards and committees, and the AMS staff. Of special note in this connection was the reorganization carried out between 1944 and 1946. It grew out of greatly magnified but similar problems to those facing meteorological workers during and after World War I and had the following results. Although retaining the AMS's academic and "pure research" interest, it effectively merged it with a greatly expanded applied research interest by rearranging the grades of membership; expanding publication facilities, commented on above; and establishing the office of executive secretary, now executive director. This office has grown physically from a few rooms to its present-day quarters in a historic house overlooking Boston Common, Boston, Massachusetts, and performs a wide variety of services for all who are interested in meteorology.

For further information, see the publications of the AMS discussed above, particularly the fortieth anniversary issue of *Weatherwise* (December, 1949), containing the following articles: Charles F. Brooks, "The Society's First Quarter Century"; and David M. Ludlum, "The American Meteorological Society"; and, in the *Bulletin, American Meteorological Society* (May, 1947), I. R. Tannehill, "The History and Status of the International Meteorological Organization (I.M.O.)." See also the undated AMS pamphlet, *American Meteorological Society, Its Purposes, Its Activities, Its Organization.*

AMERICAN MORPHOLOGICAL SOCIETY. See American Society of Zoologists.

AMERICAN MUSEUM OF NATURAL HISTORY (AMNH). For more than a century, the American Museum of Natural History has been engaged in organized curiosity. From the signing of its charter in April, 1869, to the opening of its newest permanent exhibition hall, the Gardner D. Stout Hall of Asian Peoples, in October, 1980, it has been a dynamic, active place where innovation, imagination, change, and even controversy are the rule rather than the exception.

The institution is impressive, if by its numbers alone. The museum and the adjoining Hayden Planetarium consist of twenty-two interconnected buildings that cover twenty-five acres. The museum's collections contain more than 34 million objects, which include 8 million anthropological artifacts; more than 15 million insect specimens; 8.5 million fossil invertebrate specimens; 90,000 minerals; 4,500 meteorites and more than 4,000 gems. An average of 2.5 million persons visit the museum and planetarium each year.

In terms of superlatives, the museum has more specimens of birds, spiders, fossil mammals, and whale skeletons than any other institution. It has the world's largest collection of dinosaurs, the largest meteorite (thirty-four tons) and the most complete collection of termites (one million varieties).

The American museum's scientific programs involve more than two hundred scientists and their assistants, who work on hundreds of research projects in dozens of natural sciences areas. Many scientists are internationally renowned for their discoveries and analyses in their specialty fields. The museum encourages on-site research by its scientists; and it operates research stations in Florida, Arizona, and Long Island, New York.

The museum's commitment to research was stated in its 1869 charter. In addition to providing "a Museum and Library of Natural History," the institution was organized for "advancing the general knowledge of kindred subjects." It has taken that mandate and developed eleven scientific departments that are distinguished by their activity and versatility.

The Department of Animal Behavior has concentrated on the development and evolution of behavior and the special role behavior plays in the adaptation of different species. The department's investigations have taken staff scientists to the Brittany coast to study sea hares, the Arizona deserts to view army ants and lizards, and New York's concrete canyons to study cockroaches.

The Department of Anthropology has been heavily involved in the development of many of the museum's permanent and temporary exhibitions. Its scientists have explored most of the continents and have contributed greatly to the understanding of many cultures.

The Department of Astronomy, located in the Hayden Planetarium, provides an assortment of educational programs ranging from flight training and meteorology to aviation and science fiction.

The Department of Entomology, with a collection of more than fifteen million specimens, conducts research on the behavior, distribution, and history of insects and spiders. In recent years, staff scientists have explored life histories of bees, examined North American moths, and voyaged to Asia and tropical Pacific islands to study plant bugs.

The Department of Herpetology conducts long-term, in-depth research of the growth, movement, and survival of reptiles and amphibians. Scientists examine the environmental threats to some of the more common snakes, lizards, and frogs, and they also investigate the habits and development of rare species.

The Department of Ichthyology studies fishes by using a variety of scientific disciplines—biochemistry, ecology, and geology, for example—and by collaborating with staff members of other museum departments. The department's curators continue an active teaching schedule at several New York area colleges.

The Department of Invertebrates studies the changes in the earth as inferred from invertebrate fossils as well as the history and development of the invertebrates themselves. In recent years, the department's members have engaged in fossil dating of sea urchins by measuring the half-life of applied radioactive materials, examined fossil mollusks in an effort to shed new light on marine life at the end of the Paleozoic Era, and traveled to the Red Sea to observe rare algae.

The Department of Mammalogy's collection of almost a quarter of a million specimens makes it an important resource to scientists from the museum as well as other institutions. A scientific publication based in some way on the department's collection appears on the average of every six days. Recent staff research includes the ecology of racoons, behavior of giraffes, biogeography of bats, and natural history of certain Asian and Australian rodents.

The Department of Mineral Sciences focuses on the history of the earth and the processes that have formed it. Besides studying the nature and origin of minerals, rocks, and meteorites, the department played a major role in developing a museum exhibition on volcanoes and has been cited as an authoritative source by local and national media during the eruption of Mount Saint Helens in Washington.

The Department of Ornithology has a distinguished history of research and education in the evolution, systematics, and biogeography of the world's birds. With a collection of one million specimens covering 98 percent of the world's species of birds, the department conducts research at several museum-owned field stations as well as throughout the world.

The Department of Vertebrate Paleontology studies evolution of life from the perspective of the higher animals known as vertebrates. Its collection of specimens is used by research scholars from around the world. Museum scientists continue their own research throughout the United States and on several continents.

The museum's Department of Education sponsors an annual series of lectures and film programs for adults and children; coordinates performances in the fine arts that range from puppet shows to dance demonstrations; and conducts the annual Margaret Mead Film Festival, which features works by American and foreign filmmakers and anthropologists. The education program began in 1880 for teachers, was expanded to include all adults and, by 1900, was rapidly extending to the public schools. Today, more than 120,000 New York City schoolchildren participate in the Department of Education's activities each year. The department consists of 30 professional educators and 50 volunteer teachers. More than 3,000 adults attend the department's annual fall and spring lecture series. The department operates the Alexander M. White Natural Science Center and the People Center, which host more than 200,000 visitors each year. The museum also has conducted formal programs of graduate study for more than sixty years in collaboration with local universities.

The museum's library has 325,000 volumes, which represent one of the world's finest natural science research collections. The library has an active interlibrary loan program and reference service, which assist the general public and the scientific community. Its photographic collection has approximately 500,000 catalogued black-and-white photographs and more than 60,000 catalogued color transparencies of the museum's habitat groups, exhibitions, specimens, and other subjects.

The museum publishes the monthly magazine, *Natural History*, which presents articles by experts in language that can be understood by the public. *Natural History*, with a paid circulation of 460,000 and a total readership estimated at 2 million, celebrated its eightieth anniversary in 1980 by winning the essays and criticism prize of the 1980 National Magazine Awards. Other scientific publications, such as *Anthropological Papers*, *Bulletins*, and *Novitates*, are issued, on subjects ranging from anthropology to vertebrate paleontology; *Curator*, a technical journal, is published for the museum profession; and the institution's Micropaleontology Press publishes the journal *Micropaleontology*, catalogs on foraminifera and ostracoda, and issues of the *Bibliography and Index of Micropaleontology*.

The American Museum of Natural History started with a vow by Albert Smith Bickmore, a Harvard-educated naturalist, to "work for nothing else by day and dream of nothing else by night" in developing a natural history museum for New York City. Bickmore rounded up some impressive supporters, including Theodore Roosevelt, Sr. (whose son, Theodore, politician, U.S. president and conservationist, played an important role in the institution's development); Joseph H. Choate, lawyer and diplomat; Morris K. Jesup, banker and the museum's third president; J. P. Morgan, financier; Robert Colgate, soap and paint manufacturer; and J. D. Wolfe, merchant, philanthropist, and the museum's first president.

The museum opened in the old Arsenal Building in Central Park, New York City, in 1871. Six years later, it moved to its first permanent structure. It is now located at Central Park West and Seventy-Ninth Street.

Its growth and reputation as a scientific authority accelerated through a series of expeditions from the 1880s through the 1920s. These included Joel A. Allen's efforts in 1887 to collect mammals from the Western United States; the Department of Vertebrate Paleontology's series of expeditions in the 1890s to find Mesozoic and Tertiary vertebrates in western North America; the Anthropology Department's North Pacific studies from 1897 to 1903; the Lang-Chapin expedition to the Congo for reptiles, birds, and mammals; the 1921-30 Central Asiatic voyages led by Roy Chapman Andrews; and the 1920-29 Whitney South Sea expeditions primarily for birds. This "Golden Age of Exploration" provided the museum's scientists and anthropologists with rich collections of artifacts and specimens. It also enabled them to record the activities of and obtain information about many traditional societies that were rapidly changing due to the influence of Western technology.

As the museum's collections grew and as modern transportation made hard-to-reach places more accessible, the emphasis and style of the expeditions began to change. Today, an expedition is more likely to last a few weeks or months rather than years, to emphasize data collection and verification rather than big game hunting for an exhibition hall, and to involve several scientists rather than large caravans of people. The purpose, however, is the same: a continuing quest for understanding the natural environment and the nature of life.

The museum is constantly expanding, refurbishing, refining, and developing its permanent exhibitions. The newest one is the Gardner D. Stout Hall of Asian Peoples—an ambitious effort that took fourteen years of planning—which shows the underlying themes of traditional life amidst the cultural diversity of the largest continent. The hall, which opened in October, 1980, contains more than three thousand art works and artifacts from one of the largest collections of Asian objects outside that continent. It is the museum's most comprehensive anthropological exhibition.

One of the most popular exhibitions is the Hall of Minerals and Gems. It features the famous Star of India, the largest star sapphire in the world, and a vast assortment of diamonds, rubies, and other precious stones. The Arthur Ross Hall of Meteorites, which opened in 1981 next to the Hall of Minerals and Gems, displays the world's largest meteorite, Ahnighito (thirty-four tons), and its sister meteorite, the Woman (three tons).

The Hall of Ocean Life is dominated by a ninety-four-foot blue whale made of fiberglass and polyurethane. The whale, arched in a dive, is suspended from the ceiling at a single point, giving the impression of having no visible means of support.

The forty-five-foot long, twenty-foot tall Tyrannosaurus Rex is the featured attraction of the Hall of Late Dinosaurs (there's also a Hall of Early Dinosaurs). The neighboring Hall of Late Mammals and Hall of Early Mammals present skeletons of the many giant creatures that once roamed the earth.

The Hall of North American Mammals displays a wide variety of habitat groups, in which animals are depicted amid natural settings fighting, grazing, or stalking prey.

The Hall of African Mammals, highlighted by a group of elephants in the center of the exhibition, present fierce creatures safely behind glass panels. A corridor connects this hall to the Hall of Man in Africa, which contains fascinating ritual costumes, instruments, weapons, and tools to help explain the variety of traditional cultures and the environments that influenced them.

The Hayden Planetarium, which opened in October, 1935, houses the Department of Astronomy. The planetarium features the Guggenheim Space Theater, a circular area with twenty-two screens for projecting wraparound slide shows; the Hall of the Sun, the first and only major museum exhibit in the world devoted to the sun; and Astronomia, an eclectic display of astronomical fact, history, and fancy.

The focal point of the planetarium is the Sky Theater. Centered around the Zeiss Model VI projector and located under the planetarium dome, the theater presents sky shows and is used for special astronomy and celestial navigation classes and for the Laserium, the cosmic laser light concert.

The planetarium has a thirty-member staff of astronomers, educators, production personnel, an artist, librarian, and support personnel, plus part-time instructors drawn from schools and industry. Its Richard S. Perkin Library contains more than nine thousand volumes and subscribes to more than eighty periodicals.

The American Museum of Natural History, which is a private institution, had an operating budget of over twenty-one million dollars in 1980. Its governing board of trustees has forty-three elected members, seven ex-officio members, and fourteen honorary members. Robert G. Goelet is the AMNH's president and Thomas D. Nicholson is the director and chief executive officer.

For further information, see Geoffrey Hellman, *Bankers, Bones and Beetles: The First Century of the American Museum of Natural History* (1968). See also American Museum of Natural History, *Annual Reports* (1869 to date).

ROBERT STEYER

AMERICAN MUSICOLOGICAL SOCIETY (AMS). As early as its annual meeting of 1929, the American Council of Learned Societies* (ACLS) expressed the view that, "the history and science of music constitute an important branch of learning" and directed its executive committee "to appoint a standing committee on musicology and to take such other measures as may be calculated to promote research and education in that field."

The subsequent appointment of the committee was welcomed by U.S. musicologists because the field was new to the country and there was then no national organization to serve their needs. This committee issued surveys, reports, and bibliographies, but in a few years its members decided that the growth in strength and maturity of musicology, particularly in college and university teaching and research, called for an independent organization of national scope and membership. With committee members playing a leading role, the American Musicological Society was subsequently organized in 1934.

The AMS has stimulated research in music and disseminates musicological information in various ways. It published annually from 1936 to 1941 *Papers of the American Musicological Society*, and from 1936 to 1948 *Bulletins of the American Musicological Society*. Since 1948 it has published its triennial periodical, *Journal of the American Musicological Society* and, since 1971, a *Newsletter*, two issues annually.

One of the AMS's achievements has been its assistance in the publication of learned works that for reason of expense and limited sales could not be printed through commercial channels. Three volumes of the *Collected Works of Okeghem*, a ranking fifteenth-century composer, and others by such composers as Dunstable, are examples of works published by the AMS. In addition, the AMS has provided subventions for a variety of miscellaneous works published by university presses and commercial publishing houses.

Training and research in musicology has also been advanced through AMS regional and national meetings. Presently fifteen chapters of the AMS are distributed across the country. Each of these meets for the reading and discussion of papers, abstracts of which have been published in the *Journal.* Annual meetings have been held in the fall in various parts of the country for the entire membership.

Initially membership was open to "persons who have been nominated by any member," but now it is open to all who are simply interested in musicology. The AMS has regular, student, and institutional categories of membership, which presently totals about five thousand.

The AMS elects the customary institutional officers; it conducts its business from a central office, headed by a treasurer and executive director, located in Philadelphia, Pennsylvania.

For further information, see the publications of the AMS discussed above and letter from William J. Mitchell, Secretary, AMS, to Charles E. Odegaard, Executive Director, ACLS (October 1, 1950). This five-page letter and supporting documents was the successful application of the AMS for membership in the ACLS and provides historical information about the society.

AMERICAN NUMISMATIC AND ARCHAEOLOGICAL SOCIETY. See American Numismatic Society.

AMERICAN NUMISMATIC SOCIETY. This society was organized on April 16, 1858, in New York City, by twelve New Yorkers with the object of "the collection and preservation of coins and medals, with an investigation into their history, and other subjects connected therewith." It was incorporated in New York in 1865, under the corporate name of the "American Numismatic and Archaeological Society"; but, in 1907, the name was changed back to the original "American Numismatic Society."

Coins and medals and books about them were collected from the inception of the society. For fifty years it rented rooms to house its collection and hold meetings. Then, in 1910, through the generosity of interested members, the society erected its own museum and headquarters in upper Manhattan in New York City. The museum is unique in that it is a museum devoted exclusively to numismatics. Elsewhere coin and medal collections invariably form a department or section of museums, libraries, and similar institutions. Also, unlike comparable national collections abroad, such as the Department of Coins and Medals of the British Museum or the Cabinet des Medailles in Paris, it is not supported by our government, relying primarily on membership fees and endowments.

The collections of coins and the related library in the museum form the reason and core of societal operations. The coin collections total about one million; all ages and areas are represented; the ancient Greek and Roman,

Islamic, and Far Eastern collections are exceptional. The library consists of over seventy-five thousand books, periodicals, and pamphlets covering all facets of numismatics, together with a file of mounted illustrations of ancient coins, half a million in number, and a collection of plaster casts of coins not presently in its possession. The society makes these collections available to numismatists, archaeologists, historians, and other scholars interested in numismatics. Since 1952, a summer seminar for a limited number of graduate students has become a successful part of the society program. In addition, one dissertation fellowship is awarded each year.

The society founded the *American Journal of Numismatics* in 1866, and published articles and reports therein until it was suspended in 1923. The present major publishing activities of the society comprise five series: *Numismatic Notes and Monographs*, published intermittently, since 1920, consists of some 160 titles dealing with extensive study of some numismatic topic. *Numismatic Studies*, initiated in 1938, accommodates works requiring a larger format for illustration purposes; 15 publications have appeared in this series. The society journal, *Museum Notes*, began in 1946 as an irregular publication but is now issued annually. In 1969, the society began the systematic publication of its entire ancient Greek collection, and, to date, 5 publications of a projected 55 have appeared. *Numismatic Literature* is a semiannual abstract bibliography of the literature in the profession relying for its content on a board of contributing editors located in all of the major intellectual centers of the world. Approximately 2,500 titles are analyzed each year.

There are three regular meetings annually of the American Numismatic Society plus occasional special meetings. The annual meeting in January is devoted to the reports of officers and by staff members on outstanding accessions; lecture meetings are convened in the spring and fall.

There are four classes of membership in the society: fellows, honorary fellows, associate members, and corresponding members. Fellows are limited to 150; honorary fellows, those who have rendered special service to the society, are limited to 50. Only the fellows are eligible to vote and hold office in the society. Associate membership is open to all with an interest in numismatics. Persons or organizations abroad may be elected corresponding members, which is also honorary. Total society membership is approximately 2,000.

The society elects the customary institutional officers; it conducts its business from its museum building, headed by a director, located in New York, New York.

For further information see the publications of the society discussed above. See also the handbooks, *American Numismatic Society* (1966), and *Guide to User Service* (1979), available from the society. A detailed history of the society's first one hundred years is provided in Howard L. Adelson, *The American Numismatic Society 1858-1958* (1958).

AMERICAN ONCOLOGIC HOSPITAL. See Fox Chase Cancer Center.

AMERICAN ORIENTAL SOCIETY. Founded in 1842 by John Pickering, a cultured Boston businessman, this society is one of the oldest national learned societies in the United States. It was preceded only by the American Philosophical Society* (APS), American Academy of Arts and Sciences,* and American Antiquarian Society* (AAS). Reflecting the statement of purpose in its original constitution of 1849, the aims of the American Oriental Society from that time to the present have always been the encouragement of basic research in the language and literature of Asia. Included therein have come to be such subjects as philology, literary criticism, textual criticism, paleography, epigraphy, linguistics, biography, and the history of the intellectual and imaginative aspects of Oriental civilizations, especially of philosophy, religion, folklore, and art.

In pursuing these aims society members first concentrated on three major areas of interest; the Near East, including Africa; South and Southeast Asia; and the Far East. In 1925 it was estimated that the percentage of societal interest in these areas was, respectively, 70 percent, 20 percent, and 10 percent. Today, the interests of the society have been expanded to include Islam and Inner Asia, and the percentages of members interested in each of the five areas and fields represented are about evenly divided.

The American Oriental Society does not officially carry on research of its own, but it has been a means of encouragement for members pursuing philological studies in the ancient and modern worlds of the East through its publications. The *Journal of the American Oriental Society*, established in 1849, now appears four times a year, volume 100 being current, and presents articles and other literature in the field. In 1924 an *American Oriental Series* was set up, volume 63 being current, which provides a medium of publication for essay and book-length works.

Originally there were two classes of societal membership: corporate and honorary. The corporate members were active members who carried on its work and activities. Candidates for such membership required proposal and reception of a three-fourths vote of the members present at a meeting. Honorary membership was afforded foreigners under the same conditions. Corresponding members, in the persons of attachés and others located abroad, were admitted in the 1850s and 1860s but discontinued in 1876 because improved means of communication eliminated the benefits that had been derived from this type of membership. In the 1920s the laws were revised so that candidates for corporate membership could be proposed by any member, and an honorary associate membership (now discontinued) was added. Presently, corporate membership is open to any person in sympathy with the purposes of the society and recommended by a member, and life memberships have been added. Total membership is now approximately 1,750.

Annual meetings of the society are held between March 15 and April 30, generally in cities along the North Atlantic seaboard, with programs prepared by special committees. Officers and committees present reports there, and members read papers. Some of these papers and the business matters connected with such meetings are published in the *Journal of the American Oriental Society*.

Since 1917 a number of society branches have been established to provide for meetings for groups of members living at too great a distance to attend annual meetings. Thus, the Middle West branch, Western branch, and Southwestern branch hold annual meetings, occurring at approximately the same time as the major American Oriental Society meeting.

The society elects the customary institutional officers; it conducts its business from an office, headed by a secretary-treasurer, located in New Haven, Connecticut.

For further information, see the publications of the society discussed above, particularly the *Journal of the American Oriental Society*. See also Survey, American Oriental Society; and *Information Leaflet* (undated).

AMERICAN PHILOLOGICAL ASSOCIATION (APA). By 1869 philology had become a dominating scholarly interest in Europe, and in the United States many philologists who had been trained in Europe were at the zenith of their intellectual vigor. The catalytic agent in the formation of the American Philological Association in that year was Professor George M. Comfort of Allegheny College in Meadville, Pennsylvania. It was he, following correspondence with a considerable number of other philologists, who called a conference in New York City on November 13, 1868, where he proposed the organization of a learned society modeled on the Sammlung der Deutschen Philologen und Schulmänner, organized at Göttingen in 1837. The fifty or so scholars assembled at the conference agreed that, as in the case of the German society, the proposed APA activities should embrace the entire field of philology. Thereupon an organizing convention was agreed upon, to meet in Poughkeepsie, New York, in July, 1869, and it was there that the APA came into existence.

The APA may reasonably be designated an offshoot of the American Oriental Society,* which since 1848 had maintained a classical section. It was some twenty members of this section, including Professor Comfort, together with the members of the Greek Club of New York, who furnished the nucleus of the new APA and furnished its first officers.

The first few decades of activity of the APA were concerned with other language studies in addition to the classical languages and literature. There was a gradual concentration, however, upon the latter, and this development was accelerated by the establishment of the Modern Language Association of America* (MLA) in 1883, which drew the APA from studies in American Indian, English, modern European languages, and so on. By

1919, the APA's present object, the advancement of ancient Greek and Latin philology only, was clearly defined and pursued. Through the succeeding years it has constantly encouraged the study and teaching of the Classics in secondary schools and colleges and universities. For example, in 1951 it established the Award of Merit, since 1969 named the Charles Goodwin Award. Each year since that time the award has been given to a member of the APA for a work deemed to be an outstanding contribution to classical scholarship. In 1979 it established annual Awards for Excellence in the Teaching of the Classics. In 1960 it was largely responsible for the launching of a program for reprinting out-of-print but sorely needed Greek and Latin college textbooks and for commissioning scholars to write new commentaries on Greek and Latin texts needed for college teaching but lacking in modern commentaries. Five of the latter have been published to date.

From its founding until 1905 the APA annual meetings were held in July. At that time, as the result of the insistence of many members, particularly those from the Midwest, who maintained that most of the other learned societies held their meetings in December and that the July meetings conflicted with summer university sessions and travel plans, the time of the annual meeting was changed to the Christmas—New Year's period. Since then the annual meetings have usually been held jointly with the Archaeological Institute of America* (AIA) and, occasionally other societies, such as the MLA, American Historical Association* (AHA), and the Linguistic Society of America* (LSA). Prior to World War II, some of these meetings were held in other sections of the country, but the vast majority were convened in the East. Since that time, annual meetings have been held in rough geographical rotation in the Northeast, South, Midwest, and once per decade in Canada. A Philological Association of the Pacific Coast was affiliated with the APA in 1900, but this bond was severed by mutual consent, in 1962.

The regular publication of the APA is the annual volume which, until 1896, bore the title "Transactions" and, since then, "Transactions and Proceedings." Until 1977, each annual volume was divided into two parts: the *Transactions*, which contain papers read at the annual meetings and selected for publication; and the *Proceedings*, which contain minutes of the meetings, other administrative matters, and, until 1962, the record of the meetings of the Philological Association of the Pacific Coast. In 1977 the *Proceedings* were discontinued, the annual volume now being *Transactions*, and administrative matters have since been covered in a quarterly *Newsletter*.

In connection with its publication program, it should be noted, the APA participates in the Scholars Press, a nonprofit publishing consortium, together with the Society of Biblical Literature* (SBL) and the American Academy of Religion* (AAR).

From the beginning, APA membership has been open to "any lover of philological studies," upon a usually pro forma election by its governing board of directors. Growth in membership has been slow but steady. It stood at approximately one thousand in 1925 and presently numbers about twenty-eight hundred persons.

The APA elects the customary institutional officers; it conducts its business from an office, headed by a secretary-treasurer, presently located in New York, New York.

For further information, see the publications of the APA discussed above, particularly the following articles, all in volume 50 (1919) of *Transactions and Proceedings, American Philological Association:* Frank Gardner Moore, "History of the American Philological Association"; Paul Shorey, "Fifty Years of Classical Study in America"; Jefferson Elmore, "The Philological Association of the Pacific Coast." In volume 94 (1963), see Lucius R. Shero, "The American Philological Association: An Historical Sketch." See also Survey, APA; and Harry L. Levy, "The American Philological Association," *ACLS Newsletter* (February, 1968).

AMERICAN PHILOSOPHICAL ASSOCIATION (APA). In the decade following the 1892 founding of the American Psychological Association,* an increasing divergence of interests between psychologists and philosophers took place; the meetings of the philosophers were devoted to purely philosophical as well as psychological questions. Separate sessions for the philosophers was ultimately resorted to in the annual meeting of 1898, and in 1901 a group of philosophers at Cornell University led in the founding in November of that year in New York, of an independent American Philosophical Association (APA) with ninety-eight members. Another organization of philosophers, the Western Philosophical Association, had already been in existence since January 1, 1900, and a little later, the Southern Philosophical Association, came into being. Early in the 1920s attempts were made to amalgamate the three, and after 1924, to include the newly organized Society for Philosophy on the Pacific Coast, into a true APA. A union did not take place, but in 1927 the APA, the Western, and the Pacific associations adopted a constitution forming themselves into an American Philosophical Association but retaining their individual entities as the Eastern, Western, and Pacific divisions. Finally, in 1969, the division membership was done away with, and the APA became more centralized.

Since its beginnings, the APA has had committees at work in such areas as International Cultural Cooperation, Bibliography, and Publications. From 1969 on, however, the committee structure has greatly expanded and includes committees on Career Opportunities, Professional Rights, Teaching of Philosophy, Status and Future of the Profession, and numerous others. Its primary activity remains, however, the holding of meetings for the presentation and discussion of papers, but also with emphasis upon placement activities and the transaction of business.

Recently the APA established a program of congressional fellows in philosophy. From 1902 until 1969, the organization known as the Eastern Division met annually during the last days of December, usually at the principal university cities in the East. Throughout the same period the Western Division held similar meetings during the spring in the Midwest, and the Pacific Divison also met annually. Although the 1969 reorganization resulted in the elimination of division membership, the APA has since continued to hold three regional meetings a year, usually in March, April, and December.

None of the three divisions publish a journal. The papers presented at meetings were printed by private philosophical periodicals, which were largely dependent upon the support and contributions of APA members. However, for many years the *Journal of Philosophy* published resumes of all the meetings summarizing papers and some of the discussions, and for a time, papers, or abstracts of papers, were also published in the *Philosophical Review*. In more recent years, the *Journal of Philosophy* has published papers read at the symposia held at the Eastern meetings and the abstracts of other papers presented at the same meetings. Papers read at the Western and Pacific meetings have been abstracted and published less systematically.

The full programs of all meetings, along with the presidential addresses, official proceedings, and membership list, were originally published annually in the *Philosophical Review*, but beginning in 1928 the publication of this material was taken over by the APA in its *Proceedings and Addresses*. Since the latter does not include other papers presented at the meetings, these are usually submitted by their authors to various philosophical journals, including the two mentioned above, the *Philosophical Review* published quarterly by the Sage School of Philosophy, Cornell University, and the *Journal of Philosophy*, until 1921 the *Journal of Philosophy, Psychology and Scientific Methods*, published under the auspices of the Department of Philosophy, Columbia University.

The APA membership originally consisted almost exclusively of professors of philosophy in universities and colleges, although a few individuals interested in the subject were admitted as associate members. In 1969 the distinction between full and associate members was abolished, but the status of student membership was introduced and is open to graduate students in the field. The total membership today is approximately six thousand, and all of the states of the Union and a number of foreign countries are represented.

The APA elects the customary institutional officers; it conducts its business from an office, headed by an executive secretary, located at Newark, Delaware.

For further information, see the publications of the APA discussed above, particularly H. N. Gardiner, "The First Twenty-Five Years of the American Philosophical Association," *Philosophical Review* (March, 1926). See also Survey, APA; Robert G. Turnbull, "The American

Philosophical Association," *ACLS Newsletter* (March, 1968); and Daniel J. Wilson, "Professionalization and Organized Discussion in the American Philosophical Association 1900-1922," *Journal of the History of Philosophy* (January, 1979).

AMERICAN PHILOSOPHICAL SOCIETY. See American Philosophical Society, Held at Philadelphia, for Promoting Useful Knowledge.

AMERICAN PHILOSOPHICAL SOCIETY, HELD AT PHILADEL-PHIA, FOR PROMOTING USEFUL KNOWLEDGE (APS). Usually called the American Philosophical Society, the APS is the oldest learned society in the United States. Although some of its members in the past have argued that its date of founding was 1727, it is now generally agreed that Benjamin Franklin founded it in 1743, primarily to encourage investigation into native productions, agricultural methods, and manufacturing and mining processes that would benefit the colonies. The society lasted for two or three years, electing to membership not only Philadelphians but "philosophers" in other provinces; then it died—or became "dormant," as Franklin later preferred to believe. In 1766, in response to the Stamp Act, another society was founded. Named the American Society for Promoting and Propagating Useful Knowledge, Held at Philadelphia, its purposes were similar to the older group. Its founders and members were younger men, who neglected to ask survivors of the 1743 society to join. Feeling themselves insulted, the latter revived the original APS. Thus, between 1767 and 1769, there were two learned societies in Philadelphia, each inter-colonial in membership and interests. The two united in 1769 as the American Philosophical Society, Held at Philadelphia, for Promoting Useful Knowledge. Benjamin Franklin was elected its president and was reelected annually to that office until his death in 1790.

An initial scientific research project conducted under APS auspices was the observation of the transit of Venus in 1769. This enterprise, which was an international effort, linked the astronomers of British American colonies with those of England, France, and Russia, and established the international reputation of the APS. The observations were published in the *Philosophical Transactions* of the Royal Society of London and, in 1771, in the first volume of the APS's own *Transactions*.

Most of the founding fathers of the United States belonged to the APS, including George Washington, John Adams, Alexander Hamilton, Thomas Paine, Baron Von Steuben, and the Marquis de Lafayette. Thomas Jefferson during the years that he was president of the United States (1801-1809) also served as president of the APS (1797-1814). Jefferson wanted the APS to sponsor an exploration of the West by the French botanist Michaux. A few years later, when he sent Lewis and Clark to explore the Louisiana Territory, he called on the APS to draft scientific instructions and afterward deposited their report in its library. The records of other Western exploring parties and much of the Indian-language material, which forms the basis for the present-day program of the APS in Indian ethnohistory and linguistics, were also collected during Jefferson's presidency. In 1840 Charles Pemberton Fox presented the APS with most of the papers and correspondence of Benjamin Franklin, which Franklin's grandson had left in the care of Fox's father. From these initial acquisitions, the APS library has continued to add to its holdings, concentrating on the early history of science and learning in America. To house its collection, in excess of 160,000 books, 45,000 pamphlets, and about 5,000,000 manuscripts, the APS erected a new library in 1959 opposite its headquarters in historic Philosophical Hall.

From 1769 until 1911, the society held fortnightly meetings, except for a three-year hiatus during the American Revolution. After the latter date, monthly meetings were begun. In 1902, an annual general meeting in the spring was inaugurated, and in 1936 a general meeting in the fall was begun and the monthly meetings were discontinued. These meetings are characterized by the presentation of scholarly papers and symposia spanning all areas of knowledge.

The APS began publishing soon after its inception. The first volume of the *Transactions* was issued in 1771, and was followed by others in 1786, 1793, 1802, and 1809. The year 1818 saw the beginning of the new series of the *Transactions*, and seventy-one volumes have been published since that date. The *Transactions*, which originally contained short studies of a varied nature, is now primarily employed for the printing of monographs of a specialized nature. The *Proceedings* was founded in 1838. This journal is now issued bimonthly and contains many of the papers presented at the meetings. Prior to the establishment of the *Year Book* in 1937, the *Proceedings* also contained the minutes of the meetings, lists of members, and other APS news that now appears in the *Year Book*. The *Memoirs*, established in 1935, rounds out the publications of the APS and includes scholarly works in all disciplines.

An important APS activity, since its receipt of various bequests in the past five decades, has been a program of grants-in-aid for research in a variety of areas. Because of its grants program, the APS, which is primarily a learned society, has one of the attributes of a foundation. The largest of these bequests are the Penrose Research Fund, the Johnson Research Fund, the Daland Research Fund, and the I. Minis Hays Fund. These funds provide the APS with approximately $450,000 annually for grants in aid of research. The other endowments produce nearly $1 million annually for library acquisitions, publications, and the APS's other programs and general administrative expenses. No monies are received from public sources. In addition, the APS awards prizes, such as the Henry M. Phillips Prize in jurisprudence and the Karl Spencer Lashley Prize in neurobiology, as well as several others for outstanding essays and papers on various topics.

Membership in the APS has always been an honorary distinction, and election thereto has consequently been restricted. Prior to 1902, the number of new members elected annually was small. In that year, a limitation of 15 was imposed. Subsequently, membership was limited to 500 for residents of the United States. At present, 20 residents of the United States and 10 residents of foreign countries may be elected each year. The membership in 1980 stood at 515 residents of the United States and 126 abroad.

In the eighteenth century, the majority of the APS members were from the Philadelphia area, including the entire Delaware Valley; but from the very beginning members were elected from all of the British colonies, including the West Indies, and from Britain, France, Holland, Germany, and Sweden. Today the geographical distribution of U.S. members is widespread, with only about 10 percent residing in the Philadelphia area. The first woman was elected a member of the APS in 1788, and other distinguished women have been elected in the nineteenth and twentieth centuries.

The APS elects the customary institutional officers; it conducts its business, headed by an executive officer, from its headquarters in Philosophical Hall, which is on Independence Square (formerly the State House Yard) in Philadelphia, Pennsylvania. This plot of ground was deeded to the APS by the Commonwealth of Pennsylvania in 1785.

For further information, see the APS publications discussed above, particularly Francis X. Dercum, "The Origin and Activities of the American Philosophical Society and an Address on the Dynamic Factor in Evolution," *Proceedings, American Philosophical Society* (1927); Edwin G. Conklin, "A Brief History of the American Philosophical Society," *Year Book* (January-December, 1947); and Richard H. Shryock, "The Planning and Formal Opening of Library Hall," and "The Library of the American Philosophical Society," *Proceedings, American Philosophical Society* (August, 1960). See also G. Brown Goode, "The Origin of the National Scientific and Educational Institutions of the United States," *Annual Report, American Historical Association* (1889); Leonard W. Larrabee, ed., *The Papers of Benjamin Franklin* (1959); Carl Van Doren, *Benjamin Franklin's Autobiographical Writings* (1945); and Sidney Painter, "The American Philosophical Society," *World of the Mind* (1958). For comment on APS activity during the Revolutionary period, see Brooke Hindle, *The Pursuit of Science in Revolutionary America, 1735-1789* (1956). For the best recent brief history of the APS, see Whitfield J. Bell, "The American Philosophical Society," *ACLS Newsletter* (March, 1968). Dr. Bell, the former librarian and present executive officer of the APS, is at work on a complete history of the APS and is also preparing a biographical dictionary of its past members.

AMERICAN PHYSICAL SOCIETY (APS). During the latter decades of the nineteenth century, although physics had already become a recognized scientific discipline in Europe, in the United States it was still emerging as a separate branch of natural philosophy or science. One of the first professors of physics in an American university, and incidentally the first president of the American Physical Society, Henry A. Rowland of Johns Hopkins University, was not appointed until 1876. The primary meeting ground at that time for the growing group of American physicists was Section B of the American Association for the Advancement of Science* (AAAS). With a growth in their numbers, sentiment gradually developed among them for a separate physics society, which in 1899 resulted in the founding of the APS. The so-called father of the American Physical Society was Professor Arthur Gordon Webster of Clark University. Although he did take the lead in sending out the invitations that resulted in the organizational meeting at Columbia University on May 20, 1899, Professors Ernest Merritt and Edward L. Nichols of Cornell University and the aforementioned Professor Rowland of Johns Hopkins University also played major roles in the formation of the APS.

From the time of its founding to the present the APS has worked in various ways for the advancement of physics. In 1901 it drafted and presented a petition to the U.S. Congress endorsing the founding of a U.S. Bureau of Weights and Measures. Following the latter's establishment, the APS maintained a close relationship with it. For several decades the APS held its Washington, D.C., meetings in quarters in the bureau's building specifically designed for that purpose. Also, APS interest in and support of the bureau was a material factor in the latter's transformation into the National Bureau of Standards with an expanded and enhanced role. Similarly, the APS was one of five societies, probably the major one, responsible for the organization of the American Institute of Physics* (AIP).

The APS has stimulated interest in physics by setting up eleven divisions within the society devoted to various aspects of the discipline. Similarly, it has founded four regional sections of the parent organization in various parts of the country. The APS awards a number of prizes for research in various areas of physics. The Oliver E. Buckley Prize, for example, has been awarded, since its establishment in 1952 under a fifty thousand dollar endowment from the Bell Telephone Laboratories, for distinguished research in solid-state physics.

The APS initially published nine issues of its own quarterly *Bulletin*. This publication was discontinued in 1903, however, because of low circulation and high costs. Another factor in its cessation was the fact that Professor Nichols of Cornell University had already founded his successful and competing *Physical Review* in 1893. An arrangement was therefore worked out in 1903, between Nichols and the APS, whereby his journal became for practical purposes a societal publication and acquired APS representation on its editorial board. Ultimately, in 1913, complete editorial and corporate control of the *Physical Review* was transferred from Nichols to the APS, and it has remained an official journal of the society to the present day. Other APS publications include the weekly *Physical Review Letters*, continuing short articles, comments, and so forth, dealing with new and current topics in physical research; a revived *Bulletin*, containing abstracts of papers presented at APS meetings and official notices; and a quarterly *Review of Modern Physics*, established in 1929.

From its beginnings until 1940, the annual meetings of the APS, which are now held separately, took place with those of the AAAS. In addition to these meetings, usually held in larger cities, three to four general meetings are held each year in other cities of the United States and, occasionally, Canada or Mexico. Also, since the 1960s, the APS has sponsored divisional meetings, sectional meetings, and topical conferences. The number of persons present and the papers presented at the earlier APS meetings were few but have expanded with the growth in membership.

The APS has two categories of membership: fellow and member. The former is reserved for those who have made some distinctive contribution to the advancement of physics or performed some special service in the course of science. Fellows presently number about 3,000 out of about 28,500 APS members.

The APS elects the customary institutional officers; it conducts its business from an office, headed by an executive secretary, located in the AIP headquarters building in New York, New York.

For further information, see the publications of the APS discussed above, particularly Frederick Bedell, "What Led to the Founding of the American Physical Society," *Physical Review* (May, 1949). See also A. Wilmer Duff, "Arthur Gordon Webster—Physicist, Mathematician, Linguist and Orator," *American Physics Teacher* (August, 1938); Ernest Merritt, "Early Days of the Physical Society," *Review of Scientific Instruments* (April, 1943); and "The American Physical Society," *Physics Today* (October, 1951).

AMERICAN PHYSIOLOGICAL SOCIETY (APS). This society is one of the oldest of the biological-medical societies and the one from which a number of other societies, including the American Society of Biological Chemists* (ASBC) and the American Society for Pharmacology and Experimental Therapeutics* (ASPET), drew their founders and early members.

The study of physiology as a distinct discipline did not occur in the United States until the latter part of the 1870s. Its disciplinary establishment then was due to the influence of scholars returning from European study who located at various U.S. medical centers. Among this group, and leaders in the founding of the APS, were Drs. S. Weir Mitchell of the Jefferson Medical College, Philadelphia; Henry P. Bowditch of the Harvard Medical School; and Henry N. Martin of Johns Hopkins University. These three sent out the invitations calling for a meeting in New York City, on

December 30, 1887, of persons interested in the organization of a physiological society; a meeting which led to the formation of the APS.

Although the idea for the founding of the APS appears to have originated with Mitchell, there is no doubt that he discussed the plan with Bowditch, Martin, and other outstanding scientists, and the original twenty-eight members included some of the most distinguished names in American biological and medical science. Dr. Bowditch was elected the first APS president and served six annual terms in that office. Retaining such officers for relatively long periods was continued by the APS until shortly after the turn of the century, when the growth in membership brought about a change in policy whereby officers were continued in office for only one or two years.

A major scientific achievement of the APS has been to raise standards of teaching and research in physiology. It has established and administered prizes and fellowships for work in physiology and has appropriated sums toward defraying the costs of national and international meetings and toward the erection of memorials to prominent scientists. The APS was the prime mover in the establishment in 1913 of the Federation of American Societies for Experimental Biology* (FASEB).

Annual meetings of the APS, convened in cities all over the United States, have facilitated professional intercourse among its members. Prior to 1925 the meetings were scheduled during the last week in December and lasted from one to three days. Since that time they have normally been held in the spring and usually take up an entire week. This change was made in order to hold meetings in conjunction with other FASEB members and was also dictated by the great increase in the number and variety of papers presented on the programs. Also, in 1955 three-day fall meetings were inaugurated. These have grown to five days, emphasizing educational topics, and are usually held in conjunction with those of one or more "guest" societies. During the first fifty years of the society's existence, the programs were confined to expositions of research on specific topics. Since World War II, however, a limited number of roundtable and conference-type sessions have been set up. Attendance at the meetings is usually about 35 percent of the total membership and always includes a sizable number of nonmembers.

The need for a learned journal for the APS was recognized early in its history, and a committee to consider its establishment was named in 1894. The resulting *American Journal of Physiology*, first issued in January, 1898, was largely due to the efforts of one member of the committee, Dr. W. T. Porter of the Harvard Medical School. He offered to assume the *Journal's* financial and editorial obligations if it were issued under APS auspices, and this arrangement prevailed until 1914, when other duties made it too much of a burden for Dr. Porter. He thereupon informed the APS and offered to turn the *Journal* over to it. This generous offer was accepted, and the APS assumed control of the publication. The *Journal* has been a monthly publication except for the very early years and for a short while during both world wars when there were not enough acceptable articles to warrant monthly publication.

In 1921 the publication of *Physiological Reviews* was inaugurated as a quarterly review of progress in physiological subjects. In 1939 an *Annual Review of Physiology* was established but is no longer a part of the APS's publication program. After World War II, the need for a publication dealing with "applied" physiology became apparent, and the resultant *Journal of Applied Physiology* was launched in 1948; begun as a bimonthly it now is a monthly journal. In 1962 APS added to its list of journals with the purchase of the *Journal of Neurophysiology*, now published monthly. In 1977, the journals underwent a major reorganization. The *American Journal of Physiology* is now available as six specialty journals or as a consolidated journal containing all of the information in the individual journals. Rounding out the journals is the *Physiologist*, established in 1959, a medium for general information about physiology and physiologists as well as news about the APS.

The APS also regularly publishes two series of books and occasionally has published other books on physiology. The initial editions of the *Handbook of Physiology* series consist of twenty-four volumes in nine sections, dealing with various aspects and concepts of physiological knowledge. Revisions of the initial sections are being published, and further revisions and new sections are in preparation. Four volumes of a Clinical Physiology Series, begun in 1977 and designed to bridge basic science and clinical medicine, have been published.

Regular membership in the APS is contingent upon meritorius original research in physiology, proposal by two members, and nomination by the governing council. Candidates are balloted for at spring and fall meetings. Other categories of membership now include corresponding, for physiologists residing outside North America, as well as associate and student members. Because membership has always been honorific, particularly for regular and corresponding members, the growth in members has been slow but steady, and today there are about six thousand members in all categories, of whom about 10 percent are women.

The APS elects the customary institutional officers; it conducts its business from administrative offices, headed by an executive secretary-treasurer, located at FASEB headquarters in Bethesda, Maryland.

For further information, see the publications of the APS discussed above. The APS has had two detailed and informative histories written about it since its founding: William H. Howell and Charles W. Greene, *History of the American Physiological Society, 1887-1937* (1938); and Wallace O. Fenn, *History of the American Physiological Society: The Third Quarter Century, 1937-1962* (1963). A fourth quarter-century history of the

APS is planned with John Brobeck and Orr E. Reynolds as coeditors. See also W. J. Meek, "The American Physiological Society," *AAAS Bulletin* (June, 1945); Eugene F. Dubois, "Prefatory Chapter, Fifty Years of Physiology in America," *Annual Review of Physiology* (1950); R. W. Gerard, "By-Ways of Investigators: Thoughts on Becoming an Elder Statesman," *American Journal of Physiology* (December, 1952); "Special Issue on the American Physiology Society," *Physiologist* (August, 1968); and Alfred P. Fishman and Stephen R. Geiger, "Multiple Choice, a Publications Option for a Diverse Science," *Scholarly Publishing* (April, 1978).

AMERICAN POLITICAL SCIENCE ASSOCIATION (APSA). Preceded by the creation, largely from within American Social Science Association* ranks, of the American Historical Association* (AHA) in 1884, and the American Economic Association* (AEA) in 1885, the founding of the American Political Science Association in 1903 marked the death blow to the American Social Science Association. The same forces, particularly the movement for professionalization among the university professoriate, which had resulted in the creation of the two earlier societies, led to the creation of the APSA. Significantly the latter was founded at a joint meeting of the AHA and AEA in New Orleans, and the founders and early officers were prominent in the affairs of all three older organizations. Thus, although a past president of the APSA correctly stated that it was "the god-child of the American Historical and American Economic Associations," it could also be justly stated that all three were the children of the American Social Science Association, "the mother of associations." In any case, the AHA, AEA, and ASPA have always had close and somewhat overlapping interests, a recent measure of them being the establishment in 1971 of the Consortium of Social Science Associations, which brought together on a regular basis the executive directors of eight Washington, D.C.-based social science societies to seek ways of dealing together with problems and interests of mutual concern.

Prior to the 1940s annual meetings of the APSA were held in December, often in conjunction with the AHA or AEA. Since 1941 they have been held independently the first week in September, and, in 1961, the length of meetings was extended from three to four days. Typical of the more recent ones have been those with registration in excess of 2,000 and more than 500 participants on the official program. Three plenary sessions were devoted to the topic, the American future. Other significant events were the annual business meeting, a presidential address, and an awards ceremony honoring outstanding individuals, writings, and publications.

The APSA has always considered the dissemination of scholarly and pro-fessional information for political science a major responsibility. Thus, its quarterly learned journal, the *American Political Science Review*, has appeared since 1906. In addition, the APSA publishes a Cumulative Index, last published in 1969, to the *Review*; the *Proceedings of the Annual Meeting*, recording research reported at the annual meetings; and the *News*, a newspaper for teachers of political science. The APSA also collects and circulates information about the discipline and profession in such works as *PS*, the news journal of the APSA, and *Guide to Graduate Study in Political Science*. Finally, the APSA also publishes occasional works such as *Political Science Thesaurus* and various informational directories.

Each year, to stimulate research and recognize excellence, the APSA presents citations and cash awards to leaders in political science and authors of outstanding scholarly works in the area. Representative of the five general and eight dissertation awards established are the Charles E. Merriam Award to a person who has rendered significant contributions to the art of government through the application of social science research and the Leonard D. White Award for the best dissertation in the field of public administration.

From its founding the APSA has carried on a wide range of educational, professional, and public affairs programs. Several of its more recent and better known ones are the Congressional Fellowship Program, launched in 1953, to provide political scientists and others the opportunity to observe the workings of Congress at first hand by service as a staff member in a congressional office, and the Project for Instructional Innovation in Political Science Education, begun in 1972 under a National Science Foundation grant, which has developed and is presently, among its other numerous activities, distributing instructional material, labeled SETUPS (Supplementary Empirical Teaching Units in Political Science), to educators.

In the late 1960s the APSA went through a period of activism and reexamination. It was during this time that programs and policies were established to ensure greater protection and services for women, blacks, Chicanos, and graduate students in the field of political science. Policies were established also to ensure greater protection for the professional rights and the academic freedom of political scientists.

Membership in the APSA is open to all persons interested in the study and discussion of government and international affairs. There are five classes of individual membership: annual, life, family, student, and retired, plus institutional. The membership presently totals about fifteen thousand.

The APSA elects the customary institutional officers; it conducts its business from an office, headed by an executive director, located in Washington, D.C.

For further information, see the publications of the APSA discussed above, particularly Jesse S. Reeves, "Perspectives in Political Science, 1903-1928," *American Political Science Review* (February, 1929); and, in more recent years, the summer issues of *PS*. See also Survey, APSA, and the previously cited Thomas L. Haskell, *The Emergence of Professional Social Science* (1977).

AMERICAN PSYCHOLOGICAL ASSOCIATION (APA). Although some individuals question that a meeting took place, the founding date and place of the American Psychological Association is recorded as Clark University, Worcester, Massachusetts, July 8, 1892. In any case, Professor G. Stanley Hall of Clark is credited with being its founder for it was he who issued invitations to a small group to consider such an organization. This group declared itself a governing council for an APA and called for its first annual meeting to be held at the University of Pennsylvania on December 27, 1892. It appears that the creation of the APA was inspired by the activities, including organizational, of foreign psychologists.

The APA for the first quarter-century of its existence tussled with such issues as methodology, content domain, and definition and the problem presented by its relationship and attitude to professional psychology. Success was achieved in the creation and use of standardized tests in this last area, but early attempts to achieve standards for personnel working in the area met with failure; the most conspicuous example in this regard being the efforts at certification of the Association of Consulting Psychologists. Such failure was due to the fact that individuals who could meet standards did not want or need certification, whereas those who wanted it couldn't meet the standards. This impasse was the major reason that the professional psychologists within the APA ultimately began to organize new organizations, such as the American Association for Applied Psychology and the Society for the Psychological Study of Social Issues, which they believed would be more attentive to their area of psychology. In 1946, however, as the result of a reorganization within the APA, led by Dr. Robert M. Yerkes, such organizations were merged as divisions into a now united APA. At that time the original constitution was revised; added to the old statement of purpose that the APA's object "shall be to advance psychology as a science," was the phrase, "as a profession, and as a means for promoting human welfare." By the early 1970s, responding to the rapid growth of professional psychology, the APA had developed its *Standards for Providers of Psychological Services* which, with periodic updating and revisions, has codified a uniform set of psychological practices that serves the needs of providers and users of psychological services. In 1975 a Council for the National Register of Health Service Providers in Psychology was formed to publish a listing of psychologists who met these specified standards. With APA support and encouragement, most states have now enacted laws regulating the practice of psychology, including the specification of standards to be met by practicing psychologists.

The divisional system, which came into being with the 1946 reorganization, has continued to play an important role in APA operation. Flexible in number and presently standing at forty, they have been established as conditions warrant. Maintaining a great degree of autonomy within their own sphere of psychological interest, the divisional representatives have the most numerous representation on the APA's governing council. Together with fifty state groups, some members contend that the most important function of the divisions has been to hold the APA together in the face of the fragmentizing tendencies that plagued it earlier and has thus been able to maintain numerous psychological subgroups within its membership. Other members, however, maintain that this proliferation of divisions has further fragmentized APA thus adding to its problem of remaining unified.

Annual meetings have always been an important part of APA activities, but their character has changed over the years. All papers presented to the APA during its early years were accepted and read at the meetings. The increasing number of papers submitted, however, first resulted in a shift from a two-day meeting to meetings lasting two or three times that long and the institution of symposia and other devices to handle the increased number. Then, despite such changes, a culling of papers was forced, and now only selected ones are presented.

Following an unsuccessful attempt to provide APA aid toward the publication of a privately owned journal, a committee to consider the APA's relationship to journals and publication was established in 1910. With various changes in nomenclature and personnel extending over two decades, this committee finally made a report in 1922, which resulted in the acquisition by the APA of five journals: *Psychological Review*; *Psychological Bulletin*; *Journal of Experimental Psychology*; *Psychological Monographs*; and *Psychological Index*. In 1926 the *Journal of Abnormal and Social Psychology* was acquired through the gift of Morton Prince, and in 1947, aided by a grant from the Laura Spelman Rockefeller Memorial, the APA set up *Psychological Abstracts*, which eventually supplanted *Psychological Index*. Today, the association publishes eighteen journals, including the *Journal of Consulting and Clinical Psychology*, *Journal of Comparative and Physiological Psychology*, *Journal of Applied Psychology*, and *American Psychologist*, and a newspaper, the *APA Monitor*, issued ten times each year.

APA criteria for membership during its early years were not clearly defined. From an original thirty-one in 1892, however, membership had increased in 1906 to the point that research and occupational qualifications for membership were adopted. In 1925 an associate grade of membership, as distinguished from fellows, was created. Fellows, henceforth, were required to have the doctoral degree and to have had extensive experience or published in the psychological field. Associate membership was afforded those with graduate training or experience in the field and devoting full time to professional or graduate work in psychology.

These categories of membership were unchanged by the 1946 reorganization, but a new group of affiliates, without membership privileges, was created, and the divisions were afforded the option of establishing additional classes of membership within their respective divisions. In 1958 a category of members was established for those who had the doctors degree in psychology but were not fully qualified to be fellows. Since 1946, when total membership in the APA totaled about thirty-two hundred, there was an increase by 1960 to about eighteen thousand, and by 1980 the total membership had climbed to more than fifty thousand.

The APA elects the customary institutional officers; it conducts its business from an office, headed by an executive officer, located in Washington, D.C.

For further information, see the publications of the APA discussed above, particularly Samuel W. Fernberger, "The American Psychological Association: A Historical Summary, 1892-1930," *Psychological Bulletin* (January, 1932) and "American Psychological Association, 1892-1942," *Psychological Review* (January, 1943). The latter article by Fernberger is one of eleven in a semicentenary issue dealing with historical and other aspects of APA development. See also Dael Wolfle, "The Reorganized American Psychological Association," *American Psychologist* (January, 1946) and "The American Psychological Association," *AAAS Bulletin* (March, 1946); and APA *Information Pamphlet* (1980).

AMERICAN SOCIAL SCIENCE ASSOCIATION. Although their names are similar, the American Social Science Association has no official or direct connection with the Social Science Research Council* (SSRC).

The association was organized in Boston in 1865 by several hundred persons interested in the betterment of society. Its membership included many eminent people, particularly in the New England area, and it patterned itself after the British Social Science Association, which had been founded in 1856. The American association through its publications, meetings, and other activities was probably one of the principal forces behind social reforms in the nineteenth century. Led by its long-time secretary, Franklin B. Sanborn, it was very active in the movements for civil service, prison, public health, and educational reform. In addition, it figured in the formation of many other social service organizations and several learned societies. These included the National Prison Association (1870), the American Public Health Association (1872), the Conference of Charities (1874), the National Association for the Protection of the Insane and the Prevention of Insanity (1880), the American Historical Association* (AHA) (1884), and the American Economic Association* (AEA) (1885).

Thomas L. Haskell, in his provocative history of the association, *The Emergence of Social Science. The American Social Science Association and the Nineteenth Century Crisis of Authority* (1977), maintains that this emasculation was the result of the drive for professionalization and specialization by intellectuals interested in what we now call the social sciences. In any case, such fragmentizing was the ASSA's undoing, and, although attempts were made to merge it with other institutions, particularly Johns Hopkins University, it finally passed out of existence in 1912.

For further information, in addition to the Haskell history of the association cited above, see "History of the American Social Science Association in a Letter to Its Present Secretary, I. F. Russell, New York, by F. B. Sanborn, of Concord, Massachusetts, a Founder," *American Journal of Sociology* (March, 1910); and Albion W. Small, "Fifty Years of Sociology in the United States," *American Journal of Sociology* (May, 1916).

AMERICAN SOCIETY FOR AESTHETICS (ASA). Aesthetics as a research branch of philosophy and a related field of study for various arts was a recognized area of study in pre-World War I Europe. In Germany a society and *Journal of Aesthetics* had been active since 1906 under the leadership of Max Dessoir. Despite excellent books on aesthetics by George Santayana, John Dewey, and others in the United States, it did not achieve significance in this country, however, until the organization of the American Society for Aesthetics on April 25, 1942.

Founded at the Catholic University of America in Washington, D.C., largely at the instigation of Dr. Felix M. Gatz, head of the Department of Art and Music at the University of Scranton, the stated purpose of the ASA was:

to promote study, research, discussion, and publication in aesthetics. The term "aesthetics" shall in this connection be understood to include all studies of art and related types of experience from a philosophical, psychological, scientific, historical, critical, or educational point of view. The term "art" shall be understood to include all the arts.

The major achievement of the ASA has been to bring together the previously scattered groups of persons interested in the philosophical approach to the arts. For example, the American Psychological Association* (APA), the College Art Association of America* (CAA), and the Modern Language Association of America* (MLA) had each held occasional sectional meetings on aesthetics. Persons attending such meetings, however, maintained that they lacked the mutual contact needed in the broad approach that is imperative for the solution of aesthetic problems and that the organization of the ASA would supply it.

Publications sponsored by the ASA have been a boon to those in the field of aesthetics. A *Journal of Aesthetics* was published at irregular intervals from 1941 to 1945, but was superseded on the latter date by the official quarterly *Journal of Aesthetics and Art Criticism* issued on a regular basis. The *Journal* has provided a publication medium for research that previously had a limited outlet due to the fact that the philosophical periodicals were loath to publish articles with references to art, whereas the art periodicals shunned articles of a philosophical or theoretical nature. In addition to publishing the *Journal* the ASA has aided in the compilation of bibliographies and the translation into English of important German works in the field of aesthetics. Also, in 1980, the ASA began publication of a *Newsletter* two times a year.

ASA membership is open to all persons interested in furthering the study and discussion of aesthetics and the publication of research in the area. Within the general membership there are a number of regional groups that have a high degree of autonomy, although the ASA national office has provided various forms of support and advice. These groups elect their own officers, collect their own dues, and conduct programs of their own. At the present time ASA membership totals about eight hundred.

The ASA elects the customary institutional officers; it conducts its business from an office, headed by a secretary-treasurer, located in Greenvale, New York.

For further information, see the publications of the ASA discussed above, particularly "American Society for Aesthetics: Historical Note," *Journal of Aesthetics and Art Criticism* (January, 1949). See also a letter from George Boas, President, ASA, to Charles E. Odegaard, Executive Director, American Council of Learned Societies* (ACLS) (November 16, 1949). This three-page letter and supporting documents was the successful application of the ASA for membership in the ACLS; it provides historical information about the society.

AMERICAN SOCIETY FOR EIGHTEENTH-CENTURY STUDIES. A group of interested persons in attendance at the December, 1968, meeting of the Modern Language Association of America* (MLA) deemed the time to be ripe for the formation of a multidisciplinary and interdisciplinary society devoted to the advancement of study and research in the history of eighteenth-century culture. They hoped that such a society would foster interest, among all scholars, in the achievements of that century, in the way that the Medieval Academy of America* (MAA) and the Renaissance Society of America* had in earlier periods of history. Accordingly, a provisional constitution was adopted and an executive board named for an American Society for Eighteenth-Century Studies.

Eighteenth-Century Studies, a quarterly journal originally established on September 2, 1967, at the University of California, Davis, has been associated with the society since 1970 and published by it since 1975; it contains articles, book reviews, and professional notes and correspondence. The other publications of the society include selected papers delivered at its annual spring meetings, and collected in an annual volume, *Studies in Eighteenth-Century Culture*; until July, 1979, an annual bibliography, *The Eighteenth-Century: A Current Bibliography*, since that date published by AMS Press; an annual *Directory* of members; and a quarterly *News Circular*.

The American Society for Eighteenth-Century Studies awards two annual prizes, one for the best article published in the field of eighteenth-century studies (named for the late James L. Clifford of Columbia University, the society's third president) and one (named after the late Louis Gottschalk of the University of Chicago, the society's second president) for the best scholarly book in the same field. The society carries on a number of other scholarly activities, the most significant in recent years being an exploratory study leading toward an eighteenth-century short-title catalogue of English books, the largest humanistic compilation of its kind ever undertaken. It also has an annual meeting in the spring of each year, as well as seven affiliated regional societies, which have their own meetings.

Since 1970, the society has been affiliated with the International Society for Eighteenth-Century Studies and, in January, 1976, the society became the forty-second constituent society of the American Council of Learned Societies* (ACLS).

Membership, open to all interested persons, falls into four categories: regular, student, sponsoring (those wishing to make a special contribution to the society), and institutional (universities, museums, and so on). From an initial several hundred, membership has grown to approximately eighteen hundred in all categories.

The society elects the customary institutional officers; it conducts its business from an office, headed by an executive secretary, located in Columbus, Ohio.

For further information, see "New Constituent Society: the American Society for Eighteenth-Century Studies," *ACLS Newsletter* (Fall and Winter, 1975-1976). See also the Society's *Bulletin of Information* (1980).

AMERICAN SOCIETY FOR EXPERIMENTAL PATHOLOGY. See American Association of Pathologists, Inc.

AMERICAN SOCIETY FOR LEGAL HISTORY (ASLH). Efforts to organize a learned society dedicated to the study of legal and constitutional history began in December, 1933, with the establishment of the short-lived American Legal History Society. After an initial flurry of interest, which resulted in two hundred members, the society faded into oblivion during the Depression and World War II. However, it constituted the inspiration for a renewed organizational attempt by a group of law professors headed by Erwin C. Surrency of Temple University and William Jeffrey, Jr., then of Yale University. After more than a year of planning the American Society for Legal History was founded on December 28, 1956, at a meeting of the Association of American Law Schools* (AALS). Mr. Surrency was elected the first president of the society, and the establishment of an official quarterly journal, the *American Journal of Legal History*, was approved. The first issue of the new journal appeared in February, 1957, under the joint sponsorship of the ASLH and Temple University School of Law. Continuously published since then, the *American Journal of Legal History* remains a significant part of the scholarly publications program of the society.

Since 1970 the ASLH has experienced a substantial increase in its membership, which now stands at approximately 650 individual and institutional members, and a diversification of its activities. In October, 1971, it held its first annual meeting at Boston, and since that time it has held two-day annual meetings in major cities throughout the United States. The society has also joined with other scholarly institutions and professional organizations in cosponsoring conferences on specialized legal history topics. A series of book-length monographs initiated in conjunction with Harvard University Press in 1970, and now published in association with the University of North Carolina Press, has been added to the publications program of the society. Entitled Studies in Legal History, this series has facilitated the publication of ten volumes in the years from 1970 through 1977. A third portion of the society's publication program, the *ASLH Newsletter*, serves as a clearinghouse for society business and for the exchange of information concerning legal history.

The ASLH was elected a member of the American Council of Learned Societies* (ACLS) in 1973, and it is a participant in the activities of the Joint American Historical Association* (AHA)-ASLH Committee on the Littleton-Griswold Fund. It is also an affiliated society of the AHA, and special joint sessions at the AHA annual meeting are held periodically. At the international level the society is a member of the International Association for the Study of the History of Law and Its Institutions.

Membership in the ASLH is open to any individual having an interest in the history of law. The ASLH is dedicated to the study of all legal systems and all chronological periods of legal development. A program of honorary fellowships has been established to honor distinguished legal historians; there are currently six fellows (residents of the United States) and nine corresponding fellows (residents of nations other than the United States).

The ASLH elects the customary institutional officers; it conducts its business from an office, headed by an executive officer, located in San Diego, California.

For further information, see the publications of the ASLH discussed above, particularly Earl F. Murphy, "The American Society for Legal History," *American Journal of Legal History* (January, 1957). See also "American Society for Legal History," *ACLS Newsletter* (Winter, 1973); and Herbert A. Johnson, "A Look at the American Society for Legal History," *American Bar Association Journal* (January, 1974).

AMERICAN SOCIETY FOR MICROBIOLOGY (ASM). The agent in the creation of the ASM, who also figured prominently in the creation of several other societies, was Dr. Franklin P. Mall. It was in response to his suggestion as to the need for an ASM, at an 1898 meeting of the American Society of Naturalists, that Drs. A. C. Abbott, H. W. Conn, and E. O. Jordan constituted themselves a committee to proceed with the organization of such a society. They sent out letters in the fall of 1899 to about forty prominent bacteriologists informing them of the projected society and requesting their attendance at the upcoming 1899 meeting of the Society. Following affirmative responses from thirty-seven, an organizational meeting was scheduled for December 28-29, 1899, at Yale University, and it was there that the ASM, then designated the Society of American Bacteriologists, was founded. A constitution was adopted, Dr. William T. Sedgwick was named president, and Drs. Abbott, Conn, and Jordan were elected, respectively, vice-president, secretary-treasurer, and member of a governing council of the new organization, by the fifty-nine persons in attendance.

The object of the society, as stated in its original constitution, was "the promotion of the science of bacteriology, the bringing together of American bacteriologists, the demonstration and discussion of bacteriological methods, and the consideration of subjects of mutual interest." Although revisions have made this statement of purpose more explicit, it did go far to establish bacteriology as a fundamental discipline and yet left its members much latitude in their range of interest. Thus, the extension of the interest of many members into the field of microbiology was accomplished within the framework of the Society of American Bacteriologists. This advancement of science in the microbiological area, furthermore, resulted in the 1960 change in the name to its present American Society for Microbiology.

The ASM contributed to the organization and support of the American Institute of Biological Sciences* (AIBS). It has shared in the management of the American Type Culture Collection and has aided in the preparation of various bacterial classification systems. Another contribution of the ASM has been its publications. The monthly *Journal of Bacteriology* is the best known and oldest, first appearing in 1916. A year later *Abstracts of Bacteriology* was established, to be merged, in 1925, with other publications of similar nature in *Biological Abstracts*. In 1936-1937 the quarterly *Bacteriological Reviews*, now called *Microbiological Reviews*, and a monthly *Newsletter*, now called *ASM News*, were added to the list of publications. Since 1953, the following publications have been established: *Applied Microbiology*, now called *Applied and Environmental Microbiology*, monthly; *Antimicrobial Agents and Chemotherapy*, monthly; *Infection and Immunity*, monthly; *Journal of Clinical Microbiology*, monthly; *Journal of Virology*, monthly; and *International Journal of Systematic Bacteriology*, quarterly, published by ASM for the International Association of Microbiological Societies.

Annual ASM meetings have been held since its founding, with the exception of two years during World War II. They now span an entire week, Sunday through Friday. Held in locations all over the United States, attendance, which has been on a constant rise, now includes over ten thousand persons. At these meetings there is the customary presentation of scientific papers and social and professional intercourse among members. The abstracts of the papers presented at the annual meeting were published for a number of years in *Science* and then in the *Journal of Bacteriology*. Beginning in 1949 they were published separately, under varying titles—including *Bacteriological Proceedings*—but the present title is now *Abstracts of the Annual Meetings of the American Society for Microbiology*.

Since 1961 the ASM has also sponsored conferences each year on various topics in microbiology. These conferences, currently four or five per year, are usually held on college campuses and are attended by from 100 to 250 persons. The proceedings of these conferences have been published in a series of volumes as *Microbiology 1979*, *Microbiology 1980*, and so on. The exception to this rule is the annual fall Interscience Conference on Antimicrobial Agents and Chemotherapy. Proceedings of the ICAAC are no longer published in their entirety but only in the form of abstracts in combination with the ICAAC program.

An additional feature of the annual meetings has been the presentation of a number of awards. These include the Eli Lilly Award to a young individual for outstanding research; the Carski Foundation for Distinguished Teaching Award; the Wyeth Award for a distinguished career in clinical microbiology; and the Fisher Award for meritorious research in applied and environmental microbiology.

In addition to the annual, ICAAC, and other conference meetings, the local ASM branches hold at least one or two meetings annually. Beginning in 1917 with a branch located in the Northeast, there was little activity among them until, in 1934, they were given representation on the ASM governing council and encouraged in other ways. They have subsequently increased to a total of thirty-eight; thirty-three branches located in the continental United States, and five abroad.

In 1955 the ASM sponsored the formation of the American Academy of Microbiology. The academy promotes programs of professional recognition and acts to foster the professional and ethical standing of microbiologists. Members are designated as fellows and there are now over one thousand. The academy sponsors subgroups such as the American Board of Medical Microbiology, which judges by examination the competence of microbiologists who apply for certification in public health and medical microbiology and in diagnostic specialty areas. Also, the academy established the National Registry of Microbiologists to recognize microbiologists at specific levels including the bachelor degree level.

Societal membership was originally restricted to persons who had engaged in and published research in bacteriology and was limited to a fixed number. During the period 1913-1916, because of increasing interest among students plus a desire to make the newly established *Journal of Bacteriology* available to as many as possible, these restrictions were eliminated, and membership was opened to all persons interested in furthering societal objectives. In 1959, however, this policy was slightly reversed, and new membership is now limited to persons holding a bachelor's degree in microbiology or possessing its equivalent in training or experience.

In addition to the usual active members, there are honorary members, restricted to eminent, elected scientists; student members, in 1971 the society authorized student chapters, and there are now about six in existence; emeritus members; and sustaining members, research or industrial organizations interested in aiding and furthering the work of the ASM. The latter group comprises approximately one hundred of a total membership of over twenty-five thousand.

The ASM elects the customary institutional officers; it conducts its business from a six-story office building of its own located in Washington, D.C., with a staff of approximately sixty-five persons headed by an executive director.

For further information, see the publications of the ASM discussed above, particularly H. J. Conn, "Professor Herbert William Conn and the Founding of the Society," *Bacteriological Reviews* (December, 1948); C. E.-A. Winslow, "Some Leaders and Landmarks in the History of Microbiology," *Bacteriological Reviews* (June, 1950); and the following articles by Dr. L. S. McClung, ASM archivist, in the *ASM News:* "Oral History for Archives of the American Society for Microbiology" (April, 1969), "Diamond Jubilee Archives Exhibit" (August, 1974), "The American Society for Microbiology/Society of American Bacteriologists: A Brief History" (September, 1978), and "The ASM Archives Collection of Books, Laboratory Manuals, Theses, and Reprints" (September, 1978). See also C. E.-A. Winslow, "The First Forty Years of the Society of American Bacteriologists," *Science* (February, 1940); Leland W. Parr, "The Society of American Bacteriologists," *AAAS Bulletin* (April, 1946); and Barnett Cohen, *Chronicles of the Society of American Bacteriologists, 1899-1950* (1950).

In large part due to the efforts of the ASM archivist, Dr. L. S. McClung, the extensive archives of the ASM have been placed on deposit in the special collections of the library of the University of Maryland, Baltimore County.

AMERICAN SOCIETY FOR PHARMACOLOGY AND EXPERIMENTAL THERAPEUTICS (ASPET).

This society was the result of the interest in and work of Dr. John J. Abel in pharmacology. Following a six-year period of graduate study in the leading German and French medical schools, he returned to the United States in 1891, when he was named the first full-time professor of materia and therapeutics at the University of Michigan, his alma mater. This appointment was based on the recommendation of Professor Oswald Schmiedberg, the leading pharmacologist in Europe. Abel's appointment marked the beginning of pharmacology as an independent discipline in the universities of the United States. In 1893 he was named professor of pharmacology at John Hopkins University and worked at that institution until his retirement in 1932.

Dr. Abel soon saw the need for a learned society devoted to pharmacology and experimental therapeutics, and he was primarily responsible for calling the organizational meeting for such a society in Baltimore, Maryland, on December 28, 1908. At that time the eighteen scientists in attendance adopted articles of agreement, which called for the formulation of a permanent constitution. Dr. Abel was named president, other officers were elected, and Dr. Abel announced that arrangements had been made for the publication of a monthly *Journal of Pharmacology and Experimental Therapeutics*.

The following year a permanent constitution was adopted, and a corporation, composed of Drs. John J. Abel, Reid Hunt, and C. Voegtlin, was formed for the publication of the *Journal*. This arrangement, with Dr. Abel as editor, prevailed until 1933, when, upon his retirement, control of the *Journal* was transferred to ASPET with a new editor and editorial board in charge of the publication. It was voted at that time that the front cover of the *Journal* should contain a statement to the effect that it had been founded by Dr. Abel. In addition to the *Journal*, ASPET has, since 1949, established and published the following: *Pharmacological Reviews*, quarterly; *Clinical Pharmacology and Therapeutics*, monthly; *Rational Drug Therapy*, monthly; *Drug Metabolism and Disposition*, bimonthly; *Molecular Pharmacology*, bimonthly; and the *Pharmacologist*, quarterly.

ASPET administers four awards for outstanding research in pharmacology and therapeutics: the John J. Abel Award in Pharmacology, donated by Eli Lilly and Company; the Torald Sollmann Award in Pharmacology, sponsored by Wyeth Laboratories; the ASPET Award for Experimental Therapeutics, donated by Hoffmann-La Roche Inc.; and the Theodore Weicker Memorial Award in Pharmacology and Therapeutics, sponsored by the Theodore and Elizabeth Weicker Foundation. In addition, the family of the late Harry Gold donated the Harry Gold Award for the purpose of honoring excellence of teaching in this area. All of these awards consist of a sum of money plus a medal or certificate.

Semiannual meetings of ASPET, to facilitate communication among members, have been held regularly, and ASPET was one of the groups instrumental in the founding of the Federation of American Societies for Experimental Biology* (FASEB).

Membership in the society includes active members, who are investigators in pharmacology and experimental therapeutics, honorary members, and corporation associates; presently it totals about three thousand.

ASPET elects the customary institutional officers; it conducts its business from offices, headed by an executive officer, located in FASEB headquarters in Bethesda, Maryland.

For further information, see the detailed history of ASPET: *The American Society for Pharmacology and Experimental Therapeutics: The First Sixty Years, 1908-1969*, edited by K. K. Chen. (1969). See also E. M. K. Geiling, "Milestones in the Life of John J. Abel," seminar paper (November, 1959).

AMERICAN SOCIETY FOR PROFESSIONAL GEOGRAPHERS. See Association of American Geographers.

AMERICAN SOCIETY FOR PROMOTING AND PROPAGATING USEFUL KNOWLEDGE, HELD AT PHILADELPHIA. See American Philosophical Society, Held at Philadelphia, for Promoting Useful Knowledge.

AMERICAN SOCIETY FOR THEATRE RESEARCH (ASTR). This society was founded in 1956 to increase knowledge of and appreciation for the history of the theatre and to serve the needs of theatre historians. ASTR has published the semiannual *ASTR Newsletter* since 1957, and *Theatre Survey* since 1960, as well as occasional volumes such as the *Index to the Portraits in Odell's Annals of the New York Stage* (1963), *Memoir of John Durang* (1966), *Innovations in Stage and Theatre Design* (1972), and *American Popular Entertainment* (1979).

Since its founding ASTR has represented the United States in the International Federation for Theatre Research. In 1969 the society cosponsored with the Theatre Library Association the Sixth International Congress for Theatre Research at Lincoln Center, New York City. A Conference on the History of American Popular Entertainment was similarly sponsored there by the two organizations in 1977. In 1975 the ASTR was admitted to membership in the American Council of Learned Societies* (ACLS).

Membership in the society is open to qualified individuals and institutions and currently numbers about six hundred. The society holds annual meetings, usually in November, for the presentation and discussion of scholarly papers. Most of these meetings have been held in New York. Current policy, however, favors moving meetings around the United States to cities with important theatre collections.

The ASTR elects the customary institutional officers; it conducts its business from a secretary's office located in Flushing, New York.

For further information, see the publication of ASTR mentioned above. See also Information Statement ASTR, undated; and "Forty-First Constituent Society," *ACLS Newsletter* (Winter, 1975).

AMERICAN SOCIETY OF ARCHITECTURAL HISTORIANS. See Society of Architectural Historians.

AMERICAN SOCIETY OF BIOLOGICAL CHEMISTS (ASBC). Founded in December, 1906, this society was an offspring of the American Physiological Society* (APS), organized nineteen years before, in 1887. At the time the APS was created, relatively few scientists were working in biological or physiological chemistry, as it was then called. The period 1887-1906 saw an increase in their number and a corresponding increase in the sentiment that the chemical side of physiology was of equal importance to physical or so-called pure physiology. It is around this question of the relative emphasis to be placed on these categories of physiology that the discussions attendant on the formation of a new society centered; for when the subject was broached many physiologists maintained that their discipline was a broad study of function and that to divorce physiological chemistry from it would weaken not only the APS but also physiology as a science. These objections were heightened by the problem of where, exactly, physiological or biological chemistry fit into academic organization: within the department of physiology or chemistry? New discoveries in biochemistry opening new fields of inquiry and accelerating interest in it as a specialty, however, finally culminated in 1905 in the event that led to the formation of a new society: the founding of the *Journal of Biological Chemistry* by Drs. John J. Abel and C. A. Herter. The establishment of the *Journal* was followed, the next year, by their successful launching of the American Society of Biological Chemists. Dr. Abel sent out a circular letter to a group of biological chemists in October, 1906, calling for a meeting that was held on December 26, in New York City, with twenty-nine persons present. The ASBC came into being at that time.

The *Journal of Biological Chemistry*, although not controlled by the ASBC until later, always had close ties to it because Drs. Abel and Herter had founded the one and led in the founding of the other. Although the original idea for the founding of the *Journal* appears to have been Abel's, they were one in their belief in the project, and Herter carried it through to completion by setting it up as a nonprofit corporation in New York State, managing and coediting it with Dr. Abel, and defraying its initial deficits out of his own pocket until his death in 1910. His untimely demise resulted in a crisis for the *Journal* that was met by the creation of a supporting Christian A. Herter Memorial Fund by relatives and friends of Dr. Herter; eventual transfer of the publication offices in 1914 to quarters in the Rockefeller Institute, where they remained until 1925; and a drive to increase the numbers of subscribers by offering sets of excess back numbers free with new subscriptions. As a result, the *Journal* was continued as an independent publication of the ASBC, although several organizations, including the American Chemical Society* (ACS), had offered to take over its publication. It was not until 1919, however, that the ASBC assumed full responsibilities for the *Journal*. Changes in the constitution were made at that time providing for the *Journal's* continuation as a corporation but controlled by the ASBC. Finally, in 1942, because of the possible imposition of a New York State income tax, the corporation was dissolved, and assets, including the Christian A. Herter Memorial Fund, were turned over to the ASBC.

Among the ASBC's accomplishments, it was a member of the conference committee that resulted in the creation of the Federation of American

Societies for Experimental Biology* (FASEB) in 1913. The ASBC has been active in furthering research in biochemistry. Its Committee on Protein Nomenclature, for example, cooperated with a committee of the APS in making a report on that subject. Its outstanding achievement, however, according to Dr. Russell H. Chittenden, past president and author of an early (1945) history of the ASBC, has been its publication of the *Journal of Biological Chemistry*. Dr. John T. Edsall, also an ASBC past president and the author of a 1980 history of the *JBC* offers substantiation for this view with observation therein that "to present a panorama of the discoveries in the Journal would be an impossible task. . . . Yet one may note, more or less at random, a few of the vast number of achievements recorded in the Journal." Dr. Edsall goes on to point out and briefly discusses some of them. Some are articles presented by ASBC members, others are not, for the pages of the *JBC* have always been open to papers based on their merit and regardless of origin.

The society has always been very active as an organizer of annual scientific meetings from its beginnings to the present. They have usually been held in the spring of the year and follow the usual pattern of the presentation of papers, discussion, conduct of business, and so on. They have been convened all over the United States and Canada.

In 1906, eighty-one persons constituted the charter membership of the ASBC. Since that date membership has been opened only to biological chemists who have conducted and published original and independent investigations in the field. Thus, the standards for election to membership in the ASBC are rigorous. The sponsors of the candidates, who must be nominated and seconded by ASBC members, must also provide documentation as to their research. Such nominations are reviewed by a membership committee, which recommends nominations for approval. The ASBC governing council reviews the recommendations, and the ASBC members, at the business session of the annual meeting, elect the recommended and reviewed members. Usually the membership committee's recommendation is accepted.

Until 1961 there was only one class of membership in the ASBC, with the exception of a brief period from 1922 to 1925, when a few "clinical members" were admitted. In 1961 honorary membership was opened to distinguished foreign scientists elected by the ASBC. Their number, however, may not exceed a fixed percentage of the present approximately five thousand ASBC members. Also in 1961, because of the growth in membership and in order to stimulate the recruitment and training of biochemists at the graduate level, the ASBC named a full-time executive officer in addition to the customary institutional officers. The executive officer is also the manager of the *Journal of Biological Chemistry* insofar as its business affairs are concerned. The society and *JBC* offices are located at FASEB headquarters in Bethesda, Maryland.

For further information, see the publications of the ASBC discussed above, particularly Hans T. Clarke, "The Journal of Biological Chemistry," *Journal of Biological Chemistry* (October, 1955). See also W. J. Gies, "American Society of Biological Chemists," *Science* (January, 1907); Russell H. Chittenden's now outdated *The First Twenty-Five Years of the American Society of Biological Chemists* (1945); and A. N. Richards, Donald D. Van Slyke, and R. J. Anderson, *The Journal of Biological Chemistry: 1905-1953* (1953). The following articles on the fiftieth anniversary of the ASBC, appearing in *Federation Proceedings* (July, 1956), are historically informative: J. Murray Luck, "Introductory Remarks"; Phillip A. Shaffer, "Origin and Development of the American Society of Biological Chemists"; and A. N. Richards, "Journal of Biological Chemistry: Recollections of Its Early Years and of Its Founders."

An up-to-date history of the *Journal of Biological Chemistry*, John T. Edsall, "The Journal of Biological Chemistry After Seventy-Five Years," *Journal of Biological Chemistry* (October 10, 1980), by the editor-in-chief of the *JBC* from 1958 to 1967, also provides much insight into the history and operation of the ASBC. This same seventy-fifth anniversary issue of the *Journal* also contains an appendix in which the 1953 history of the *Journal* by Richards, Van Slyke, and Anderson is reprinted.

AMERICAN SOCIETY OF INTERNATIONAL LAW. This society was organized in 1906 as the natural outgrowth of the movement in this country and abroad to prevent or limit war by recourse to arbitration resting on international law. Dr. James Brown Scott, an internationally recognized scholar on the subject, played a leading role in the founding of the society, and its offices were located in his Washington, D.C., home until 1911, when Dr. Scott became the chief administrative officer of the newly created Carnegie Endowment for International Peace. The offices were moved at that time to quarters provided in the endowment buildings. A virtual "who's who" in business, diplomacy, law, and academia were associated with Dr. Scott in the launching of the society, including Andrew Carnegie, Elihu Root, and William Howard Taft.

The exploratory meetings calling for the founding of the society also called for the establishment of a journal of international law in connection therewith. At that time it was pointed out that there was no publication in English devoted exclusively to international law. The original and present constitution of the society stated that its purpose is "to foster the study of international law and to promote the establishment and maintenance of international relations on the basis of law and justice." It occasions no surprise, then, that within a few months of the society's birth, on June 1, 1906, Dr. Scott's proposal for the establishment of a quarterly *American Journal of International Law* was approved together with his appointment as its editor. In addition to articles, book reviews, international law decisions, and news and notices, a special feature of the *Journal* was a supplement of important treaties, diplomatic notes and documents, and so forth. This was particularly valuable during the early years of the *Journal*—the first issue appeared on January 1, 1907—because at that time published U.S. State Department diplomatic documents were some fifteen to twenty years behind the times. Indeed, the society was eventually instrumental in obtaining congressional appropriations for the State Department to remedy this situation. Through the years of Dr. Scott's editorship and down to the present, the *Journal* has maintained an influential position in the circles that it serves. In addition to the *Journal*, the society also published an account of annual meetings in a *Proceedings*; a bimonthly current documentary, *International Legal Materials*; a quarterly *Newsletter*; and, intermittently, books written under its auspices.

The first annual meeting of the society was held in Washington, D.C., on April 19-20, 1907. With the exception of several wartime lapses, they have been continued down to the present, in April, usually in Washington. From the beginning, the society has followed the practice of maintaining an open forum for discussion of all sides of controversial questions and of not adopting resolutions and measures that might be viewed as binding upon its members. Although there was originally some sentiment for restricting membership to lawyers and members of the diplomatic service, it was opened and remains open to all persons interested in its objectives.

In the early 1960s, with support from the Ford Foundation, the society began a studies program, which focused initially on commissioning books by individual authors working outside the society. This activity has evolved into a wide-ranging research and study program that has received support from a variety of private and public foundations and other agencies. The program works mainly through interdisciplinary panels and working groups drawn from the university, government, international organizations, and other professional communities and planned and managed by the society for each project. To a lesser extent it relies on small research teams employed by the society and housed at its headquarters. Research often is directed to international policy issues with a strong international legal component. In 1972, the society began an occasional paper series, *Studies in Transnational Legal Policy*, designed primarily for the program's work product, which is also published in the form of books and articles in learned journals.

From an initial membership of about 850 members, the society has grown to its present approximately 5,500 members. It elects the customary institutional officers; it conducts its business from an office, headed by an executive director, located in Washington, D.C.

For further information, see an early account of the founding of the

American Society of International Law by James B. Scott, "History of the Organization of the American Society of International Law," *Proceedings* (April, 1907). For a later brief history of the society, see George A. Finch, "The American Society of International Law," *American Journal of International Law* (April, 1956).

AMERICAN SOCIETY OF PARASITOLOGISTS (ASP). Although Dr. Joseph Leidy did pioneer work in parasitology in the nineteenth century and has been called the founder of American parasitology, parasitology as a separate discipline in the United States dates from the turn of the twentieth century. Some scientists, such as Drs. C. W. Stiles of the U.S. Public Health Service, C. A. Kofoid of the University of California, and Henry B. Ward of the University of Nebraska and later the University of Illinois, were engaged at that time in parasitological research, and in the 1920s scientists of the Zoological Division, Bureau of Animal Industry, U.S. Department of Agriculture, became increasingly active in the area of parasitology. During this same period, too, the newly established School of Hygiene and Public Health at Johns Hopkins University began to supply increasing numbers of parasitologists and public health officers.

The need for a publication outlet for this early activity in parasitology resulted in the establishment of the *Journal of Parasitology* in September, 1914, by Dr. Henry B. Ward. Dr. Ward was influenced in founding the *Journal* by his graduate training in Germany and by the establishment in 1908 in England of *Parasitology* by Dr. George H. F. Nuttall. The *Journal* was a complete success, due in large part to the increase in the number and activity of parasitologists in the United States following World War I. These developments served to inaugurate a movement, particularly among the members of the Helminthological Society of Washington, D.C., known as Helmsoc, for a national organization of parasitologists. A self-constituted committee from the Washington, D.C.-Baltimore area took the lead in calling an organizational meeting for December 30, 1924, in Washington, and it was there that the American Society of Parasitologists was organized, with Dr. Ward elected its first president.

By 1932 membership in ASP had increased to about six hundred persons, and its stability seemed assured; Dr. Ward thereupon transferred ownership and control of the *Journal* to the ASP. Following the transfer the *Journal* shifted from being a quarterly and became a bimonthly periodical.

One of the major accomplishments of the ASP in recent years was the important role it played in organizing programs to combat the parasitic diseases encountered by Allied combat forces, particularly in the Pacific, during World War II. The ASP was one of the biological organizations instrumental in the formation in 1947 of the American Institute of Biological Sciences* (AIBS) and has since worked closely with the AIBS. In

1940 the ASP established an endowment fund, now known as the Stoll-Stunkard Fund in honor of the two parasitologists who founded it, which presently totals about $106,000. Income from the fund is used for special projects of value and interest to the ASP.

Prior to the creation of the AIBS in 1947, annual meetings of the ASP were held the last week in December in conjunction with those of the American Association for the Advancement of Science* (AAAS). After that time and until 1962 they were scheduled in late summer or early fall with other member societies of the AIBS. From 1962 on, however, the ASP has essentially held meetings on its own with joint meetings every third year with the American Society of Tropical Medicine and Hygiene. Held all over the United States, they have featured the customary reading of papers, transaction of ASP business, and social forgathering.

Following discussions in the 1940s and 1950s as to the desirability and feasibility of establishing regional affiliates of the APS, the year 1957 saw the authorization by the society of their establishment. Subsequently, eight have been founded. These are active groups that hold their own annual meetings, the Southwestern Association of Parasitologists being the largest.

ASP membership originally consisted of two classes: active, open to anyone interested in parasitology; and foreign honorary, open to distinguished foreign parasitologists. Qualifications for active membership were slowly tightened, however, so as to include only those with an adequate academic background and a record of activity in the field of parasitology. Also, the AST enacted restrictions on the number of foreign honorary members. Today, the three categories of members are active, honorary (both foreign and domestic), and emeritus. Again, however, there are restrictions on the numbers included in the last two categories. The present membership of the ASP in all categories is about sixteen hundred.

The ASP elects the customary institutional officers; it conducts its business from an office, headed by a secretary-treasurer, located in New Orleans, Louisiana.

For further information, see a detailed history of the ASP by Joseph C. Kiger, "The American Society of Parasitologists: A Short History," *Journal of Parasitology* (October, 1962). For other articles of historical interest appearing in the same *Journal*, see Henry B. Ward, "The Founder of American Parasitology, Joseph Leidy" (September, 1923); W. W. Cort, "Professor Henry Baldwin Ward and the *Journal of Parasitology*" (December, 1932); Asa C. Chandler, "The Making of a Parasitologist" (June, 1946); Eloise B. Cram, "Stepping Stones in the History of the American Society of Parasitologists" (October, 1956); and Donald V. Moore, "Fifty Years of American Parasitology" (August, 1976). See also J. T. Culbertson, "American Society of Parasitologists," *AAAS Bulletin* (June, 1944).

AMERICAN SOCIETY OF ZOOLOGISTS (ASZ). In the 1950s a zoologist observed that the history of the American Society of Zoologists was interesting, charming, and somewhat confused. A great deal of this confusion can be traced to the series of changes during the formative years of the ASZ, including inadequate or nonexistent records and changes in its title, and to the often conflicting statements about the society by various early officials. The following historical account attempts to present a reasonably accurate resolution of these problems in historical interpretation.

The ASZ was founded in December, 1890, at an annual meeting of the American Society of Naturalists in Boston, Massachusetts. Originally designated the American Morphological Society, it was organized because its founders, some twenty academic biologists and zoologists particularly interested in comparative anatomy and animal morphology, believed that existing organizations, including the American Society of Naturalists, did not meet their professional needs.

Parenthetically, the American Society of Naturalists, which had been set up in 1883, has been referred to as the grandmother of scientific societies with a score or more, including the ASZ, tracing their origin to it. Such fragmentization, reminiscent of the American Social Science Association* in the social sciences, had a similar effect upon the American Society of Naturalists in that it was undoubtedly a major factor in retarding its growth. Later, the emergence of new biological groupings, such as the Federation of American Societies for Experimental Biology* (FASEB) and the American Institute of Biological Sciences* (AIBS), terminated the American Society of Naturalists's role as a coordinating body for biology. Nevertheless, it is still in existence with a membership of about 650 and publishes the bimonthly *American Naturalist*.

H. Burr Steinbach maintains that, by 1899, the American Morphological Society had changed its name to the Zoological Society of America; more recent historians of the ASZ can find no record of the ASZ calling itself by this title. In any case, 1902 saw the emergence of the Society of American Zoologists, with an Eastern and a Western branch. Finally these two branches, which had been holding separate annual meetings for two years and a joint one every third year, merged and formed the ASZ in 1914.

Some of the early accomplishments of the ASZ were its support for holding the 1907 International Zoological Congress in this country; its assistance in creating and promoting the Division of Biology and Agriculture within the National Research Council (NRC) during the World War I period; and the role its members played, along with those of the Botanical Society of America* (BSA) in the founding in 1922 of the Genetics Society of America* (GSA). It should be noted, however, that the ASZ did not join in the movement for the establishment of the FASEB, although many members of the ASZ endorsed the FASEB's creation. More recently the ASZ has cooperated with such organizations as the FASEB,

AIBS, National Institutes of Health, Office of Naval Research, and National Science Foundation. The ASZ has sponsored a number of summer institutes for college teachers and various regional conferences. It has set up several committees to study and report on the teaching of the zoological sciences and, in that connection, has prepared and distributed booklets on career opportunities in the zoological and biological sciences.

Since the reorganization of 1902-1903, annual meetings have been held in cities all over the United States. Since that time, too, the ASZ has sometimes met with the AIBS in the summer and the American Association for the Advancement of Science* (AAAS) at its winter meeting. These meetings are characterized by the customary presentation of papers, demonstrations, and conduct of business. Prior to 1960, the meetings were reported in and published as supplements to the *Anatomical Record*; since that date they have been published in the *American Zoologist*. In 1919 the ASZ assumed editorial responsibility for the *Journal of Morphology*, published by the Wistar Institute of Anatomy and Biology,* and some papers presented by members at meetings are published in that *Journal*. Also, the ASZ has issued a *Newsletter* on an intermittent basis.

Membership in the ASZ has always been selective, and presently there are four categories: members, those who have the doctorate or its research equivalent and are active in the zoological field; student; emeritus; and corresponding. The last category consists of distinguished foreign scientists whose number may not exceed 1 percent of the total number of members. The total membership of the ASZ today is about four thousand.

The ASZ elects the customary institutional officers; it conducts its business from an office, headed by a business manager, located in Thousand Oaks, California.

For further information, see the following articles, presented at a symposium on the history of the ASZ, and appearing in volume 19, number 4, of the *American Zoologist* (1979): C. Edward Quinn, "Introduction to the Symposium"; James W. Atkinson, "The Importance of the History of Science to the American Society of Zoologists"; C. Edward Quinn, "The Beginnings of the American Society of Zoologists"; Ralph W. Dexter, "C. O. Whitman and the American Society of Zoologists"; and Anthony C. Clement, "Edwin Grant Conklin." For earlier historical accounts of the ASZ, see "Historical Review," *Anatomical Record* (January, 1917); Edwin C. Conklin; "Fifty Years of the American Society of Naturalists," *American Naturalist* (September-October, 1934); and H. Burr Steinbach, "Brief Unpublished History of the ASZ" (1958). See also various newsletters and information pamphlets published intermittently by the ASZ.

AMERICAN SOCIOLOGICAL ASSOCIATION (ASA). This association (until 1959, American Sociological Society) was formed at the December, 1905, annual meeting of the American Historical Association* (AHA),

American Economic Association* (AEA), and American Political Science Association* (APSA), which were held together in Baltimore, Maryland. Some forty members of the three older organizations, together with a few from the almost moribund American Social Science Association,* led by Professor C. W. A. Veditz and including such prominent social scientists as Lester H. Ward, Charles A. Ellwood, William Graham Sumner, Edward A. Ross, Walter F. Wilcox, Albion W. Small, Charles H. Cooley, and Franklin H. Giddings, created the ASA. They defined its aims as the promotion of sociological research and discussion and the fostering of intercourse among persons engaged in the scientific study of society.

Up until the 1940s, ASA annual meetings were held during the last week in December, often with the AEA; since that time they have been scheduled for the last week in August, and the place of meeting has included cities all over United States. During its first three decades, all of the activities of the ASA meetings, save the reports of committees and the business session, were centered on one central topic in sociology, such as "The Trend of Our Civilization," "The City," or "The Problem of Democracy." This topic was selected in advance, and all papers and discussions dealt with it. Since this early period, however, the programs at the meetings have been arranged so that the papers and discussions cover a wide variety of topics.

Publication has been an important ASA activity. Until 1936 the principal papers presented at the meetings were published either in full or in abstract, along with business matters and the reports of committees, in the annual *Publication and Proceedings of the American Sociological Society*. The ASA played an important part in the production of the bimonthly *American Journal of Sociology*, which, although founded in 1895 and published by the University of Chicago, operated under the guidance of an advisory council composed of ASA officers. This connection was severed in 1936, however, by the establishment of ASA's *American Sociological Review*. In addition, ASA now publishes *Social Psychology Quarterly, Sociology of Education, Journal of Health and Social Behavior, American Sociologist*, and various monographs and bulletins.

Because of the extremely diverse interests of its members, the splintering of ASA into independent societies has been an ever present possibility. Reflecting these interests some sixteen sections have been developed within the organization, such as Criminology, Family, and Medical Sociology, which have a considerable degree of latitude within the ASA's operation. Each, for example, are given control, within ASA guidelines, of a part of the program for annual meetings. A procedure has been developed, too, to provide for establishment and disestablishment of sections with the waxing and waning of members' interest. Also, a loose affiliation or relationship was developed with nine regional societies, such as the Eastern Sociological Society and Southern Sociological Society, together with the Rural Sociological Society and the Society for the Study of Social Problems.

Nevertheless, a number of societies were organized—the Association for Sociology of Religion and the Sociological Research Association—that frequently meet at the same time and place as does ASA but are completely independent of it.

Membership in ASA is divided into members and associates. Members are broken down into members, international members, and student members. They must hold the Ph.D. in sociology or a closely related field; in lieu of the doctorate there must be a demonstrated commitment to the field. Student members must have completed all work for the Ph.D. except the dissertation.

Associates are broken down into associates and student associates. The first need have only an interest in the discipline but the latter must be students in sociology who do not yet qualify for the student member category. Voting and holding office within ASA is limited to those in the member category.

From the original membership of forty in 1905, ASA grew to about thirteen hundred members in 1926, sixty-five hundred in 1960, and about thirteen thousand in 1980.

The ASA elects the customary institutional officers; it conducts its business from an office, headed by an executive officer, located in Washington, D.C.

For further information, see Survey, ASA; Robert E. L. Faris, "Development and Functioning of the American Sociological Association," *ACLS Newsletter* (April, 1969); Mary O. Furner, *Advocacy and Objectivity, A Crisis in the Professionalization of Social Science, 1865-1905* (1975); and Thomas L. Haskell, *The Emergence of Professional Social Science: The American Social Science Association and the Nineteenth Century Crisis of Authority* (1977).

AMERICAN SOCIOLOGICAL SOCIETY. See American Sociological Association.

AMERICAN STATISTICAL ASSOCIATION (ASA). One of the oldest national social science organizations in the United States, the American Statistical Association was founded in 1839. It resulted from the interest in the establishment of statistical societies evident between the years 1830 and 1840 in France, Germany, Italy, and the United States, but more than anywhere else in England, there being no less than six such societies founded in Great Britain in the 1830s. The first to be established here was the New York Statistical Society, incorporated in 1836, but like numbers of those abroad it had an ephemeral existence.

The ASA founded in Boston in 1839, was doubtless inspired largely by and copied the form of organization of the London (now Royal) Statistical Society, founded in 1834. An 1840 statement of the field and aim of the

ASA, however, shows a familiarity with German statistics and indicates that it intended to cultivate this type, developed in the German universities, rather than the earlier English studies, largely of political arithmetic.

At ASA's organizational meeting held in Boston on November 27, 1839, it was announced that its object would be "to collect, preserve, and diffuse statistical information in the different departments of human knowledge" and indicated that it construed "statistical" in the sense of including all information related to the structure of society and not merely that susceptible of mathematical interpretation. From the first ASA sought to avoid the danger of remaining or becoming a local organization. Its bylaws provided that "the operations of this Association shall primarily be directed to the statistics of the United States; and they shall be as general and as extensive as possible and not confined to any particular part of the country." Although all but two of the fifty-four active members of ASA in its first year of existence were New Englanders, contact with a wider field was at once sought through corresponding and foreign members in the United States and abroad.

Of ASA's founders, Lemuel Shattuck, its first secretary, is renowned in the history of statistics in this country. The first adequate and scientific city census, that of Boston in 1845, was taken under his direction. It was primarily at his suggestion that the U.S. Congress created the census board for planning the census of 1850, and he designed five of the six schedules used in that census.

The nature of statistics has brought ASA into continuous and close contact with local, state, and federal government. It has urged on state legislatures the creation of sanitary commissions, state boards of health, and similar bodies; the extension of registration areas; and the need to collect and compile statistical information. It is at the federal level, however, that ASA has left its mark. The Shattuck census of 1850 determined the direction of subsequent ones, and he and the ASA were largely instrumental in the establishment thereafter of the Bureau of the Census as a permanent institution. Invariably ASA members have been directors of the census and members of the bureau. In 1933, ASA was instrumental in the establishment of the Federal Central Statistical Board, now Office of Federal Statistical Policy and Standards. This is now the central statistical office, which plans and coordinates the federal statistical system.

Some sixty-four local groups of ASA have been established in most of the principal cities from coast to coast and in Canada. They are semiautonomous organizations and meet regularly for discussion. Members now belong to one or more of eight national sections: Biometrics, Biopharmaceutical, Business and Economic Statistics, Statistical Education, Statistics in the Physical and Engineering Sciences, Social Statistics, Statistical Computing, and Survey Research Methods. These sections are responsible for most of the program sessions held at the annual meetings.

The ASA has had at least one meeting in every year since 1839. During its early years, it met quarterly except during the summer, the principal meeting being that held in December of each year. This was practicable so long as all meetings were in Boston and the membership was primarily from the Northeast, but with an expansion and broadening of membership annual meetings became inevitable. At the present time these annual meetings are held in August, often in conjunction with the Biometric Society and the Institute of Mathematical Statistics* (IMS). As a substitute for the quarterly meetings there are now meetings of the local chapters or one or more of ASA's sections, or regional meetings in conjunction with other societies.

The first ASA publication appeared in 1843, when it brought out part 1 of the *Collections of the American Statistical Association*. Parts 2 and 3 followed in 1845 and 1847; all three parts were eventually bound into one volume. For twenty years thereafter only desultory papers appeared, and it was not until 1888 that ASA undertook the regular production of a quarterly journal. In that year appeared number 1 of volume 1 of the *Publications of the American Statistical Association*, which has appeared, under varying titles, ever since. In 1915 it became the *Quarterly Publication of the A.S.A.*, and in 1922 the present *Journal of the A.S.A.* It is devoted to articles and book reviews. The ASA also publishes the quarterly, the *American Statistician*, which includes articles of general interest as well as discussions of professional problems; a monthly newsletter, *Amstat News*; *Technometrics*, a quarterly initiated jointly with the American Society for Quality Control; and *Journal of Educational Statistics*, jointly with the American Educational Research Association. An annual *Current Index to Statistics* is published jointly with the IMS. Five *Proceedings* volumes are published after each annual meeting, containing the papers from the Business and Economic Statistics, Social Statistics, Statistical Computing, Survey Research, and Statistical Education sections.

The earliest ASA members were termed fellows: ordinary, honorary, corresponding, and foreign. Throughout the nineteenth century this nomenclature obtained, except that for a time the terms *fellow* and *member* were used interchangeably. In the 1910s the title *member* was adopted as applying to the four groups named above, and fellow became a distinct classification. Since that time, the only qualification for membership is that the candidate be "interested in statistics," but fellows have to be elected and not more than 1 percent of the members can be so elevated in any one year. In practice the percentage so elected has been much smaller, and the number so elected has never exceeded thirty-five in any one year.

For the firsty fifty years of its existence, ASA's membership rarely exceeded one hundred, and it was confined primarily to New England residents. In the 1880s and 1890s, there was an influx of college and university teachers from our burgeoning academic institutions, so that by 1897 the association numbered over five hundred. At present ASA has over fourteen thousand members, residing in all parts of the United States and most foreign countries. Today, almost all of the members have had formal university training in statistics, and those engaged in teaching number about 40 percent of the membership. The other 60 percent are statisticians employed in government bureaus, business, industry, international agencies, and other organizations.

The ASA elects the customary institutional officers; it conducts its business from offices, headed by an executive director, located in Washington, D.C.

For further information, see the publications of the ASA discussed above, particularly the following articles appearing in the *American Statistician:* Paul J. Fitzpatrick, "The Early Teaching of Statistics in American Colleges and Universities" (December, 1955), "Statistical Works in Early American Statistics Courses" (December, 1956), and "Statistical Societies in the United States in the Nineteenth Century" (December, 1957); and Abe Rothman, R. S. Barker, and E. M. Bisgyer, "Characteristics of the American Statistical Association Membership, 1964" five consecutive articles appearing December, 1965, through October, 1966. See also Survey, ASA; Edwin W. Kopf, "American Statistical Association," *Proceedings of the Casualty Actuarial Society* (November, 1924); and "American Statistical Association," *AAAS Bulletin* (August, 1944).

AMERICAN STUDIES ASSOCIATION (ASA). This association was founded in 1951 to provide an organization whereby American culture and civilization could be studied as an entity rather than within the context of one discipline.

The ASA holds biennial national conventions, which provide an overview of the most current scholarship in the field. It has eighteen regional chapters within the United States. ASA members are automatically enrolled in these chapters. The latter operate autonomously, however, electing their own officers, calling meetings and conferences, and conducting other functions.

The study of American civilization and culture in other countries has been a primary concern of the ASA. It played a role in the establishment in various nations of comparable scholarly organizations, such as the British Association for American Studies and the Japanese Association for American Studies. It has also arranged for meetings and conferences between American studies scholars abroad and their counterparts in the United States.

Members of the ASA receive: the *American Quarterly* (published by the University of Pennsylvania), which presents articles in American studies; *American Studies International* (published at George Washington University), dealing with the activities of the various national associations; an opportunity to purchase *Prospects* (published by Burt Franklin Co.), an annual publication in the field; and the *ASA Newsletter*. Membership in the

ASA, open to all who are interested in American studies, grew from about fifteen hundred in the early 1960s to approximately twenty-five hundred in 1980.

The ASA membership elects the customary institutional officers and a governing board; its business office, headed by an executive director, is located in Philadelphia, Pennsylvania.

For further information, see the publications of the ASA discussed above, especially *American Quarterly* (Bibliography Issue, 1979), which features a thirty-year retrospective of the field. For an account of American studies activities abroad in the 1960s, see "A Decade of American Studies," *ACLS Newsletter* (June, 1970).

ARCHAEOLOGICAL INSTITUTE OF AMERICA (AIA). Harvard University Professor Charles Eliot Norton's desire to stimulate classical scholarship and learning in the United States was the catalyst in the founding of the AIA in Boston in 1879. As an initial step in achieving these ends, Norton successfully urged the establishment of a school in Greece for Americans where study could be undertaken at first hand with the original monuments of antiquity. Thus, the American School of Classical Studies in Athens was founded under AIA auspices in 1881. A similar school was established at Rome in 1895, In 1900 the work spread to Jerusalem, with the organization there of the School of Oriental Research. Also during these early years, with Professor Norton serving as AIA president for its first eleven years, the AIA directly subsidized individual explorers and organized archaeological expeditions of its own, primarily to classical sites, such as the investigation of Assos, a Greek city in Asia Minor.

Even at the time of its establishment, however, some members of the small group that participated in the founding of the AIA did not share Norton's almost exclusive concern with classical archaeology. They urged that the AIA also involve itself with American archaeology. Despite such sentiment and despite the labors of individuals, such as the Swiss-American archaeologist Bandelier, who did notable work in the 1880s under AIA auspices in the U.S. Southwest and Mexico, it was not until the twentieth century, after what Institute Archivist Phoebe S. Sheftel calls "many years of benign neglect," that American archaeology really got some AIA attention. A School of American Archaeology, now School of American Research, was founded at Santa Fe, New Mexico, in 1907; in 1921, the AIA, in collaboration with the American Anthropological Association,* established the American School of Prehistoric Research. Subsequently, with varying degrees of involvement on the part of the AIA and varying degrees of success, an American Research Center was opened in Egypt in 1951, and support was provided for an American Research Institute in Turkey in 1964 and an American Institute of Iranian Studies in 1968. Also, when the American Institute of Nautical Archaeology was founded in 1973, the AIA voted support for it. Although the Old World continues to be its major area of archaeological concern, the AIA is continually broadening its support of work in all parts of the world.

The AIA began to establish affiliated groups and societies in 1884; in that year local organizations were formed in New York and Baltimore. Since that time, eighty-four affiliated groups and societies, extending from coast to coast on the North American continent, have been established. Each local society works to meet the needs and interests of its members as well as those of the AIA. In this way, the local groups maintain their autonomy within the parent organization. The AIA provides support to the groups through the disbursement to them of a portion of membership dues; sponsors a variety of lecture programs and symposia for the membership, including the Charles Eliot Norton Lectureship established in 1909; and honors distinguished work in archaeology by the awarding, since 1965, of an award of merit (a gold medal), which is supported by Leon and Harriet Pomerance.

Through the years the AIA has awarded a number of fellowships for archaeological research, usually conducted at AIA schools. Recent awards are those funded by the Olivia James Trust and one in memory of Harriet Pomerance. Also, the AIA now maintains an archive of over ten thousand archaeological slides for the use of scholars and publishes an annual *Fieldwork Opportunities Bulletin* for those interested in doing archaeological fieldwork.

Annual meetings were begun by the AIA in 1899, and have been held during the last week in December since that year. The meetings, conducted in various cities, are often held jointly with other societies, such as the American Philological Association,* and are devoted to the reading of papers and routine business matters.

The AIA publishes the *Bulletin*, which contains the reports of officers, committees, and the affiliated schools and societies; it superseded the *Annual Reports* published from 1879 to 1908. The *American Journal of Archaeology and of the History of Fine Arts* was founded as a semi-independent AIA publication in 1885. Through the years, however, its relationship to the institute grew closer, and in 1896-1897 the AIA took over the *Journal* and at that time brought it out as volume 1 of the *American Journal of Archaeology*. In 1914 *Art and Archaeology* was established for the public. It was published until the depression of the 1930s caused its cessation. Revived in 1948 as the quarterly, now bimonthly, *Archaeology*, this illustrated journal has proved to be a major attraction for nonprofessionals and professionals in many other fields.

Because of the large group of nonprofessionals interested in its work, particularly its publications, the AIA has a wider variety of membership than most learned societies. At one time there were eleven different categories of members; today there are eight. Membership in one or another category is open to all interested persons and has grown from about twenty-five hundred in 1960 to approximately eighty-five hundred today. Women play an important part in the activities of the affiliated societies and in the AIA's general affairs.

Representatives of the local groups and societies of the AIA meet as part of its governing council, which elects the customary institutional officers. AIA business is conducted from an office headed by an executive director, located in New York, New York.

For further information, see the publications of the AIA discussed above, particularly a recent article by Phoebe Sherman Sheftel, "The Archaeological Institute of America, 1879-1979: A Centennial Review," *American Journal of Archaeology* (January, 1979). See also a biography by Kermit Vanderbilt, *Charles Eliot Norton: Apostle of Culture in a Democracy* (1959), which discusses Norton's relationship with the AIA.

ARGONNE UNIVERSITIES ASSOCIATION (AUA). This association came into being on July 1, 1965, with the signing of the AUA founders agreement. As stated in the preamble of that agreement:

Each Signatory University recognizes (1) that it shares a mutual responsibility for cooperating with other persons, agencies and institutions in order to stimulate scientific and technological advancement in the Midwest community and in the nation and for promoting the maximum scientific progress and engineering development made possible by public funds and facilities, and (2) that this responsibility can be furthered by continued emphasis on recruiting and retaining on the staff of the Argonne National Laboratory the most competent and creative administrators, scientists and engineers available, by affording such staff full assistance and support and by making the facilities of the Laboratory broadly available to the scientific community of the Midwest and the nation.

AUA is a not-for-profit corporation incorporated in the State of Illinois. Since shortly after its beginning, it has included thirty major research-oriented universities, primarily located in the Midwest.

An initial six-member board of trustees was soon expanded to a board having, at various times, between seventeen and twenty-three members. The founders agreement stipulates that the board must include no less than twelve individuals affiliated with the member universities in at least one of the following capacities: (1) a principal administrative officer, which over the years has come to be understood as a dean of a college or school, a graduate dean, a vice-president or vice-chancellor for research or academic affairs, or a provost, chancellor, or president of a university; (2) a chief business officer (such as a vice-president for finance or business affairs); a professor of (3) biology; (4) chemistry; (5) engineering; (6) mathematics; (7) physics. These twelve must include at least one professor from each of these disciplines and at least six principal administrative or chief business officers.

Further required are: (8) at least two individuals from technological industry; (9) an ex officio trustee designated by the president of the University of Chicago; and (10) the chief executive officer of the AUA as an ex officio trustee. Originally there was also a requirement for (11) two individuals nominated by the Associated Midwest Universities. The AMU was a consortium of Midwestern universities created in 1958 to facilitate the use of Argonne National Laboratory by qualified personnel and students of the member institutions. This organization merged into the AUA within the first few years of AUA's existence.

The primary purpose for which AUA was created was to enter into a tripartite contract, together with the University of Chicago and initially the U.S. Atomic Energy Commission (AEC), more recently the U.S. Energy Research and Development Administration, and presently the U.S. Department of Energy (DOE), for the direction, management, and operation of Argonne National Laboratory. The first tripartite contract went into effect on November 1, 1966.

The Argonne National Laboratory itself was formed under the Atomic Energy Act of 1946 as one of the peacetime successor organizations resulting from the World War II Manhattan Project, the code name for the atomic bomb development effort. In early 1942 the Metallurgical Laboratory was established at the University of Chicago as part of the Manhattan Project. The Met Lab undertook the nuclear physics research required for the production of plutonium and the development of the chemical processes necessary to separate plutonium from uranium and fission products. The first milestone was reached on December 2, 1942, when Enrico Fermi and his colleagues achieved the world's first controlled nuclear fission chain reaction under the west stands of Stagg (football) Field at the University of Chicago.

On July 1, 1946, after the end of World War II, the name of the Met Lab was changed to Argonne National Laboratory, after the Cook County (Illinois) forest preserve in which one branch of the laboratory had been located since 1943, and the University of Chicago entered into a contract with the AEC for the operation of the laboratory. The present site in DuPage County, Illinois, was selected in 1947 as a permanent home for the laboratory. In 1948 the AEC decided to center its nuclear reactor development work at Argonne, and this has remained a major focus of the ANL for nearly thirty years.

Ever since its inception, Argonne has maintained ties with the university community. In 1946 a Council of Participating Institutions, consisting of thirty universities and two research organizations, was established to advise the government on matters of general research policy for the laboratory. The council evolved into the Associated Midwest Universities in 1958.

The creation of the AUA and the tripartite contract is rooted in the development of high energy physics research in the United States in the post-World War II period. By the mid-1950s the particle accelerators and associated facilities required for experimental research were becoming so big, sophisticated, and expensive to build and operate that organizations too large and complex to be encompassed within individual university departments of physics were required; thus consortia of several universities and national laboratories were seen as useful organizational frameworks.

Centered in Madison, Wisconsin, a Midwest Universities Research Association (MURA) was created in the early 1950s for the purpose of designing and proposing to the AEC a large Midwestern particle accelerator. At about the same time separate studies for a similar purpose—sometimes competing, sometimes interacting—were going forward at the ANL. The Zero Gradient Synchrotron, in an energy range competitive with a then recently announced Soviet machine, was approved for construction at the ANL in the latter 1950s. Thereafter in 1962 and 1963, it became clear that funding for a MURA-sponsored machine would not be made available by the AEC. Subsequently, complex negotiations resulted in decisions leading to the contract for the direction, management, and operation of the laboratory being recast into the tripartite contract.

Thus the tripartite contract itself is the product of governmental decisions responsive to competing claims and interests; it was created to smooth over and heal disagreements about the location and governance of high energy physics facilities in the Midwest. It is noteworthy that neither the text of the founders agreement that created the AUA in 1965 nor that of the tripartite contract specifically refers to a high energy physics facility; both address the direction, management, and operation of the whole laboratory.

The tripartite contract is a unique instrument in the governance of national research and development facilities. The conventional prime contractor role for a national laboratory is divided between two separate, independent, and dissimilar institutions, the University of Chicago and AUA. It is thus an extraordinarily difficult document to execute effectively.

The basic provisions of the tripartite contract state that the University of Chicago shall employ the staff and operate the laboratory in accordance with policies and programs formulated, approved, and reviewed by the AUA. The laboratory's facilities are owned by the U.S. government. The current contract runs to some fifty articles and approximately one hundred typewritten pages. At the heart of it is article 5, which spells out the "General Responsibilities of the Parties" in four sections: basic considerations, DOE's (Department of Energy) responsibilities, the association's responsibilities, and the university's (of Chicago) responsibilities. Each section has several paragraphs of specifics. The original tripartite contract was entered into for a five-year period ending on September 30, 1971, extended for one year, then renewed for three years through September 30, 1975, followed by a two-year renewal, and another three-year renewal through September 30, 1980. The current extension, with no substantive change in the assigned responsibilities among the parties, extends for three years through September 30, 1983.

When AUA was created, each member university provided a $10,000 contribution and committed itself to make available additional amounts not to exceed another $15,000 total when called upon to do so by the board of trustees; no such call has been made to date. The principal income of the association is an annual allowance paid by the DOE for AUA's role in the contract. For the ten years ending with fiscal year 1980, this allowance was $450,000 per year: for the current contract extension it is set at $1 million per year.

A brief description of each of the four principal programmatic functions of AUA shown in the fiscal year 1981 budget follows.

AUA review committee operations for the ANL. Currently there are eighteen review committees to provide expert examination and constructive appraisal of the technical activities of the ANL for the AUA trustees, University of Chicago, ANL laboratory director, and DOE. Each review committee concentrates on evaluating the effectiveness of one ANL division or major laboratory programmatic segment, the quality of the staff and its performance during the review year, the quality of the programs, and, insofar as the committee is able to do so, the relevance of activities to the long-range goals of the laboratory and the mission of the DOE.

Each review committee consists of six to nine members whose specialties generally subsume the division's programs. Members are appointed for three-year terms and may not serve more than two consecutive terms; they are appointed by AUA with the concurrence of the University of Chicago and the laboratory. A liaison trustee serves with each review committee. Reviews are conducted annually and normally last two to three days.

AUA special committee operations. The special committees provide the board of trustees and the laboratory with advice and counsel on specific programmatic areas in the laboratory, such as reactor development, fusion, high energy physics, and the Intense Pulsed Neutron Source. Whereas the review committees provide independent peer evaluation of the technical activities of the laboratory, the special committees assist the AUA and laboratory in addressing specific problems, developing long-range objectives, formulating and overseeing programs, and establishing and attaining particular goals. The committees meet as needed, generally three or four times each year. The membership includes experts in the relevant technical areas, as well as some individuals whose broad backgrounds and experience give them general insights useful to the particular committee.

Institutional interactions and support. Under this function are the range of activities aimed at nurturing interactions between the member universities and the laboratory, as well as between the laboratory and other outside institutions, such as industrial firms. Support is provided for selected conferences and workshops of interest to the laboratory and the scientific community.

The board of trustees operations. The whole board generally meets four times each year. Its standing committees, including a planning committee, an executive committee, a nominating committee, and an assessment (of the president) and budget (of the AUA) committee meet several times each year as needed. The board is served by a small AUA staff currently consisting of three full-time professionals (president, vice-president for administration, and executive officer), a part-time treasurer, and a half dozen secretaries.

In fiscal year 1980, ANL had an operating budget in excess of $250 million; some $70 million of that was "pass through" money spent for major procurements and subcontracts. Its capital assets presently exceed $500 million. Currently ANL employs approximately fifty-three hundred people, of whom more than eighteen hundred are scientists and engineers; more than one thousand hold doctoral degrees. Some seven hundred of all employees are located at the "Argonne-West" Laboratory site near Idaho Falls, Idaho. There the laboratory operates the Experimental Breeder Reactor No. 2 (EBR-II), a small liquid-metal-fast-breeder reactor which for more than sixteen years has successfully demonstrated electric power generation through use of a breeder reactor system.

For further information, see Leonard Greenbaum, *A Special Interest: The Atomic Energy Commission, Argonne National Laboratory, and the Midwestern Universities* (1971). See also "Argonne Universities Association: Access to Argonne" (1980); published by the AUA, this booklet reproduces the founders agreement and provides other similar documentation about AUA operations.

HENRY V. BOHM

ARMOUR RESEARCH FOUNDATION. See IIT Research Institute.

ASPEN INSTITUTE FOR HUMANISTIC STUDIES. The Aspen Institute is a nonprofit international enterprise—international in its programs, participants, sources of support, governance, and affiliates. Headquartered in New York City, its activities are not confined to just one season of the year, nor anchored to just one place. They go forward around the year, and they employ facilities over what has become an expanding geographical base.

The institute's original campus in Aspen, Colorado, still serves as its focal point for summertime traditional seminars and for conferences that deal with issues central to the institute's "thought-leading-to-action" programs. But the Wye Plantation in Maryland's countryside outside Washington, D.C., is now the seat of endeavor focused on critical problems of governance in both the domestic and world arena. At the same time, a facility in Hawaii and a new one at Baca, Colorado, are other important bases for action. On top of all else, the institute's international concerns are vivified by its permanent presence in West Berlin, its facility in Tokyo, and its work in the Middle East, as well as its evolving special efforts in Asia and Latin America.

The institute was an outgrowth of the international Goethe Bicentennial Convocation held in Aspen, Colorado, in the summer of 1949. That convocation, organized on the joint initiative and division of labor among three Chicagoans, Walter Paepcke, University of Chicago President Robert M. Hutchins, and Professor Guiseppe Borgese, brought together renowned humanists from ten countries, and included Albert Schweitzer and José Ortega y Gasset. The excitement the event generated carried over into a proposal Ortega made to Walter Paepcke: to create in Aspen something like a *hochschule* of the humanities, but not a research center. Its educational mission would be to promote a synthesis of human life and to forge a single discipline out of the humanities, the social sciences, and the natural sciences.

In a follow-through on this seminal suggestion, Paepcke proceeded with the help of other Chicagoans to organize the Aspen Institute for Humanistic Studies—whose expansive title initially covered only a very small operation. It consisted in the main of the Executive Seminar, organized by Professor Mortimer Adler, offered for the first time in 1951, and confined to a few summer months. The Executive Seminar, with its intimately related offspring, remains to this day at the core of all of the institute's activities.

Each seminar session brings together senior corporate executives and leaders from other sectors of society the world over for a period of intensive reading, discussion, and interaction. Participants begin with a study of the intellectual foundations of Western civilization and with an eye on other civilizations as well. They then move on to examine their own values, attitudes, and responsibilities in a rapidly changing world. More than five thousand men and women at the front of affairs in the United States and overseas have participated in the Executive Seminar, which in recent years has been supplemented by other core seminars, such as those on the corporation and society, governance, and international corporate leadership. They also include special seminars addressed to major humanistic issues in parts of the world caught in the tensions between tradition and modernization: Iran, the Arab world, China, Japan, and Korea.

In 1957, the presidency of the Aspen Institute, which had been in the hands of Walter Paepcke since its formal birth, passed to Robert O. Anderson. Anderson, a former student of Professor Adler at the University of Chicago, was at that time rapidly emerging as a business leader of the first rank and as a patron of high-risk enterprises in education and the arts. In retrospect, it is doubtful that the Aspen Institute, small as it was, could have survived its many problems were it not for the lifeline it found in Anderson.

The institution had no endowment, its summertime activities never paid for themselves, and there were recurrent moments when it seemed that its future was limited to two prospects. Either it must liquidate itself out of existence, or, alternatively, its land and modest facilities must be taken over by a major university—at risk of the institute losing its distinctive identity as the only contemporary American institution dedicated to the promotion of humanistic values among the leaders of states and societies. Despite many discouragements, Anderson not only kept the institute alive and independent by covering its deficits but lent support to its innovative conferences on specific issues such as business school education, civil rights, disarmament, environmental protection, and the impact of science on society.

These conferences, however, had no coherent order, were not interrelated, and tended to be confined to a single season and have no follow-up. As Anderson himself later commented, "We shot at every bird that came along." The institute could contribute to an understanding of the human problems of the day, and to the alternative policy choices they posed, only if they were dealt with systematically in a process of consensus building. If the need here was plain, the means for meeting it proved elusive until 1969.

In that year, Anderson joined forces with a like-minded individual widely experienced in the world of government and philanthropy. This was Joseph E. Slater, who assumed the presidency of the institute in 1969, when Anderson moved into the new role of chairman of the board of trustees. It was Slater's conviction that the traditional dividing lines between domestic and foreign affairs had become as indistinct as lines drawn in water; that the salient problems of human existence were transnational and transregional; that to light up the parameters of these issues and to formulate the humanistic policy choices they posed called for an integrated approach among all the disciplines.

Slater further observed that, although important research always went forward within the academic world, in government circles, and under the direct auspices of foundations, institutional walls tended to separate what was done in one place from what was done in another. What was needed was a common ground where scholars and policy makers could meet in workshops held the year round to exchange information, test perceptions, and formulate alternative choices among value-oriented policies. The Aspen Institute could not only provide that common meeting ground and help bridge the distance between existing foundations so that each could best serve a common interest, but it could mobilize diverse intellectual resources for the institute's own "thought-leading-to-action" programs.

These programs, as Slater outlined them in a five-year plan that the institute's trustees approved, were initially centered in six areas, but are presently confined to four: communications and society; education for a changing society; justice, society, and the individual; and science, technology, and humanism.

Two of the initial programs—environment and the quality of life, and international affairs—were eventually merged and later absorbed into the institute-wide activities bearing on the problems of governance. Under its own name, however, the program on the environment and the quality of life worked closely with the United Nation's Secretariat in laying the conceptual basis for the United Nation's conferences on the environment, population, and food. The program in international affairs, as well as the one on science, technology, and humanism, were linked through their participants with the Aspen Institute-based activities of the university consortium on arms control that helped prepare the ground for SALT I.

The Aspen Program on Communications and Society, aside from its direct impact on legislation enacted by Congress in the ever changing realm of electronic communications, had made a major contribution to the development of communication policy analysis as a subject for university study. The series of books that emerged from the program workshops now comprise the essential texts in an increasing number of institutions of higher learning that offer programs in communications. The program on education for a changing society has exhibited a feature common as well to the program on justice, society, and the individual and to all other institute activities. At its inception, it sought out the most promising men and women in the field of education, brought them together for work on common tasks, and by enriching their perceptions helped prepare them for major governmental posts.

In line with Slater's five-year plan, elements of all the programs he envisioned were in place and in operation by the end of 1974. At the same time, the international character of the institute's board of trustees was more strongly accented. Since the birth of the institute, the board had included citizens of countries besides the United States. Albert Schweitzer, for example, had served as the honorary head of the first board. But increasingly, from the start of the 1970s to the present, the board has been composed of working trustees drawn from leaders in education, communications, science, government, and business in different regions of the globe. In addition, the institute is now served by new special advisors, also representing an international mix. The trustees and advisors alike have all been members or moderators of the core seminars and are active participants in various institute programs.

Slater, with the support of the trustees, always called the attention of the program directors to the word *humanistic* in the title of the institute and stressed the importance of approaching all specific issues from the standpoint of humanistic values. He also underlined the need to integrate the activities of one program with those of others for a coordinated, wide-angle approach to humanistic issues of common concern. In the latter respect, however, although the object in view was agreed to around a program-planning table, go-it-alone habits tended to reassert themselves when planning sessions adjourned. This hard truth was faced up to in July, 1980, coincident with a change in the institute's financial condition that led to what Slater had recognized all along as a logical step in the development of the institute's structure.

Individual "thought-leading-to-action" programs had drawn many affiliated individuals and organizations into a consensus network, but a point had been reached where it seemed that the Aspen Institute's own contributions had reached their maximum utility. If so, then the resources of the institute would have to be applied to other matters that were in need of clarification. It also became apparent that, although institute-wide approaches were necessary to many national and international governance issues, such approaches were not always forthcoming despite expressions of cooperation from various program directors. At the same time, only the program on communications and society had secured sustained support from outside foundations. The others, although supported by outside grants for short-term undertakings, were primarily sustained by whatever general funds were available to the institute itself.

The institute had made many attempts to dispose of its property in Aspen on a sale or lease-back arrangement so as to secure a stable nest egg of funds on which it could draw up a budget and plan its program accordingly. All such attempts, however, fell through until the summer of 1980. At that time, the sale of the institute's facilities and land in Aspen to a buyer was consummated on terms that permitted the institute to use the existing campus facilities on an agreed schedule. The event worked in its own way to spur a restructuring of institute activities in relation to financial resources.

As a consequence, all existing program directors were made fellows of the institute. The activities in which they had been engaged would continue, but the scale would depend on the extent to which they could mobilize outside funds for their support. The institute, which had always lived with deficits over and above what it received from foundations and individual gifts, was henceforth expected to live within its income. Its traditional core Executive Seminar had at least come to produce a modest surplus to the institute, and other core seminars such as the one on the corporation and society were breaking even. But the decision was made to focus the institute's own immediately available funds in support of institute-wide activities grouped under the heading of "governance."

These included projects bearing titles such as "The First Twenty Years of Life," "Financing the Future," "Tradition and Modernization," "Food, Climate, and the World's Future," "Jobs and Work," "Energy: A Challenge to Governance," "Arms Control," "Cities and Foreign Working Populations," "International Governance," "The Future of the Nonprofit Sector," and "International Corporate Leadership." Capping all activities of the institute in the broad realm of governance was a project known as the Wye Papers, after the Wye Plantation, which was becoming an important conference center for the institute. The Wye Papers, taking their model from *The Federalist*, start with a "circle of correspondents" whose members initiate papers on major national and international issues of governance, circulate the papers for comments and criticism among fellow correspondents, and incorporate these into redrafts, which are then published for wide distribution as Wye Papers. One such paper on the presidential nominating process has already had a major impact on the form and focus of a nationwide movement for reform.

For further information, see Sidney Hyman, *The Aspen Idea* (1975), which provides a history of the institute up to that date. See also the following publications of the Aspen Institute: *Brief Overview* (1978); Joseph E. Slater, *Governance* (1979); and various issues of the *Chronicle*.

SIDNEY HYMAN

ASSOCIATED UNIVERSITIES, INC. (AUI). A nonprofit corporation chartered in 1946 for educational and research purposes under the education laws of New York, AUI's organization was sponsored by nine Northeastern universities: Columbia, Cornell, Harvard, Johns Hopkins, Massachusetts Institute of Technology, Princeton, the University of Pennsylvania, the University of Rochester, and Yale.

The founders of AUI, with the financial support of the federal government, set out to create a multidisciplinary research institution, a primary purpose of which was to provide facilities essential for basic research in the nuclear and related sciences, facilities so large, complex, and costly as to render inadvisable their operation on the campus of a single university. The facilities were to be available on a competitive basis to all qualified scientists without regard to affiliation as well as to a resident scientific staff. For this institution a university-type management was deemed most conducive to the prosecution of the research program. The original plans of the founders resulted in the establishment in Upton, New York, of Brookhaven National Laboratory (BNL), in 1947.

In light of the success of Brookhaven, the governing body of AUI accepted responsibility in 1956 for the establishment and operation of another institution of a similar character, the National Radio Astronomy Observatory (NRAO), with its initial research facilities located at Green Bank, West Virginia.

The broad outlines of the Brookhaven research program, particularly its multidisciplinary character, were determined at its inception. The research staff is organized into eight departments: Physics, Accelerator, Biology, Chemistry, Mathematics, Medicine, Nuclear Energy, and Energy and Environment. The multidisciplinary program and staff and the highly flexible character of the laboratory's principal research facilities have proved to be major strengths.

The laboratory has designed and built a series of large research devices. The first generation of these, the Cosmotron and the Brookhaven Graphite Research Reactor, have already completed long and useful programs of research and have been replaced by newer machines. Today the Alternating Gradient Synchrotron (AGS) accelerates protons to energies up to 30GeV and continues as one of the nation's primary devices for high energy physics research. The High Flux Beam Reactor provides intense beams of neutrons for fundamental experiments in nuclear and solid-state physics, chemistry, and biology. The Medical Research Reactor serves for activation analyses and for medical dosimetry studies. The Tandem van de Graaf installation provides beams of many varieties of ions at energies up to several hundred MeV for fundamental research in nuclear physics. Several smaller accelerators are also employed for solid state physics and nuclear research. A sixty-inch cyclotron and the linac injector to the AGS produce many special isotopes, primarily for medical research and treatment. A scanning transmission electron microscope provides extremely high resolution for investigation of biological molecules and subcellular structures. A pulmonary toxicology facility allows the study of animals exposed to atmospheres of hazardous substances.

In each of these facilities a core of Brookhaven scientists and engineers performs research and oversees the maintenance and upgrading of the facility. Scientists from universities, other laboratories, and industry also use the facilities, sometimes in collaboration, and often independently. At many of the facilities the visitors outnumber the Brookhaven users substantially. At the AGS, for example, about 80 percent of the research is done by visitors.

In furtherance of this role of providing research machines, the laboratory has under construction new devices designed to meet developing needs of science: The ISABELLE colliding beam storage accelerator will provide intersecting beams of protons at energy up to 800 GeV in the center of mass system (equivalent to protons impinging on a fixed target with energy of 340 TeV). This machine will allow deeper studies into the nature of matter and the fundamental forces that hold it together. The National Synchrotron Light Source will provide intense beams of ultraviolet light and X-rays for experiments in physics, chemistry, the life sciences, and technology.

The National Radio Astronomy Observatory is the second national research facility to be established and managed by AUI. Funded by the National Science Foundation (NSF) since its establishment in 1956, it is charged with the responsibility of providing forefront radio telescopes and auxiliary instrumentation for the use of the radio astronomy community. In recent years up to 70 percent of the observing time on the telescopes has been used by visiting scientists from colleges and universities throughout the United States who come to the NRAO for periods of a few days to several months to conduct their own research programs.

The original NRAO twenty-seven hundred-acre site in Green Bank, West Virginia, was acquired in 1957. In this initial year, work started on the design of the 140-foot telescope, which was to be the largest and most accurate equatorially mounted telescope ever built. Initial research programs used a standard 85-foot telescope, operating as a single unit. Subsequently, an interferometer system of three 85-foot telescopes was designed and built.

During this period, a 300-foot transit telescope was constructed, which for many years was to be the world's largest movable telescope. In succeeding years, a 36-foot millimeter wave telescope was constructed on Kitt Peak, near Tucson, Arizona, where the six thousand-foot altitude and dry climate minimized the absorption of radio waves by water vapor, and a new headquarters and research center were established in Charlottesville, Virginia, on the University of Virginia campus.

The next big step for the NRAO was the Very Large Array (VLA), which is located near Socorro, New Mexico. The VLA is a synthesis array designed to give high resolution "pictures" of radio sources, rapidly and with high sensitivity. Initial funding was received in 1973, partial operation began in 1977, and full operation began in 1981.

The VLA telescope consists of twenty-seven antennas, each having a diameter of twenty-five meters, distributed along three arms of railroad tracks arranged in the shape of an equiangular "Y." Each arm is about twenty kilometers long. The railroad tracks will permit the antennas to be transported to and from the various observing stations along the arms. The array will be under the control of a central computer.

The great flexibility, versatility, and power of the VLA will make it the premier instrument in the world for scientific research on the physics of radio sources beyond the Milky Way, on cosmology or the structure of the universe, on the structure and evolution of stars, and on the chemical constituents of gas clouds that lie between the stars. Investigation of radio galaxies and quasars carried out by scientists using the VLA promises to increase our understanding of the mechanisms by which these sources produce such large energies and of the physical processes and laws relating to gravity, magnetic fields, and plasma.

The corporate organization created by AUI's founders in 1946 to provide overall policies and guidance for Brookhaven National Laboratory and later for the National Radio Astronomy Observatory has functioned well. In fact, AUI's success in the establishment and operation of BNL and later the NRAO provided a background of experience for the establishment of other university consortia to conduct government-financed research in much the same manner as AUI.

The governing body of the corporation is a board of trustees, which originally numbered eighteen, of whom two must be designated by each of the nine sponsoring universities.

With the establishment of the NRAO in 1956, the board was increased to twenty-four elected members by the addition of up to six trustees-at-large, to permit the addition to the board of representatives of any field of endeavor in which the corporation might become involved.

The bylaws provide for the board of trustees to elect officers with the "duties which usually pertain to their offices." The president is described as the "principal executive officer of the corporation" and, if not already a member of the board, becomes a trustee ex officio. The bylaws also provide for the selection by the trustees of a director to have charge of "each major scientific, educational, and research activity of the corporation" in accordance with policies established by the board, its committees, and officers.

The first two presidents of the corporation, Mr. Edward Reynolds and Dr. Frank Fackenthal, received no salary and in view of other responsibilities were not expected to perform personally the duties of principal executive officer.

In January, 1951, the board elected Dr. Lloyd V. Berkner as the first full-time president of the corporation. The board also indicated that the corporation would engage in other activities besides the operation of BNL and would establish its corporate headquarters in New York City.

During the next ten years, under Dr. Berkner's leadership, AUI's horizons broadened. In 1951, the corporation undertook a study for the Defense Department on optimum civil defense measures and, in 1956, contracted to operate the NRAO, as described above.

During the four years following Dr. Berkner's resignation on November 30, 1960, AUI had five presidents, all of whom either were or had been closely connected with the organization. Three of the five were drawn from the board. The remaining two were Drs. Leland J. Haworth and Gerald F. Tape. The former, who also served with great distinction as director of BNL, resigned from both positions on April 15, 1961, to accept membership on the Atomic Energy Commission. The latter resigned as president on July 10, 1963, also to become an AEC commissioner. On October 1, 1965, Dr. T. Keith Glennan, who came to AUI from the presidency of Case Institute of Technology and who was formerly head of NASA, assumed the presidency of AUI. He held this office until July 1, 1968. Dr. Glennan devoted much time to a study of the AUI organization and stimulated discussion of possible changes to increase its efficiency and to enhance AUI's standing as a national institution. To facilitate contact with the contracting agencies, he moved the corporate office from New York to Washington, D.C. In addition, he was instrumental in the preparation of formal proposals to the National Science Foundation for the establishment of two institutions to be managed by AUI, a Tropical Marine Science Center to be established in Puerto Rico and an Institute for Information Systems in Higher Education. However, the budgetary climate at the time proved unpropitious for either venture, and the first did not receive strong support from the scientific community.

Several months after Dr. Glennan's resignation, Dr. Gerald F. Tape resigned as a member of the AEC and for a second time accepted the presidency of the corporation. His election, on March 20, 1969, brought to AUI and its operating organizations wide experience and sound objective judgment combined with thorough knowledge and sympathetic understanding of the entire organization and its personnel.

Dr. Tape served in a most outstanding manner as AUI's president until he relinquished the post in October, 1980. He was succeeded by Dr. Robert E. Hughes, professor of chemistry at Cornell University and formerly assistant director of the National Science Foundation. The transition of the AUI presidency occurred on a most appropriate date, at the dedication of NRAO's new Very Large Array telescope, a project for which Dr. Tape had worked most earnestly and successfully.

For further information, see two historical brochures published by AUI: *Associated Universities, Inc. 1946-1971* (1971); and *A Report from Associated Universities, Inc.* (1977). See also Norman F. Ramsey, "Early History of Associated Universities and Brookhaven National Laboratory," *Brookhaven Lecture Series* (1966).

CARL B. AMTHOR

ASSOCIATION FOR ASIAN STUDIES (AAS). The Far Eastern Association, the predecessor organization of the Association for Asian Studies, was organized on June 9, 1941, with the primary purpose of publishing the *Far Eastern Quarterly*, by a small group of scholars who were concerned with the Far East and felt that the existing means of publication about this area were not sufficient. The first issue of the *Quarterly* appeared in November, 1941, on the eve of U.S. entry into World War II, and publication was maintained throughout the war. For several years after the war, leaders in the association, the American Council of Learned Societies* (ACLS), and other interested individuals discussed the possibility of changing the association to an active-membership learned society, which could sponsor and engage in other activities in addition to publication. Ultimately, the Committee on Far Eastern Studies of the ACLS, as the result of a conference for all interested parties on January 3, 1948, proposed that such a society be organized, and a small committee was appointed to arrange for an organizational meeting. On April 2, 1948, at a meeting at Columbia University attended by about two hundred persons, a constitution and bylaws were adopted, providing for officers, membership, publications, and meetings, that is, the usual organizational structure of a learned society. The original name, "Far Eastern Association," was retained, and the association continued to operate under this constitution until 1956.

By 1956, although the majority of the members of the association continued to be mainly interested in Japan, China, and Southeast Asia, there had been a buildup of interest within and without the association in the history and culture of South Asia. Also, there appears to have been some sentiment for the founding of a separate society to concern itself with that area. A decision was eventually reached, however, that it would be in the best interest of all concerned if the association were to extend its range of interest to include South Asia. Thus in 1956 the necessary constitutional revisions were made to reflect this broadening of scope, and the name of the association was changed to its present Association for Asian Studies; the *Quarterly*, correspondingly, being changed to the *Journal of Asian Studies*.

During the 1950s and 1960s, the AAS probably had more than its share of problems associated with the operation of a learned society. In the former decade, they centered around the relationship of certain leaders and members of the AAS to the Institute of Pacific Relations and the institute's role or attitude in the struggle for power in China between the Kuomintang and Chinese Communists. In the latter decade, they centered around the degree of political activism to be engaged in by the AAS. In 1968, an AAS policy statement was issued that it had always been a "nonpolitical" organization and that it "cannot endorse any position regarding specific foreign policy issues." At that time, a Committee of Concerned Asian Scholars (CCAS) was organized by those scholars dissenting with this position, and although there is still adherence to the nonpolitical policy, the AAS has been under intermittent pressure since to take a more aggressive stand, particularly on political issues.

Regardless of dissensions within its ranks, a major achievement of the AAS has been its role in making Americans realize the importance to us of Asia in the context of the U.S. world position. A more specific contribution of the AAS was the large number of members who served as language and area specialists during the initial stages of combat in World War II and also in the Korean and Vietnam wars.

Numerous AAS committees have been established to carry out its objective of promoting interest in and scholarly study of Asia. Among them, the Committee on Southeast Asia and the South Asia Committee have been particularly active. Libraries in the United States have been helped by the establishment of a Committee on East Asian Library Resources.

In addition to the *Journal of Asian Studies*, the AAS in 1949 established a monograph series, which has presented scholarly studies by its members. In 1955 a *Newsletter* was founded and an *Annual Bibliography of Asian Studies* (formerly *Far Eastern Bibliography*) was issued for many years even before the appearance of the *Far Eastern Quarterly*, which in 1941 incorporated these listings; in 1956 the *Bibliography* began to appear as a separate publication because its size, reflecting the great expansion of scholarly publication on Asia, had made that necessary. It continues to be published as a large separate volume each year. It is interesting to note, regarding publications, that nonmember subscriptions—particularly foreign subscribers—bulk larger in the AAS's subscription list than is ordinarily the case among learned journals, in recent years accounting for 40 percent of the total.

Membership in the AAS, of which about 50 percent of the total has always been academicians, has climbed from an initial six hundred in 1948 to approximately five thousand today. Within the United States, from 30 to 50 percent of the members have always been located in the region in and around Boston, New York, and Washington, D.C., with the Chicago and Pacific Coast areas accounting for the overwhelming majority of the remainder. The Southern and Rocky Mountain areas have fewer members. The annual AAS meetings, held since 1948, are now being rotated among East Coast, Midwest, and West Coast locations. In addition to regular membership, which also included students, the AAS offers membership in the following categories: patron, supporting, associate, and honorary. Over 90 percent of the total membership, however, falls in the regular category.

The AAS elects the customary institutional officers; it conducts its business from an office, headed by a secretary-treasurer, located in Ann Arbor, Michigan.

For further information, see a detailed and authoritative history of the AAS by Charles O. Hucker, *The Association for Asian Studies. An Interpretive History* (1973). In addition to this volume, by an informed participant in the first two decades of the AAS's history, see, by the same author, "The Association for Asian Studies, Inc., at the Age of Twenty," *Journal of Asian Studies* (November, 1968). For earlier histories, see Earl H. Pritchard, "The Association for Asian Studies, Inc., A Brief History," *Journal of Asian Studies* (August, 1957); and Robert I. Crane, "The First Ten Years of the Association for Asian Studies, 1948-1958," *Journal of Asian Studies* (August, 1958). See also Wilma Fairbank, "The Association for Asian Studies," *World of the Mind* (1958).

ASSOCIATION FOR SYMBOLIC LOGIC (ASL). The objective of the ASL has always been to bring together mathematicians and philosophers concerned about problems of logic. Before the 1935 organization of the ASL, mathematicians interested in problems of foundations and philosophers interested in symbolism did not have an organization to bring them together or an effective medium of publication. Thus a group of philosophers/mathematicians, including Professors C. A. Baylis, Alonzo Church, H. B. Curry, and C. J. Ducasse, became convinced by the early 1930s that the situation warranted the creation of a medium of publication for papers devoted to symbolic logic, papers that were not usually welcomed by the existing philosophical or mathematical journals. Professor Ducasse was the scholar, at the 1935 annual meeting of the American Philosophical Asociation's* (APA) Eastern Division at Columbia University, who led in the founding of the ASL for the express purpose of underwriting a learned journal, and he was elected the first president of the new association. The ASL's quarterly *Journal of Symbolic Logic* was established the following year with Professors Alonzo Church and C. H. Langford as editors.

The *Journal* is conceded to be the major accomplishment of the ASL. In addition to presenting articles, reviews, and notes, it has provided a bibliography of all known publications on symbolic logic since Leibnitz (1666).

This bibliography, published in 1936 (volume 1, number 4, of the *Journal*), with additions and corrections in 1938 (volume 3, number 4, of the *Journal*), has been supplemented by a continuing review section to the present. It should be noted that this bibliography and the review section was long the almost single-handed work of Professor Alonzo Church. The *Journal* is financed largely from membership dues, but subventions have been received from various universities, and, more recently, it has received support from UNESCO through the International Council of Scientific Unions* (ICSU).

Membership in the ASL is open to all who are interested in symbolic logic, with approximately 30 percent of its eighteen hundred members living abroad.

Annual meetings of the ASL have usually been held in December. They provide a forum for research reports of members together with addresses by invited speakers. These meetings are often held in conjunction with the American Mathematical Society* (AMS) or the APA. Also, the ASL maintains close contact with and is a member of the American Association for the Advancement of Science* (AAAS) and the International Union of History and Philosophy of Science.

The ASL elects the customary institutional officers; it conducts its business from offices, headed by a secretary, located at Providence, Rhode Island.

For further information, see C. J. Ducasse and Haskell B. Curry, "Early History of the Association for Symbolic Logic," *Journal of Symbolic Logic* (September, 1962). Information about the ASL and its history has also been provided through correspondence with Professors C. A. Baylis, Alonzo Church, H. B. Curry, C. J. Ducasse, and S. C. Kleene. See also *Bulletin of Information* published intermittently by the ASL.

ASSOCIATION OF AMERICAN ANATOMISTS. See American Association of Anatomists.

ASSOCIATION OF AMERICAN GEOGRAPHERS (AAG). This is a learned society, organized for the purpose of bringing professional geographers together where they could hear each others papers and carry on a discussion of problems with a group of specialists. The AAG is very different from the American Geographical Society* (AGS), founded in 1851, which was originally intended to serve a widespread popular interest in the scientific study of geography in this and other countries and to provide government offices and business houses with useful information. The American Geographical Society is known for the many excellent research studies that it has conducted since its founding. The AAG is also different from the National Geographic Society,* which was originally organized in 1888 to provide a meeting place for scientific and literary people in

Washington, D.C. But the National Geographic Society decided in 1897 to write about geography "in language that could be understood by the general public." Their success in this undertaking is well known; however, this policy ended any possibility that it could serve specialized professional geographers.

In 1903 Professor William Morris Davis of Harvard proposed the organization of a learned society strictly for professional geographers. Davis, who in that year was the vice-president of the American Association for the Advancement of Science* (AAAS), Section E, Geology and Geography, gave the annual vice-presidential address on "The Essential in Geography." He pointed out that geology had gained recognition as a learned profession after the organization of the Geological Society of America* (GSA), where membership was restricted to scholars who had made original contributions to the field. Because of the widespread popular interest in what is commonly called geography, it was essential, he thought, to establish standards of professional work—original contributions and ample publication—as a basis for election to membership in a new organization. Davis's address to Section E met with immediate support, mostly from geologists who were interested in the earth as the home of man, an often quoted general description of the field of geography. A year of organizational effort by a cluster of scholars who supported Davis's ideas resulted in the formation of the AAG in Philadelphia in 1904.

The AAG was formed, therefore, to provide a national organization that would bring its 48 founding members, 22 holding academic positions and 26 in a variety of jobs outside the universities, into association and provide a medium for the exchange of views on geographical matters. Because of the widespread, popular, nonscientific interest in geography, Professor Davis and other AAG leaders insisted on the necessity of restricting membership, by election, to those persons who had done original and high-quality work in some branch of geography and had published widely. Consequently, the AAG grew from 48 in 1904 to only about 275 by 1948.

Meanwhile, during the 1920s and 1930s, more and more Ph.D. degrees in geography were awarded, and by the middle of the decade the nonmembers were sufficiently numerous so that when special sessions, for members only, were announced at AAG meetings arrangements had to be made for the meetings of nonmembers for the discussion of various topics. The problem became more critical during World War II, when large numbers of geographers carried out classified work in geography but could not use the results to qualify for AAG membership. In 1943, when the annual meeting was held in Washington, D.C., there were more nonmembers than members in attendance, and it was at this time that the American Society for Professional Geographers (ASPG) was established, including many who were already members of the AAG. Between 1943 and 1948 there was much discussion about the roles of the two societies. Despite vigorous opposition to a merger and heated discussion as to a title, in 1948 the two were merged into one, retaining the title of the older organization but with modifications in its rigid provisions for membership. Since the merger the AAG has had a swift growth in membership and today numbers about six thousand persons; more than one-half are college and university instructors or teachers in geography.

Before 1911, AAG members published papers in various journals, particularly the *Bulletin* of the AGS. In 1911 the *Annals* of the AAG was established. Its first few years were supported by grants from the AGS and by personal donations from a small group of AAG founders. By 1922 the AAG had become strong enough to cover the costs of its *Annals* without outside assistance and at that time the *Annals* was changed to a quarterly. In addition to articles, the *Annals* includes abstracts of papers and, since 1956, a special reviews section. In 1943 the *Professional Geographer* was founded as the official publication of the ASPG. Upon the merger in 1948 it was originally carried on as an AAG publication containing short articles, reviews, research reports, and so forth, together with news of interest to members, schedules of meetings, committee reports, and the like. With the establishment in 1965 of a *Newsletter*, the last functions have been transferred there from the *Professional Geographer*. Volumes in a *Monograph Series* were first published in 1959, but were temporarily discontinued in 1976. In 1968, with a grant from the National Science Foundation, the AAG launched a Resource Paper Series. These papers are concerned with important topics of modern geography and are designed to complement a variety of undergraduate college geography courses. Several issues are published annually.

Annual AAG meetings have been held each year since 1904, with the exception of the war years, 1917, 1942, and 1944. During the early years of its existence, reflecting general control of the AAG by members from the Eastern seaboard, these were usually held in the East. By the early 1920s, there was a substantial increase in the number of members with advanced degrees from Midwestern universities. Reflecting their desire for the convening of meetings in the Midwest, a policy was adopted at that time of alternating annual meetings in Eastern and Midwestern cities. This policy prevailed until 1946; since that time, meetings have also been held in the South, Canada, and the Far West.

The presentation of technical papers by members has always been the major component of AAG meetings, although there have been recent meetings in which there were some panels and special interest sessions where no formal papers were presented. Also, there are a variety of field trips, workshops, book exhibits, and poster sessions, which are characteristic of contemporary AAG meetings.

Although the AAG has always been interested in the teaching of geography, its activities and programs have been built around the results of research. These have been aided by the creation of various research funds and prizes.

The AAG elects the customary institutional officers; it conducts its business from its own office building, purchased in 1971, located in Washington, D.C. The staff there is headed by an executive director.

For further information, see the publications of the AAG discussed above, particularly Preston E. James and Ralph Ehrenberg, "Original Members of the AAG," *Professional Geographer* (May, 1975); and Preston E. James, "The Process of Competitive Discussion," *Professional Geographer* (February, 1976). Dr. James is also the author of an account of the formation and history of the AAG appearing in the *ACLS Newsletter* (Spring-Summer, 1975); and he and Geoffrey J. Martin have jointly published a detailed history, under AAG auspices, entitled *The Association of American Geographers: The First Seventy-Five Years 1904-1979* (1979).

In addition to the works cited above, see Albert P. Brigham, "The Association of American Geographers, 1903-1923," *Annals of the Association of American Geographers* (September, 1924); and Charles C. Colby, "Changing Currents of Geographic Thought in America," *Annals of the Association of American Geographers* (March, 1936).

ASSOCIATION OF AMERICAN LAW SCHOOLS (AALS). Following the Civil War, various leaders in the legal profession began to seek some means to upgrade the nineteenth-century bar in general and legal education in particular. Initially, local bar associations were organized for this purpose, and by 1878 there were sixteen state, city, and county bar associations in existence, located primarily in the Northeast. In August of that year, at Saratoga Springs, New York, some seventy-five prominent attorneys met together and formed the national American Bar Association (ABA). One of the original ABA committees set up at that time was the Committee on Legal Education and Admission to the Bar, later (1893) Section on Legal Education, and it was this section and its members that became the parents of the Association of American Law Schools.

Meeting, as it did, at the same time as the annual ABA meetings, the committee/section members discussed and passed resolutions aimed at uplifting legal education. It periodically recommended, for example, more stringent standards for the admission of students to law schools, an adequate number of full-time professors, better law school libraries, and so on. Despite two decades of such activity, however, very little was accomplished. In large measure, this was due to the fact that any action by the section was subject to the control of the parent bar association, and there were enough members in the latter with a vested interest in blocking such measures.

By 1899 dissatisfaction over this stalemate reached the point that, Henry Wade Rogers, John C. Gray, and George M. Sharpe, all active instructors in prestigious U.S. law schools, took the lead in drafting and issuing an invitation to various leading law schools calling for a meeting to organize a separate organization. Forty-seven delegates from thirty-five law schools assembled in response at Saratoga Springs, New York, on August 29, 1900, and it was there that the AALS was founded. With James B. Thayer of Harvard as its first president, its stated purpose was and continues to be "the improvement of legal education in America."

The constitution adopted by the AALS laid down certain qualifying standards that law schools must meet in order to become members. Of the thirty-five schools represented at the meeting, twenty-seven met these standards and, together with five more recommended for admission, became charter members.

Through the years, the AALS has amplified and broadened this standard-setting function. More recently this has included provision for the elimination of all aspects of sexual and racial discrimination by member institutions, enforcement of the principles of academic freedom and tenure, clarification of library standards, the setting up of a visitation program to assist member institutions in self-improvement, and the institution of a general accreditation program for them.

The original constitution also provided that the AALS should meet at the same time and place as the annual meeting of the American Bar Association, and up until 1914 it did so. By that time, however, differences over the best time and place of meetings plus a desire on the part of law school representatives for a lengthier meeting of their own saw a parting of the ways. Thereafter the AALS began the practice of holding independent annual meetings during the Christmas holidays and, primarily, in Chicago. In 1965, however, the practice was established of rotating the annual meetings among the Eastern, Midwestern, and Western portions of the country. In 1979, a decision was reached that the annual meetings would be held during the first week in January.

Whether meeting together or separately the two associations have always had a close relationship. Leaders in both, for example, figured prominently in the 1923 creation of the American Law Institute, which, from that time to the present, has done so much for the study and statement of American law in various fields and the ascertainment of defects in our legal system.

Much of the activities of the AALS is carried on through standing and special committees. The traditionally active ones are the Committee on Academic Freedom and Tenure, Accreditation Committee, Library Committee, and Government Relations Committee. There is a standing joint committee with the Canadian Association of Law Teachers. In 1972 the association established "sections," professional interest groups of the faculty of member schools who wish to join together to present a program at an annual meeting or to conduct other activities. Anyone may become an associate member of a section, and its membership selects its own presiding officers. There are presently forty-seven sections, and they have been pointed to as one of the most significant developments in the association's history.

In addition to the discussions and reports presented at its annual meetings and published annually in its *Handbook* and *Proceedings*, the AALS has, through the years, published essays, monographs, and books in such areas as legal history, philosophy of law, and constitutional law. Because of the number of academic and commercial publishers in the field, however, it was not until 1950 that a quarterly *Journal of Legal Education* was established. In addition to articles and book reviews, the *Journal* contains parts titled "Comments" and "Law School Developments" designed to promote an interchange of ideas.

Other publications include a quarterly *AALS Newsletter*; since 1976, a *Research Bulletin*, alerting law schools and law teachers to available research grants and fellowships; a *Legal Affairs Manual* (copublished with the Law School Admission Council), discussing the impact and possible reaction to federal statutes and regulations on the operation of law schools; and a *Placement Bulletin*, published six times a year, listing the openings for law teaching positions in our colleges and universities. In connection with the latter the AALS has, since 1974, convened an annual faculty recruitment conference for deans and others seeking to interview candidates for their faculties.

Other recent services undertaken by the AALS include the preparation of a memorandum containing suggestions for planning law school buildings together with the assembling of floor plans for law school buildings constructed in recent years; both items are available for nominal fees. Annually, it offers law teaching workshops devoted to the teaching of various subjects in the law school curriculum. From its initial membership, the AALS now totals 139 member U.S. law schools.

The AALS elects the customary institutional officers; it conducts its business from an office, headed by an executive director, located in Washington, D.C.

For further information, see the publications of the AALS discussed above, particularly an early brief history of the AALS by Manon R. Kirkwood, *Handbook* (1935). For later brief histories, see "Concerning the Journal," *Journal of Legal Education* (Autumn, 1948); Warren A. Seavey, "The Association of American Law Schools in Retrospect," *Journal of Legal Education* (Winter, 1950); and Michael Cardozo, "The Association Process, 1963-1973," *Proceedings* (June, 1975).

ASSOCIATION OF BIBLICAL INSTRUCTORS IN AMERICAN COLLEGES AND SECONDARY SCHOOLS. See American Academy of Religion.

ASSOCIATION OF UNIVERSITIES FOR RESEARCH IN ASTRONOMY, INC. (AURA). Cooperation in research has been an absolute necessity in most branches of modern astronomy. The International Astronomical Union, founded at the end of World War I, was the first of the international scientific unions devoted primarily to encouraging and facilitating cooperation in research. As early as 1940 Otto Struve, director of the Yerkes and McDonald observatories, proposed a cooperative observatory to be operated and used by a group of five or six universities, with capital funding from private foundations. World War II prevented this from becoming more than a good idea.

On May 15, 1952, the University of Arizona, Indiana University, and Ohio State University submitted a proposal to the two-year-old National Science Foundation for funds to conduct a one-year site survey near Tucson to find a good location away from city lights for the Steward Observatory thirty-six-inch reflector. The proposed budget was $21,200. After the move to the new site the telescope was to be shared by the three universities. The proposal suggested the possibility of setting up a nonprofit corporation and inviting other universities to join. Additional funding would be requested from the NSF to pay the cost of moving the telescope and the first year of joint operation. It was expected that the cooperating institutions would share the maintenance costs after the first year.

The National Science Foundation convened an Ad Hoc Meeting of Astronomical Consultants on August 1, 1952. The next year this group was renamed the Advisory Panel for Astronomy; it was the first NSF advisory panel in any discipline. The Arizona-Indiana-Ohio State proposal was discussed at this meeting and was declined. However, several panel members urged the NSF to look into the needs of astronomy for modern facilities. The NSF responded by appointing an Ad Hoc Panel on Astronomical Instrumentation (Robert R. McMath, chairman, I. S. Bowen, Otto Struve, and A. E. Whitford; Roger L. Putnam, trustee of the Lowell Observatory,* also participated as a guest). This group proposed that NSF sponsor a conference on the need for facilities for photoelectric photometry. The needs in this field had been stressed by John B. Irwin of Indiana University in a paper published in *Science*, February 29, 1952. The conference was organized by a committee chaired by A. E. Whitford, and was held at the Lowell Observatory, August 31-September 1, 1953.

The recommendation of the Flagstaff Photoelectric Conference to the National Science Foundation was that a panel be appointed to study the need for a national optical astronomy observatory not limited to photoelectric photometry and to conduct a site survey for a suitable location if the need was found to exist. This panel consisted of the members of the original Ad Hoc Committee on Astronomical Instrumentation plus Bengt Stromgren. A group of six consultants to the panel was also appointed, including Leo Goldberg, who had played an important role in the Flagstaff conference. His role in the work of the panel proved to be even more important. NSF funded the work of the panel, including the site survey, through several grants to the University of Michigan because this was the home base of the panel chairman, Dr. McMath. The administration of these grants was handled by Leo Goldberg using the facilities of the Astronomy Department office. A decision was made at the first meeting of the panel of November 4-5, 1954, to employ Dr. Aden B. Meinel, then on the staff of the Yerkes Observatory, to serve as the executive secretary of the panel and to conduct the day-to-day operations of the site survey.

The National Science Foundation was also supporting a site survey and planning for a national radio astronomy observatory. The site survey was conducted by Associated Universities, Inc.* (AUI). After the site at Greenbank, West Virginia, had been chosen, the NSF selected AUI to be the contractor to build and operate the radio astronomy observatory, ultimately named the National Radio Astronomy Observatory (NRAO).

A suitable consortium to operate the optical observatory did not yet exist, but it had been clearly understood from the beginning of the site survey that an operating agency of some sort would be created and the McMath panel and the NSF grants to the University of Michigan would be phased out before the actual construction of the optical observatory began.

Leo Goldberg, acting for the panel, arranged for representatives from universities with a faculty of at least four astronomers conducting active Ph.D. programs in astronomy and with experience in operating research telescope facilities to meet in Ann Arbor on March 29, 1957, to discuss forming a corporation that could build and operate the optical observatory under contract with the National Science Foundation. Representatives of seven universities (California, Chicago, Harvard, Indiana, Michigan, Ohio State, and Wisconsin) attended the meeting and approved an agreement to form a corporation under the laws of the State of Arizona. The agreement was formally signed by the seven universities a short time later. The articles of incorporation were signed, and the first meeting of the board of directors of AURA took place in Ann Arbor on October 28, 1957. Each university has two representatives on the board, a scientist and an administrator. There is also provision for several director-at-large appointments for terms of three years.

Yale University became a member in 1958, and Princeton University joined in 1959. The present membership of sixteen also includes the University of Arizona, California Institute of Technology, University of Colorado, University of Hawaii, University of Illinois, Massachusetts Institute of Technology, and University of Texas at Austin.

The site survey was nearly finished at the time AURA came into existence. The final choice was between several sites in the Hualapai Mountains near Kingman, Arizona, and Kitt Peak to the southwest of Tucson. Kitt Peak is on the Papago reservation and is one of the tribe's holy mountains. Special permission from the Schuck Toak District Council and the tribal council was required before the site tests on the mountain could be carried out. Professor Edward Spicer of the Anthropology Department at the University of Arizona was especially helpful in the negotiations that led to permission for site testing being granted. The final report on the site survey was evaluated by the Scientific Committee of the AURA board, and Kitt Peak was formally chosen by the AURA on March 1, 1958. NSF approval was announced March 14. A lease for the use of Kitt Peak for the observatory then had to be negotiated with the Papago tribe. Enabling legislation to make a long-term renewable lease possible was passed by the Eighty-Sixth Congress on August 28, 1958. The lease was signed on October 24, with the National Science Foundation as lessee. The name "Kitt Peak National Observatory" was proposed by the AURA board on December 8, 1958, and approved by the National Science Foundation on January 23, 1959.

AURA has also built and operates the Cerro Tololo Inter-American Observatory, near La Serena, Chile, under contract with the National Science Foundation. This project was started by Gerard P. Kuiper at the University of Chicago, with U.S. Air Force funding. Chicago asked AURA to take over the project when Kuiper moved to the University of Arizona in 1960. Jurgen Stock completed the site survey under AURA auspices, and NSF funding replaced Air Force funding.

A 150-inch telescope had been funded for Kitt Peak by a line item in the NSF budget. In late 1966 the Ford Foundation offered to provide up to five million dollars toward the cost of an identical telescope for Chile, if NSF could get a matching five million dollars from Congress in the fiscal year 1968 budget. This offer came so late in the budget process that the personal approval of President Lyndon B. Johnson was required to add it to the NSF budget request. Congress appropriated the money, and AURA was able to go to bid for two identical mountings, saving about one million dollars compared with separate purchases.

The cooperation of the University of Chile has been an important factor in the success of the Cerro Tololo Inter-American Observatory. Staff members of the Observatorio Nacional were active participants in the site survey from the beginning. The rector and other officials of the university have been supportive in many ways. One of the director-at-large positions on the AURA board is used to give the University of Chile active participation in AURA.

AURA also operates the Sacramento Peak Observatory near Cloudcroft, New Mexico, under a third contract with the NSF. This solar research facility was originally established by the U.S. Air Force. NSF took it over when Air Force budget cuts led to plans to close the observatory.

AURA was given a major new responsibility when the National Aeronautics and Space Administration announced on January 16, 1981, that AURA had been selected to establish and manage the new Space Telescope Science Institute. The AURA proposal had included the selection of the Johns Hopkins University as the site for the institute, and the university will construct a new building to house the institute on its main campus. The ninety-six-inch telescope will be launched in early 1985 using the space shuttle. Data from the telescope will come to the institute via a data link to the

Goddard Space Flight Center. The permanent staff of the institute is expected to be about 150, including 40 astronomers. It is anticipated that some 200 other astronomers will visit the institute each year to make observations with the space telescope and to analyze data.

At the time of incorporation all AURA officers except the treasurer were elected from the university representatives on the board and served without additional compensation. The treasurer was an officer of the Valley National Bank, and his services were provided at no cost to AURA. The associate director for administration of the Kitt Peak National Observatory held a parallel appointment as secretary of AURA from 1960 to 1972.

As AURA and NSF grew, both in dollars and administrative complexity, the time finally arrived when a full-time, paid president of AURA became a necessity. This position was created in 1972, and the board member who had been president became chairman of the board. The title of vice-president of AURA was changed to vice-chairman of the board, and the position of vice-president was eliminated. The president is the chief executive officer of the corporation, and he is assisted by a small corporate staff. An executive committee of nine, including the president, chairman, and vice-chairman, has authority to act for the board and handles the ongoing activities of the corporation. The directors of the three observatories report to the president.

The full board holds one meeting per year. The work of the board is distributed among a number of standing and ad hoc committees. There is also a visiting committee, which gives the board an independent view and outside evaluation of the work of the observatories and the corporation.

The three observatories are national research facilities and are open to qualified investigators from all institutions. Proposals for telescope time and other uses of the facilities are judged solely on the basis of scientific merit. Many meritorious proposals for telescope time have to be turned down owing to the limited number of telescopes now in operation.

In the absence of published historical accounts about AURA, the foregoing brief history is based upon a study of archival material, particularly NSF files; Bentley Historical Library Archives, Ann Arbor, Michigan; AURA files, Tuscon, Arizona; and oral tape-recorded interviews with more than fifty persons conducted by Frank K. Edmondson. Professor Edmondson is presently engaged in the preparation of a detailed history of the AURA.

FRANK K. EDMONDSON

ASTOR LIBRARY. See New York Public Library, Astor, Lenox and Tilden Foundations, The.

ASTRONOMICAL AND ASTROPHYSICAL SOCIETY OF AMERICA. See American Astronomical Society.

_B_

BATTELLE MEMORIAL INSTITUTE (BMI). The history of Battelle Memorial Institute is the story of a man, of an idea, and of an organization that grew out of that idea to become a pioneer in contract research and one of the world's largest independent research institutes.

The man central to the history of BMI is Gordon Battelle. Gordon Battelle died on September 21, 1923, leaving a will which provided that the bulk of his estate be used to create "a Battelle Memorial Institute . . . for the encouragement of creative research . . . and the making of discoveries and inventions." BMI, to be governed by a self-perpetuating board of trustees, was to serve as a memorial to his family—pioneers in Ohio and its early steel industry.

Two years later (1925) Gordon's mother, Annie Norton Battelle, died and left the balance of the Battelle family fortune to the same purpose, making the total a sum of about $3.5 million.

The Battelle board of trustees, in the four years following incorporation of the institute in 1925, acquired a site of about ten acres in Columbus on King Avenue adjacent to the Ohio State University, and carried out plans for a laboratory, which was built and opened for use in October, 1929. To begin operations, the board chose a director, Dr. Horace W. Gillett, who was considered by his peers the "dean of American metallurgy." It was Dr. Gillett who determined that the work of the BMI should initially be concerned primarily with metallurgy.

At the time BMI began operations, it had a staff of about thirty people, and annual research expenditures in the first year totaled $71,000. Five years later, annual expenditures for 1935 had risen to $198,000, and the staff approached one hundred. And although BMI's research activities throughout the 1930s must be characterized as almost completely concerned with materials technology, including coal research, the philosophy of diversification of capabilities was constantly at work.

Significantly, BMI's first sponsored project was the preparation of a number of volumes on metallurgy known as the Alloys of Iron Research

Monograph Series. Work on this classic series marked the beginning of BMI's continuing and—over the years—vast contribution to technical literature.

Doubtless one of the most important events in the history of BMI in the 1930s was the decision by Dr. Gillett in 1934 to ask the board of trustees to relieve him of administrative duties and to name Clyde E. Williams as director. During William's years as director—the title in his later years was president—BMI's capabilities and interests were extended far beyond materials technology to serve the changing research needs of industry and, through industry, the public. He and the BMI board recognized this need for diversification, and, accordingly, expertise was acquired in chemistry, physics, engineering, and economics.

One example of BMI's efforts to broaden its capabilities was in nuclear research. It became involved in the Manhattan Project of World War II because of its international reputation in the field of metallurgy and was asked to study the fabrication of the then almost unknown metal uranium. In the next decade, it became one of the country's outstanding centers for nuclear research, and at times over four hundred of its staff members were engaged in research in this area. Thus, in the early 1950s, BMI purchased a large tract of land at West Jefferson, just west of Columbus, and built what was the first privately owned nuclear research center in the world, including a research reactor, critical assembly facility, and hot cells.

Also during this period, BMI was, by fortuitous circumstances and remarkable foresight, pursuing the development of "xerography"—a development that would later have a far-reaching effect on Battelle and the entire business world.

The postwar years were a period when BMI not only expanded its range of research interests but also established its presence outside the United States. It was in the early 1950s that it build research centers in Frankfurt, Germany, and Geneva, Switzerland, and both quickly became self-sustaining operations, bringing to Europe the concept of sponsored research. These years, too, saw a corresponding period of amazing growth. Thus, in 1957, at the time of Williams's retirement, the total worldwide BMI staff stood at thirty-one hundred, and total annual research expenditures were just over twenty-five million dollars.

Williams's retirement, and the appointment of his longtime associate, Dr. B. D. Thomas, as president, coincided closely with a rather dramatic shift in science policy in the United States and elsewhere as the space age began. One important factor in the growth of BMI under Dr. Thomas's leadership was its selection by the U.S. Atomic Energy Commission to operate the former Hanford Laboratory in Richland, Washington. With the stroke of a pen, as the transfer was made in January, 1965, BMI acquired 1,959 new staff members, at what was designated Battelle's Pacific Northwest Laboratories—bringing the total staff to a new all-time high of 5,500.

Other facilities, as well, were added by BMI during Dr. Thomas's years as president. New buildings were constructed at almost all of its established research centers. In the fall of 1964, it assumed responsibility for management and operation of the William F. Clapp Laboratories in Duxbury, Massachusetts. Long noted as a world center for the study of marine biological attack on materials, the Clapp Laboratories complemented BMI's Florida Marine Research Facility, which it had established near Daytona Beach in 1946. Later in the 1960s, BMI was to acquire a 120-acre site at the mouth of Sequim Bay in the State of Washington for a marine research facility. Finally, there was the acquisition of an 18-acre wooded site near the University of Washington that was transformed into the Battelle Seattle Research Center—a cluster of quietly handsome buildings to house conferences and offices and provide living quarters for visiting scientists and scholars.

These years of building and expansion for BMI reflected the mood of the space age and the continuing demand for its research services, but they also reflected additional financial income from its endowment and from the commercialization of xerography.

The BMI's board of trustees and officers elected to use the money derived from its investments to enhance its established capabilities and to reach out into new areas of research. Indeed, with Dr. Thomas's leadership, BMI sought a broader approach to its mission than contract research and its traditional involvement in education. Extending its contract research efforts in the 1960s into such areas as oceanography, regional planning, health care, ecology, pollution control, and urban problems was only part of Dr. Thomas's strategy.

During this period, for example, BMI embarked on a far-reaching program, known as the Battelle Institute Program, through which it sought to make significant contributions to human knowledge and to the professional development of researchers. The program, funded by BMI, provided support for a cadre of fellows appointed from outside sources as well as from existing BMI staff to conduct work of a basic or scholarly character.

Following later was another major program conceived in the same spirit in which BMI used its own resources for the public good: the Battelle Energy Program. This program, championed by Dr. Sherwood L. Fawcett, Dr. Thomas's successor, was a multimillion-dollar effort to provide research leadership in dealing with the energy crisis. Significantly, this program was begun in 1973 in advance of the embargo by the Organization of Petroleum Exporting Countries (OPEC).

Dr. Sherwood L. Fawcett, the fourth and current chief executive at BMI, brought the presidency a generation forward when he assumed the post in 1968. His three predecessors had had careers spanning World War I and the Great Depression and had worked together closely throughout BMI's formative years. Dr. Fawcett, by contrast, served in World War II as a young Navy officer and did not begin his career as a nuclear physicist at BMI until 1950, following graduate school.

Under Dr. Fawcett's leadership, BMI has continued to grow and diversify its activities. For example, total sponsored research revenues, which were $116 million in 1970, surpassed $350 million in 1979. And the staff total had climbed from 5,602 at the end of 1970, to over 7,000 at the end of 1979. Through foresight and planning, the BMI has carried out a much expanded research effort in those areas where demand is strong, for example, energy and environmental work and the life sciences.

At the same time, BMI's two subsidiaries for putting technology to work—the Battelle Development Corporation and Scientific Advances, Inc. (SAI)—have launched new efforts to capitalize on the intellectual property of the BMI.

With respect to the future, the authorization in the spring of 1978 by the U.S. Department of Energy (DOE) for the BMI to manage a major program on commercial nuclear waste isolation, and BMI's creation of a new operating division for this and other subsequent development programs are indicative of its intent to formalize and expand efforts in the management of large development-type programs. The emphasis in these programs is on demonstration of new technology, as opposed to the research and development that precedes demonstration.

The strongest promise of BMI's future, however, is the continuing line of research achievements: development of the world's largest operating solar-powered irrigation pump; a new simplified underwater arc-welding process; improved food products; a simple hand water pump for use in developing nations; a novel fluidized-bed coal combustion process for industrial boilers.

For further information, see an earlier history by George A. W. Boehm and Alex Groner, *The Battelle Story—Science in the Service of Mankind* (1972); and James R. Hunkler, *Science Serving Human Needs—A History of Battelle Memorial Institute* (1979). The latter is a booklet prepared for distribution during BMI's fiftieth anniversary. Also, for two works dealing with the histories of the BMI and similar not-for-profit research institutes, see Harold Orlans, *The Nonprofit Research Institute* (1972); and Harold Vagtborg, *Research and American Industrial Development* (1976).

JAMES R. HUNKLER

BERNICE P. BISHOP MUSEUM. When Charles Reed Bishop thought of establishing a museum, he contemplated a memorial to his wife that would incorporate her collection and encourage public interest in the Hawaiian heritage. This concept was greatly broadened, and today the Bishop Museum, founded in 1889, is the paramount museum in Oceania and the leading museum concerned with Pacific Basin collections and research in cultural and natural history.

Princess Bernice Pauahi Bishop (1831-84), as the last survivor of the founding (Kamehameha) dynasty of the Hawaiian monarchy, inherited family treasures that constituted important collections of ethnographic and historical items. These she bequeathed to the care of her husband, C. R. Bishop (1822-1915), who came to Hawai'i from the United States in 1846, and soon became one of the kingdom's most successful businessmen and bankers and a leading philanthropist.

Besides Princess Bernice's possessions, the first base of the museum's collections was formed by the historical collections of Queen Emma, wife of Kamehameha IV, who died soon after Bernice, and the contents of the (Hawaiian) National Museum, which had become entirely inactive by 1887.

Bernice P. Bishop left her wealth to support the education of Hawaiian children. This trust became the Bishop Estate, which supports the Kamehameha Schools. Schools and museum had the same trustees initially, later modified to a largely overlapping trusteeship. However, the two trusts were entirely separate financially, and the more modestly endowed museum could not receive support from the Bishop Estate. In 1975, a petition by the trustees for a change in governance was granted. The Bishop Museum became a private charitable corporation with a board of trustees, now numbering twenty-one, that is representative of the community and entirely separate from the Bishop Estate.

The trust formalized in 1896 mandated that the Bishop Museum would be "a scientific institution for collecting, preserving, storing, and exhibiting specimens of Polynesian and kindred antiquities, ethnology, and natural history . . . and the publication . . . of the results of such investigation and study." This fortunate extension of C. R. Bishop's first concept was most significantly effected by Bishop and another American.

William Tufts Brigham (1841-1926) was the first curator and then the first director (1898-1918) of the Bishop Museum. He came from Boston in 1864 to study Hawaiian botany and geology and stayed into the following year. When he settled in Hawai'i in 1888, it was with Bishop's support and the care of the planned museum in view. Brigham influenced the extension of its mandate to include emphasis on natural history, as well as cultural materials, to cover the Pacific broadly, and to stress research and publication. Bishop responded to the views of the scientific curator, but he also had an informed interest in the sciences that directly affected the breadth of the mandate. When Bishop resigned as trustee in 1897, having moved to California in 1894, the scope of the museum had been basically established.

The museum has had only five other directors after Brigham, each of whom has significantly influenced its progress: Herbert E. Gregory (1919-1936), Peter H. Buck (1936-1951), Alexander Spoehr (1952-1961), Roland W. Force (1962-1976), and Edward C. Creutz (1977 to present).

R. C. L. Perkins came to Hawai'i from England (1892-97, 1900-01) to conduct a faunal survey, and in 1895 the museum joined in supporting his work by providing the major financial backing to the resulting *Fauna Hawaiiensis* (1899-1913), and its collections were enriched by approximately one-third of the survey specimens. In keeping with the intent of Pacific coverage, a collector was sent to Guam and the Philippines in 1900, and continued work in the southern and western Pacific between 1901 and 1903. Exchange arrangements with other institutions also were begun early (1893 with the Australian Museum).

However, it was not until the 1920s and 1930s that the museum sponsored a number of large-scale expeditions to other parts of the Pacific. One of the first was the Bayard Dominick expedition (1920-1922) to Tonga, the Marquesas, and the Austral Islands, planned in consultation with four American universities and museums and with leading anthropologists. This approach reflected the philosophy of Director Gregory, who saw interinstitutional cooperation as essential in carrying out scientific exploration in the vast and changing Pacific. Gregory convened the First Pan-Pacific Scientific Conference in Hawai'i in 1920, the beginning of the Pacific Science Association and Congresses and of a continuing role of the museum in their proceedings. The museum has continued to seek cooperation in Pacific research. For example, a program administered by it, the University of Hawaii, and Yale University was funded in 1953 by the Carnegie Corporation of New York and for eleven years supported work on cultural growth and social change.

The museum is located on ten acres a few miles west of the center of Honolulu. The first building, which continues as the public entrance, was started in 1888 and constructed of cut lava stone with beautifully carved koa wood interiors. Other buildings were completed in 1894, 1903, 1911, 1926, 1961, 1964, 1977, and 1980. Further construction is planned and necessary to provide adequately for collections, research, and exhibits. Off-campus activities include a museum ship, the *Falls of Clyde*, and a branch office in Waikiki, united since 1972 by the museum's London double-decker buses.

The research collections of nearly twenty million specimens are curated and studied in the five scientific departments discussed below. Several other departments also hold research materials, including the library, with the leading Pacific collection in the Western hemisphere.

Anthropology. The museum has been best known to the general public through its exhibits and publications in Pacific anthropology and history. Ethnological and historical artifacts number over one hundred thousand, including an extraordinary concentration of Hawaiian materials, along with good to excellent representation from other parts of Polynesia, Micronesia, and Melanesia. Archaeological research is stressed, and there are forty-two thousand accessioned artifacts. Other sections concern ethnobotany, ethnomusicology, and oral history. The Hawai'i Immigrant Heritage Preservation Program relates to the diverse groups who came to Hawai'i in the past two hundred years.

History. Although authorized much earlier, a separate Department of History was not activated until 1966. History now encompasses archival materials, historic paintings, architectural and marine history, and restoration of the *Falls of Clyde*.

Botany. The Herbarium Pacificum contains over 420,000 plant specimens, including more than 5,500 types, the largest assemblage of Hawaiian material and among the largest for Oceania and for New Guinea.

Entomology. Among the several largest in the nation, with 12.5 million specimens and over 11,000 type specimens, the worldwide collections emphasize the Pacific in a broad sense, including East and South Asia, Australasia, and Antarctica, as well as Oceania.

Zoology. There are four divisions with over 1,750 primary types. Invertebrate Zoology covers all invertebrates except those in malacology and entomology, with emphasis on the marine fauna of the Indo-Pacific and with primary strengths in decapod Crustacea, echinoderms, polychaete annelids, and corals. The collections in malacology consist of 6 million shells, of which 2 million are marine and the rest are land gastropods—the largest assemblage of the rich Pacific land snail fauna. For Vertebrate Zoology, the two most significant collections are the historically unique Hawaiian Birds and the Papuan region vertebrates, particularly mammals and birds. Ichthyology is in the process of incorporating the holdings of the Honolulu Laboratory, National Marine Fisheries Service, which will bring the collection to perhaps forty thousand lots and make it second only to that of the United States National Museum in Indo-Pacific fishes.

Among recent exhibitions, the assemblage from thirty-seven museums and other collections of items taken on the three Pacific voyages of Captain James Cook was a unique museological event, open from January to August, 1978, for the bicentennial of Cook's first Hawaiian landfall. The museum's "Hawai'i: The Royal Isles," which expresses the continuity of Hawaiian culture, toured museums in eight U.S. cities from January, 1981 to January 1982.

The Bishop Museum Press has had an important role in transmitting research results and in making the institution known to the global scientific community. There have been 236 *Bulletins*, 24 volumes of *Occasional Papers*, and 66 *Special Publications*. Two anthropology series (e.g., *Pacific Anthropological Records*) and five entomology series (e.g., *Journal of Medical Entomology*) are issued through the press but edited within the departments.

Income from the museum's endowment covers a lesser part of the operating expenditures. The largest single source of funding is from grants and contracts. Admissions and shop sales have become increasingly important, and other major support is from gifts by individuals and corporations. The museum has received several specifically appropriated amounts from the State of Hawaii but not sustained funding to date.

The staff of the museum now exceeds two hundred. Principal administrative officers are Dr. E. C. Creutz, director, and Dr. F. J. Radovsky, assistant director.

For further information, see Donald D. K. Mitchell, "The Educational

Practices of the Bernice Pauahi Bishop Museum" (Ph.D. dissertation, University of California, Berkeley, 1963); Brenda Bishop, "The Bright Light of Knowledge," *Conch Shell* (1964-1965); Frank J. Radovsky, "Bernice P. Bishop Museum," *ASC Newsletter* (1979). See also *Wills and Deeds of Trust: Bernice P. Bishop Estate, Bernice P. Bishop Museum, Charles R. Bishop Estate*, 3rd ed. (1957); and the Bishop Museum *Annual Reports* (1898-1980).

Roger G. Rose has written a historical account entitled "A Museum to Instruct and Delight: William T. Brigham and the Founding of the Bishop Museum," to be published by the Bishop Museum Press.

FRANK J. RADOVSKY

BIBLIOGRAPHICAL SOCIETY OF AMERICA (BSA). An outgrowth of the Bibliographical Society of Chicago, the Bibliographical Society of America was founded in 1904 in Saint Louis and is now one of the constituent members of the American Council of Learned Societies* (ACLS), its object being "to promote bibliographical research and to issue bibliographical publications." Most of the early officers and members of the BSA were librarians and members of the American Library Association. The relationship between the two was close until World War I. Between the World Wars the BSA also established close ties with the American Historical Association* (AHA), and until about 1940 the BSA held its biannual meetings jointly with both the American Library Association and the AHA. In 1940 the BSA consolidated its activities in the New York area, where the annual meeting is held toward the end of January. From time to time additional meetings have taken place, but not on a regular basis.

The BSA provides a forum for the testing of newer bibliographical techniques; it is a source for answers to bibliographical questions; and it has sponsored many noteworthy bibliographical indexes. It has, for example, completed the twenty-eight volume *Bibliotheca Americana, A Dictionary of Books Relating to America* and the second and third editions of *Incunabula in American Libraries*; and it has sponsored a ten-volume *Bibliography of American Literature* (still in process), and a supplement to the *Census of Medieval and Renaissance Manuscripts*, which lists the thousands of manuscripts that have been brought into the United States since 1940. The BSA's major and continuous publication endeavor, however, is the *Papers*, a quarterly journal, which has appeared since 1907. These contain articles and notes on all aspects of bibliography: analytical, historical, textual, and enumerative.

Membership in the BSA is open to all who are interested in bibliography and bibliographical research and presently numbers about sixteen hundred persons.

The BSA elects the customary institutional officers; it conducts its business from an office, headed by an executive secretary, located in New York, New York.

For further information, see the publications of the BSA discussed above, particularly Henry B. Van Holsen, "The Bibliographical Society of America—Its Leaders and Activities, 1904-1939" *Papers of the Bibliographical Society of America* (December, 1941); and J. M. Edelstein "The Bibliographical Society of America 1904-1979" *Papers of the Bibliographical Society of America* (December, 1979). See also William A. Jackson, "The Bibliographical Society of America," *World of the Mind* (1958).

BISHOP MUSEUM. See Bernice P. Bishop Museum.

BOTANICAL SOCIETY OF AMERICA. The official date for the founding of the Botanical Society of America, is 1906, but its origins go back to 1893. It was on the former date that the Botanical Society of America, founded in 1893, merged with the Society for Plant Morphology and Physiology, founded in 1896, and the American Mycological Society, founded in 1903, to create the Botanical Society.

The oldest of the trio, the Botanical Society of America, grew out of the American Botanical Club, organized in 1883 as a part of the American Association of the Advancement of Science* (AAAS). At the 1892 meeting of the club, a committee was set up to consider and report on the feasibility of a separate botanical society. Eight members of this committee of ten, including the chairman, reported unfavorably on the proposal; one favored it but offered no suggestions as to implementation. The final member, Dr. C. R. Barnes, disagreed with the majority report and urged the creation of a separate society. He detailed specifications for carrying it out, whereupon they were adopted by a two-thirds majority of the members of the club.

Subsequently twenty-five botanists were invited to become charter members of the Botanical Society of America, and from this group a committee was designated to draft a constitution. The committee, among other provisions, recommended that membership should be restricted to "American botanists engaged in research, who have published work of recognized merit" and that persons elected to membership should actively participate in its program or forfeit membership. It also called for relatively high admission fees and dues. The constitution, with the rather stringent provisions included, was adopted in 1894.

In part because of these provisions and in part because of the societal policy of holding summer meetings, opposition developed from botanists along the Atlantic seaboard, which resulted in the 1897 founding of the Society for Plant Morphology and Physiology and in 1903 of the American Mycological Society. By the latter date, however, many leading botanists were regretting such action and were urging the re-union of botanists. This movement was crowned with success at a December, 1906, meeting in New York City. A new and more mutually agreeable constitution was adopted by the members of the three societies as a result, and the organization opted for the name, "Botanical Society of America," later incorporated in Connecticut.

Since the merger the Botanical Society has played an important role in the botanical sciences. It has concerned itself with the teaching of botany and has sponsored many symposia on the subject; it has named committees to study various aspects of botanical research; it has surveyed and enumerated employment opportunities in botany; and it has aided the defense efforts in both World Wars. More recently, it has sponsored summer institutes of botany under grants from the National Science Foundation and, in 1956, established the Certificate of Merit, which is awarded annually to one or more outstanding botanists.

The publications of the society include the *American Journal of Botany*, which has been published monthly, excepting August and September, since 1914, the *Plant Science Bulletin*, established in 1955, and an irregularly published *Guides to Graduate Study*. The *Journal* contains articles and monographs by botanists and some of the papers presented at annual meetings of the society; the *Bulletin* is devoted to news and notes of interest to all workers in the botanical field.

The annual meetings of the Botanical Society have been held all over the United States and Canada; early in its history in conjunction with AAAS meetings and more recently with the American Institute for Biological Sciences* (AIBS). Also, the society has set up geographical sections in various parts of the United States, which meet intermittently.

Membership has grown from an original 119 in 1906, and now numbers about 3,500, including regular members, graduate students, and some 50 corresponding members elected from among distinguished foreign botanists.

The BSA elects the customary institutional officers; it conducts its business from the offices of the secretary, located in Lexington, Kentucky, and the treasurer, located in Davis, California.

For further information, see the publications of the Botanical Society of America discussed above, particularly Oswald Tippo, "The Early History of the Botanical Society of America," *American Journal of Botany* (December, 1956). See also Paul R. Burkholder, "The Botanical Society of America, Inc.," *AAAS Bulletin* (August, 1943).

BROOKINGS INSTITUTION. It may seem peculiar that an institution renowned for "liberal" political and economic views should have been founded by a Horatio Alger-style Midwestern industrialist—peculiar, that is, until you realize that the liberal reputation is recent, only comparative, and often misleading. Whereas Richard M. Nixon and his aides saw the Brookings Institution as a refuge for liberal "enemies," Franklin D. Roosevelt was mad at this think tank for harboring conservatives who criticized his New Deal. No matter what its perceived reputation for public policy views, though, Brookings's main attribute is its record of producing high-quality research about social, political, and economic issues of the day. Robert S. Brookings (1850-1932), a Saint Louis businessman and an organizer of the institution, believed that thinking through such issues would do more good for people than all charities.

The Brookings Institution was incorporated in 1927 to merge three complementary enterprises: the Institute for Government Research, founded in 1916 as the country's first private organization devoted to public policy issues at the national level; the Intitute of Economics, established in 1922 to study economic problems; and the Robert Brookings Graduate School of Economics and Government, organized in 1924 as an experiment in training candidates for public service.

Brookings today remains a blend of those three different pursuits. But, above all, the institution prides itself on being practical: neither an academics' enclave nor a refuge for out-of-office politicians. The place exists to aid and perfect public policy, its fourth president, Bruce K. MacLaury believes, by allowing the best minds from academe and government to concentrate on current problems. "The activities of staff members are not limited to research and writing of Brookings books," MacLaury said in his 1980 annual report. "The Institution has a long tradition of service to government," he continued, "without regard to party, through staff participation in congressional hearings, service on boards and commissions, and through individual consultation with policymakers in the executive and legislative branches." Staff members also discuss public policy issues through professional organizations and in their writing for scholarly journals. They prepare articles for the mass media. And they appear on radio and television programs that cover public affairs. Many Brookings projects also consciously promote interaction between experts in the public and private sectors with formal conferences and informal roundtable discussions.

Its (1980) annual report states:

Brookings is financed largely by endowment and by the support of philanthropic foundations, corporations, and private individuals. Its funds are devoted to carrying out its own research and educational activities; under the terms of its charter it may not make studies for private clients. Upon request it undertakes some unclassified government contract studies, reserving the right to publish its findings.

Over the years the component proportions of its funding have changed, and in 1980 its board of trustees abolished a ceiling that had limited government contract work to a fixed percent of its income. Government work provided 20 percent of its $9.4 million budget in 1980, whereas foundation support—once as much as 47 percent—was 27 percent for that year.

Research activities today are carried out through three programs:

Economic Studies, Governmental Studies, and Foreign Policy Studies. A significant feature of the Economic Studies program since 1970 is the annual *Setting National Priorities*, a collection of essays that analyze and explain the country's policy options and spending priorities as presented in the current federal budget. Another well-respected publication that has appeared since 1970 is the *Brookings Papers on Economic Activity*, a twice-yearly journal dealing with contemporary American economic performance. The Economic Studies program also promotes analysis of productivity, growth, and inflation by several scholars and former government officials and gives special attention to federal programs and the alternative ways to achieve their results privately.

The Governmental Studies program has recently sponsored research on such topics as Washington's press corps, the role of Congress in contemporary politics, bureaucratic behavior, federal programs to aid the family, immigration policies, and the politics of deregulation in the airline, trucking, and telecommunications industries. Most of the governmental studies take advantage of Brookings's location in Washington, D.C. They are usually empirical and deal with actual problems of governance rather than the more abstract notions of political theory that many university scholars pursue. Also, research activities concentrate more on public than private institutions, an emphasis that is expected to shift in the future.

Foreign Policy Studies have focused consistently on national security problems and the political implications of international economic activity. Understandably, study of the Soviet Union—recently its diplomatic style and leadership, for example—has continued to be important. Works on nuclear nonproliferation, nuclear strategy, and U.S. military personnel policies are other current study topics. But, increasingly, energy issues and international economics have gained in importance.

Besides these three research programs, Brookings offers a variety of special study forums on critical policy issues for federal, business, and labor executives; seminars for state legislatures; and conferences for foreign delegations. Three issues now dominate the advanced study programs for professional and academic participants: business-government relations; public institutions and economic change; and the role of the United States in international economic and political orders.

The institution has a full-time staff of about 230 persons at its Washington, D.C., office, including some 35 senior fellows, 15 research associates, and 20 research assistants. Conference organizers, editors, computer specialists, administrators, librarians, secretaries, and service workers comprise the rest of the full-time employees. Another two dozen visiting scholars and government experts conduct research at Brookings while maintaining professional affiliations elsewhere.

Publications, a Brookings mainstay, undergo rigorous critical scrutiny—normally by three anonymous outside critics and several staff members—

before they appear, and they are noted for their high quality. In a typical year the institution publishes fifteen to twenty new books, two issues of *Brookings Papers*, four technical reprints, ten general reprints, four bulletins on current activities, and twenty-five reprintings of backlist titles. Foreign publishers produce about ten translation editions each year.

The institution hired its first fund raiser in 1978, to compensate for stock market declines in its endowment portfolio and the shrinkage of foundation funding. Through new revenue and expanded government contract work, the income has continued to grow—from about $7 million in 1975 to $10 million in 1982—although adjusted for inflation the level of expenditures actually dropped in those years. Although its near neighbor and aggressive younger rival, the American Enterprise Institute for Public Policy Research,* has exceeded Brookings's operating budget, it is still Brookings that sets the standard for Washington think tanks. Indeed, other younger operations publicly pride themselves as being "a conservative Brookings," or "a radical Brookings," according to their policy persuasions. The Brookings model has also attracted imitators abroad, with less ambitious results.

It is difficult to gauge Brookings's influence on public policy, but several studies of the past decade have had a visible effect: for example, a thirteen-volume series on economic regulation laid the technical foundation for the current movement toward deregulation; early editions of *Setting National Priorities* proposed improvements in the congressional budget process, several of which were adopted in the Congressional Budget Act of 1974; and the report of a Brookings study group was the point of departure for President Carter's peace initiatives with Egypt and Israel.

Since the Brookings Institution does not take public policy positions itself, a history of the place is actually a history of its distinguished associates. Similarly, accounts of the institution are most often concerned with the people it attracts and the work they do rather than with the organization as a whole.

For further information, see Charles B. Saunders, Jr., *The Brookings Institution: A Fifty Year History* (1966). A chapter about Brookings appears in Leonard and Mark Silk *The American Establishment* (1980). Several accounts about the institution have appeared in the following periodicals: "Inside Brookings," *RF Illustrated* (September, 1977); "The 'Shadow Cabinets'—Changing Themselves as They Try to Change Policy," *National Journal* (February 25, 1978); and "Brookings, Flattered by Rivals," *Economist* (March 3, 1979).

WILLIAM J. LANOUETTE

BUREAU OF MUNICIPAL RESEARCH. See Institute of Public Administration.

C

CARNEGIE ENDOWMENT FOR INTERNATIONAL PEACE. The Carnegie Endowment for International Peace was established in 1910 by Andrew Carnegie with an endowment of ten million dollars in 5 percent first mortgage bonds of the U.S. Steel Corporation. In his letter of December 14, 1910, to the trustees whom he had selected to administer this foundation, Carnegie had written that the revenue from this gift "is to be administered by you to hasten the abolition of international war, the foulest blot upon our civilization." So optimistic was Carnegie that the enlightened leadership of his self-appointed trustees, backed by his millions, could achieve world peace that he provided when

war is discarded as disgraceful to civilized men, the Trustees will please then consider what is the next most degrading remaining evil or evils whose banishment . . . would most advance the progress, elevation and happiness of man, and so on from century to century without end, my Trustees of each age shall determine how they can best aid man in his upward march to higher and higher stages of development unceasingly.

The creation of the Carnegie Endowment marked the successful conclusion of a long campaign by several American peace leaders, including Edwin Mead, Hamilton Holt, Edwin Ginn, and Nicholas Murray Butler, to persuade Carnegie to give monetary substance to his frequent pacifistic pronouncements. The men to whom Carnegie turned to direct his peace foundation, most notably Elihu Root, Joseph Choate, and Butler, were not the "radical opponents of war" that would satisfy such activists as Benjamin Trueblood, Oswald Garrison Villard, and such young Turks of the peace movement as Norman Angell. From its inception, the endowment was to be dominated by the conservative philosophy of Root and Butler, who saw the attainment of world peace "not by great demonstration but by that quiet resistless influence," as Root so aptly expressed his aspirations for the foundation he was to head. Butler even wanted to drop the word *peace* from the name of the endowment, calling it instead, the Carnegie International Institute, for he envisioned an organization that would stress the education of the public through lectureships, scholarly treatises, and the international exchange of academicians and international lawyers. Although Carnegie insisted that his name for his endowment stand as he proposed it, Root's and Butler's underlying philosophy was to prevail.

At the first meeting of the trustees, the objectives of the endowment were declared to be the promotion of a thorough and scientific investigation and study of the causes of war; assistance in the development of international law; the diffusion of information to educate public opinion; the cultivation of friendly feelings between the inhabitants of different countries; and the promotion of a general acceptance of peaceable methods in the settlement of international disputes. To achieve these genteel goals of persuasion through education, the work of the endowment was compartmentalized into three major divisions: the Division of Intercourse and Education, headed by Butler with the largest share of the annual income from the endowment; the Division of International Law, directed by James Brown Scott; and the Division of Economics and History, directed by John Bates Clark.

With former Secretary of State Root as its first president, it was to be expected that the endowment would cooperate closely with the State Department and eventually allow the latter to lead it during the years 1914 to 1917 from first espousing neutrality to later giving active support to American participation in World War I. Immediately after the entry of the United States into the war in April, 1917, the Carnegie Endowment offered the services of its Division of International Law to the government, an offer which was gratefully accepted by Secretary of State Robert Lansing. At the conclusion of the war, the secretary of the endowment, James Brown Scott, who also headed the Division of International Law, and four of his staff members accompanied President Wilson and the American delegation to the Versailles Peace Conference as advisors in negotiating a peace treaty. The endowment also made effective use of its funds in helping to restore some of the cultural centers of France and Belgium damaged in a war that the endowment's "quiet influence" had been powerless to prevent.

In 1925, Elihu Root retired from the presidency of the endowment and was succeeded by his heir apparent of long standing, Nicholas Murray Butler. In 1929-1930, the Carnegie Endowment became incorporated under the laws of the State of New York, but its new corporate status and its new president brought no essential change in either the philosophy, organization, or activities of the endowment from that which Root had established. In 1923, the endowment had been largely instrumental in the founding of the Academy of International Law at the Hague, and in many respects the endowment's most impressive contribution to the concept of world order continued throughout the Butler years to be in the field of international law. Under the able editorship of James T. Shotwell, who became director of the

Division of Economics and History in 1924, the endowment embarked upon its most ambitious single publishing venture, a 154-volume study of the *Economic and Social History of the World War.*

To commemorate its thirtieth anniversary of operations, the endowment issued a "Summary of Organization and Work" in 1941. This report could point with pride to the work of each of its three divisions over the past three decades, to the one million copies of its various publications that it had distributed gratis to libraries around the world, to the 1,219 international clubs it had sponsored in high schools and colleges from China to Newfoundland, to its Visiting Carnegie Professorships, to its European centers in Paris and Geneva, to the international law journals it helped support, and the many other peace societies to which it made monetary contributions up until the mid-1930s. But the date of publication for this summary of accomplishments, 1941, was a tragically ironic reminder of how far distant still was that day when the trustees could heed Carnegie's second request after "war is discarded . . . please consider what is the next most degrading remaining evil."

In 1945, the coincidence of the ending of World War II and the resignation of Butler after twenty years of service as president at last enabled the trustees to make major revisions in both the organization and direction of the endowment. A new office, that of chairman of the board, was created in 1946, with John Foster Dulles as the first occupant. A new president for the endowment, Alger Hiss, the first to be given a salary, was chosen the following year. Hiss's tenure proved to be brief. In 1949, he resigned the presidency because of the charges of espionage that had been brought against him by a former Communist, Whittaker Chambers. During his two years in office, however, Hiss was able to effect major changes in the endowment. The old three-divisional structure was abandoned. Much of interest and concern of the organization was now directed toward the United Nations and its various international agencies as representing the best hope of realizing the goal of the endowment's founder for the abolition of international war. Perhaps symbolic of the change from its former attachment to the State Department to its new allegiance to a supernational organization, the endowment began to make plans to shift its center of operations from its old headquarters at 700 Jackson Place, N.W., in Washington, D.C., to a new Carnegie International Center, which was to be located on the United Nations Plaza in New York City. During his tenure as president, which exceeded in length even that of Butler's, Joseph E. Johnson, from 1950 until his resignation in 1971, developed new programs of research studies and conferences in the designated areas of diplomacy, international law, the changing role of military force, international organization and the advancement of international relations research. Although maintaining its European center in Geneva, the endowment increasingly in the decades of the 1950s and 1960s turned its attention away from the old power centers of Europe to the new developing nations of Asia, Africa, and the Middle East. It promoted the improvement of international law training by supporting the Hague Academy External Program for developing countries and by the publication in 1968 of *A Manual of Public International Law*. Through its programs in diplomacy the endowment also provided special training in international affairs to the foreign service officers of those nations which had recently achieved independence.

In 1971, Thomas L. Hughes succeeded Johnson in the presidency, and under Hughes's leadership the endowment became even more flexible in organization and program development in order to cope with the problems of understanding an ever more unstable and volatile world. Under his and Chairman of the Board John W. Douglas's leadership, the rigidity that had resulted from having only a few specified areas of program development was dissolved. Increasingly, the endowment turned its attention to specific issues as they arose on the various continents of the planet. It ended tenure for its professional staff and inaugurated a new practice of term appointments, bringing in professional experts to work on one- or two-year projects. It developed such new techniques as the Face-to-Face program, which involved direct communication between government officials and private citizens, and Project Dialogue, a series of conferences between students and the general public organized by the Student Committee on International Affairs. In 1972, the endowment began to provide financial support for *Foreign Policy* magazine and six years later became the magazine's sole owner and publisher. Increasing budgetary pressures on its fixed endowment forced the Carnegie Endowment in the late 1970s to close its European center in Geneva. It also sold its headquarters building at the United Nations Plaza in New York and moved into new quarters at 30 Rockefeller Plaza. At the same time, however, it reestablished an office in Washington, D.C., at Du Pont Circle.

Hughes best summarized the role of the endowment as developed by his predecessors when he wrote:

Comparatively speaking, we have been the archetypal symbol over sixty years of the value-free approach to international peace. With minor lapses here and there, we have chosen to identify ourselves with symbolically dispassionate institutional-instrumental programs like international law, international organization, training diplomats and examining "the changing role of force." [Carnegie Endowment *Report* (1974)]

Neither Root nor Butler could quarrel with that historical summary of the Carnegie Endowment for International Peace.

For further information, see Burton J. Hendrick, *The Benefactions of Andrew Carnegie* (1935); *Carnegie Endowment for International Peace: Summary of Organization and Work, 1911-1941* (1941); Michael A. Lutzker, *The Formation of the Carnegie Endowment for International*

Peace (1972); and *Carnegie Foundation for International Peace in the 1970's* (1979). See also Burton J. Hendrick, *The Life of Andrew Carnegie* (1932); Joseph Frazier Wall, *Andrew Carnegie* (1970); and Carnegie Endowment for International Peace *Annual Reports* (1911 to present).

JOSEPH FRAZIER WALL

CARNEGIE INSTITUTION OF WASHINGTON. On January 4, 1902, in Washington, D.C., John Hay, Andrew D. White, John S. Billings, Charles D. Walcott, and Carroll D. Wright incorporated the Carnegie Institution, which is now known as the Carnegie Institution of Washington. Andrew Carnegie—for whom the institution is named—had retired from the steel business the year before and wanted to use his fortune, estimated at four hundred million dollars, for various philanthropic purposes. In devising the idea of the institution, Carnegie enjoyed the advice of such men as Andrew D. White, Charles D. Walcott, Daniel C. Gilman, and John S. Billings. Unfortunately, each man held a somewhat different vision of what the institution should be. In the end, Carnegie created a trust deed stating that the money provided would be used to aid basic research, discover the exceptional man, increase facilities for higher education, increase the efficiency of universities and other institutions of learning, and enable students to best use the government facilities then located in Washington D.C. To make this work possible, Carnegie provided the new institution with ten million dollars worth of U.S. Steel bonds. He asked Gilman to become its first president and appointed his other three advisors to the board of trustees. This board consisted of twenty-one men selected from around the country plus five ex officio members. The ex officio members included the president of the United States, the president of the Senate, the speaker of the House of Representatives, the secretary of the Smithsonian Institution,* and the president of the National Academy of Sciences* (NAS).

Unfortunately, the Carnegie Institution discovered two years later that it had failed to conform to the statutes of the District of Columbia when it was incorporated. To avoid further problems, it sought and was granted a charter from Congress. However, as a result, Congress forced it to drop those aspects of the original trust deed that gave the institution a quasi-governmental and educational appearance. Thus, the institution dropped the parts dealing with the ex officio membership on the board of trustees as well as the statements on increasing facilities for higher education and increasing the efficiency of universities.

The Carnegie Institution began its work by providing small grants ranging from five hundred to fifteen thousand dollars for either the support of research or for promising research candidates, just beginning their career, who could work as research assistants. In addition, the trustees appointed eighteen advisory committees to look into what could be done for the fields of anthropology, astronomy, bibliography, botany, chemistry, economics, engineering, geography, geology, history, mathematics, meteorology, paleontology, physics, physiology, psychology, and zoology.

A combination of factors, including the early resignation of Daniel C. Gilman as president, the revised charter, dissatisfaction with the grants program, the advisory committee reports, and the preference of the trustees, contributed to a shift in the institution's methods of support. Instead of only giving minor grant support, it established eleven of its own departments, laboratories, and observatories by 1913. These included the Department of Plant Biology, Mount Wilson Observatory, Department of Terrestrial Magnetism, Department of Genetics, Geophysical Laboratory, Department of Embryology, Department of Historical Research, Department of Economics and Sociology, Department of Marine Biology, Department of Meridian Astronomy, and Nutrition Laboratory. Nevertheless, a program of individual small grants continued, although in greatly diminished proportions.

To support these activities and avoid financial problems introduced through postwar inflation, the Great Depression, and other economic changes, the institution secured two more gifts from Andrew Carnegie totaling another twelve million dollars. In addition, the Carnegie Corporation of New York donated about eight million dollars between 1911 and 1943. Today, the institution maintains assets of more than eighty-five million dollars and has an operating budget of about nine million dollars.

In both World Wars, the Carnegie Institution heavily committed its staff and resources to assist the American effort. In World War I, it developed optical glass and used the glass to manufacture optical equipment needed by the military. It worked on antisubmarine devices, made navigation in fledgling aircraft safer, and helped create magnetic mine warfare. Staff members translated numerous German periodicals for the government, and others took over teaching duties at medical schools or made sanitary conditions at military camps safer.

At the start of World War II, Vannevar Bush—the president of the institution—also became the chairman of the National Defense Research Committee. Later, this committee became part of the Office of Scientific Research and Development, and Bush became the director of the office while remaining president of the institution. This office had responsibility for the entire program of civilian scientific research and development, both for weapons and for all fields of military medicine. The headquarters for the office were located in the institutions's Administration Building. Carnegie Institution departments contributed to many of the war efforts, including the development of the atomic bomb and the proximity fuze, the commercial production of penicillin, the elimination of gun erosion, the development of radar and worldwide radio transmission, the creation of devices for the blind, the design of aerial cameras, the monitoring of shock in patients, and the expansion of Western grazing lands to increase food production. In both wars, the institution paid the salaries of staff members engaged in war research and did not charge the government for overhead.

In the course of its history, the institution discontinued the minor grant program and terminated several of its large groups. Today, it operates the Geophysical Laboratory and Department of Terrestrial Magnetism in Washington, D.C.; the Department of Embryology in Baltimore, Maryland; the Mount Wilson and Las Campanas observatories in Pasadena, California, and La Serena, Chile, respectively; the Department of Plant Biology in Palo Alto, California; and a Developmental Biology Research Group in Pasadena, California. Each department supports a small permanent staff along with predoctoral, postdoctoral, and trainee students. Occasionally, departments make funds available to selected senior fellows and visiting investigators for work at the department itself.

The departments in biology have surveyed a wide range of problems. The Department of Plant Biology has studied the growth of plants in arid and tropical regions, ecology, and mechanisms of photosynthesis and plant development. The Department of Embryology led investigations into human fetal development, primate and human reproduction, regulation of cell growth, endocrinology, and the physiology of the placenta. Today, the department concentrates on membrane biogenesis, cell surface biochemistry, fertilization in lower organisms, nervous system regeneration, the development of human embryos, and gene transcription.

The departments of physical science have also held extensive interests. The Mount Wilson and Las Campanas observatories have historically studied astronomical and astrophysical phenomenon, ranging from the distance and chemical composition of the stars to the expansion of the universe. In earlier years, the Geophysical Laboratory emphasized mineralogy, volcanology, glass production, geophysics, geochemistry, and petrology. Today, many of those same studies continue with particular emphasis on high-pressure research. The Department of Terrestrial Magnetism has worked on terrestrial and solar magnetism, oceanography, atmospheric and terrestrial electricity, cosmic rays, meteorology, seismology, nuclear and atomic physics, astronomy, biophysics, astrophysics, and geochemistry. Today's efforts range from the physics and chemistry of the Earth to the evolution of galaxies, stars, and planetary systems.

While continuing to emphasize basic research, with staff scientists being kept free of teaching and administrative responsibilities, the institution has contributed significantly to a host of important discoveries and development, including special optical glasses, hybrid corn, oil and mineral prospecting, weather forecasting, large-scale production of penicillin, radar development, radio transmission, navigation, devices for monitoring human birth, earthquake prediction, atomic energy, ecology, Portland cement, animal and plant genetics, and numerous scientific instruments and devices used today around the world. It has also contributed directly and indirectly to the growth of science in South America.

Former presidents of the Carnegie Institution include Daniel C. Gilman, Robert S. Woodward, John C. Merriam, Vannevar Bush, Caryl P. Haskins, and Philip H. Abelson. Today James D. Ebert serves as its seventh president. Ebert formerly directed its Department of Embryology and then was president and director of the Marine Biological Laboratory* (MBL) at Woods Hole, Massachusetts. As president, Ebert has general charge of all matters of administration and supervision for research and other work undertaken by the institution or with its funds. His actions are subject to the control of the board of trustees and the executive committee.

William R. Hewlett is the chairman of the board of trustees, which now consists of twenty-four members. The institution's executive committee, consisting of six trustees, has general control of the administration of its affairs when the board of trustees is not in session. Carnegie Institution headquarters are located at 1530 P Street, N.W., in Washington, D.C.

For further information, see J. Harland Paul, *The Last Cruise of the Carnegie* (1932); Helen Wright, *Explorer of the Universe* (1966); Caryl P. Haskins, ed., *The Search for Understanding* (1967); Nathan Reingold, "National Science Policy in a Private Foundation: The Carnegie Institution of Washington," *The Organization of Knowledge in Modern America, 1860-1920* (1979); and Franklin H. Portugal, "The Good Ship Carnegie," *Carnegie Magazine* (1980). See also the annual *Year Book* published by the Carnegie Institution. Dr. Franklin H. Portugal has completed a full-length history of the Carnegie Institution of Washington, based primarily on extensive archives located at its Washington headquarters, which will be published shortly under the title *The Scientists*.

FRANKLIN H. PORTUGAL

CENTER FOR ADVANCED STUDY IN THE BEHAVIORAL SCIENCES. The 1949 report of the *Study for the Ford Foundation on Policy and Program* was the genesis for the Center for Advanced Study in the Behavioral Sciences. Specifically, program area five of that report called for the Ford Foundation, which had acquired several billions of dollars in assets following the death of Henry Ford, to support research and activities in the behavioral sciences "designed to increase knowledge of factors which influence or determine human conduct, and to extend such knowledge for the maximum benefit of individuals and society." In the early 1950s the foundation named a committee to implement these objectives, and it recommended the establishment of the center.

The latter was envisioned as a place, with a specially designed physical setting, where scholar-scientists could gather and work toward the goal of understanding the principles of human behavior. Thereupon, the Ford

Foundation provided an initial grant of $3.5 million and appointed the first board of directors for the center. During 1953-1954, the board developed program plans and compiled an initial list of scholars, each considered a leader in his or her discipline, who might be appointed for study under center auspices.

By September, 1954, buildings had been erected on a California hilltop overlooking Stanford University. They were designed by the distinguished San Francisco architect William Wurster. It should be noted that they have continued to serve their original purpose admirably and have been awarded many architectural prizes. The landscape architect Thomas Church designed the grounds to take full advantage of the oak-studded hilltop setting. It was there that the first group of center fellows assembled in 1954. At the same time Ralph W. Tyler was named the first director, to be succeeded in July, 1967, by O. Meredith Wilson, who was succeeded by Gardner Lindzey, the present director, in September, 1975.

Conceived initially to be operational on a five-year experimental basis, at the end of its third year the center had proved such a success that the Ford Foundation made an additional grant of five million dollars for its continuation. Subsequently, additional operating funds were obtained from other sources, which enabled the center to carry on through 1969. Following an extensive review of its activities up to that year, the Ford Foundation made a four million-dollar endowment grant to the center plus another three million dollars in further operating funds. With this endowment base, plus another of one million dollars given it later by the Andrew W. Mellon Foundation, the center has been able to attract increasing support from an ever widening group of agencies in the private and public sector.

In recent years significant grants have been made to the center by the Exxon Education Foundation, Ford Foundation, Foundations' Fund for Research in Psychiatry, Henry J. Kaiser Family Foundation, John D. and Catherine T. MacArthur Foundation, Andrew W. Mellon Foundation, National Endowment for the Humanities, National Institute of Mental Health, National Science Foundation, Alfred P. Sloan Foundation, and Spencer Foundation. The current annual operating budget of the center is about $2.5 million, with about 80 percent of this amount expended for payments and services to fellows.

The activities of the center from its origin to the present revolve around its conduct of a residential postdoctoral fellowship program for scholars and scientists. Some forty-five to fifty fellows per year have been selected with a wide range of disciplinary backgrounds, from home and abroad, and with ages ranging from twenty-six to eighty. In the past few years increased diversification has been achieved through the inclusion of more minority scholars, more women, and representatives of a broader spectrum of institutions.

The selection of fellows for any one year at the center begins with a careful look at the scholarly achievements or promise of several hundred men and women; it ends with a group of forty-five to fifty scholars, each of whom is part of the environment in which the others will study. Therefore, one consideration in assembling a cohort of fellows is the likelihood of their creating and reinforcing the intellectual environment for each other. Each year a few people are invited whose own specialities lie in physical science or in literature, music, or art, because their interests offer promise for stimulating the other scholars with whom they will interact. Most fellows, however, are drawn from the fields of anthropology, biology, economics, history, linguistics, political science, psychology, and sociology, complemented by representatives from education, law, medicine, philosophy, psychiatry, and statistics.

The selection process is moderately complex. Any scholar may nominate another person for consideration as a fellow, but most nominations come from well-known behavioral scientists, academic administrators, and former fellows. Periodically, requests for nominations are sent to former fellows, graduate deans of most universities, and heads of major behavioral science departments, as well as selected additional institutions. Nominees are asked if they are interested in spending a year at the center, and if they respond affirmatively they are asked to provide certain background information and a short list of professional references. The names of nominees are submitted regularly in lists by field or area to panels (rotated over time) of scholars in each field, who rate the persons on the list. The final decision with regard to eligibility is made by the board of trustees of the center, typically with heavy reliance on the panel ratings and letters of evaluation supplied by nominees' references, sometimes supplemented by additional letters solicited by the center. In the case of certain less visible scholars, such as the very young, panel ratings may be dispensed with and the decision based upon recommendations, publications, and the candidate's educational and professional record.

Nominees approved by the board are notified of their eligibility and asked their preferences concerning the timing of their fellowship. In most cases the interval between nomination and residence at the center is at least two years. The process of composing a group of fellows for any given year involves a set of recommendations made by the staff of the center and approved by the board of trustees. In determining the composition of the cohort, a variety of criteria are considered, including age and sex distribution and diversity in terms of institutions, disciplines, and ethnic background, as well as the special needs of any collaborative project planned for a particular year.

The fellowship award entails a period of residence in the vicinity of the center, normally beginning in September and extending from seven to twelve months. In most cases the fellow contributes to the cost of the stipend, which is based on the academic salary for the year preceding residence at the center.

Each fellow is provided with a modest study containing a desk, bookshelves, typewriter, filing cabinet, and no telephone. The absence of a telephone is an intentional protection against interruption—a relatively convenient telephone is available if needed. Most journals and a number of standard reference works are available in the library. More important, the center librarian is ready to obtain from Stanford, or elsewhere, whatever library materials are required.

The most significant aspect of the fellowships appear to be the opportunity to devote an extended period of time to intellectual development at an advanced level and stimulated by the company of other scholars from a variety of disciplines. This is accompanied by congenial surroundings for the fellow's family and almost complete scheduling freedom.

In its more than a quarter of a century of operation one of the center's major accomplishments has been facilitating the publication of more than eight hundred books, together with thousands of scholarly articles, stemming directly from the fellows' stay at the center. Although more difficult to document, the scholarly-scientific trends and intellectual developments that have originated or evolved out of center activities are also noteworthy. The increased sophistication in mathematical methods on the part of behavioral scientists, the new specialty of behavior genetics, and the interrelationship of law and the behavioral and social sciences, are a few examples of this process. In this connection the center is placing some emphasis upon similar topics of high scientific and social priority for exploration by center fellows. An Advisory Committee on Special Projects assists in their formation and evaluation. In assessing its relative success, however, center officials overwhelmingly cite the quality and accomplishments of the some thirteen hundred scholar-scientists it has attracted as fellows. Also, they point to the center replication by other organizations, such as the National Humanities Center at the Research Triangle in North Carolina.

The center is governed by a board of trustees, which appoints the customary officers and staff. The program, administered by a director, is conducted from offices of the center located in Stanford, California.

For further information, see the *Annual Reports* of the center together with an information brochure published in 1977. See also for a listing of books conceived, initiated, or completed by fellows while at the center, *The Ralph W. Tyler Collection, 1954-1979* (1979).

CENTER FOR APPLIED LINGUISTICS (CAL). The catalytic agent in the founding of the Center for Applied Linguistics was the Modern Language Association of America* (MLA). In 1957, in assaying projected needs for modern foreign-language research and training in the United States and abroad, the MLA called for the establishment of an organization such as the CAL. By 1959 the MLA had enlisted the support of the Ford Foundation and in its annual report for that year the foundation announced a two hundred thousand-dollar grant to the MLA for the establishment of "a Center for Applied Linguistics to disseminate research findings and information on training methods concerning English as a second language."

The center began operations on February 16, 1959, in leased quarters in the old American Council on Education* (ACE) building at 1785 Massachusetts Avenue in Washington, D.C., with Charles A. Ferguson as its first director. Since then CAL has had two full-term directors (John Lotz and Rudolph Troike) and two interim directors (Martin Joos and Albert Marckwardt). The present director is G. Richard Tucker.

In 1960 the MLA received a five-year grant from the Ford Foundation for the support of the center. In 1964 the center became a separately incorporated nonprofit organization, and from that period down to 1982 the Ford Foundation continued to supply it with additional operating funds, which by then totaled about eight million dollars. Another major source of funding for CAL operations during its first two decades of existence was the U.S. Office of Education, which awarded it some thirty-five contracts during that period.

Since its founding the center has sought to expand understanding of the role of language in education and society. It has functioned in an advisory capacity to a host of government agencies on such problems as the teaching of English as a second language. For example, it trained or assisted in the training of American Peace Corps Volunteers in foreign languages. It has assisted in the preparation and distribution of linguistic teaching aids for a wide range of foreign languages. The creation and refinement of the TOEFL test, widely used as a proficiency test for foreign students who want to study in the United States, was greatly facilitated by the initial and continuing efforts of the center. In accomplishing the coordinating and clearinghouse function for linguistics, the center in 1966 established an Educational Research Information Center (ERIC), which has since cooperated in a national network of information analysis centers. From its very first year of operation, the CAL has reported these and a myriad of other activities and developments of interest to the linguistic community in its newsletter, the *Linguistic Reporter*, published nine times a year.

The center is governed by a board of trustees, which appoints the customary officers and staff. The program, administered by a director, is conducted from offices of the center located in Washington, D.C.

For further information, see the *Linguistic Reporter* mentioned above, particularly the April, 1979, issue. There is no history of the Center for Applied Linguistics.

CENTER FOR THE STUDY OF DEMOCRATIC INSTITUTIONS. See Robert Maynard Hutchins Center for the Study of Democratic Institutions.

CHARLES F. KETTERING FOUNDATION. The Charles F. Kettering Foundation of Dayton, Ohio, is a nonprofit, research-oriented private foundation established June 24, 1927, by the inventor-industrialist, Charles F. Kettering.

Born on a farm in Loudonville, Ohio, in 1876, Kettering graduated from the Ohio State University with a degree in engineering in 1904, and immediately joined the inventions staff of the National Cash Register Company (NCR) of Dayton, Ohio, where he led the research team that developed the first successful electrically powered cash register.

In 1911, Kettering and a group of friends calling themselves the Dayton Engineering Laboratories Company (Delco) developed an electric self-starter for automobiles and sold it to the Cadillac Motor Company, which first marketed it on the 1912 Cadillac. General Motors hired Kettering to direct the General Motors Research Laboratories in 1919, and in 1920 he was named vice-president for research. Many of his best-known inventions or developments—among them the refrigerant freon, ethyl gasoline, and fast-drying automobile lacquers—grew out of his work at General Motors, where he served until his retirement in 1947.

Throughout his life, however, Kettering pursued a variety of interests in addition to industrial research. He was convinced of the value of cooperative education, or work study programs, and contributed substantially to such efforts at numerous colleges and universities in Ohio and the Midwest. From his early years he had believed that the secret of unlimited energy resources could be revealed by studying the process of photosynthesis, for which he established several laboratories, including one on the campus of Antioch College in Yellow Springs, Ohio.

In his later years, Kettering became interested in medical research, receiving the Legion of Honor Award in 1937 for his work in fever therapy, an early cure for venereal disease. For many years the Kettering Foundation made large grants to cancer research, including several to the Sloan-Kettering Institute for Cancer Research of New York. Now a part of Memorial Sloan-Kettering Cancer Center,* the institute was founded in 1945 by Alfred P. Sloan, first president of General Motors, and Charles Kettering. The early history of the foundation reflects very clearly his support for all of the above interests, as well as others.

During the 1960s and 1970s, the Kettering Foundation underwent a number of significant changes. Late in 1963 the board of trustees began to discuss the desirability of finding more significant ways of directing its spending for education. Rather than giving many grants for a variety of projects that were largely unrelated, they decided, the foundation should direct its resources toward specific long-term educational goals. As a result, the Institute for Development of Educational Activities (/I/D/E/A/), was incorporated in 1966. This affiliate became the "operating" arm of the foundation; that is /I/D/E/A/ initiated its own educational projects, which were then carried out by its staff in cooperation with public and private school administrators and teachers. Although the Kettering Foundation as a whole had always had some aspects of an "operating foundation," it was not officially designated as such until September 1 of 1979, at which time /I/D/E/A/ dropped its separate incorporation and became the educational division of the foundation. (The Charles F. Kettering Research Laboratory in Yellow Springs, Ohio, which was also incorporated separately for a time, is presently the Science and Technology division of the foundation.)

In 1971, Robert G. Chollar left a position as vice president and group executive at NCR Corporation in Dayton to become president and chairman of the board of the Kettering Foundation. A Kettering board member since 1956 and friend of the late Charles Kettering, Chollar, who had begun his career as a research chemist, resolved to apply some of the techniques of industrial research to the pursuit of social objectives. Under his guidance the institution intensified its "mission" orientation, establishing long-term goals for each of its programs and supporting research and outside collaboration designed to aid their realization. Chollar encouraged the formation of interdisciplinary teams and interprogram cooperation and provisions for frequent monitoring and reassessment of progress. The international affairs and urban affairs programs initiated during his tenure were united with education in 1979, under the administrative umbrella of social sciences, and there is a high degree of crossover among activities in all the foundation's programs, including those of the Kettering Laboratory.

The Charles F. Kettering Research Laboratory in Yellow Springs, Ohio, is one of the best known of its kind in the world. Although it continues the studies in photosynthesis started by Charles Kettering, the laboratory has become better known in recent years for its work in nitrogen fixation, the process whereby nitrogen is converted into a form that plants can use as fertilizer. Scientists and researchers from countries around the globe are devoting themselves to studies of both chemical and biological nitrogen fixation at the Kettering Laboratory.

On the biological side, Kettering researchers have made considerable progress in understanding and elucidating various stages of the nitrogen-fixation process within individual plant cells; for example, in cooperation with scientists at Stanford University they are using the Stanford Linear Accelerator to gain insight into enzymatic nitrogen fixation.

The laboratory's work with plants that live in symbiotic association with nitrogen-fixing bacteria offers considerable promise for increasing world food supplies. Kettering researchers have begun to learn how to speed up the infection of soybean roots by *Rhizobium* bacteria, and they are now able to inoculate alder seedlings with nitrogen-fixing organisms, thereby producing healthy, rapidly growing plants without the aid of applied fertilizers.

Approaching nitrogen fixation from another standpoint, the laboratory has developed a relatively small unit, about the size of a normal desk, that can extract nitrogen from the air and convert it to a form usable for fertilizer, reviving an old technique known as the electric-arc process. At present the scientists and technologists are working to upgrade the efficiency and lower the cost of the machine, testing it at sites where the climate is comparable to that of countries in need of such technology.

One of the outstanding contributions of the Education Program is the /I/D/E/A/ Change Program for Individually Guided Education (IGE). This program, which grew out of the special interests of /I/D/E/A/ staff (working with educators in several other institutions) is a plan by which elementary and secondary schools can tailor an individual plan of study for each student. Heavy emphasis is placed on participation by students and parents, as well as teachers and administrators, in formulating, carrying out, and monitoring each student's program of study. The IGE plan is currently in use by over two thousand public and parochial schools in the United States and several dozen schools for American dependents abroad. In keeping with the Kettering Foundation philosophy, much of the administration of IGE was given over in 1979 to a separate, independent organization called the Association for Individually Guided Education (AIGE), although the foundation continued to provide support for IGE in the form of newsletters and other publications.

Several other education projects of the foundation have proven outstanding over the years, among them the /I/D/E/A/ Fellows Program, a weeklong seminar for educational administrators that takes place each summer in four widely scattered U.S. locations, and the Annual Gallup Poll of Public Attitudes Toward the Public Schools, which has given rise in the past two years to a separate Kettering-sponsored Gallup Youth Poll on Attitudes Toward Schools.

In the spring of 1979, the twelfth annual Dartmouth Conference was convened at Williamsburg, Virginia. The 1979 conference was cosponsored by the Rockefeller Foundation, with partial financial assistance from the U.S. International Communication Agency. So named because the first meeting took place on the campus of Dartmouth University, this conference was designed to bring together influential citizens from the United States and the Soviet Union to discuss problems of mutual concern. Because the meetings are private and unofficial, they provide an excellent forum in which representatives from both countries can offer opposing perspectives, air grievances, and arrive at some point of agreement on possible solutions.

Topics of discussion over the years have included Soviet and American influences in Africa, Asia, and the Middle East, SALT I and SALT II, and scientific cooperation to eliminate world hunger. A spinoff of the Dartmouth Conference is the Soviet-American Writers' Conference, convened in 1977, 1978, and 1979, to bring together writers of note from both countries to discuss the role of the artist in society, differing attitudes toward censorship, and other related issues.

The International Affairs Program has also sponsored numerous projects designed to raise global awareness in U.S. schools and communities. For example, in cooperation with the Education Program of the Kettering Foundation and the North Central Association of Schools, it has developed materials for helping elementary and secondary school teachers from educational units on global interdependency.

Helping to restore and revitalize America's urban centers is the underlying goal of all activities in the foundation's Urban Affairs Program. These activities range from highly individualized studies about how to create and support more neighborhood industries in specific neighborhoods, to training programs designed to help city council members in any city improve their decision-making processes, to suggestions for a national urban policy.

The Negotiated Investment Strategy (NIS), a plan by which federal, state, local, and private interests can negotiate priorities and coordinate allocations for a given urban area, was developed by the Urban Affairs Program in cooperation with a number of individuals and institutions, including SRI International,* the National League of Cities, the U.S. Conference of Mayors, the Academy for Contemporary Problems, the Miami Valley Regional Planning Commission, and the Federal Regional Councils. Currently, the Federal Regional Council of the Midwest region, assisted by a grant from the Department of Housing and Urban Development, is supervising tests of the NIS in three cities: Saint Paul, Minnesota; Columbus, Ohio; and Gary, Indiana.

Over the last five years, the Urban Affairs Program has sponsored several National Urban Policy Roundtables, in cooperation with the Academy for Contemporary Problems, Columbus, Ohio, exploratory forums which bring together individuals from industry, government, and academia to discuss possible approaches to urban problems. The importance of encouraging communication among these three segments of society is axiomatic to most of the foundation's urban activities.

The bulk of the foundation's operating capital is income from stocks, bonds, and securities acquired as the result of its original endowment from Charles F. Kettering. The value of these assets fluctuates with the market, but current assets are approximately seventy million dollars. For several years, however, the foundation has pursued a vigorous program of collaboration with other institutions and agencies, receiving considerable financial support for specific activities as a result of grants and contracts with its collaborators. The foundation's annual report clearly indicates the amount of such outside support.

The foundation employs approximately 150 professional and clerical staff members at four locations: the headquarters at 5335 Far Hills Avenue in Dayton, Ohio; the Charles F. Kettering Research Laboratory in Yellow Springs, Ohio; and two small offices of the Education Division in Melbourne, Florida, and Los Angeles, California. Its activities are directed by a committee made up of the senior executive staff and chaired by the chief executive officer. (From January, 1971, until February 1, 1981, Robert G. Chollar, a former research director and vice president of NCR corporation served as both president and chairman of the board. In preparation for Mr. Chollar's retirement in June, the position of president was assumed by David Mathews, former president of the University of Alabama and secretary of the U.S. Department of Health, Education and Welfare under President Ford.) The foundation's activities are also reviewed by a board of trustees, which meets formally twice a year and in various subcommittees throughout the year.

For further information, see Charles F. Kettering Foundation, *Review for Years 1927-1960* (1960); *A Fiftieth Anniversary Prospectus, Statement of Collaboration* (1970); *New Ways* (1971 to present); and *Annual Reports* (1961 to present). See also Marcus Franda, "Kettering's Nitrogen Fixers. Parts I, II, and III," *University Field Staff Reports* (1980); and /I/D/E/A *Annual Reports* (1968-70).

The following biographies of Charles F. Kettering provide information about him and his life and the founding and early history of the Kettering Foundation. Thomas Alvin Boyd, *Professional Amateur: The Biography of Charles F. Kettering* (1957); Sigmund Lavine, *Kettering: Master Inventor* (1960); Rosamond McPherson Young, *Boss Ket, a Life of Charles F. Kettering* (1961); and Gladys Zehnpfenning, *Charles F Kettering; Inventor and Idealist; a Biographical Sketch of a Man Who Refused to Recognize the Impossible* (1962).

PATRICIA PIETY

COLLEGE ART ASSOCIATION OF AMERICA (CAA). The founding of the College Art Association of America grew out of various meetings in the early 1900s of the Western Drawing and Manual Training Association, the Eastern Art Teachers' Association, and the Eastern Manual Training Association. College art instructors who were members of these associations formed a committee which, in 1910, reported that their subject was still in an experimental stage at the college and university level and recommended "the formation of a permanent organization of college art-workers."

In May of 1912, the Western Association held its annual meeting in Cincinnati, and it was there that the CAA was organized. Its first annual meeting was held in Pittsburgh during the Christmas holidays that same year. The stated purpose of the new organization was "the furtherance and promotion of the study and appreciation of art," including all media, periods, and cultures. It has held annual meetings, in January or early February, in all parts of the United States, at which papers are read and discussed, information exchanged, and business conducted. In recent years, these meetings have also become the focal point of the academic placement service organized by the CAA for its members. Although membership is open to anyone interested in its objectives, the CAA consists predominantly of teachers of the history of art, artist-teachers, and art museum professionals.

Since 1917, the CAA has published the quarterly *Art Bulletin*, which contains authoritative articles and reviews on the history of art. From 1929 until 1941, it also published the monthly *Parnassus*, which in 1942 was succeeded by the *College Art Journal*, designed specifically for the collegiate art world (as of January, 1961, the name was changed to the *Art Journal*.) In addition, the CAA publishes the *CAA Newsletter* (since 1976). In cooperation with the Archaeological Institute of America* (AIA), the CAA has published a series of scholarly monographs in book form. Its most recent publishing venture has been the sponsorship of RILA *(Répertoire international de la littérature de l'art)*, an international English-language abstracting service of current scholarly writings in postclassical European and postconquest American art, the first issue of which appeared in July, 1976.

An early CAA activity was its cooperation with the study conducted by Priscilla Hiss and Roberta Fansler to determine the status of education in the fine arts in American colleges and universities. More recently, a subsequent study of similar scope, sponsored by the Ford Foundation, was conducted by Andrew C. Ritchie. The CAA has established a number of awards for excellence in art historical scholarship, art criticism, and teaching. It also has endeavored to formulate standards of professional practice and conduct for both art historians and studio teachers. Through its Millard Meiss Publication Fund, the CAA subsidizes the publication of scholarly books in the history of art. Membership, including institutional, presently totals about eighty-five hundred.

The CAA elects the customary institutional officers; it conducts its business from an office, headed by an executive secretary, located in New York, New York.

For further information, see the publications of the CAA discussed above, particularly Holmes Smith, "Problems of the College Art Association," *Bulletin, College Art Association of America*, no. 1 (1913); and W.

L. M. Burke, "Early Years of the College Art Association," *College Art Journal* (May, 1942). See also Priscilla Hiss and Roberta Fansler, *Research in Fine Arts in the Colleges and Universities of the United States* (1934); Joseph C. Sloane, "The College Art Association of America," *World of the Mind* (1958); and Andrew C. Ritchie *The Visual Arts in Higher Education* (1966).

COLUMBIAN MUSEUM OF CHICAGO. See Field Museum of Natural History.

COUNCIL ON FOREIGN RELATIONS, INC. The council was started by a group of Americans at the Versailles Peace Conference who felt that the U.S. delegation had not been as well prepared for some of the problems that came up as it ought to have been and that in the years to come there would be a growing need for Americans to understand international issues. In May and June, 1919, they met with a group of British colleagues and agreed to form a binational Institute of International Affairs. This did not work out, but it did lead to the creation of two separate national bodies, the Royal Institute of International Affairs (known as Chatham House) and the Council on Foreign Relations, Inc., which was established under the laws of the State of New York in August, 1921. The American body was made up of the Paris group, somewhat enlarged, and an informal organization that had met in New York since late 1918 to discuss international events. The purpose of the organization was and is to improve the understanding of international issues and thereby to contribute to the shaping of enlightened American policy.

The group that met in Paris included leading academic experts who had been attached to the "Inquiry," the expert staff organized by Colonel House to advise President Wilson at the peace conference (such as George Louis Beer, Archibald C. Coolidge, Clive Day, Charles Haskins, Manley Hudson, Charles Seymour, and James T. Shotwell), and also people of business and political background who had been working on the Commission to Negotiate Peace, such as General Tasker H. Bliss, Herbert Hoover, Thomas W. Lamont, Christian A. Herter, Whitney H. Shepardson, and Colonel House himself. The group in New York with which they merged had a strong business orientation. This mixture of people of differing backgrounds and activities has continued to characterize both the membership of the council and the makeup of its study or discussion groups. In its publications, as well, the council seeks to combine high scholarly standards with the additional dimension of understanding that comes from firsthand experience. With rare exceptions, council publications are the work of individual authors. The council itself does not take positions on public issues. It is strictly nonpartisan and has in its membership leading people from both major parties in the United States.

From the beginning, the council planned to publish a journal. Volume 1, number 1 of *Foreign Affairs* appeared on September 15, 1922, with Archibald Cary Coolidge, professor of history at Harvard, as editor and Hamilton Fish Armstrong as managing editor. The latter was a young journalist nominated by Edwin F. Gay, an economic historian then editing the New York *Evening Post*, who continued to play an important part in shaping council work until the 1940s. When Coolidge died in 1928, Armstrong succeeded him as editor and remained in the post until 1972, just a few months before his death. He was succeeded by William P. Bundy. *Foreign Affairs* has from the first been conducted as an independent journal whose editors have complete freedom of action. They have published the works of famous authors and unknowns, who sometimes became famous, articles reflecting official positions of governments and opposing them. A substantial bibliographical section has been an important feature of the journal, combining brief book reviews by members of the council staff and outside experts with a listing of "source material" compiled by the council's librarian, including government reports, pamphlet literature, and other fugitive material. Five bibliographies have been published covering a decade each; the *Foreign Affairs 50-Year Bibliography* published in 1972 contained a reassessment of major works by experts in many fields. A fifty-year index to *Foreign Affairs* was published in 1973.

A second major activity of the council has been the organization of meetings primarily for the benefit of its members. These range from large gatherings to hear prominent American or foreign speakers to specialized discussions among ten or a dozen people. There are occasional conferences of a day or longer. The council sponsors two sets of lectures, which are sometimes published: those named after Elihu Root are given by Americans, whereas the Russell C. Leffingwell Lectures are given by eminent foreigners. With a few exceptions, council meetings have always been private and conducted under a rule of nonattribution to encourage free and frank discussion.

The third major activity of the council is its studies program, research and publication in a variety of forms. Between 1928 and 1931 four volumes surveying *American Foreign Relations* appeared under the editorship of Charles P. Howland of Yale with contributions by members of the council staff and outside experts. This led to the inauguration of the *United States in World Affairs*, an annual survey of U.S. foreign policy, which began in 1931 under the editorship of Walter Lippman, who was succeeded by Whitney H. Shepardson and William O. Scroggs. The series was suspended between 1940 and 1945, and the gap partially filled by two later volumes by William L. Langer and S. Everett Gleason, *The Challenge to Isolation* (1952) and *The Undeclared War* (1953). The series was resumed with volumes covering the years 1945 to 1949 written and edited by John C. Campbell, who was succeeded by Richard P. Stebbins who wrote all but a few of the volumes until the series ended in 1970. From 1952 on the council also published a volume of documents, which in 1971 was merged with the annual survey. The last of these volumes covered 1978. Since that year *Foreign Affairs* has published a special annual issue which to a degree substitutes for the original survey.

Starting in 1927, Walter H. Mallory, then the executive director of the council, edited an annual *Political Handbook of the World* containing basic data on the government and press of most countries. He was succeeded by Richard P. Stebbins, who considerably expanded the issue for 1970, which was followed by several supplements. Since then the volume has been sponsored by the council and the State University of New York, Binghamton, where annual revisions are made. *American Agencies Concerned with International Affairs*, edited by Ruth Savord, the council's librarian, was published in 1931; four revised editions followed, the last, by Donald Wasson, her successor, in 1964.

In addition to these serials the council has been responsible for the appearance of a large number of individual studies of U.S. foreign policy and international developments. These were sometimes written by members of the council staff but more often by visitors who spent a year or more at the council and occasionally by others. Usually these authors worked with a study group made up of council members and others who discussed issues put to them by the author who was, however, completely free to form his own conclusions. The council's responsibility for the publication of these books has been limited to the judgment of their quality, a decision made by the Committee on Studies.

Although individual authors not on the council staff contributed some of the volumes during the 1920s and early 1930s, the practice of bringing visiting fellows to the council began in 1938 under a grant from the Rockefeller Foundation. It was part of an expansion of the studies program under the council's first director of studies, Percy W. Bidwell, an economist with academic and governmental experience. Other types of fellowships followed after the war with grants from the Carnegie Corporation of New York and Ford Foundation. There was also some expansion of the council's regular studies staff, especially during the period that Philip E. Mosely was director of studies, 1955-1963.

A major element in the council's work has been a series of special projects, each separately financed by foundation grants. In the 1950s these included studies of U.S. relations with the United Kingdom, India, and the Soviet Union. In the 1960s, there were two major projects concerning Atlantic relations and China. In the 1970s the primary example of this kind of activity was the 1980s Project, in which an effort was made to look ahead for ten or fifteen years at the kinds of issues that would be of particular concern to the United States and the world at large. Africa and U.S.-Soviet relations have been the focus of projects begun in 1977-1978. In 1980 and 1981 the council sponsored statements on American policy toward China, the Soviet Union, and Western Europe made on the responsibility of groups of individuals.

The council's War and Peace Studies (1939-45) was unique in a number of ways. Immediately after the Nazi invasion of Poland, some leading members of the council began looking for ways in which it could contribute to a better postwar settlement than the one that gave birth to the council. With support from the Rockefeller Foundation, five groups of experts were set up to identify economic, political, and security issues that would arise, suggest solutions to them, and call attention to immediate measures that should be taken, or avoided, because of their long-run effects. The papers prepared by these groups were sent to the State Department and sometimes distributed to other official bodies. As the government's postwar planning work developed, individuals working in the council groups took part in it, but the groups remained wholly autonomous in deciding what issues to study and what to say about them. Later a number of reports were given wider distribution in mimeographed form and a book based on some of them was published. After the project ended most of the reports were deposited in some fifty libraries around the country and abroad. The remaining documents along with the reports of the discussions at meetings became publicly available in 1975, when the council's archives were opened under a twenty-five-year rule. People using the archives (which include reports of other council meetings) may not attribute views to living people without their written permission, but otherwise there are no restrictions.

From the beginning the council's library has been essential to its studies and other work. For a long period it was an unrivaled specialized collection, but the growth of international studies in the postwar period and the constraints of space and funds have changed the emphasis to make it a working collection of current and reference material. There are extensive clipping files covering foreign and domestic newspapers and magazines.

The council has long had cooperative relations with foreign institutes concerned with international affairs. Bilateral and multilateral conferences have been held from time to time, some of which have led to publications. As of 1980, an annual conference brings together representatives of the Committees on Foreign Relations in over thirty cities across the country. Begun in the late 1930s largely to elicit regional views of U.S. foreign policy, these bodies have become active centers of discussion in their communities, and several books and pamphlets have been based on their work. The committees set their own programs and membership, but the council helps them in planning programs and provides some speakers. Council members are drawn from all parts of the United States, and in recent years the council has organized conferences in several Southern and Western cities. A number of meetings are held in the Washington, D.C., office of the council, where some of its discussion and study groups also hold sessions. Most activities, however, take place at the council's headquarters, 58 East Sixty-Eighth Street, New York, New York.

In addition to the regular staff and visiting scholars there are usually resident at the council on fellowships, two military officers, a State Department official, and a journalist. Walter Levy Fellowships bring foreign visitors to the council for short stays. Since 1967 the council has conducted an International Affairs Fellowship program to help bridge the gap between theory and practice. Young scholars are given opportunities to work in government or international organizations, and people from government are able to take a year off for writing or research. Some of these spend all or part of their time at the council.

As a private nonprofit organization the council has over the years drawn financial support from a variety of sources. Its members pay dues and in addition many of them contribute to annual fund campaigns or make other gifts and bequests to the council. Much of the work of the studies program and some other activities have been financed by grants from foundations. A corporation service, under which the council organizes conferences and meetings for interested business firms, provides another important source of income. The council does not do contract work or accept government funds. Its total budget in the fiscal year ending June 1980 was just under four million dollars.

Members of the council form the corporation under the laws of New York State. They elect annually eight of the twenty-five members of the board of directors. The board's executive committees and its finance and budget committees are both made up entirely of members of the board. Committees on membership, member's programs, nominating, and studies include both members of the board and other coopted members of the council. From time to time in the past there have been other committees, such as the one concerned with the library. The chairmen of the council's board have been: R. C. Leffingwell (1946-1953), John J. McCloy (1953-1970), and David Rockefeller (1970 to date). Until 1971 the presidency of the council was a part-time office held by John W. Davis (1921-1933), George W. Wickersham (1933-1936), Norman H. Davis (1936-1944), R. C. Leffingwell (1944-1946), Allen W. Dulles (1946-1950), Henry M. Wriston (1951-1964), and Grayson Kirk (1964-1971). The chief full-time executive officer was then called executive director: Hamilton Fish Armstrong (1922-1928), Malcolm W. Davis (1925-1927), Walter H. Mallory (1927-1959), and George S. Franklin (1953-1971). In the overlapping years during the period 1922-1971, both executive officers carried the title executive director. Since 1972 the full-time presidents have been Bayless Manning (1971-1977), and Winston Lord (1977 to date).

The staff grew from 3 or 4 people in the early days to a top figure approaching 100 in the early 1970s. As of 1980 the staff numbered about 80. The basic membership of the council is limited to 1,750 people, but certain special categories are not included in that total, such as people under thirty elected for terms of five years and members over seventy.

For further information, see the *Annual Reports* of the council, printed since 1940. These reports list council members and staff and give a full account of activities and finances. They also include a list of council publications. See also the following accounts published by the council: *The Council on Foreign Relations. A Record of Fifteen Years, 1921-1936* (1937); *The War and Peace Studies of the Council on Foreign Relations. A Record of Twenty-Five Years, 1921-1946* (1947); and Joseph Barber, *These Are the Committees* (1964). For a history of the early council, see Whitney H. Shepardson, *Early History of the Council on Foreign Relations* (1960).

There have been a number of books about the council, many of a highly critical nature and none of which can be regarded as wholly reliable, much less definitive. There have also been a number of newspaper and magazine articles devoted to the council including, for example, a long one by Elisabeth Jakab, "The Council on Foreign Relations," *Book Forum*, no. 4 (1978).

WILLIAM DIEBOLD, JR.

CRERAR LIBRARY. See John Crerar Library, The.

_D_

DUMBARTON OAKS RESEARCH LIBRARY AND COLLECTION.
This institution was established as a center for research in the areas of early
Christian, Byzantine, and medieval humanities and was conveyed to Har-
vard University in 1940. It is located on the property in Georgetown,
District of Columbia, long known as the Rock of Dumbarton, after the
rock formation of that name near Glasgow in Scotland, with a house built
in 1800 and known as the Oaks, which was acquired in 1920 by Mr. and
Mrs. Robert Woods Bliss, who renamed the estate Dumbarton Oaks. The
Blisses remodeled the house and made four major additions: first, the
Music Room in 1929, where the Dumbarton Oaks Conferences at which the
United Nations was planned were held in 1944; second, the museum wing,
with exhibition rooms for the Byzantine and medieval collection, surrounding a courtyard, which was opened in 1940; and third and fourth, the two
wings built to accommodate Mr. Bliss's pre-Columbian collection and Mrs.
Bliss's Garden Library, which were both completed in 1963. Mr. and Mrs.
Bliss meanwhile embarked on the creation of a magnificent garden, designed by the noted landscape gardener Beatrix Farrand and taking the
form of a series of terraces and "rooms" extending down the slope to the
north and east of the house. This garden was more or less complete in 1940,
when the grounds were divided into two parts, one of which was given to the
District of Columbia as a park and the other, including the garden and some
additional land, to Harvard University. Sections of the garden were later
remodeled, partly as a result of the building of the two new wings, but its
basic design remains at it was in 1940, and it is generally regarded as one of
the finest gardens in the country. Mr. and Mrs. Bliss themselves lived at
Dumbarton Oaks for only seven years, from 1933, when Mr. Bliss retired
from the diplomatic service, until 1940, when they moved to a nearby
house. They continued to take a keen interest in Dumbarton Oaks and all of
its activities until their deaths in 1962 and 1969, respectively. During their
lifetimes the institution was supported by their generosity and still derives
most of its income from their endowment.

Both Mr. and Mrs. Bliss were avid collectors and assembled, principally in the 1930s, a collection of Byzantine and early Christian art, together with some fine pieces from antiquity and the Western Middle Ages. They were above all interested in acquiring items of the highest artistic quality in all media, and the collection includes examples of silver and ivory work, jewelry, textiles, glass, ceramics, and a few icons and manuscripts, as well as sculptures and mosaics. It has continued to grow since 1940, although increasingly slowly in recent years owing to the cost and rarity of first-rate works of art and to the policy of acquiring only items that are known to have left their country of origin legally or a long time ago. Catalogs of all parts of the collection except for the sculpture and textiles have been published. Dumbarton Oaks also has large collections of Byzantine coins and seals, of which catalogs are in the course of preparation and publication. Mr. Bliss's collection of pre-Columbian art was started in Paris before World War I and was added to both during his years in the diplomatic service and after Dumbarton Oaks was conveyed to Harvard. It is marked, like the Byzantine collection, by his taste and discrimination and also his desire to show the aesthetic value as well as the ethnographic and archaeological interest of pre-Columbian works of art.

The Garden Library was put together by Mrs. Bliss primarily after World War II and reflected both her interest in the history of gardening and her desire for a wider recognition of the importance of this field both in scholarly work and in practical garden design. The library, which is added to regularly, is now the center of a scholarly enterprise designed to show the interest not only of landscape design and plant illustration but also of man's relation to nature as part of the history of civilization.

Finally, in addition to these more specialized collections, Mr. and Mrs. Bliss also acquired a number of autographs, music manuscripts, and rare books, not related to the three principal research areas, and put together a collection of works of art and furniture, now known as the House Collection. Although some of these were disposed of (partly by Mr. and Mrs. Bliss during their lifetimes) as the result of the expansion of the research activities, many of the finest pieces, including El Greco's *Visitation*, Riemenschneider's *Madonna and Child*, and Dégas's *Répetition de Chant*, are on exhibition in the Music Room and Garden Library. Others decorate parts of the building that are not open to the public.

Each of the specialized collections became the nucleus of a research activity that formed the basis of the present scholarly programs at Dumbarton Oaks. Most important is the Byzantine library, which has grown over the years to almost ninety thousand titles, including over eight hundred periodicals. It is the finest specialized library in the world in the area of Byzantine studies and also has notable holdings in late antique, Western medieval (especially art), and Slavic studies, which enables scholars to take a broad approach, as the founders intended, to the study of Byzantine civilization.

The Byzantine research facilities also include the Author Index of Byzantine Scholarly Literature (on which the *Dumbarton Oaks Bibliographies* are based), a large photograph collection, and a copy (one of the four outside Princeton) of the Princeton Index of Christian Art, which together form a link between the books in the library and the objects in the collection and permit scholars to engage in studies covering every aspect of the history of the Eastern Empire. The pre-Columbian collection also has a notable, although less comprehensive, library, concentrating on the artistic aspects of pre-Columbian studies, and the Garden Library has, in addition to its holdings of rare books, a growing research library of books dealing with the history of all aspects of landscape architecture. In addition to the manuscripts and autographs already mentioned, there are small archival collections (as yet not properly catalogued) of the papers of a few notable Byzantinists (including Hayford Pierce and Francis Dvornik), material relating to the history of Dumbarton Oaks, and records arising from field work sponsored by it.

Both Mr. and Mrs. Bliss took an interest in field work and archaeology and supported the Byzantine Institute, which was founded by Thomas Whittemore, after whose death in 1950 Dumbarton Oaks took over many of the institute's activities. At first these concentrated principally on the restoration, cleaning, preservation, and study of works of art *in situ*, especially mosaics and frescoes in buildings in Istanbul and elsewhere, but in the 1960s Dumbarton Oaks undertook two major architectural and archaeological enterprises in Istanbul and in the 1970s an investigation of a site soon to be flooded in Syria. Other major long-term fieldwork projects are an architectural survey of Santa Sophia in Istanbul and two studies of the medieval mosaics in Sicily and, with the support of the National Endowment for the Humanities, in San Marco, Venice, and the North Adriatic area. Although it is doubtful that Dumbarton Oaks will be able in the future to sponsor other enterprises of this size, it will continue to support a number of more limited field work projects, in addition to other projects, such as the Index of Byzantine Literature mentioned above and the Index of Catalogues of Greek Manuscripts, which is sponsored by Dumbarton Oaks but is centered at the Pontifical Institute of Mediaeval Studies in Toronto, with help from the National Endowment for the Humanities.

Research activities are carried on not only by members of the staff and fellows appointed to work on particular projects but also by qualified "outside" scholars, who are welcome to use the research facilities at Dumbarton Oaks. There are at present on the staff three professors (two in Byzantine studies and one in the history of landscape architecture), two senior research associates, and four research associates (three on joint appointments with universities in the Washington, D.C., area) in addition to several scholars holding administrative positions in the collections and libraries. The categories of fellows include nonstipendiary associate fellows, who hold positions at local universities, postdoctoral fellows, and predoctoral junior fellows. As a rule, between ten and twelve fellows are appointed each year in Byzantine studies and two to three in each of the other two fields. A few appointments of more than one year, or part-time appointments for several years, have been made. In 1980 a program of summer appointments of between four and ten weeks and two joint fellowships with the American Academy in Rome and the American School of Classical Studies at Athens were initiated. The basic annual stipends (prorated for shorter periods) are seven thousand dollars for fellows and five thousand for junior fellows, with five hundred dollars added for each dependent accompanying the fellow. Accommodations, a research expense account, and lunches on weekdays are also provided.

Dumbarton Oaks is governed by the trustees for Harvard University (the president and fellows of Harvard College, separately incorporated in the District of Columbia) and by an administrative committee chaired by the president of the university, who is advised by a rotating board of advisors concerned with the institution as a whole. The chief executive officer is the director, who is assisted by an assistant director and, in scholarly matters, by three rotating external committees, one in each area, which are responsible for the selection of fellows and other aspects of the scholarly programs. The staff includes five curators, sixteen librarians, bibliographers, and photoarchivists, three editors, two photographers, thirteen gardeners, eighteen members of the building and security staff, two engineers, two cabinet-makers, four members of the staff of the Fellow Building (where lunch is served and guests accommodated), and various others, making up a total staff of about ninety people not including the fellows.

In addition to these scholarly activities, which are inevitably addressed to a comparatively limited audience, Dumbarton Oaks also has a more public face in the form of the gardens, which are open daily from 2 to 5 P.M. throughout the year (except on national holidays and in inclement weather) and which attract upwards of two hundred thousand visitors a year, especially in spring and fall when the tulips and chrysanthemums are in bloom, the collections, which are open daily except Monday from 2 to 5 P.M., and the series of concerts given in the Music Room for the Friends of Music. Mr. and Mrs. Bliss were patrons of music and the tradition of giving concerts in the Music Room has been continued. Seven or eight concerts are given each year, usually on two successive evenings in order to accommodate a greater number of listeners, and for many people these concerts are among the most valued aspects of Dumbarton Oaks's activities.

A link between the research and public faces of Dumbarton Oaks is also formed by its traditional concern for the dissemination of learning. The first volume of the Dumbarton Oaks Papers, which contained the lectures given at the inauguration of the new buildings in 1940, came out in 1941, and volume 34 was published in 1980. Two series of books concerned with

Byzantine studies are the Dumbarton Oaks Studies, of which eighteen volumes have been published to date, and the Dumbarton Oaks Texts, of which five volumes have been published and which constitutes the Washington Series of the international *Corpus Fontium Historicae Byzantinae*. There are parallel, although less extensive, publications in pre-Columbian studies and the history of landscape architecture. No less important than the publications are the symposia held in each field (pre-Columbian in the fall and Byzantine and history of landscape architecture in the spring), which have proved a major stimulus to research and means of communication among interested scholars. In addition, Dumbarton Oaks sponsors throughout the year a series of public lectures in the various fields with which it is concerned, including music, and also a series of informal talks, addressed primarily to specialists, by members of its own scholarly community and by visiting scholars. More recently, it has embarked on a program of small seminars and discussion courses, limited to fifteen members and open to students from institutions of higher learning in the Washington area. Two of these were offered in the year 1979-1980 and six in 1980-1981. In these various ways Dumbarton Oaks carries its mission as defined by its founders "to clarify an everchanging present and to inform the future with wisdom."

For further information, see "An Introduction to Dumbarton Oaks," *Harvard Library Bulletin* (January and April, 1979); and Dumbarton Oaks *Annual Reports*. On the history of the building, see Walter M. Whitehill, *Dumbarton Oaks. The History of a Georgetown House and Garden, 1800-1966* (1967). On the development of the gardens, see Georgina Masson, *Dumbarton Oaks, a Guide to the Gardens* (1968); Noelle Blackmer Beatty and Ursula R. Pariser, *The Dumbarton Oaks Gardens. Their History, Design and Ornaments* (1978); and Diane Kostial McGuire, ed., *Beatrix Farrand's Plant Book for Dumbarton Oaks* (1980).

GILES CONSTABLE

_E

EAST-WEST CENTER. The East-West Center (known formally as the Center for Cultural and Technical Interchange Between East and West) is a national educational institution established in Hawaii in 1960 by the U.S. Congress.

Hawaii's citizens had long realized the special role their islands play in bringing together the diverse peoples and cultures of Asia, the Pacific, and the United States. In the late 1950s they could see potential for an even greater contribution. The road to formalizing this role became wider and shorter with the achievement of statehood for Hawaii in 1959, and the bond of friendship that developed between John A. Burns and Lyndon B. Johnson. Burns, Hawaii's territorial delegate to Congress in the 1950s, and later governor, had worked long and hard for statehood. In the process, he and then Senate Majority Leader Johnson came to know and respect each other.

As statehood became a certainty, they considered how Hawaii's unique resources could best be used for the nation's benefit. Johnson first publicly suggested the concept of an international center during a speech in 1959. He proposed that the nation establish an international university in Hawaii as a meeting place for East and West. He observed that we should remove the barriers between ourselves and the people who should be our friends.

Midway through 1959, Congress passed a bill establishing the center, and President Dwight D. Eisenhower signed it on May 14, 1960. The mandate given to the center by Congress was to promote better relations and understanding among the nations and peoples of Asia, the Pacific, and the United States through cooperative study, training, and research.

Congressional funding was approved the next year. Congress designated the secretary of state to prepare a plan for establishing the center. Eventually, a grant-in-aid agreement was approved by the Department of State and the University of Hawaii to enable the university to establish and operate the center. Johnson, as vice-president of the United States, visited Hawaii in 1961 for groundbreaking ceremonies.

In the first year the university established an International College, which provided programs and services for degree students and international scholars. Also associated with the center were an English Language Institute, an Institute of Advanced Projects, a Translations Bureau, an Institute of American Studies, an Asian Studies Program, and an Overseas Operations Program. An International Training Agency was established to provide short-term practical training projects for participants from Asia and the Pacific. The state-administered International Cooperation Center also was incorporated into the East-West Center.

In 1961, on the advice of the Department of State and the University Board of Regents, a small group of nationally known educators was invited to Hawaii to evaluate the center and provide recommendations for improving its operations. The group recommended that the International College be disbanded and that several of the other programs be carried out by the university under appropriate colleges or administrative units.

The center was reorganized by establishing administrative units to implement its three mandated functions: to provide for cooperative study, training, and research. The center then operated mainly as a grant-administering agency, coordinating the academic work of students at the University of Hawaii, arranging for the training of nondegree participants by various State of Hawaii agencies, and providing support for the research activities of senior scholars.

In 1964, a national review board was appointed to review the operation of the East-West Center on a continual basis. Governor Burns was named chairman and served until his death in 1975.

A joint East-West Center/University of Hawaii task force in 1966 recommended a problem-oriented approach for center programs. This approach was defined by the center's then new deputy chancellor, Dr. Everett Kleinjans, as not duplicating university programs. Thus, in the East-West Center, scholars would be grouped in programs centering around a problem and be drawn from several disciplines.

The thrust of each center program would be—and is today—cooperative action: bringing together from different countries, cultures, disciplines, and professions men and women equipped to generate knowledge about the problem, to propose alternative solutions, and to develop materials potentially useful to policy makers in solving similar problems.

The national review board endorsed the problem-oriented approach. In 1970, the three former administrative units of the center were replaced by problem-oriented programs in communication, culture learning, food, and technology and development, joining an existing program in population. An office of open grants also was established to provide flexibility and innovation.

After extensive deliberation, the national review board in 1974 recommended the establishment of an entity independent of the University of

Hawaii to operate the center. On May 14, 1975, Governor Ariyoshi signed into law the act creating the public, nonprofit, autonomous corporation that continues today to operate and administer the East-West Center.

The center's programs focus on major world problems, especially potential or actual sources of difference, misunderstanding, and conflict among cultures and nations, East and West. Staff and participants seek to generate and share knowledge about alternative approaches and solutions to problems; to produce, share, and test policy aids and materials; and to educate people to reconcile differences, clarify misunderstandings, and avoid or resolve conflict. In order to plan research and to disseminate knowledge generated by the center's programs, workshops, seminars, and conferences are held throughout the year.

The style of each program is cooperative, bringing together from different countries, cultures, disciplines, and professions, older and younger scholars, practitioners, and policy makers to seek solutions to the problems being tackled. The problem provides a focus around which people from East and West can interact as they study, give and receive training, exchange ideas and views, and conduct cooperative activities.

The center's programs are organized into five institutes, open grants, and special projects. The institutes focus on the following problem areas: communication, culture learning, environment and policy, population, and resource systems.

The Communication Institute investigates the various patterns of communication that bind individual societies together and analyzes how these different patterns facilitate or retard better relations and understanding among nations.

The Culture Learning Institute focuses on the special set of problems that arise when different cultures come into contact, specifically when people of Asia, the Pacific, and the United States interact.

The Environment and Policy Institute explores ways to integrate environmental factors into a broad range of policy considerations so that activities designed to meet human needs will not be counterproductive among different sectors of society and over time.

The Population Institute contributes to the knowledge and understanding of the facts of rapid demographic change, its causes and effects, and policy alternatives.

The Resource Systems Institute concentrates on the interrelationship of food, energy, and raw materials, which influence the lives of people and relations among nations.

In addition to international staffing, participants, and teamwork, the center has international financial support and an international board of governors.

The staff includes more than 250 men and women of numerous nationalities, diverse academic backgrounds, and wide practical experience.

The "participants" number approximately fifteen hundred men and women each year and include scholars, leaders, public officials, professionals, and graduate students. They come to the center from the United States and more than forty countries and territories ranging from Korea to Iran on the Asian continent and from Japan to Australia in the Pacific. For each participant selected from the United States, two are selected from the Asia-Pacific area.

Participants, chosen in relation to center objectives, are invited to join center projects. They bring with them varying degrees of knowledge and awareness about a problem area. They begin working with center staff and with each other in the production, testing, and dissemination of knowledge and in applying skills to respond to problems. Their contributions to the projects vary depending on their backgrounds and skills and on the responsibilities assigned to them by the project leaders. In the process, they develop bonds of friendship, collegiality, and trust that serve to promote better relations and understanding.

The center is supported not only by appropriations from the U.S. Congress ($18,338,000 est. 1982) but also by contributions from more than twenty governments of Asia and the Pacific. Such international support creates a true sense of partnership, the essential foundation for mutual understanding and better relations.

Since 1975, the center has been operated by a quasi-public, educational, nonprofit corporation with an independent, international board of governors. Board members come from the United States, Fiji, India, Japan, the Philippines, and Singapore.

The center maintains close and cooperative relationships with the University of Hawaii. Staff and participants have access to its libraries, computer center, and other resources. The center provides reciprocal access for University of Hawaii faculty and students to facilities and resources.

The center's twenty-one-acre campus is adjacent to the university. There are three residence halls, housing five hundred participants. One hall has self-contained apartments; the other halls are dormitories. The center also has a three hundred-office program building, a conference building with a cafeteria, and garden, recreation, and performance areas. A Thai Pavilion and a Japanese Garden are among facilities contributed by governments, organizations, and businesses in Asian countries.

For further information, see the following publications of the East-West Center: *East-West Perspectives Magazine* (quarterly); *East-West Center Programs* (annually); and *East-West Center President's Review* (annually).

JOHN H. WILLIAMS

ECOLOGICAL SOCIETY OF AMERICA (ESA). An ecological society composed of botanists and zoologists was first advanced by Professor

Robert H. Wolcott at the University of Nebraska in a letter dated March 27, 1914, to Professor V. E. Shelford of the University of Chicago. Professor Wolcott stressed fieldwork as one of the major reasons for organizing such a society, and in order to facilitate such work at meetings he suggested the restriction of membership to the Mississippi Valley area. Professor Shelford responded favorably but broached the possibility of making the society a national one and added that others favored the plan. He urged that "the thing be started" at the American Association for the Advancement of Science* (AAAS) meeting in Philadelphia scheduled for December, 1914. Some twenty men met at the AAAS meeting, and an organizing committee was set up which, by December, 1915, successfully carried through the founding, in Columbus, Ohio, of the Ecological Society of America. A constitution was adopted, officers were elected (Professor Shelford being named the first president), and the newly formed ESA agreed to hold a meeting the following December in conjunction with the AAAS meeting in New York City.

Major activities of the ESA over the years have been carried on through the establishment of various committees, a number of which have evolved into sections. Committees have included, for example, the Study Committee, Public Affairs Committee, and Education Committee. Sections have usually been devoted to specific aspects of ecology; for example, there are present-day sections of the ESA on Applied Ecology, Physiological Ecology, and International Affairs, which have their own officers, budgets, programs, and so on. There has been interest in regionalization within the ESA, and there are presently Western and Southeastern chapters; Oregon and Minnesota chapters have also functioned.

In 1946 the Ecologists Union (changed to the Nature Conservancy in 1951) was founded when the ESA adopted the policy of not attempting to influence legislation. From that time forward, however, many members of the ESA have worked with this group on conservation problems. Both the Nature Conservancy and the Institute of Ecology, established in 1971, arose primarily over the question of whether land acquisition, for natural area purposes, was a legitimate function of a learned society.

Since its founding a number of awards have been established by the ESA. These include the George Mercer Award, made annually to the writer of an outstanding paper in ecology; Eminent Ecologist Award; Murray F. Buell Award, awarded to students; William S. Cooper Award, for publication; Robert H. MacArthur Memorial Lectureship; and Distinguished Service Citation.

The major ESA publication was the earlier quarterly and, since the 1960s, bimonthly *Ecology*. The founding of such a journal was discussed by members in 1917, but it was not until 1919, largely through the efforts of Barrington Moore and Norman Taylor, that it was accomplished. These gentlemen also arranged for the owners of the previously published *Plant World* to transfer their rights, including subscription lists, to the ESA with a few inconsequential stipulations, for example, the cover of *Ecology* should carry the words "Continuing the *Plant World*" for five years. Finally, Taylor, who at the time was a staff member of the Brooklyn Botanic Garden, was able to secure the Botanic Garden's financial backing and cooperation in the publication of *Ecology* until 1948. Since that time Duke University Press has cooperated with the ESA in its publication. *Ecological Monographs*, which contains longer papers on ecological topics, was established as a quarterly in 1931, and it and *Ecology* constitute the major publications of the ESA. Publications also include a quarterly *Bulletin*, published continuously since 1917, containing general news about the ESA, commentary, letters, records of ESA business, and abstracts of papers presented at the national meetings, and every three or four years a special directory number with names and addresses of all members.

Annual meetings of the ESA were held with the AAAS until several years after the 1947 founding of the American Institute of Biological Sciences* (AIBS). Since 1949, however, although the ESA has continued to partic- ipate in the AAAS meetings, the annual business meeting and most field trips of the ESA have been scheduled with the annual meeting of the AIBS, which normally is held in late August. These annual meetings include the election of officers, reports, presentation of awards, presentation of papers, and field trips.

Membership in the ESA grew from an initial 286 charter members to 687 by 1937. After climbing in the 1950s and 1960s, membership reached 4,000 by 1970. It stands today at about 6,000. Although there are presently eight categories of membership, such as active, student, and life, a majority are in the active category and receive *Ecology* and the *Bulletin*.

The ESA elects the customary institutional officers; it conducts its busi- ness from an office, headed by a secretary, located in Norman, Oklahoma.

For further information, see the following earlier histories appearing in *Ecology:* V. E. Shelford, "The Organization of the Ecological Society of America, 1914-1919" (January, 1938); Norman Taylor, "The Beginnings of Ecology" (April, 1938); and Barrington Moore, "The Beginnings of Ecology" (October, 1938). See also William A. Dreyer, "The Ecological Society of America," *AAAS Bulletin* (February, 1945). For later histories of ESA, see Tania Simkins, "Association Profile: The Ecological Society of America," *Association and Society Management* (1971); Robert L. Burgess, "The Ecological Society of America: Historical Data and Some Preliminary Analyses," in F. N. Egerton and R. P. McIntosh, eds., *The History of Ecology* (1977); and Robert L. Burgess, "Developments in Ecology in the United States, 1945-1979: The Institutional Framework," in E. J. Kormondy and J. F. McCormick, eds., *Handbook of Contemporary World Developments in Ecology* (1980).

ECONOMETRIC SOCIETY. A general description of econometrics appears in the constitution of the Econometric Society which explains that the association

is an international society for the advancement of economic theory in its relation to statistics and mathematics. The Society shall operate as a completely disinterested, scientific organization without political, social, financial, or nationalistic bias. Its main object shall be to promote studies that aim at a unification of the theoretical-quantitative and the empirical-quantitative approach to economic problems and that are penetrated by constructive and rigorous thinking similar to that which has come to dominate in the natural sciences. Any activity which promises ultimately to further such unification of theoretical and factual studies in economics shall be within the sphere of interest of the Society.

Two nineteenth-century Europeans, Leon Walras and Antione A. Cournot, had pioneered in mathematical economic studies, and, by 1912, a small number of men in Europe and the United States were interested in and advocating a furthering of such work. At about that time Professor Irving Fisher of Yale University made an unsuccessful attempt to get the American Association for the Advancement of Science* (AAAS) to sponsor an organization of an econometric nature. Although Wesley C. Mitchell, Arthur L. Moore, and a few others expressed interest in the idea, it was not until 1926-1927 that the activities of Professors Charles F. Roos of Princeton University and Ragnar Frisch of the University of Oslo led to the founding of the Econometric Society. Specifically, Roos had submitted a paper at that time to an American economics journal and was told that it could be published if the mathematical and statistical aspects were deleted; an inquiry to a mathematical journal elicited an offer to publish if the economic and statistical aspects were deleted; a statistical journal offered to publish if the mathematical and economic aspects were deleted. Roos brought this impasse to the attention of Professor Edwin B. Wilson of Harvard University, who was then a member of the AAAS executive committee, and it was a material factor in the creation of Section K of the AAAS, to be devoted to the development of economics and sociology as sciences, and with Roos as secretary of the section.

Meanwhile in Europe, Professor Frisch was urging the creation of an Econometric Society, and in a September, 1926, letter to Professor François Divisia of the École Nationale des Ponts et Chaussées, Paris, France, suggested the establishment of a periodical to be called *Econometrica*. In the spring of 1928 Frisch came to the United States under the auspices of the Laura Spelman Rockefeller Memorial and soon met Professor Roos. In agreement as to the need for an Econometric Society, the two tried to enlist Professor Fisher's support. Although sympathetic to the idea, Fisher was pessimistic because of his earlier experience and agreed to help only if one hundred supporters could be enlisted. Although Roos and Frisch came up with only seventy names, this so far exceeded Fisher's expectations that he agreed to cooperate anyway. After a year of discussion and consultation with others, the three sent out invitational letters to attend an organizational meeting to be held in Cleveland, Ohio, on December 29, 1930, where several other learned societies were meeting. Twelve Americans and four Europeans attended this founding meeting of the society; Professor Fisher was elected its first president, and Professors Roos and Frisch were elected members of a nine-member governing council.

Meanwhile, Alfred Cowles III, an investment counselor of Colorado Springs, Colorado, had become interested in the possibilities for economic forecasting that he saw in the activities of the society and its members. Following discussion with President Fisher and other American leaders of the society, including Roos, Cowles offered to underwrite many of its activities, including publication of a learned journal. Although a few European members raised questions concerning the propriety of such aid, all eventually were convinced that Cowles's motives were disinterested and scientific. Early in 1932, therefore, it was agreed that a research organization would be set up in Colorado Springs, the Cowles Commission for Research in Economics, under society sponsorship and operating under an advisory council appointed by it. It was also agreed that Cowles would defray the costs of publication of a societal journal.

When the official society journal, *Econometrica*, was established, Cowles became its circulation manager as well as treasurer of the Econometric Society, and from 1932 to 1937 joint offices of the society and the Cowles Commission were maintained in Colorado Springs. By the latter date, dissatisfaction with this location distant from academic centers resulted in a move to the University of Chicago. In 1955, the society and Cowles Commission headquarters were moved to Yale University. Then, in 1976, the links between Cowles and the society were severed, when the appointment of a new secretary and treasurer led to the transfer of offices to Northwestern University.

The Econometric Society and its allied Cowles Commission have been important centers for econometric research and publication. Many of its officers and members have played influential roles in this area. For example, the fifth, sixth, and seventh presidents of the society have been, respectively, Joseph A. Schumpeter, Wesley C. Mitchell, and John Maynard Keynes.

Beginning with only 16 in 1930, society membership grew to 163 in 1931, 671 in 1939, and stands at approximately 2,700 today. Early on, however, it was decided that the character of the society would not be altered by the press of numbers. Consequently, two categories of members have been provided for: regular and fellows. The latter are distinguished in the econometric field; charged with the control of the society; and, significantly, few in number. At the present time, for example, there are only 310 fellows in the total society membership.

Reflecting its international origins, the European membership has always comprised an important section within the Econometric Society. As a result, the practice developed of alternately naming presidents from different regions; usually, not always, a European and American alternate. Although all members recognized the importance of convening meetings on an international basis, pecuniary considerations eventually forced separate European and American annual meetings of the Society. The American meetings have usually been held in December, often in conjunction with those of the American Economic Association* (AEA) or American Statistical Association* (ASA). The European ones have tended to be separate, often held at European universities. In the late 1940s and 1950s, the society also held summer meetings in the United States, often jointly with the American Mathematical Society* (AMS) and Mathematical Association of America* (MAA). A world congress has been held every five years since 1965.

The Econometric Society elects the customary institutional officers; it conducts its business from an office, headed by a secretary and treasurer, located in Evanston, Illinois.

For further information, see the following articles appearing in *Econometrica:* Charles F. Roos, "A Future Role for the Econometric Society in International Statistics" (April, 1948); Ragnar Frisch, "Editorial" (January, 1953); and François Divisia, "La Société d'Économetrica a Atteint sa Majorité" (January, 1953). See also "The Econometric Society," *AAAS Bulletin* (July, 1945); and *Economic Theory and Measurement: A Twenty Year Research Report, 1932-1952* (1952), providing a history of the work of the Cowles Commission.

ECONOMIC HISTORY ASSOCIATION (EHA). During the 1920s and 1930s, the study of economic history was beginning to transcend the traditional limitations of political economy. Scholars like Edwin F. Gay and his students Abbott P. Usher, Norman S. B. Gras, and Julius Klein and a score of other individuals acting independently, such as Herbert Heaton, started to concentrate their efforts on analyzing economic issues, events, and institutions in and of themselves rather than as reflections of the political environment. The establishment of the Economic History Society in England (1926), with its *Economic History Review* and the publication of the *Journal of Economic and Business History* (1928), illustrated the growing consciousness of scholars interested in economic history. Although events such as these were promising for the future, some American historians felt that the editors of the journals were more interested in publishing articles on European economic history, and, with the demise of the *Journal of Economic and Business History* in 1932, there seemed to be dwindling opportunities for publishing works on economic development generally. More importantly, the outbreak of World War II in 1939 raised serious doubts about the future of the growing discipline. With travel to war-torn Europe interrupted and with the increasing uncertainty as to whether or not scholars could continue their work in the midst of a world war, a group of concerned Americanists decided to do something to prevent a complete blackout of scholarly productivity in the area of economic history.

At the American Historical Association* (AHA) convention in Washington, D.C. in 1939, Dr. H. A. Kellar led a group of interested scholars in forming an Industrial History Society. Despite the best of intentions, however, the society did not materialize. Almost simultaneously, Professor Earl J. Hamilton, meeting with a group of scholars at the American Economic Association* (AEA) convention in Philadelphia, decided to set up a steering committee to investigate the possibility of forming an organization promoting the study and teaching of economic history. With World War II very much in their minds, the Hamilton group set up a fairly large steering committee and a much smaller and workable executive committee including Arthur Cole (chairman), Herbert Heaton (vice-chairman), Ann Bezanson (secretary), and Earl J. Hamilton. This committee was charged with forming an independent organization that would cooperate with existing organizations in economic history but, at the same time, enroll its own members and consider the possibility of publishing its own journal. Aided by Edwin Gay, Joseph Willits, Harold Innis, Edward Kirkland, and Federick Lane, Cole, Bezanson, and Hamilton worked prodigiously, arranging meetings to coincide with the annual conventions of the AHA and AEA in New York and New Orleans in December, 1940. They also wrote to over five hundred prospective members so as to determine the feasibility of financially supporting such an organization. By September, 1940, they had arranged the meetings in New York and New Orleans, had drafted a constitution, were already drawing up a slate of officers, and had decided upon an editor for the journal and the amount of the annual dues. By November, Edwin Gay had agreed to serve as the president of the new organization and Professor Shepard Clough as secretary-treasurer. On December 27 at the AHA convention and on December 30 at the AEA convention, the Economic History Association was officially established, and a commitment made to publish a *Journal of Economic History* with E. A. J. Johnson as editor and Shepard Clough as assistant editor. After resolving the financial and publishing problems normally associated with any new organization, the first issue of the *JEH* was published on April 26, 1941.

From its inception to the present, the purpose of the Economic History Association has been the same. As stated in the 1977 *Handbook* of the association, the EHA has been set up to "encourage and promote teaching, research, and publication on every phase of economic history" and to aid in the preservation and administration of valuable archival materials. To achieve these goals, the association has not only cooperated with other organizations committed to the study and teaching of economic history but has utilized the *Journal of Economic History* as a primary medium to publish the results of original research done by committed and professional scholars in economics, history, and other related disciplines. From 1941 to 1950, the *Journal* was published on a semiannual basis with a third issue/ supplement known as the *Tasks of Economic History*, devoted to the publication of papers delivered at the annual convention. Since 1951, the *Journal* has been published on a quarterly basis with the *Tasks* supplement still intact. Today, the membership rolls of the EHA and subscriptions to the *Journal* have exceeded 3,000, approximately 1,200 representing individual memberships and 2,000 library or institution subscriptions. Of the 2,000 library or institution subscriptions, nearly 950 are from institutions in foreign countries. Since it was originally designed to promote studies in economic history generally, the *Journal* has encompassed a wide variety of themes. Articles on American, modern European, and medieval to early modern economic history have typically graced the pages of the issues, along with studies on economic thought, methodology (especially with the cliometrics approach), theories of economic growth, the importance of cooperation between historians and economists, and developments in Asia, Africa, and Latin America. Maintaining very high standards of academic excellence, the editors of the *Journal* normally accept a small proportion of the manuscripts submitted for publication. In 1980, for example, only fifteen percent of all manuscripts submitted were accepted for publication. Similarly, the presidents, secretaries, secretary-treasurers, and treasurers of the EHA and the editors of the *Journal* have consistently been among the leaders and pioneers in the study of economic history, including such well-known scholars as Edwin Gay, Arthur Cole, Carter Goodrich, George Rogers Taylor, Harold Williamson, William Parker, Alfred Chandler, Douglass North, Thomas Cochran, Herman Krooss, Robert Gallman, Robert Fogel, Richard Easterlin, and Stanley Engerman. Today, the EHA and the *JEH* are internationally recognized for their outstanding contributions to the study and promulgation of economic history.

The *Journal* has served as the principal means of the organization to foster the study of economic history; however, the association has acted in this regard in another way. In recent years, the EHA has taken control of and supervised the Committee on Research in Economic History. Established in 1940 and financed by a Rockefeller Foundation grant of $250,000 the CREH was created to aid in developing the field of economic history. The brainchild of Joseph Willits and Anne Bezanson at the Rockefeller Foundation, the committee, under the able chairmanship of Arthur Cole, sought to aid scholars financially with grants-in-aid for release time from teaching, secretarial help, travel expenses, and publication costs. Acting as a committee technically under the jurisdiction of the Social Science Research Council* (SSRC) and independent of the EHA, the committee originally defined four areas of research to support: the role of the government in the economy, the role of entrepreneurship, the growth of the corporation, and the development of banking. Parceling its money out carefully, the committee supported in whole or in part the completion of scholarly studies in these areas that are still considered classics. The list of individual scholars helped by the committee was impressive, including such prominent individuals as Oscar Handlin, Fritz Redlich, James Hedges, Ralph Hidy, and scores of others. In addition, the committee also helped in the preparation of the first *Historical Statistics of the United States* compilation and sympathetically supported the founding of the Research Center in Entrepreneurial History at Harvard University. Financed by a separate grant and acting independently of the CREH and/or the EHA, the center was molded and led by Arthur Cole until its demise in 1958. In the same year, the Committee on Research in Economic History underwent a radical transformation. All of its board members resigned en masse, its name was changed to the Council on Research in Economic History, and a new board of directors was appointed. Under the direction of George Rogers Taylor, Harold Williamson, Oscar Handlin, Hugh G. J. Aitken, Rondo Cameron, John Dales, David Landes, and Douglass North, the new council changed the direction of the old CREH by establishing an open competition for research awards to scholars in economic history. From 1959 to 1968, moreover, the council continued this program and acted independently of the EHA, although there was cooperation. In 1968, the council was officially taken over by the EHA and its name changed again to the former Committee on Research in Economic History. Since then, the committee has continued to finance with grants-in-aid scholarly studies in economic history by promising young individuals.

The EHA has held annual meetings since its founding and published the proceedings of such meetings in a separate yearly *Tasks* issue. Supported by membership dues primarily, it has five categories of membership: regular, student, joint, sustaining, and life. All categories of membership carry voting privileges in elections and subscriptions to the *Journal of Economic History.*

The EHA elects the customary institutional officers; it conducts its business from an office, headed by a secretary-treasurer, located in Wilmington, Delaware.

For further information, see the following articles in the *Journal of Economic History:* Herbert Heaton, "The Early History of the Economic History Association" (December, 1941); S. B. Clough, "The Economic History of a Young Corporation" (December, 1941); Arthur Cole, "A Report on Research in Economic History" (May, 1944); Herbert Heaton, "Twenty-Five Years of the Economic History Association: A Reflective Evaluation" (December, 1965); Arthur Cole, "Economic History in the United States: Formative Years of a Discipline" (December, 1968); Shepard

Clough, "A Half-Century in Economic History: Autobiographical Reflections," (March, 1970); and Arthur Cole, "Committee on Research in Economic History: An Historical Sketch" (December, 1970). See also Herbert Heaton, *A Scholar in Action: Edwin F. Gay* (1952); the *Handbook* of the EHA (1967 and 1977); and E. A. J. Johnson, *American Imperialism in the Image of Peer Gynt: Memoirs of a Professor-Bureaucrat* (1971). Professor Rondo Cameron, editor, *Journal of Economic History*, provided historical information and assistance in the preparation of this article.

MICHAEL V. NAMORATO

ELECTROCHEMICAL SOCIETY, INC. The American Electrochemical Society, forerunner of the Electrochemical Society, was organized in 1902 as a result of the burgeoning worldwide scientific interest in the relationship of chemistry and electricity. Similar groups, such as the Bunsen Society of Germany (1894) and the Faraday Society of England (1903) were springing into existence at about the same time.

The immediate incentive for the founding of such a society in the United States, however, was the belief on the part of a small group of Philadelphia engineers and chemists that their needs were not being met by existing learned and scientific societies. This group, led by Joseph W. Richards, Carl Hering, and C. J. Reed, sent out a circular letter to some thirty persons presumed to be interested in electrochemistry, calling for an organizational meeting on November 1, 1901, in Philadelphia. Eleven persons attended this meeting, and it was there decided that if the names of seventy-five persons pledging membership could be obtained, a society should be formed. Also, it was at this initial meeting that the name "American Electrochemical Society" was adopted, not to be changed to "Electrochemical Society" until 1930.

The response from prospective members was unexpectedly and overwhelmingly favorable, 337 membership pledges were received from thirty-six states and eight foreign countries, and another organizational meeting was convened in Philadelphia on April 3, 1902, with fifty-two persons present. Officers were elected; a constitution was adopted; and some twenty scientific papers were presented at this first meeting. Since this meeting the society has continually sought to stimulate interest and research in electrochemistry. It has sponsored essay and other publication contests, and various members have endowed research and publication awards to be administered by it. Various divisions dealing with major aspects of electrochemistry have been established, and each of them is responsible for its own programs at the now semiannual societal meetings.

During the first decade of its existence, in order to economize, serious thought was given to printing the society's papers and reports in another learned journal. Such an action was not taken, however, and it published its own semiannual *Transactions* from 1902 to 1948. At that time it was superseded by the monthly *Journal*, which, in addition to papers and reports, provides more news about the society and its members. Much of the value of these journals is that they provide a repository of reports of investigations, successful and unsuccessful, that prove of value to later investigators.

Another medium whereby members stay abreast of the activities of their colleagues is the semiannual meetings. These meetings, held for five-day periods in May and October, are the occasion for the presentation and discussion of papers; social activity; and the usual attention to societal business affairs. Also, the society has always encouraged the development of regional groups in the United States and abroad. Some nineteen of them now hold periodic meetings and complement the work of the parent organization.

Outstanding contribution to the scientific fields of interest of the society have been recognized by four major awards, each of which are given every two years: Edward Goodrich Acheson Award founded in 1928 for contribution to society objectives; Olon Palladium Medal Award founded in 1950 for contribution in the fields of electrochemical science and corrosion; Vittorio de Nora-Diamond Shamrock Medal and Prize founded in 1977, succeeding a society award established in 1971, for contributions in the field of electrochemical engineering and technology; and Solid State Science and Technology Award founded in 1971 for contributions in the field of solid-state science and technology.

Originally there was only one class of membership in the society, and it was open to all who had a scientific interest in electrochemistry. Through the years the membership regulations were revised, and now there are two different categories of regular membership: active and student, turning upon qualifications and age; plus emeritus, honorary, life, patron, and sustaining membership. Well over 50 percent of the present membership of fifty-seven hundred, however, falls into the regular active category.

Earlier members were almost all from the Northeastern section of the United States, particularly New York and Pennsylvania. With the passage of years, however, the membership has become much more diversified geographically. This membership includes and has included practically every scientific, educational, and industrial leader in the electrochemical field.

The Electrochemical Society elects the customary institutional officers; it conducts its business from an office, headed by an executive secretary, located in Pennington, New Jersey.

For further information, see the publications discussed above, particularly, Carl Hering, "The American Electrochemical Society," *Transactions* (1907); and Charles F. Burgess, "Early Days in Our Society," *Transactions* (1942).

See also the fiftieth anniversary issues of the *Journal* (1952), which contain much historical information about the founders, early days, and histories of the committees of the society. See particularly therein, R. M. Burns, "The First Decade: An Account of the Founding and Early Days of the Society" (January, 1952); and Ralph M. Hunter, "The Electrochemical Society—Past and Future" (July, 1952). Also, in connection with the observance of its seventy-fifth anniversary, the society published *A History of the Electrochemical Society, 1902-1976* (1977).

ELEUTHERIAN MILLS-HAGLEY FOUNDATION. The genesis of this foundation is to be found in the preparations for the sesquicentennial celebration in 1952 of the founding of E. I. du Pont de Nemours & Company. Early on the officials of the company decided that they wanted a permanent memorial to the occasion. They noted that the early buildings of the company on the Brandywine River in Delaware, powder mills, offices, and a du Pont family residence, were still in a remarkable state of preservation after the passage of 150 years, although no longer owned by the company. Led by Pierre S. du Pont, retired company president and honorary chairman of its board of trustees; Crawford H. Greenwalt, president; and Lammot du Pont Copeland, secretary, plans were made for the reacquisition and development of this historic site.

The instrument established for the execution of these plans was the Eleutherian Mills-Hagley Foundation, a not-for-profit corporation, which was chartered in 1952. At that time the foundation acquired 160 acres of land, since expanded to about 220, which included the Eleutherian Mills property, acquired in 1802 by Eleuthère Irénée du Pont and the Hagley estate, bought by du Pont in 1814. Also, an initial endowment for the foundation of six million dollars was provided by the Du Pont Company. The foundation began operations under Luther D. Reed, its first managing director. Walter J. Heacock joined the foundation in 1954 as director of research and interpretation. He became director of the Hagley Museum when it opened in 1957, and general director of the foundation in 1966.

In its first years, the foundation concentrated upon the preservation and restoration of the historic site entrusted to its care and the interrelated establishment of an industrial museum as the basis for a program in the origin and development of American industry and its significance in our history. The foundation's Hagley Museum, formally established in 1957, evolved from these concepts.

Integral to this program was the establishment in 1954 of the Hagley Fellowship Program. Conducted as a joint effort since then by the foundation and the University of Delaware, the program from its inception has been viewed as one providing training leading to the M.A. and Ph.D. in American history for prospective college teachers and museum personnel. With courses conducted by university, museum, and foundation personnel and with internships, travel, and other learning experiences provided, the foundation from the beginning made several fellowships available annually to outstanding students. Their number was gradually increased to about ten per year and, since 1967, has been augmented by funds provided by the National Museum Act, which supported some three to five fellows. Although the program has undergone modification and change of emphasis in its over twenty-five-year existence, its continued excellence is attested by the enviable placement record of its graduates.

During the restoration of museum buildings and the preparation of accompanying exhibits, the research staff compiled and analyzed voluminous and extensive documentation. Using as a base the extensive records dealing with the property holdings of the foundation, collections from other libraries were examined, archaeological excavations were made, and oral interviews were held with those who had worked or been associated with the company fifty or more years earlier. The first of the museum's exhibit buildings was opened to the public in 1957. Since then stabilization and restoration has continued on the some dozen industrial and domestic structures and appurtenances open for visitation. Dams and mill races, powder mills and textile buildings, and the du Pont family complex-home, office, barn, workshop, and gardens, were all restored with the idea of concretely illustrating, in microcosm, the story of the nation's industrial development.

Despite its relatively extensive acreage, the museum properties were confined to a narrow strip extending for about a mile on the banks of the Brandywine River and separated by steep hills, so an early decision was made to ban automobiles. Consequently, trips through the museum complex are provided by buses with appropriate stops where visitors disembark and proceed on foot. Interpretive signs and previously distributed guide books aid them in charting and comprehending earlier and now almost forgotten manufacturing processes. By 1977 more than two million visitors had toured the museum property, for which no admission fee was charged. In that year, however, it became necessary to charge a small admission fee, and there was an approximately 25 percent fall-off in the number of visitors for that year. Since then heightened publicity, new exhibitions, and rerouting of visitor traffic have combined to reverse this attendance drop.

The collecting of books, manuscripts, records, and archives for a research library for the study of American economic history had not figured in the founding and early operation of the foundation or the Hagley Museum. Yet the small library that the museum staff had amassed in the 1950s in support of its restoration projects was to be transformed into a library and, ultimately, research center for the study of the technological, industrial, and economic history of the mid-Atlantic region in particular and U.S. industrial development generally. The catalytic agent in this process was again the du Pont family.

Pierre Samuel du Pont de Nemours, founder of the du Pont family in the United States, brought his books and papers with him when he emigrated from France in 1800. In 1815 he returned to France and brought back more.

Various individuals in successive generations of the du Pont family kept the by then growing collection together. Prior to his death in 1954, Pierre S. du Pont had brought together almost all of this collection at his home in Longwood, Pennsylvania. In 1955, the Longwood Foundation, established by du Pont in 1937, implemented his plan for a library to care for the family collection by founding the Longwood Library. As in the parallel case of the Hagley Museum properties, the first years of the library's operation were taken up with the processing of the du Pont collection, although the acquisition of the Lukens Steel Company papers (1790-1890) and Northern Liberties Gas Company records (1839-1900) were harbingers of the program to follow. The decision to press forward in earnest with a well-rounded regional collection, however, dictated the removal of the Longwood Library, renamed the Eleutherian Mills Historical Library when it became an operating division of the foundation, to the foundation site on the Brandywine where a modern library building and administrative quarters could be constructed with easier access by scholars than was the case at the Longwood site. Also, the existence at the foundation of an organization whose museum facilities could uniquely tie in and complement the library contributed to the move there in 1961.

Commencing with almost 35,000 Longwood volumes and 3,000 from the Hagley Museum, plus the du Pont papers and other records, the Eleutherian Mills Historical Library holdings now stand at about 150,000 volumes, approximately 18 million manuscripts, plus about 270,000 pictorials and other materials, which together superbly trace and illustrate the growth of business and industry in the mid-Atlantic region. During this process, in addition to its continued acquisition of private papers and other materials, the library increasingly located and acquired the archives of mid-Atlantic businesses and industries. These included, for example, the archives of the Sun Oil Company, Alan Wood Steel Company, Poole Foundry and Machine Company, Union Canal Company, and First Pennsylvania Banking and Trust Company.

A measure of the success of the library's acquisition program was the establishment by the foundation in 1975 of its Regional Economic History Research Center. Working in close cooperation with the library and assisted by an academic advisory board consisting primarily of specialists in economic and technological history, the center embarked on an initial program that focused on the transition from the rural, agrarian society of the mid-Atlantic states to the early phases of an industrial society during the general chronological period 1750 to 1850. Following receipt of a grant from the National Endowment for the Humanities in 1976, the center inaugurated a variety of research fellowships for the utilization by scholars of center, library, museum, and foundation resources. At the same time the center continued its annual sponsorship of a number of scholarly conferences, colloquia, and lectures. Several volumes of *Working Papers* have been published, and in 1981 a joint undertaking was begun with the Johns

Hopkins University Press to issue a book series, Studies in Industry and Society, edited by center director Glenn Porter. The center has also engaged in a number of other projects, such as collaborating with the Hagley Museum in developing exhibits and mapping transportation systems in the mid-Atlantic region to 1860.

In 1962 the foundation appointed an advisory committee, which meets annually to review and evaluate the foundation's plans and projects for its twelve-member board of trustees. This committee has had a continuing influence on foundation affairs. For example, the inauguration of a publications program by the foundation was one of its first recommendations, and in 1967 a foundation director of publications was appointed. The relatively small publication program has since published a number of noteworthy items, including, for example, Carol Hoffecker, *Wilmington, Delaware: Portrait of an Industrial City* (1974), Richard L. Ehrlich, *Immigrants in American Industry* (1977), and *Water Power* (1979), by Louis C. Hunter, the first of a projected three-volume history of industrial power in the United States from 1780 to 1930.

The Tax Reform Act of 1969 imposed certain handicaps upon private operating foundations, including a four percent excise tax on endowment income. As permitted under the law, the Eleutherian Mills-Hagley Foundation in 1974 filed for a change in its status to that of a public charity. Following Internal Revenue Service approval and a sixty-month probationary period, this new designation was approved in 1980. At the same time that the foundation began this process to change its status, the formation of the Hagley Associates was announced. Consisting of some six hundred members, this group has helped to strengthen the foundation's financial base as it moves into the 1980s. More recently a new category of corporate membership in the associates has been established.

For further information, see John Beverley Riggs, *A Guide to the Manuscripts in the Eleutherian Mills Historical Library* (1970); and Maureen Quimby, *Eleutherian Mills* (1974). There is no book-length history of the foundation. See also, the foundation *Newsletter*, published since 1972 and foundation *Annual Reports* 1972 to date. The *Annual Report* for 1972 contains a short history of the foundation from 1952 to 1972. The one for 1975 has a set of photographs together with an accompanying commentary on some twenty years of the Hagley Museum's restoration program.

ENTOMOLOGICAL SOCIETY OF AMERICA (ESA). Although preceded by many local entomological societies, the first one to be founded, in 1875, and operated on a national basis was the Entomological Club of the American Association for the Advancement of Science* (AAAS). This club was discontinued in 1891, however, because of the 1889 organization of the American Association of Economic Entomologists. The latter, which was first known as the Association of Official Economic Entomologists, originally restricted its membership to those in the U.S. and Canadian departments of agriculture and their experiment stations. When this restriction was dropped its membership expanded, and it began to hold meetings and engage in other activities. The forgoing developments, however, left those entomologists who were not primarily interested in the economic side of entomology bereft of an organization, and, in 1906 they organized the Entomological Society of America to meet their needs.

One of the ESA's first activities was the establishment, in 1908, of a journal, the *Annals of the Entomological Society of America*. In the same year, the American Association of Economic Entomologists, which up to that time did not have an official publication of its own, founded the *Journal of Economic Entomology*. There was always a close connection between the two societies, and they often held joint meetings. As a result, sentiment developed for a merger of the two, and finally, in 1953, the societies were combined into the ESA.

An important feature of the new organization was the sectional grouping that was developed under the 1953 constitution. These now include: Section A, Systematics, Morphology, and Evolution; Section B, Physiology, Biochemistry, and Toxicology; Section C, Ecology, Behavior, and Bionomics; Section D, Medical and Veterinary Entomology; Section E, Extension and Regulatory Entomology; and Section F, Crop Protection Entomology.

These sections cover the fields of interest of both predecessor organizations and combined with the geographical branches, discussed below, form the basis in the ESA for representation upon the governing board, control of its various publications, and the arrangement of annual meeting programs. The sections are so weighted as to reflect the predominating interests of the academic or economic-professional groups.

Geographical branches were organized by both predecessor societies. The ESA retained and expanded these branches, and the five present-day branch memberships include the United States, Canada, and Mexico. Their activities parallel those of the national society and provide a local and regional point of contact for all entomologists. Their political composition is similar to that of the sections in that officers in both are elected by the members.

In other words, the branches are coequal political entities with the sections. The branches provide a common rallying point for geographical groups. The sections provide a professional subject-matter grouping. Not all members are in sections, section membership being voluntary. All ESA members, except foreign ones, are automatically members of a branch. Both groups have representatives on all decision-making bodies, including the ESA's governing board. To summarize, the sections and branches are the organizational methods whereby the differing and yet related interests of these subject matter and geographical groups within the ESA have been balanced and protected.

One of the major accomplishments of the ESA and its predecessors has been the sponsorship of publications. In addition to the *Annals of the Entomological Society of America* and *Journal of Economic Entomology*, both of which were continued after the merger of the ESA and American Association of Economic Entomologists, a quarterly *Bulletin of the Entomological Society of America*, containing items of current and general interest to the members, was established in 1955. In 1972, a new journal entitled *Environmental Entomology* was launched. The society also publishes the Thomas Say Foundation Monographs; since 1955, it has cooperated in the distribution of the *Annual Review of Entomology*; in 1959 it inaugurated publication of the irregular Miscellaneous Publications to provide an outlet for articles of less than book length but more than twenty printed pages; in 1974 the biennial publication of the *Pesticide Handbook—Entoma* was begun, and in 1976 the biennial publication of the *Pesticide Index*. Also, a new publication, *Insecticide and Acaricide Tests*, was established in 1976.

Another major ESA activity has been the holding of annual meetings in most of the major cities of the United States. Initially, these meetings were held in conjunction with those of other groups, such as the AAAS. Since 1953, each branch and the ESA have conducted independent annual meetings.

In the ESA, the ratio of applied entomologists to those with a more academic interest is approximately sixty to forty. There are three classes of membership: active, all persons engaged in or having training or interest in entomology and approved by the governing board; honorary or distinguished, member entomologists who must be nominated and elected, limited in number to 1 percent of the membership; and student. In December, 1970, the ESA formed the American Registry of Professional Entomologists (ARPE) to provide a certificate process for the membership. Entry on the registry is through examination, education, and experience. The total ESA membership is presently about eight thousand.

The ESA elects the customary institutional officers; it conducts its business from an office, headed by an executive director located in College Park, Maryland.

For further information, see L. O. Howard, *A History of Applied Entomology* (1930); and Herbert Osborn, *Fragments of Entomological History* (1937). See also Clarence E. Mickel, "The Entomological Society of America," *AAAS Bulletin* (June, 1943); E. G. Linsley, "Consolidation of the Entomological Society of America and the American Association of Economic Entomologists," *Annals of the Entomological Society of America* (June, 1952); "Preface," *Annual Review of Entomology* (1959); and the ESA *Information Pamphlet* (1976).

_F_

FAR EASTERN ASSOCIATION. See Association for Asian Studies.

FEDERATION OF AMERICAN SOCIETIES FOR EXPERIMENTAL BIOLOGY (FASEB). This organization was formed in 1912 by delegates from the American Physiological Society* (APS), founded in 1887; the American Society of Biological Chemists* (ASBC), founded in 1906; and the American Society for Pharmacology and Experimental Therapeutics* (ASPET), founded in 1908. The American Society for Experimental Pathology* (ASEP), founded in 1913, now American Association of Pathologists, Inc.* (AAP), joined the federation in 1914. Since that time two other societies have been admitted to membership in FASEB. The American Institute of Nutrition* (AIN), founded in 1928, joined the federation in 1940, and the American Association of Immunologists* (AAI), founded in 1913, joined the federation in 1942.

The purposes of the federation, as set forth in its constitution, are:

To bring together investigators in biological and medical sciences represented by the member Societies; to disseminate information on the results of biological research through publications and scientific meetings; and to serve in other capacities in which the member Societies can function more efficiently as a group than as individual units.

Administratively, FASEB was originally a loosely knit organization with executive functions vested in an executive committee composed of the president and secretary of each member society. It was found at an early date, however, that one person could best handle the logistics of the meetings, and, until 1946, this task was performed by Dr. D. R. Hooker. In 1947 a new full-time position, executive officer, was created, and programming and other functions were assigned that officer. Dr. Milton O. Lee, then editor of the _American Journal of Physiology_, was named the first executive officer, a position which he held until his retirement in 1965. His successors were Dr. J. F. A. McManus, 1965-1970; Dr. E. L. Hess, 1971-1979; and the incumbent Dr. Robert W. Krauss, since 1979.

The constitution and bylaws, adopted in 1952, provided for a governing board composed of three delegates from each of the six member societies. Since 1965, an executive committee, formerly advisory committee, consisting of one member of the board from each society, has also functioned. A veto provision of this almost thirty-year-old constitution proved an increasing problem for FASEB, as it allowed a single society to block any new proposal made to the board and is generally conceded to be the reason why there has been no expansion in the number of member societies since 1942. Changes in the constitution and bylaws were adopted January 31, 1980, abolishing the veto power, and thus, making more probable future expansion of the federation membership.

Despite the constitutional obstacle to external growth, FASEB has had remarkable internal growth. Statistics on the annual meetings provide a dramatic illustration. There was an attendance of 242 at the 1923 meeting. This had increased to about 2,500 by the 1946 meeting, and over half of those in attendance that year were not members of any constituent society. In 1973, out of a total registered attendance of about 21,000 more than two-thirds were nonmembers. Approximately 450 sessions were scheduled at the 1973 meeting in which about 4,500 papers were presented; the 1979 meeting saw 6,600 papers presented at approximately 550 sessions. By the late 1970s, too, the number of scientific exhibits displayed had grown from a dozen or so to a total of about 450 requiring over seven hundred display booths.

For a lack of a permanent staff, meeting sites during the early years were chosen proximate to major universities to permit handling of arrangements by local committees. Later on arrangements were handled by Dr. Milton O. Lee, and in 1953 a permanent separate Convention Office was established. The Convention Office was redesignated the Office of Scientific Meetings in 1968. In addition to the FASEB annual meeting, the Office of Scientific Meetings manages the meetings of individual constituent societies. The Office of Scientific Meetings also manages a growing number of meetings sponsored by nonmember organizations with interests allied to those of the FASEB societies. In 1981 the federation instituted a new thematic meeting component to the FASEB annual meeting. The Placement Service, operating under the auspices of the Office of Scientific Meetings, acts as a clearinghouse for information between employers and individuals seeking positions in the disciplines represented by the federation societies. The Placement Office also manages interviewing facilities for meetings of several other societies.

Scientific publication has been an important function of FASEB since the establishment of the then quarterly *Federation Proceedings* in 1942. In 1962 this was changed to a bimonthly and in 1973 to a monthly journal. At present, it publishes primarily symposia from FASEB and society meetings, as well as abstracts of FASEB and society meetings. In addition, the FASEB Office of Publications is responsible for a membership *Directory* and redactory services for other organizations. The FASEB *Directory* is a separate annual publication that includes society and geographic membership listings.

Since World War II, FASEB has increasingly contracted to provide information and advice to various agencies of the federal government. The year 1962 witnessed the creation within FASEB of the Life Sciences Research Office (LSRO) established as a unit of the federation to analyze specific problems in biology and medicine confronting research program administrators in federal agencies. The office furnishes expert evaluation of scientific issues through a mechanism involving ad hoc review of the study topic by qualified scientists who are actively engaged in research. Documented reports are prepared that provide scientific and technological assessment of the subject, identify new research opportunities, incorporate a comprehensive and critical literature review, and reflect the opinions of knowledgeable scientists who participate in the ad hoc review. Emphasis is placed on evolving a factual basis for subsequent administrative decisions by the sponsors. By 1979, LSRO had produced-fifty-five reports for several different governmental agencies.

The 1960s also saw the creation of the Office of Public Affairs, which provides constituent societies and their members with information about legislative and executive acts affecting the biomedical community and keeps governmental agencies informed as to the latter's attitude and position on scientific questions. The office recently named its sixth congressional science fellow. The Congressional Science Fellow Program was started as a public service to foster cross-education between Congress and the scientific community. The chosen fellow spends a year working on the staff of a member of a congressional committee, and upon completion of the tour becomes a member-at-large on the FASEB Public Affairs Committee. The federation's Public Information Program also falls under the auspices of the Office of Public Affairs. There are two main components. The FASEB Feature Service provides lay-language translations of research reports in usable form for mass media representatives. The Public Information Committee screens abstracts to determine which have a combination of scientific worth and potential news value. Summaries are made available to the press in the form of press releases, and the investigators whose work is the subject of a press release may be scheduled to meet with the press to discuss his work.

All of the forgoing activities are now carried on from the 11.2-acre Beaumont campus, which was purchased by FASEB in 1954. Named for the distinguished American physician and pioneer physiologist, William Beaumont (1785-1853), the campus is part of an old estate with beautiful grounds and furnishes a pleasant yet functional setting for FASEB activities. The Beaumont campus centers around a stone mansion, the main structure of the old estate; the Milton O. Lee Building, constructed in phases from 1962 to 1967; and several smaller buildings. This headquarters for FASEB is located at 9650 Rockville Pike, Bethesda, Maryland 20014.

For further information, see FASEB publications discussed above, particularly *Federation Proceedings*. There is no definitive history of FASEB. See also an *Information Pamphlet*, published by FASEB.

FIELD COLUMBIAN MUSEUM. See Field Museum of Natural History.

FIELD MUSEUM OF NATURAL HISTORY (FMNH). Within its short history the FMNH has attained a distinguished position among the natural history museums of the world, and it now occupies perhaps the largest and finest of all museum buildings. It is a nonprofit institution, supported largely by private funds. This museum, like other great museums, is concerned with the accumulation and preservation of specimens of natural history for exhibition and research. The scope includes anthropology, botany, geology, and zoology. The museum was primarily an outgrowth of the World's Columbian Exposition held in Chicago in 1893.

An important aspect was the material assembled for the Exposition, which was too important to be dispersed and provided a core for the new museum. A committee was formed early in 1893 "to adopt measures to establish in Chicago a great museum that shall be a fitting memorial to the World's Columbian Exposition." On September 16, 1893, a charter for the Columbian Museum of Chicago was granted, and various exhibitors transferred their exhibits to the museum. In 1893 Marshall Field contributed one million dollars for the establishment of the museum. This was followed by other contributions, which together with donations of exposition stock totaled one and a half million dollars by the end of 1894. On January 22, 1894 the board of trustees of the museum was formed and selected a president and a director. The Palace of Fine Arts of the exposition became the first location of the museum. Various experts with museum training from other institutions were called in to assist, and most became the first departmental chairmen. On May 21, 1894, the trustees voted to change the name to "Field Columbian Museum," in recognition of the founding of the museum by Marshall Field. In 1905 the name was changed to "Field Museum of Natural History." The museum was opened to the public on June 2, 1894; the main lines of future activities were established, and departmental heads were named.

The need for a permanent building for the museum was fully recognized by Marshall Field, and by the terms of his will he left four million dollars for the construction of a new building and an additional four million dollars for the endowment of the institution. After much controversy and legal battles, the present site in an area south of Grant Park was finally selected and approved. The cornerstone was laid on September 28, 1917, and the doors to the new museum were opened on May 2, 1921.

In 1922 an era of extensive expeditions was inaugurated. Some eight expeditions to South Africa were carried on during 1922. The paleontological expedition to Argentina lasted nearly three years and then, after a gap, continued until 1927. Geological expeditions to Brazil were also in two installments. One of the zoological expeditions remained in Chile and Peru until 1923, and another continued until 1924. Archaeological investigations in Colombia were conducted for nearly two years. Botanical explorations were mainly devoted to Peru and British Guiana. There were ethnological studies in Malaysia during 1922-1923, and, in cooperation with Oxford University, excavations were carried out at the ancient city of Kish, Mesopotamia, in 1922. Other expeditions were to China in 1923 and to central Africa from 1923 to 1926, in cooperation with the American Museum of Natural History* (AMNH). From 1924 to 1930 a new set of expeditions was begun, particularly to the equatorial and Arctic zones. Expeditions were led by Colonel Theodore Roosevelt and his brother Kermit Roosevelt in 1925 and again in 1928. They explored southern Asia, where they collected zoological material, southern China, and little-known parts of French Indochina. In 1926 expeditions to Labrador, Greenland, and Baffinland brought much zoological material, ethnological material of the Naskopi Indians, and geological specimens from Baffinland. It is impossible to list all the expeditions; suffice it to say that the active explorations were carried out up to the time of the Great Depression. After World War II field activities continued, but the nature of the expeditions changed. The earlier expeditions were widespread with broad interests and limited selectivity, which is understandable because the museum was young and had many gaps to fill. Now the collecting does not emphasize collecting as such. It is, instead, interested in obtaining information directed at some particular aspect or problem. Due to political and economic realities in a changing world, the focus of field work has shifted to an increased emphasis on problem-oriented fieldwork and on obtaining data rather than artifacts. Building great collections has been a sustained goal of the FMNH for more than eighty years, and the collections have grown until they now number more than twelve million specimens. These collections represent major stages in the history of the Earth and of human societies and are concerned with the composition and evolution of the Earth, its nearest neighbors, and all forms of life, past and present, nonhuman and human.

Two names stand out in the history of the FMNH: One, the founder Marshall Field; the other, E. Leland Webber, who served as director from 1962 to 1976, as president and director from 1976 to 1980, and as president since

1980. Webber directed all his energy to an unparalleled broadening and strengthening of the museum programs in exhibition, education, collection maintenance, and research. This he accomplished by a radical increase of income.

In the early 1960s the collection of fossils of the University of Chicago, among the finest university collections in existence, was transferred to the FMNH. In order to house this wealth of material the museum secured a grant of $875,200 from the National Science Foundation. This appropriation, one of the largest federal grants ever made to a privately endowed museum, initiated all natural history museums into a new era of growth and expansion with the help of federal funds. The money was used to construct the first major addition to the museum's physical facilities since the completion of the building in 1921. In the following years this was augmented by additional NSF grants and other money to enlarge further the space and facilities of other departments. The 1971 capital campaign to match $12.5 million provided by the state legislature was successful and permitted a considerable renovation of the building and the construction of new facilities for collections and research. All museum collections are now housed in modern storage areas.

It is difficult to give a brief history of the scientific contributions of the museum. Research by its own scientists or research associates based on study of the great collections is published in 225 volumes of four series of Fieldiana—anthropology, botany, geology, and zoology—and unknown numbers of scientific articles and books. For example, in 1978-1979, the staff of geology alone published over seventy-five scientific papers including three books. Each of the four scientific departments has had a different historical pattern of research development and emphasis. Anthropology has focused on selected areas of primitive cultures and high civilizations of the past. Botany specializes on the vascular plants of Latin America. Geology's main research interest was and is in paleontology, and zoology developed active research programs in several taxonomic groups.

The renowned Franz Boas—who had worked for Frederic Ward Putnam in gathering materials for the exposition—became the first curator of anthropology at FMNH. At the end of 1894 Boas had already published 185 articles and was on his way to becoming one of the world's greatest anthropologists and a generally acknowledged founder of the field. Boas was succeeded in 1894 by William H. Holmes, an archaeologist, who undertook important pioneering excavations in Yucatan and elsewhere in southern Mexico in the context of an interdisciplinary botanical-archaeological expedition. His work resulted in the addition of Maya, Aztec, and Teotihuacan artifacts to the museum's collections. While at the Museum he published his famous work on the Maya civilization in the first two volumes of Fieldiana: Anthropology. The Museum has remained active in Latin American archaeology since Holmes's day. George A. Dorsey, another of Putnam's former assistants, followed Holmes in 1896 and remained as chief curator until 1915. His administration saw a sharp increase in funds and staff available for fieldwork and the evolution of a carefully articulated methodology for collecting objects. Under Dorsey's tenure monographs of the Tinguian, Philippine, and Melanesian tribes were published. Berthold Laufer succeeded Dorsey and remained chief curator until his death in 1934. Laufer became the most distinguished American Sinologist and wrote extensively on ancient jades, pottery, and plant distribution. More than 250 publications include 150 books and monographs, of which his *Jade: A Study in Chinese Archaeology and Religion*, and *Sino-Iranica: Chinese Contributions to the History of Ancient Civilizations in Iran* are most influential. Paul S. Martin became chairman in 1934 and stayed in that post for the next thirty years. American anthropology was born in the museums, and all the leaders of the field until the time of Martin were museum men. With the aid of National Science Foundation and other grants Martin developed a close relationship with many universities and trained about fifty individuals in professional archaeology. Martin published enormous amounts of work, 150 popular articles alone! His main contributions were, in the study of archaeology of the Southwest. A system of rotating chairmen was instituted after Martin's retirement. Donald Collier, James VanStone, and Phillip Lewis have each occupied the chairmanship for several years during the past decade and a half. Lewis and Bennet Bronson are currently cochairmen. Collier was probably the only undergraduate student whose research paper (on peyote and the Indian peyote religion, in 1932) became a part of the Congressional Record. James VanStone, who became a chairman after Collier in 1971, publishes extensively on the peoples of the Arctic and sub-Arctic regions of North America, and on the early Russian and American activities along the West Coast of North America.

The work of museum botanists has always been associated with problems of naming and classifying plants. This work falls into two general headings: studies of specific taxonomic groups resulting in monographs or revisions; and studies of particular geographic regions resulting in floristic accounts. Botany at Field Museum has tended to emphasize the latter. These floras, like dictionaries and encyclopedias, perform an important service as primary access routes to information about the natural environment. Botanical work at Field Museum has concentrated on the American tropics. C. F. Millspaugh began the pattern with his studies of the Yucatan peninsula, the Bahamas, and Bermuda. J. F. Macbride initiated the monumental *Flora of Peru*, now nearing completion with over seven thousand pages already published. P. C. Standley worked on the floras of Belize, Honduras, and Costa Rica and began the flora of Guatemala. The Guatamalan project, another encyclopedia-like endeavor of sixty-five hundred pages, was completed by L. O. Williams and his associates. The detailed and definitive *Flora of Missouri* was written by J. A. Steyermark while at the FMNH.

Floristic work continues with efforts to complete the *Flora of Peru*, an ongoing international program with Mexico on the vegetation and flora of Veracruz under the leadership of L. I. Nevling, Jr., who in 1980 became director of the museum, and the initiation of a detailed study of flora of Costa Rica by William C. Burger. Monographs and revisions have also been an important part of the Botany Department's output. The more important examples include Standley's work on the family Rubiaceae, B. E. Dahlgren's survey of the Palm family, and F. Drouet's studies of myxophycean algae.

The first chief curator of geology was Oliver C. Farrington, who published over one hundred papers in mineralogy, with particular emphasis on meteorites. He built these collections into worldwide importance, and today the department's meteorite collection is virtually without peer. Henry W. Nichols, a mineralogist, became the second chief curator, followed by Sharat K. Roy. Bryan Patterson, on the staff from 1926 to 1955, published on one of the first significant Paleocene fossil vertebrate faunas. His publication on the Mesozoic metatherian-eutherian grade mammals from North Texas is now a classic. Rainer Zangerl became head of the department in 1962 after serving seventeen years as curator of fossil reptiles. His main areas of research are the lower vertebrates: he has published extensively on fossil turtles and chondrichthyian fishes. Zangerl extended his interests to Pennsylvanian paleoecology, and his now classic memoir on the paleoecology of Pennsylvanian black shale was coauthored with Eugene Richardson. Zangerl presided over the First North American Paleontological Convention held at the Field Museum in 1969. Zangerl was succeeded by Edward J. Olsen in 1974, an authority on meteorites, who received a National Science Foundation medal for his work in Antarctica. David M. Raup joined the museum as chairman in 1978. Raup's contributions to paleontology have been recognized by his election to the National Academy of Sciences. His work concerning crystallography as it relates to life, computer-based paleobiometrics, and modeling in paleontology has clearly established him as a major figure in evolutionary biology and paleontology. During the last few years Raup has vigorously and with vision tackled fundamental and difficult problems of the geological record and the diversity of life. In 1980 Raup was appointed dean of science at FMNH.

At the founding of FMNH a Department of Zoology was contemplated that would include all animal life, for which the divisions of Ornithology, Mammalogy, Herpetology, Ichthyology, Entomology, Conchology and Osteology were set up. However, when it was possible to acquire the nineteen thousand-specimen bird collection of Charles B. Cory in exchange for creating a Department of Ornithology with Cory as curator, that step was taken, and the two departments were formed together, one as Department of Ornithology, the other with the cumbersome title of Department of Zoology, Except Ornithology. This name it bore for twelve years until in 1906 ornithology was returned to the fold as a division.

During the early years of the department, the staff consisted of the curator, D. G. Elliott, an eminent ornithologist and mammalogist, and as many assistants as he could wangle. The first two, O. P. Hay and S. E. Meek, serving consecutively, were both ichthyologists, but Meek was noted in one annual report as relabeling the shell collection. The first person to receive a formal appointment in a given division was W. J. Gerhard, who was made assistant curator for entomology in 1900; his tenure had spanned half a century when he retired in 1950. In the meantime, the Department of Ornithology was developing under Cory and his assistant curators, G. K. Cherrie and N. Dearborn. In 1906 Ornithology was brought back into Zoology. Elliott resigned to return to the American Museum of Natural History* (AMNH) in New York. At that time the wealthy Cory lost his fortune and was forced to seek a paying job. The problem was resolved by uniting the departments and making Cory curator of zoology, where he was extremely productive, publishing books on the birds and mammals of Wisconsin and Illinois and starting publication of the *Catalogue of the Birds of the Americas*, eventually completed in eleven parts, and comprised of fifteen volumes. During his tenure most of the divisions received their own or a shared assistant curator. E. N. Gueret took over Osteology in 1906; W. H. Osgood, Mammalogy and Ornithology in 1909; and Carl Hubbs, briefly Ichthyology and Herpetology in 1916, to be succeeded by A. C. Weed in 1920. During Osgood's thirty-two years at the museum, he became the leading authority on Neotropical mammals, but his interests were worldwide and he also collected and published on mammals of Africa and Indochina. On the death of Cory in 1921, there was considerable change and expansion with dual appointments being ended. Osgood was made curator, and he was replaced in Birds by J. T. Zimmer and in mammals by E. Heller. Weed was restricted to Fishes and was replaced the following year in Reptiles and Amphibians by K. P. Schmidt. Schmidt was not only a first-rate herpetologist but a world-renowned ecologist. His influence extended well beyond his published works, for he was devoted to young students and inspired many to adopt careers in science. Upon his retirement in 1955, he was elected to the National Academy of Sciences, the first member of the museum staff to be so honored. In 1922 came the appointment of the first associate curator, C. E. Hellmayr in the Division of Birds, who was hired to complete the *Catalogue of Birds of the Americas* that had just been started by Cory. Hellmayr was at that time the preeminent student of Neotropical birds, and he brought with him a first-hand knowledge of European collections and of the types of Neotropical birds that was unsurpassed. Although he returned to Europe in 1931, he remained on the staff and continued to submit manuscripts for the catalogue. He was forced to flee Austria to Switzerland when Germany invaded, but he continued his work as best he could, and the four volumes were completed in collaboration with Boardman Conover, research associate in the division. Conover, a wealthy young sportsman from Chicago, had been guided into scientific ornithology by Osgood, starting in 1920, and had formed a superb collection of game birds of his own, housed in the museum and eventually becoming part of the museum's collections. The completed catalog, the joint product of Cory, Hellmayr, and Conover between 1918 and 1949, is still the basic taxonomic text for the New World birds. In 1938 the final division received its own curator when Fritz Haas, another Hitler refugee, was appointed in Lower Invertebrates (originally Conchology). Haas was a world-renowned authority on fresh water clams, and he maintained a prodigious productivity during his years at Field Museum. By the late 1940s the form and size of the department were pretty much what they are today. The only basic change since the war occurred in 1970, when the position of chief curator was placed on a rotating basis and its title changed to chairman.

The present is but the first step in the museum's future development. Since its conception the research of the museum scientists (consisting of forty-two Ph.D.'s) ranged from intensive coverage of a geographic area, biotic groups, or single cultures to extensive coverage of a world biota or a broad culture area. The museum's commitment to the future is a better understanding of the impact of scientific discovery upon our civilization and a need for more knowledge of man and his world. The FMNH accepts its obligation to serve this need.

For further information, see Oliver C. Farrington, "A Brief History of Field Museum from 1892 to 1930," *Field Museum News* (January 1930-May 1931); Chesly Manley, *One Billion Years at Our Doorstep* (1956); Donald Collier, "Men and Their Work," *Field Museum Bulletin* (September, 1972); Matthew H. Nitecki, "Featured Institution—Field Museum of Natural History," *Newsletter* (October, 1980); and Alan Solem, "A Curatorial Legacy," *Field Museum Bulletin* (January, 1981).

MATTHEW H. NITECKI

FOLGER SHAKESPEARE LIBRARY. The creation of the Folger Shakespeare Library in Washington, D.C., was a reflection of the personality and tastes of the founder, Henry Clay Folger, sometime president and later chairman of the board of the Standard Oil Company of New York. As a student at Amherst College he had developed an abiding interest in English literature, especially the works of William Shakespeare, and, when he acquired sufficient income to so permit, he became a book collector. Ultimately he began to think of founding a library that would house his collections and provide a research facility where scholars might concentrate on Shakespeare and his time. In the years that followed, the Folger Shakespeare Library vastly broadened its activities and became one of the nation's most important resources for the study of Tudor and Stuart literature and history.

Folger was born in New York City on June 18, 1857, the son of a wholesale milliner. His ancestor was Peter Folger of Martha's Vineyard and Nantucket, maternal grandfather of Benjamin Franklin. After attending Adelphi Academy in Brooklyn, young Henry Clay Folger entered Amherst College. A classmate was Charles M. Pratt, son of one of John D. Rockefeller's associates in the Standard Oil Company. The friendship of the two boys was important, for when they finished college, in the class of 1879, Pratt's father found jobs for both of them in Standard Oil. There Folger made the modest fortune that enabled him to establish his library.

In 1885, Folger married Emily C. Jordan, a graduate of Vassar College who shared his interest in book collecting—and in Shakespeare. With her help he assembled the collection, which he kept in safe storage until a library could be built.

Folger decided that Washington D.C., would inevitably become an important research center, and he quietly bought up property on the corner of East Capitol and Second streets. There he began to erect a white marble building designed by Paul Cret, which was completed in 1930. Two weeks before Folger died on June 11, 1930, the cornerstone of the library was laid, and it was formally opened in 1932.

Under Folger's will, the management of his endowment was left to the trustees of Amherst College, with a provision that the income should be used in perpetuity for the maintenance of the Folger Shakespeare Library. A substantial proportion of the income from his estate he left to Amherst in compensation for the trustees' management of the trust. Mrs. Folger survived her husband for six years and took a personal interest in the development of the library. At her death, she left the bulk of her fortune to the library.

Folger took intense interest in the erection of the library building and provided the architect and the contractor with detailed instructions. Although the plans called for a small replica of a typical theater of Shakespeare's period, it did not attempt to reproduce any particular Elizabethan playhouse. Nor did Folger intend for it to be used for the performance of plays. In a letter dated May 20, 1929, to the consulting architect, Alexander B. Trowbridge, Folger specifically stated, "We must keep in mind that our enterprise is, first of all, a Library, and while there are other features which we hope will be interesting to the public, that of the 'Library' is all important." Again, in letters to Paul Cret, he repeated his injunction to remember that "our enterprise is primarily a Library and all other features are supplemental." In reply to an inquiry from Cret as to whether the replica of an Elizabethan theater should be "fitted for Moving Pictures," Folger replied, "No. The Theatre is to show the conditions under which the Elizabethan plays were presented, primarily, and any other use by us will be supplemental." It was Folger's intention for the theater to be an exhibition and not an active playhouse. The most use he conceived for it was for academic lectures and perhaps an occasional musical program. He insisted that the space allotted to the theater not encroach on the library. Consequently the maximum capacity was limited to 250 seats. Since the 1970s, however, the operations of the Folger Library have been expanded to encompass other cultural activities, including play performances in the theater.

The Folger Shakespeare Library opened its doors in 1932. The first two years were devoted to transforming an inchoate collection into an operating library. The most significant event of 1934 was the appointment of Joseph Q. Adams, a distinguished professor of English at Cornell University, as director, a position he held until his death on November 10, 1946. Stanley King, elected president of Amherst College in 1932, served as liaison officer between the Folger Library and the college's managerial board of trustees. He worked closely and sympathetically with Adams and has left a record of the early days in a charming essay, *Recollections of the Folger Shakespeare Library*, published as a small monograph in 1950.

The collections that Folger bequeathed to the library were not confined strictly to Shakespeariana, for he realized that Shakespeare could not be studied in a vacuum. Already before his death he added the nucleus of a general Tudor and Stuart library of historical works. But Folger's obsession with the collection of copies of the first folio of 1623 and of subsequent folio editions of Shakespeare's plays resulted in distorted journalistic accounts of the library and earned for Folger a certain amount of unfair criticism as a "miser of books." Actually, his accumulation of early editions had a serious bibliographical purpose.

As director, Adams decided that his most important duty was the acquisition of rare books that might never be available again. He became a shrewd and discriminating searcher for Tudor and Stuart books, and the wisdom of his decision was amply proved, for during his lifetime opportunities arose that will never be repeated.

In 1938 the Folger Library managed to acquire one of the largest collections of Tudor and Stuart books remaining in private hands, the library of Sir Leicester Harmsworth, the English publisher. Folger had concerned himself chiefly with belles lettres. Harmsworth was interested primarily in the history of all aspects of culture. The purchase of his collection completely transformed the focus of the Folger Shakespeare Library. Overnight it changed from an institution centered upon Elizabethan literature as such to a research library containing material for the investigation of the entire conspectus of sixteenth- and seventeenth-century life. The story of the negotiations that enabled the Folger to procure the Harmsworth books is related with some humor in Stanley King's monograph.

During the next few years, Adams was able to procure further additions from Harmsworth's estate, both rare books and manuscripts. He also purchased the Dobell Collection of John Dryden, which strengthened the later seventeenth-century material in the library.

After Adams's death, the trustees of Amherst College decided that the time had come to broaden the activities of the Folger Library and to emphasize its utility to the scholarly profession. Adams's concentration upon the search for rare books and manuscripts had left him little time to organize the library into an efficient working institution for scholars.

In March, 1947, Charles W. Cole, then president of Amherst, made a visit to the Huntington Library* in San Marino, California. The Huntington's reputation as an active research institution had attracted widespread publicity on both sides of the Atlantic, and Cole had been advised to consult Louis B. Wright, then a member of the research group at the Huntington and chairman of its fellowship committee. His duties had resulted in contacts with many scholars in the United States and abroad. Cole sought his advice about possible candidates for director of the Folger Library. Cole also outlined a variety of problems that the Folger faced and discussed means of correcting them.

Wright provided the president of Amherst with a list of names of possible candidates for the post and described the methods that the Huntington Library had employed in transforming a ducal private collection into an efficient research library. It had deliberately set out to encourage active and promising scholars to utilize its materials and had established a publication program. A part of the Huntington's income was devoted to subsidizing visiting scholars and research fellows in a variety of fields. To a discreet inquiry as to whether Wright might be interested in being considered for the directorship of the Folger, he emphatically ruled himself out. His situation at the Huntington made a move unthinkable.

Cole made notes and returned to Amherst. Later, in the summer, Eustace Seligman, a member of the legal firm of Sullivan and Cromwell and chairman of the Amherst trustee committee for the Folger Library, asked Wright if he would serve as consultant to the board of trustees and would come to a meeting of the board in New York City. At this meeting, Wright outlined a formidable list of improvements that the Folger required and suggested that the board seek someone who would be willing to implement such a program. Before the meeting was ended, the chairman called Wright back and asked: "If we agreed to all of your suggestions, would you be willing to accept the directorship?"

Wright has described his surprise and later agony of decision in an autobiographical volume, *Of Books and Men* (1976). He had no desire to leave the Huntington and move East, but after pondering the problem for a month he wired Cole his acceptance. He later asserted that the strongest influence on his decision was his highly favorable opinion of Cole and Seligman as well as other members of the board of trustees of Amherst College. Wright was to remain at the Folger for the next twenty years carrying out the program that the trustees had approved and adopted.

Much had to be done to make an efficient institution. Folger had believed that a reference collection would be unnecessary because the Library of Congress was accessible across the street. That of course proved impractical, and an effective reference collection had to be acquired. Folger books had been classified under an absurd system based on the name *William Shakespeare* invented by an eccentric member of the staff. Quickly a reclassification of books under the Library of Congress system was undertaken. The acquisition of scholarly books was accelerated to strengthen the Folger's sources for the study of Tudor and Stuart history. By 1968 the Folger had more than trebled the original collection of books and manuscripts, at least half of the new acquisitions classified as rare or scarce. To accomplish this, Wright brought from the Huntington Library an expert book buyer, Eleanor Pitcher, who maintained a residence in England for approximately half of each year and diligently searched rare bookshops throughout Western Europe.

The Folger Library established a visiting scholar and fellowship program and invited to its reading rooms eminent Tudor and Stuart scholars from this country and abroad. New publications included Folger Documents of Tudor and Stuart Civilization and a series designed for a more popular audience, Folger Booklets on Tudor and Stuart Civilization.

During this period the Folger added a new wing, designed by Paul Cret's original architectural firm, that increased both stack space and offices and conference rooms. The Amherst trustees also authorized the purchase of a block of buildings on Third Street, opposite the original Folger building, for eventual expansion when necessary.

In 1968 Wright retired as director and was succeeded by O. B. Hardison, an English professor from the University of North Carolina. The president of Amherst at the time, Calvin H. Plimpton, believed that a change in Folger activities would increase its popular appeal, especially in the local community. Subsequently the Folger Library organized a dramatic company and began offering plays, most of them modern and "experimental," in the little theater. It expanded its other activities to include poetry readings by local amateurs as well as more professional authors, lectures on a wider variety of subjects, and more extensive musical programs. The library also appealed to corporations and the National Endowment for the Humanities to subsidize a traveling exhibit, "Shakespeare: The Globe and the World," which has been shown in several American cities. In the 1970s the Folger Library, like many other institutions, has been the recipient of substantial funds provided by the National Endowment for Humanities, various foundations, and a few private donors to foster its diverse programs.

After attempting to raise money to build an addition on its Third Street property, the Amherst trustees authorized a remodeling of the original Folger building, at a cost of several million dollars. The reading rooms were to be closed for an indefinite period while the interior was being altered and enlarged, although it was not found necessary to interrupt play performances. The Folger *Newsletter* for October, 1980, announced, "Reader services are now expected to resume March 2, 1981, two months later than previously had been planned."

For further information, see Joseph T. Foster, "Folger: Biggest Little Library in the World," *National Geographic Magazine* (September, 1951); Louis B. Wright, *The Folger Library: Two Decades of Growth* (1968) and *Of Books and Men* (1976); and Betty Ann Kane, *The Widening Circle— The Story of the Folger Shakespeare Library and Its Collections* (1976).

LOUIS B. WRIGHT

FOREIGN POLICY ASSOCIATION (FPA). The FPA had its origin in the disillusionment and frustration brought about by U.S. participation in World War I. Except for the terrible experiences of the "Great War," few Americans seemed interested in world affairs. Even as President Woodrow Wilson set off for Europe to win the "just peace" he had advocated in his Fourteen Points, no organized support group had arisen in the United States to mobilize public opinion for President Wilson's principles.

In April, 1918, Paul U. Kellogg, the editor of *Survey*, joined with eighteen like-minded publicists and academicians in New York to plan for the peace. This progressive group, calling itself the Committee on Nothing at All, viewed the war as a struggle for democracy and pledged to help Wilson realize a postwar world of open diplomacy, national self-determination, recognition of rights of colonial areas, and open door economic exchange. For the next six months this impromptu body worked to give liberal purpose to unformed public opinion.

In November, 1918, on the eve of the armistice, the committee and other intellectuals formally organized themselves into the League of Free Nations Association, with an initial membership of 141, including such distinguished Americans as Charles A. Beard, Mary Beard, John Dewey, James T. Shotwell, Felix Frankfurter, Judge Learned Hand, and Ida M. Tarbell. Initially, the association existed to promote a "universal and democratic" league of nations that would uphold peace by guaranteeing individual national security and equality of economic opportunity. Hardly pacifistic, these liberal-minded Americans accepted the necessity of collective force. Unabashed progressive nationalists, they praised the league idea as American in conception and saw the American experiment in government now poised at the threshold of worldwide success.

The statement of principles of the association stressed many elements of maturing liberal internationalism. It argued that the United States must take the lead in organizing a predictable world order that would preserve democracy and nationalism while avoiding the threat of socialist class war or reversion to great-power imperialism. The association favored "the establishment of some sort of international organization, some sort of league of free and self-determining nations, as a substitute for international anarchy and international hatred."

Confident in the American way, liberal proponents of some new international machinery to maintain the peace wanted to replace the widespread ignorance of world affairs with facts and correct principles. The League of Free Nations Association was convinced that international affairs were passing under democratic control, and it suggested the need to control the danger of unpredictable popular passions by cultivating an objective understanding of world politics among the public. As "absolutely requisite" to the development of sound American foreign policy, the association stressed a careful study of all sides of every international question affecting the United States to the end that the American people might understand fully what U.S. problems were and how they might be dealt with most effectually.

With a cause, ideology, and the support of leading liberals, the association began the search for members. It sponsored a series of luncheon discussions under the direction of prominent authorities in New York, and this practice quickly spread to other cities. National membership was soon boosted to a thousand by the middle of 1919, and contributions to the association reached twenty thousand dollars. Although the luncheon discussions were successful, they demonstrated the dependence of the organization upon cultivating the nation's urban liberal elite and the restrictive effect doing so had on the growth of the association. Such practices precluded successful drives for mass membership.

The final rejection of Woodrow Wilson's League of Nations by the Senate forced the League of Free Nations Association to shift its emphasis to the arena of citizen education in world affairs. In the early years of its existence, the association had sponsored several foreign policy studies outside its primary area of concern as advocate for the League of Nations. A succinct analysis of U.S.-Mexican relations and a documentary record of U.S. relations with the new Soviet regime were among these commissioned studies. They enjoyed immediate public acceptance. These endeavors led the association toward new nonpartisan goals and the renaming of the League of Free Nations Association to the Foreign Policy Association in 1921. The FPA, although still liberal in orientation, ceased its activities as advocate of any particular solution to international affairs and became a nonpartisan institution devoted exclusively to citizen education and research in world problems.

In its first decade the FPA emphasized research on foreign policy concerns and communicating the results to writers, editors, and educators. A News Bulletin, later the Foreign Policy Bulletin, was begun in 1921. In 1924 the Editorial Information Service, later known as Foreign Policy Reports, was initiated. The FPA also utilized the radio to discuss foreign affairs, first broadcasting the New York luncheon meeting and later presenting fifteen-minute weekly talks on "The World Today." Through these varied means the association summarized developments overseas and helped ensure coverage of foreign news in the American press. Relying on the mass media, the FPA succeeded in reminding Americans of foreign affairs.

Although the FPA promised to study all sides of every issue, liberal internationalists in the association favored American entry into the League of Nations, opposed U.S. interventionism in Latin America, and called for the restoration of normal relations with Russia and Germany. As early as 1921 the FPA worked for naval arms limitation.

As the tenth anniversary of the FPA approached in 1928, the association had a nationwide membership of nine thousand, branches in fourteen cities and an increasing number of international studies that broadened the nation's understanding of foreign policy. However, the homogeneity and the East Coast orientation of the FPA made it difficult for the internationalist membership to comprehend public attitudes on foreign affairs. They believed that they were converting the American people to a commitment to international cooperation; however, events of the 1920s often convinced them that the people were confirmed isolationists who would deny the United States the right to play a significant role in world developments. FPA members often failed to realize that the majority of Americans were neither intensely isolationist nor internationalist but simply uncertain about the growing complexity of foreign policy.

The depression decade of the 1930s ushered in a domestic crisis so severe that foreign policy issues paled by comparison. But the economic collapse fostered the rise of totalitarianism in Europe and Asia, and overseas events stimulated the FPA in 1935 to add the bimonthly *Headline Series* pamphlets to its list of regular publications. The association argued that foreign policy was inextricbly tied to national policy and that prosperity and internal stability at home depended upon knowledge and understanding of international developments. By 1938, membership in the FPA had reached seventeen thousand, and its services were in increasing demand.

The outbreak of World War II shattered American provincialism once and for all. During the war years the FPA devoted attention to problems in the occupied countries of Europe, the economic and political impact of total war in both hemispheres, the problems of postwar reconstruction, and building support for a new international organization. FPA members made well-publicized speaking tours in support of American leadership in establishing institutions to maintain peace. FPA membership peaked in 1946, with 32,800 members and an additional 8,000-10,000 subscribers and with local branches in Boston, Philadelphia, Saint Louis, San Francisco, and a number of other cities.

With U.S. membership in the United Nations assured, the postwar years were a time of innovation and change for the FPA. The onset of the Cold War and the attendant threat of nuclear annihilation generated a host of new publications and institutes dealing with foreign policy concerns. Improvements in mass media, principally television, dramatized to the American people crisis situations that heightened national insecurity. In this age of uncertainty the FPA goal of citizen education in foreign affairs shifted away from mobilization of urban intellectuals to an emphasis on reaching large numbers of citizens.

The attempt to reach the widest possible audience and to explain principal alternatives for U.S. foreign policy meant the retrenchment of some established FPA programs along with expansion in new directions. Because the mass media increased its dissemination of news and analysis of foreign policy problems, the FPA discontinued its *Foreign Policy Reports* in 1951, the Speakers Bureau in 1960, and the *Foreign Policy Bulletin* in 1961. The FPA broadened its scope, however, by establishing five regional offices in other cities in 1952, and developing a World Affairs Center at the national headquarters in New York in 1956. It gave up general membership, allotting the over twenty thousand members to local branches. The branches were asked to function as independent community groups using the name "World Affairs Council." The FPA regional staff devoted themselves during this period to organizing and aiding community World Affairs Councils, of which there are now about seventy in principal cities across the country. Perhaps the most imaginative innovation to increase foreign affairs awareness was the Great Decisions program, first tried in a pilot project in 1955. Presently an annual, nationwide program, it brings together interested citizens who are provided factual background material on foreign policy issues for discussion. To help publicize and coordinate programs, the FPA utilized community organization, education institutions, and mass media.

Beginning in 1965, the FPA initiated a national effort to improve the teaching of international affairs in the nation's school systems. This attempt to broaden its prior adult-oriented emphasis was aided by a major foundation grant. The associaton maintained a staff of school service experts in its regional offices as well as the New York headquarters to provide information and assistance to teachers and for curriculum development. To support its youth education program, the FPA sponsored a series of publications to assist in classroom instruction and a nationwide workshop program for educators. This program of special services to schools was terminated in 1971, when grant funds were no longer available.

Although the FPA ceased to be a general membership organization in 1957, it has developed into an institution that influences the lives of millions of Americans. Because much of the association's present work is developed through the mass media or in cooperation with other organizations, it is difficult to measure the total impact of the FPA on the formulation of American public opinion. However, by utilizing the Great Decisions program only, the following figures may serve as a rough guide to the reach of the FPA. Some 150,000 students and adults gather once a week each, largely in February and March, for the association's Great Decisions program; an additional 4 million to 6 million listeners follow Great Decisions discussions on National Public Radio, and about the same number watch the Great Decisions television series on the educational television network. It is estimated that 1.5 million Americans read background articles on Great

Decisions topics written for client newspapers each year by United Press International and the Christian Science Monitor News Service in cooperation with the FPA.

During the tumultuous 1960s, the association had approximately 125 employees but now operates with about 25 employees on an annual budget in excess of one million dollars. Roughly half that amount is raised from individual and corporate donors, nearly one-third from forums and publications, and the rest from limited foundation grants.

For further information, see the publications of the FPA discussed above and, particularly, the following histories published by the association: *Twenty-Five Years of the Foreign Policy Association, 1918-1943* (1943); and *Fifty Years: The Story of the Foreign Policy Association, 1918-1968* (1968). See also *A Cartoon History of United States Foreign Policy, 1776-1976* (1975); and, the following recent general account of American foreign policy, Ralph B. Levering, *The Public and American Foreign Policy, 1918-1978* (1978).

LARRY D. GIVENS

FOREIGN POLICY RESEARCH INSTITUTE (FPRI). Founded in February, 1955, by Dr. Robert Strausz-Hupe, former U.S. ambassador to Sweden, Sri Lanka, and NATO, the FPRI was part of the University of Pennsylvania until January, 1971, when, under the leadership of Dr. William R. Kintner, it was established as an independent, public operating foundation, exempt from federal taxation.

The Foreign Policy Research Institute began operations in the context of a nationwide attempt to bring intellectual resources to bear on critical national problems. It was especially important that this be done in the foreign policy area. The issues facing the United States after World War II were far more numerous and complex than those faced before. The political, economic, military, and technological forces affecting American foreign policy were of a long-term character, but their immediate demands tended to occupy fully the regular foreign policy apparatus of the U.S. government, which was unprepared for the challenge. It was urgent to inform both policy makers and public about the international issues facing the United States.

The purpose of the FPRI was, therefore, to examine the major issues of American foreign policy, with special emphasis on the longer-term problems, and to provide analyses for use by government and for broad public dissemination. A group of experts, primarily with academic background, was assembled to consider a select group of problems. This procedure was found to be very effective in bringing academic talent to bear on foreign policy issues, especially in relating current events to the fundamental and long-term strategic problems. An additional objective was to enrich both the academic discipline of international relations and the training of personnel for government service through a dialogue between academic theorists and foreign policy practitioners.

The ideas and findings developed by the FPRI have been disseminated through several outlets. It has always sought some contractual relations with government in order to develop the formal and personal channels whereby ideas could be conveyed to the highest levels of policy formation and decision making. Since 1957, the institute has provided a forum for the scholarly discussion of policy problems through its quarterly journal, *ORBIS*. In addition, a monograph and book series have served to make the FPRI's work available to the intellectual community and broader public. These vehicles have been supplemented from time to time by conferences, occasionally in collaboration with other organizations.

The leadership of the FPRI has always emphasized a broad approach to the study of foreign policy problems in which the political, strategic, military, and economic factors were placed in an integrated framework. Although the institute has maintained experts in geographical regions (including the Soviet Union and Eastern Europe, Western Europe, the Middle East, Latin America, Southeast Asia, and the Far East) and functional subjects (such as arms control), it prefers to relate both regional and functional issues to a larger global perspective. The range and complexity of foreign policy issues makes it difficult for government agencies to avoid the preoccupation with urgent and largely tactical problems; the academic world tends to be isolated from the more practical considerations that underlie foreign policy. The FPRI has attempted to bridge the gap between the "urgent" and the "irrelevant" by emphasizing the long-term strategic considerations of American foreign policy and their implications, without neglecting shorter-range problems. In fact, the FPRI has always had the capability of responding rapidly to immediate problems presented to its staff by outside groups for analysis.

During the first decade of its existence, the FPRI concentrated upon analyses of Communist strategy and the Atlantic Alliance. Several major works were published: *Protracted Conflict* (1959), *A Forward Strategy for America* (1961), and *Building the Atlantic World* (1963). These books had a sharp impact upon the policy debate. During the last half of the 1960s the FPRI addressed major efforts to the problems of limited war, revolution, and arms control. One of the publications resulting from these programs was *Peace and the Strategy Conflict* (1968). Beginning in 1969, the FPRI, in cooperation with other groups, organized a series of International Arms Control Symposia. The results have been issued in such books as *SALT: Implications for Arms Control in the 1970s* (1973); and *Contrasting Approaches to Strategic Arms Control* (1974).

When William R. Kintner, the FPRI's current president and director, became U.S. Ambassador to Thailand in 1973, Robert L. Pfaltzgraff, Jr., served as director. Dr. Kintner resumed the presidency of the institute in 1976.

In 1979, General Alexander M. Haig, Jr., the retired Supreme Allied Commander in Europe, initiated and served as a director of a program of Studies in Western Security that addressed (1) the West's commitment to defense in an age of "welfare statism" and slow economic growth; (2) the ability of the United States and its allies to coordinate their approaches to the energy challenge; and (3) the need for a coherent national strategy ranging from the political level to military doctrine and weapon systems. In 1980, as a result of this program, FPRI published *Oil Diplomacy: The Atlantic Nations in the Oil Crisis of 1978-79.* A major work on the future of NATO and the crisis of Western defenses is in preparation.

For further information, see the publications of the institute discussed herein, and the FPRI's *President's Report and Program 1979* (1979). The foregoing brief history of the FPRI was compiled by past and present staff members of the institute.

FOX CHASE CANCER CENTER. A history of the center begins with the establishment and growth of the Lankenau Hospital Research Institute (LHRI), which later became the Institute for Cancer Research (ICR) and is now part of the Fox Chase Cancer Center located in northeast Philadelphia. It is a nonprofit organization, privately funded at its outset, now operating on an admixture of private and government support.

Dr. Stanley Reimann, a pathologist, had the novel conviction in 1925 that the way to solve the problem of abnormal growth, cancer, was to unearth the little-known facts about how cells grow normally. He persuaded Rodman Wanamaker, the Philadelphia merchant, to finance a research building on the grounds of the old Lankenau Hospital in Philadelphia. Frederick Hammett, Ph.D., a physiological chemist, was the first scientific director of LHRI. In 1927 the staff also consisted of Mary A. Bennett, Ph.D., a biochemist, and several technicians. In 1929 they were joined by the organic chemists, Gerrit Toennies, Ph.D., and Theodore Lavine, Ph.D., who synthesized the pure compounds needed. By 1930 their studies on the effects of organic sulfhydryl (-SH) compounds in stimulating cell division in plants and chick embryos was extended to wound healing in animals with dramatic effects on humans that gave this small research institute a worldwide reputation.

The death of Wanamaker in 1928 and the onset of the Depression precipitated in 1930 the institute's first crisis for survival. The board of trustees doubted the relevance of the LHRI work to cancer and appointed a committee of scientists outstanding in cancer research to determine if it was worthwhile to continue. Professors Francis Carter Wood and A. B. Macallum and Drs. James B. Murphy and Alexis Carrel were adamant that the research be continued and expanded. The board agreed to support the institute, but it was only by Reimann's continuous effort at fund raising, including his own piano recitals, that the institute kept going. In 1931 Irénée du Pont's gift of ten thousand dollars made up more than one-third of the budget. Reimann's appreciation of the ability of women, not only as scientists but as organizers, helped save the institute.

In a fiscal emergency in 1933 Reimann's friend, Mrs. Alfred Gray, formed a Women's Auxiliary. They immediately found money to feed the inbred mice and gave card parties and dances to raise funds to keep the lab running. In addition, they organized yearly (for eighteen years) Cancer Forums, where capable speakers disseminated facts about cancer to the public. The work in the institute was thereby publicized and contributions came in. This auxiliary was particularly active in supplying fellowships for work at the institute's Marine Experimental Station at North Truro, Massachusetts.

Hammett in 1930 had persuaded Reimann to build a one-room laboratory on Cape Cod so that work could be done on the many flora that grew in ponds there. This lab was used by professionals from within and without the institute until 1947, when the area became so highly populated and polluted that the sea animals began to die. Hammett was increasingly unwell and died in 1953. He was well known for testing the effects of a variety of biological chemicals and carcinogens on the well-defined growth stages of some of the marine organisms. He started the journal *Growth* in 1937 and the symposia on "Development and Growth" in 1939, which led to the society of that name.

It was in the decade 1937-47 that the institute started to change from a relatively small organization into a large cancer center. New sources of income, both private and public, permitted an increase in personnel from eighteen to forty-six. Funds were obtained from the Blanche and Frank Wolf Foundation and from the International Cancer Research Foundation (Donner). In 1943 an inheritance of over fifty thousand dollars annually came from a trust (Anna C. Burr), and in 1947 the first government grants were obtained from the National Institutes of Health (NIH). Grace Medes, Ph.D., a biochemist, had previously joined the staff, and the scope of the work was broadened later by the appointments among others of Irene Diller, Ph.D., a cytologist; Robert W. Briggs, Ph.D., an embryologist; Theodore Hauschka, Ph.D., a protozoologist; Jack Schultz, Ph.D., a geneticist, Hugh J. Creech, Ph.D., an immunologist; Philip White, Ph.D., a plant tissue culturist; Andrew J. Donnelly, M.D., a pathologist; and H. Donald Putney as administrative director. In 1946, sixty-seven projects were under investigation with a yearly budget of only $106,000.

The formation of the Institute for Cancer Research (ICR) came about at the suggestion of Philip Sharples, an industrialist, who in 1942 was elected chairman of the research committee of the board of trustees of the Lankenau Hospital. He persuaded Reimann that funds from outside Philadelphia would be easier to obtain if an organization with the word *cancer* in it were formed and the local hospital name dropped. In 1945 the ICR was incorporated with Sharples as president and a board of directors that included Ethel Pew. In 1947 her brother, J. Howard Pew of Sun Oil, became chairman of the board. The LHRI and ICR existed under the same roof for thirteen years until the LHRI name was dropped to avoid confusion with the Clinical Research Institute at the Lankenau Hospital, which had moved to Overbrook, Pennsylvania.

By 1945 the Wanamaker building had become overcrowded, and the Pew family provided $1 million for a new building on land given by the Society of Friends, trustees of the adjacent Jeanes Hospital in Fox Chase (north Philadelphia). The four-story building and separate animal colony structure designed by Vincent Kling were completed in 1949. A grant of $149,000 had been obtained from the NIH for movable equipment, as had a biennial appropriation from the Commonwealth of Pennsylvania for supportive services, including building maintenance. Thus public funding began to play an increasing role in the institute.

More space in the new building permitted further appointments, among them: A. Lindo Patterson, Ph.D., an X-ray crystallographer; Jakob Stekol, Sc.D., a biochemist; Sidney Weinhouse, Ph.D., a biochemist; Thomas J. King, Ph.D., an embryologist; and a librarian and a purchasing agent. To finance these appointments, there were grants to individuals from the NIH and from the American Cancer Society and an inheritance of a considerable estate from a member of the Women's Auxiliary, Elizabeth Nax.

Notable work in the 1950s included that of Briggs and King on nuclear transportation in frog's eggs (subject of a later award by the French Academy of Sciences); Bennett's nutritional studies on rats that led to the discovery by others of vitamin B-12; the synthesis by Creech and his colleagues Peck and Preston of antitumor nitrogen half-mustards (ICR compounds); Hauschka's and his guest, George Klein's establishment of lines of ascites tumors (pure cultures of cancer cells) in mice; and use of the isotope ^{13}C first in cancer research by Medes and Weinhouse on fatty acid metabolism for which Medes received in 1955 the Garvan Medal of the American Chemical Society* (ACS).

Disagreements at the board level in the period 1953-1957 twice resulted in proposals for physical separation of LHRI and ICR, which really were one institute as far as work was concerned. Sharples wanted to force the ICR "people" to work entirely on testing compounds for anticancer activity, whereas the Lankenau Hospital board backed Reimann's program of basic research. Again an evaluation committee of outside experts (Drs. Shields Warren, Sidney Farber, and Albert Tannenbaum) was brought in. They solidly supported Reimann's program. But the ICR board persisted in their ideas. After Hanuschka (1954) and Briggs (1956) resigned, Anthony Whitaker, a lawyer on the Lankenau board, realized that the staff would not work under Sharples and prevailed upon Ethel Pew to persuade Sharples to resign. Whitaker took over as president of the ICR; the institutes remained together and were soon revitalized.

Reimann retired in 1956 at age sixty-five (died in 1968) and was replaced in 1957 by Timothy R. Talbot, Jr., M.D., who had an excellent background in clinical research. Talbot quickly realized the strength of the staff and their "loyalty to an institution that was designed to serve creative science and to nurture the innovative spirit of individual scientists of quality." His first move was to appoint a scientific advisory committee of outstanding scientists from other institutions. Such committees are continued to this day. Then in 1962 a formal agreement of affiliation was signed between the ICR and the University of Pennsylvania. Many of the staff accepted secondary appointments and gave lectures there, and these interactions stimulated the attraction of graduate students to the ICR laboratory for research for their Ph.D.s.

It had been one of Reimann's desires that clinical research be set up at the institute, and this was one of Talbot's primary objectives. A grant was awarded by NIH for support ($2.25 million over five years) of a ten-bed unit in hospital space rented to the ICR by the Jeanes Hospital trustees. The grant included the salary of a director for the new Division of Clinical Research. Talbot searched for "someone acquainted with medicine, biochemistry and genetics." Baruch Blumberg, M.D., D. Phil., was appointed in 1964. His receipt of the Nobel Prize in Medicine in 1976 confirmed the wisdom of this choice. The isolation by his group of Hepatitis-B virus led to a method used worldwide for testing donor blood for carriers of the virus.

Notable also among appointments made by Talbot were those of Thomas F. Anderson, Ph.D., phage geneticist and electron microscopist; Robert Perry, Ph.D., a biophysicist; Beatrice Mintz, Ph.D., a geneticist; and Irwin Rose, Ph.D., a biochemist. All have since been elected to the National Academy of Sciences* (NAS).

Further diversification of the research required new funds and physical expansion of the laboratories. With an NIH grant of $750,000 and matching money, a new laboratory wing and animal colony were constructed in 1965. Also the first "core" grant in the nation was given by NIH to ICR in 1962 to cover supportive services and salaries of key personnel who received their own grants. In 1966 the assets ($2.1 million) of the Biochemical Research Foundation of Newark, Delaware, were awarded by the courts to ICR.

Talbot had long been discussing with the board of trustees of the American Oncologic Hospital of Philadelphia (AOH) the possibility of a move of the hospital to Fox Chase adjacent to ICR. The AOH since 1905 had been a well-established Philadelphia hospital, first at Forty-Fifth and Chestnut streets, then at Thirty-Third Street and Powelton Avenue. It was the first institution devoted exclusively to the study and treatment of cancer and is now one of only nine in the country. Thirteen prominent Philadelphians founded the hospital, and George H. Stewart, Jr., of Ardmore,

Pennsylvania, served as president of the hospital board of trustees. In 1905, the AOH had twenty-four beds and admitted 206 people for treatment. clinical research developed slowly; it was the first facility in the country to use radium in therapy and also later to use a supervolt X-ray therapy unit. AOH pioneered in developing surgical techniques for head and neck cancers. Dr. George Morris Dorrance, one of the greatest American surgeons, for years was medical director of the AOH, and his son, G. Morris Dorrance Jr., is now chairman of the Fox Chase Cancer Center board of trustees. In May of 1963 it was agreed that AOH would affiliate with ICR, and late in that year $1.5 million was awarded under the Hill-Burton Authority toward the construction of a new fifty-five-bed AOH adjacent to the ICR. The hospital moved in 1967. In 1974 a new corporation was formed, the Fox Chase Cancer Center, made up of ICR and AOH. Talbot was made its president, and in 1977 Alfred G. Knudson Jr., M.D., Ph.D., a pediatrician and geneticist interested in the genetics of human cancer, took over as director of the ICR. The wide range of Knudson's knowledge in medicine and biology and his experience as an administrator made him an ideal choice for this position. The ICR and AOH were physically joined by a new building in 1977, financed largely by a contribution from the Pew Memorial Trust. It houses a new expanded library, laboratories, administrative offices, facilities for epidemiology, computation, and the training and outreach activities of the center.

Thus Stanley Reimann's dream of a research institute devoted to fundamental studies of normal and abnormal growth working with an adjacent cancer hospital has come to fulfillment. The yearly budget of twenty-eight million dollars might well have exceeded his expectations. But without his insight and tremendous effort to establish and maintain the original LHRI none of this would have been possible.

For further information, see the following articles appearing in *The Institute for Cancer Research—Scientific Report 1977-1978:* Elizabeth K. Patterson, "Early History of the Institute for Cancer Research, 1927-1957"; and Timothy R. Talbot, Jr., "Recent History of the Institute for Cancer Research, 1957-1976."

ELIZABETH K. PATTERSON

FRANKLIN INSTITUTE, THE. The Franklin Institute was established in Philadelphia in 1824. It grew out of the mechanics' institute movement then just beginning in Great Britain, and the men behind its creation called upon Old World precedents to justify their action. But, in fact, the organization provides a nice example of the way European institutions were modified to suit American needs and tastes and of the relationship among industry, applied science, and some of the country's most important social values.

At its beginning, the institute's founders linked the organization's objectives to great national purposes. The institute would address itself to the educational needs of working people, so that they might rise to "their proper place in a republican society," and to the improvement of manufacturing industry, so that the nation might enjoy an economic independence commensurate with its political status. The essential mechanism for both these ambitions was a kind of training that would unite scientific theory and craft practice. A knowledge of the basic principles of science would give the artisan the ability to break out of traditional patterns of craft training, which not only limited his career possibilities but fixed his social status as well. That concept of a dynamic relation between scientific laws and craft skill led the institute's board of managers—a group composed of Philadelphia manufacturers, professional men, educators and a few skilled craftsmen—to schedule regular evening lecture classes in natural philosophy and in chemistry, to begin a mathematics school as well as one for mechanical drawing, to publish the *Franklin Journal and American Mechanics' Magazine*, and to sponsor annual exhibitions of American manufacturers.

This remarkable array of activities, designed as a program of democratic social reform and as a means to create healthy domestic manufactures, was extended in the decade after 1824 to include the analysis of patents, original technological research, and the formation of a special Committee on Science and the Arts, whose task was to identify the most compelling needs and opportunities of American technology. During that same decade, however, it became apparent that there were serious flaws in the idea that instructing workmen in the principles of science would improve their status and advance the state of their art.

For instance, Dr. Thomas P. Jones, editor of the *Journal of the Franklin Institute* (as the magazine was called after 1828) ultimately discovered that most craftsmen could only understand scientific language so elementary that it lost both precision and relevance. Thus, although the concept of uniting theory and practice had ideological power, in actuality, scientific principles proved of little utility to artisans, either in their work or in their lives. In a similar fashion, the institute's board of managers discovered that if evening lectures in science were to be pertinent, especially to the apprentices for whom they were originally designed, the students needed a better educational background than they usually had. To correct that problem, the managers tried to establish an evening school in mathematics and one for general science. Despite repeated efforts to place them on a secure financial basis, though, both these schools failed, and a college-level School of Arts to train engineers never got past the planning stage. One of the results was that the institute's evening lecture program became more general in content and more popular with middle-class audiences of both sexes than with young apprentices.

Although the Franklin Institute never succeeded in establishing schools of its own, apart from night classes in mechanical drawing conducted for almost a hundred years, its efforts marked an important transition in the history of American scientific and technical education. The board of managers recognized that industrial progress required different forms of education, both for workers and for superintendents, and experience taught them that the voluntarism of mechanics' institutes did not provide sufficient structure or rigor. In Philadelphia, the most immediate effects of their campaign were the establishment of Central High School, which soon became a model for science-oriented secondary schools, and the creation within the University of Pennsylvania of a scientific and technical course of study. Beyond the city, the vision of public education in science and its practical applications led directly to a broad movement culminating in the Morrill Act of 1863, which provided for the establishment of agricultural and mechanical colleges throughout the union.

The same Philadelphia industrialists who perceived the need for new forms of technical training also came to realize the value of a scientific style of research to solve important technical problems. That awareness, too, flowed from a set of activities at the institute that were originally educational in purpose. The organization's founders imagined that the study of new patents would be an especially instructive way to identify fruitful areas of technical advance, and they formed a Committee on Inventions for that purpose. Just as in other educational activities, however, it soon became apparent that, although the committee performed a useful service by publicizing the novel features of new inventions, its work still did not answer the need for the systematic solution of recognizable technical problems. Steam power, for instance, was a technology of great significance in America, especially as applied to transportation. Yet in 1830, when its potential worth in the exploitation of the entire Mississippi River Valley drainage basin was already apparent, increasing numbers of steamboat boiler explosions threatened the industry's future development, and that was a matter of particular concern in Philadelphia, the country's leading center of steam engine building.

What led the institute in 1830 to begin a five-year investigation into the causes of steamboat boiler explosions was, however, not simply the economic interests of local industry. Besides Philadelphia's heavy concentration of machine industries, the city was also still one of the country's most active scientific centers, and the institute's research project grew out of an unusual alliance between a small group of industrialists at the beginning of their business careers and a few ambitious young scientists. The principal figures behind the enterprise were Alexander Dallas Bache, a great grandson of Benjamin Franklin and a man who would go on to a brilliant career as America's most important science administrator in the years before the Civil War; and Samuel Vaughan Merrick, a young manufacturer whose wealthy and literate family had been influential in Revolutionary-era politics and science. From the outset, the investigation reflected their joint concerns.

With financial support from the federal government, the institute created a research laboratory in Philadelphia for a wide variety of experiments having to do with boiler explosions and concluded their investigation in an 1836 report that featured several recommendations, which were incorporated into a model law Bache drafted. These tests were paralleled by an equally remarkable investigation into the strength of materials used in boiler construction, carried out by Walter R. Johnson. His work depended upon novel test apparatus and also resulted in an important publication (1837), which for the first time systematically analyzed the characteristics of American iron and copper.

One of the things the institute's steam boiler investigation demonstrates is that there was industrial research in the United States much earlier than is usually imagined. In fact, a Merrick-instigated and industry-financed experimental inquiry into waterwheel efficiency had preceded the institute's boiler study, which in turn served as a frequent precedent for a number of other technical investigations scattered through the middle years of the nineteenth century. From these kinds of activities scientists discovered the rewards of government-financed, mission-oriented research, and entrepreneurs learned how to use science profitably. Contrary to the ideas with which the institute started, it was not the principles of science that would advance the mechanic arts, but the methods of science that proved so full of potential.

The Franklin Institute's early research projects established other links between science and technology that also proved highly significant. Besides bringing experimental methods to the solution of technical problems, Bache and Merrick fashioned a professional style for the advancement of technology that emphasized systematic knowledge and the creation of engineering specialties. Thus, for example, they changed the format of the *Journal of the Franklin Institute* in order to publish translations of important foreign technical articles and the original research of American engineers. Because of those measures, the institute came to serve as a focal point for engineers, an occupational group just beginning to emerge as a distinct profession in the 1840s and 1850s.

From its inception, the Franklin Institute had reflected the interests of Philadelphia's industrialists and indeed became the mechanism by which their concerns were integrated into the larger framework of American social values. On one hand, knowledge of science and its applications was made the basis for a society in which anyone could rise to the level of his or her talents; on the other hand, the promotion of internal improvements and manufacturing was made the means by which the United States would rise to assume its rightful place in the family of nations. It was a system ideally designed to rationalize individual pursuit of wealth, to make industrial progress an act of patriotism, and to enshrine inventiveness, efficiency, and a labor-saving approach to technical problems as national virtues.

William Sellers, president of the institute and the country's preeminent machine tool manufacturer, articulated most of those ideals in his 1864 proposal for a standard American screw thread. He aimed at uniformity with the least possible labor costs and the greatest potential for adoption by designing a system that would allow intelligent mechanics to construct it without special tools. It sounded democratic, it saved labor compared with the British screw standard, and it served the national interests of American industry.

These traditional concerns to link theory and practice for the benefit of industry continued throughout the nineteenth century. In 1877, for instance, the institute conducted a series of dynamo tests to establish comparisons of efficiency as that new technology was emerging, and its 1884 International Electrical Exposition led directly to the adoption of some fundamental units of electricity as well as to the formation of the American Institute of Electrical Engineers. But increasing specialization in both science and engineering created other institutions better able to deal with the problems of those fields, and the Franklin Institute gradually became an essentially local organization whose affairs centered around evening lectures on science for the general public, a lending library, its *Journal*, and an annual ceremony at which prizes were awarded for meritorious scientific and technical accomplishment. By the beginning of the twentieth century, the Franklin Institute had not only lost the national importance it enjoyed in the preprofessional era of American science and technology, it had also lost its sense of purpose. Still housed in the 1825 building it had started with, the organization lacked space, funding, and vitality.

An awareness of the need for regeneration was behind a vigorous fund-raising campaign of the early 1930s, and with Munich's Deutsches Museum as their model, the managers moved the institute to a large new building on Benjamin Franklin Parkway that incorporated a museum of science and technology and a planetarium. They had hoped for enough money also to add space for research laboratories, but the Great Depression made that impossible. Still, a 1918 bequest that the institute administered had led to the creation of the Bartol Research Foundation at Swarthmore College in 1925, to engage in research in the physical sciences and to investigate problems of a scientific nature arising in industries. And in 1935, the foundation was made trustee of another legacy, to establish the Biochemical Research Foundation at the University of Delaware. These activities yielded some sense of connection to science, although their absorption with pure research and their physical separation from the institute made the relation somewhat abstract.

It was World War II that finally gave the institute its long-hoped-for permanent research facilities, which took on formal status in 1946 with the establishment of the Franklin Institute Laboratories for Research and Development. The sustained demand for those kinds of services in the postwar era, heightened by the Korean War, led to the construction of a large new laboratory and the expectation that the Franklin Institute would be able to conduct a substantial research program, the income from which would also help defray other expenses—an attractive concept for an organization that had always been financially dependent upon membership dues, a small endowment, and, because those were never enough to meet expenses, the periodic charity of a few wealthy supporters. Indeed, by the 1960s the laboratories brought in over four million dollars of contract work, mostly on behalf of the federal government and, as a result of another contract with the Office of Naval Research, had taken over operation of the Center of Naval Analyses in Alexandria, Virginia.

But that heavy dependence on federal funding, which had created such an air of prosperity and mission in the 1960s, left the organization vulnerable when the government initiated the sharp cutbacks associated with its withdrawal from the Vietnam War. In a way reminiscent of its earlier years, the Franklin Institute was then forced to look back to local industry for its financial support and to attempt an accommodation with the changed social values of that period.

For further information, see Sidney L. Wright, *The Story of the Franklin Institute* (1938); Henry Butler Allen, "Alexander Dallas Bache and His Connection with the Franklin Institute of the State of Pennsylvania," American Philosophical Society *Proceedings* (May, 1941); Mary Williams Brinton, *Their Lives and Mine* (1973); Bruce Sinclair, *Philadelphia's Philosopher Mechanics: A History of the Franklin Institute, 1824-1865* (1974); and Bowen C. Dees, "The Franklin Institute," *Interdisciplinary Science Review* (June, 1980).

BRUCE SINCLAIR

FRANKLIN INSTITUTE OF THE STATE OF PENNSYLVANIA FOR THE PROMOTION OF THE MECHANIC ARTS, THE. See Franklin Institute, The.

_G

GENERAL MEMORIAL HOSPITAL FOR THE TREATMENT OF CANCER AND ALLIED DISEASES. See Memorial Sloan-Kettering Cancer Center.

GENETICS SOCIETY OF AMERICA (GSA). The forerunners of the Genetics Society of America were the Joint Genetics Sections of the American Society of Zoologists* (ASZ) and the Botanical Society of America* (BSA). The Joint Genetics Sections was set up in December, 1921, following an annual meeting of the American Association for the Advancement of Science* (AAAS), and was organized on the basis of proportional official representation from the ASZ and BSA. Many geneticists, however, were not satisfied with the sectional arrangement, desiring a common and separate meeting ground with their fellow geneticists. In 1927 therefore, the Joint Genetics Sections appointed a committee to consider the matter, and, as the result of its study and subsequent reports, it was resolved at a 1931 AAAS meeting that the Joint Genetics Sections be reorganized as an independent GSA. A constitution was thereupon adopted; officers were elected; and invitations were extended to all geneticists to join the new society.

The GSA has retained its connection with the AAAS over the years and, since its founding, the American Institute of Biological Sciences* (AIBS). The earlier arrangement whereby abstracts of the papers presented at meetings of the Joint Genetics Sections were published in the Wistar Institute of Anatomy and Biology's* *Anatomical Record* was terminated, and an agreement was reached to publish them in the *American Naturalist*. This arrangement prevailed until 1937, when the abstracts were transferred to *Genetics*, and all subsequent abstracts have been published in that journal. An official GSA publication, *Records*, appeared annually from 1932 until 1962, and contained abstracts of papers, directories, obituaries, and GSA business items. In 1961 the GSA voted to take over the publication of *Genetics*, which became its official organ on January 1, 1963. The *Records* were discontinued at that time, and the material previously published there has since been published each year as a supplement to *Genetics*.

With the exception of the World War II years, annual meetings have been held since 1932, first in conjunction with the AAAS, then with AIBS, and, since 1965, independently. Meetings are usually held in late summer on a university campus. In addition, the GSA has sponsored other meetings of a special nature. In 1950, for example, it cosponsored, in conjunction with the AIBS, a golden jubilee meeting on genetics at the Ohio State University that resulted in the publication of *Genetics in the 20th Century*, a book of essays by leaders in the field. In 1965 a Mendel Centennial Symposium was held at Colorado State University with a resultant publication entitled *Heritage from Mendel* (1967).

The main functions of the GSA at the present time are its annual meetings and the publication of *Genetics*. Accessory functions, handled through committees, representatives, or its officers, are concerned with monitoring and providing for the preservation of genetic stocks of various research organisms; providing expert advice on matters of public interest, such as recombinant DNA research; participating in matters dealing with genetics on the international level, such as those involving the International Congress of Geneticists; and nominating representatives to various agencies, such as the AIBS and National Council on Radiation Protection and Measurement.

Membership is open to persons interested in genetics. They must be recommended by two members and elected by the board of directors. The GSA has grown from an initial 338 to its present 2,500 members.

The GSA elects the customary institutional officers; it conducts its business from an office, located in Austin, Texas, and the office of its elected secretary, located in Vancouver, British Columbia.

For further information, see the GSA publications discussed above, particularly P. W. Whiting, "History and Organization," *Records, Genetics Society of America* (1933) and (1934). See also B. P. Kaufmann, "Genetics Society of America," *AAAS Bulletin* (July, 1944). GSA records of an archival nature have been deposited in the library of the American Philosophical Society* (APS).

GEOCHEMICAL SOCIETY (GS). In the early 1950s a small group of earth scientists, led by Drs. Earl Ingerson and John A. S. Adams, advanced the need for the establishment of a society concerned with the application of chemistry to the solution of geological and cosmological problems. Following discussions along this line at the 1955 annual meetings of other groups, such as the American Geophysical Union* (AGU), a formal meeting was held in that same year at the annual November meeting of the Geological Society of America* (GSA). It was there that the Geochemical Society was organized with the election of provisional officers and the naming of a committee to draft a constitution.

Following adoption of a constitution and incorporation the following year (1956), an agreement was made with the Pergamon Press for the establishment of *Geochimica et Cosmochimica Acta* whereby the GS exercised editorial control and the press retained financial control of the publication. At that time, too, the GS began publication of *Geochemical News*, containing book reviews, notices, and so on. More recently, with funds provided by the National Science Foundation, the GS has set up a translation program for Russian-language books and journals in the geochemical area.

The GS has, over the course of its existence, set up various committees to carry out specific functions. For example, a Standards Committee aided the U.S. National Bureau of Standards in supplying standard samples for isotope abundance; a Research Committee has compiled and looks into possible geochemical research projects; and an Education Committee concerns itself with pedagogical questions.

Annual GS meetings are held in conjunction with those of the GSA. Also, the GS has sponsored and cosponsored national and international meetings. For example, it cooperated with the International Geological Congress in the latter's 1956 meeting in Mexico; and in 1959 a Coonamessett, Massachusetts, conference on the geochemistry of carbonates was held under GS auspices.

GS membership is confined to those persons with an interest in its purpose and activities and who can present evidence of scholastic or technical attainments in the physical sciences. There are presently about fifteen hundred members with about one-third of that number residing outside the United States, from whom many of the GS officers, including presidents and members of the governing council, have been drawn.

The GS elects the customary institutional officers; it conducts its business from an office headed by a secretary, located in Tempe, Arizona.

There is apparently no published material dealing with the history of the GS. The brief history of the GS furnished here was primarily based on an account of its history and activities furnished the author by Dr. Earl Ingerson.

GEOLOGICAL SOCIETY OF AMERICA (GSA). There were no serious geological studies made in this hemisphere prior to the nineteenth century. Thomas Jefferson was interested in vertebrate paleontology, and Benjamin Silliman had some interest in aspects of geology, but it was not until the publication of William Maclure's "Observations on the Geology of the United States, Explanatory of a Geologic Map," in the American Philosophical Society* (APS) *Transactions* (1809) that a study of note was produced here. It was not until the 1830s and 1840s that college and university courses in geology were offered, and it was then, on April 2, 1840, that the Association of American Geologists was formed. The association was our first national society devoted solely to the earth sciences, and it was the ancestor of the Geological Society of America. It was founded because of the need for coordination among New York, Pennsylvania, and New England geologists whose survey work often carried them across state lines.

In 1843 the newly founded association widened its scope, and its name was changed to the Association of American Geologists and Naturalists. By 1847 a movement was under way to broaden the membership and activity still further, and in 1848 the association metamorphosed into the American Association for the Advancement of Science* (AAAS), with Geology and Geography as Section E of the new AAAS.

From 1848 to 1881, geologists were most active in AAAS affairs; ten of their number served as AAAS presidents during the period. By the latter date, however, there was sentiment expressed for the creation or recreation of an independent and separate society, much of this sentiment stemming from dissatisfaction with the AAAS practice of holding summer meetings, which interfered with geologists' summer field seasons. Although a committee to consider the matter had been set up and there was some discussion and correspondence, no action was taken until 1888, largely because of a reluctance to do something that might weaken the AAAS. Finally, however, a plan was agreed upon whereby the officers of Section E of the AAAS would be the same as those of the projected society, and it was also agreed that the meetings of the AAAS section and the society would be held jointly. Thereupon, a separate American Geological Society was organized on August 14, 1888; at its next annual meeting on August 28, 1889, it changed its name to the "Geological Society of America." It has been advanced that the reason for this abrupt change in nomenclature can be traced to the anticipation that fellowship in the society, following European custom, would be indicated by the initials FAGS following a member's name. When it was realized that such initials had an unpleasant connotation, the society's name was changed so that the initials FGSA could be utilized.

The GSA recognized the importance of publication at its founding; a committee on publications was named at the organizational meeting and the establishment of the then quarterly and now monthly *Bulletin* followed the next year. The *Bulletin* includes the records of GSA meetings and many of the papers presented there. An annual *Proceedings* was established in 1933 but was discontinued in 1968. Since then *Memorials* to deceased members are published in a separate series; other material formerly in the *Proceedings* is published in the *Bulletin*, in a news and information section in the monthly journal *Geology*, established in 1973, or in the seven-part periodical *Abstracts with Programs*, established in 1969. The last covers the annual meetings of the GSA and of each of its six sections. The *Bibliography and Index of Geology*, established in 1934, (formerly *Bibliography and Index of Geology Exclusive of North America)* was published monthly in conjunction with the American Geological Institute* (AGI) until 1979, when the GSA withdrew and turned over this publication completely to the AGI. The GSA also publishes, intermittently, *Special Papers, Memoirs, Maps, Charts* and *Treatise on Invertebrate Paleontology*. Founded in 1948, the last is copublished with the University of Kansas and consists of comprehensive volumes on each of the principal fossil groups. Finally, the GSA publishes an annual *Yearbook*, now called *Membership Directory*.

The GSA has always followed the practice of holding winter meetings, in recent years in October or November. Until 1908 these meetings were held jointly with the AAAS, being discontinued at that time because of the problem of accommodations. Since then, however, the GSA has met with associated societies, first with the Paleontological Society* and later (1920) also with the Mineralogical Society of America and the Society of Economic Geologists, these three being directly descended from the GSA. In more recent years, the Society of Vertebrate Paleontology, Cushman Foundation, Geochemical Society,* National Association of Geology Teachers, and Geoscience Information Society have also become associated societies and meet with the GSA regularly or intermittently. Meetings have been held in all sections of the country, usually in large cities and preferably where there are large concentrations of geologists and also opportunities for instructive field trips. A Cordilleran Section was created in 1899 for members in the Far West; since 1947 the Rocky Mountain, Southeastern, Northeastern, North Central and South Central sections have been added. Each of these geographic groups holds its own annual meeting, commonly in late winter or early spring. In addition to these, there are now seven topical or specialistic divisions—Archaeological Geology, Coal Geology, Engineering Geology, Geophysics, History of Geology, Hydrogeology, and Quarternary Geology and Geomorphology. These hold scientific sessions within the framework of the GSA's annual meetings.

In comparison with the majority of learned societies, the GSA is in an enviable position due to the fact that it was named the recipient of the $3,884,345 Penrose Bequest in 1931 by the late Dr. R. A. F. Penrose, Jr. Dr. Penrose also gave the GSA his personal library and provided funds for the Penrose Medal which the GSA awards in addition to other medals and prizes. This endowment has grown significantly, and the income from it has provided for many GSA activities, particularly publications and research grants.

Initial GSA membership consisted of 112 fellows. Since that time, membership as a fellow has been extended on a selective basis from among researchers and teachers in geology. Since 1947 member status was extended to those persons interested in geology but not meeting the qualifications for election as a fellow. Although the constitution provided for election of distinguished foreign scientists as correspondents, now called honorary fellows, it was not until 1909 that the first of this group was named, and their number has never been more than 50. Total membership is presently about 12,500: 3,300 fellows, 6,800 members, and 2,400 student associates. Women were admitted to the GSA at an early date, and a number have served in official capacity.

The GSA elects the customary institutional officers; it conducts its business from an office, headed by an executive director, located in Boulder, Colorado.

For further information, see a now outdated history by Herman L. Fairchild, *The Geological Society of America, 1888-1930* (1932). Edwin B. Eckel, former executive secretary of the GSA, has completed a new and updated GSA history. See also the following articles appearing in the *Bulletin, Geological Society of America:* Alexander Winchell "Historical Sketch of the Organization" (February, 1890); J. J. Stevenson, "Our Society" (February, 1899); and C. H. Hitchcock, "Supplementary Note on the Organization of the Geological Society of America" (December, 1910); as well as H. R. Aldrich, "The Geological Society of America," *AAAS Bulletin* (June, 1943); and Frederick Betz, Jr. "The Geological Society of America," *GeoTimes* (May-June, 1961).

_H_

HALL LIBRARY. See Linda Hall Library.

HASTINGS CENTER, INSTITUTE OF SOCIETY, ETHICS AND THE LIFE SCIENCES. All organizations begin in someone's mind; however, it is by no means always easy to trace one's way back to an ultimate source. Moreover, later developments tend to obscure the memory, inviting the creation of an imaginary past, much tidier than the forgotten reality. In this case, Daniel Callahan can no longer identify a single moment that would mark the real beginning. During much of 1968, he was spending his time writing a book on abortion, with the support of grants from the Ford Foundation and the Population Council.* That subject was then, as now, controversial and difficult, all the more so in his case because he wanted to look at the problem from a variety of disciplinary perspectives—ethics, law, medicine, demography, and public policy. He was trying to be a one-man interdisciplinary band and had to work his way, more or less unassisted, through a wide range of literature, most of it unfamiliar. But that effort was one source of the idea for an institute: the need for interdisciplinary work on controversial moral questions. The other source of the idea came out of that effort as well. Abortion, it became clear, was simply one of a wide range of medical and biological problems facing society. That was the era when the "biological revolution," the first heart transplants, speculations about genetic engineering, and efforts to modify human behavior by surgical and electrical means were just beginning to surface. Despite widespread media interest and a number of conferences, there were no organizations devoted to exploring those problems in a serious and systematic way.

During the latter part of 1968, Callahan talked with a number of people about the idea of forming an organization devoted to ethical problems in the life sciences. It was not clear exactly what was needed, and there were no models to draw upon. At a Christmas party in 1968, Callahan mentioned the idea to a Hastings neighbor, Dr. Willard Gaylin, a psychiatrist and psychoanalyst on the faculty of the College of Physicians and Surgeons, Columbia University. Gaylin was taken with the idea, and over the next couple of months they talked intensively. Each then set about talking further with various friends and colleagues. Having been trained in philosophy, Callahan knew a number of potentially interested people in the theological and philosophical communities, and Gaylin had a variety of contacts in the medical and biological communities. In March of 1969—with the assistance of a loan from Callahan's mother—they organized a small meeting of people interested in the idea of forming a research and educational organization. That, probably, was the public beginning, and for well over a year the center was located in Callahan's house (with a mimeograph machine in the home of Will Gaylin). At that point, of course, it was not a "center" at all, but it did have nice stationery and a part-time secretary. And although the official name is the "Institute of Society, Ethics and the Life Sciences," it is more informally referred to as the Hastings Center.

Incorporation came quickly, and during 1969 and early 1970 the search began for financial support. The main obstacle initially encountered was the use of the word *ethics*. Even today, the term means many things to many people, but a very general reaction at that time was that, however important the issues, no real progress could be made on problems of morality. They were thought to be "soft," elusive, and not subject to rational analysis or resolution. Potential donors had to be persuaded that the founders believed just the opposite to be the case and that, in any event, however difficult, the emerging moral problems of medicine and biology had to be confronted.

By the end of 1969, the first financial support came from Elizabeth K. Dollard and John D. Rockefeller III, together with a matching grant from the National Endowment for the Humanities and the Rockefeller Foundation. Just as importantly, a good deal of support was being gained from various professionals and others. They were willing to pay their own way to early meetings and do a good deal of work without any financial return and were enthusiastic about developing a solid core of people in the country who would take on these ethical problems in a systematic way. In the fall of 1970, office space in Hastings-on-Hudson (where Callahan and Gaylin lived) was rented, and the first full-time staff member was hired, Dr. Robert M. Veatch, who was just then graduating from Harvard with a degree in medical ethics.

Initial center efforts were concentrated in four general areas: death and dying, genetics, the control of behavior by medical and technological means, and population limitation. More informally, there was concern with human subject research and the ethics of social science investigation. In each case, the focus was on the moral problems but construed so as to include not only philosophical analysis but also the social, legal, and policy implications of different moral positions. In addition, an education program was initiated, one-week intensive summer workshops were organized, publication of the *Hastings Center Report* was begun, work was launched with a variety of medical schools aimed at introducing courses in medical ethics, and a student intern program was established. In addition to these formal programs, the center was quickly deluged with a variety of requests for assistance—for legislative testimony, for help in setting up teaching programs, for advice on drafting legislation, and for counsel on moral problems.

All of that activity led to a growing staff and budget, and by 1976 the full-time staff had grown to its current twenty-six. By 1977 the center's budget had reached $1 million, and by 1981, $1.3 million. Over the years the Hastings Center has been served by a distinguished board of directors, among them Nobel laureates James D. Watson and David Baltimore, eminent legal scholars such as Paul Freund, by such leading philosophers and theologians as Paul Ramsey, James M. Gustafson, and Sissela Bok, by medical educators such as Stanley S. Bergen, Jr., and by corporate executives such as Edwin C. Whitehead. Since the beginning, Willard Gaylin has served as president and Daniel Callahan as director.

An unusual feature of the Hastings Center is its structure. One of the first questions considered at the beginning was how the work would get done. Would all of the work be carried out by permanent staff members, or would heavy reliance be placed upon outside consultants? The center's solution to that problem was to invent a two-tiered structure. On the one hand, there are the permanent staff members; on the other, there are some one hundred elected fellows. It is the function of the latter to work very closely with the staff, take part in the research and educational programs, and form the broad intellectual base for the work of the center. The fellows of the center are elected by the board of directors.

All organizations change somewhat over time. In the case of the Hastings Center, the scope of issues examined has been expanded to include ethics and health policy, to take on in a more formal way ethical problems in the social sciences, and, most recently, to expand into the area of professional ethics and the teaching of ethics to both undergraduate and professional students. The center's main publication, the *Hastings Center Report*, goes to 10,000 associate members, and an additional publication, *IRB: A Review of Human Subjects Research*, is a major source of information for institutional review boards. Over the years, some 1,400 people have taken part in center summer workshops, 110 students have spent periods of time at the center as part of the internship program, and the postdoctoral and visiting scholars program has brought dozens of others for periods of one month to a year.

The Hastings Center is supported by grants from private foundations and the federal government, by corporate and individual contributions, and by the income from its membership and educational programs. The center has done very little contract work, and most of its research projects have been initiated by the center, with grant support then being sought to carry out the proposed projects. In recent years, the center has considerably intensified its efforts to find individual and corporate support, and plans are now being formulated to begin an endowment campaign.

In 1975, the center moved its offices from downtown Hastings (a town of ninety-five hundred people, approximately fifteen miles north of Manhattan) to what is locally known in Hastings as the Burke estate, a large tract of land owned by the Hastings Board of Education. There a building is rented from the board on what was the site of an estate owned by Flo Ziegfeld and actress Billie Burke.

What has the Hastings Center accomplished over the years? It appears to have been a major force in stimulating the teaching of medical ethics and bioethics in both professional schools and at the undergraduate level. Its various publications, as well as testimony by its staff before legislatures, have had a significant effect upon public policy. Most importantly, in terms of early ideals, a genuinely interdisciplinary organization has been created, one where professionals of a variety of fields work together effectively and productively. Most pleasingly, perhaps, the center helped to rescue the word *ethics* from its earlier aura of suspicion and doubt. Although the specific issues of medical and biological ethics change from year to year, the continuing rapid scientific advances appear to guarantee a constant flow of fresh and difficult problems. The center hopes to remain in the forefront in responding to them and to see if it can make sense of a society that is complex, difficult, and going through constant change.

For further information, see the following articles about the Hastings Center: Kenneth L. Woodward, "The Ethics of Miracles," *Newsweek* (September, 1977); Dava Sobel, "The Hastings Center: Think Before You Act," *RF Illustrated* (September, 1978); Jane Stein, "The Bioethicist: Facing Matters of Life and Death," *Smithsonian* (January, 1979); Gene I. Maeroff, "The Hastings Center— A Cool Look at Hot Issues," *Change* (February, 1979); and Charles Laroux, "Independent Think Tank Takes Theoretical to Limits," *Chicago Tribune* (February 26, 1979).

DANIEL CALLAHAN

HENRY FRANCIS DU PONT WINTERTHUR MUSEUM. Chartered in 1930, the Winterthur Museum operates a complex of properties and programs at two sites in Delaware: Winterthur (six miles northwest of Wilmington) and Odessa (twenty-three miles south of Wilmington). The properties at Winterthur consist of 960 acres and ninety-six buildings, at Odessa 13 acres and nine buildings. The programs include curatorial, conservation, library, research, museum visitation, teaching, publication, and horticultural activities.

The 960 rolling acres at Winterthur form a beautifully landscaped park of meadows, streams, ponds, hillsides, woodlands, and gardens. This park had its origin in the estate established here in 1839 by Evelina Gabrielle du

Pont (1796-1863), daughter of E. I. du Pont, who founded the Du Pont Company in 1802, and her husband James A. Biderman (1790-1865), who served as second head of the company. The estate was steadily enlarged by the next three generations of du Ponts until it reached 2,500 acres: General Henry (1812-1889), who owned but did not live at Winterthur; Colonel Henry A. (1838-1926); and Henry Francis (1880-1969). It was the latter who transformed Winterthur from a distinguished private home into a prestigious public institution. Marked by the discrimination and taste of the connoisseur, the organizational skill and drive of the born manager, and the zeal of the perfectionist, H. F. focused his remarkable energies on three achievements for which he attained nationally recognized excellence: a prize-winning herd of Holstein-Friesian cattle; a large, beautiful garden; and an unequalled collection of American decorative arts. The farm and herd were a private avocation and were discontinued at his death in 1969; the garden and collection were opened to the public in 1951 and have been steadily extended since then.

Of the 960 acres of grounds, some 200 are under cultivation in bulbs, rhododendrons, azaleas, and mixed shrubs and trees. Another 60 acres are intensely cultivated show gardens, and these constitute the center of Winterthur's extensive horticultural activity. In the midst of these grounds and gardens are located some ninety-five buildings made up of residences, barns, shops, greenhouses, and the three chief structures of the museum complex: the visitor center with cafeteria and lecture facilities for 350 persons; the H. F. du Pont House, which was the principal home of the family from 1951 to 1969, and is now being remodeled as the Winterthur Gallery; and a large structure rising above the banks of Clenny Run occupying 4 acres of land and enclosing 210,404 square feet of floor space, which serves as the central hub of Winterthur's activities. This structure is made up of five units. The Main Museum, which was Mr. du Pont's home from 1927 until 1950, is a nine-story building housing two hundred period rooms, alcoves, and passages displaying Winterthur's main collections. Joined to it is the Washington Wing, built in 1959, which contains eighteen chronologically arranged period rooms and display areas, the main administrative offices, four classrooms, photo studio, staff lunchroom, and conference area. A two-story textile and service area, constructed in 1948 and enlarged in 1962, and the Glass Corridor join these two units to the five-story Louise du Pont Crowninshield Research Building, dedicated in 1969, which includes the library and the conservation laboratories. The Main Museum, which incorporates architectural elements of three earlier du Pont homes going back to 1839, was placed on the National Register of Historic Places in 1971. The Odessa properties include five historic structures and their dependencies: the Collins-Sharp House (c. 1700), the Warner-Wilson House (1769), the Corbit-Sharp House (1772), John Janvier Stable (1791), and the Brick Hotel (1822). The last four are open to the public. These buildings form a major part of Historic Odessa, a district registered under the National Register of Historic Places.

The grounds and gardens are the setting, and the buildings the base for Winterthur's many-sided activities designed to promote the study and teaching of early American culture. The origin of this program is to be found in Mr. du Pont's third area of interest and achievement—the American decorative arts. As early as 1923 he formed the resolve to collect American furniture and furnishings to 1840, and soon thereafter decided to assemble and display these in appropriately contemporary architectural interiors secured from American residential structures from Maine to Georgia. His motivation, he wrote, was the realization "that early American arts and crafts had not been given the recognition they deserved," and his objective became "to afford all those interested an opportunity to view and to study the conditions surrounding early American home life." By the mid-1930s Mr. du Pont was recognized as America's foremost collector of antiques. In 1951 the former curator of the American Wing of the Metropolitan Museum of Art described his collection as "the largest and richest assemblage of American decorative arts ever brought together." Over the next eighteen years Mr. du Pont installed twenty-five additional rooms furnished with hundreds of new objects.

It was one of H. F.'s distinctions that he knew how to find and use the expert advice of many specialists. It was one of them, Charles F. Montgomery, who formed the conviction that Mr. du Pont's collection should be made the foundation of a nationally recognized center for the study and teaching of early American culture; that this study should begin with the home and the objects made to furnish, embellish, and equip it; and that these objects should be examined and interpreted as art, as examples of craftsmanship, and as artifacts conditioned by and implementing their culture and thus serving as basic nonverbal documents. He found Mr. du Pont ready and eager to support this ambitious dream and the steps necessary to implement it.

The Winterthur collections constitute an archive of the material culture of the chiefly Anglo-American society of the eastern seaboard of North America between 1640 and 1850. Emphasis is on artifacts relating to the home made by artisans and artists. These artifacts, numbering about fifty thousand, might be loosely classified as representing the practical arts (tools, utensils, instruments), the decorative arts (furniture and furnishings made of ceramics, glass, textiles, and metals—silver, pewter, brass, copper, iron, and tin), folk art, and the fine arts (exterior and interior architecture, painting, sculpture, and the graphic arts). It is probably the largest and most comprehensive collection of such arts made in America and imported from Europe and Asia. The special strengths of the collections are in American furniture (about four thousand pieces), lighting devices, Pennsylvania folk art, Chinese export porcelain made for the American market, and textiles made after 1600. Also outstanding are its holdings in American metalwork (about five thousand examples), especially silver and pewter; American pottery, glass, prints, and paintings; English delft and Oriental rugs. Supplementary to the main collections are, at Winterthur, the Textile Study Collection, the Maps and Prints Collections, the Ineson-Bissell Collection of Small Silver Objects, the study collection of reproductions, forgeries, broken objects, and antique objects not on display; and, at Odessa, the four house museums.

The objects in the collections are given daily care by the housekeeping staff. In addition, the collections are cared for by the conservation staff, which at present represents seventeen people who specialize in six different areas: paint, glass and ceramics, metals, furniture, paper, and textiles. These areas also receive support from the conservation photographer and a well-equipped analytical laboratory. The latter aids the conservation and curatorial staffs in both assessing the provenance, age, and maker of museum objects and identifying the materials used in fabricating and finishing them. The types of analysis carried out include chemical, X-ray fluorescence, infrared, ultraviolet, gas chromatography, and related methods.

The segment of American material culture represented by the collections —as conserved by the conservation laboratories and identified by the data from the analytical laboratory and the files of the registrar's office—is illumined and amplified by the verbal and visual documents in the museum library. This complex occupies two and a half floors and five stacks in the Research Building and contains approximately 52,000 bound volumes, 325 periodical subscriptions, 6,241 lots of manuscripts, 3,612 reels of microfilm, 5,000 microfiche cards, 120,000 photographs, and 84,000 slides. The general scope of the library is American fine and decorative arts, their social setting and European backgrounds to the Armory Show in 1913. Included are several thousand volumes of rare books which include what is probably the finest collection of British architectural and design publications in this country, American architectural books, trade catalogs, cabinetmakers' and architects' price books, American illustrated books before 1860, and early children's books. Special collections include the Waldron Phoenix Belknap Jr. Research Library of American Painting, established in 1958, containing books, prints, manuscripts, and photographs emphasizing the relationship between American painting and its European background; the Edward Deming Andrews Memorial Shaker Collection; and the Joseph Downs Manuscript and Microfilm Collection, established in 1955, containing material bearing on American arts, artists, and craftsmen before 1914. The Slide Library specializes in the history of art in the United States and its European origins. The province of the Photographic Index of American Art and Design (25,000 photos) is American paintings, sculptures, and graphics produced before 1914; of the Symonds Collection (10,000 photos), English furniture and clocks collected by the English scholar R. W. Symonds; of the Decorative Arts Photographic Collection (85,000 photos), American decorative art with special emphasis on documented furniture and metal objects. The latter also maintains the Woodworking Craftsmen and Silversmiths Files, each having more than 15,000 names and dates, the Touchmark File of American Silversmiths' Die Marks (4,500 marks), and the Prime File, 20,000 cards recording newspaper advertisements of craftsmen from 1721 to 1800. Special information retrieval systems include "Termatrex" in the manuscript collection, the McBee Keysort System in the Decorative Arts Photographic Collection, and a cross-reference file in the library based on "The Outline of Cultural Materials" developed by the Yale Human Relations Area File.

The publications program serves both those who visit the museum and a national audience by publishing books, periodicals, films, filmstrips, and slides bearing on the collections and subjects related to them. Forty-seven titles were published between 1963 and 1980. One objective has been to issue well-researched catalogs of the museum's holdings, such as *American Furniture: Queen Anne and Chippendale Periods* (1952). Another has been to publish the papers read at the Winterthur Conference, a professional meeting held annually from 1954 to 1975 and every two years since 1975. An even broader commitment to encouraging the study of American culture is represented by the *Winterthur Portfolio*, first published in 1964, an annual collection of scholarly articles contributed by academic and museum scholars nationwide. From 1968 through 1978, the publication was distributed by the University Press of Virginia. In 1979 it became a quarterly journal published for the museum by the University of Chicago Press. Substantive book reviews became a regular feature, and the journal adopted the subtitle "A Journal of American Material Culture."

Two publications serve as channels of communication in the Winterthur community and among the museum's growing constituency. The *Winterthur Newsletter*, issued monthly from 1955 through 1977, and since then six times a year, evolved from an in-house publication to become the major carrier of news and events to the membership of the Winterthur Guild (five thousand three hundred members by the end of 1980) and other friends of the museum. Since 1977, in-house news has been circulated in the *Reporter*. Both the *Newsletter* and the *Reporter* began appearing quarterly in 1981.

With the collections, libraries, and laboratories as study and research resources, Winterthur offers a broad program of educational services for every level of age and interest. There are four graduate study programs, three of them taught and administered jointly with the University of Delaware, which prepare students for careers in academic, museum, and historical-cultural agency positions: the two-year Winterthur Program in Early American Culture established in 1952; the three-year Winterthur Program in the Conservation of Artistic and Historic Objects, established in

1974; an interdisciplinary program in American Material Culture offered within the History of American Civilization Ph.D. course of study, established in 1979; and the Winterthur Summer Institute on the Decorative Arts in America to 1950, established in 1967. At the museum's Odessa properties and in collaboration with the American studies program of the University of Delaware, a semester course in community studies and a winter session seminar explore the role of this community in developing a distinctive regional culture between 1750 and 1850. Winterthur also sponsors a series of conferences and symposia. At the popular education levels, Winterthur offers to the public forty-three different tours conducted by a staff of 112 professional guides. In 1979 some 130,000 persons participated in 250,000 of these tours.

In addition to the research continuously in progress by its staff, graduate students, and visiting scholars, Winterthur offers three postdoctoral NEH research fellowships to provide six to eleven months in residence at Winterthur.

Winterthur has long been one of the foremost teaching museums in the United States. Its first graduate program was planned before its museum was opened to the public. Its M.A. and M.S. courses of study are two of the nation's outstanding graduate programs in museum studies. An average of fifty graduate students are in residence at Winterthur every year. Sixteen members of its staff serve as adjunct professors on the University of Delaware faculty. In 1979 this long tradition of scholarly activity was recognized by the National Endowment for the Humanities, when it designated Winterthur as one of twelve Centers for Advanced Study, the only museum in the United States to receive this distinction.

Winterthur is administered by a director operating through three deputy directors. Winterthur's four directors have been Charles F. Montgomery (1954-1962), Edgar P. Richardson (1962-1966), Charles van Ravenswaay (1966-1976), and James Morton Smith (1976 to date). Authority is vested in a thirty-member, self-perpetuating board of trustees. Winterthur employees number 350: 123 full-time, and 227 part-time, including 103 professional guides at the museum and 9 at Odessa. The Winterthur Corporation is a private, nonprofit foundation supported by investment income, gifts, government and foundation grants, program-generated income, and a marketing program creating and selling authentic reproductions of objects in the collection. Gifts include those made by the Friends of Winterthur, founded in 1964 and numbering about 275, and the Winterthur Guild, founded in 1976 and numbering about 5,300.

For further information, see Charles F. Montgomery, "The Henry Francis du Pont Winterthur Museum," *Museum* (1957); John A. H. Sweeney, *The Treasure House of Early American Rooms* (1963); E. McClung Fleming, "Accent on Artist and Artisan: The Winterthur Program in Early American Culture," *American Quarterly* (Summer, 1970); Frank H.

Sommer, "A Large Museum Library," *Special Libraries* (March, 1974); and James Morton Smith and Charles F. Hummel, "The Henry Francis du Pont Winterthur Museum," *Antiques* (June, 1978). See also the following Winterthur publications: *Four Month Reports* (1952-62) and *Annual Reports* (1962 to date); *Winterthur Newsletter* (1955 to date); *Reporter* (1977 to date); and *The Winterthur Story* (1965).

E. McCLUNG FLEMING

HIGH ALTITUDE OBSERVATORY. See University Corporation for Atmospheric Research.

HISPANIC SOCIETY OF AMERICA. The founder of the Hispanic Society of America was Archer M. Huntington, the adopted son of railway magnate Collis P. Huntington. The former was privately tutored and as a young man spent years in travel and study in Spain, which resulted in his assembling one of the world's finest collections of Hispanic manuscripts, books, paintings, and other works of art. In 1904 he founded the Hispanic Society of America in order to make his collection available to the public. His deed of foundation provided for an endowment of land and money for the erection of a free public museum and reference library to present the culture of Hispanic peoples. A building to carry out these purposes was erected in 1905, with an addition in 1930, for a collection that now contains thousands of manuscripts and over 150,000 books dealing with Spanish, Portuguese, and Latin American art, history, and literature.

Membership in the society is by invitation. It is limited to 100 honorary members chosen from 300 previously elected corresponding members. Election as a corresponding member is based on recommendations from the Hispanic Society's research staff, members, and others to the governing board of trustees. Honorary members are elected from "scholars and creative workers of recognized achievement in the fields of Hispanic arts and letters." Proposed members are presented to the board of trustees only after extensive screening with respect to "recognized achievement," which includes an exhaustive and factual report by the membership librarian of the society. Membership, in both categories, is open to residents of the United States as well as foreign countries. In 1975 there were 134 members resident in the United States and Canada, 188 in Europe, 68 in Latin America, and 10 elsewhere.

Since its founding the Hispanic Society has carried on an impressive research and publication program. Approximately four hundred volumes have been published under its auspices together with the production of a number of films and recordings. A large proportion of the publications and films and recordings deal with the society's collections and were written or directed by present or former staff members. Currently, this staff numbers nine persons, including one Ph.D., several doctoral candidates, and seven persons with a master's or professional degree.

The Hispanic Society makes five different awards periodically for scholarly distinction in Hispanic literature and art. Also, beginning in 1970, it has been the contributing sponsor to the *Hispanic Review.*

The society elects the customary institutional officers; it conducts its activities and programs, headed by a director, from offices in its museum and library located in New York City.

For further information, see *A History of the Hispanic Society of America, 1904-1954, with a Survey of the Collections* (1954). See also *The Hispanic Society of America. Catalogue of Publications* (1943); and *The Hispanic Society of America: Archer M. Huntington (1870-1955), In Memoriam* (1972). For a brief account of the society, see "The Hispanic Society of America," *ACLS Newsletter* (Winter, 1973). See also "Archer Milton Huntington," *The National Cyclopedia of American Biography* (1962).

HISTORICAL SOCIETY OF PENNSYLVANIA, THE. A number of state historical societies have achieved the status of major research institutions, and one of the most important in the country is the Historical Society of Pennsylvania, founded in Philadelphia on December 2, 1824.

Reasons and motives for founding historical societies in the United States have varied. The spirit of the Enlightenment and the Puritan tendency toward a theistic interpretation of history probably helped launch the first, the Massachusetts Historical Society,* in 1791. Not until the decade of the 1820s did such societies begin to proliferate, primarily under the stimulus of nationalism and patriotism. In some instances, too, the force of a single personality played a vital role in bringing them into existence, for example, that of Jeremy Belknap in Massachusetts, John Pintard in New York, and Jonathan Peter Cushing in Virginia. In the founding of the Historical Society of Pennsylvania, certain members of the American Philosophical Society* (APS) and the Pennsylvania bar were the catalytic agents.

On March 17, 1815, the American Philosophical Society created a committee on "History, Moral Science, and General Literature," to be chaired by a scholarly Philadelphia lawyer named Peter Stephen DuPonceau (1760-1844). The committee and its chairman defined history in a broad and inclusive fashion so as to include such present-day disciplines as geography, economics, and sociology, together with some in the natural sciences. The group collected materials on the early history of Pennsylvania, and DuPonceau eventually published two works in history and three on Indian languages, one of his major interests.

By late 1824, DuPonceau and several other Philadelphians, mostly lawyers, decided to form a separate historical society. The founding meeting took place at the home of Thomas Wharton (1791-1856), a lawyer and member of the APS. In February of 1825, William Rawle (1759-1836), also a lawyer and member of the Library Company of Philadelphia,* assumed office as the group's president. In its first year, the new organization adopted a constitution which declared that the society's purpose was to elucidate and study the natural, civil, and literary history of the state, and the Commonwealth of Pennsylvania granted the fledgling society a charter of incorporation in June of 1826. Following the pattern established by the Massachusetts Historical Society, the Pennsylvanians received no public support for operations, and ever since the society has depended almost entirely on paid memberships, contributions, and bequests for its support.

Starting any new organization is difficult, and the Historical Society of Pennsylvania had its share of problems. Initially, the society limited membership to persons who had lived in Pennsylvania for ten years. Because the principal source of income was the paid subscription from members, this restriction worked to limit the income and the early activities of the society. In the depression of the late 1830s, membership fell to a low of 24, and this brush with extinction motivated the society to stronger efforts to attract members, including modification of the earlier residency requirement for membership. By 1846, the number of members had grown to 146; and, by 1854, it had climbed to 402.

In the post-Civil War years the society maintained a slow but steady growth in membership, and their dues plus a number of bequests and philanthropic grants, such as the 1875 bequest of sixty thousand dollars from the estate of Henry D. Gilpin, put it on a sound financial footing. For its present-day operations, the society relies primarily on its income from such endowments plus contributions from about three thousand members. The membership fees range from a twenty-five-dollar general membership to a thousand-dollar benefactor membership.

From its founding the Historical Society of Pennsylvania devoted itself to collecting and publishing historical source material. From 1826 to 1895, fourteen volumes of *Memoirs* were published. Also in the nineteenth century, in conjunction with the American Philosophical Society* and the State of Pennsylvania, the society cosponsored the publication of sixteen volumes of *Colonial Records* and twelve volumes of *Pennsylvania Archives*. This preservation through publication of selected documents was quite popular in the nineteenth century, but the practice gradually disappeared because of the expense involved and because of the rising influence of the professional historians, who opposed the selective editing and publication of documents as unscientific.

One of the Historical Society of Pennsylvania's major achievements has been the issuance, beginning in 1877, of the *Pennsylvania Magazine of History and Biography*. Certainly one of the best of the state historical journals, the architect in its founding was Frederick D. Stone, who served as librarian of the society from 1877 to 1897. The most recently retired editor is Nicholas B. Wainwright, who had served in that capacity since 1952 and was also director of the society from 1965 to 1974. His successor and the incumbent editor is J. William Frost.

Another major achievement of the society has been the gradual creation of a large and important research library. In 1844, its holdings totaled only sixty volumes. Today the number of volumes has expanded to a quarter of a million, and the society has accumulated over fourteen million manuscript items. The collections cover the whole span of American history from 1492 to the present. The most notable manuscripts include collections of the papers of the Penn family, the American Negro Historical Society, John and William Bartram, Joel Poinsett, the Bank of North America, James Buchanan, and Jay Cooke. In general, the holdings are especially strong in business history, church history, and genealogy.

The society lacked permanent quarters throughout the nineteenth century and was forced to move four different times in the decades prior to the Civil War. Following that conflict, it was successively located at the "Picture Building" and then the Patterson House at 1300 Locust Street. Finally the Commonwealth of Pennsylvania provided $150,000 in 1910 toward the construction of a permanent building for the society at 1300 Locust Street, on the site of the razed Patterson House where it is presently located. Adjacent is the building that houses the Library Company of Philadelphia.*

The governance of the society is carried out by an elected president, two vice-presidents, a secretary, a treasurer, and a number of councillors serving staggered terms. The chief executive officer is presently titled director, and the incumbent is Dr. James E. Mooney, 1975 to the present.

For further information, see Hampton L. Carson, *A History of the Historical Society of Pennsylvania* (1940); Leslie Dunlap, *Historical Societies in the United States, 1790-1860* (1944); Walter Muir Whitehill, *Independent Historical Societies* (1962); and Clifford L. Lord, ed., *Keepers of the Past* (1965).

ROGER D. TATE, JR.

HISTORY OF SCIENCE SOCIETY (HSS). This society traces its origins to a general increase in interest in the historical aspects of science during several decades before and during World War I. Some of the foremost figures in its founding in 1924 were a group centering in the American Association for the Advancement of Science* (AAAS) and the American Historical Association* (AHA): F. E. Brasch, L. J. Henderson, David Eugene Smith, Lynn Thorndike, and, particularly, George Sarton, a Belgian scholar who had devoted years of study to the relationship of history to science prior to coming to this country in 1915 and had, in 1912, founded the journal *Isis* devoted to the subject.

The primary purpose of the HSS was and is to promote the study of the history of science. One of its earliest undertakings, in 1924, was the naming of the quarterly *Isis* as its official journal. George Sarton, who remained its editor down to 1945, had supported it almost single-handedly during its early years; as late as 1933, he estimated that of the first eighteen volumes issued he had given as many as half outright to subscribers. Nevertheless, the measure of financial support stemming from HSS sponsorship made its position much less precarious. *Isis* contains articles, book reviews, and news of interest to historians of science together with exhaustive annual bibliographies of books and articles dealing with the subject. An equally important recent publication is the multivolume *Dictionary of Scientific Biography*, published with the cooperation of the HSS under the auspices of the American Council of Learned Societies* (ACLS) and with the support of the National Science Foundation. Also, since 1972, a quarterly *Newsletter* has been issued.

Up until 1929, annual HSS meetings were held in conjunction with those of the AAAS. Subsequently, however, the policy has been followed of meeting alternately with the AAAS and the AHA, although in recent years this schedule has not been followed strictly.

The HSS confers a number of annual prizes: the Henry Schuman Prize for the best undergraduate or graduate paper in the history of science; the Pfizer Award for the best book on the subject published during the year previous to the award; and the Sarton Medal for distinguished contributions in furthering the history of science. Recently, the Zeitlin-Ver Brugge Prize was instituted to encourage the publication in *Isis* of original research of the highest standard. Consisting of $250 and a certificate, this prize is also given annually to the author of the best article in *Isis* in the three years prior to the year of the award. Also, in connection with its fiftieth anniversary celebration in 1974, the HSS established an Endowment Fund; the income from the fund is used for various societal purposes, such as supporting lectures, and special issues of *Isis*.

The HSS brings together in its membership persons of the widest academic, professional, business, and governmental backgrounds. Membership is open to persons interested in the history of science and to libraries, museums, and other institutions. Within a year of its founding, HSS membership totaled 505 individuals and 61 institutions. From that point on, however, growth was slow, and it was not until 1962 that individual membership climbed to about 1,000 and institutional to about 900. At the present time there are about 1,450 and 1,600 members, respectively, in each category.

The HSS elects the customary institutional officers; it conducts its business from an office, headed by a secretary, located in Syracuse, New York.

For further information, see various historical articles appearing in *Isis* (December, 1975), in connection with the fiftieth anniversary celebration of the HSS. See also Dorothy Stimson, "History of Science Society," *World of the Mind* (1958); and Henry Guerlac, "Address of Retiring President," *Isis* (March, 1961).

HOOVER INSTITUTION ON WAR, REVOLUTION AND PEACE. The Hoover Institution at Stanford University dates back to 1919, when Herbert Hoover, a Stanford alumnus, offered a gift of fifty thousand dollars for collecting documents on the World War. Stanford President Ray Lyman Wilbur sent Professor Ephraim D. Adams to Europe to direct a team of young scholars who, at Hoover's request, were released from military service to become "historical sleuths." The Adams team concentrated its efforts on Western Europe; a second effort, led by Professor Frank A. Golder, focused on Central and Eastern Europe. A third core collection, dealing with Germany, Central Europe, and the Paris Peace Conference, was amassed by Professor Ralph H. Lutz. Golder later acquired twenty-five thousand volumes and sixty thousand pamphlets on tsarist Russia, the Bolshevik revolution, and the new Soviet regime. When Nobel laureate Alexander Solzhenitsyn used these materials in 1975, he observed that these documents were outstanding and unique; they comprised the kind of material that the Soviet Union, in order to change history, had either destroyed or made unavailable to scholars.

At the outbreak of World War II, the collecting effort was expanded to include Japan and East Asia. After the war, collections dealing with Africa, the Middle East, and Latin America were begun. Subsequently, each of these areas was placed under the supervision of a full-time curator, and considerable sums were devoted to building these collections.

As a result the Hoover Institution today is the world's largest private repository for documentation on twentieth-century political history. Its 25 million documents, in nearly 4,000 separate collections, include the papers of diplomats, military officers, politicians, journalists, and scholars, as well as the records of American and foreign organizations whose activities dealt with war and peace, revolution, resistance to tyranny, and relief for the victims of war and famine. The holdings include an immensely rich collection of "ephemera"—leaflets, tracts, broadsides, photographs, posters, and banners—that is essential for understanding the growth and appeal of radical and revolutionary movements in this century. These materials are supplemented by a specialized library containing more than 1.3 million books, as well as 24,000 magazines and 6,000 newspaper files.

During the middle and later 1950s, the institution curtailed its publishing activities due to difficulties in attracting sufficient gifts to cover operating expenses. Fund raising was a necessity because Stanford University, under President Wilbur, had accepted Hoover's blueprint for the institution: that it always was to have a separate identity and endowment. Each of the first four directors—E. D. Adams (1920-1925), Ralph Lutz (1925-1944), Harold H. Fisher (1944-1952), and C. Easton Rothwell (1952-1959)—had been historians who viewed the institution's primary function as collecting documents but placed less emphasis on having them interpreted. By the late

1950s, Hoover wanted the institution to play a more active role in contributing to the discussion of major issues of public policy. In 1959, at the suggestion of Raymond Moley, Hoover nominated W. Glenn Campbell, a young Canadian-born, Harvard-educated economist, to become the institution's fifth director. Campbell had previously served as a research economist for the U.S. Chamber of Commerce and then as research director for the American Enterprise Institute for Public Policy Research* (AEI).

During his first years as director, Campbell made very few new appointments to the staff; he concentrated, instead, on building a cash reserve to cover three years of operating expenses so that the institution would not be vulnerable again. Campbell's fund-raising efforts proved successful: by 1963 he already had obtained two million dollars in cash or firm pledges for future gifts. Since that time, the institution has been able to attract scholars of national and international reputation. Among the best-known scholars have been sociologist Seymour Martin Lipset, political theorist Eric Voegelin, economists Milton Friedman, Martin Anderson, and Thomas Sowell, physicist Edward Teller, philosopher Sidney Hook, and historians Bertram D. Wolfe and Robert Conquest.

A decade ago, the institution began to strengthen research on domestic affairs as a counterpart to its traditional emphasis on international affairs and diplomatic history. The Domestic Studies Program, headed by Thomas Gale Moore, focuses on research and publication on issues such as income redistribution, regulatory reform, taxation, nuclear energy, social security, the welfare system, and the economics of crime and punishment.

In 1966, the International Studies Program, headed by Richard F. Staar, began publishing an annual *Yearbook on International Communist Affairs*, a project inaugurated by Richard V. Allen. Since 1978, the program has undertaken four new monograph series: on Latin America, on defense, on the ruling Communist parties of the world, and a general series, Hoover International Studies, whose first volumes have dealt with the Panama Canal controversy, the future of South Africa, security in the Persian Gulf, modernization in China, and Yugoslavia after Tito.

The National Fellows Program, begun in 1971, and headed by Dennis L. Bark, enables the institution to invite a dozen younger scholars for a year of postdoctoral research, free from any teaching responsibilities. Several, designated as 'public affairs fellows,' spend a second year in Washington, D.C., working as aides to members of Congress or serving on the staffs of congressional committees.

Originally housed in a separate wing of the Stanford University library, the institution did not possess its own building until the construction, in 1941, of the fifteen-story Hoover Tower. Less than a decade after Campbell became director, a second building was needed, and in 1967 the Lou Henry Hoover Building, honoring Hoover's wife, was opened. A third structure was built using seven million dollars of federal funds on a matching grant basis. In 1975, President Gerald Ford signed a bill authorizing the Herbert Hoover Memorial Building as the sole federal memorial to the former president, and in 1978 Ford went to Stanford to dedicate the new facility.

The institution's rapidly growing publications program has helped to extend its impact on public policy analysis. The Hoover Institution Press now publishes more than thirty-five books a year. By far the best-known work is *The United States in the 1980's*, edited by Peter Duignan and Alvin Rabushka. It consists of specially commissioned essays on the domestic and foreign policy decisions that confront America. In the domestic essays—written by Milton Friedman, Martin Anderson, Alan Greenspan, Murray L. Weidenbaum, and others who served on President-elect Ronald Reagan's transition teams—the authors stress the importance of releasing the creative energies of the private sector. They urge strict spending limits at all levels of government and massive deregulation of the American economy. Their analysis is applied to a broad range of issues, including taxation, welfare, housing, urban problems, health care, energy, economic stability, inflation, regulation, environmental protection, and higher education. Their theme was prominently reflected in President Reagan's inaugural address in January, 1981.

Similarly, the writers on foreign affairs—including Fred Charles Iklé, Ray S. Cline, Edward Teller, Richard J. Whalen, and Robert A. Scalapino —emphasize the need for realism after a decade of despair and disillusionment about America's waning power in world affairs. They argue that détente has not reduced Soviet expansionism, that the United States has lost military superiority to the Soviet Union and must regain it, that foreign aid cannot wipe out poverty, and that different cultural values and political traditions in foreign nations make it difficult, perhaps even impossible, to export democratic ideas and institutions. They caution the United States to avoid the twin perils of inflated expectations and embittered frustrations and to concentrate on what must be done to restrain Soviet power and influence in world affairs.

The *New York Times* in 1978 called the Hoover Institution the "brightest star" in the constellation of conservative think tanks, and in 1981 Ronald Reagan commented that he drew more people from the Hoover Institution to help with his presidential campaign than any other institution. As his chief advisors on national security affairs and domestic policy, he chose two scholars—Richard V. Allen and Martin Anderson—long identified with the institution. It is a remarkable development for an institution in only twenty years.

For further information, see the following articles: Kenneth L. Woodward, "Conservative Brain Trust," *Newsweek* (January 12, 1976); Peter H. King, "Hoover's Tower of Power: Domestic Influence Grows," San Francisco *Examiner* (May 9, 1978); Kenneth Lamott; "Right-Thinking Think

Tank," *New York Times Magazine* (July 23, 1978); Stewart McBride, "Leaning to the Right," *Christian Science Monitor* (April 2, 1980). See also Charles G. Palm and Dale Reed, *Guide to the Hoover Institution Archives* (1980); Peter Duignan and Alvin Rabushka, eds., *The United States in the 1980's* (1980); W. Glenn Campbell, "Herbert Hoover and the Hoover Institution," in *Herbert Hoover Reassessed* (1981); and Hoover Institution *Annual Reports*, particularly those for 1963 and 1980.

ROBERT HESSEN

HUDSON INSTITUTE. The Hudson Institute was founded in 1961 by Herman Kahn and Max Singer, both of whom had been with the Rand Corporation.* Their purpose was to create a small independent research organization that would concentrate on broad public policy issues as distinct from narrow technological problems. Thus the motto of the institute is "policy research in the public interest." Independence has several connotations for Hudson. First, although it works for many U.S. and foreign government agencies, its existence is dependent on no outside group. Second, it adopts no "official" position or doctrine on substantive issues. Its findings and recommendations reflect the views of specific researchers or teams of researchers working on particular problems. This is not to say that the institute does not sometimes develop an identifiable outlook on certain issues that reflects a consensus among its staff, but such a consensus is not mandated, nor would Hudson take on a contractual obligation in which it was. As a corollary, the Hudson staff includes a cross section of ideological and political viewpoints. The expression of independent positions is encouraged; intellectual and professional competence are the only criteria upon which the institute judges its own work.

In the early years of its existence, the institute concentrated almost exclusively on national security issues, and its principal client was the U.S. Department of Defense. This focus reflected inter alia the professional interests of its director, Herman Kahn, who had published *On Thermonuclear War* in 1960.

Hudson's work in this area has been wide ranging. Early military studies included such topics as civil defense, arms control, missile defense, and the American national interest in international order. Emphasis shifted later to counter insurgency and the U.S. role in Vietnam. More recent studies in this area have included future military technology, the Strategic Arms Limitation Treaty, nonnuclear wars, and nuclear proliferation. A Defense Issues Program was founded in 1980 to analyze relevant problems for a small group of major firms that specialize in military hardware.

Although the institute's single largest research concentration remains national security issues, by the mid-1960s its attention had begun to broaden into other areas. Thus economic development studies commenced in 1965 with a contract with the government of Colombia. Over the years, similar work has involved Algeria, Angola, Thailand, Mexico, Brazil, and such advanced economies as France, the United Kingdom, and the United States. Much of this work is summed up in Herman Kahn, *World Economic Development* (1979).

In 1970, the institute began its Corporate Environment Program. This program alerts participating companies to important social, political, and economic trends that are likely to affect the business environment in the mid- and long-term future. The program has been supported by over 100 corporations and other organizations.

With publication of Herman Kahn's and A. J. Weiner's, *The Year 2,000* (1967), the institute launched a series of future studies. In addition to exploring future prospects for the world and regional, national, and other entities, these studies have explored and applied a methodology of studying the future. Among these techniques is the creation of alternative scenarios as a basis for speculation and policy assessment. Since 1967, Hudson has carried out studies on the future of Japan, Canada, Brazil, Australia, Arizona, and Westchester County in New York State. In addition, Herman Kahn, William M. Brown, and Leon C. Martel, in *The Next 200 Years* (1976), argued that—contrary to widespread concerns about population growth, resource shortages, and pollution—mankind can face the future with hope and even confidence.

Since 1971, the institute has devoted intensive and increasing attention to energy and food studies. In general, it has taken a relatively optimistic position regarding these problems. In 1977, a comprehensive report made recommendations for a national energy policy. Two comprehensive volumes have summarized the institute's work on food issues: Marilyn Chou, David P. Harmon, Herman Kahn, and Sylvan Wittwer, *World Food Prospects and Agricultural Potential* (1977), and Marilyn Chou and David P. Harmon (eds.), *Critical Food Issues of the 1980's* (1979).

Since the early 1970s, the institute has devoted increasing attention to American domestic problems, primarily the economy and urban affairs. Such studies have included policy analyses of legalized gambling, drug abuse, federal poverty programs, the economic development of the United States and its regions, U.S. public opinion, and the crisis in U.S. public education. In general, Hudson has adopted a neoconservative stance in dealing with contemporary socioeconomic problems.

To assess the accomplishments of the Hudson Institute over nearly twenty years is no simple task. It has certainly been successful in opening up the field of future studies and in bringing many key policy positions to the attention of the public, government agencies, and business leaders. More specifically, Hudson was almost alone in forecasting the spectacular economic success of Japan and the economic strength of France—not to mention the relative economic decline of the United Kingdom. Although many of its studies have concretely affected government and other policy decisions, others have had little apparent impact. For example, Hudson has long emphasized the production of coal and synthetic fuel as key components of U.S. energy policy; these ideas are now espoused by the Department of Energy. Quite apart from its specific policy impact, Hudson has for many years conducted a series of lecture seminars on policy issues that are attended by influential people from government, business, the military, the media, and other vocations. These sessions have undoubtedly served to disseminate Hudson's views and to stimulate discussion of the issues presented.

A basic attribute of the institute is its small size. Thus its professional staff of mathematicians, physicists, economists, lawyers, journalists, engineers, political scientists, and others has never exceeded fifty people. Roughly speaking, social scientists have outnumbered physical scientists by about three to one. Analysts are not compartmentalized into separate areas. In addition to authors and officers identified elsewhere in the essay, Hudson's professional staff has included Frank Armbruster, Paul Bracken, B. Bruce-Briggs, Lewis Dunn, Raymond Gastil, Colin Gray, Irving Leveson, Jane Newitt, William Overholt, Robert Panero, Thomas Pepper, William Pfaff, William Schneider, Jr., and Edmund Stillman. Many consultants have participated in Hudson studies.

The institute is managed by researchers rather than professional administrators. Since 1961 it has had five presidents (Donald Brennan, Max Singer, Clifford L. Lord, Ruby Ruggles, Jr., and Gail Potter) and one director (Herman Kahn). It has evolved an organizational structure that consists of four elements: trustees, members, management, and employees. The basic constituency of the institute is its members, who are divided into three categories. Public members are prominent persons in such fields as business, politics, and education; fellow members are primarily noted scholars; and employee members are drawn from the senior staff of the institute. The members elect the board of trustees, who oversee and are responsible for institute activities. The board chooses its own chairman and elects the president, who appoints the other officers at the institute.

The Hudson Institute is a nonprofit organization. It is supported primarily by contract work for government agencies and private firms and by annual subscription fees paid by participants in its multiclient programs. In addition, a small but growing amount of supplementary support is provided by foundations and private individuals. In the early years of its existence, the bulk of its income was derived from the U.S. Department of Defense. However, since the early 1970s, only about a third of the institute's income has been provided by government defense contracts. The remaining two-thirds has come from nondefense government contracts, policy studies for private industry, various institute programs, and grants. Hudson Research Services, Inc., a wholly owned, taxable subsidiary of the institute, performs proprietary services for the United States and for public and private sectors abroad.

The headquarters of the Hudson Institute are in Croton-on-Hudson, New York. Two independent affiliates, Hudson Research Europe, Ltd., and Hudson Institute of Canada, are located in Paris and Montreal. An Asia-Pacific office is located in Tokyo.

For further information, see Mark J. Smith, *A Short History of Hudson Institute, 1961-1972* (1972); and a 1979 institute information pamphlet, both published by Hudson Institute. See also Hudson Institute *Annual Reports*, particularly 1975, 1977, and 1978.

ERNEST E. SCHNEIDER

HUNTINGTON LIBRARY, ART GALLERY, BOTANICAL GARDENS. This privately endowed research institution is situated on 207 acres of beautifully landscaped grounds in the residential suburb of San Marino, twelve miles east of Los Angeles. Its origins can be traced to a pleasant day in 1892, when its founder visited Southern California on his way from New York to San Francisco, where he was to join his uncle, Collis P. Huntington, in operating the Southern Pacific Railroad. One high point of his stopover was a visit to the 600-acre ranch of J. de Barth Shorb, where he feasted his eyes on the sun-dappled San Gabriel Valley, checkerboarded with orchards and framed by two mountain ranges. From that moment Mr. Huntington was determined to make his home in that modern-day paradise.

His dream came true ten years later when, shortly after his uncle's death, he returned to Los Angeles to launch a career in urban and interurban transit that was to amass a sizable fortune. Shorb was dead by this time, and his ranch fallen into disrepair; but his heirs were willing to sell, and Mr. Huntington was eager to buy. In 1903 the sale was arranged, and Mr. Huntington turned his genius into its improvement. This included extensive gardens, orange and avocado groves, and a stately mansion that was completed in 1910 and today houses the extensive collections of French furnishings and English art that he was already beginning to acquire.

Even this early Mr. Huntington envisioned his estate as an eventual public institution. "I am going to give something to the public before I die," he told a friend in 1906. When he told architects designing his San Marino home to reinforce the second floor to hold a large number of people he was obviously thinking of his dwelling as a future art gallery where his treasures could be shared by the public.

He was even more concerned with the future of the rare books and manuscripts that he had been collecting since the 1890s. Increasingly he centered his purchases in English and American history and literature with an eye to a library that would be of use to specialists, not one simply to satisfy his own whims. These purchases mounted year after year, particularly after 1910, when he divorced himself from his more pressing business obligations to concentrate on buying books and paintings. His success was remarkable. Whole libraries were imported from Europe and the East, rare book was piled on rare book, priceless manuscript on priceless manuscript

—always with an eye to their future use. The advancement of humanistic learning, not his own satisfaction, was Mr. Huntington's guiding principle.

That he moved steadily in this direction was due partly to the influence of a world-famed astronomer, George Ellery Hale, a neighbor in nearby Pasadena and member of the staffs of the Mount Wilson Observatory and the fledgling school soon to be known as the California Institute of Technology. Hale, a dreamer of grandiose dreams and a promoter who could make them come true, saw Southern California as the future Athens of the United States, where scientific and humanistic studies would spark a national cultural outpouring. The observatory and university were already recruiting the world's most eminent scientists; an outstanding library in the humanities would lure scholars needed to crown this edifice in glory.

Hale was a gadfly who pestered Mr. Huntington with suggestions, some of them absurdly bad (such as a proposal that the books be housed in a four million-dollar marble replica of the Parthenon), some of them eminently practical—such as his insistence that a usable library be fashioned from the donor's collections. "The books," Hale wrote in 1914, "would then serve not merely as rare and interesting curiosities appreciated by the few, but as a continual source of literary and historical study." With his usual good sense, Mr. Huntington sifted the wheat from the chaff and by the summer of 1919 had perfected a workable plan for the Huntington Library. It would be located on his San Marino estate, not in New York or an ersatz Parthenon, and administered by a self-perpetuating board of five trustees. Its primary purpose would be to serve the needs of scholarship rather than the curiosity of the passerby. The trust indenture that gave legal substance to these plans was signed on August 30, 1919, and in 1922 his books, paintings, and estate were transferred to the trust, with the stipulation that they be used "to assure the advancement of learning."

Mr. Huntington's major holdings of books and manuscripts, long housed in New York, were transferred to San Marino in 1920, to be housed in a newly completed library building adjacent to his home. With their presence as an incentive, he devoted his remaining years to an unparalleled collecting spree. The famed art dealer, Sir Joseph Duveen, and the premier seller of rare books and manuscripts, Dr. A. S. W. Rosenbach, were frequent visitors at his home, arriving from the East with whole freight-car-loads of priceless books and paintings. As these treasures accumulated they were turned over to the trustees: $2 million worth in 1922, $7.5 million in 1923 and 1924, $3.5 million in 1925. Step by step, Mr. Huntington was building a collection of rarities that would rival those of the greatest cultural institutions of the East or Europe.

One more step remained, and that was of the utmost importance. The donor must be convinced that some of his fortune be used to transform his collection of rare books and manuscripts into a workable research library. This meant funds for the tools of scholarship—reference books, journals, government documents, and the like—and even larger sums for an endowment to provide for administration, future acquisitions, and grants to scholars.

Hale, who had been named a trustee, carried the banner here. For a time the cause seemed hopeless; as long as tempting books or paintings were available Mr. Huntington's collecting instincts could not be checked. Why put money aside for the future when a once-in-a-lifetime opportunity arose to buy a Gainsborough painting or a collection of Shakespeare first folios? Hale's one hope was to convince Mr. Huntington that his treasures would remain unknown unless prepared for publication by competent scholars and that those scholars must have the tools of their trade. This was on his mind when he persuaded the donor to invite a well-known historian and administrator, Dr. Max Farrand, to San Marino as the library's first senior research associate. Let the donor see a real scholar at work and he might recognize the needs of the profession.

Dr. Farrand spent the summer of 1926 at the library, busily engaged in editing for publication one of its most precious manuscripts: Benjamin Franklin's autobiography. Day after day Mr. Huntington watched him work and listened to his needs. By the end of that summer he had learned his lesson so well that Farrand was invited to remain as permanent director of research, and the benefactor had agreed to provide funds for administration, a permanent research staff of eminent scholars, and short-term grants to visiting researchers.

Mr. Huntington still had to be convinced that no paltry sum would do, and that a sizable endowment was necessary. A long memorandum from Farrand in January, 1927, stated the case bluntly: at least $7 million would be needed, and $17 million would be a more suitable figure. Mr. Huntington agreed in principle, but more fascinating ways of spending his fortune proved irresistible. During the early months of 1927 he spent more than $450,000 on works of art, then in April added another $380,000 to buy Sir Thomas Lawrence's famed painting of "Pinkie." He had not, he assured Hale and Farrand, forgotten his pledge to endow research properly; he might even be able to set aside $20 million for that purpose.

Alas such hopes. Mr. Huntington died unexpectedly in May, 1927, after a minor operation. When the trustees calculated the value of the endowment that he had set aside it totaled some $10.5 million for Huntington Library support. This was not what Hale and Farrand wanted, but it was far from an insignificant sum in those days. Even George Ellery Hale was forced to confess that "we can do very well with what we have."

The trustees "did very well" indeed over the next years. Their first step was the physical alteration of the library to assure proper care for the books and proper accommodations for readers; in the months after Mr. Huntington's death a reading room lined with twenty-five thousand reference works was installed, additional stacks built and equipped with steel shelves to reduce the fire hazard, temperature and humidity controls added, and a photographic department inaugurated to provide photocopies of rare materials to readers. Work was also begun on a usable catalog; by 1937, 615,000 cards guided scholars to the books and manuscripts they sought. The reference collections were built rapidly as collections of secondary works were purchased each year and a scout was employed to roam the West in search of manuscripts.

By the time Max Farrand retired as director in 1941, the library was a fully equipped research institution with a small group of well-known scholars serving on its permanent research staff, an efficient grants program to lure outstanding professors for year-long stays, and funds available for lesser awards to younger scholars who needed a month or two amidst its treasures. The permanent staff over the next years included such academic luminaries as Frederick Jackson Turner, Godfrey Davies, Collins Baker, Edwin Gay, Dixon Wecter, Robert G. Cleland, Allan Nevins, and A. L. Rowse.

For some years after Farrand's retirement a committee of these scholars and staff members administered the library's affairs, but the need for a permanent director was soon felt. J. E. Wallace Sterling assumed that post in 1948, only to be replaced by John E. Pomfret a year later when Sterling resigned to become president of Stanford University. On Pomfret's retirement in 1966 the post was assumed by James Thorpe, an eminent literary scholar from Princeton. All built well; during their administrations the rare book and manuscript collections were increased, the reference books kept up to date, new stack wings constructed, the buildings air-conditioned, the grounds beautified, and an imposing new wing added to house nonlibrary functions.

The institution today is administered by a director operating through four department heads: a librarian, a curator of art collections, a curator of the botanical gardens, and a director of administration and public services. Authority is vested in a five-person, self-perpetuating board of trustees, supplemented by a twenty-five-person board of overseers to aid in financial matters. More than two thousand friends of the library contribute to its support, as do nearly two hundred library fellows who pledge one thousand dollars yearly and a group of corporate fellows who give a still larger sum. In addition the library leans heavily on gifts from foundations and government agencies. These sums allow an extensive educational program in which well-trained volunteer docents offer instruction to some thirty-five hundred primary and secondary school students yearly.

The Huntington library's collections, still concentrated in English and American history and literature but with a fine collection of rare Continental books to illuminate the background of the British Renaissance, attract more than thirteen hundred scholars annually from all over the world; in addition nearly half a million visitors each year admire its spectacular gardens and the rich collections of French furniture and English paintings in the art gallery. Available to scholarly users are historical and literary riches ranging from its 5,400 incunabula to the papers of Wallace Stevens and Conrad Aiken. These include among the rare books nearly complete holdings of all titles printed during the sixteenth and seventeenth centuries, and among the manuscripts such essential collections as the Ellesmere, Hastings and Stowe papers (the latter of 525,000 items), as well as the papers of 455 British writers. Its book collections in American history are uniquely strong in the colonial, Revolutionary, and Civil War periods, and in the history of the West; manuscript holdings in these areas are surpassed only by the Library of Congress.

Its manuscript collections are described in *Guide to American History Manuscripts in the Huntington Library* (1979), and *Guide to Literary Manuscripts in the Huntington Library* (1979); there is one additional volume on the holdings in British history and another on medieval and Renaissance materials scheduled for publication by 1983.

The library also sustains a permanent staff of senior research scholars and annually awards grants to thirty or more qualified investigators who need to spend from a few weeks to a year among its collections. Its publications program is responsible for a scholarly journal, the *Huntington Library Quarterly*, and for six to ten volumes yearly based on its resources.

For further information, see the Huntington library *Annual Reports*, 1927 to date. For early histories of the library and its founder, see Robert O. Schad, "Henry Edwards Huntington: The Founder and the Library," *Huntington Library Bulletin* (May, 1931); and Godfrey Davies, "The Huntington Library as a Research Center, 1925-1927," *Huntington Library Quarterly* (May, 1948). For a later full-length history, see John E. Pomfret, *The Henry E. Huntington Library and Art Gallery: From Its Beginnings to 1960* (1969). See also James Thorpe, Robert E. Wark, and Ray A. Billington, *The Founding of the Henry E. Huntington Library and Art Gallery: Four Essays* (1969); and James Thorpe, *A Place of Learning: An Introduction to the Huntington Library, Art Gallery, Botanical Gardens* (1977).

RAY ALLEN BILLINGTON

HUTCHINS CENTER FOR THE STUDY OF DEMOCRATIC INSTITUTIONS. See Robert Maynard Hutchins Center for the Study of Democratic Institutions.

_I_

IIT RESEARCH INSTITUTE (IITRI). An independent, not-for-profit organization that applies science and technology to solve problems for industrial and government clients, IITRI is dedicated to the advancement and use of knowledge to meet the needs of society through the performance of contract research. Its research activities encompass virtually all of the physical sciences and their related technologies.

Established in 1936 by the trustees of Armour Institute of Technology, the Research Foundation of Armour Institute of Technology (as IITRI was originally called) was set up as the first not-for-profit research institute in the country. Its purpose was to help industry by providing facilities and staff to stimulate growth through technological development. The foundation consolidated the research activities of institute personnel. Early project work centered on the problems of efficient combustion of high volatile Illinois-Indiana coals, the design of coal stokers for domestic use, chemical filtration, heat flow and exchanges, and the chemistry of oils.

One of the most dramatic projects during the foundation's early years was the design and construction of the Snow Cruiser, a large mobile laboratory for Admiral Byrd's third Antarctic expedition. The completed body was fifty-five feet long, twenty feet wide, and sixteen feet high, with tires almost three feet wide. Its top speed was thirty miles per hour.

After a brief trial run in the dunes near Gary, Indiana, the Snow Cruiser began its slow journey to Boston, the expedition's embarkation point. Public interest in the vehicle was so extraordinary that twenty miles outside Boston seventy-two thousand automobiles filled with curiosity seekers created one of the world's largest traffic jams!

Back in Chicago a young Armour student working with the foundation developed the first commercially practical tape recorder in 1944. This work resulted in over two hundred patents, which for many years covered all recorders sold in the United States and in many other countries. Perhaps only the development of the transistor and integrated circuitry have surpassed in impact the work on magnetic recording.

In 1943 the Armour Institute merged with the Lewis Institute to form the Illinois Institute of Technology, and the foundation changed its name to the Armour Research Foundation (ARF). Throughout the World War II years the ARF expanded its staff and facilities to help meet the demands generated by the international conflict. By 1944, it employed 350 individuals who conducted projects representing an annual volume of $1.7 million.

After the war, ARF realigned its priorities for peacetime industrial development. By 1949, research volume reached $4.25 million—a 250 percent increase in only five years.

In the 1940s former IITRI directors were instrumental in setting up several new research organizations, most notably Midwest Research Institute* (MRI) in Kansas City, Missouri; Southwest Research Institute* (SwRI) in San Antonio, Texas; and SRI International* (SRI) in Palo Alto, California.

Following the Korean conflict, the development of a new generation of defense weapons became a high national priority. The ARF was commissioned by the Department of Defense to help this development, and it was responsible for some major accomplishments, including high-speed weapons and new types of ammunition. The ARF's work on rocket boosters solved the problem of inaccurate trajectories. The development of consumable cartridge cases solved the problem of cartridge disposal and consumption of scarce metals. Work on nuclear weaponry lead to safer bombs in transit, the detection of enemy fire, and the determination of the effects of blasts on buildings. One outcome of research in the Sputnik era was the development of a special paint to coat space vehicles permitting them to withstand the extremely high temperatures generated by solar radiation in outer space.

In 1961, the Department of Defense awarded the ARF a two million-dollar contract to establish and run the Electromagnetic Compatibility Analysis Center (ECAC). The ECAC, which is still run by IITRI, assures that all communication, control, and electronic detection activities of the military operate without interference from armed forces or civilian electronic equipment.

In 1963 the ARF changed its name to "IIT Research Institute," by which it continues to be known today. IITRI made dramatic progress during the 1960s, as evidenced by a research volume of almost thirty million dollars at the close of the decade.

During the 1970s, IITRI continued to grow, changing its emphasis and activities with the changing demands of the times. Among its notable achievements were the development of lightweight brick aggregate, flexible ceramic coatings, fiber metal, computer-programmed tooling, automatic packaging and labeling machines, a surgical stapler, and a fiber optic ear probe.

IITRI also installed the first industrial research nuclear reactor and has played an important role in atomic weapons testing, olfactronics, microencapsulation, nondestructive testing, plasma physics, biomedical engineering, and man-machine communications.

Today energy, health, and productivity have emerged as important national concerns, and IITRI has taken a leadership position in these areas. For example, IITRI researchers have proved the feasibility of using radio frequency technology to obtain oil from shale and tar sand deposits. In field tests, this approach has been shown to be environmentally safe because little premining and no rubblization are necessary. The process is also energy efficient, with the ratio of energy returned to energy used equal to or better than such ratios for alternative processes.

Cancer research receives major attention at IITRI. An extensive testing program provides performance and evaluation data on hundreds of substances for potential use in cancer chemotherapy. Ongoing research is also devoted to the study of retinoids (a derivative of vitamin A), which have effectively prevented and remitted some cancerous tumors in laboratory animal tests.

The 1970s saw major commitments at IITRI toward improving the nation's productivity. A one-million-dollar laser center was set up to educate industrial clients in the uses of advanced production techniques. The automation of IITRI's 15 kW CO_2 laser enables such operations as welding, heat treating, and laser-assisted machining to be in progress simultaneously.

The Manufacturing Productivity Center, established in 1976, is a multiclient activity addressing the nation's productivity problems through conferences, information exchange, and productivity studies.

IITRI presently employs almost sixteen hundred individuals, most of whom work in the headquarters facility, a five-building complex on the campus of the Illinois Institute of Technology (IIT) in Chicago. IITRI also maintains an acoustics research laboratory in Geneva, Illinois; a fire research laboratory in Gary, Indiana; and an explosives-testing facility in LaPorte, Indiana. One IITRI division, the Electromagnetic Compatibility Analysis Center in Annapolis, Maryland, employs over six hundred individuals. Parts of the Applied Technology Division are located in Rome, New York, at Griffiss Air Force Base, and in Dayton, Ohio.

Through the years IITRI has maintained its position at the forefront of scientific and technological innovation. At the beginning of the 1980s, IITRI's research volume had reached fifty million dollars despite a slowing national economy and curtailments in both government and industrial research and development expenditures. Continual additions to its experienced research staff and reinvestment in equipment and facilities assure IITRI the ability to meet a diversity of client requirements. Furthermore, its policy of developing new thrusts and phasing out areas no longer responsive to the needs of government, industry, or society provides the flexibility necessary for IITRI to grow and prosper in the future.

For further information, see Irene Macauley, *The Heritage of Illinois Institute of Technology* (1978); and Harold Vagtborg, *Research and American Industrial Development* (1978). See also the IITRI *Annual Reports* 1946 to 1965, and 1977 to date, and the following IITRI monthly publications; *ARF News* (1949-1963); *Industrial Research Newsletter* (1950-1967); *Spectra* (1962-1970); *IITRI Staff Newsletter* (1972-1980), particularly the special fortieth-anniversary issue (1976); and, quarterly, *Frontier* (1938-1969).

PAULA C. NORTON

INDEPENDENT RESEARCH LIBRARIES ASSOCIATION (IRLA). Founded in 1972, the IRLA is an informal confederation of major American independent, privately supported, research libraries. As of 1981, the membership consisted of fifteen institutions that support major collections or research materials in the humanities, science, and medicine: the American Antiquarian Society,* Worcester, Massachusetts; American Philosophical Society* (APS), Philadelphia; John Crerar Library,* Chicago; Folger Shakespeare Library,* Washington, D.C.; Linda Hall Library* (LHL), Kansas City, Missouri; Historical Society of Pennsylvania,* Philadelphia; Huntington Library, Art Gallery, Botanical Gardens,* San Marino, California; Library Company of Philadelphia*; Massachusetts Historical Society,* Boston; Pierpont Morgan Library,* New York City; Newberry Library,* Chicago; New York Academy of Medicine,* New York City; New-York Historical Society,* New York City; New York Public Library, Astor, Lenox and Tilden Foundations,* New York City; and the Virginia Historical Society,* Richmond.

The members possess several common characteristics, which together constitute the criteria for membership. All of them house superb collections that are capable of supporting sustained research in a variety of interrelated subjects and of attracting scholars from all over the world. All are organized as privately endowed, independent institutions, each with its own instrument of incorporation or charter, its own board of trustees, and a full-time professional chief executive officer. The primary purposes of all the members are to collect and to preserve the records of the past, to promote research in them, and to interpret those materials to scholars and to the public.

Several preliminary meetings preceded the official organization of the IRLA. The first was called by the American Academy of Arts and Sciences,* the American Antiquarian Society, and the Massachusetts Historical Society and was held at the academy's headquarters in Brookline, Massachusetts, on September 30 and October 1, 1970. Attending the Brookline conference were representatives of the fifteen present IRLA members and of several learned societies and library organizations. The purpose of the meeting was to assess the role of independent, privately supported, research libraries within the nation's structure of higher education and to examine their relationships with federal, state, and local governments and with private funding agencies. A continuing committee was elected from among those present to study the problems facing independent research libraries and to recommend appropriate remedial actions. Representatives of nine of the libraries met for further discussions at the Newberry Library on May 11 and 12, 1972, at which meeting the actual establishment of the Independent Research Libraries Association took place. Fourteen of the fifteen participants in the 1970 Brookline conference joined within a short time of the founding of IRLA; the New-York Historical Society became the fifteenth member sometime later.

The IRLA has from the beginning remained a relatively informal organization. There are no bylaws, no permanent office, and no paid officers. Meetings are held as necessary, usually once or twice a year. There is no formal dues structure, although all members pay an assessment to support the expenses of the association's temporary, floating office. A membership committee, using IRLA's criteria, passes on any applications for membership that are received. The chairmanship has rotated among several persons: Marcus A. McCorison, American Antiquarian Society, 1972-1973; O. B. Hardison, Folger Shakespeare Library, 1973-1975; Lawrence W. Towner, Newberry Library, 1975-1978; McCorison again, 1978-1980; James Thorpe, Huntington Library, 1980 to the present.

The IRLA was established in reaction to a number of developments in the late 1960s and early 1970s of ominous portent to the executive officers of the major independent research libraries. At bottom, the libraries were concerned about their very survival in a world that placed increasing demands on them for services but failed to provide adequately for their needs. For years the libraries' endowments had generally been adequate to support their modest activities and the demands for services placed on them. Since World War II and the Soviets' launching of Sputnik, the increased demands of the American people for self-advancement through formal or informal education had greatly enlarged the role in scholarship that the independent libraries chose, or were asked, to play. Unfortunately, however, these libraries did not share in the relative prosperity that more formal educational establishments enjoyed during the 1960s. As privately endowed libraries not formally affiliated with degree-granting institutions, they were not eligible for governmental assistance through programs created by the Library Services and Construction Act or the Higher Education Act. Not being classified officially as educational institutions, the independent libraries faced problems of potentially destructive taxation, especially in the wake of the passage of the Tax Reform Act of 1969. Although the intent of the act was to curtail fraudulent philanthropies, it inadvertently jeopardized the tax-exempt status of several of the major independent libraries. The main problem from the libraries' standpoint was that the tax legislation established sources of income rather than functions as the basis for an institution's tax-exempt status. Furthermore, the libraries every year had to prove to the Internal Revenue Service that they were not private operating foundations (thus subject to federal taxation)—an annual burden of proof not required of formal educational institutions that possessed students and teachers. Most but not all independent libraries remained tax-exempt through administrative decisions within the IRS, but the letter of the law held a Damoclean threat of potentially devastating consequences for all of them. Meanwhile, severe inflationary trends placed debilitating financial burdens on all not-for-profit institutions, including independent libraries. Unlike other, kindred institutions, however, independent libraries possessed few ways of passing on those increased costs to their "clients" (such as the options of raising tuition or admission fees open to colleges and museums). In short, by 1970 the endowments of most of the major independent research libraries were no longer capable of withstanding inflationary pressures and enlarged responsibilities. As a consequence, with no existing agency able fully to represent the interests of independent research libraries, IRLA was founded for self-protection, self-promotion, and the airing and resolution of common problems.

For most of its brief history, then, the IRLA has been largely engaged in ensuring that the role its members play in American cultural life is fully recognized by the agencies that wield power and dispense money. To that end, the IRLA, in concert with other organizations, has twice influenced the filing of legislation in the Congress to classify independent research libraries statutorily as educational institutions for the purposes of the IRS and thus permanently exempt them from taxation. As of 1980, these complex efforts had not succeeded.

The IRLA has enjoyed some successes on other fronts, however, most notably in the encouragement of major foundation and governmental support for their activities. Although an effort to persuade the Ford Foundation to provide independent libraries with what would have amounted to "second endowments" failed, the IRLA did succeed in pressing its members' case before the Andrew W. Mellon Foundation. The immediate result was a round of Mellon capital awards in 1972 to seven IRLA institutions. Since then, the Mellon Foundation has been one of the most sympathetic of the major private foundations to the needs of independent research libraries.

IRLA institutions have also fared comparatively well with the National Endowment for the Humanities. Several member libraries have received one or more NEH grants for the support of specific projects in such traditional library activities as processing collections, developing new collections, and promoting focused research in collections, and for various public-oriented educational or cultural programs.

A truly impressive innovation was the establishment in 1978 of a program of challenge grants at NEH, a development in which IRLA played a substantial role. Two IRLA libraries were among the three recipients of experimental challenge grants that tested the viability of the program. Nine IRLA members later received challenge grants in the first two regular rounds of the program. These grants to IRLA members totaled nearly $3.5 million, requiring the grantees to raise over $10 million to qualify for the matches. This the libraries managed to do in comparatively speedy fashion. For the IRLA members participating, the challenge grant program was highly valuable, not only because it provided the stimulus for much new outside giving but because the funds awarded could be used for general operating expenses, not just for specific, discrete programs.

Meanwhile IRLA efforts to secure an amendment to the Library Services and Construction Act to permit independent libraries to apply for governmental assistance under this act succeeded in the mid-1970s.

The IRLA also serves as a forum for sharing nuts-and-bolts information about the problems independents face. Members have compiled common statistics and have discussed fund-raising techniques, the advantages and disadvantages of "friends" support groups, problems of the conservation of library materials and their security, and group collection insurance.

The advocacy element in IRLA's activities continues to be important, but it is beginning to be joined by some more purely creative initiatives. In this light IRLA at its meeting in the fall of 1978 established an ad hoc Committee on Standards for Rare Book Cataloguing in Machine-Readable Form, chaired by McCorison of the American Antiquarian Society. The committee, which secured a chairman's grant from the NEH to support its operation, issued its final report in December, 1979. The report consisted of a number of recommendations for augmenting or modifying the MARC format for automated cataloguing in order to serve the detailed needs of libraries holding specialized research collections. Several of the recommendations were subsequently adopted as the national standard by the appropriate library agencies.

The IRLA remains an informal organization. Whether it will tighten its structure, establish a permanent office, or hire a full- or part-time representative in Washington, D.C., remains to be seen. IRLA has been successful in general in voicing in the national forum the concerns of a small but crucial part of the American library establishment and in particular in helping to bring about several concrete developments that advance the interests of its members. Much remains to be done, particularly in regard to encouraging the federal government and private agencies to assume an enlightened and coherent policy toward independent research libraries. Enough had been accomplished, however, to encourage the custodians and well-wishers of these libraries "to persevere," in the words of the Newberry's Towner, "confidently believing that the American people, individually and collectively, would value their unique holdings and their unique services much too much to let them disappear."

For further information, see William S. Budington, "To Enlarge the Sphere of Human Knowledge: The Role of the Independent Research Library," *College and Research Libraries* (1976); and James Thorpe, "The Role of Independent Research Libraries in American Society," *ACLS Newsletter* (Summer-Fall, 1980). See also a 1980 information brochure about IRLA, together with IRLA *Annual Reports* from 1976 to the present appearing in *ALA Yearbook*. IRLA archives are presently placed in the custody of the incumbent chairman.

JOHN B. HENCH

INSTITUTE FOR ADVANCED STUDY (IAS). The institute is devoted to the encouragement, support, and patronage of learning—of science, in the old, broad, undifferentiated sense of the word. It partakes of the character of both a university and a research institute, but it also differs in significant ways from both. It is unlike a university, for instance, in its small size—its academic membership at any one time numbers about 175. It is unlike a university in that it has no scheduled courses of instruction, no commitment that all branches of learning be represented in its faculty and members. It is unlike a research institute in that its purposes are broader, it supports many separate fields of study, it maintains no laboratories, and above all it welcomes temporary members, whose intellectual development and growth are one of its principal purposes. The institute, in short, is devoted to learning, in the double sense of the continued education of the individual and of the intellectual enterprise on which he is embarked.

The Institute for Advanced Study was founded in 1930, by a gift from Mr. Louis Bamberger and his sister, Mrs. Felix Fuld. The founders entrusted the general supervision and furthering of the institute's purposes to a board of trustees of fifteen members, and to a director elected by them, who should have primary responsibility for its academic affairs. The first director was Abraham Flexner; he was succeeded in 1939 by Frank Aydelotte; in 1947 by Robert Oppenheimer; in 1966 by Carl Kaysen; and in 1976 by Harry Woolf. In a letter addressed by the founders to the first trustees of the institute, their original purposes were set forth. The founders had in mind the creation of a graduate school in which the students would have an opportunity to pursue work qualifying them for a higher degree and in which the faculty, unburdened by the teaching of undergraduates, would be free to devote themselves to their researches and the training of graduate students. In actual fact, from the very first, the institute has developed in a rather different way. It has awarded no degrees and usually admits to membership those who have already taken their highest degree. Its members are characteristically at once teacher and student. It thus carries even further than originally contemplated the typical features that were to distinguish it from the college or the university. For its course had been defined in the founders' letter: "The primary purpose is the pursuit of advanced learning and exploration in fields of pure science and high scholarship to the utmost degree that the facilities of the institution and the ability of the faculty and students will permit."

The academic work of the institute opened with the appointment of its first professors, eminent in pure mathematics and mathematical physics. A little later, appointments were made in various fields of archaeological and historical study and in economics. These initial appointments, like the faculty appointments to be made later, helped to define—but did not limit —the fields of study at the institute. On the one hand, the inevitable and desirable limitation on the size of the faculty and the importance of some partial community of interest among its members have clearly foreclosed the possibility of representing all academic disciplines. On the other hand, although no policy was adopted of excluding members whose interests are remote from those of any member of the faculty, the institute tends to support with special emphasis fields in which it has some tradition of fruitful activity.

The institute has for the most part sought to work without experimental facilities. In part this is because its limited funds could not adequately support such facilities; but it is also a natural consequence of an emphasis on, and solicitude for, temporary members, who manifestly cannot by themselves make feasible the operation of experimental programs.

At present the academic work of the institute is carried out in four schools: Mathematics, Natural Sciences, Historical Studies, and Social Science, the faculty consisting of those holding appointments as professors in these four schools, twenty-three in number. The members of the School of Mathematics are for the most part pure mathematicians; and the members of the School of Natural Sciences, theoretical physicists, astrophysicists, and astronomers. In the past there have been members who have worked in other sciences—chemistry, biology, and psychology, for example. The School of Historical Studies is broader still in scope and includes in principle all learning for which the use of the historical method is a principal instrument. The work of the school tends to reflect the interests of the faculty: Greek archaeology, epigraphy, Greek philosophy and philology, Roman history, palaeography, medieval history, the history of art, modern history, the history of modern philosophy, American intellectual history, and the history of mathematics and the sciences. Here again there have been members, working alone or in concert, in disciplines not represented on the faculty. The School of Social Science brings together a small number of scholars using methods and perspectives of the social sciences to examine historical and contemporary materials with the aim of elucidating the processes of social change. Visitors under this program have been drawn from the disciplines of history, sociology, anthropology, economics, and political science. Scholars working on a variety of related problems discuss common perspectives and approaches, but there is no attempt at an integrated project approach.

A principal function of the institute is to provide for members who come for short periods, for a term of a year or, in the schools of Mathematics and Natural Sciences, occasionally for two years. There are currently some 180 such members in residence. Selection of visiting members is made on the basis of applications sent to each school. All visiting members are chosen on the basis of open competition. The faculty of each school constitutes a permanent search and selection committee. Through wide reading and personal contact, each faculty member identifies the most promising and distinguished scholars in his or her particular field and in the larger realm of the school's interests. Selected scholars are encouraged to apply for membership.

This has traditionally been an important way of bringing members to the institute, but it is relied on now to a decreasing degree. Nor is it true that an invitation to submit an application is tantamount to appointment; solicited applications go through the same process of discussion and election by the entire faculty of each school as do the unsolicited. Final selections for each school are made by each school's faculty.

The largest number of applications arrives unsolicited. The most powerful force for bringing in such applications is word-of-mouth recommendation throughout the scholarly world by former visiting members. Perhaps half of the annual total of applications is made because candidates have been inspired by former members. The other forces that bring in applications are the institute's well-established reputation and direct notification in several directories and scholarly journals.

Inevitably there is a real competition for memberships because both the physical limitations of the institution and the desire to preserve a community small enough to be a true community restrict the number of members admissible. The institute maintains and always has maintained a nondiscrimination policy of member selection with respect to sex, race, and creed. It has in its history always had members of both sexes and members from every country, approximately one-third coming from Europe, Asia, and Latin America.

About half of the members are supported by grants-in-aid from funds available to the schools and supplementary institute funds; the other half are supported by the members' own institutions, by the United States and foreign governments, and by private foundations.

The institute maintains some of the facilities necessary for academic life and relies on a fortunate symbiosis with Princeton University, from which it is organically and administratively separate but with which it enjoys close academic and intellectual relations. Thus the institute has a small working library, partially adequate for the fields represented; but inevitably it relies on the libraries of Princeton University, to which institute members have full access.

The institute occupies about a square mile of land; most of this is farm and woodland. Its buildings, in Princeton, New Jersey, house libraries, dining hall, common rooms, offices for faculty and members, and seminar and lecture rooms. It operates a housing project for temporary members. It serves lunch and tea and provides transportation between its buildings and the town of Princeton and the university. The institute's academic year is divided into two terms, from September 1 to December 31, and from January 1 to June 30. Residence during July and August is handled by special arrangement in each case. During a period from late September until just before Christmas and a period from early January until early April, it is expected that members will be in residence.

The self-perpetuating governing board of trustees of the institute present-ly consists of twenty members. The corporation elects the principal admin-istrative officers. The director serves as the principal executive officer of the institute.

For further information, see "Some Introductory Information" (1980), an information pamphlet about the IAS on which this account is primarily based. See also *Annual Report* (1980); and, for accounts of the founding of the institute, see Abraham Flexner, *I Remember* (1940); and Frances Blan-shard, *Frank Aydelotte of Swarthmore* (1970).

INSTITUTE FOR CANCER RESEARCH. See Fox Chase Cancer Center.

INSTITUTE FOR GOVERNMENT RESEARCH. See Brookings Insti-tution.

INSTITUTE FOR SEX RESEARCH. The institute grew out of a course at Indiana University at Bloomington for students newly married or con-templating marriage soon. In 1938, the Association of Women Students recognized the value of such a course and successfully petitioned the univer-sity to put it in the curriculum. Alfred C. Kinsey, a zoology professor who had supported the petition, was asked to assist in teaching the class. Dr. Kinsey, who had no formal training in human relations, had directed most of his professional experiences toward a study of an evolutionary species of wasps and in writing biology textbooks. Because of his genuine interest in people, his students confided in him privately concerning some of the more intimate fears about or experiences in marriage. In order to expand his own understanding of their problems, he began to question the students systematically and to record the information in a code that only he could interpret.

Professor Kinsey decided to expand his research beyond the Bloomington campus to include other sociological levels of people. Improving his interview techniques, he observed that one's socioeconomic class had a statistically measurable influence on sexual attitudes and behavior. Each new discovery impelled Dr. Kinsey to go deeper into research, until human sexual behavior became the prime focus of his professional energies.

Early research was carried on at Dr. Kinsey's own expense, but when the cost of the project he envisioned began to develop beyond his financial means he applied for a grant to the National Research Council's Committee for Research on Problems of Sex. In 1941, the committee awarded Kinsey a grant of sixteen hundred dollars from funds provided by the Medical Division of the Rockefeller Foundation. With this meager grant he was able to employ Clyde Martin, a biology student assistant, to help him with the research. The following year, the committee sent three of its members to observe Kinsey's operation firsthand. Favorably impressed by Kinsey and his associates, the Rockefeller Foundation awarded a second grant of seventy-five hundred dollars. In 1943, the grant was increased to twenty-three thousand. Thereafter, grants were raised each year: twenty-five thousand, twenty-eight thousand, thirty-five thousand, and, beginning in 1947, forty thousand dollars, a figure that remained constant until 1954.

With substantial monetary assistance, Dr. Kinsey was able to enlarge the program and his staff. Wardell Pomeroy joined the research team in 1943, and helped in collecting case histories, chiefly in colleges, prisons, hospitals, medical schools, and other institutions in Northern and Midwestern states.

In 1946, Dr. Kinsey decided to change the direction of his work from purely gathering data to analysis with the anticipation of publishing a "report." Dr. Paul Gebhard was added to the staff that year to help in this shift of emphasis. In 1947, in order to determine the legal possession of any royalties that might accrue from a published report and to establish ownership and confidentiality of interview records, the Institute for Sex Research was established by the State of Indiana as a nonprofit corporation. Kinsey, Martin, Pomeroy, and Gebhard were named trustees.

Indiana University trustees and President Herman Wells supported the work of the institute from its inception, despite the criticism it received. The university made available six rooms, including Kinsey's office in Biology Hall, for the researchers.

The first "Kinsey Report," *Sexual Behavior in the Human Male*, was published in 1948 by W. B. Saunders of Philadelphia and became a best seller. The response was not all in favor of the publication. Although some regarded it as a significant contribution to understanding humankind, others saw it as a blatant invasion into an area regarded tabu by Judeo-Christian moralists. The success of the first "report" heightened anticipation of the second in 1953, *Sexual Behavior in the Human Female*. The publicity that accompanied the publication of this volume catapulted the work of the Institute for Sex Research into international prominence. The work was no longer that of an obscure professor and his associates in a small Midwestern town. The demands made for Dr. Kinsey's appearance in conferences around the world were nearly beyond the point of human endurance. Unbelievably long hours at work and globe-trotting took its toll, and the indefatigable Kinsey developed a heart ailment.

Before his death, Dr. Kinsey and the institute became the focus of a bitter attack that led to the loss of some of the grants that had made his work possible. University President Wells was able to fend off local attacks on the institute from lay religious organizations and the governor of the state. It was the attack by the federal government that was most damaging to the institute. The Customs Bureau confiscated shipments of erotic materials to the institute. Senator Joseph McCarthy also warned foundations about funding organizations or persons whose American loyalties were suspect. The distribution of erotic reading material was regarded by the senator as a part of the Communist plot to weaken the morals of the nation. A member of Congress called for the "Kinsey Reports" to be barred from the mails, and a special congressional committee intensified its investigation of the institute. A professor of some repute who was critical of Kinsey's work attempted to discredit the institute in a House committee hearing. Trustees of the Rockefeller Foundation were interrogated as to its support of the Institute for Sex Research. The House committee decided that the institute's research was not scientific and that its effect was to weaken U.S. morality and make the nation more susceptible to a Communist takeover.

The support of the Rockefeller Foundation was terminated in 1954, and for the next two years the only grant the Institute for Sex Research received was that given by the National Research Council of from three to five thousand dollars annually as a token of the council's belief in the worthiness of the institute's labors. Dr. Kinsey literally exhausted himself in a fruitless search for funds. The royalties on the two published reports and the dedication of a determined staff enabled the institute to survive those lean years. Intensive interviews were taken among prison inmates in anticipation of the publication of a report on sex offenders. The sexual behavior of chimpanzees was scientifically monitored, and the erotic art of Peru was photographed and studied. In the meantime, Dr. Kinsey's health worsened, yet he insisted on honoring engagements and searching for funds. Death came in August, 1956.

The staff of the institute had been inspired by their mentor's example and were determined to maintain and even enlarge the program. Dr. Paul Gebhard was made head of the institute, two new trustees were appointed, and Dr. Wardell Pomeroy was put in charge of field work. The institute filed a suit against the U.S. Customs Bureau, and Indiana University entered the case as *amicus curiae*. In 1957, the federal district court in New York ruled in favor of the institute. This ruling permitted the importation of erotic materials for research purposes and allowed such materials to be sent through the mail. The decision has become a landmark in the history of the relationship between science and law.

The National Institute of Mental Health made the first of a series of substantial grants to the institute, which constituted its major financial support for research for several years. With both the legal and financial problems resolved, the institute decided to temporarily forgo gathering new data by interviewing and to concentrate on analyzing and publishing the results of that already accumulated. The third volume, *Pregnancy, Birth, and Abortion*, was published in 1958, followed by *Sex Offenders: An Analysis of Types*, in 1965. In addition, the staff concentrated on publishing journal articles and book chapters. The trustees decided to make the institute's library and collections available to other scholars wishing to do legitimate research.

The institute diversified its program during the decade of the 1960s with several simultaneous projects headed by different individuals. Interviewing techniques were improved and were taught to graduate assistants, who could relieve the work load of senior staff members to give them more time to apply their analytical skills and supervision.

The institute founded the monograph series entitled Studies in Sex and Society, originally intended as publications of scholars who had done most of their research in the institute's library. Later, scholars who wished to publish worthwhile books on research done elsewhere were included in the series.

The National Institute of Mental Health encouraged the institute to begin a program on sex education in medical schools. The first seminar for psychiatrists was held in 1962 at the Indiana University School of Medicine and has since become a general sex education course for all medical students. The institute has sponsored a summer program since 1970 for psychiatrists, physicians, educators, social workers, and other professionals.

The primary function of the institute is to conduct research on human sexual behavior by gathering and analyzing data and making available the resultant information to those who need it through publications, lectures, consultations, and correspondence. The institute also purposes to collect and preserve library and archival materials relevant to human sexuality for the benefit of serious researchers.

Dr. Paul H. Gebhard has served as the director of the institute and member of the board of directors since 1956. Although the institute is in theory autonomous under its eight-member board of trustees, it is dependent on Indiana University, which supervises finances, makes all staff appointments, pays the salaries of permanent staff members, and provides a fund for consultants. The institute is directly responsible to the vice-president and dean for research and advanced studies. The university provides rooms, utilities, and furnishings, which are located presently in Morrison Hall on the Bloomington campus. There are four permanent researchers, a librarian, a computer programmer, and several office workers, including twenty-seven work-study university students on the staff.

Major funding of the institute is from federal sources: the National Institute of Mental Health and the National Endowment for the Humanities. Private foundations, such as the H. M. Hefner Foundation and the Ledler Foundation, have helped subsidize some research.

More recent projects have been in the areas of public attitudes toward homosexuality and sexuality of the spinal-cord injured. A basic philosophy that the institute seeks to maintain is that no behavior is strictly abnormal and that an enlightened society will become more tolerant.

For further information, see Cornelia V. Christenson, *Kinsey, A Biography* (1971); Wardell B. Pomeroy, *Dr. Kinsey and the Institute for Sex Research* (1972); and Martin S. Weinberg, *Sex Research: Studies from the Kinsey Institute* (1976). See also the institute books cited above.

RAYMOND L. MUNCY

INSTITUTE OF EARLY AMERICAN HISTORY AND CULTURE. The institute was founded in 1943 in Williamsburg, Virginia, by the College of William and Mary and Colonial Williamsburg, Inc., for "the furtherance of study, research, and publications bearing upon American history approximately to the year 1815." The institute considers this a broad mandate. Although historical studies have always been central to its program, the institute also encourages the complementary scholarly activities of anthropologists, economists, and geographers, as well as students of the fine arts, literature, religion, and the history of science. Moreover, although it has concentrated on the colonial and early national history and culture of the thirteen original states, the institute has also recognized the relevance for its work of the history of Canada and the West Indies, as well as the European and African background and relations of white, black, and native Americans. Chronologically, the institute has emphasized the study of the seventeenth, eighteenth, and early nineteenth centuries, but it has not allowed artificial limits to prevent it from ranging both earlier and later in order to treat subjects fully and effectively.

A small organization with no more than twenty staff members at any time since its establishment, the institute and its programs have been shaped by the personalities, objectives, and concerns of its directors. Its history, in consequence, falls conveniently into five eras. The first was a time of uncertainty and indecision before the appointment of the first director, the next three were periods of developing and changing programs coinciding with the tenures of Carl Bridenbaugh (1945-1950), Lyman H. Butterfield (1951-1954), and Lester J. Cappon (1954-1969), and the fifth has been a time of increasing financial pressures during the terms of Cappon's successors, Stephen G. Kurtz (1960-1972) and Thad W. Tate (1972 to date).

After several months of preliminary inquiry, Colonial Williamsburg's Advisory Committee of Historians and the editorial board of the *William and Mary Quarterly* met in joint session in December, 1943, to discuss a proposal to create an early American research center. Called together by President Kenneth Chorley of the historical restoration and President John E. Pomfret of the college, the two panels, which included such distinguished scholars as Charles M. Andrews, Samuel Eliot Morison, Arthur M. Schlesinger, and Earl Gregg Swem, responded favorably to the initiative and agreed to unite as a council to oversee the activities of the new center. By January 8, 1944, press releases heralded the institute's establishment.

The integration of four research and publishing projects previously operated by its sponsors produced the core of the new organization's program. Colonial Williamsburg provided an associate from its research department, its program of grants-in-aid for research, and the Williamsburg Restoration Historical Studies series, initiated in 1940; the college contributed the *William and Mary Quarterly*, a periodical devoted to Virginia history and genealogy but transformed by the institute into "A Magazine of Early American History, Institutions, and Culture." Both sponsors also opened their research facilities to the new center and offered major financial support.

With the publication of the January, 1944, issue of the *Quarterly*, under the editorship of Richard L. Morton, the institute commenced operations. Until the end of World War II, wartime conditions and the absence of a director prevented it from pursuing other projects, but in the autumn of 1945 Carl Bridenbaugh was named to lead the institute, and Lester Cappon became editor of publications. Within a year the institute had awarded its first grants-in-aid, and in 1947 it published its first book.

The institute's original activities provided the basis for a strong program, but as early as 1946 Bridenbaugh and other staff members had begun to consider the advantages of expanding into new areas. A number of alternatives seemed attractive. Bridenbaugh envisioned the institution as "the research center of Early American History and Culture for the whole country." He foresaw a facility with major collections of monographs, microfilms, and other resources for research. Another proposal, advanced at a meeting in May, 1946, would have instructed the institute to hire several young historians to conduct research on assigned topics.

None of these proposals had been completely realized by 1950, when Bridenbaugh resigned, but the institute had recorded a number of achievements. Rising subscription figures appeared to show that the *Quarterly* had won the respect of scholars in early American studies; the research publications program had issued seven titles; seven scholars had received grants to support their research; and a small library of microfilms had been started. In addition, Cappon and Stella F. Duff had compiled the *Virginia Gazette Index, 1736-1780*, the first comprehensive subject guide to a major newspaper of the colonial era.

Bridenbaugh had developed a coherent and growing program, but the appointment in 1951 of Lyman Butterfield to the directorship produced important changes. Although he considered the editing and publishing of books and the *Quarterly* central to the institute's mission, Butterfield advocated alternatives to the most ambitious of the other projects proposed and initiated during his predecessor's tenure. The new director believed that an extensive library of primary source materials was beyond the institute's means, and he doubted the feasibility of a center for the writing of scholarly monographs. Instead, in keeping with the example set by the *Virginia Gazette Index*, Butterfield noted that scholars of early America had "special need of guides, manuals, indexes, calendars, and bibliographical aids of many sorts," and he urged that the institute "could render great service by planning, stimulating, and working at the preparation of such aids."

Butterfield's term as director was brief, but he had already taken steps to reshape the institute when he resigned in 1954. Although Butterfield encouraged research by individual staff members, the institute itself became, through his efforts, increasingly a service organization for scholars rather than the research center that Bridenbaugh had proposed. Under Butterfield the institute undertook two continuing activities, both of which were designed to serve the scholarly community at large. A series of conferences on "Needs and Opportunities for Study," initiated in 1952, led to the publication of historiographical essays and annotated bibliographies on a variety of early American subjects, including science, the decorative arts, and education.

A *News Letter* was also started in 1952 to serve as a clearinghouse for information on conferences, fellowships, archival acquisitions, and similar matters of interest. However, believing that its benefits had not matched its costs, Butterfield terminated the grants-in-aid program in 1954.

Lester Cappon succeeded Butterfield in 1954. Drawing from the proposals and policies of each of his predecessors, Cappon brought the institute into a new era. Under Cappon's leadership it sought to combine service with scholarship. To be sure, several continuing programs remained devoted almost exclusively to serving the scholarly world. Among these, publishing activities were the most prominent. The *Quarterly* grew in influence under the editorships of Douglass Adair (1947-1953, 1954-1955), Lawrence W. Towner (1956-1962), William W. Abbot (1962-1966), and Thad Tate (1966-1972). As a twentieth-anniversary appraisal noted, although the *Quarterly* modestly styled itself "A Magazine of Early American History," by the 1960s it was "rightly regarded as *the* magazine of early American history." Meanwhile, between 1954 and 1969, under the supervision of James Morton Smith and Stephen Kurtz, editors of publications from 1955 to 1966, and 1966 to 1969, respectively, the institute issued more than fifty monographs and other books. Among these were *White over Black: American Attitudes Toward the Negro, 1550-1812* by Winthrop D. Jordan, which received the National Book Award for History and Biography, and *The Creation of the American Republic, 1776-1787* by Gordon S. Wood, the recipient of a Bancroft Prize. New projects also served scholars. Following a suggestion from Professor Lawrence H. Gipson of Lehigh University, a series of Conferences in Early American History was introduced in 1955. By 1980 thirty-nine of these symposia had been held in various locations across the United States. And in 1966 a training program in historical editing for graduate students was undertaken in cooperation with the Department of History at the College of William and Mary.

Other activities, however, produced the synthesis of service and scholarship that Cappon sought. Through his efforts the institute strengthened one program, its research associateships, and undertook two major new ones, the *Papers of John Marshall* and the *Atlas of Early American History*, each of which combined the two objectives.

The reshaping of the research associateship was Cappon's first significant achievement as director. Between 1956 and 1958 he added a second position and transformed the appointment into a postdoctoral fellowship, a change recognized by the adoption in 1958 of a new name for the associateship, the Institute Fellowship. Under its current terms the fellowship is a two-year appointment for a promising young scholar. Fellows teach a one semester course each year at the College of William and Mary and devote the rest of their time to their own research.

Work began on the papers of Chief Justice John Marshall in 1966, after seven years of planning and searching for funds. When the last of the projected ten to twelve volumes appears in the mid-1980s, scholars will have at their disposal reliable texts, expertly edited and annotated, of the correspondence and writings of one of the leading figures in American legal history. Preparation of the *Atlas of Early American History*, published in 1976, began in cooperation with the Newberry Library* in 1970, after more than a decade of preliminary planning. The atlas provides scholars with 286 maps describing all aspects of American life between 1760 and 1790.

Cappon's most enduring contribution to the institute was his synthesis of service and scholarship; since his retirement, however, his successors, Stephen Kurtz and Thad Tate, have had to devote their time and energy primarily to matters of money rather than program. Although Colonial Williamsburg and the College of William and Mary have continued to provide the institute with major funding, financial questions have required increasing attention. During the late 1960s and early 1970s, Kurtz pursued foundation grants to fund new projects; by the mid-1970s the draining effects of inflation and rising energy costs on the resources of the institute's sponsors forced Tate to seek support from new sources to maintain existing programs. Grants from the Andrew W. Mellon Foundation and the National Endowment for the Humanities, as well as smaller donations from the Institute's associates, an organization of scholars and laymen founded in 1977 and numbering about three hundred in 1980, have eased pressures to a degree, but in 1980 finances remained a subject of concern.

Despite financial constraints, Kurtz and Tate managed to maintain established programs intact throughout the 1970s, and to record a number of important achievements as well. Colloquia during Kurtz's tenure included a major symposium on the American Revolution, held in 1971 in anticipation of the bicentennial celebration; since Tate's appointment conferences have included important sessions on such issues as the development of the American economy and seventeenth-century Chesapeake society. Significant publications supervised by James H. Hutson and Norman S. Fiering, editors of publications from 1969 to 1972, and 1972 to the present, respectively, have included three-volume sets of the *Circular Letters of Congressmen to Their Constituents*, edited by Noble Cunningham, and *The Works of Captain John Smith*, edited by Philip Barbour. Meanwhile, under the editorship of Michael McGiffert (1972 to present), the *Quarterly* was a leading force in the emergence of the new quantitative social history.

Presently, a small staff, including eight historians and four professional editors, operates the institute. The director administers the institute; separate departments are responsible for the *Quarterly*, book publications, and the Marshall papers. The program remains a joint project of the College of William and Mary and Colonial Williamsburg, responsible to both sponsors and to its seventeen-member council, the successor to the two panels that originally supported its establishment in 1943.

For further information, see the institute's *Handbook*, 3rd ed. (1967) and its *News Letter*, published irregularly two or three times each year. For an appraisal of the *William and Mary Quarterly*, see Keith B. Berwick, "A Peculiar Monument: The Third Series of the *William and Mary Quarterly*," *William and Mary Quarterly* (January, 1964).

CONRAD E. WRIGHT

INSTITUTE OF ECONOMICS. See Brookings Institution.

INSTITUTE OF MATHEMATICAL STATISTICS (IMS). *Annals of Mathematical Statistics*, a quarterly journal established by Professor H. C. Carver of the University of Michigan in 1930, preceded the founding of the Institute of Mathematical Statistics by five years. During this period the *Annals* was affiliated with the American Statistical Association* (ASA). By 1935, however, Professor Carver and a small group of persons interested in mathematical statistics had come to the viewpoint that the existing mathematical and statistical societies did not meet their needs. Consequently, during the joint meeting of the American Mathematical Society* (AMS) and the Mathematical Association of America* (MAA) in Ann Arbor, Michigan, on September 12, 1935, this group set up the IMS. In

1937 the *Annals* became the official journal of the IMS, and by 1941, aided by a previous subvention from the Rockefeller Foundation, it was able to assume full editorial and financial responsibility for the *Annals*, a responsibility which Professor Carver had previously assumed.

The *Annals*, issued as a bimonthly from 1965 to 1972, presented articles containing new results in statistical theory and methodology, probability, and related fields. In the latter year, two journals, *Annals of Probability* and *Annals of Statistics*, jointly superseded the *Annals of Mathematical Statistics*. The two journals are bimonthlies, issued in alternate months. In addition, since 1948 a committee on special invited papers periodically selects and publishes papers that are of particular interest and merit. Other publications of the IMS include a series entitled *Statistical Research Monographs*; a series of *Mathematical and Statistical Tables*, translations of Russian papers in statistics and probability; and a *Bulletin*. Another contribution of the IMS in this area was its editing and resultant publication in 1955 of *Selected Papers in Statistics and Probability* by Abraham Wald.

Another activity of the IMS has been its designation of members to serve on intersociety committees, councils, and other scientific groups such as the American Association for the Advancement of Science* (AAAS) and the National Research Council. It has established the Rietz Lecture, named for its first president, and biannually designates a distinguished scientist to deliver it.

The IMS has held annual meetings since 1935; in earlier years these were usually in the fall, but now they are usually held in August, often jointly with the AMS and the ASA. The programs of these meetings consist of the presentation of research papers, addresses of a more general nature, the transaction of business, dinners, and other social affairs. A distinctive feature of the annual meetings, since 1956, has been the presentation of a sequence of three or four one-hour expository lectures by one lecturer on some phase of work in progress that is of considerable interest to members. The specialist selected to present the lectures has sufficient time to develop his material in some detail and thus makes it accessible to people not particularly conversant with his specialty. This annual lecture series is designated the Wald Lectures in honor of Abraham Wald. Since 1949, groups in the Eastern, Central, Western, and Southern regions of the United States have held regional meetings of their own, each under the aegis of an associate secretary, and this has provided additional means of communication and intercourse among IMS members. Also, during the period 1962-1976, the IMS held European regional meetings. Since that time, similar meetings have been held under the sponsorship of the European-based Bernovilli Society.

Membership is open to those interested in mathematical statistics and includes primarily students and faculty members in colleges and universities and persons in government and industry. Although 70 percent are located in the United States, the membership is international. Members with outstanding reputations may be elected fellows, a distinction presently held by 425 members. In addition, there is provision for retired members and institutional members. The latter comprise organizations desirous of contributing $165 or more annually toward the support of the IMS. The total membership is presently about 3,000.

The IMS elects the customary institutional officers; it conducts its nonfinancial and noneditorial business from an office, headed by an executive secretary, located in East Lansing, Michigan.

For further information, see the following articles appearing in the *Annals of Mathematical Statistics:* Willford I. King, "The Annals of Mathematical Statistics" (February, 1930); and "Notice of the Organization of the Institute of Mathematical Statistics" (December, 1935). See also "The Institute of Mathematical Statistics," *AAAS Bulletin* (March, 1945); and an IMS pamphlet, *An Introduction to the Institute of Mathematical Statistics.*

INSTITUTE OF PUBLIC ADMINISTRATION (IPA). Founded in 1906 as the Bureau of Municipal Research, the Institute of Public Administration is the oldest center for research and education in public management and public policy analysis in the United States. Its founders, William H. Allen, Henry Bruere, and Frederick A. Cleveland, often referred to collectively as the "ABCs," sought to bring emerging concepts of scientific management to the field of government.

The founding of the bureau was a response to reform movements that included criticisms of municipal governments by the muckrakers. Public exhortations for "efficiency" and "economy" coincided with the entry of the municipal government into health and welfare functions that had been the province of charitable organizations and foundations. The founders of the bureau went beyond the reformers of their time by stressing the importance of better results to be achieved through scientific means. The bureau had little in common with the burgeoning taxpayer protection groups. It maintained a strong faith in the potential of improved government; its early reports stressed better services attained by better administration. The approach taken by the bureau was pragmatic and factual and came to be the hallmark of the American analytical style.

The bureau's early work made contributions to public financial administration. Typical of the time, New York City made appropriations without reference to revenues and comprehensive expenditures. In 1907, at the urging of the bureau, a modern budget-making procedure was introduced to the New York Health Department and subsequently was extended to all city departments. From the bureau there emerged the concept of an executive budget that centralizes responsibility for financial planning for all executive agency programs in the chief executive's office.

The management survey was another contribution of the Bureau of Municipal Research. Surveys were conducted for a variety of municipalities. The basic technique of the survey consisted of gathering data and information on existing municipal conditions, analyzing the data, and proposing constructive solutions and recommendations.

Demand for the services of the bureau and its experienced research staff grew. To meet this demand the bureau established its Training School for Public Service in 1911, with generous assistance from Mrs. E. H. Harriman. Charles A. Beard, educator and historian from Columbia University, became the director of the training school in 1914. In 1921 the training school and the Bureau of Municipal Research were reorganized as the National Institute of Public Administration. Luther Gulick, then twenty-nine years old and an alumnus of the training school, succeeded Charles A. Beard as director of the new organization. Thanks to substantial grants from the Rockefeller, Harriman, Rosenwald, and Carnegie foundations, the institute built up its endowment. This enabled the organization to expand its mission and extend its field of activity beyond the New York municipal scene. Survey and consulting services could be provided to interested governments at cost, and NIPA staff members could concentrate on research and publications when they were not actively involved in direct technical support to governments.

With Luther Gulick's encouragement, the Maxwell School of Citizenship and Public Affairs was created at Syracuse University, and the NIPA training school was gradually transferred to it. NIPA staff supervised candidates for masters degrees at Maxwell until 1930.

At this time NIPA's surveys emphasized developing administrative procedures for specific government functions: tax administration, law enforcement, health administration, and other special areas. Experts like Bruce Smith, famous for his work in police administration, were brought to the institute.

In 1932 the organization developed a close affiliation with Columbia University, where the first American chair of public administration was established. In that same year the organization was granted an absolute charter by the Regents of New York State as a nonprofit educational institution and became the Institute of Public Administration.

IPA participated in the government reforms of the 1930s, when Luther Gulick was appointed to the president's Committee on Administrative Management with Louis Brownlow and Charles Merriam. The collection, *Papers on the Science of Administration*, edited by Luther Gulick and L. Urwick, was prepared as background material for the president's committee. Gulick's article on the theory of organization (which summarized the functions of the chief executive under the acronym POSDCORB—planning, organization, staffing, direction, coordinating, reporting, and budgeting) became a classic in the field.

The committee recommended that the Office of the President be transformed systematically so as to enable the president to perform those executive functions. The committee proposed an executive office of the president to include a Bureau of the Budget and a National Resources Planning Board. The committee also proposed that a small cadre of assistants serve the president in staff capacities, although not to exercise a policy role. President Roosevelt's adoption of these recommendations changed the character of the executive branch of the government.

Since 1950 IPA has concentrated on emerging problems in the fields of urban administration, organization and planning, public policy research, and the communication of research. IPA works with interdisciplinary teams. Its staff includes economists, political scientists, engineers, lawyers, and planners, as well as public administration specialists. IPA's direct consulting services to governments have continued to grow. After Lyle C. Fitch became president of IPA, the scope of its international work was broadened, particularly for training in public management, research, and advisory services for urban government. IPA's major international urban studies project—a ten-year effort undertaken in fifteen nations—was jointly sponsored by the Ford Foundation and the United Nations.

IPA's overseas projects have taken it to Latin America, Africa, Europe, Asia, and the Middle East. The institute's international operations have addressed the improvement of national government organization and management as well as development planning, budgeting and financial administration, and urban service delivery.

In its work within the United States, the institute has concentrated less on developing new methods of administration and shifted its attention to direct technical support of government agencies in the resolution of problems attendant to urban growth and expansion of the suburbs. IPA has become particularly involved in problems of urban transportation, government organization (including public enterprise, charters, and agency structures), and planning.

In 1961 the Kennedy administration commissioned IPA to do a background study of urban transportation with particular attention to possible forms of transit subsidies and the organizational location of any new federal transit agency. The report was published as *Urban Transportation and Public Policy*. A Ford Foundation grant to IPA financed a survey and influential report on the feasibility of public assumption of rail commuter transportation in the New York region. The report was published in 1963 as *Suburbs to Grand Central*. In 1965 IPA opened an office in Washington, D.C., where policy research and consulting on urban transportation continued, with increased interest on the part of the federal government in balancing its support of highway construction with funds for mass transit, an area in which IPA has recently prepared a handbook for transit officials and legislators on transit finance. In 1980, IPA began a joint project with the Netherlands National Ministry of Transport to devise techniques for ascertaining the levels of transit service appropriate to particular social and economic needs and formulas allocating to cities the funds that the parliament authorizes for transit subsidies.

Studies of government organization and management have been a mainstay of the institute throughout its life. During the 1960s and 1970s, IPA was involved in several major reorganization studies including the Pennsylvania Department of Transportation, the District of Columbia government, New York City's executive branch, the Jacksonville Port Authority, Greenville, South Carolina, and individual federal, state, and local departments and agencies. One recent target of IPA's organization studies has been the government corporation. *The Public's Business*, by Annmarie Hauck Walsh, has been recognized as the most authoritative work on the subject of government corporations to be published to date. Subsequently, IPA has been asked to provide consulting services to several public authorities. An example is a public corporation in the State of Washington constructing five commercial nuclear power plants that retained the institute to address specific questions of organization and management. These included the role and organization of the board of directors, deployment of staff resources, central management structure, and external relations. A critical part of the IPA work was in fostering improved communication between the corporation and the Bonneville Power Administration, the federal energy agency charged with distributing much of the output of the plants when they come on line. Another major study was Ruth Mack's *Planning on Uncertainty: Decision Making in Business and Government Administration* (1971).

The legal framework of government has also been a major concern to the staff of the institute. IPA participates in constitutional and charter revisions as well as reorganization of governments and evaluations. Howard N. Mantel, IPA's general counsel, served as the technical draftsman for the 1975 New York City charter. He participated in drafting the constitution and plan of government for the Commonwealth of the Northern Mariana Islands and in preparing new health and mental health codes for the states of New York and Connecticut; and he has been engaged in significant efforts to improve the structure of governments and their management.

The problem of communication among the research community, community groups, business, and government administrators was the focus of an experimental series of briefings in a major economic policy issue under a grant from the Rockefeller Brothers Fund.

Innovation and technological transfer also is a recent manifestation of IPA's tradition of focusing on emerging issues of public policy. Starting in the late 1960s and continuing to date the institute has taken on projects and published several works in the field of technological research and innovation and its application to the private market. Convinced that federal research activities, particularly in the energy field, took insufficient account of the problems associated with producing and marketing new products or technologies, IPA sought to identify practical means of fostering incentives for innovation and of facilitating communication between federal researchers and private businessmen on the subject of commercial application of the results of technological research. Eldon Sweezy and Sumner Myers penned the results of their study of the impediments to innovation on behalf of the National Science Foundation in a paper entitled "Federal Incentives for Innovation: Why Innovations Falter and Fail, A Story of 200 Cases." Further findings on innovations were contained in "Successful Industrial Incentives," written by Sumner Myers and Donald Marquis for the National Science Foundation.

IPA maintains a research library of more than eighty thousand books, pamphlets, and other documents dealing with politics, law and government, planning, and other fields related to public policy and administration. The library serves the staff and is available for use by other institutions and researchers. In addition, as part of the institution's overseas technical assistance program, Xenia Duisin, IPA librarian, has helped establish public administration libraries and trained librarians in a number of countries, including Nigeria, Peru, Liberia, and Egypt.

IPA maintains offices in New York City and Washington D.C., with branches in California and Puerto Rico. It is governed by a board of trustees, of which Luther Gulick is chairman, and Lyle C. Fitch, president. In 1981 Annmarie Walsh became director of IPA. Staff support and overhead require project support to supplement endowment income.

For further information, see a thorough account of IPA's early years by Jane S. Dahlberg, *The New York Bureau of Municipal Research: Pioneer in Government Administration* (1966). See also general informational brochures published by IPA, particularly the ones for 1971 and 1976, and one for 1976 dealing with IPA international programs.

PHILIP J. GAMBACCINI

INTERNATIONAL COUNCIL FOR PHILOSOPHY AND HUMANISTIC STUDIES (CONSEIL INTERNATIONALE DE LA PHILOSOPHIE ET DES SCIENCES HUMAINES) (CIPHS). Prior to the 1948 organization of the CIPHS the major humanistic organization operating at the international level was the International Union of Academies (Union Académique Internationale (UAI). Founded in 1919 in Paris on the initiative of the French Académie des Inscriptions et Belles Lettres, the UAI began operations in 1920 when delegates from seventeen countries, largely chosen by their national academies and councils, such as the American Council of Learned Societies* (ACLS) for the United States, assembled in Brussels. From that time until World War II the UAI engaged in a number of important collaborative humanistic enterprises, which included, for example, the compilation and publication of volumes in such works as the

Corpus Vasorum Antiquorum, Monumenta Musicae Byzantinae, and *Tabula Imperia Romani.*

Following World War II, officials of the UAI participated in the 1947-1948 movement within the United Nations Educational, Scientific, and Cultural Organization (UNESCO) for the creation of an international humanistic organization similar to that of the previously founded International Council of Scientific Unions* (ICSU), which operated in the natural science area. The outcome was the creation of the CIPHS, which held its first meeting in Brussels in January, 1949. The founding members were the UAI; International Federation of Philosophic Societies, now International Federation of Societies for Philosophy; International Committee of Historical Sciences; Permanent International Committee of Linguists; International Federation of the Societies of Classical Studies; and International Commission on Folk Arts and Folklore, now International Union of Anthropological and Ethnological Sciences.

There were and have been two levels of generality among the institutions represented in the CIPHS. The UAI, in which various humanistic societies and academies were already associated on a national scale through such organizations as the United States ACLS and the original five and presently twelve international organizations of individual humanists such as the International Committee of Historical Sciences. The UAI was afforded two-fifths of the total number of delegates and votes in the CIPHS governing assembly. Since then, the following seven organizations have been admitted to membership in the CIPHS: International Committee for the History of Art; International Association for the History of Religions; International Federation for Modern Language and Literature; International Union for Oriental and Asian Studies; International Musicological Society; International Union of Prehistoric and Protohistoric Sciences; and International Congress of African Studies.

The CIPHS and its members have promoted international cooperation in research projects, organized the international distribution of information bearing on the humanities, and provided continuity in the convening and conducting of international meetings and congresses. For example, the *Codices Latini Antiquores,* a guide to Latin manuscripts prior to the ninth century A.D., edited by the late Elias Howe of the Institute for Advanced Study* (IAS), was brought to completion under CIPHS auspices in 1972.

As this project title and those cited earlier indicate, the earlier enterprises of both the UAI and the CIPHS were generally European-oriented and concerned with the classical-medieval-Renaissance axis. In the late 1960s and early 1970s, a new policy was inaugurated, called geographical extension, under which more of their efforts and activities were concentrated on other continents, Asia, Africa, and Latin America, and other periods. A major reason for this shift was a similar and slightly earlier one on the part of UNESCO. Because CIPHS projects, meetings, publications, and administration have been supported in large part by subventions from UNESCO, along with smaller appropriations from its member organizations, the desire on the part of the CIPHS to harmonize and dovetail its activities with the current general program of UNESCO is understandable. Thus, a project presently being carried on by CIPHS and its members aims at a compilation of the sources of African history, the *Fontes Historiae Africanae*. There are several under way that concern Asia, for example the *Corpus Inscriptionum Iranicarum*, and in Latin America studies are being conducted of those objects of art produced in the old civilizations of Central America and Peru.

A continuing and noteworthy activity of the CIPHS has been its quarterly journal *Diogenes*. Founded in 1953 and edited, until his death in 1979, by Roger Caillois, this publication has been widely acclaimed for its international and interdisciplinary scope. Appearing in three language editions (English, French, and Spanish), as well as anthologies in other languages, the articles published in *Diogenes* are written by scholars and intellectuals from all over the world. They shed new light on variegated aspects of the past and present. Titles of articles, for example, range from "Was Homer a Liar?" and "The Stone Man of the Canadian Arctic" to "Islam Facing Development" and "Art in Today's Society."

The CIPHS elects the usual institutional officers who are normally rotated among members of its various adhering organizations. A permanent secretariat-headquarters is maintained in Paris under the direction of an appointed secretary-general.

For further information, see the CIPHS *Bulletin*, which has been published every two years since 1949. The *Bulletins* for the years 1954-1955, 1964-1965, and 1970-1971 are particularly helpful in describing CIPHS reorganizations and changes in policy. See also the following articles: William Berrien, "The Founding of an International Council for Philosophy and Humanistic Studies," *ACLS Bulletin* (March, 1949); Richard McKeon, "Waldo G. Leland, 1879-1966, A Memorial," *ACLS Newsletter* (November, 1966); and Rensellaer W. Lee, "Union Académique Internationale," *ACLS Newsletter* (Summer-Fall, 1976).

INTERNATIONAL COUNCIL OF SCIENTIFIC UNIONS (ICSU). The first organization formally devoted to international scientific research and cooperation apparently was a Magnetic Union organized initially in Germany in 1828, which soon became international in scope. This union sponsored the first international studies of the earth's magnetism. During the period 1898-1900, German initiative also led to the founding of an International Association of Academies, and most of the leading European academies, together with the U.S. National Academy of Sciences* (NAS), joined this organization. The association, however, had no permanent headquarters and was inadequately financed. World War I saw the suspension of its activities and ultimate dissolution.

The victorious Allies of World War I, particularly the United States and

Great Britain who had engaged in a great deal of wartime collaboration, desired a more effective postwar organization than the old association. They led, therefore, in the 1918-1919 formation of a new international scientific organization, the International Research Council. The fifteen founding members of the IRC included the Allied powers plus some neutral powers of World War I but excluded Germany and the other Central powers. Each of the IRC members could name delegates to the council's governing body, the general assembly. The scientific unions, international groupings of scientists in particular disciplines (astronomy, chemistry, and so on), some already in existence and some projected, were not formally represented in the assembly. They were envisaged as and actually were, however, the organizations through which the IRC would act. Thus, the objects of the IRC, as formulated at its first meeting in 1919, were to coordinate international activities in the various areas of science and its applications; encourage the creation of international unions needed to advance science; guide international scientific activities in fields where no adequate organizations existed; and establish relations with the governments represented in the unions in order to interest them in scientific projects.

One of the major accomplishments of the IRC in 1919 and the 1920s was its role in the reconstituting or establishment of seven scientific unions: International Astronomical Union, International Union of Geodesy and Geophysics, International Union of Pure and Applied Chemistry, International Union of Radio Science, International Union of Pure and Applied Physics, International Union of Biological Sciences, and International Geographical Union. These same unions, however, became increasingly dissatisfied in the 1920s with an IRC that did not admit all nations to council membership and, because council membership was a prerequisite to union membership, prevented these same nations from assuming union membership.

Although several unsuccessful attempts were made in the 1920s to change this situation, it was not until 1931, when the IRC was dissolved and replaced by an International Council of Scientific Unions, that membership in the new council and the unions became open to all nations. The change in name reflected, too, a simultaneous change in relationship between ICSU's governing general assembly, its executive committee, and the unions. From this time forward the unions assumed complete autonomy in the management of their affairs, including the admission of members irrespective of whether the country applying for union membership was a member of ICSU. Furthermore, not only were the unions afforded representation in ICSU's governing general assembly and its executive committee, but the latter was formed to a large extent by union delegates. It is for this reason that the present executive secretary of ICSU states:

> The structure of ICSU with its dual membership, both National and Scientific, . . . is unique in the international field. The Council is a federation of International

Scientific Unions, each of which has its own national membership. The majority of National Members adhere to the Council through a scientific academy or national research council. Both types of members, scientific and national, help to guide the general policy of the Council through representatives at the General Assembly and in the General (Executive) Committee. [F. W. G. Baker, "The International Council of Scientific Unions," *Transnational Associations* (June, 1979), p. 235]

Although ICSU was active in the 1930s (it created, for example, a Committee on Science and Social Relations, which conducted several world surveys), the outbreak of World War II in 1939 saw a practical cessation of activities until 1945. December of that year saw a resumption of ICSU work with the opening of discussions with the Preparatory Commission of the United Nations Educational, Scientific and Cultural Organization (UNESCO), which was to result in a 1946 agreement whereby UNESCO recognized ICSU as the coordinating and representative body for the intellectual organization of science, and, reciprocally, ICSU recognized UNESCO as the principal U.N. agency in the international scientific area. This far-reaching agreement was concluded for an unlimited period and, with minor revisions to bring it in line with similar agreements made between UNESCO and other organizations, has persisted to the present time. Over the years, UNESCO has supplied significant financial and personnel support for many ICSU ventures.

One of the key factors in the postwar development of ICSU was its organization of the International Geophysical Year (1957-1958). The IGY was followed by the creation of committees and programs in the later 1950s and on into the 1960s and 1970s whose titles reflect the variegated nature of their endeavors: Committee on Space Research (1958); International Biological Year (1959), which became the International Biological Programme; Committee on Water Research (1964); Committee on the Teaching of Science (1968); and Global Atmospheric Research Programme (1968).

One of the most significant of such projects was the establishment in 1966 of the ICSU's Committee on Science and Technology in Developing Countries. Gaining experience of development needs through the work of this committee, ICSU was instrumental in the calling of the unique Singapore Symposium on Science and Technology for Development, which was sponsored by nineteen nongovernmental organizations representing world science in the broadest sense. This symposium proved of considerable value in the deliberations of the U.N. Conference on Science and Technology for Development, which was held in Vienna in August, 1979. These meetings are still too close for a detailed assessment of their impact, but it already appears that they will provide a considerable impetus for scientific progress in Third World countries.

Today there are sixty-seven national members and three national associates of ICSU. Since 1919 and the 1920s the following eleven additional unions have been formed and joined the first seven: International Union of Crystallography; International Union of Theoretical and Applied Mechanics; International Union of the History and Philosophy of Science; International Mathematical Union; International Union of Physiological Sciences; International Union of Biochemistry; International Union of Geological Sciences; International Union for Pure and Applied Biophysics; International Union of Nutritional Sciences; International Union of Pharmacology; and International Union of Immunological Societies. Also, since the setting up in 1968 of scientific associates, sixteen have been accepted for such membership in ICSU.

The work of the scientific committees and programs of ICSU has been carried on with the closest cooperation and support of disciplinary-oriented unions, associates, and ICSU. What then is and has been the role of ICSU's national members, the other part of the ICSU federation? Again, quoting from F. W. G. Baker, they are:

First, the provision of some of the ideas for new scientific programmes; second, the contribution of dues which provide a major portion of ICSU's working budget; third, a source of talent for the membership of the Unions, Associations, Committees, Commissions, and Permanent Services; fourth, as hosts to the many Assemblies, Congresses, Conferences and meetings which take place throughout the world at all times of the year. [F. W. G. Baker, "The International Council of Scientific Unions," *Transnational Associations* (June, 1979), p. 237]

ICSU elects the usual institutional officers, who are normally rotated among the various member nations and unions. A permanent secretariat-headquarters is maintained in Paris under the direction of an appointed executive secretary.

For further information, see the following recent accounts by the present executive secretary of ICSU, F. W. G. Baker: "The International Council of Scientific Unions," *Transnational Associations* (June, 1979); and "The International Council of Scientific Unions: A Brief Survey," a 24-page pamphlet published by ICSU in December, 1979. There is no book-length history of ICSU. For an earlier history that highlights the role of the scientific community in ICSU operations, see Harold Spencer Jones, "The Early History of ICSU, 1919-1946," *ICSU Review* (1960). Also, for earlier works dealing with the histories of ICSU and other international organizations, see Katherine O. Murra, *International Scientific Organizations* (1962); and Joseph C. Kiger, *American Learned Societies* (1963). See also a 182-page booklet, *International Council of Scientific Unions, Organizations and Activities* (1976), which includes an explanatory organization chart, and the ICSU annual *Year Book*, 1954 to date.

INTERNATIONAL RESEARCH COUNCIL. See International Council of Scientific Unions.

INTERNATIONAL SOCIAL SCIENCE COUNCIL (ISSC). Following World War II, the United Nations Educational, Scientific, and Cultural Organization (UNESCO) was largely responsible for setting up, under its auspices, a number of international, disciplinary associations in the social sciences. In 1951, at the Sixth Session of the General Conference of UNESCO, a resolution was passed calling for the creation of an international, interdisciplinary body to coordinate and further the work of the associations. The following year (1952) the ISSC was founded to draw together these associations, together with the different branches of knowledge they represented, and to speed up intellectual communication, particularly in the social sciences, among the nations of the world.

At the time of its founding the ISSC consisted of ten members, two from each of the five following associations: International Economic Association, International Committee of Comparative Law, International Political Science Association, International Union of Psychological Science, and International Sociological Association. In 1953, the International Union of Anthropological and Ethnological Sciences joined the ISSC, and, accordingly, it nominated an additional two members to the council. At this same time, six other members were coopted, that is, the twelve members nominated by the associations selected six other persons for membership in the ISSC.

From the 1950s on, the ISSC, with funds provided largely by UNESCO, engaged in such activities as the creation (1953) of an International Bureau for Research into the Social Implications of Technical Progress, which, in 1961, was merged with the council; the founding (1963) in Vienna of a European Co-ordination Centre for Research and Documentation in Social Sciences; the establishment (1965) in Paris of an International Center for Intergroup Relations jointly with the École Pratique des Hautes Études. These bureaus and centers were and have continued to be active in promoting cooperation among social scientists internationally and in amassing and interpreting social science data and documents. During this period, too, the ISSC founded *Social Science Information*, a periodical providing news and informative articles of interest to ISSC members, the disciplinary associations, and social scientists generally, particularly those concerned with the international ramifications of the social sciences.

In 1961 four additional international organizations were designated for representation in the ISSC with the addition of the International Committee for Social Science Documentation, the International Union for the Scientific Study of Population, the World Association for Public Opinion Research, and the World Federation for Mental Health.

In 1972-1973 the organizational structure of the ISSC was transformed into a federation of international disciplinary organizations consisting of three categories of members: regular (the eleven disciplinary associations); coopted (five); and associate (ten). At the same time a Committee and later

Conference of National Social Science Councils and Analogous Bodies of the ISSC was set up. In 1979, at the Thirteenth General Assembly of ISSC, this conference, with a change in name to the International Federation of Social Science Organizations, was admitted as the twelfth regular member of the ISSC, with the agreement that the federation would provide eight delegates to represent national councils in socialist, developed, and developing countries and regions. This agreement provided for a heavier representation (eight) for the federation than that (two) afforded each of the other eleven regular members of the ISSC. The ISSC at this same Thirteenth General Assembly had changed the status of the International Institute of Administrative Sciences from associate to regular member.

The above organizational change, which was taken with the expressed hope that close cooperation would now develop between the ISSC and the federation together with the national councils comprising the federation, brought the organizational structure of the ISSC much closer to that of the International Council of Scientific Unions* (ICSU) and International Council for Philosophy and Humanistic Studies* (CIPHS). An important result of the change was that it facilitated the work of ISSC members that overlapped that of the other two international councils and served to increase the rapport and cooperation among the three. By this time, for example, some of the members of the three councils held dual or sometimes triple affiliation with the others.

The ISSC elects the usual institutional officers, who are normally rotated among members of its adhering organizations. A permanent secretariat-headquarters is maintained in Paris under the direction of an appointed secretary-general.

For further information, see the ISSC publications cited above and, since December, 1974, a *Newsletter* published by the council. Also, since 1972, the ISSC has been publishing an information booklet every two years, which contains statistical information about itself, the member associations, publications, and so on.

__ *J* _____

JOHN CRERAR LIBRARY, THE. This library is one of a small group of significant institutions frequently overlooked in identifying the nation's research resources. Libraries are generally considered to be functional components of educational institutions or tax-supported, public circulation libraries. The Crerar Library is a privately supported, independently incorporated, nonprofit institution with its own self-perpetuating board of directors. It was established in 1894 under provisions of the will of a wealthy Chicago railroad officer and vendor of railroad supplies, who named the first board from among his prominent friends. That board set the scope of the collections as including (at research levels) the natural and physical sciences, including engineering. To these, medicine was added in 1905. From its beginning, the library has been freely open to the public for reference and research and is (with certain exceptions) noncirculating. In its ninety years, Crerar has grown to stature as one of the nation's major library resources in the disciplines covered. It has available collections of well over one million volumes and receives nearly ten thousand current periodicals and other serial publications.

Conventional library services have always been provided: assistance in using the various catalogs and bibliographies; suggestions as to research procedures; responses to some fifteen thousand telephone inquiries each year; answers to hundreds of questions received by mail. In addition, the library has developed a variety of specialized services. Photocopy service has been provided since 1912 (second in time only to the Library of Congress); specialized filming and copying facilities were added in 1946. Over thirty thousand items annually are now sent out to users in all fifty states and some two dozen other countries who have submitted requests by mail, telephone, teletype—and even satellite. In 1948, Crerar established the first fee-based research service in the country, offering extensive and competent literature searching and analysis for individuals or organizations without the time, facilities, or expertise to undertake the work themselves. Research Information Service (RIS) results may include bibliographies, abstracts and digests, and photocopies and may utilize both conventional printed sources as well as the scores of computer data bases now accessible on line. The RIS also scans daily the thousands of books and periodical issues received by the library, selecting material that fits the specific, respective interest profiles of its clients. Again, these findings can be reported by lists, abstract bulletins, photocopy, punched card, or whatever format and at whatever frequency a client wishes.

Since 1953, Crerar has operated the National Translations Center (1953-1968: Special Libraries Association Translations Center). The center solicits and receives deposits of unpublished translations, prepared originally by industrial firms, universities, government agencies, and others. Retrieval files are prepared (author, original citation, patent number, etc.). The center is also notified of the availability of translations available through some thirty other cooperating national centers and sources abroad and in the United States. A monthly listing, *Translations-Register Index*, is available by subscription. The center's own collection now includes some 260,000 items, and the files record another 300,000 available elsewhere. Annual additions amount to over 20,000 with nearly 10,000 availability inquiries processed each year. The objective is to prevent the unneeded duplication and expense of translating.

With the advent in recent years of cooperative networks of libraries, Crerar has functioned as a contract resource in the Illinois Library and Information Network and in the Midwest Health Science Library Network. From 1968 to 1979, the latter network was administered by Crerar under contract to the National Library of Medicine.

In its earliest years, 1894 to 1919, the library was housed in rented space in the Marshall Field building. A ten-story home of its own was occupied in 1920, at the corner of Randolph Street and Michigan Avenue in Chicago. In 1962, the library moved again to a new, fully air-conditioned building on the campus of the Illinois Institute of Technology. By agreement with the IIT, Crerar also operates the Kemper Library (in the same building) and the branch Stuart Library of IIT, being reimbursed for the operating costs. Thus, Crerar took on the additional role of serving a closely affiliated academic community, while continuing all of its public library and special service functions.

About 60 percent of Crerar's users come from various academic institutions, about 30 percent from industry, and the balance are private consultants, professionals, and other users. Its $2,011,800 budget (1980) is supported about 31 percent from endowment, 20 percent from memberships and contributions, and 48 percent from contract and other reimbursable services. The staff numbers seventy-five, of whom twenty-five are professionals in various library and other specialties.

The administrative heads over the years have combined both subject and bibliographic/library backgrounds. The first librarian (1895-1928) Clement

W. Andrews had been librarian and chemistry professor at Massachusetts Institute of Technology. J. Christian Bay (1928-1946) brought a background in botany as well as worldwide scholarly and bibliographic contacts. Serving from 1947 to 1965 was Herman H. Henkle, nationally recognized authority in the history of science with academic credentials in biology. The present librarian, William S. Budington, was trained in electrical engineering. It has been policy to recruit, as far as possible, a professional staff with scientific and technical backgrounds, in order to enhance the level of service to users and the selection of publications for the collections.

Although nearly all disciplines in science, technology, and medicine are well represented, particular strength is to be found in biology, chemistry, physics, and the various branches of engineering (civil, mechanical, electrical, metallurgical, chemical) and applications of the physical sciences in communication, transportation, and manufacturing industries. Included in medicine are related basic sciences—anatomy, biochemistry, physiology, pathology—and such medical specialties as cardiology, pediatrics, ophthalmology, and radiology. With respect to agriculture, the engineering aspects are emphasized, together with insecticides, fertilizers, and other agriculture-related industries, such as foods and food processing. The collections include not only currently published information; they are also rich in the landmark works of historical significance to the development of science.

The library is open from 8:30 A.M. to 5:30 P.M., except Sundays and usual holidays. Because some older materials are housed in special facilities elsewhere and serviced twice weekly, out-of-town visitors may wish to confirm in advance the availability of needed material, as well as specific hours of opening.

For further information, see C. W. Andrews, "The John Crerar Library," *Wisconsin Library Bulletin* (December, 1916); J. C. Bay, *The John Crerar Library* (1945); H. H. Henkle, "John Crerar Library: A Complex of Special Collections and Special Services," *Illinois Libraries* (1963); W. S. Budington, "To Enlarge the Sphere of Human Knowledge: The Role of the Independent Research Library," *College and Research Libraries* (July, 1976); and O. W. Tuthill, "The John Crerar Library," *Commerce* (1980).

WILLIAM S. BUDINGTON

K

KETTERING FOUNDATION. See Charles F. Kettering Foundation.

_L_

LANKENAU HOSPITAL RESEARCH INSTITUTE. See Fox Chase Cancer Center.

LEAGUE OF FREE NATIONS ASSOCIATION. See Foreign Policy Association.

LENOX LIBRARY. See New York Public Library, Astor, Lenox and Tilden Foundations, The.

LIBRARY COMPANY OF PHILADELPHIA, THE. Located at 1314 Locust Street in Philadelphia, Pennsylvania, the Library Company with over 400,000 volumes and in excess of 162,000 manuscripts includes an extensive collection of rare books and manuscripts dealing with science, technology, history, architecture, agriculture, natural history, and education. Special areas of interest are records of the Revolutionary and Federal era, Afro-Americana before 1906, materials dealing with the woman's rights movement, and prints and photographs of Philadelphia.

The Library Company was formed on July 1, 1731, by Benjamin Franklin and a group of friends who were members of the "Junto." The Junto was a discussion society, organized by Franklin in 1727, in which the members considered literary and scientific topics of the day. As the majority of the Junto's members were not men of means, few had large personal libraries at their disposal. A board of directors was selected, and in November, 1731, fifty members agreed to pay forty shillings each for a share in the Library Company and to contribute ten shillings a year thereafter for dues. Franklin's "Mother of all North American Subscription Libraries" was on its way to success.

In March, 1732, the members sent their first order for books to London. The list was unusual in that it did not contain the standard emphasis on theology, a staple of the academic libraries in colonial America. Included were works dealing with science, architecture, history, literature, and mathematics. In addition, as most members did not have a mastery of foreign or classical languages, the books they sought were in English. Indeed, from the beginning, books on the Library Company's shelves were an indication of the intellectual tastes of the individual members, most of whom were self-taught men. The fledgling library also received books and money from members and friends. Franklin gave several volumes, as did the library's first librarian and its secretary. A planter in Antigua sent a monetary gift, even though he had never visited the library.

In its first years, the Library Company was given a number of nontextual items. Few of these materials survive, but one gift, an ''air pump,'' sent by John Penn, a son of the original proprietor of Pennsylvania, was of such importance as to prompt the library's directors to commission a cabinet to house the device. The cabinet, now located in the Library Company's ''Logan Room,'' is considered the earliest extant example of American-made Palladian architectural furniture.

At first situated in private quarters, the library's increasing size made it necessary to find more spacious accommodations. In 1739, books, air pump and cabinet, and other scientific equipment and curiosities were moved to the second floor of the west wing of the State House, where they would remain until 1773. In that year, the library's books and materials were transferred to rented quarters on the second floor of Carpenters' Hall.

In September, 1774, the Library Company served the reference needs of delegates to the First Continental Congress, and later of those attending succeeding congresses and the Constitutional Convention. Thus, the Library Company was the de facto Library of Congress prior to the time that there was one de jure and acted in that role until the government moved to Washington, D.C., in 1800.

By the late 1780s, the Library Company's rented quarters were becoming cramped. A lot was purchased on Fifth Street near Chestnut, and on New Year's Day, 1791, it opened its new handsome and commodious Palladian red-brick structure designed by the amateur architect, Dr. William Thornton, who later drew the preliminary plans for the U.S. Capitol.

As the Fifth Street building was being constructed, James Logan, Jr., was contemplating the future of his father's fine but esoteric library. The elder Logan had come to America in 1699, as the secretary to William Penn. Even as a young man, James Logan had had a passion for collecting books. But he was more than a mere collector; he mastered the contents of most of the volumes in his library. He was an accomplished linguist and wrote detailed notes and comments (usually in Latin) in the margins of many of his books. When Logan died in 1751, he had intended to leave his library, numbering over twenty-five hundred volumes, for the use of the public. A building was constructed on Sixth Street in Philadelphia to house the library, and the Loganian Library opened in 1760 under the guidance of a board of trustees composed of certain of his heirs and several friends.

James Logan's children did not share their father's enthusiasm for books, and, as a result, in the thirty years after 1760, little attention and direction were given to the library's affairs. Although the extensive medical library of William Logan, James's physician brother, was added to the Loganian Library in 1776, because of the overwhelming number of texts in Latin and Greek, the collection was not much used by the public. Consequently, James Logan, Jr., urged that the Library Company take over the management of the Loganian Library. The negotiations for the trusteeship were successful; the Library Company took custody of the Loganian Library, which was then moved to a newly constructed wing on the Library Company's new Fifth Street building.

In the first years of the nineteenth century, the Library Company received a number of other substantive gifts from individuals. One of the more unusual occurred in 1799, when Henry Cox, a native of Ireland, came to the Library Company and gave it a miscellany of books and manuscripts including records that he claimed had been passed to him by his grandfather. They were all duly listed in the library's minutes but remained little consulted until 1866. In that year, a British historian recognized the manuscript records as the long lost documents relating to the political affairs of Ireland during the reigns of Queen Elizabeth I and James I. The Library Company returned the documents to the British government. This act was noted by British officials, and a number of historical publications were sent to the Library Company from London as a gesture of appreciation. Of far greater importance was the return of the Mayflower Compact to Massachusetts in 1897. The London *Times* noted that the British government's decision to send the document to the United States was in part influenced by the return of the Cox papers by the Library Company some years before.

Several other important acquisitions came to the Library Company, either by gift or purchase, in the first portion of the nineteenth century. In 1803, the Reverend Dr. Samuel Preston of Kent, England, bequeathed twenty-five hundred volumes to the library. In 1828, William Mackenzie, Philadelphia merchant and the first American "rare book" collector, died, by his will assuring the acquisition of his whole library by the Loganian Library and Library Company.

In 1832, James Cox, artist and bibliomaniac, offered his library of six thousand books to the Library Company. Cox was somewhat eccentric. He devoted a modest inheritance to the accumulation of books, mainly works relating to literature. When he was in his eighties, Cox agreed to transfer his collection to the Library Company for an annuity of four hundred dollars. As Cox lived but two years after the bargain was struck, the arrangement proved profitable for the Library Company.

Prior to the Civil War, as private residences began to disappear from the old area of Philadelphia, some thought was given to a new location for the Library Company, one that would be more convenient to the members' homes and places of business. A small amount of money was raised to fund a new structure, and lots were considered, but nothing further was done for several years.

However, the matter was dramatically brought to the attention of the entire membership in 1869, when Henry J. Williams, a Library Company director and brother-in-law and executor of the estate of Dr. James Rush, announced that Dr. Rush had made arrangements in his will to leave the Library Company nearly one million dollars, providing certain explicit stipulations were met.

The main part of the will noted Dr. Rush's intentions to leave his estate to the Library Company and his desire that a new building be constructed to house its books. However, codicils rambled on about the type of material the library should contain, discouraging the reading of "every-day" novels, and even speaking scornfully of cushions on the library chairs. Furthermore, while on his deathbed, Dr. Rush informed Williams exactly where he wanted the new building sited. In June, 1869, Williams told the Library Company directors that Dr. Rush had chosen as the location for the new building a block in South Philadelphia, far from where the members lived and worked. Williams stated that to receive the bequest from the Rush estate the shareholders of the Library Company would have to comply with every aspect of Dr. Rush's wishes.

With little enthusiasm, the membership accepted the bequest, and, after years of legal arguments, the Ridgway Branch, named after Mrs. Rush's family, was finally accepted by the Library Company in 1878. The building, located at Christian and Broad streets, was a magnificent Doric temple built of solid granite, but with its huge drafty spaces it was more impressive than utilitarian.

The Library Company kept the old Fifth Street property until 1880, when a new building at Juniper and Locust was completed. A decision was made to place the more valuable and lesser used books in the Ridgway Branch. The Locust and Juniper location, closer to where the members resided, was the place they preferred for the circulation and use of current works.

With the rise of public libraries supported by tax monies after the Civil War, the dominant position of private subscription libraries, such as the Library Company was threatened. By the 1890s, there was a noticeable drop in the circulation and use of the Library Company's books. Recognizing that conditions had changed in the city after the opening of the Free Library of Philadelphia in 1894, which provided new sources of books for a wide reading public, the library's directors reported in 1903 that the institution might very well have to rethink its place and function in Philadelphia. The directors further stated, however, that the Library Company's position as a "library for the student and the thoughtful reader" remained unchallenged.

The fortunes of the Library Company, nevertheless, began a descent at the beginning of this century. The descent accelerated during the depression years of the 1930s. Income from the Ridgway investments dwindled, and in 1940 the directors considered it wise to consolidate all the library's holdings in the Ridgway Branch at Broad and Christian. The library building at Locust and Juniper was vacated, torn down, and turned into a parking lot.

During World War II, because of this continued deterioration of its financial position, the Library Company entered into an operating agreement with the Free Library of Philadelphia. The Free Library was given administrative control over the Library Company, and the Ridgway Branch became a branch of the city public library system. But by the early 1950s, the income from a parking garage built on the Juniper and Locust lot enabled the Library Company again to stand on its own financially; the agreement was amicably terminated in 1955.

Several studies of the Library Company and its operations were made in the 1950s by outside experts, all of which concluded that the Library Company's future was as a research library. With this in mind, in 1952 the present librarian, Edwin Wolf 2nd, was asked to perform a survey of the library's holdings. A plan was adopted to determine exactly what was there and then gradually to cull the post-1880 volumes that did not directly bear on the earlier collections. Mr. Wolf, formerly associated with the rare book firm of Rosenbach, found a state of physical disarray. Irreplaceable books and manuscripts that had been buried for years in the stacks were located. Mr. Wolf, who became librarian in 1955, continued the process of bringing order out of chaos. It became apparent that the Library Company could not remain indefinitely at the Broad and Christian street location. Situated in a deteriorating part of the city, the once magnificent Ridgway Building was in a state of disrepair, and there simply was not adequate space to store the library's holdings. Consequently, negotiations in the 1960s led to the sale of the Ridgway property to the city and the erection of the present building on Locust Street in 1965.

The library's holdings were moved to the new Locust Street building in February, 1966. This structure, also called the Ridgway Branch in recognition of the substantial funds for its construction that came from the remains of the Ridgway estate, is located next to the Historical Society of Pennsylvania.* There is ample cooperation between the two institutions. An arrangement made the Historical Society custodian of the Library Company's manuscript collections, and the Library Company became responsible for the Historical Society's rare books. In addition, being located physically next to one another enables both organizations to share common exhibition facilities.

Although the Library Company has modified its mission since its founding 250 years ago, the devotion to scholarly excellence Franklin envisioned has never been forgotten. Surveying the future, Librarian Wolf concludes that the Library Company's role as a research library of national significance seems assured.

For further information, see a brief history of the Library Company by its current librarian, Edwin Wolf 2nd, *At the Instance of Benjamin Franklin, A Brief History of the Library Company of Philadelphia* (1976). Two previous librarians of the Library Company have written earlier histories: George Maurice Abbott, *A Short History of the Library Company of Philadelphia* (1913); and Austin K. Gray, *Benjamin Franklin's Library, A Short Account of the Library Company of Philadelphia 1731-1931* (1937). For the recent history of the Library Company, see its *Annual Reports*, 1955 to date. See also, for a discussion of the association of the Historical Society of Pennsylvania with the Library Company, Walter M. Whitehill, *Independent Historical Societies* (1962).

JOHN SOBOTKA

LINDA HALL LIBRARY (LHL). Herbert F. Hall, founder and executive of a Kansas City, Missouri, grain company, died in February 1941, three years after the death of his wife, Linda Hall. Their wills placed the bulk of their estate into a trust fund dedicated to establishment and maintenance of a public library on the fourteen-acre plot where they had lived in the house they had built in Kansas City in 1907. A board of five trustees was named in both wills, with instructions that, when a vacancy on the board occurs, the remaining trustees are to elect a replacement. Responsibility for governance of the library and for management of the trust rests with the board of trustees. Soon after Mr. Hall's death, the trustees sought advice and guidance from four prominent and respected American librarians about the kind of library that would most suitably meet pressing library needs in the Kansas City area. The trustees had wisely decided that the new library should complement existing local resources.

The four consultants, independently and without discussion among themselves, each recommended that the new institution be a noncirculating research library serving the community's needs for scientific and technical information. Acting upon this consensus, the trustees announced in October, 1945, that Linda Hall Library would specialize in science and technology, and also that they had hired Joseph C. Shipman to serve as the first librarian. The Halls' house, a fine open plan of graceful design, was adapted for library use during the winter of 1945-1946; the LHL was opened to the public there in May, 1946. For ten years the house served as the library building, with some material going into temporary warehouse storage and many of the current acquisitions being shelved in the Halls' garage and coach house across the drive from the back entrance to the house. Shipman served as head librarian through 1973, and then as curator of the History of Science Collection until his death in 1977. He was succeeded as director of the LHL in 1974 by Thomas D. Gillies.

In 1956 the library was moved into a new 90,000-square-foot building just east of the house, to which it was connected by an open courtyard. The collection grew rapidly, and in 1964 a west wing was added, primarily for additional stack space. This necessitated razing the Halls' house, although many architectural details were salvaged and incorporated into the new wing. In 1973 the LHL was given funds from the Helen F. and Kenneth A. Spencer Foundation for a room and vault to provide additional shelving for the History of Science Collection. In 1978 another addition to the main building, this time to the south, was completed, bringing the total space for library use to approximately 180,000 square feet.

From the beginning it had been emphasized that the Linda Hall Library collection would be international in scope, although it was perhaps not then foreseen that the LHL's services would also become international. Through an extraordinarily happy coincidence, one that must have seemed almost providential for a new library just ready to open its doors, the trustees were able in 1946 to buy the library of the American Academy of Arts and Sciences.* The LHL thus acquired a collection that was especially rich in retrospective holdings and represented many of the world's most distinguished scientific academies and societies. During the LHL's first twenty-five years it acquired back files of many scientific journals to broaden the coverage already provided by the American Academy's collection. During the late 1950s and early 1960s, the LHL had also begun to expand its exchange program with foreign institutions, most notably those in the Soviet Union, Japan, the People's Republic of China, and Eastern European countries. Among its many foreign acquisitions, Russian-language and Japanese journals are currently in second and third places, respectively, after English. In all, more than forty languages are represented in the collection. Although the LHL has always strongly emphasized the acquisition of current scientific serials, it has also regularly acquired significant scientific monographs, reference works, and bibliographic aids and especially has stressed the regular acquisition of proceedings of scientific symposia and conferences. There are now approximately 500,000 volumes in the library, 650,000 microforms, 90,000 engineering specifications and standards, as well as 33,000 titles in the serials collection, of which more than 16,000 are currently received.

An early decision had been made that within the sciences and technology all subjects would be germane to the collection save surgical and clinical medicine, the field of medicine being already well served in the Kansas City area. Subjects most thoroughly covered in Linda Hall Library holdings include applied mechanics, mathematics, physics, chemistry and chemical engineering, geology, the engineering sciences, biochemistry, plant science, and agricultural engineering. There is also a considerable collection of original works important in the study of the history of science. The earliest of these is the *Naturalis Historiae* of Pliny printed by Jenson in 1472; there are several more incunabula in the collection in addition to other significant historical items from the sixteenth century to present times. Research in the history of science is also well served by holdings of the earliest scientific society journals, such as the *Philosophical Transactions* of the Royal Society of London, *Mémoires de l'Académie des Sciences, Acta Eruditorum, Journal des Scavans*.

As the holdings of the American Academy had been regularly reported to the *Union List of Serials*, Linda Hall Library became recognized early on as a national source. Linda Hall Library reported holdings to the third edition of the *Union List of Serials* as well as to *New Serial Titles*. From the first, it had reported pertinent holdings to the "List of Periodicals Abstracted" of *Chemical Abstracts*. By mid-1950, library holdings were thus identifiable nationally as well as locally. Requests for interlibrary loan of journals to other institutions were sufficiently frequent that in 1957, in order to make materials available as inexpensively as possible, Linda Hall Library elected not to loan journals but to fill requests for articles with microfilm copies. Subsequently, of course, the advent of improved photoduplication equipment altered the medium but not the procedure. During the 1960s the LHL had issued a list, updated from time to time, to advise users about what serial titles were being currently received. Expanded under the title *Serials Holdings in the Linda Hall Library*, the list has been issued annually since 1966 as a comprehensive holdings list for all serials held, both current and noncurrent.

The use of Linda Hall Library is about equally divided between local users and those who are geographically removed. The number of books and journals used locally is only a little higher than the number used through interlibrary loan procedures. Users outside the Kansas City metropolitan area range geographically throughout the world and include governmental research agencies, various kinds of information research services, industrial and other special libraries, academic institutions, as well as individual research scientists and engineers. In 1979 the public service departments had over 137,000 transactions.

It was the intent of Mr. and Mrs. Hall to establish a trust fund whose sole purpose and objective would be to provide library service to the public. This intent has been conscientiously adhered to and has thus benefited thousands of people. Careful and judicious reinvestment of undistributed funds has enhanced the trust sufficiently for the library to expand collections and services, to keep pace with inflationary pressures, and to build the physical plant needed to provide proper storage and adequate work space. This it has been able to do without seeking user support in the way of gifts and without vying for governmental support in the way of grants or other funds made available through federal programs. Unfortunately, regulations of the Internal Revenue Service classify Linda Hall Library as a private operating foundation rather than as an educational institution. The library is therefore subject to taxes under the Tax Reform Act of 1969. Although the LHL continues to serve as broad a public as it can within the limitations of available funds, the erosion of resources by federal taxes threatens its ability to expand services in new specialized areas of science and technology as aggressively as the LHL's commitments would otherwise merit.

For further information, see the following articles by the LHL's first librarian, Joseph C. Shipman, "Linda Hall Library," *Library Journal* (November, 1946), "Linda Hall Library," *College and Research Libraries* (April, 1955) and "Linda Hall Library and Its Distinctive Collections," *Missouri Library Association, MLA Quarterly* (March and June 1963). See also two articles by J. R. Ball, "The Linda Hall Scientific Library, Kansas City, Missouri," *Science* (April, 1949), and "Linda Hall Combines Beauty and Science," *Library Journal* (November, 1956); Eugene H. Mueller, "Kansas City's Linda Hall," *Library Journal* (May, 1957); Malcolm G. Wyer, "In Kansas City, Missouri," *Books and People* (1964); John Walsh, "Linda Hall Library: Kansas City Institution Builds a Reputation with Operations Outside Its Region," *Science* (May, 1965); Bruce Bradley, "Linda Hall Library's History of Science Collection," *Show-Me Libraries* (December, 1979); and Paul Ingrassia, "Look in Kansas City," *Wall Street Journal* (November 10, 1980).

THOMAS D. GILLIES

LINGUISTIC SOCIETY OF AMERICA (LSA). One of the founding fathers of this society, Leonard Bloomfield, stated in the 1920s that it had been organized so that linguists could meet and know each other. He added that a science of language did not exist and that students of language needed a professional society as much as adherents of any other disciplines. It should be added that Bloomfield's statement of the mid-1920s reflected a belief that there was not at that time any term for the scientific study of language other than *philology*, and that was not satisfactory because philology was viewed as ancillary to literary study. Hence, the founding of the Linguistic Society of America in 1924 was viewed as a step toward making known the term *linguistic* and the science it designated.

An initial contribution of the LSA in the field of linguistics was the founding, in 1925, of its quarterly publication, *Language*. It was devoted exclusively to research in the nature, structure, and history of language rather than its use. Following surveys of opportunities for linguistic training, a comparable or even greater one was the establishment, in 1928, of the Linguistic Institute.

Spearheaded by the efforts of Professor Edgar H. Sturtevant of Yale University, these summer institutes were created in order to foster the interchange of ideas, more so than for the holding of courses, although the latter were not excluded. Supported at first by the self-sacrifice of members together with small subventions from the American Council of Learned Societies* (ACLS), in spite of its scholarly success, the Great Depression forced the cessation of the institute in 1932. Resurrected in 1935, primarily through the efforts of Professor Charles C. Fries of the University of Michigan, five consecutive sessions of the institute were held at that institution.

Carried on through World War II at Michigan and other universities, the institute and the LSA helped the United States to carry out the various government language-training programs that were so vital in that conflict. With our global involvement in the postwar decades, the skills developed by LSA members have become of ever increasing importance to industry as well as to government. Reflecting this broadening national and international linguistic interest, institutes have been held continuously at a variety of major U.S. institutions.

Other significant linguistic developments in the past several decades were the setting up, in 1941, of the ACLS Committee on Language Programs and, in 1959, the Center for Applied Linguistics* (CAL). The former came into being to administer various World War II and postwar language programs and has provided assistance to the Linguistic Institute. The latter, although an independent organization, is dedicated to the application of the findings of linguistic science to the solution of educational and social problems. The center carries out policy studies, research, and development and works to promote cooperation between linguistics and other disciplines. The center's activities are recounted and documented in its serial publication, the *Linguistic Reporter*.

The LSA has held annual meetings since its beginnings, during the week between Christmas and New Year's. Occasionally other learned societies, including the American Association for Applied Linguistics, have met in conjunction with the society. In addition, summer meetings of the LSA are normally held with the Linguistic Institute.

Membership in the LSA is open to those persons interested in language and linguistics and to libraries, museums, and similar institutions. Total membership at the present time is approximately sixty-one hundred, of which about two thousand are institutions.

The LSA elects the customary institutional officers; it conducts its business from a secretariat headed by an associate secretary located in Washington, D.C.

For further information, see detailed accounts of the Linguistic Institute and the more recent history of linguistics in general and the LSA in particular appearing in the *ACLS Newsletter:* Archibald A. Hill, "History of the Linguistic Institute" (March, 1964); and Thomas A. Sebeok, "Linguistics Here and Now" (January-February, 1967). See also a series of papers by Einar Haugen, Martin Joos, J. Milton Cowan, Archibald A. Hill, Thomas A. Sebeok, and Arthur S. Abramson and published under the title "Golden Reminiscences: Fifty Years of the Linguistic Society of America," *LSA Bulletin* (March, 1975). Hill and Joos have also prepared a manuscript history of the LSA from its founding to 1969. See also Leonard Bloomfield,

"Why a Linguistic Society," *Language* (March, 1925); and Albert H. Marckwardt, "The Linguistic Society of America," *World of the Mind* (1958).

LOWELL OBSERVATORY. Percival Lowell (1855-1916), a member of the illustrious Boston Lowell family, founded his private observatory at Flagstaff, Arizona, in 1894. Lowell had been seriously interested in astronomy from boyhood and graduated from Harvard in 1876 with highest honors in mathematics. He was the elder brother of Amy Lowell, the poetess, and A. Lawrence Lowell, the president of Harvard University from 1909 to 1933.

After six successful years in the business world, first managing trust funds in the office of his grandfather, John Amory Lowell, and then as executive head of a large cotton mill, he became financially independent. Following this, he spent the next ten years intermittently in the Far East studying language, culture, and religious customs, first in Japan, and then in Korea. Out of this came four scholarly books, which are still classics of their time. Lowell had been interested in astronomy since early childhood, as he was given a small 2.25-inch portable telescope, which he carried on most of his worldwide travels. That he was well read in astronomy became evident in 1893, as he was aware that G. Schiaparelli, an Italian astronomer of Milan, due to age and failing eyesight, would not be able to observe Mars at the forthcoming opposition of 1894. The fine lines and markings that Schiaparelli had observed on the surface of Mars in previous years intrigued Lowell greatly. Finally, the smoldering interest in astronomy broke out. He decided he wanted to see for himself, firsthand, what Schiaparelli had seen.

From his studies and experience observing with his small telescopes all over the world, he realized that the selection of the observing site for a telescope was very important. Advice and help for site testing was obtained from his old friend, Professor W. H. Pickering of Harvard College Observatory. The consensus reached was that the best observing conditions might be found in the relatively cloudless, arid Southwest. Pickering recommended a promising young assistant, A. E. Douglass, later to distinguish himself by founding the analytical study of tree rings, to make the site studies in the Southwest.

Douglass arrived in Tombstone, Arizona Territory, on March 8, 1894, to make the first "seeing" tests. A month later, he arrived at Flagstaff, and by April 16, Lowell made the decision to try Flagstaff for the 1894 opposition of Mars. While Douglass was making the seeing tests, Dr. Lowell placed an order for a twenty-four-inch refractor "of the highest optical perfection possible" from Alvan Clark and sons of Cambridgeport, Massachusetts, and arranged for the use of the eighteen-inch refractor they had just completed for the Flower Observatory of the University of Pennsylvania for the coming opposition of Mars. The first observations of Mars with this telescope and a twelve-inch Clark refractor borrowed from Harvard were made by Lowell, Pickering, and Douglass at Flagstaff on May 31, 1894. The twenty-four-inch refractor was delivered in 1896, and has been in continuous use ever since; it was designated a Registered National Historic Landmark in 1966.

Although Lowell was responsible for what has been called the "Mars furor," he ably directed astronomical research at his observatory through creative imagination to stimulate important work by extremely capable assistants. Thus Lowell directed the development of planetary photography by C. O. Lampland, who received the Gold Medal of the Royal Photographic Society in 1907 for his development of planetary cameras. Later, under E. C. Slipher, this type of photography resulted in the systematic accumulation of many hundreds of thousands of planetary photographs. These photographs formed the nucleus for an international repository for planetary photographs and the support of a Planetary Research Center by NASA in 1964. A systematic photographic planetary patrol on a worldwide basis from seven strategic longitudes was maintained for many years in support of direct exploration of the solar system.

One of the most significant observational efforts stimulated by Percival Lowell was the spectrographic study of galaxies begun by V. M. Slipher in 1913. Slipher was the first to document the large recessional velocities of galaxies, data fundamental to the concept of the expanding universe. The record also shows that Slipher later pioneered in many other areas of astronomical spectroscopy, such as planetary rotation, comet spectra, light of the night sky, emission nebulae, nuclei of active galaxies, and planetary atmospheres.

As early as 1902, Percival Lowell became interested in searching for a trans-Neptunian planet by employing both theoretical and observational techniques, which ultimately led to the discovery of Pluto in 1930 by C. W. Tombaugh. A byproduct of the search provided comprehensive knowledge about faint moving objects in the solar system and basic material for a twenty-year proper motion survey by H. L. Giclas that identified many thousands of nearby stars.

In 1921 the temperature of Mars was determined from radiometric techniques developed at the Lowell Observatory. These techniques were the precursor of further infrared investigation by A. Adel, who discovered nitrous oxide, deuterium, and the "twenty-micron" window in the Earth's atmosphere in 1941.

In 1948 the first financial support outside the Lowell endowment was negotiated, first with the U.S. Weather Bureau and later with the U.S. Air Force, to investigate planetary atmospheres and systematically compare the Sun's light reflected from Uranus and Neptune with nearby solar-type stars in an effort to check the constancy of solar output in limited wavelengths— an ongoing program at the present time.

V. M. Slipher, the director since the death of Percival Lowell in 1916, retired in 1955, and the observatory's sole trustee, Roger L. Putnam, nephew of Percival Lowell, appointed John S. Hall of the U.S. Naval Observatory as director in 1957. Following the postwar years, government support of scientific research became a national policy, and it became possible to upgrade observing facilities and institute new innovative programs. The most fundamental was the agreement to move the sixty-nine-inch Perkins reflector telescope of the Ohio Wesleyan and Ohio State Universities to a dark-sky site twelve miles southeast of Flagstaff in 1961. This move was made possible by a National Science Foundation grant that included, several years later, modernization and a new, low-expansion glass primary mirror seventy-two inches in diameter. About this time also, exploration of the moon began. First an agreement was entered into with the Aeronautical Chart and Information Center of the U.S. Air Force to produce maps of the moon as seen through the telescope. Later competent staff trained for this project made more detailed maps that the astronauts used on the moon from the Ranger and Orbiter data telemetered back to Earth from these vehicles.

As mentioned previously, the Lowell Observatory had accumulated the most extensive collection of planetary photographs in existence; therefore, it was not surprising that at the Berkeley meeting of the International Astronomical Union it was recommended that the observatory be made one of the two international repositories of planetary photographs. In anticipation of its exploration of the solar system, NASA agreed to support such a repository in connection with a Planetary Research Center. In 1964, a nine thousand-square-foot native stone building, architecturally compatible with the old historic administration and library building completed in 1916, was funded by NASA. It has operated since that time under the direction of W. A. Baum as an integral part of the Lowell Observatory.

Also in 1964, an IBM 1130 computer was added for the use of staff astronomers, and plans were formulated to replace the old forty-two-inch reflector built in 1909 with a new, modern Ritchey-Chrétien type of the same aperture at the dark-sky site mentioned in connection with the moving of the sixty-nine-, later seventy-two-, inch Perkins reflector telescope. A few years later, the thirteen-inch wide-field search telescope located at the original observatory site, with which Pluto was discovered, was moved to this dark-sky site with funds from the Lowell endowment.

At the present time, three telescopes are still used on Mars Hill in Flagstaff: two reflectors and the historic Clark twenty-four-inch refractor. At the dark-sky site southeast of Flagstaff, three reflectors and the thirteen-inch A. Lawrence Lowell "Pluto" refractor are in operation. In 1979 the IBM 1130 computer was replaced with a PDP-11/55-based system.

The twenty-five persons now employed at the Lowell Observatory are involved in research covering a wide range of astronomical topics, with emphasis on solar system problems. The observatory is still a private institution, a corporation-sole in the State of Arizona, and is still managed by a single trustee. Professor Michael Putnam, a grandnephew of Percival Lowell, became the trustee in 1980. In July, 1977, upon the retirement of John S. Hall, the trustee appointed Arthur A. Hoag as director of the observatory. The operating funds are provided by income from the Lowell bequest and by competitive research grants. Current research topics include the history of astronomy, laboratory and observational spectroscopy, lunar occultations and stellar diameters, solar variations, planets, planetary rings, satellites, asteroids, comets, stellar motions, double stars, interstellar matter, evolution of galaxies, and discovery of quasars.

The Lowell Observatory maintains a public program including lecture tours and telescope viewing that now accommodates about fifteen thousand guided students and public visitors each year.

For further information, see A. Lawrence Lowell, *Biography of Percival Lowell* (1935); and Edward Weeks, *The Lowells and Their Institutes* (1966). See also Henry L. Giclas, "Lowell Observatory: A History of Discovery," *Plateau* (1978).

HENRY L. GICLAS

___M ___

MARINE BIOLOGICAL LABORATORY (MBL). While serving as the first director of the Marine Biological Laboratory in Woods Hole, Massachusetts, zoologist Charles Otis Whitman wrote for the *Atlantic Monthly* (June, 1893): "The ocean is now regarded as the original home of life on this planet and its present inhabitants furnish records of life histories and evolution phases which are absolutely indispensable to a deeper insight into the phenomena and laws of life."

Whitman was reflecting upon what was the chosen mission of an institution that has come to stand as the model biological station and one of the top intellectual gathering places in the United States, the "MBL." Then, as in the decades since, the Marine Biological Laboratory was international in character, for students and investigators from Maine to California worked side by side with those from England, Germany, and Japan. Arising from the spiritual antecedent of Louis Agassiz's Anderson School for Natural History on Penikese Island, the practical antecedent of Alpheus Hyatt's summer school in Annisquam, Massachusetts, sponsored by the Boston Society for Natural History and the Women's Educational Association of Boston, the MBL was founded in 1888 as a private, nonprofit corporation, a station for research and teaching in biology and natural history.

The MBL has viewed itself and has been viewed through its first century as a center for secondary-school and university-level biological educators (through about 1930), as a summertime intellectual "club" for high-ranking and aspiring biologists (until about 1965), and as a year-round "think tank" and training ground for interdisciplinary approaches to biological problems (most recently). Always, it has been a meeting site for current leaders in the life sciences and allied fields. It has been a place owned, governed, and at times zealously defended from peril, by established scientists who have each spent at least two summers there and who have met academic standards for corporation membership. These now number about 650 and more than 70 of them belong to the National Academy of Sciences* (NAS). Thirty-seven Nobel Prize winners have been associated with the laboratory.

In his 1944 history of the MBL, Frank R. Lillie, who served as MBL director and president during most of the first half of the twentieth century, identified the following fields in which work done at the MBL in its first twenty years greatly expanded the horizons of biological research: animal morphology; embryology, regeneration, fertilization and parthenogenesis; cytology; genetics and evolution; general physiology; animal tropisms and behavior; botany; and medical sciences. Thus, it would be difficult to find any branch of the twentieth-century life sciences whose roots could not be traced back to lectures, arguments, or experiments at the MBL early in its development.

Embryology and what has become cellular, developmental, and reproductive biology were brought out of nineteenth-century observational zoological studies to modern experimental status by now legendary researchers, many of whom spent their summers working at the MBL. C. O. Whitman, Jacques Loeb, Thomas Hunt Morgan, E. G. Conklin, and Edmund Beecher Wilson were among them. Loeb was the first person to demonstrate artificial parthenogenesis, and Whitman, Wilson, and Conklin were the first to trace embryonic cell lineages in *Clepsine*, *Nerei*, and *Crepidula*.

Morgan and his graduate students, the "Fly Room Boys," retreated to the MBL each summer to test and to clarify the ideas generated in the previous winter's research in *Drosophila* at Columbia University. It was at the MBL, too, that Morgan, together with these graduate students and knowledgeable colleagues, directed the work that gave birth to the new discipline of genetics.

W. C. Allee, Bostwick Ketchum, Alfred C. Redfield, V. T. Bowen, and John Ryther are also a few of the many scientists who have lived in Woods Hole, frequented the MBL, and brought botany, chemistry, natural history, zoology, and physics to bear on the hybrid science of ecology decades before its popular applications emerged.

Albert P. Mathews, having studied centrioles with E. B. Wilson at MBL during the summers of the early 1890s, went on to hold the first faculty position in physiological chemistry in the United States at the University of Chicago. His biochemistry text, first published in 1915, was used worldwide for the next three decades.

Frank Lillie, studying *Nerei* at MBL at the turn of the century, gave a complete description of the penetration of sperm into egg that was unsurpassed for thoroughness into the 1960s. Later, at the University of Chicago, he provided the original description of the actions of hormones in embryological development, thus giving rise to the new discipline of developmental endocrinology.

E. E. Just was a graduate student, hired by Frank Lillie out of his own pocket, to collect *Nerei* in Woods Hole's Eel Pond during the summers prior to World War I. Just went on to distinguished international studies in physiology. He is, moreover, widely remembered as an early proponent of the importance of scrupulously clean apparatus and strict temperature control, two concepts which were then far from accepted as significant aspects of experimental procedure.

Engineering science has not escaped the influence of MBL research. Twenty-nine papers presented at a neuromorphology seminar in 1898 foreshadowed deepening interest in the study of nerves at the laboratory. Beginning in the 1930s Kenneth S. Cole, Alan Hodgkin, Andrew Huxley, H. K. Hartline, and Stephen Kuffler, meeting regularly together and with others, taught MBL courses and applied emerging electronics technology to physiological studies. Their work on the eggs of the sea urchin, *Arbacia*, and on giant axons, particularly in the Woods Hole squid, *Loligo pealei*, was followed by the work of a number of their students who became leaders in neurophysiology and biophysics. This, in turn, led to a cross fertilization of ideas and to basic research that contributes today to advancements in clinical medicine and in developing fields such as cybernetics and artificial intelligence.

In writing to report the results of his work at the University of Pennsylvania and the MBL, Herbert Spencer Jennings effectively founded the study of behavioral psychology with his book *Behavior of the Lower Organisms* (1906). Animal behavior was a hotly contested topic at that time, and other MBL regulars who wrote on the subject were Whitman, Loeb, Edward L. Thorndike, R. M. Yerkes, Gilman A. Drew, Walter E. Garrey, S. J. Holmes, E. P. Lyon, Raymond Pearl, and Adele M. Field. It is interesting to note that at about this same time (1910-1921) Princeton University philosopher E. G. Spaulding was giving a widely attended course of lectures at Woods Hole on the "Philosophical Aspects of Biology and Allied Sciences."

Still other distinguished scientists who have spent many summers working and teaching at the laboratory include Victor Heilbrunn, Cornelia Clapp, E. G. Gardiner, William Morton Wheeler, Otto Loëwi, Ross G. Harrison, Alfred H. Sturtevant, Edgar Zwilling, and Katherine Foot. Most served terms as trustees of the MBL. Married couples whose contributions are known around the world and whose summers and often active retirement years have been spent at the laboratory include E. Newton and Ethel Browne Harvey, Katsuma and Jean Clark Dan, and Lester and Lucena Barth.

Documentation for many more biological-scientific advances attributable to MBL people can be found in the archival documents, books, and other material in its library, in itself a treasure trove of American science. Originally established by the MBL at its founding to serve its own students and investigators, the collections of the neighboring Woods Hole Oceanographic Institution,* the Woods Hole laboratory of the National Marine Fisheries Service, and the U.S. Geological Survey's Atlantic–Gulf of Mexico Branch Headquarters have been merged with it. Thus, the MBL repository has, through the years, become the common ground of this wider scientific community. The NAS's summer conference center is also nearby, and participants there often employ the MBL library's extensive collection of scientific journals and other holdings.

Current activities of the MBL have been described in a twenty-page descriptive pamphlet by its present director, Paul R. Gross, as:

a perfectly continuous spectrum, the microscopic end represented by submolecular biology (for example the structure and conformation of biopolymers and related condensed systems) and the macroscopic end by earth-wide exchanges of matter and energy between the biosphere and the non-living features of our planet (for example the world carbon budget).

Programs that compose that spectrum embrace Ecology and Ecosystems Analysis; Neurobiology, Biophysics, and Physiology; Cellular, Developmental, and Reproductive Biology; and Marine Biomedicine. The laboratory is active year-round now, with a permanent population of about 250, which grows in summer to more than 1,000 workers. Conferences, seminars, the library, and educational courses bring hundreds more visitors for shorter stays throughout the year.

Funding for the operations of the MBL has come from a wide variety of personal, governmental, corporate, and foundation sources over the years. Grants and contracts from federal and state government have been important, particularly in recent years. Yet, part of the money to found the MBL was raised by the presentation in Boston of a series of popular lectures and a now forgotten operetta. Members of the Crane, Clark, Meigs, and Swope families have been joined by numerous corporation members and MBL associates in rendering support to the MBL. Their munificence together with that of such philanthropic organizations as the Ford Foundation, Rockefeller Foundation, and Carnegie Corporation of New York have well nigh meant survival on occasion and the only opportunity for growth at other times.

Collaboration and fellowship at the MBL and Woods Hole extends beyond science. Friendships and romances have flourished there, particularly in Cape Cod's "good old summertime" activities. Sharing meals together in the dining hall or nautically designated "mess," living together in proximity in the dormitories, or inhabiting adjoining homes, has promoted and helped many efforts requiring cooperation—and a number of marriages. Dances, musicals, and dramatic performances, many centering around the MBL Club, have all been popular diversions through the years. Some Woods Hole scientists, including Leonor Michaelis, Ralph S. Lillie, and E. B. Wilson, have been, concurrently, professional musicians. There are, of course, the outdoor recreations of swimming, fishing, and sailing; and tennis courts and golf links are readily accessible. A summer Children's School of Science has operated at Woods Hole for more than sixty-five years under the leadership of mothers in the scientific and village community. It, of course, is one of the key focuses of beneficial interaction between the MBL and the townspeople of Woods Hole. Denis Robinson, who was inducted into the Order of the British Empire for his work in developing RADAR during World War II, has called the MBL a modern Athens. Lewis Thomas, the physician-philosopher chancellor of the Memorial Sloan-Kettering Institute for Cancer Research,* has written glowingly of the laboratory's character and promise. Such testimonials as these are examples, from among numerous others that could be provided, of the esteem in which the MBL is held by the thousands of scientists who have engaged there in research and teaching.

For further information, the definitive, although now outdated, history of the MBL is Frank R. Lillie's *The Woods Hole Marine Biological Laboratory* (1944). For an early account of the MBL, see Dallas L. Sharp, "The Marine Biological Laboratory," *Science* (1893). For later accounts, see E. G. Conklin, "The Story of Woods Hole and the Marine Biological Laboratory," *Collecting Net*, supplement, (1929); John E. Pfeiffer, "Woods Hole in 1949," *Scientific American* (September, 1949); and Lewis Thomas, "The MBL" in *The Lives of a Cell* (1974). See also Paul R. Gross, et al., *Marine Biological Laboratory* (1980), a twenty-page information pamphlet about the laboratory.

ANNE CAMILLE MAHER

MASSACHUSETTS HISTORICAL SOCIETY. This society was founded in Boston, Massachusetts, on January 24, 1791, during the first administration of President George Washington. It was the first historical society to be established in the United States and in the New World. A private institution, it was incorporated by the state legislature on February 19, 1794.

The society was founded by a handful of learned, historically minded Bostonians under the leadership of the Reverend Jeremy Belknap (1744-1798), a Harvard-trained Congregational minister. Because of his achievements, Belknap has been called the "father of American historical societies." (At present, there are over ten thousand historical societies in the nation.)

The founders set forth the aims of the society in its constitution:

The preservation of books, pamphlets, manuscripts, and records, containing historical facts, biographical anecdotes, temporary projects, and beneficial speculations, conduces to mark the genius, delineate the manners, and trace the progress of society in the United States, and must always have a useful tendency to rescue the true history of this country from the ravages of time and the effects of ignorance and neglect.

A collection of observations and descriptions in natural history and topography, together with specimens of natural and artificial curiosities, and a selection of every thing which can improve and promote the historical knowledge of our country, either in a physical or political view, has long been considered as a desideratum.

Collecting historical materials (principally primary sources), preserving them, and communicating historical information by means of publications—these became the three main missions of the fledgling intellectual agency.

The founders began the society's collection with contributions of manuscripts and printed works from their private holdings. Thereafter, they sought other materials to augment the collection through a campaign of active importuning of friends and likely contributors. Belknap, who led this effort, set the tone for this aggressive collecting policy in these words: "We intend to be an *active*, not a *passive*, literary body; not to lie waiting, like a bed of oysters, for the tide (of communication) to flow in upon us, but to *seek* and *find*, to *preserve* and *communicate*, literary intelligence, especially in the historical way."

Because of its active collecting policy, as well as a lack of competition, the society was able to acquire a significant corpus of materials bearing upon the history of the young nation, especially of New England. In subsequent years, the collection grew to the point where it now ranks as one of the most comprehensive and important historical collections in the United States. According to the authoritative *Harvard Guide to American History*, a standard bibliographical tool of the historical profession, only the Library of Congress's collection is superior to that of the society.

The society's manuscript holdings are especially noteworthy. The magisterial Adams Family Papers tops the list. There are also large collections of manuscripts that were produced by such prominent figures as Edward Everett, Thomas Jefferson, Henry Knox, Benjamin Lincoln, Horace Mann, Francis Parkman, William H. Prescott, William Ellery Channing, Theodore Parker, Timothy Pickering, and the Revere, Hancock, Winthrop, Saltonstall, and Lodge families. The society also owns many individual documents of singular significance: two copies of the Declaration of Independence; Paul Revere's three manuscript accounts of his famous "midnight ride"; George Washington's Newburgh Address; Samuel Sewall's diary; and John Winthrop's journal.

The institutional character of the society has markedly changed over the years. From its founding until the early twentieth century, it functioned in the manner of an eighteenth-century English gentlemen's "culture club." It was the private preserve of the members, a select group of Bostonians (all male) who comprised an intellectual and social elite. These learned men were "amateur" historians. On occasion, outsiders were permitted to use the society's resources, but they were a select few. Membership was limited by its constitution to a small number (less than one hundred), and administrative control was exercised by a self-perpetuating council. The organization acquired the reputation of being the most exclusive historical society in the nation.

The social transformation of the nation in the Progressive Era affected the society as well. Elitist, male-dominated cultural organizations were no longer in harmony with the spirit of the times. Then, too, the character of historical study in the United States underwent a profound change, and this development had a pronounced effect upon the society. With the advent of graduate history programs in the nation's colleges and universities, and the concomitant development of a class of "professional" historians, the society's rich holdings assumed a special significance. It was difficult for the organization to maintain itself as a "closed corporation" under these changed circumstances.

In 1910, the society's council issued a report that proclaimed a dramatic shift in policy with respect to the use of its materials:

It is generally admitted that the relations of the Society, not only to the outside public but to the scholars, are far from what they should be, and demand a radical improvement. To accumulate and bury was never the intention of the founders of this Society. To collect and hold rigidly for the use of the Society would be a suicidal act. The book or the manuscript which enters the doors of this Society has been lost to investigators, on the double plea that it was [a] private society and that its collections should be held for the use of its members or its own publications. The Society has lost by cultivating such an impression, and, by what is probably an unconscious narrowness of policy, permitting that impression to become general . . . Your Council believes in perfect freedom in the use of the Society's accumulations and in giving every facility to those who come to consult them. In this way only can the neglected available qualities be developed and the proper functions of the Society be fulfilled.

From this point on, the society's library became accessible to a growing number of historical researchers. Graduate students and professional historians were now able to use these materials. It was a gradual process, but by the 1940s all barriers had been lifted. Today, the Massachusetts Historical Society functions like a public institution. Any serious researcher (beyond high school age) can utilize the library.

Membership in the society has always been kept to a small number. At its founding, its constitution called for no more than 30 resident members. By 1980, the number of resident members had been increased to 175. The limit for corresponding members is currently 150. A major criterion for membership is distinguished service in the field of history, either as a writer, teacher, collector, or library administrator.

The society's governance also has undergone change in modern times. Until well into the twentieth century, the officers were drawn from a narrow social base. For the past two decades, there has been a considerable broadening of this base. There has been one other significant development: once a solid male phalanx, the council now includes two women.

The society's physical quarters have improved dramatically in recent years. For the first century of its existence, it occupied space in a number of buildings located in the heart of Boston. These constant changes of abode (six) worked a serious hardship on the collections. In the 1880s plans were laid for a permanent home. The dream was finally realized in the period 1897-1899. A large, handsome headquarters building was constructed in the Back Bay area, adjacent to the Fens. But, alas, within a few decades the building was bulging with materials, and there was an acute need for more space.

A resolution finally came in the early 1970s with the construction of a six-story wing, which was attached to the older building. The union was an artful blending of the old and the new. The society now enjoys spacious quarters that are equipped with a sophisticated climate-control system for the preservation of its precious paper materials. Although a research library, it has the physical appearance of a museum, with many historical paintings on the walls and exhibits positioned in different areas of the two main buildings.

From its founding to the 1950s, the society was wholly sustained by private funds. The early years were characterized by extreme poverty. For the first sixty-three years of its existence, the society had no endowment whatsoever. Gradually, an endowment was developed, and a number of special funds created for specific purposes.

Since the 1950s, the society has applied for and received state and federal grants for library projects. It has also received support from private foundations. The bulk of its support at this writing, however, is still derived from private sources (that is, a modest endowment).

A lack of funds has had a profound effect on society staffing. In the early years, there was no paid staff. The holdings were administered by volunteers drawn from the membership. When the funding situation improved in the early twentieth century, a librarian and a few support personnel were hired. From the 1920s to 1976, the staff was enlarged to about a dozen employees. But this group was not able to manage the library in a proper fashion. Many essential tasks were ignored for lack of time. The principal function of what was really a skeletal staff was to service the needs of patrons, and this it did in an heroic manner.

A major personnel breakthrough occurred in 1976 when the society was awarded two sizable grants (each three years in duration) by the National Endowment for the Humanities, which provided funds to hire seven professional personnel, increasing the staff to twenty-two. The grants terminated in late 1979, but the society has been able to retain five of these seven people on its payroll. It should be underscored that the present staff is of a highly professional order. Most employees are trained librarians and historians.

Since the 1950s, the society has had a special unit (now numbering five people) editing the Adams Papers. They are technically society employees, but they operate as a semi-autonomous administrative unit.

In 1991, the society will be celebrating its bicentennial. The history of this venerable Boston institution spans the life of the new nation, and its rich holdings document America's colonial origins. It is a unique cultural treasure house that performs the same tasks today as it did in the eighteenth century.

For further information, see Jane Belknap Marcou, *Life of Jeremy Belknap* (1847); Stewart Mitchell, "Historical Sketch," *Handbook of the Massachusetts Historical Society* (1949); Stephen T. Riley, *The Massachusetts Historical Society, 1791-1959* (1959); and *Stephen Thomas Riley: The Years of Stewardship* (1976).

LOUIS L. TUCKER

MATHEMATICAL ASSOCIATION OF AMERICA (MAA). The founding fathers of the Mathematical Association of America in 1915, were Professors W. D. Cairns, E. R. Hedrick, and, particularly, H. E. Slaught. It was Slaught who, in 1907, took over the editorial direction and management of the *American Mathematical Monthly*, launched in 1894 by B. F. Finkel. A number of colleges and universities began to provide financial support for the *Monthly*, and increasing attention was given to articles of interest to teachers as contrasted with researchers in mathematics. This trend in the magazine buttressed a developing sentiment on the part of Slaught and others that, although the needs of those interested in pure mathematical research were met by existing organizations, the teaching aspects of mathematics were being overlooked. At the April, 1914, meeting of the American Mathematical Society* (AMS), Slaught and his associates organized a committee that in 1915 made a report to the governing council of the AMS urging the latter to take over publication of the *American Mathematical Monthly*. The AMS decided that, although it would not be wise for it to take over publication of the *Monthly*, the founding of a separate organization for this purpose was in order.

Thereupon an organizational meeting was called for and held in Columbus, Ohio, on December 30, 1915; it resulted in the creation of the MAA. Hedrick was elected the first president; Cairns, secretary-treasurer, a position which he occupied until 1942; Slaught was named the MAA manager, and, when the *American Mathematical Monthly* was acquired in 1916 as the MAA's official publication, he was retained as editor and continued in these positions until his death in 1937. Due to the prominent role he played in the founding and activities of the MAA, Slaught was honored in various ways. Elected president in 1919, in 1933 he was made honorary president and member for life, and the 1938 publication of the *Monthly* was dedicated to him and featured two articles in his memory.

In addition to the outright publication of the *Monthly*, the MAA, from 1916 to 1943, provided subsidies to the *Annals of Mathematics*, wherein that journal published mathematical papers of a historical nature. In 1925

funds for the publication of the first four volumes of the Carus Mathematical Monographs were supplied by Mrs. Mary H. Carus. Succeeding volumes
in this series have been published with appropriations from the MAA. Also,
a series of pamphlets, entitled the Slaught Memorial Papers, has been
published by the MAA since 1947. In recent years the MAA has instituted a
number of other publications. Two are supported by gifts similar to the
Carus gifts: the Dolciani Mathematical Exposition, begun through a gift
from Mary P. Dolciani; and the Raymond W. Brink Selected Mathematical
Papers, supported by a gift in memory of a former president by his wife,
Carol R. Brink. Also, since the 1960s, it has published *Mathematics
Magazine* and the New Mathematical Library, a series of twenty-nine
paperback books designed for high school and college students. Finally,
since 1974, the MAA has published the *Two-Year College Mathematical
Journal*.

The MAA holds an annual meeting in January and a summer meeting in
August. They have often been convened in conjunction with the AMS and
other societies. A feature of the summer meetings has been the Earle Raymond Hedrick Lectures on topics of current mathematical interest. These
meetings have been held all over the United States and Canada. Also, the
MAA has established twenty-nine sections in the United States, which hold
one- and two-day meetings for members in their regions consisting of the
presentation of papers, discussions, and social activities.

Other noteworthy MAA activities include the work of its famous National Committee on Mathematical Requirements, which studied and
reported on the whole problem of mathematical education at the secondary
and collegiate levels; its sponsorship of visiting lecturers for secondary
schools and colleges; and its Committee on the Undergraduate Program in
Mathematics, which worked for curriculum reform and revitalization in the
1960s and 1970s. Its work has been summarized in the two-volume *Compendium of CUPM Recommendations*, published by the MAA in 1975.

Membership is open to anyone interested in mathematics. From 1,045
charter members the MAA has grown to over 18,500 members, resident in
all the states of the Union and including more than 800 abroad.

The MAA elects the customary institutional officers; it conducts its
business from an office, headed by an executive director, located in
Washington, D.C.

For further information, see the biography of Professor Slaught, which
also provides a great deal of historical information about the MAA, by
Harris Jeremiah Dark, *The Life and Works of Herbert Ellsworth Slaught*
(1948), and the following articles appearing in the *American Mathematical
Monthly:* Herbert Ellsworth Slaught, "Retrospect and Prospect for
Mathematics in America" (November, 1920); W. D. Cairns, "Herbert
Ellsworth Slaught—Editor and Organizer" (January, 1938); and G. A.

Bliss, "Herbert Ellsworth Slaught—Teacher and Friend" (January, 1938). See also W. D. Cairns, "Mathematics in Education," *AAAS Bulletin* (January, 1944); and the MAA *Bulletin of Information*.

MEDIEVAL ACADEMY OF AMERICA. A major catalyst in the establishment of the Medieval Academy in 1925 was the presidential address of Professor John M. Manly to the 1920 meeting of the Modern Language Association of America* (MLA), in which he stressed the need for organization for research with greater specialization regarding subject matter. The creation of a medieval Latin studies group resulted from such observations, and the academy with a broader statement of purpose, evolved from it. This purpose is, according to its bylaws:

To conduct, encourage, promote and support research, publication and instruction in mediaeval records, literature, languages, arts, archaeology, history, philosophy, science, life and all other aspects of mediaeval civilization, by publications, by research and by such other means as may be desirable, and to hold property for such purpose.

The major contribution of the Medieval Academy to scholarship has been its publications. The quarterly journal *Speculum*, published since 1926, provides articles and book reviews dealing with the medieval period. An index to volumes 1 through 49 of *Speculum* will be published in 1982; it will include subject and manuscript indexes to the articles and a list of books reviewed.

The academy also publishes three book series. Medieval Academy Books, begun in 1928, now numbers ninety-one volumes on all facets of the Middle Ages, among them a series of editions of the commentaries of Averroes on Aristotle. Speculum Anniversary Monographs, established at the fiftieth annual meeting in 1975, is intended especially for young scholars who are publishing their first books, but others are welcome to write for the series as well. Seven volumes have so far been published. Medieval Academy Reprints for Teaching is published in cooperation with the University of Toronto Press. Since 1978 it has reprinted in paperback ten books needed for teaching courses in the medieval field. The academy occasionally sponsors works that are published elsewhere, such as Edgar B. Graves's *A Bibliography of English History to 1485* (a revision of Gross's *Sources*) and a revision of Paetow's classic *A Guide to the Study of Medieval History*, prepared by Gray Boyce.

The Medieval Academy makes several awards. A gold medal award established in 1939, the Haskins Medal, is awarded annually for an outstanding book in the medieval field. The award is highly prized and has been a stimulus for research in the medieval areas of study. The Elliott Prize, consisting of three hundred dollars, was established in 1972. It is awarded annually to a young scholar publishing his or her first article in the field of medieval studies. Articles appearing in any journal (American, European, or other) are welcomed for consideration provided their authors are residents of the United States or Canada. The John Nicholas Brown Prize, consisting of five hundred dollars, was established in 1978 and is awarded annually to a young scholar publishing his or her first book or monograph on a medieval subject judged to be of outstanding quality; the author must be a resident of North America.

The academy holds an annual meeting in the spring. These meetings have been held in various sections of the United States and Canada, with the greater number being convened in the Eastern section of the United States.

The Medieval Academy has a combination of elective and open membership. The fellows and corresponding fellows are distinguished domestic and foreign medievalists, respectively, and are elected by the existing fellows. The number of fellows and corresponding fellows may not exceed one hundred in each category, and there are presently eighty-five fellows and sixty-three corresponding fellows in the academy. The other categories of membership are open to all who are interested in medieval studies, and at the present time there are about four thousand members in all categories.

The Medieval Academy elects the customary institutional officers; it conducts its business from an office, headed by an executive director, located in Cambridge, Massachusetts.

For further information, see George R. Coffman, "The Medieval Academy of America: Historical Background and Prospect," *Speculum* (January, 1926); and Bartlett J. Whiting, "The Medieval Academy of America," *The World of the Mind* (1958).

MEMORIAL HOSPITAL FOR THE TREATMENT OF CANCER AND ALLIED DISEASES. See Memorial Sloan-Kettering Cancer Center.

MEMORIAL SLOAN-KETTERING CANCER CENTER. Memorial Sloan-Kettering Cancer Center is the world's largest privately operated, nonprofit cancer center. It includes the Memorial Hospital for Cancer and Allied Diseases and the Sloan-Kettering Institute for Cancer Research. An institution dedicated to cancer treatment, research, and education, Memorial Sloan-Kettering is also the oldest cancer center in the United States. Its history dates back nearly one hundred years to a time when most general hospitals were reluctant to accept patients with cancer and there was no special hospital in the country devoted exclusively to the disease.

In 1884, surgeon-gynecologist J. Marion Sims and a group of supporters founded the New York Cancer Hospital, renamed Memorial in 1899. Plans for the institution arose out of controversy at the New York Woman's Hospital, founded by Sims in 1854, where the board of supervisors opposed the admission and treatment of women with cancer. John Jacob Astor, a member of the institution's board of governors, had proposed the erection of a separate pavilion adjacent to the Woman's Hospital for cancer patients. Sims chose, however, to resign in order to promote the founding of a specialized cancer hospital.

In a powerful letter to Mr. Astor's lawyer, John Parsons, Sims argued for such a hospital "on its own foundation, wholly independent of all other hospitals,"with a medical board "composed of those who go into it with zeal, determined not only to give temporary relief to human suffering but to do something toward discovering better methods for treatment." Sims continued:

> It is time we turned a listening ear to the cries of humanity. If there are those who favor a special hospital for cancer (and I hope there are some) let me beg you to take steps at once to inaugurate a movement which must culminate in a great work so much needed here and now. The subject of cancer is too large and its interests too great to be lodged in a pavilion subsidiary to any other hospital.

Sims received financial support from Mr. Astor, his wife Mrs. Astor, a cousin, Elizabeth Hamilton Cullum, and other members of the board of governors of the Woman's Hospital who had stood behind Sims's efforts to treat women with cancer at that institution. Determined in their resolve to find more effective means of cancer therapy, they spearheaded a movement to conquer the fear, ignorance, and indifference surrounding treatment of the disease.

Staffed by a dedicated group of doctors who had worked with Marion Sims, the New York Cancer Hospital formally opened in December of 1887, with the completion of the Astor Pavilion for Women on Eighth Avenue in New York City. John Parsons became the first president of the hospital board.

The speed with which available beds were filled highlighted the need for the facilities, but the institution encountered economic problems from the very start. Over the course of the first year, 278 patients were admitted and 180 operations performed. The admission rate increased as time passed. However, almost half the patients admitted were unable to pay the full costs of treatment, and protracted stays by indigent patients drained the resources of the hospital. The pavilion for men was completed in 1891, but could not be opened until 1898 for lack of means.

The hospital and its staff were also subject to public hostility, indifference, and disapproval. The circular towers of the hospital provided more light and air than was usual for hospitals of the day. Nevertheless, the castle-like appearance of the structure, along with the somewhat forbidding and hopeless prognoses accorded the patients by the general public, led many people to refer to Memorial as the "Bastille of Central Park." Because of their association with the "Bastille," staff members were often shunned and denied recognition for the many cases in which life was lengthened, distress changed to comfort, and normal routines restored.

Despite the extraordinary efforts of the medical staff and the personal devotion and fund raising efforts of John Parsons, economic necessity began to erode the initial concept of the hospital. In 1890, the rules were relaxed to admit patients with diseases allied to cancer, and the staff soon began to admit their own private surgical patients to rooms unoccupied by cancer patients.

The early efforts of Memorial's staff had been limited to cancer surgery and the improvement of surgical techniques, but events at the turn of the century signalled the beginning of a new era for the institution. In 1902, the family of Collis P. Huntington, founder of the Southern Pacific Railroad and a former patient at the hospital, established at Memorial a Fund for Cancer Research, the first such fund in the United States. Because of limitations in the facilities at Memorial, the pathology research called for by the fund was begun at the Loomis Laboratory for Research in Experimental Pathology at the Cornell University Medical College. That same year, Mrs. Huntington provided two Roentgen ray machines that allowed the hospital to begin its pioneering role in the use of X-rays in cancer therapy.

The research supported by the Huntington Fund and the initially promising results with radiation therapy at Memorial attracted the attention of Dr. James Ewing, a highly respected pathologist at Cornell who became the next leader of Memorial. While at Cornell, Ewing had developed a deep interest in cancer research. He had also envisioned the establishment of a cancer center where clinical research together with treatment activities and the education of doctors and scientists would lead to unprecedented progress in cancer medicine. In 1910, Ewing was introduced to Dr. James Douglas, a scientist and leader in the copper mining industry whose interest in supporting research into new therapies for cancer had resulted from his daughter's death from the disease. Together, they approached board members at Memorial with plans for a "rebirth" of the hospital. Douglas offered to contribute close to one-third of a million dollars, including several grams of radium, contingent upon Dr. Ewing's appointment to the staff and the hospital's return to the exclusive treatment of cancer patients. An agreement was reached in 1912. Ewing became pathologist and head of the rejuvenated cancer hospital.

Under Ewing's leadership, from 1913 to 1939, Memorial became an internationally known and respected center for the study and treatment of cancer. Ewing recruited collaborators in every area of cancer medicine, who were to become leaders in their respective fields. The hospital assumed the research that had been carried on at Cornell and established new laboratories for studies in pathology, immunology, biochemistry, and nutrition. Radiation therapy was transformed from a promising technique to a professional discipline, and Memorial opened the first radiation research laboratory in the country. Memorial also became known for its bold and imaginative use of surgery. In addition, Ewing completed a classic treatise on *Neoplastic Diseases*, the first complete collection and classification of tumors, which became a standard reference work in many translations around the world.

During Ewing's tenure, public response to Memorial changed dramatically. The expansion of facilities could not keep pace with the growing demand for treatment, and as early as 1920, hospital reports made reference to the number of professional visitors who came to Memorial from other parts of the United States and foreign countries. At this time, Dr. Ewing became involved in the establishment of the American Cancer Society, an institution which became a potent factor in arousing public and professional interest in cancer research and treatment.

In the late 1920s, with the generous support of John D. Rockefeller, Jr., education became a major thrust of the institution. Six clinical fellowships established in 1927 formed the basis for more extensive resident training programs, and Memorial soon became a world-renowned cancer training facility.

By 1939, Memorial had begun to strain the capacity of its facility, and with support from the Rockefellers and Edward S. Harkness, a new twelve-story hospital was erected and equipped on a site donated by John D. Rockefeller, Jr. The site was bounded by York and First avenues and East Sixty-Seventh and Sixty-Eighth streets in Manhattan. This first unit of the present center opened with a bed capacity of 240 and the most up-to-date facilities then available for therapy and research; it was the largest of all institutions devoted to cancer and included the first ward for children in a cancer hospital.

After the retirement of Dr. Ewing in 1939, Memorial found a leader in Dr. Cornelius P. Rhoads, a dedicated physician and scientific investigator from the Rockefeller Institute for Medical Research. C. P. Rhoads was committed to improving medical diagnosis and treatment at Memorial and also to developing a more effective means of cancer prevention and control.

The growing conviction that research and improved treatment must go hand in hand led in 1945 to the founding of the Sloan-Kettering Institute for Cancer Research, the research affiliate of Memorial, with the generous support of Alfred P. Sloan, Jr. and Charles F. Kettering. Dr. Rhoads became its first director.

Within the institute, programs were established for the systematic testing of possible anticancer agents, and investigators began work in steroid chemistry, virology, immunology, endocrinology, nuclear acid chemistry, carcinogenesis, toxicology, and nutrition. The spinoffs of research were many. In the 1940s, work with radioactive isotopes formed the basis for improvement of diagnostic tools. In the 1950s, Dr. Rhoads pioneered the development of chemotherapy—or the treatment of cancer with drugs—now one of the most effective means of cancer control for many patients. In 1954, the first computerized radiation treatment planning system was developed at the institute and made available to hospitals throughout the country. In the late 1950s, work with viruses and immunotherapy in laboratory animals opened new avenues of exploration in the field of human cancer.

During the tenure of Dr. Rhoads, from 1939 to 1959, the Memorial expanded with the addition of an outpatient building, a pavilion for children, and a forty-bed chemotherapy ward. New educational programs were also established for medical students and nurses, and investigators began to study the early stages of cancer with an eye toward prevention of the disease.

The Memorial Sloan-Kettering Cancer Center was incorporated in 1960 to oversee and coordinate the work of the growing Memorial Hospital and the Sloan-Kettering Institute. Over the next twenty years, the center supported research and treatment activities that improved established techniques for the diagnosis and treatment of cancer and opened the way to new advances in prevention, early detection, and other areas of cancer control. Relatively few could be successfully treated for cancer in 1884, but today the chances of surviving the disease have greatly improved. Throughout its history, Memorial Sloan-Kettering has assumed a leadership role in the fields of cancer medicine and biomedical research; and it continues to maintain its strong threefold commitment to patient care, research, and education.

In 1961, recognition of increased pressure on existing facilities led to the initiation of a program of expansion and modernization that established the center as it stands today. Eleven buildings with nearly 1 million usable square feet of space include a sophisticated twenty-story, 565-bed hospital that admits more than 15,700 patients annually, a surgical pavilion with fifteen operating rooms, an outpatient facility that handles 138,000 outpatient visits per year and houses a Diagnostic Radiology Center, over one hundred laboratories in four buildings, and residences for staff.

A board of overseers composed primarily of business and civic leaders who serve voluntarily is charged with overseeing the direction of the center. In addition, each of the three corporations, the institute, hospital, and center, has its own board of managers, drawn from the membership of the board of overseers. The three boards are composed of essentially the same individuals in order to achieve greater unity of the institute, hospital, and center, while at the same time preserving the status of each as a separate corporation. The boards of managers set policies and monitor the activities of the three corporations.

The president of the center acts as chief executive officer of all three corporations. In addition, there is a director of the Sloan-Kettering Institute and general director and chief operating officer of Memorial Hospital.

The work of the center is carried out by a staff of more than five-thousand, including research scientists, attending physicians, physicians-in-training, postdoctoral fellows, nurses, technicians, and a full staff of administrative, clerical, and service personnel.

Treatment within the hospital includes surgery, radiation therapy, chemotherapy, immunotherapy, and experimental methods such as hyperthermia and bone marrow transplantation. A multidisciplinary team approach is employed to provide each patient with the most effective therapy.

At the institute, research is presently conducted in molecular biology and genetics, cell biology, developmental biology, carcinogenesis, immunobiology and transplantation biology, tumor immunology and virology, developmental therapeutics, biophysics, and radiation biology and biostatistics. Research results are available without delay to clinicians at the center. In fact, many of the researchers are themselves physicians who also treat patients, thus ensuring the patient of the best and newest treatment.

Memorial Sloan-Kettering has continued to expand its role in training doctors and scientists and providing continuing education for those who seek to update their knowledge and skills. Today, more than five thousand physicians and researchers and many thousands of other health workers who have trained at the center are active in cancer treatment and research at leading institutions in many countries.

In patient care, research, and education, Memorial Sloan-Kettering has developed close working relationships with its neighbors, the New York Hospital-Cornell Medical Center, the Rockefeller University, and the Hospital for Special Surgery. The center also maintains extensive relations with other major biomedical centers throughout the world.

For further information, see the following articles and monographs published by the Memorial Sloan-Kettering Cancer Center: Bob Considine, *That Many May Live* (1959); Reginald G. Coombe, *The Evolution of a Center for Cancer Research* (1962); Guy F. Robbins, "James Ewing—The Man," *Clinical Bulletin* (1978); *A Singleness of Purpose* (1978); and *Historical Highlights, Memorial Sloan-Kettering* (1981). See also C. P. Rhoads, "Cancer University," *Reader's Digest* (August, 1956); Francelia Butler, *The Sun Dial* (1959); and unpublished archival material located at the center.

SHELLEY S. LOTTER

METAPHYSICAL SOCIETY OF AMERICA (MSA). The establishment of the Metaphysical Society of America (MSA) was largely due to the efforts of Professor of Philosophy Paul Weiss, at Yale University. He had been disturbed by the tendency of philosophers to split themselves into small groups on the basis of religion, doctrine, or region. He called for the creation of a society that would negate this tendency and devote itself to the pursuit of those questions which have perplexed mankind from the beginnings of its career of reflective thinking.

A few years before the 1950 founding of the MSA, Professor Weiss established the *Review of Metaphysics*, a quarterly journal which has had close, historical, and informal ties with the MSA and publishes the annual presidential address of the MSA. The stated policy of the *Review*, however, is that it is not associated with any school or group nor the organ of any association or institution and is interested in inquiries into root questions regardless of a writer's affiliation.

Thus, the list of *Review* authors is international in scope, and about as many non-MSA as MSA members have published in the journal. An MSA newsletter, prepared by the secretary-treasurer, keeps the membership informed of pertinent matters.

The MSA has held annual meetings since its founding. The earlier ones were usually convened at Eastern or Midwestern universities. Latterly, however, they have been held in institutions located in other sections of the country. The MSA elects the customary institutional officers; it conducts its business from an office, headed by a secretary-treasurer, located in Columbia, South Carolina.

For further information, see a brief unpublished history of the MSA from 1950 to 1970, by Professor Paul G. Kuntz. Professor Kuntz is presently updating this history for publication. See also an address by Professor Weiss appearing in the *Review of Metaphysics* (September, 1950); and "The Philosophy of Paul Weiss," *Review of Metaphysics* (June, 1972).

MIDWEST RESEARCH INSTITUTE (MRI).† Kansas City, Missouri, is the locale for one of the more unusual founding histories of any research institution in the country. Of the handful of independent, not-for-profit institutes in the country, MRI is the only one to be started by a diverse group of regional business and civic leaders. It had no endowment, foundation, or university money behind it and operates largely from research contracts. It also is the only institute started to do research for a defined region initially and to grow gradually into national and international research.

The regional leaders were a nucleus of concerned citizens who sought ways to bring modern industrial development to the Midwest. They sought to keep skilled technicians and professionals as well as attract new ones to the region. World War II caused a rapid buildup of industry in the mainly

---

†Reprinted with permission of Midwest Research Institute.

agricultural Midwest and halted somewhat the migration of residents to the industrialized coasts. Those industries had to be converted into peacetime activities to keep the trained scientists and engineers in the region and to continue the economic growth.

Leaders in education, science, business, and industry were brought in from a six-state area to design the best approach. They hit upon the expanding frontier of technology and industrial research as a viable solution. It would use the existing facilities of the region and develop the natural resources available to allow the region to develop many products imported from the East at higher costs.

The group sought advice from research institutes, geologists, university presidents, and Midwesterners prominent in science and related fields. They studied data on the area to determine the strengths, weaknesses, and capabilities of its people and resources. They also contacted other regional businessmen and prominent citizens in search of financial backing. Their idea to build an independent research institute designed specifically to help solve problems inherent to the Midwest received widespread acceptance. A charter was drawn up for a not-for-profit independent research institute, and on June 17, 1944, Midwest Research Institute was incorporated. By 1945, $500,000 had been donated by local and regional organizations and individuals for initial operational costs.

The founding purpose of MRI was to support the Midwestern region of Missouri, Kansas, Iowa, Nebraska, Arkansas, and Oklahoma by developing new industry, finding profitable uses for products, and acting as a regional research center. Limited operations began in July, 1944, under the direction of W. T. Rinehart, a chemist on leave from the Armour Research Foundation in Chicago. Harold Vagtborg, director of Armour Research, had been a key advisor during the inception of the institute, and he took over officially as president on January 1, 1945.

Nine men who were most influential in making MRI a reality comprised the first board of trustees and governing council for the institute. All were leaders in education, science, business, and industry from the Kansas City area; all were dedicated to developing the organization. Vagtborg attracted a small group of professional researchers to form his staff. In the spring of 1945, MRI's staff consisted of eleven professionals and four administrative personnel. Offices and laboratories for the small group were housed in a former bakery laboratory owned by the Campbell-Taggart Research Corporation. The building was leased to the institute by C. J. Patterson, president of Campbell-Taggart and a founder of MRI. This initial facility was limiting from the outset of operations, and expansion proliferated into nearby buildings and residences. By the end of 1945, the staff had increased to thirty-one and by 1948 MRI had acquired six structures in the Westport area. Various off-site locations were also used around the city.

The first research project done by MRI was in chemistry, adapting munition compounds developed for military use during World War II for use in agriculture. Equipment and expertise used for the chemical research in the beginning dictated the direction of research in following years, and the institute continued to build a strong national reputation in the chemical field. Many of the projects were concerned with developing ways to upgrade resources so that they could be used to higher efficiencies by manufacturers and thus reduce costs.

Vagtborg left the institute in September, 1948, to become the president of the newly founded Southwest Research Institute* in San Antonio, Texas. For the next two years, MRI operated under the direction of an advisory group of trustees.

Dr. Charles N. Kimball, technical director for Bendix Corporation's central research laboratories in Detroit, became MRI's second president in June of 1950. Over the next twenty-five years, Dr. Kimball was influential in raising contributions from all sectors of the country and in expanding the facilities, equipment, staff, capabilities, and reputation of MRI. It was financially stable by 1951 and has continued to run in the black ever since. The 1952 fiscal year shows an operating volume of over one million dollars, and that steadily increased to over twelve million dollars by 1975.

One of the first major fund drives Dr. Kimball instigated was to raise contributions for a new facility to be built for MRI. The board of trustees had the wisdom and insight to purchase 11.5 acres of land in the late 1940s for future growth. This tract was located in the cultural center of Kansas City, just south of the Nelson Art Gallery and to the west of what is today a state university and a private college. The land also was near the new six-million-dollar Linda Hall Library* (LHL), one of the largest privately endowed science libraries in the country.

Construction for the new facility began in 1953, and operations were moved from the overtaxed Westport facilities to the initial seventy thousand-square-foot structure in 1955. The institute rapidly outgrew even those facilities, and by 1959 an east wing had been added with new laboratories devoted to the health sciences. Also, three private school buildings adjacent to its land were acquired in the late 1950s, and the social and engineering departments were moved into the revamped classrooms. A west wing was built onto the original structure in 1962 primarily for biochemical research.

As the institute continued to outgrow additions, Dr. Kimball again was instrumental in soliciting funds for a second new building. A half-million-dollar donation by Helen F. Spencer, widow of Kenneth A. Spencer, who was a founder of MRI, was augmented by the institute and used to build the Kenneth A. Spencer Laboratories in 1970. Funds were also contributed in 1970 by the children of C. J. Patterson, another MRI founder, to help construct and equip the Patterson Library adjoining the new building.

The institute also expanded off site. William N. Deramus, an MRI trustee from 1945 to 1965, donated forty acres of his property in south Kansas City in 1957, and, in 1964, thirty acres were added by his son William N. Deramus III, also a trustee. The L. Russell Kelce Memorial Laboratory and the Speas Memorial Laboratory were built on the Deramus site from contributions given to honor two MRI trustees. The Deramus Field Station now has six special purpose laboratories and a large lake, which is used as a field station for health research and for testing hazardous materials.

Another major step in the expansion of MRI came in 1975, when MRI merged with the North Star Research Institute in Minnesota. North Star was established in 1963 in a former school building under many of the same auspices as MRI. It became the North Star Division of MRI after the merger, and a new North Star facility was built in Minnetonka, Minnesota, in 1976. Today, North Star's emphasis and expertise is in regional economics and marketing as well as analytical chemistry.

MRI opened an office in Raleigh, North Carolina, in 1978 as part of a project for the Environmental Protection Agency. The contract calls for MRI to assist the EPA in developing standards for hazardous air pollutants and to compile recommendations for new stationary source performance standards.

The institute has been represented in Washington, D.C., since 1953 by liaisons working with governmental agencies and trade associations. A permanent office was opened there in 1965 as more and more national and governmental research programs were developed.

As the institute expanded, so did its capabilities. The initial spectrum of chemical research evolved into agricultural chemistry, organic and inorganic chemistry, biochemistry, and chemical engineering. Contracts for research in the ballistics field augmented the engineering division in the early years. The biological life sciences division began to grow rapidly in 1948, when cancer research was first initiated at MRI. In the late 1950s and 1960s the life sciences field grew dramatically and comprised an ever increasing proportion of MRI's research. Economic and marketing research also began expanding rapidly in the late 1950s and 1960s.

MRI has consistently advanced modern technology through its research in such areas as cancer, the environment, and materials. It was a pioneer in efforts to identify the role of the automobile as a cause of smog. It also was responsible for getting the National Aeronautics and Space Administration (NASA) interested in technology transfer. In 1962, it set up the first program in the United States designed to apply NASA's inventions, processes, and techniques to industry. The initial program led to widespread research in technology transfer not only at MRI but in universities and institutions throughout the country.

Research in pharmacology, toxins, energy, and waste recycling are newly developing areas, reflecting the national emphasis on environmental concerns. MRI has gained a national reputation for its research in solar energy, cancer, environmental health, and law enforcement.

The institute continues to place major importance on regional research. The Kimball Fund, named for Dr. Charles N. Kimball, was established in 1970 to underwrite public service projects of local and regional importance. It is now over one million dollars and provides money for special research not contracted by outside organizations but considered important to the institute's purpose and growth.

Dr. Kimball retired as president of MRI in 1975, becoming chairman of its board of trustees. In 1979, he was elected president emeritus. John McKelvey, who has been on the MRI staff since 1964 in key research management and executive positions, moved into the position of president in 1975.

Under McKelvey, the institute has doubled in volume and staff by obtaining a contract from the Department of Energy to manage and operate the Solar Energy Research Institute. SERI, located in Golden, Colorado, is the major center for research and development of solar energy technology in the United States. The project got under way in 1977 with about a dozen professionals. By 1979 its staff numbered over seven hundred.

SERI administers more than $60 million in solar energy research, which is subcontracted to other institutions and industries around the country. The research is aimed at developing both passive and active forms of solar energy that are economically feasible for use by both industrial and private sectors.

McKelvey also has actively steered MRI into international research. Programs have been established in Riyadh, Saudi Arabia, as part of a contract from the Department of the Treasury to set up laboratories and develop quality controls for food imported into the Middle East. The project also calls for training Saudis so that they eventually can operate the program independently. SERI is expanding its operations into Saudi Arabia with project plans to set up the world's largest photovoltaic power system near Riyadh and develop an information data base.

MRI has a board of approximately 140 trustees who are national and civic leaders, businessmen, and industrialists. Twenty of those trustees are on the executive committee of the institute and are the governing body of over 1,200 employees for all branches of MRI. The committee continues to keep MRI operating independently and with a balance of governmental and private sector contracts. It also continues to keep much of the focus at MRI on its founding role as a convener and developer of regional programs for civic and professional groups.

For further information, see George E. Ziegler, "Midwest Research Institute—A New Scientific Research Institution," *Journal of Applied Physics* (August, 1946); "Midwest Banks on Research," *Business Week*

(September, 1946); "Research Progress at Midwest Research Institute in 1946-1947," *Chemical and Engineering News* (November, 1947); John Temple Graves, *History of Southern Research Institute* (1955); and Harold Vagtborg, *Research and American Industrial Development* (1976). See also MRI *Annual Reports*, 1945 to date.

CHARLES N. KIMBALL

MISSISSIPPI VALLEY HISTORICAL ASSOCIATION. See Organization of American Historians.

MODERN LANGUAGE ASSOCIATION OF AMERICA (MLA). A former executive secretary of the Modern Language Association of America, Professor John Hurt Fisher, has stated that the approximately forty scholars who participated in the founding of the MLA at Columbia University in December, 1883, were chiefly motivated by the need to assert the value of the study of English and the other modern languages in the face of a dominance of Greek and Latin in the schools and colleges. Another major factor leading to the MLA's establishment was the influence of the German universities. Increasingly in the late nineteenth century, associations had been formed in Germany by academicians for this purpose, and they provided examples for American scholars, many of whom had been trained there.

Prior to the turn of the nineteenth century, members of the MLA devoted considerable attention to pedagogical problems, and in 1899, in cooperation with the National Education Association, the MLA prepared a report on foreign-language teaching and study. From this time on, however, there was a shift of emphasis to research coupled with an interest in the production of well-qualified graduate students. By the 1920s, MLA's interest in the actual teaching of modern languages and particularly foreign languages in secondary schools had declined to the point of abandonment, and pedagogical concerns became the province of a number of new organizations established primarily for that purpose. Coincidentally, interest in and study of modern foreign languages declined at a rapid rate in these same schools.

Various MLA officials and members called attention to this situation and maintained that, although the study of English as a subject was ever increasing, the decline in interest in the problems connected with the teaching of modern foreign languages, particularly at the secondary level, boded ill for the MLA, scholars in the modern language field, and the nation. Officially, however, the MLA did not become involved. In 1923, for example, although three past presidents participated in and played an important role in a five-year study of the problem, the MLA did not officially participate. In the 1930s the tide turned, and in 1939 an MLA Commission on Trends in Education was established. This commission, and a succeeding committee dealing exclusively with modern foreign languages, emphasized the responsibilities of the MLA in these areas. In 1950 the committee declared that the MLA could not remain aloof; its future rested upon the quality and amount of work carried on in the schools and colleges of the country. The promotion and support of the study of English and of foreign languages at all scholastic levels must, therefore, be a matter of concern to the MLA.

An early manifestation of this reappraisal was the setting up, in 1952, of the MLA Foreign Language Program. Operating under a grant from the Rockefeller Foundation, the program proved to be a boon to foreign-language teaching and programs. Work done under the program provided the statistical support, rationales, and pedagogical principles that were later incorporated into the 1958 National Defense Education Act (NDEA), which provided support for teaching and research in foreign languages. In 1967, the MLA helped to create the American Council on the Teaching of Foreign Languages. Then, in 1969, it founded the Association of Departments of Foreign Languages (ADFL) to provide a means of communication among the chairmen of college and university modern language departments. All of these efforts were designed, of course, to counter and possibly reverse the continuing decline in foreign-language enrollments in the secondary schools of the United States.

During the same period the MLA also supervised many projects on the teaching of English. The Cooperative English Program was begun in 1957, in conjunction with the National Council of Teachers of English. In 1963 the Association of Departments of English was founded, which provided an earlier model for the work of the ADFL in foreign languages. Although these projects never had access to the specialized funds available in the foreign-language areas, they did serve to revitalize English-language teaching.

Despite this increased pedagogical activity there was no decrease in other MLA activities. *PMLA*, its learned journal established in 1884, is now issued six times a year. Four issues are devoted to scholarly articles; the other two are directory and program issues. Circulation has continually increased and now stands at about thirty-five thousand annually. In 1921 the MLA began publication of an annual bibliography of works by American scholars. Expanded, following World War II, into the *MLA International Bibliography*, it now appears annually in three volumes containing about fifty thousand entries. A computerization program, begun in 1964, has been of material aid in this effort. An *MLA Newsletter*, together with other books and pamphlets dealing with research and pedagogy in language and literature, rounds out the MLA's publications. Best known of the latter is the *MLA Style Sheet*, a writing guide used by many humanistic scholars. First published in 1951, over two million copies of the *Style Sheet* have been printed, and it has been a steady source of revenue for the organization.

In the 1960s the MLA launched a program calling for the publication of definitive text editions of noted American authors. Plans were laid for an initial ten such editions, and, in 1963, a Center for the Editions of American Authors (CEAA) was founded by the MLA. In 1964, the U.S. Office of Education contracted to support the first of such editions. Then, following the creation of the National Endowment for the Humanities in 1965, the MLA, in 1966, received one of the first NEH grants in the amount of three hundred thousand dollars for this work, followed by a like sum the next year.

Membership in the MLA has been open to all interested persons. Beginning with approximately four hundred members in its first ten years of existence, the MLA membership more than tripled by the time of World War I, climbed to over four thousand in 1932, about seven thousand in 1953, and eleven thousand in 1960. During the 1960s and early 1970s, it experienced the phenomenal growth characteristic of other national learned societies, and membership now stands at nearly thirty thousand. The vast majority of the past and present MLA members are members of college and university faculties or graduate students at such institutions.

Since its founding, annual meetings of the MLA have been held in various sections of the country. Prior to World War II, colleges and universities generally acted as hosts, but the vast increase in members since that time forced the transfer of such meetings to convention hotels in large cities. The annual meetings have almost always been held during the Christmas week. Because of its large membership and the range of interests represented, MLA programs at the meetings have included a bewildering variety of subjects. The 1976 annual meeting in New York, for example, had more than five hundred separate meetings, with more than two thousand participants, and approximately ten thousand members in attendance.

The tremendous growth in members and activities in the 1960s and 1970s saw an increase in office space and funds needed for operation. Since the 1920s, New York University had housed the MLA rent free on its campus. Despite augmentation of such space by the university and the leasing of additional space at 70 Fifth Avenue in the 1960s, such growth eventually resulted in the move of the headquarters of MLA to 62 Fifth Avenue. There was, of course, a corresponding increase in the permanent and temporary staff of the MLA. All of this activity and growth took money, and the late 1960s were years of barely balanced budgets.

In addition to such financial problems engendered by growth, there was the danger of concentration upon funded projects to the relative neglect of matters of interest to the members themselves. As early as 1963, for instance, there was criticism that the MLA's foreign-language programs were simply extensions of the NDEA being run by government officials connected with the NDEA. At the same time, allegations were made that the organization had become so big and complex that the annually elected officers did not have enough familiarity with what was going on to do an effective job. In other words, it took them a year to acquaint themselves, and by that time they were out of office. This has been, of course, an inevitable problem for any organization resorting to full-time appointed officials as its size and scope increase. In any case, to counter such criticism, MLA raised dues in the 1960s to cover the costs of expansion and also to provide more of its own monies for operations. It also amended the constitution whereby the annual election of a second vice-president was provided for who would automatically move on to become the first vice-president and then president in successive years. At the same time, the six regional affiliates were urged to take similar measures to cope with the problems associated with growth.

In the late 1960s more serious problems surfaced. By then the MLA was being urged to take stands on current political and social issues. The following year, led by Edmund Wilson and Lewis Mumford, the CEAA activities were attacked on the grounds that the editions being produced were pedantic and of little interest or use. These were the opening guns in the open attack and rebellion on the MLA itself, which occurred at the New York annual meeting in 1968. Led by Noam Chomsky, Louis Kampf, Richard Ohmann, and other members of the newly organized New University Conference (NUC), this group engaged in activities at the meeting hotel that caused the arrest of some of them by police on the request of hotel officials. There followed sit-ins, demonstrations, and protests. Finally, a settlement was worked out with the hotel and charges were dropped. Then in the business session on the closing day of the meeting, those present nominated and elected Louis Kampf second vice-president and passed a number of resolutions from the floor, including a condemnation of the Vietnam War and support for draft resistance. Although a resolution to abolish the CEAA was voted down, a resolution passed to move the 1969 meeting site from Chicago in protest against the incidents connected with the Democratic convention recently held there.

These events and the continuing debate that ensued in the following months did not seriously curtail the scholarly and pedagogical activity of the MLA. They did result, however, in various measures to democratize the MLA's governing process and the setting up of a number of projects that the dissidents advocated.

The primary organizational changes, which went into effect in 1971-1972, were the creation of a delegate assembly and an enlargement in the powers of the executive council, which performed the function of the prior annual business meeting. Specifically, this reorganization placed the administration of the MLA in an executive council, consisting of 3 elected officers, president, first vice-president, and second vice-president, an executive director, and deputy executive director or directors, who are appointed, and 12 members, 3 of whom are elected annually for four-year terms by the MLA membership. Candidates for second vice-president and for the council are chosen by a nominating committee, which is elected by the delegate assembly, with the membership at large having the right to add names by petition. The delegate assembly is an elected, representative body charged with advising the executive council on MLA's policies, direction, goals, and future. Composed of some 240 members, including 108 representatives from seven electoral regions, 39 at-large delegates to represent special interests, and 1 delegate from each of the divisions, the assembly meets every December during the annual meeting. In addition to its advisory role to the executive council, the assembly determines dues, elects the nominating and elections committees, and, subject to ratification by the entire membership, initiates constitutional amendments, debates, and acts upon resolutions and elects the MLA's honorary members and fellows.

Among the program and project responses to the dissidents were the addition to the 1969 annual meeting program of thirty-three sessions devoted to social issues relating to teachers and students of language and literature. A Commission on the Status of Women in the Profession was set up and, by the early 1970s, had been allocated over $42,000 for use in making various studies and has been a continuing and active entity of the MLA on into the 1980s. In 1969 a Commission on Minority Groups and the Study of Language and Literature was also established. It undertook studies of problems caused by bilingualism in the United States, surveys on minority college enrollments and faculty percentages, and, from 1974 to 1977, with the aid of an NEH grant of $180,000, a series of national seminars, regional conferences, and institutes to promote the study and teaching of minority literature.

Louis Kampf became the MLA president on schedule in 1971, and another NUC member, Florence Howe, was then elected second vice-president. Other measures were taken: the establishment of an aforementioned *Newsletter* to speed communication, a survey on "The Training of Teaching Assistants," and the publication of an expanded Job Information List every two months. Also, the old sections and groups at the annual meetings were reorganized into some seventy new divisions, the better to reflect newer conceptions of areas of learned inquiry. In addition, easy and speedy methods were devised for the organization at the annual meetings of discussion groups and special sessions for as few as fifteen members.

Although there is still some contention within the MLA over these controversies and changes, its activities continue with needed modifications. The CEAA, for example, carried on, receiving NEH grants through mid-1976 totaling about three million dollars, but with a new title, Center for Scholarly Editions. In early 1980 a Commission on the Future of the Profession was set up to explore the nature and needs of the profession and the MLA during the 1980s and 1990s. Consultants, members of an advisory board, and three working groups have been named, and local and regional hearings have been scheduled. In September 1981 the commission issued a "Working Paper" on its findings and plans to follow up with a report on its ultimate findings and recommendations which will be published in *PMLA* late in 1982.

The MLA elects the customary institutional officers in the manner described above; it conducts its business from offices, headed by an executive director, located in New York City.

For further information, see the following articles appearing in *PMLA:* Carleton Brown, "A Survey of the First Half-Century" (Supplement, 1933); Percy Long, "The Association in Review" (March, 1949); William R. Parker, "The MLA, 1883-1953" (September, 1953); Louise Pound, "Then and Now," (March, 1956); and George W. Stone, Jr., "The Beginning, Development, and Impact of the MLA as a Learned Society," (December, 1958). For a more recent brief history, see John Hurt Fisher, "Modern Language Association of America, 1883-1968," *ACLS Newsletter* (March, 1969). See also George W. Stone, Jr., "The Modern Language Association of America," *World of the Mind* (1958); and for detailed accounts of MLA activities from 1960 to the present see annual reports of the executive director of the MLA, usually appearing in the May, sometimes September, issues of *PMLA*.

MORGAN LIBRARY. See Pierpont Morgan Library.

_N

NATIONAL ACADEMY OF SCIENCES (NAS). Although the American Association for the Advancement of Science* (AAAS) from its beginning was an all-inclusive organization spanning all of the natural sciences, with most of the professional scientists and increasing numbers of those interested in the advancement of science as members, it did not completely satisfy its early leaders. Alexander Dallas Bache, for instance, who was to become the first president of the National Academy of Sciences, stated in an 1851 presidential address to the AAAS that a scientific institution supplementary to existing ones was much needed in order to guide public action in reference to scientific matters. In 1858 Louis Agassiz sketched a plan for a highly selective scientific academy but acknowledged that there would be opposition to it as being aristocratic.

In the period between these two calls for a new organization, a group of scientists intimately associated with the creation of the AAAS came into being. Centering initially in Cambridge, Massachusetts, they began to meet informally, dubbing themselves the Florentine Academy. Eventually, they changed their label to the "Scientific Lazzaroni" or, simply, the "Lazzaroni"—the facetious title being derived from the Neapolitan vagrants and beggars.

With Bache in Washington, D.C., emerging as their acknowledged "chief," by the late 1850s members of the Lazzaroni were strung along the Eastern seaboard from the capital to Cambridge. They included Bache and Joseph Henry in Washington, D.C., John F. Frazer and Fairman Rogers in Philadelphia; Wolcott Gibbs in New York City; Benjamin A. Gould in Albany, New York; James D. Dana in New Haven, Connecticut; and Louis Agassiz, Benjamin Peirce, and Cornelius C. Felton in Cambridge, Massachusetts. Although always an informal network, the members kept in constant touch with each other through correspondence, attendance at the meetings of such organizations as the American Philosophical Society* (APS) and the AAAS, and on other occasions.

The Civil War saw the Lazzaroni dreams of a new and selective organization to guide national scientific activity become a reality. The catalyst was the flood of ideas, suggestions, gadgets, and so forth for the successful prosecution of the war with which the government was inundated. Initially, the more promising were routed to the Smithsonian Institution* for examination and appraisal. As the volume swelled, however, Henry and Bache, together with Admiral Charles H. Davis, a former student of Peirce's at Harvard and former subordinate of Bache's in the Coast Survey, conceived the idea of a scientific advisory commission of larger scope. The outcome was the February 11, 1863, naming of a permanent commission in the Navy Department composed of Davis, Henry, and Bache to "which all subjects of a scientific character on which the government may require information may be referred." Although the commission began operations, Agassiz, Bache, and Davis continued their ruminations about a permanent academy along the lines advanced by Agassiz. The upshot, following correspondence between them and Senator Henry Wilson of Massachusetts, was a meeting at Bache's home on February 19, 1863. In addition to Bache and Wilson, those present included Agassiz, Benjamin A. Gould, and Benjamin Peirce. The plan drafted there, and introduced in the Senate by Wilson on February 21, succeeded in gaining quick congressional and presidential approval, and the resultant National Academy of Sciences was chartered on March 3, 1863. Henry, who initially opposed the idea and was not included in the planning of the NAS, eventually came around to support it.

The charter of the NAS, which was surprisingly brief, named fifty scientists who were to be its incorporators. It specified that it could make its rules for governance and operation and provide for the election of additional members. It called for an annual meeting and stated, as its sole, stipulated function:

The Academy shall, whenever called upon by any department of the Government, investigate, examine, experiment, and report upon any subject of science or art, the actual expense of such investigations, examinations, experiments, and reports to be paid from appropriations which may be made for the purpose, but the Academy shall receive no compensation whatever for any services to the Government of the United States.

Originally, a limitation of 50 members was imposed by Congress in the NAS's charter. This provision was removed by Congress in 1870, and, since that time, limits on total membership and on number of members elected annually have been set by NAS. In 1916 it set a limit of 250 on the total membership, which was periodically raised until it was removed in 1949. The NAS has always set a limit on new members elected annually, however, which is currently 60. In addition, 12 foreign associates may now be elected annually. Officers and members have always insisted on rigorous standards for election to membership. As a result, although there are presently approximately 1,300 members, membership in the NAS is considered one of the highest scientific honors.

During Bache's presidency (1863-1867) the committee system, devised by him, was inaugurated; committees being named to investigate the scientific questions posed by government. These then included such variegated committees to investigate weights and measures, corrosion of ship bottoms, charts for naval usage, counterfeiting of currency, purity of whiskey, and the effect of the expansion of steam upon machinery. Also, it was during Bache's incumbency that initial rules and bylaws were adopted.

With Bache's death in 1867, the infant NAS elected Joseph Henry as its second president. His presidency (1868-1878) saw it through a threatened dissolution. During the ensuing decades, although it carried on with the appointment of various committees to consider scientific questions, the calls for its services by the government were desultory and infrequent; it did not have any quarters of its own—occupying rooms in the Smithsonian building; and, in the last analysis, its continued existence was due to the vision for the future of its leaders, particularly the presidents who served during this period: William Barton Rogers (1879-1882); O. C. Marsh (1883-1895); Wolcott Gibbs (1895-1900); Alexander Agassiz (1901-1907); and Ira Remsen (1907-1913).

Thus matters stood with the outbreak of World War I in 1914. Scientific leaders of the country, within and without the NAS, knew that a better method of organizing the scientific and technical competence of the country was needed than that provided by the NAS as then structured if the United States became involved.

At the urging of George E. Hale, director of the Mount Wilson Observatory, he and NAS President William H. Welch (1913-1917), together with Edwin G. Conklin, Robert S. Woodward, and Charles D. Walcott, met with President Woodrow Wilson on April 16, 1916, to offer the NAS's services in the event of war. Following the president's suggestion, the NAS appointed a Committee on the Organization of the Scientific Resources of the Country for National Service, consisting of Hale, Conklin, Simon Flexner, Robert A. Millikan, and Albert A. Noyes. This group devised the plan for a National Research Council (NRC), as an operating arm or agency of the NAS, which was approved by President Wilson on July 24, 1916.

Subsequently, various NRC divisions, committees, conferences, and so on, contributed materially to the war effort. For example, the Research Information Committee, later Service, secured and exchanged Allied and U.S. scientific, technical, and industrial information. The NRC sponsored conferences to develop scientific responses to German submarine attacks on Allied shipping. A Committee on Noxious Gases aided in the research effort on gas warfare. An NRC group under Robert M. Yerkes pioneered in the use of intelligence testing and worked on methods of psychological testing for use in the armed services. Consequently, several months before the armistice, on May 11, 1918, President Wilson issued Executive Order No. 2859, which requested the NAS to continue the NRC as a permanent body and constitutes the charter of the council. The general purposes of the

NRC, as stated in the order were "to stimulate research in the mathematical, physical, and biological sciences, and in the application of these sciences to engineering, agriculture, medicine and other useful arts, with the object of increasing knowledge, of strengthening the national defense, and of contributing in other ways to the public welfare."

Retained as a part of the NAS's structure after World War I, the postwar NRC's membership, grouped under various administrative and scientific divisions, was made up of the representatives of the learned and technical societies of the country, which were invited to nominate representatives for appointment by the president of the NAS. Initially designated by some 40 societies, by the 1960s those named in this way totalled approximately 175 persons from some 110 societies. There were in addition, varying numbers of members—at-large and representatives from governmental agencies—making the total membership of the NRC at that time about 250.

During the period between the two world wars, the NAS-NRC made multitudinous and varied contributions to the advancement of science. A few outstanding examples were the fellowship program in the natural sciences, launched with grants from the Rockefeller Foundation; the role of the NAS-NRC in the 1919 formation of the International Research Council (IRC) and its 1931 reorganization, which saw the emergence of the present-day International Council of Scientific Unions* (ICSU); and during the Depression-New Deal period of the 1930s, the creation and operation of the Science Advisory Board. During this period, too, in 1934, the NAS finally acquired a home. Funded by a $1.35 million grant from the Carnegie Corporation of New York together with an accompanying endowment of $3.65 million for the maintenance and support of the NRC, a magnificent building was erected between Twenty-First and Twenty-Second streets on Constitution Avenue; the nucleus there of the present-day NAS complex.

World War II, however, witnessed another restructuring of the U.S. scientific community. It would appear that the NAS-NRC should have been sufficient to meet the need for U.S. scientific coordination and mobilization in the 1940s. Even at that time, however, the chairman of the NRC observed that it seemed that each national crisis, although taking advantage of the past, still needed a special organization particularly suited to the immediate situation.

Retrospectively, here is the explanation for the restructuring provided by Dr. Vannevar Bush, the man largely responsible for the creation and operation of the National Defense Research Committee (NDRC) and later the Office of Scientific Research and Development (OSRD), which became the scientific mobilizing agency for World War II:

I think perhaps there is an opportunity here to straighten out a point which I believe is still in confused condition in the minds of a good many Academy members. Unless I am mistaken some of the members feel that when NDRC was formed and later when OSRD was formed there was a situation where a few of us who might have operated within the Academy structure operated outside of it for some strange reasons of our own. As a matter of fact it was the closest cooperation throughout the war. The real reason that the structure was set up for war purposes in the way that it was became essential for two reasons. First we had to obtain large sums of money, and toward the end directly from Congress. Second, we had to have an organization which reported directly to the President and it had his delegated authority to operate as an independent agency in our relations with the military structure. . . . Frank Jewett, the President of the Academy, worked closely in bringing this all about. . . . I feel that far from injuring the Academy we really gave it some opportunity to operate effectively which it might not have had. [Rexmond C. Cochrane, *The National Academy of Sciences—The First Hundred Years 1863-1963* (1978), p. 390]

Thus, the NAS-NRC, in addition to entering into numerous war-related contracts with various other governmental agencies, established very close operating ties with the OSRD during the war years. To cite a few examples, the latter's Committee on Medical Research built its program around the personnel in the NRC's Division of Medical Sciences. An OSRD contract provided for the setting up of the Office of Scientific Personnel within the NRC. The NAS-NRC's War Metallurgy Committee directed the expenditure of some $6.5 million provided by the OSRD and War Production Board and furnished them with over a thousand metallurgical reports during the period 1941-1946. The OSRD, working in this close harmony with and through the NAS-NRC, wrought a revolution in the relationship of science to all segments of U.S. society during the period from its creation in 1941 to its formal dissolution in 1947. What emerged was "big science," with its national and international scope, ranging over all of science, enlisting the efforts of ever growing numbers of scientists, financed on a previously undreamed of scale, particularly by government, and developing such revolutionary administrative mechanisms as the research contract. The augmented role of science in the late 1940s and 1950s saw the creation of numerous governmental scientific agencies, such as the Atomic Energy Commission, Office of Naval Research, and the National Science Foundation. During these years, the NAS-NRC, with the election of Dr. Detlev W. Bronk (1950-1962) as president of the NAS, played a prominent role in their setting up and operation. There was a consequent broadening of NAS-NRC activities, some projects conducted for government agencies and some independently. Such projects included, for example, creation and operation of the Atomic Bomb Casualty Commission, study of the disposal of atomic wastes, conduct of the International Geophysical Year, and involvement in many portions of the burgeoning U.S. space program.

In the conduct of such projects the NAS and the NRC increasingly meshed. In effect the NAS members came to act as a large board of directors or trustees for the NRC. The executive body of the two was a governing board composed of the eleven-member council of the NAS and the eight chairmen of the eight divisions of the NRC. The undertakings of the NAS-NRC were carried out by these eight divisions, operating through boards, institutes, committees, and special ad hoc groups. There were also several interdivisional offices, such as the Office of Scientific Personnel and the Office of International Relations. Until the 1950s, however, the NAS and the NRC had, respectively, a president and a chairman, the latter acting as chief administrative officer for the NRC. At that time, at the urging of Dr. Bronk, these offices were merged, and after 1954, the president of the NAS also served as chairman of the NRC. At that time, too, a new full-time post of executive officer was created.

Thus, at the time of Bronk's retirement, he turned over a transformed NAS-NRC to his successor, Dr. Frederick Seitz (1962-1969). In response to the ever closer NAS relations with the government, for example, the Committee on Science and Public Policy (COSPUP) was set up in 1962 within the NAS itself. Composed of fourteen NAS members, COSPUP has, since that time, made many influential studies and reports on topics of special interest to both government and the NAS, including population growth and basic research. In 1964 a semiautonomous National Academy of Engineering (NAE) was set up, within the corporate structure of the NAS, as a vehicle for input of engineers into national science and technology policy.

Dictated by the sheer growth in the scope, quantity, and complexity of the scientific activities of the NAS by the late 1960s, a set of far-reaching administrative changes were launched under the presidency of Dr. Philip Handler (1969-1981). More specific reasons for the changes were: (1) the need for better representation within the NAS structure of the social sciences and of the engineering and medical professions; (2) recognition of the increasing number of scientific questions and problems that could only be addressed by multidisciplinary groupings; and (3) in the projects devoted to such questions and problems, the need for greater participation by more qualified scientists, more public access to the way they were conducted, and a more vigorous review process in their conduct.

In part the result of the jockeying within the NAS in working out its relationship with the NAE, in part in response to pressures to create an Academy of Medicine and in order to provide a special means of contributing to national health policy, an Institute of Medicine (IOM) was created within the NAS in 1970, but much more circumscribed as to membership, function, operation, and so on than the NAE. Within the corporate entity of NAS, all three (NAS, NAE, IOM) elect members. The NAS presently numbers about thirteen hundred, the NAE about eight hundred, and the IOM about four hundred; each has an elected governing council of its own. Since 1974, these three membership bodies, in turn, have exercised joint supervision of the activities of the NRC through a governing board consisting of seven members of the council of the NAS; four members of the council of the NAE; and two members of the council of the IOM.

In 1973-1974, in order to facilitate the conduct of large multidisciplinary projects and to increase participation in these projects by the members of the NAS, NAE, and IOM and of the scientific community at large, the concept of an NRC "membership," designated primarily by learned societies, to carry out its work was abolished. Replacing the old disciplinary divisions were eight new constituent parts consisting of four assemblies and four commissions. Today, therefore, a diagrammatic representation of the organizational structure of the NAS is as follows:

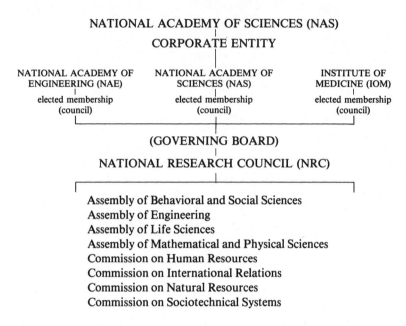

NATIONAL ACADEMY OF SCIENCES (NAS)

CORPORATE ENTITY

NATIONAL ACADEMY OF ENGINEERING (NAE)	NATIONAL ACADEMY OF SCIENCES (NAS)	INSTITUTE OF MEDICINE (IOM)
elected membership (council)	elected membership (council)	elected membership (council)

(GOVERNING BOARD)

NATIONAL RESEARCH COUNCIL (NRC)

Assembly of Behavioral and Social Sciences
Assembly of Engineering
Assembly of Life Sciences
Assembly of Mathematical and Physical Sciences
Commission on Human Resources
Commission on International Relations
Commission on Natural Resources
Commission on Sociotechnical Systems

The assemblies, like the former divisions, follow traditional disciplinary lines, but they address problems that can validly be conducted along these lines. The commissions, as their titles indicate, are concerned with broad, interdisciplinary, contemporary problems. They are a recognition that these problems cannot be attacked within neat disciplinary confines. Each assembly and commission consists of twenty-one members appointed by the chairman of the NRC (the president of the NAS) who are responsible for decisions concerning the program of that entity. Both the assemblies and commissions draw from a mix of disciplines appropriate to the work they conduct. Thus, during the year ending June 30, 1975, nearly 7,500 individuals, including 611 members of the NAS, NAE, and IOM, were serving within these various units and their subunits of the NRC.

Despite these changes, there were criticisms in the 1970s that scientists who had made significant contributions in their fields had been overlooked or bypassed by the NAS. Perhaps the harshest criticism at that time was directed at an alleged "electoral inbreeding" process whereby the NAS reproduced itself from the same universities—and even the same departments therein—within the same regions of the United States year after year. The rebuttal of the NAS has been that its membership is not claimed to be representative of society or science as a whole but it does claim to try to represent the best U.S. scientific achievement and scientists. While acknowledging that the selection process has communicative and procedural faults and while making changes to remedy the situation, President Handler maintained that the NAS was not elected by "participatory democracy"; it was an elite organization by its very nature because science itself is elitist. His position was that the NAS cannot be an open organization but that it can and must work to be certain that it represents the best of the scientific elite. When addressing technical questions of concern to the entire nation, however, it seemed appropriate that the membership of the NRC committees be not only highly competent but also broadly representative.

Accordingly, at approximately the same time that the assembly-commission system was set up, a special office was created in the NRC to ensure that, in addition to being highly qualified, those requested to serve in the system would represent a reasonable balance with respect to geography, age, and minority groups. Also, particularly when the nature of the subject studied warranted it, a system designed to avoid improper "bias" was set up and put into effect. Thus, a systematic procedure has been followed to obtain diverse, albeit not necessarily "extreme" points of view in scientific deliberations. Finally, a comprehensive process for the critical review of completed reports before their publication and release and a broad policy of public access to work of NRC committees were adopted.

Such changes buttressed the respect with which the recent studies and reports prepared under NAS auspices have been received. To cite a few examples from the mid-1970s: the salary structure of physicians in teaching hospitals; standards for drinking water; the utilization of our national scientific and technical capabilities to increase world food production and decrease world hunger and malnutrition; and future policy concerning nuclear energy and alternative energy sources. It should be noted that, on average, the NRC presently releases one report each working day.

Reflecting these changes and concomitant increase in activity, the headquarters building at 2101 Constitution Avenue, Washington, D.C. 20418, was enlarged beginning in the early 1960s, by a multimillion-dollar building program. A new conference hall was erected which, among a number of other facilities, included an auditorium seating 697 persons, and the leasing of a new office building, appropriately named the Joseph Henry Building, made it possible for offices previously situated in twelve other different office buildings to be centrally located therein. Also, the NAS's Summer

Study Center in Woods Hole, Massachusetts, acquired in 1971, has proved invaluable to the work of the NRC.

The NAS holds an annual meeting in the spring at its headquarters in Washington, D.C., as does the IOM; the NAE also holds its annual meetings there in the spring. Principal officers of the NAS include a president, vice-president, home secretary, foreign secretary, treasurer, and executive officer. The NAE's principal officers consist of a president, vice-president, and secretary, whereas the IOM's include a president and executive officer.

For further information, see the *Annual Reports* and *Proceedings* of the NAS. Rexmond C. Cochrane's *The National Academy of Sciences—The First Hundred Years 1863-1963* (1978), and an earlier work by F. W. True, ed., *A History of the First Half Century of the National Academy of Sciences, 1863-1913* (1913), are the standard histories of the NAS. See also Vernon Kellogg, "The National Research Council," *International Conciliation* (1920), and *A History of the National Research Council* (1933). For autobiographies and biographies of early NAS leaders, see Walter S. Adams, *Biographical Memoir of George Ellery Hale* (1939); Merle M. Odgers, *Alexander Dallas Bache: Scientist and Educator, 1806-1867* (1947); Thomas Coulson, *Joseph Henry: His Life and Work* (1950); Robert A. Millikan, *Autobiography* (1950); Edward Lurie, *Louis Agassiz: A Life in Science* (1960). For a work that is highly critical of the NAS, particularly on grounds that it is elitist, see Phillip M. Boffey, *The Brain Bank of America* (1975). For a rebuttal see the essays in the NRC *Current Issues and Studies 1976-78*, and Philip Handler's "Handler Defends Academy Elitism," *Science* (1976).

NATIONAL ASSOCIATION OF BIBLICAL INSTRUCTORS. See American Academy of Religion.

NATIONAL GEOGRAPHIC SOCIETY. When the National Geographic Society was founded in 1888, geography was regarded as one of the dullest of subjects, something to inflict upon schoolboys and avoid in later life. Today—thanks to the unstinting efforts of generations of talented, dedicated men and women working for the society—that 1888 definition is as obsolete as the gas lamp. It has transformed a dull subject into a unique vision of the world.

Organized for the increase and diffusion of geographic knowledge, the society has fulfilled the sweeping mission with scientific precision and journalistic genius. For more than eight decades, it has been at the leading edge of scientific exploration, taking man's past back more than three million years, unlocking the secrets of the oceans, lifting men into the stratosphere, mapping the very boundaries of the sky. In order to convey this invaluable body of knowledge to an ever growing membership, National Geographic staff members have pioneered the latest advances in communication from color photography to high-speed printing, setting a standard of accuracy and graphic excellence in the production of magazines, maps, books, and films.

National Geographic, the official journal of the society, has earned a worldwide reputation as the leading source of accurate, often definitive, information about the world and its peoples. With a present-day circulation of 10.3 million, its yellow-bordered cover is a familiar sight in millions of homes, libraries, and schools. Everyone from schoolchildren writing reports to scientists seeking information has learned to rely upon the *Geographic*. It is the society's prime means of fulfilling its mission of increasing and diffusing geographic knowledge.

Now one of the world's largest scientific educational institutions, the society had modest beginnings. It was started in January, 1888, when thirty-three public-spirited men met in Washington, D.C. The guiding spirit behind the enterprise was Gardiner Greene Hubbard, a Boston lawyer and philanthropist who had helped organize the first telephone company for his son-in-law, Alexander Graham Bell. Mr. Hubbard was elected president of the new society.

In October, 1888, the first *National Geographic* magazine appeared. A slim, highly technical journal bound in a drab terra-cotta cover, it went to 165 charter members, who presumably enjoyed such articles as "The Classification of Geographic Forms by Genesis" and similar abstruse discourses. This was not exactly what Mr. Hubbard had in mind. He wanted a magazine that would appeal to intelligent laymen as well as geographers, but he died before he could fulfill his dream.

Mr. Hubbard was succeeded in 1898 by Dr. Bell, who devoted much of his prodigious intellect and energy to making *National Geographic* a better journal. The inventor made two key decisions that were to have a profound effect on the future course of the society.

One was to stop trying to increase circulation by newsstand sales and offer the journal to anyone who wanted to become a member of the society, thus drawing upon people who believed in its work and wanted to contribute to it. Dr. Bell believed people from all walks of life would join the society if their interest were aroused by a lively journal. He was right.

Through the years, right up to the present, the National Geographic Society has been sustained by loyal members, who are not merely subscribing to a magazine but are adding their support to an organization of which they feel a part. The familiar stories of members who cannot bear to part with their ever growing stacks of *National Geographics* and of memberships continuing through several generations of one family testify to the wisdom of Dr. Bell's decision. After all, not many scientific societies inspire the kind of personal identification that caused one *National Geographic* member to write: "As you know, there is no such thing as a 'tin roof,' and many years ago you promised me you would watch that error."

Dr. Bell's second major decision was to hire a promising young man to put some life in the magazine and promote membership. That man turned out to be Gilbert H. Grosvenor, a twenty-three-year-old schoolteacher who reported for work on April 1, 1899. His innovative leadership transformed the *National Geographic* from one of cold geographic fact into a vehicle for conveying the living, breathing truth about the world, at the same time leaving a lasting imprint upon American journalism.

Young Grosvenor moved into an office that consisted of half of one small room with a few sticks of furniture and six enormous boxes crammed with magazines returned by newsstands. Within a year, he had more than doubled the membership in the society, raising it from one thousand to two thousand, and had begun publishing articles of general interest. It was a start. The young editor's major breakthrough came when he decided to fill eleven pages in the January, 1905, issue with photographs of the mysterious city of Lhasa in Tibet. He expected to be fired for this unprecedented move. Instead, he recalled that society members congratulated him on the street.

The layout and introduction of color photographs five years later set the pattern for *National Geographic's* pioneering in photojournalism. The historian of American magazines, Frank Luther Mott, maintained that this use of color made the *Geographic* a kind of periodical never before known.

The pages of the magazine have brought the world in all its diversity to millions of people, broadening their horizons and making no small contribution to world understanding. African tribesmen and Iowa farmers, the heights of Mount Everest and the depths of the Pacific Ocean, the turbulent eruption of a volcano and the quiet blooming of a flower, a whale breaking the surface of the sea and an eagle soaring in the sky—all these and many more reflections of the incredible variety of the world have appeared in *National Geographic*.

At the same time it was reporting about faraway places, the National Geographic Society was playing a major role in discovering and understanding them. Almost from its very beginning, it has sponsored expeditions and research projects. The first expedition, in 1890 and 1891, explored and mapped Mount Saint Elias along the then unknown border of southern Alaska and Canada and discovered Canada's highest peak, 19,850-foot Mount Logan. The mountaineering tradition was still alive in 1963, when the society was the principal sponsor of the first American ascent of Mount Everest. Barry C. Bishop of its staff was one of the six members of the expedition to reach the top of the world's highest mountain.

National Geographic grants also helped Robert E. Peary to reach the North Pole, Richard E. Byrd to fly over the South Pole, and a stratosphere balloon to set an altitude record of 72,395 feet that stood for twenty-one years. These feats combined adventurous exploration with science, but the society long has supported pure science. One of the most significant of these projects was the enormous effort, cosponsored by the California Institute of Technology, of systematically photomapping the night skies, revealing objects up to one billion light-years distant, including tens of thousands of vast, remote clusters of galaxies.

The society's Committee for Research and Exploration is made up of distinguished experts who evaluate and pass on research projects. Their support has helped hundreds of scientists add to man's knowledge of the world around him. Aided by National Geographic grants, the famed Leakey family of Africa has uncovered man's deepest past. Field studies by three researchers have revealed hitherto unknown facts about primates. Jane Goodall has observed chimpanzees; Dian Fossey, gorillas; and Birute M.F. Galdikas, orangutans. The search for early man in Alaska has been intensified in a major joint effort with the National Park Service.

In a related field, the National Geographic Society has long been in the forefront of the conservation movement. When lumbering threatened the giant sequoias of California in 1915, the society and its members contributed one hundred thousand dollars to help preserve 2,239 acres in Sequoia National Park. The society also was active in the effort to save the national parks, a campaign culminating in the landmark National Park Service Act of 1916. Since then, the society's interest in protecting the environment has been reflected in many magazine articles and such books as *Vanishing Wildlife of North America* and *As We Live and Breathe*. Entire issues of the magazine have been devoted to conservation-oriented topics such as energy and the national parks.

Books are one of the many varied means the society has to diffuse geographic knowledge. The Book Service and Special Publications divisions prepare lavishly illustrated books ranging over a broad spectrum of interests from ancient Greece and Rome to the exploration of space. As a public service, the National Geographic also contributes the services of editors, writers, and photographers to publish official guides to the White House, the U.S. Capitol, the Supreme Court, and the Washington Monument. More than ten million copies have been sold.

The society's cartographers are world renowned for the quality of their maps and since 1918 have been doing special supplements for the magazine. A definitive map of China, the first since 1945, appeared in the July, 1980, issue, along with an ethnic map showing the diversity of that country's peoples and languages. The National Geographic *Atlas of the World* has become a standard reference since the first edition in 1961. A revised, fifth edition was published in the fall of 1981. The society's first world globe appeared in 1961, and now is in homes and schools around the world.

The society did not rush into television, but when its first programs appeared in 1965-1966, they immediately elevated the standards of documentary television. Geographic programs have won dozens of awards, including the coveted George Foster Peabody prize for "outstanding television education." The society also produces highly praised educational films and filmstrips and a series of multimedia kits designed to teach science and social studies and to reinforce reading comprehension skills in young learners.

National Geographic World, the society's newest magazine, proved to be an instant success when it was introduced in September, 1975. Produced for children aged eight through twelve years, the colorful magazine is edited with the same attention to detail and regard for accuracy that has made the parent magazine world famous. *World* obviously filled a need, for in a little more than three months after it was launched circulation reached 1 million, and it now totals 1.8 million. A series of books for children of the same ages has proved equally as stimulating and successful, as has a series of books for children between the ages of four and eight.

In August, 1980, Gilbert M. Grosvenor became president of the society, the fourteenth in a distinguished line. Robert E. Doyle, Mr. Grosvenor's predecessor, is a vice chairman of the board, and Dr. Melvin M. Payne is chairman. Dr. Melville Bell Grosvenor is chairman emeritus of the board, and editor emeritus of *National Geographic*; and Dr. Thomas W. McKnew is advisory chairman of the board. All are members of the board of trustees. The affairs of the society, incorporated in Washington, D.C., as a nonprofit scientific and educational institution, are directed by the board of trustees. The trustees meet regularly to act as a budget bureau, a promotions board, an appropriations commission, and an advisory board—all rolled into one.

For further information, see *The National Geographic Society and Its Magazine: A History by Gilbert Grosvenor* (1957). This 117-page history was written by the chief executive of the NGS from 1899 to his retirement in 1954. The forgoing account of the NGS is primarily based upon a brief history of the NGS prepared by its news service (August, 1980). For a biography that deals tangentially with the founding and early years of the NGS, see Robert V. Bruce, *Alexander Graham Bell and the Conquest of Solitude* (1973). See also *National Geographic Index 1947-1969* and *National Geographic Index 1947-1976*. For works that discuss the history of the *National Geographic Magazine* see Frank L. Mott, *A History of American Magazines* (1957); and Edwin C. Buxbaum, *Collector's Guide to the National Geographic Magazine* (1971).

NATIONAL INSTITUTE OF ARTS AND LETTERS. See American Academy and Institute of Arts and Letters.

NATIONAL INSTITUTE OF PUBLIC ADMINISTRATION. See Institute of Public Administration.

NEWBERRY LIBRARY, THE.† The Newberry Library is a privately endowed, independent research library situated in Chicago, Illinois. Concentrating in history and the humanities, its holdings comprise some 1.4 million volumes and 4,110 running feet of manuscripts, plus 2 large railroad archives, the archives of the Pullman Company, and 13,000 separately printed pre-1900 maps. The collections embrace Western civilization from the late Middle Ages to the end of the Napoleonic era in Europe; from the era of discovery to the age of revolution in Latin America; and to modern times in North America.

To know the history of the Newberry Library is to understand its collections and its character. Unlike its nearest analogs, the Folger Shakespeare Library* and the Huntington Library, Art Gallery, Botanical Gardens,* both based on great collections gathered by their founders, the Newberry Library began, from scratch, as a collection of money made available in the great era of institution building during the Chicago Renaissance.

Walter Loomis Newberry, under whose will the library was founded, died at sea in 1868. He had been an early Chicago pioneer involved in shipping, commerce, banking, and real estate, the latter being the true foundation of his bequeathed estate. It was not until the death of his two surviving daughters, Mary and Julia, and later, in 1885, of his widow, Julia Clapp Newberry, however, that a contingent provision of his will, providing for a library, became operative because his children died without issue. Half of his estate was assigned to the purpose. The surviving trustees of the estate proceeded to establish the library, hire its first librarian, William Frederick Poole, get it incorporated in 1892, and construct the present building at 60 West Walton Street.

Events—equally real and symbolic—between Newberry's death in 1868 and the death of founding librarian Poole in 1894 significantly shaped, and still shape, the Newberry's collections and its character. First, the Chicago Public Library was established, in 1876, so that the Newberry trustees in 1887 were free to create a reference and research library rather than a circulating library. Second, shortly after the Newberry opened its doors, the John Crerar Library* was established, in 1893. Between them, the trustees of the Newberry and the Crerar shortly divided up the world of knowledge then deemed relevant to research and reference libraries. The Newberry disposed of its materials in medicine, science, technology, and the hard social sciences, such as they were in those days, and left those fields to the Crerar and other institutions. The Newberry then focused more sharply on

---

†Reprinted, with revisions, from Lawrence W. Towner, "The Newberry Library" in *Encyclopedia of Library and Information Science*, ed. Allen Kent, Harold Lancour, and Jay E. Dailey, vol. 19 (New York: Marcel Dekker, Inc., 1976), pp. 450-56, by courtesy of Marcel Dekker, Inc.

the humanities and established a traditional willingness to dispose of duplicate and out-of-scope materials. The Chicago Public Library, in addition to general circulating library responsibilities, also agreed to collect in business, law, patents, and fine arts. The third event was the purchase by the Newberry of the rare book collection of Henry Probasco of Cincinnati, Ohio, in 1889, before it opened its doors. This collection, some twenty-five hundred volumes, purchased for $52,924, included incunabula, Shakespeare folios, and other rarities. The Newberry would henceforth collect rare books as well as general research and reference materials.

Although the purchase of the Probasco collection certainly established rare books as a field of collecting at the Newberry, by both individual and en bloc acquisitions (as late as 1964, an even greater collection than Probasco's, that of Louis H. Silver, was also purchased), the Edward E. Ayer collection is more characteristic of Newberry acquisitions because it focuses on a broad subject field rather than on books as artifacts, even though it contains thousands of rarities. Ayer was a member of the first board of trustees. An avid collector of works relating to the pioneer period in America, he extended his collecting back into Europe and the age of discovery; southward to Central and South America; and westward to the Pacific Coast, Hawaii, and the Philippines—always focusing on the early contacts between aboriginal peoples and the European and on discovery, settlement, and emergence to statehood, a major theme running throughout the Newberry's Americana collections. He gave his collection (then about 14,000 volumes) to the library in 1911, continued to add to it himself, and later provided for its maintenance by endowment funds, until today it numbers 97,797 volumes, some 78,000 of which have been chosen by successive curators and bibliographers. It is a true—and great—research collection.

Ayer's gift attracted other collections of note that were closely related in subject matter. First came trustee William B. Greenlee's excellent gathering of working books on the Portuguese empire to about the 1830s, a gift in 1937, with a small endowment later established by his widow. Subsequently, trustee Everett D. Graff bequeathed his notable collection of Western Americana, along with a purchase fund, in 1964. These gifts and bequests were followed by the purchase of the Frank Cutter Deering collection of early Americana which, among other fields, increased the Newberry's Indian captivity narratives by 50 percent, making it the best collection in the world, and the Franco Novacco collection of sixteenth-century Italian printed maps (1967), which fit well with Ayer's early map collecting.

The early decision to shape the collections by transferring out-of-scope books, in that case to the John Crerar Library, also took root and flourished, in part because the purchase of collections resulted in duplicates and out-of-scope materials, in part because the Newberry sought and still seeks to avoid competition with major libraries in its community, and in part because the explosion in scholarship and publication now places an immense burden on private libraries with limited means.

Thus the Newberry has never hesitated to dispose of either duplicates or books deemed outside its scope. Free both to buy collections en bloc (or receive them as gifts or bequests) and to sharpen the collections by disposal of unwanted items, a long series of librarian-scholars has been encouraged to build massive subject-oriented collections—in the history of printing (the John M. Wing Foundation, which holds, for example, most of the Newberry's nearly two-thousand incunabula), the history of cartography, the history and theory of music, the Italian Renaissance, colonial Brazil and other Latin Americana, the history of the family, local history, and the history of Indian-white relations, to name only a few of the stronger areas of collecting. At the same time they built and maintained a solid foundation in the general history and literature of the areas and periods in which the more specialized collections fall. Bibliographies, journals, documentary sets, monographs, biographies, publication series of learned societies, antiquarian and out-of-print works, modern works, and newspapers all help make the Newberry Library a complete reference and research library in its fields as much as a collection of collections.

By the early 1940s, the chief librarians—William Frederick Poole, 1887-1894; John Vance Cheney, 1894-1909; William N. Carleton, 1909-1919; and George B. Utley, 1920-1942—had directed, with the aid of a highly skilled staff, the building of a very substantial collection of some 900,000 titles. Their successor, the late Dr. Stanley Pargellis, 1942-1962, a historian trained at Oxford and Yale and a great bookman, perceived for the library three tasks building on those collections.

First, Pargellis sought to augment the collections, building primarily on already developed strengths. In doing so, he bought imaginatively and well, taking advantage of the books and manuscripts available at low prices in postwar Europe and England. Second, he reversed a long-standing policy that had kept the library from acquiring manuscripts in large numbers. He did this not only by encouraging the purchase of texts in the Renaissance but also, and more importantly by literally inventing two new fields at the library: the history of the Chicago literary Renaissance, whose anchor is now the seventy thousand-piece collection on Sherwood Anderson; and the history of business, in which field Pargellis was a founding father. He persuaded two great railroads, the Illinois Central and the Chicago, Burlington & Quincy, to place their early records on deposit for use by scholars. Third, he perceived that the library's often unknown resources had to be brought to the attention of scholars worldwide. To do this he created the *Newberry Library Bulletin,* a modest fellowship program, and a series of brilliantly conceived and executed conferences, all focusing on the library's great collections.

Beginning in 1964 the Newberry capitalized on what Pargellis had achieved by the time of his retirement. That is to say, it adopted as policy the desirability of helping scholars, wherever they may be, to use the Newberry if they need the Newberry. It achieves this goal not only in the traditional manner—cooperation with national and international bibliographies and checklists, publication of catalogs and checklists and exhibit catalogs based on its own collections, publication of primary resources, microfilm and xerox, and extensive telephone and written response to reference questions—but also by bringing scholars to the library.

To accomplish this second purpose, beginning in 1964, the library created a series of programs and centers designed to increase the effective use of its collections. The first of these was the Kenneth Nebenzahl, Jr., Lectures in the History of Cartography, a series that led eventually, in 1971, to the endowed Hermon Dunlap Smith Center for the History of Cartography. There followed the Humanities Program of the Associated Colleges of the Midwest, later enlarged to include the Great Lakes Colleges Association; the Center for the History of the American Indian; the Family and Community History Center, and, most recently (1980), the Renaissance Studies Center. The Research and Education Division, established in the early 1970s, also administers a large fellowship program and an adult education program and has become a center for nontraditional education. Since 1964, to sum up, the annual budget for research and education has grown from twenty thousand to one million dollars, and several endowed funds have been established to support the division.

The library has always had a close, symbiotic relationship with its small board of trustees. Formerly elected for life and self-perpetuating, they have taken a strong interest in the library's activities since its founding. Officers, although elected annually, have tended to serve for life. This interest in the library was often stimulated by the fact that there have always been "bookmen" on the board, some of them scholars in the first instance, others businessmen who were book collectors.

An amendment in 1973 to the enabling legislation of 1892 permitted the trustees to enlarge their numbers from thirteen up to a maximum of twenty-five. Subsequent revisions in the bylaws changed the term of trustees from life to five years, renewable; set seventy-five years as the retirement age; changed the titles of officers from president and vice-presidents to chairman of the board and vice-chairmen (necessitating a change in the designated title of the director and librarian to president and librarian, the incumbent Dr. Lawrence W. Towner being the first to bear these titles). These changes recognized the evolution, culminating under President Hermon Dunlap Smith (1964-1975), and continued by his successors Edward F. Blettner (1975-1979), and Chalkley J. Hambleton (1979 to present), of placing administrative responsibility on the professional staff, reserving to the board the role of policymaking.

One major area of board policymaking concerns the institution's finances. The original endowment by Walter Loomis Newberry paid not only for the construction of the building and the early purchases of books but also continues to provide approximately 75 to 80 percent of the current endowment income. At approximately $19.4 million (1980), the total endowment now includes twenty-six additional funds: some designated for books, some for research and education, some for general purposes. Until 1964 the library had lived well within its endowment income and had little occasion to raise money on a regular basis. Its total annual gifts amounted to something over $4,000 in 1962, for example. However, with the purchase of the Louis H. Silver collection, the drive to upgrade and professionalize the library's staff, and the development of research and education programs, the trustees now had to play a much larger and more active role in the library's finances than had hitherto been the case. In 1964-1965, the first fund drive in the library's history resulted in gifts totaling $1.5 million. In 1965, the Newberry Library Associates was created and now gives some $100,000 per year. Other gifts, grants, and bequests have raised the annual level of giving to well over $1 million and in some years to over 2.5 million. The total annual budget of the library is over $3 million (1980).

Other policy decisions include the momentous one of electing to continue as a privately endowed independent research library, in the present location, a decision made in the period 1959-1962. During those years, the library invested more than $1 million in renovating the building, and in establishing air-conditioning and fireproofing to protect its collections. Because it is a research library with major irreplaceable collections, the trustees also adopted a policy early in the 1960s of supporting the developing field of book conservation, both in practice and in research, so that the Newberry has become an important center in this much-needed effort.

In the early 1970s, planning for the future intensified; the 1959-1962 decision to remain independent was reaffirmed; and plans were developed for a ten-story bookstack building. The twofold purpose is to provide the best environment for the collections that can be devised and to create adequate space for research and education programs and for public programs in the existing structure. Construction of the bookstack was authorized by the trustees and begun in September of 1980. Renovation of the present building began in 1981.

Bibliographic access to the Newberry's collections is best gained through consultation of its general and special card catalogs. However, various published checklists and catalogs are available in university and research libraries throughout the world. Further, since 1944 the irregularly issued *Newberry Library Bulletin* and, since 1973, a *Newberry Newsletter* have carried articles and notices, respectively, on more important collections and acquisitions.

There is no book-length history of the Newberry Library. Dr. Lawrence

W. Towner is the author of the following articles, which deal with varied aspects of Newberry history: "The Newberry Library: A Research Opportunity in Library History," *Journal of Library History: Proceedings* (1968); "Every Silver Lining Has a Cloud," in A.N.L. Mumby and Lawrence W. Towner, *The Flow of Books and Manuscripts* (1969); "The Library and the Collector: The Newberry Library," *Louisiana State Library Lectures* (1971); and *An Uncommon Collection of Uncommon Collections: The Newberry Library* (1976).

For further information, see the following accounts of the founding and early history of the library: Paul Finkelman, "Class and Culture in Late Nineteenth-Century Chicago: The Founding of the Newberry Library, "*American Studies* (Spring, 1975), and Helen L. Horowitz, *Culture and the City* (1976). A biography of the first librarian, William L. Williamson, *William Frederick Poole and the Modern Library Movement* (1963), is also valuable on this score. See also the publications of the Newberry Library discussed above; the library's *Annual Reports*, 1893-1938, and 1978 to date; and the unpublished "Annual Reports to the Trustees," 1962 to 1977.

LAWRENCE W. TOWNER

NEW YORK ACADEMY OF MEDICINE, THE. Formally organized in January, 1847, this is the oldest existing and largest academy of medicine in the United States. It was incorporated by special act of the New York State Legislature in 1851. Its purposes were to improve medical education and practice, encourage measures that would improve the public health, establish a library, and fight quackery.

The conception of the academy occurred on November 18, 1846. On that evening a group of outstanding physicians gathered in a restaurant on lower Broadway to celebrate the fourth anniversary of the Society for the Relief of the Widows and Orphans of Medical Men. Dr. Valentine Mott, world-famous surgeon and president of the New York University Medical College, proposed a toast to the older College of Physicians and Surgeons. Dr. Alexander H. Stevens, president of the College of Physicians and Surgeons, returned the compliment in a stirring address. He urged the assembled group to establish a medical hall with ample meeting rooms and a library. Dr. Stevens suggested that such an institution be independent of the medical schools and hospitals, stating that it would bring together eminent members of the profession to correct the deplorable standards of medical education and medical practice existing at that time.

The decade of the academy's creation was a vivid one in the young nation's history. The Mexican War was in progress. In 1848 revolution burned through European governments, gold was discovered in California, and the sweep westward began. Bernard De Voto's book *The Year of Decision* refers to this period. In these bold times the graceful manners of the English colony were largely gone, and Winston Churchill's remark that the English people were without hot baths and central heating for over fifteen hundred years from A.D. 400 to the end of the nineteenth century applied also to this side of the Atlantic. Dirt, squalor, impure water, epidemic infestation, and the lack of adequate sewage disposal all characterized New York in the 1840s. The members of the new organization set about to combat these evils.

The latest (1956) text of the constitution of the academy has this succinct statement of its goals: "The advancement of the science and art of medicine, the maintenance of a public medical library, and the promotion of public health and medical education." How it strives toward these goals can only be partially described in the limits of this presentation.

Today the administration of the academy is subject to a governing council consisting of twenty-one elected officials: the president, three vice-presidents, the treasurer, the secretary, ten trustees, and the chairpersons of five major standing committees: Admission, Public Health, Library, Medical Education, and Medicine in Society. Its day-to-day affairs are delegated to a salaried staff of some ninety persons under a director who is appointed by the council.

Candidates for admission to fellowship must be nominated and sponsored by three fellows and screened by an elected Admission Committee. After approval by the Admission Committee, names are submitted to the governing council for approval. The present aggregate membership of about twenty-seven hundred includes a limited number of associate fellows, who are not physicians but are involved with the health professions, usually as teachers in medical schools or as officials of medical centers or health agencies.

The activities of the academy are accomplished in various ways. All fellows on election identify with one or another section depending on professional interest. At present there are eighteen sections: Anesthesiology and Resuscitation; Biomedical Engineering; Clinical Nutrition; Dermatology and Syphilology; Geriatric Medicine; Historical Medicine; Medicine; Obstetrics and Gynecology; Occupational Medicine; Ophthalmology; Orthopedic Surgery; Otolaryngology; Physical Medicine and Rehabilitation; Plastic and Reconstructive Surgery; Psychiatry; Radiology; Surgery; and Urology.

These sections each have a chairperson, a secretary, and a council of five, usually former section officers who are responsible for arranging monthly meetings during the period October through May. Occasionally these meetings are held jointly with another professional organization in the particular specialty. The meetings are regularly open to nonfellows and are usually free.

The announcements and in-house arrangements for section meetings are handled by the staff and executive secretary of the Committee on Medical Education. This committee meets monthly, except during the summer, to discuss topics of general interest in medical education. Each fall it conducts a full-day symposium on a currently interesting or troublesome phase of medical education. In recent years, state and national requirements have emerged requiring that physicians must verify participation in some form of continuing education in order to continue to be licensed or certified. This has contributed to the burden of record keeping because academy programs have been approved or accredited by both state and national authorities.

The Public Health Committee, the oldest of the major standing committees, has a long history of involvement in a vast array of problems affecting the public health. Over the years, its opinion has often been sought on health legislation because of its reputation for objectivity. Thus it was instrumental in drafting the first health code for New York City and in replacing the coroner system with the Office of Medical Examiner.

In the early part of the century national and local organizations made many unsuccessful attempts to create a nomenclature of disease that would be adopted by medical institutions throughout the country. In 1928 the Committee on Public Health called a conference of twenty national societies, representing special fields of medicine and surgery, and effected a National Conference on Nomenclature of Disease. The result was an eight-year academy study, which produced a Standard Classified Nomenclature of Disease. The influence of this publication on accuracy of medical terminology and public health records is inestimable.

The committee also carried out landmark studies on maternal mortality and perinatal mortality, which led to improvements in both of these vital areas. It also studied the procurement and distribution of blood for transfusion. Over sixty recommendations emerged covering every aspect of blood transfusion. The study resulted in major positive changes in blood distribution in the metropolitan New York area.

Recently, at a time when the problems regarding the environment are mounting, it has embarked on a series of symposia on environmental problems, such as Sulphur Oxides and Related Particulates; Non-Ionizing Radiation; Health Aspects of Automotive Emissions.

The Committee on Medicine in Society concerns itself with social, political, economic, and legal aspects of health care. In addition to monthly meetings, during the fall, winter, and spring, through the years this committee has sponsored a variety of extended seminars and symposia. Since 1940 an annual two-day conference in the spring has been devoted to an important current topic, such as "Cost Containment and Resource Allocation in Health Care," "Health Policy: Realistic Expectations and Reasonable Priorities," "Planning for Community Health Services," and "Toward a National Health Policy."

Participants come from various parts of this country and abroad. The committee has also sponsored a series of closed seminars on "Social Policy for Health Care"; a series of seminars on long-term care and problems of nursing homes; lectures to the laity (on medical topics); and a program for teaching health education in inner city public schools. Programs in cooperation with the Association of the Bar of New York City on topics of joint interest, such as psychiatric testimony in family court proceedings, continue a tradition of cooperation with the bar, which in the past has led to endeavors to establish better psychiatric and legal determination of insanity.

Transactions of many of the seminars and studies referred to in the preceding paragraphs have been published in book form. Most have been published in the monthly *Bulletin of the New York Academy of Medicine*. The *Bulletin* also publishes selected papers presented at various meetings held on academy premises and occasionally significant papers that were not presented there. Offering the advantages of permanent record and worldwide readership, the *Bulletin* plays an important role in the educational activity of the academy.

The library, from the point of view of space occupied and share of budget, is the major activity of the academy. It stands among the world's greatest collections of medical and related literature, housing over 450,000 bound volumes, over 180,000 catalogued pamphlets, over 25,000 catalogued illustrations, almost 250,000 catalogued portraits, and receiving over 4,000 serials.

The only medical library in New York City open to the public, it has, besides the usual holdings in medical and allied fields, excellent holdings in psychology, public health, medical economics, psychoanalysis, foods, and cookery. It is particularly strong in foreign monographs, encyclopedias, indexes, bibliographies, and biographies. The Michael M. Davis Library of articles, memoranda, correspondence, and clippings compiled by Dr. Davis over a fifty-year span is a valuable reference for anyone studying the economic and social developments in medical care and the background of medicare and medicaid in the United States.

The historical collection of over fifty thousand volumes with its most valuable books housed in the Rare Book Room is an exciting trove of medical and scientific thought through the ages. First editions of most of the landmark publications in medicine and allied sciences are to be found there. Perhaps the greatest treasure and surely the earliest item is the Edwin Smith Surgical Papyrus of 1500 B.C. concerning diseases of the head and neck. The collection of Harvey, who first described the circulation of the blood, is one of the most extensive in the world, including two copies of rare first editions of his works.

The library has been the referral library for medicine and allied subjects in the New York State Interlibrary Loan Network since 1967, and is the Regional Medical Library of the National Library of Medicine's national network for New York and New Jersey. The library houses archives not only of the academy itself but also those of a number of other medical organizations.

Relying on its rare library collection, the academy has published in its History of Medicine series some fifty reprints of medical classics. These limited editions include such treasures as: (1) the classical anatomical atlas of Andreas Vesalius "Icones Anatomicae" from the original woodcuts, which were destroyed in Munich in World War II; (2) the landmark work in pathology, Giovanni B. Morgagni's "De Sedibus et Causis Morborum"; this reprint sold out, is being printed again because of many requests; (3) a hitherto unknown revision of Claude Bernard's *Introduction to the Study of Experimental Medicine*; (4) *The Confederate States Medical and Surgical Journal 1864-65*; and (5) Bernardino Ramazzini's *Diseases of Workers*.

Each year a plaque for distinguished service to the academy and a medal for distinguished contribution to science are awarded. The academy also awards a Valentine Medal in Urology and a Salmon Medal in Psychiatry. It administers endowed lectureships, including the Salmon Lectures in Psychiatry, the Fox Lecture in Dermatology, the May Lecture in Ophthalmology, and a number of lectureships that do not carry such restrictions on subject matter. In addition it awards, from special endowment, fellowships in urology (Valentine Fund) and neurosurgery (Elsberg Fund) and fellowships for travel and study abroad (Glorney-Raisbeck and Bowen Brooks scholarships). These awards range from ten thousand to twenty thousand dollars. There are also other smaller or unendowed awards.

The academy does not receive any subvention from local, state, or federal governments. It is supported by dues of its fellows, endowment income, gifts and bequests, and grants for specific studies and services.

In 1890, at the New York Academy of Medicine, Oliver Wendell Holmes said that the academy that fulfills its function is a working body. He added that it deals with living subjects and unsettled questions; provides help to its members; and, by providing a standard of excellence, should judge their work and performance.

The academy cherishes the hope that it will continue to live up to Dr. Holmes's prescription.

For further information, see Phillip Van Ingen, *The New York Academy of Medicine, Its First Hundred Years* (1949), a detailed book-length account of the academy down to 1949; and E. H. L. Corwin, *Thirty Years in Community Service* (1942); Bernard A. DeVoto, *The Year of Decision 1846* (1943); H. D. Kruse and Lois Stice, *Pioneering in Public Health for Fifty Years* (1962); and Stephen Smith, *The City That Was* (1973). See also the following articles: Gertrude L. Annan, "Our Greatest Material Heritage, the Library," *Bulletin of the New York Academy of Medicine* (January, 1967); and Marvin Lieberman, "The New York Academy of Medicine," *Journal of Health Politics, Policy and Law* (Summer, 1978).

JAMES E. MCCORMACK

NEW YORK CANCER HOSPITAL. See Memorial Sloan-Kettering Cancer Center.

NEW-YORK HISTORICAL SOCIETY. The New-York Historical Society is housed in a large granite building in New York City overlooking Central Park. There it seeks to implement the mission charged to it by its founders, the "collection, preservation, and dissemination of history—that of New York City and New York State and United States history in general." Membership in the society is nominally elective but actually open to anyone who applies and pays a membership fee; special patron and fellow members are elected from those who have given generously of funds or added to the society's collection.

The society was founded in the Picture Room of City Hall in New York on the evening of November 20, 1804. The moving spirit on this occasion was John Pintard, a merchant who had made a vast fortune but had lost it through unwise trust in his associates and had at one point been in debtors prison. Many of the founders were clergymen, but the society was lucky to have then New York Mayor De Witt Clinton among the original members. He was able to procure for the group rent-free quarters in City Hall. The society is the second oldest U.S. historical society in continuous operation since its founding. It was incorporated in 1809 by the state legislature. The hyphen was inserted into the name in that act and has been retained to this day.

The society led a vagabond existence in its early years. Finding itself unable to house its library properly in City Hall, it moved to Government House in 1809, and then got control of the New York Institution, formerly Alms House, in 1816. After being evicted from this building, the members rented the Peter Remsen Building for the sum of five hundred dollars per year. The society could not afford this money, and the building was deemed inadequate to house the growing collections of research materials and art. By this time, both the newly established New York University and the Stuyvesant Institute were willing to offer the society free quarters. The latter unfortunately was chosen, and the society moved again in 1837. The panic that struck that year bankrupted the institute, and the society was forced to move again, in 1841, to New York University on Washington Square, where it remained until 1857.

The collections that the New-York Historical Society now possessed were very valuable, and the building in which they were housed was not fireproof. Many members were worried that their books, papers, and works of art might be lost through some accident. In the intervening years, contributions had given the society some financial leeway, and the members decided to build their own building on the corner of Second Avenue and Eleventh Street. The cost of this fireproof building was $85,000, but the society was able to pay for it in cash. As the turn of the century approached, the expansion of the city northward had made lower Second Avenue neither a desirable nor a convenient place for a museum and library. Therefore, in 1891, it was decided to purchase a site on Central Park West for $286,500. Ground breaking for the new building took place in September, 1902, and the central wing of the present building was opened for its first exhibition and for members' inspection on May 4, 1909. The building cost $421,150, with much of this money being contributed by Henry Dexter in honor of his late son. While construction was taking place, disaster almost struck the society. The Second Avenue building was sold by the city for taxes and water fees in 1905. Fortunately for the society's financial position, this mistake was soon rectified. Between 1935 and 1943, the society received a bequest of $3 million from the wills of Elizabeth Gardiner Thompson, Charles Griswald Thompson, and Mary Gardiner Thompson. The money made available by these benefactors allowed the society to expand its facilities greatly, adding the north and south wings, which tripled the museum's display space. The building was closed for renovation on May 1, 1937, and reopened to the public on April 1, 1939.

The New-York Historical Society has throughout its history been faced with varying kinds of problems. In the 1820s, a group of physicians attempted to gain control, causing much dissension among the members. At one point during this era, the financial situation became so bad that the society voted to sell off the library in order to raise funds. President David Hosack, a founder of Bellevue Hospital, resigned in protest, but the New York state legislature provided the money to save the collection.

Between 1914 and 1921, Mrs. John Van Rensselear launched an attack on the leadership of the society. When her bid for control failed, she and her backers seceded and attempted to create a new one called the Society of Patriotic New Yorkers. This group collected materials for a museum, but they began to quarrel, and the group fell apart. After Mrs. Van Rensselear's death, that collection became the basis for the Museum of the City of New York.

The great events of the twentieth century have not left the society untouched. During the Depression the society suffered hard times. Much of its income came from rents that were impossible to collect for several years. The donation of the Thompson Fund late in this period proved to be a great blessing. World War II also disrupted the activities of the society. After the Japanese attack on Pearl Harbor, many of the employees left to join the service. Because there was fear of an attack on New York City, the museum and library were closed, and many of their most valuable items were taken out into the safer countryside or stored in a vault. The glass roof designed to allow the paintings on the fourth floor to be displayed in natural light was covered. The Red Cross took over the front galleries and brought in volunteers to make surgical dressings. In all, four million were produced in the society's building. By October, 1943, the danger was deemed to be passed, the building was cleaned up, and the library was reopened. Throughout the war years, society lectures continued and the *Quarterly* was published regularly.

In the past thirty years, inflation and the energy crisis have been major problems for the New-York Historical Society, as they have for the rest of the country. In 1949, utilities cost the society a mere fourteen thousand dollars; by 1980, that cost had soared beyond two hundred thousand dollars annually. During that same era, salaries quadrupled from under two hundred thousand dollars to over eight hundred thousand. The annual budget of the society is well over one million dollars and is currently running a deficit.The society has gained considerable support from the National Endowment for the Arts, a source of funding which might be in jeopardy if the federal budget were cut. Because of its large-scale resources, the society is not in danger of bankruptcy, but it has been forced to dip into its capital to keep operating normally. As one method of gaining money, the members instituted a discretionary admission fee for nonmembers entering the museum in 1978. There is a small fee for use of the library, although readers who plan to use it extensively may purchase a "membership" at a nominal cost of ten dollars per year.

Over its history, the society has elected many distinguished members, including most American presidents. Washington was not among them because he died before the society's founding in 1804. Many distinguished statesmen, both American and foreign, have been elected, as have notable writers, artists, inventors, and industrialists. Among the great nineteenth-century historians on the rolls of the society are George Bancroft, William H. Prescott, Francis Parkman, and Charles Francis Adams.

One of the delightful aspects of the society in its early days was the tradition of holding meetings to be followed with a feast for the members. The first of these sessions came on September 4, 1809, the two hundredth anniversary of Hudson's discovery of New York. The Reverend Samuel Miller gave an address to the society, and after the ladies had gone home the men repaired to City Hall for a dinner of wild pigeon and succotash, at which many toasts were drunk. Such dinners became a continuing tradition of the society. One such dinner in 1883, attended by President Arthur and Governor Cleveland, took place at historic Fraunces Tavern and inspired the creation of the Sons of the Revolution in the State of New York. The new society's first project was to restore the historic building to its revolutionary form. Although the society welcomed women from its beginnings, it continued to fail to include them fully at the turn of the twentieth century. At the centennial celebration in 1904, the women were confined to the balcony because the men wished to smoke.

The society's main mission today is twofold: to maintain a major library and keep a museum. The library of the society was founded in 1809, with John Forbes as the first librarian. Contributions to it were supplemented by active collecting. A major acquisition was the collection of Reverend Francis L. Hawkes, which contained two thousand works, one hundred of which were quite rare. By 1900, the library consisted of one hundred thousand volumes; today that number has risen to five hundred thousand books and pamphlets. The collection of abolitionist pamphlets is considered one of the best. The library covers all of American history up to 1900, but since then has been concentrating on materials related to New York history.

The collection of newspapers is especially fine. The society has the fourth largest collection of American newspapers in the country published before 1820, and has long runs of many important papers, as well as a number not usually found in research libraries. New York City and State papers are, of course, heavily represented.

One aspect of the library that is especially valuable to scholars is the Manuscript Department, which today contains one and a half million documents of various kinds. Among the valuable materials are Dutch records for early New York, diaries of New Yorkers in the Civil War, and a good collection of Revolutionary War orderly books. Also available is the Landauer collection of business and professional literature which contains thousands of items relating to business history. The selection of maps and prints, many of them rare and beautiful, are also of interest to the scholar. The large collection of photographs amassed by the society is put on display in the museum from time to time.

The second aspect of the society's current activities, the museum, occupies most of the building. Among the most important collections are all but two of the original watercolors by James Audubon for his *Birds in America*. This collection was sold by Mrs. Audubon to the society in 1863 for four thousand dollars and is priceless today. The picture gallery on the fourth floor contains a great many paintings, including a portrait gallery with pictures of important members of the society and a number of portraits of United States presidents. A collection of colonial silverware and the photographic collection are also of interest.

Around the time that they acquired the Audubon collection, the society also purchased a collection of antiquities from ancient Egypt and the Lenox marble bas reliefs from Nineveh. These collections allowed the society to boast that it had the best art museum in New York City until the opening of the Metropolitan Museum of Art in 1872. However, artifacts from Egypt and Nineveh are not closely related to the history and natural setting of New York. In 1937 these collections were placed in the care of the Brooklyn Museum and shipped across the East River. Slightly over a decade later, the Egyptian collection was sold outright. The transfer of these artifacts puts the society museum's more in accord with its main purpose.

In addition to maintaining its library and museum, the society has also been active in publishing scholarly material. It produced the *New-York Historical Society Quarterly*, which was discontinued temporarily in January, 1980. From time to time, the society has published collections of its papers and various types of historical monographs. These functions are currently being carried on by the University of Virginia Press, which has begun to reprint some of the society's more important works.

For further information, see a history of the society by R. W. G. Vail, *Knickerbocker Holiday* (1954), then director of the society; and the *Annual Reports* of the society. See also Walter Muir Whitehill, *Independent Historical Societies* (1962), chapter 2 of which deals with the New-York Historical Society.

JACKSON TAYLOR, JR.

NEW YORK MATHEMATICAL SOCIETY. See American Mathematical Society.

NEW YORK PUBLIC LIBRARY, ASTOR, LENOX AND TILDEN FOUNDATIONS, THE. The origins and original purposes of The New York Public Library account for its uniqueness, its greatness, its complexity, and, to an extent, its problems. Established in New York City (then only Manhattan and part of the Bronx) on May 23, 1895, as a public reference library for study and research, incorporated by state law as a privately endowed, tax-exempt nonprofit institution governed by a self-perpetuating board of trustees, the New York Public Library was a product of the consolidation of three predecessor corporations, hence its official name: The New York Public Library, Astor, Lenox and Tilden Foundations. The oldest of the three was the Astor Library, founded in 1848 by terms of the will of John Jacob Astor; it was the first privately endowed public reference library in the United States and one of its largest scholarly resources. Next came the Lenox Library, incorporated in 1870 as an endowed public library by its founder, James Lenox, to house and augment his choice collections of rare books, manuscripts, Bibles (including the first Gutenberg Bible brought to this country), Americana, and works of art. Then there was the Tilden Trust, created by the will of Samuel J. Tilden to establish and maintain a free library and reading room in New York City. The financial straits and unpopularity of the Astor and Lenox libraries, combined with the loss to the Tilden Trust of a large part of its funds through a successful challenge to Tilden's will, led eventually to the merger of the three corporations into an entirely new one, The New York Public Library.

Its board of trustees aimed to build the institution into a great, free, public research library, open to all and on a par with the British Museum, the Library of Congress, and the Bibliothèque Nationale. To help achieve this goal the board, composed predominantly then and for many years thereafter of powerful, wealthy businessmen and lawyers (women were not elected to the board until 1950, and nonwhites, 1970), appointed as director (as of 1896) the distinguished physician, librarian, bibliographer, and public health specialist Dr. John Shaw Billings. Working with the trustees and his staff, Billings, a brilliant and forceful executive as well as a knowledgeable bookman, set the library's course for years to come.

Although the library was and remained an independent, privately operated institution, from the first it entered into partnership, financial and otherwise, with government. The library's own resources being insufficient to consolidate, organize, and develop the collections or to construct a badly needed new building, the trustees managed to obtain from the City of New York both a site and a building. The location finally chosen, the site of the obsolete Croton Reservoir on Fifth Avenue between Fortieth and Forty-Second streets, was ideal—in the center of Manhattan, at the crossroads of traffic, and bounded in the rear by Bryant Park. The contract with the city for the lease and occupancy by the New York Public Library of the building and its site and the maintenance of both by the municipality was signed on December 8, 1897; razing the reservoir and starting construction took several years more. All of this was not accomplished without a series of political maneuverings and struggles. But the City of New York, once committed to the library project, proved generous, whichever party occupied city hall during the many years it took to complete the building: constructed of the finest materials and with meticulous care, it cost a record nine million dollars.

The majestic marble edifice with its splendid interior was officially opened on May 23, 1911. It was hailed as one of the most important public buildings of its time, symbolic of the rise of New York to supremacy in cultural as well as economic enterprise. The design, based on a simple sketch made by Dr. Billings, was created and executed by Carrère and Hastings, the firm that won the competition for architectural plans, and is considered their masterpiece. Notwithstanding its lavish interior and classic exterior, the building was planned to be functional. The grand main reading room, said then to be, with its 768 seats, the largest in the world, was placed above the massive free-standing steel stacks in order to achieve maximum light, air, and quiet and to avoid attracting tourists. The function and location of the other rooms were based on the collections, organization, and expected use of the library. These included a circulating collection of books on the ground floor, reached directly through a side entrance on Forty-Second Street. The bulk of the collection stood in the general stacks and special reading rooms and was for reference only, never to leave the building. There were also exhibition rooms as well as spacious lobbies and halls to accommodate large numbers of visitors and to display artworks, rare books, and other holdings in an active public exhibition program.

The Fifth Avenue building, which is both a New York City Landmark and a registered National Historic Landmark, is significant not only as an outstanding example of Beaux Arts architecture but as one of the first monumental libraries in the United States to take function seriously into account in its design. This feature, generally unappreciated and not readily apparent, owes much to the active and at the time unusual participation in the planning by librarians, most notably Dr. Billings, and to the combination of practicality and aestheticism that the Beaux Arts-trained architects brought to the work.

The inclusion of a circulating department was a concession that the trustees, primarily interested in the research collections, had to make to public interest in popular library service. There were in the city a number of independent circulating libraries, some of them quite extensive, all struggling with insufficient municipal subsidies and private contributions, and altogether not constituting the efficiently run, well-planned system of central headquarters and branches that was becoming the model for public library service in the United States and that was emerging as the aim of New York City officials.

The provision of a lending library in the Fifth Avenue building was only the first step, and after the plans for the building had been secured and construction started, pressure mounted for the New York Public Library to assume responsibility for circulating library service in the boroughs of Manhattan, the Bronx, and Richmond. (The city took on its modern identity in 1898, with the formation of a new New York City comprising five boroughs, of which two, Brooklyn and Queens, each developed their own separate public library systems.)

In 1901 the New York Public Library absorbed the New York Free Circulating Library and was reconstituted as a new legal entity. Internally it was organized into two units, the primarily privately supported Reference Department and the primarily tax-supported Circulation Department, renamed in 1966 the Research Libraries and the Branch Libraries, each under a chief and with the director as chief executive over the whole. Later that year the foundation for comprehensive branch library service in all five boroughs was laid when the city accepted Andrew Carnegie's gift of funds to construct branch buildings, contingent upon municipal support for their operation. The result for the New York Public Library was consolidation with most of the independent circulating libraries in Manhattan, the Bronx, and Richmond and the creation eventually of a system of community libraries in those boroughs. The politics of this process led to the enlargement in 1902 of the board of trustees to include representation from the circulating libraries and ex officio membership of the mayor, the comptroller, and the president of the Board of Aldermen (later the City Council) of the City of New York.

These historical circumstances account for the division of the New York Public Library into two quite distinct entities, each a vast, renowned system with separate functions, administration, and sources of funding, albeit one board of trustees, one director, and, in time, the consolidation of some operations. This anomalous structure, hard to explain and hard to understand, has burdened the institution with a confused public image and has complicated efforts to raise funds.

It meant, too, that New York, unlike most American cities, had for many years no large, central, circulating collection of materials for general and student use. There was the great research library on Fifth Avenue and a network of neighborhood libraries, but nothing in between, an arrangement that seemed adequate enough at the outset but soon proved otherwise. Organized at a time when relatively few persons attended high school, much less college, and when the United States, and New York City, stood just on the threshold of enormous expansion in education, research, technology, and culture, the New York Public Library felt acutely the impact of change and growth. The result was that the Reference Department served a public much more diverse and much larger than initially expected. It early became clear that space in the central building would quickly run out, that existing income would not suffice, and that use of the Reference Department would be phenomenal. A special problem by the 1920s was the burgeoning student population, whose high schools and colleges had weak libraries and whose local communities had branch libraries designed for popular reading rather than study and reference. By 1930 overcrowding in the central building had become so overwhelming that restrictions were imposed upon student use.

The popularity of the Reference Department (with which the remainder of this article will be concerned) can also be seen as a sign of success, of the fulfillment of the founders' ambitions for the library: the acquisition and organization of an extraordinarily wide range of materials on almost every subject, in almost every form, and in virtually every language, and all available freely to the public every day and every evening of the year. Based upon the Astor and Lenox collections, the holdings were developed by Dr. Billings and then his protégé Harry Miller Lydenberg, who in nearly half a century with the library devoted himself to the collection, its growth, organization, and preservation, and who was in his time the dominant influence in the Reference Department. Together with his staff and the encouragement of the trustees and of Billings's successor, Edwin H. Anderson (1913-1934), Lydenberg (himself director after Anderson) set a model for the comprehensive collection of materials for research in a broad array of fields and including all sorts of materials—book and nonbook, print and nonprint, mundane and esoteric, rare and common. There were not only strong collections in most subjects and including periodicals, public documents, patents, newspapers, music, fine prints, and manuscripts, but an increasing number of special, unique collections.

By 1941, when Lydenberg retired, the Reference Department comprised nearly three million volumes, second in size in the United States only to the Library of Congress and among the first rank of libraries anywhere. By 1981 the collection numbered some six million volumes and twenty-two million pieces, one of the five largest research libraries in the world. This was an extraordinary accomplishment for an independent institution operating without benefit of copyright deposit, such as the Library of Congress had, or the aid of faculty members, such as university libraries had, and one which depended heavily upon private funding and whose constituency was, potentially, the entire public. Its holdings and services contributed to the production of countless publications, projects, inventions, artistic designs, and enterprises of all kinds. The staff, initially developed by

Anderson as a cadre of scholar-librarians—a number of whom were trained in the library's Library School, which functioned from 1911 to 1926, when it moved to Columbia University—not only participated in book selection and helped users to locate information and materials but were encouraged to do scholarly and bibliographical work, much of which appeared as part of the library's active publication and printing program. The library was a major force in the library world and a major resource for the scholarly community, as well as the communications, design, technical, and performing arts communities in New York City. Through its publications, its information services by mail and telephone, and, in time, an extensive photoreproduction service, its use was extended far beyond the New York metropolitan area.

Funding always presented a problem, but crises were weathered through contributions from trustees and other donors and through timely bequests. Space limitations were somewhat alleviated by the acquisition of an annex and the conversion of exhibition halls and corridors into office space. After World War II, the need for funds became chronically urgent and informal fund raising no longer sufficed. There were new pressures: rising costs, along with the necessity to raise the low library salaries; explosive growth in the number and variety of publications and fields of interest; demands for information generated by expansion of research, technology, and higher education; and increasing competition among nonprofit institutions for voluntary contributions. The trustees of the New York Public Library began dipping into endowment capital to make up the Reference Department's annual deficits; for the first time large-scale, consistent fund-raising campaigns and support groups were launched to tap corporate beneficiaries of the library's services and to acquire gifts from individuals and foundations. An increasingly important ingredient was government support, from New York State and, later, the federal government. The municipal contribution was inconsistent: the contractual obligation to maintain the central building was at times only barely met, and funds to support service to students and faculty in the new City University, a significant part of the library's clientele, were forthcoming for only a short time, victim of the city's own fiscal problems. By 1971 inflation and limited income had forced drastic reduction in opening hours in the central building, and there was talk of the library's demise.

The crisis spurred the institution to make instead a remarkable comeback. Under new leadership that impressively publicized the library's plight and stressed its significance as a national resource, new and broader sources of support were developed. Both private and governmental—mainly state and federal—contributions increased to the point where together they overshadowed income from endowment. Especially significant were the substantial grants, beginning in 1971, from the National Endowment for the Humanities in the form of matching funds, which greatly stimulated private giving.

In 1971, in order to deal more effectively with the institution's complexity, the necessity for constant fund raising, and the need to plan for the future, the New York Public Library's governance was reorganized. The board of trustees would be headed by a chairman rather than a president; the president was to be the chief operating officer of the library, with a director reporting to him. In 1972 the position of chief of the Research Libraries was endowed by the Andrew W. Mellon Foundation and thereafter known as the Andrew W. Mellon Director of The Research Libraries. The board of trustees was enlarged and made more representative of the scholarly as well as other sectors of the community, as were its committees. The first president under the reorganization, Richard Couper, resigned in 1981; his successor as of June 1, 1981, was Dr. Vartan Gregorian. Upon the retirement of John Mackenzie Cory as director in 1978, that position was eliminated.

Although the post-World War II decades were years in which financial struggle was a major theme, they were also a time of growth and accomplishment. Various surveys and studies of the use and management of the Research Libraries contributed to improvement of services and streamlining of internal organization and operations. A new, larger annex was acquired, and the opening in 1970 of the Mid-Manhattan Library on Fortieth Street and Fifth Avenue finally gave New York a large circulating collection and took some of the pressure off the main building, where the longtime need to accommodate researchers working on extended projects was met through contributions of funds to create the Frederick Lewis Allen Room and then the Wertheim Study. Another highlight was the inclusion of the New York Public Library in the new Lincoln Center complex as the Library and Museum of the Performing Arts. The distinguished Schomburg Center for Research in Black Culture, languishing in desperately inadequate quarters in Harlem, came under the aegis of the Research Libraries in 1972, and obtained grants to preserve, organize, and describe its holdings and construct a new building, opened in 1980. The card catalogs of most of the special divisions were published in book form by G. K. Hall Co., thus making information about these resources widely available.

The Research Libraries pioneered in applying computer technology to the creation of accurate bibliographic records of its holdings and also, in the process, made access to these records more widespread. On December 31, 1971, the central catalog, eleven million cards, was closed, to be continued by a computer-produced, regularly updated book catalog, first published in 1972, for new additions to the collections. Also launched was a project to restore and reproduce in book form the old catalog, a great bibliographic resource; by early 1981 two hundred out of a projected eight hundred volumes had been published. The library had from the beginning been concerned with and had led the field in preservation of materials; it operated its own bindery, carried on experiments in preserving paper and bindings, and early utilized microfilm and photostat. By the 1960s American research libraries were becoming acutely aware of the gradual deterioration of modern paper and bindings and the deleterious effects of the environment on library collections, conditions which threatened unique research materials with extinction. The New York Public Library was in the vanguard, after the Library of Congress, in establishing in 1970 a Conservation Laboratory and in 1972 a Conservation Division, which, with the aid of grants, has been trying to stem the tide of destruction.

Through the years and especially after World War II, the Research Libraries were involved in cooperative endeavors with other libraries on local, state, and national levels. Financial conditions of the 1970s—high inflation, rising salaries, and reduced real income, together with the unprecedented number and range of new and high-priced publications— propelled the New York Public Library into a new and uncharted venture. With Yale, Columbia, and Harvard universities, it founded in 1974 the Research Libraries Group, a consortium which subsequently admitted many more members (and lost Harvard). The group was designed to enable members to pool their resources to develop interrelated computerized bibliographic files that would facilitate the identification, description, and location of items; it also aimed to avoid excessive duplication in acquisition of materials through cooperative arrangements and to deal collectively with preservation problems. All this would mean sharing the use of materials and thus modifying the New York Public Library's traditional ban on loan of the Research Libraries' holdings.

For the New York Public Library, as well as other great research libraries, the era of institutional self-sufficiency and comprehensive collecting in all fields, an impossible goal by 1974, was coming to an end. Its mission would have to be fulfilled, for better or worse, in concert with other institutions.

For further information, see two general book-length histories of the library: Harry Miller Lydenberg, *History of the New York Public Library, Astor, Lenox and Tilden Foundations* (1923); and Phyllis Dain, *The New York Public Library: A History of Its Founding and Early Years* (1972).

For information on and development of the collections, see Karl Brown, *Guide to the Reference Collection of the New York Public Library* (1941); Sam P. Williams, comp., *Guide to the Research Collections of the New York Public Library* (1975); and Phyllis Dain, "Harry M. Lydenberg and American Library Resources: A Study in Modern Library Leadership," *Library Quarterly* (October, 1977).

Biographies of many of the chief figures of the library are included in Bohdan S. Wynar, ed., *Dictionary of American Library Biography* (1978). See also NYPL *Annual Reports* (1896 to date); NYPL *Bulletin* (1897-1977); and numerous handbooks; guides, newsletters, and so forth issued by the library through the years.

PHYLLIS DAIN

_O_

OAK RIDGE ASSOCIATED UNIVERSITIES (ORAU).† This private, nonprofit association of fifty colleges and universities in the southern United States conducts programs of research, education, and human resource development for a variety of governmental and private organizations. Established in 1946, ORAU was one of the first university-based, science-related corporate management groups. Based in Oak Ridge, Tennessee, it is governed by its sponsoring institutions through a board of directors elected by the ORAU council. ORAU programs are reviewed by committees of the council as well as by advisory panels drawn from academic and other appropriate groups. These programs of research and education are primarily concerned with problems of energy, health, and environment. About five hundred employees and a budget of eighteen million dollars in 1980 support ORAU activities.

The history of ORAU is woven of numerous strands: World War II, the Manhattan Project, the creation of the secret city of Oak Ridge and its sophisticated scientific facilities, the desire of universities in the South to develop high-quality graduate programs in the sciences—and the extraordinary career of ORAU's principal creator and first executive director, Dr. William G. Pollard.

The institution that Dr. Pollard built is a complex one. It began as the Oak Ridge Institute of Nuclear Studies (ORINS) with clear mandates: to train university researchers in the use of radioisotopes and to act as liaison between universities and what was to become Oak Ridge National Laboratory (ORNL). In the passage of three and a half decades, ORAU has become a leader in the development of nuclear medicine, administered the highly successful Atomic Energy Commission (AEC) National Fellowship Program, created a national energy museum, developed a program of na-

---

†This contribution is based, in part, on *ORAU: From the Beginning*, by W. G. Pollard, 1980. ORAU-162, xi-140 pp., Oak Ridge, Tennessee.

tional and international traveling exhibits in science and energy, and established an important energy analysis institute. Much of this is possible by virtue of a series of five-year contracts with the U.S. Department of Energy and its precursors.

An early guiding principle was stated by David Lilienthal, first chairman of the AEC, who was director of the Tennessee Valley Authority (TVA) at the time he played a role in the creation of ORAU. Lilienthal argued then that a sharp distinction should be drawn between management and participation: participation should be open to everyone without any element of regional bias, but the sponsorship should draw upon the strengths and coherence represented by the common aspirations and endeavors of the southern universities. That principle has endured—only the number of governing universities has changed from fourteen founding institutions to a current membership of fifty universities. Subsequent experience has shown that the decision in favor of regional management was wise. During more than thirty-four years of corporate progress, the organization has successfully conducted its programs with the sustained and cooperative support of the members, this a direct result of their regional coherence and identity.

One of the early programs, initiated in 1948, was the four-week radioisotope technique courses. Their success greatly enhanced atomic science in universities, and this and similar professional short courses in science and technology continue to be offered. For twelve years the Manpower Education, Research, and Training Division has also pioneered a highly successful industrial skills training program. Welding, machining, drafting, and related skills are provided to undertrained young people, and over 90 percent of these graduates are placed in industrial jobs. Similiar programs have been assisted in other states. To better understand the labor market and to forecast the need for critical skills for new technologies, a manpower analysis group conducts analyses of job trends.

Also in 1948, the AEC sought (and a conference of twenty medical schools recommended) that a clinical research facility be established to explore medical applications of radioisotopes. Contributions to the development of nuclear medicine, particularly the diagnosis of cancer and other diseases, continue. These applications, such as Ga-67 and the accompanying scanning technology, are the basis for a thriving radiopharmaceutical industry. To take advantage of radioisotopes that are positron emitters, the Medical and Health Sciences Division is using a new instrument known as an emission computerized axial tomograph (ECAT). This capability permits tagging of body functions.

The Medical and Health Sciences Division conducts biomedical research and training in studies of respiratory and gastrointestinal diseases and cancers related to occupational exposures to chemical toxicants and ionizing radiation involved in energy production. Immunobiology, biological chemistry, cell biology, radiopharmaceutical chemistry, nuclear medicine, experimental pathology, cytogenetics, and epidemiology are the main research disciplines from which pragmatically targeted task groups are structured to enhance efficiency. Predoctoral and postdoctoral training are provided in these areas. Besides newly refurbished laboratory units, the division has two unique facilities: the Radiation Emergency Assistance Center/Training Site (REAC/TS), maintained for the U.S. Department of Energy as a demonstration and training unit for medical preparedness for radiation accidents; and the Marmoset Research Center (MRC), which is a source of primates for research in the division and elsewhere in the United States.

As a result of the opening of Oak Ridge to the public in 1949, an energy museum was created to portray the discoveries of nuclear sciences. A new building was occupied in 1975, and exhibits about all forms of energy represent an important basis for public understanding of energy technologies. The Museum Division also manages the National Traveling Exhibit Program for the U.S. Department of Energy.

To further enhance public understanding of energy issues, the Energy Education Division (beginning in 1973) provides science enrichment and demonstrations to schools throughout the United States with funding from private energy companies. The public and private funding efforts combined to reach about twelve million people in 1979. An energy audit and building management training activity is also under way.

The Institute for Energy Analysis was established in 1974 as an ORAU division to examine broad questions of energy policy. More specifically, it assesses energy policy and energy research and development options and analyzes alternative energy supply and demand projections from technical, economic, and social perspectives. The institute focuses primarily on national energy issues, but it is also concerned with regional and international energy questions and their implications for domestic energy problems. Under the able leadership of Dr. Alvin M. Weinberg, this institute has already contributed to national energy policy formation, particularly regarding a lowered U.S. energy demand projection; criteria for nuclear siting acceptability; and atmospheric carbon dioxide accumulation from fossil fuel combustion. As a "think tank," the institute seeks to tap expertise throughout the nation and to synthesize the pertinent facts about a policy issue.

Sharing of experimental facilities by faculty and students is exemplified by University Isotope Separator at Oak Ridge (UNISOR), a consortium of sixteen universities operated by ORAU. Funding for multicampus experiments is provided by the U.S. Department of Energy and the universities. The accelerator beam line is provided by ORNL. The atomic nucleus is held together by strong forces, one of the four basic forces known to govern the behavior of the physical universe. Atoms whose nuclei are unstable—that is, held by relatively weaker forces—tend to decay and are of quite short life. UNISOR studies nuclei far from stability in order to better understand nuclear structure and behavior. User groups have been initiated around other specialized experimental equipment in such areas as materials science.

A major accomplishment growing out of these ORAU programs was its contribution to the development of the natural sciences in southern universities to a level comparable with that of universities elsewhere in the nation.

Thus ORAU was a part of and contributed to the scientific discoveries and technological applications made during the decades since World War II. Much of this achievement was made possible through federal funding for basic research to scientific organizations. Beginning in the early 1970s, however, the scientific community experienced an abrupt change in the momentum of federal funding for basic research. By the time of the Arab oil embargo in 1973, a radical shift in public expectations of science was evident. There is an insistent demand that science serve the immediate and pressing needs of society. Research in many frontier fields of experimental science has become very expensive and must compete with rising public demand for solutions to the energy crisis and other social issues. Thus, the spirit of the post-Sputnik era, which stimulated expanded government support, is waning. In its place has arisen a period of uncertainty and anxiety as we pass on to a new stage in human history.

ORAU is probably much more fit than most institutions for a successful course through this period. This fitness results from the dual role that has characterized ORAU from the beginning. The liaison function that ORAU exercises between ORNL and universities is independent of shifting ORNL program emphasis by the government. The nature of ORAU programs over the last three decades has left it far less committed than either the national laboratories or the universities to the preservation of the past. Its wide range of educational activities has been addressed to pressing needs of the time. These activities have endeavored both to eradicate false hopes and to calm unnecessary fears by holding as close to reality as possible. As the needs and opportunities in higher education, particularly in scientific research, emerge in a decade of falling enrollment, ORAU continues to seek the means to do better together.

For further information, see the ORAU *Annual Reports,* 1946 to date. The tenth *Annual Report* contains an account of the first ten years of operation. For a later full-length history, see William G. Pollard, *ORAU: From the Beginning* (1980). This brief history is based, in part, on the Pollard history.

PHILIP L. JOHNSON

ORGANIZATION OF AMERICAN HISTORIANS (OAH). Clarence S. Paine of the Nebraska State Historical Society together with the secretaries of other state historical societies in the Mississippi Valley were responsible for the organization, in 1907, of the Mississippi Valley Historical Association, predecessor of the Organization of American Historians. The major reasons for the creation of the association were: travel difficulties encountered by historians from the Mississippi Valley in attending the annual meetings of the older American Historical Association* (AHA); a belief that better outlets for research and interpretation in American history, particularly the West, were needed than was being provided by the AHA; and the conviction of Paine and his fellow secretaries that a new and independent association would provide a regional cooperative medium for them in their state historical endeavors. Thus, a new historical society came into being, despite suggestions at the time that the creation of a Midwest Branch of the AHA comparable to its recently formed Pacific Coast Branch might be a better alternative.

Although state historical society representatives held many of the offices and the association did play the cooperative role envisaged for it, within a few years after its founding historians from educational institutions became ever more numerous and influential and molded the role of the association primarily to their ends. Thus, despite its original title, the association became, at a very early period, national rather than regional in its scope and emphasis: national, in that its membership and office holders were attracted from the entire United States and that it eschewed Hispanic American history in its purview, although including Canadian. As early as the 1930s, for example, members of its executive committee had been elected who were residents of Georgia and New York. Also, the *Mississippi Valley Historical Review,* established in 1914 as its official quarterly journal and eventually superseding an earlier *Proceedings*, reveals this trend. An examination of the articles in the first five volumes of the *Review* with those of several decades later reveals a striking decline in the number of articles dealing with the Mississippi Valley as compared with those concerned with other areas. Association acknowledgment of this change was implicit in its adoption, in 1938, of the *Review's* subtitle, "A Journal of American History."

The first moves to recognize this change officially, however, went down to defeat. As early as 1943 a committee was set up to make recommendations on restating the purpose and scope of the association; it unsuccessfully urged a change in the name of the association and the *Review.* Almost similar attempts failed in the early and late 1950s. Finally, in 1962, an eighteen-member Committee on the Future, with Thomas D. Clark as chairman, was appointed by the executive committee of the association with the mandate to "study its future." The committee first recommended that the name of the *Review* be changed to *Journal of American History.* Following approval in 1964 of this recommendation, a change in name of the association to "Organization of American Historians" followed. This was accomplished in 1965, and in 1970 the American Council of Learned Societies* (ACLS) officially recognized the national status of the OAH by voting to admit it to membership in the ACLS.

Publication of the earlier *Proceedings,* later *Review,* now *Journal,* have always been one of if not the most successful functions of the OAH, which was particularly fortunate in its successive choices for editor of these journals. Beginning with Clarence W. Alvord and extending to the incumbent, Lewis Perry, they have set a standard for scholarly periodicals. The OAH has encouraged historical publication by the establishment of six annual awards for scholarship in American history: the Louis Pelzer Award; Frederick Jackson Turner Award; Binkley-Stephenson Award; Merle Curti Award; Charles Thomson Prize; and Ray Allen Billington Prize.

Initially, it was proposed that two annual meetings of the association be held, one in conjunction with the AHA in December and another in June. Such joint meetings with the AHA were eventually abandoned because the AHA changed its policy in this regard, and annual OAH meetings have since been held in the spring or early summer. Up until the 1950s these meetings were held at sites in the Mississippi Valley, where there was enthusiastic academic sponsorship for them. Since that time, such support has no longer been a factor in choosing the location for annual meetings, and they have often been held in other sections of the country.

From a handful of founding members at the turn of the century, the OAH grew to about one thousand members in the 1930s, about three thousand in the 1950s, and now stands at about eighty-three hundred members, together with approximately thirty-four hundred institutional subscribers.

The OAH elects the customary institutional officers; it conducts its business from an office, headed by an executive secretary, located in Bloomington, Indiana.

For further information, see the following articles, all appearing in the *Mississippi Valley Historical Review:* Theodore C. Blegen, "Our Widening Province" (June, 1944); James L. Sellers, "Before We Were Members—the MVHA" (June, 1953) and "The Semi-Centennial of the Mississippi Valley Historical Association" (December, 1957); and John W. Caughey, "Under Our Strange Device: A Review of the 'Review'" (December, 1957).

For a recent cogent and brief history of the OAH, see William D. Aeschbacher, "The Mississippi Valley Historical Association, 1907-1965," *Journal of American History* (September, 1967). See also the following reminiscences about the OAH by two older members, both articles appearing in the *Journal of American History* (June, 1978): Ray Allen Billington, "From Association to Organization: The OAH in the Bad Old Days"; and Thomas D. Clark, "Our Roots Flourished in the Valley."

P

PALEONTOLOGICAL SOCIETY. This society was an offspring of the Geological Society of America* (GSA) and has continued to maintain rapport with the latter organization. The initial move for a society separate from the GSA occurred at the latter's 1907 meeting when a committee, headed by Charles Schuchert, met to discuss the matter. It agreed that opinion would be obtained from paleontologists on such matters as the nature of the proposed society, its proper relationship to the GSA, and publication policy. Having accomplished this a meeting was held on December 31, 1908, in Baltimore, at which thirty-four charter members formed the Paleontological Society, including the naming of an executive committee with powers to proceed with organization. At a subsequent meeting in February, 1909, a proposed constitution was ratified by the executive committee, and a conference was held with the GSA to spell out the relationship between the two. It was decided that the Paleontological Society, although nominally independent, would be affiliated with and form a section of the GSA and that the latter, within certain financial limits, would provide for publishing the research papers and other material of the paleontologists. During that same year inclusion in Paleontological Society membership was offered to all members of the existing Society of American Vertebrate Paleontologists. Because a large number of members availed themselves of this offer, the latter society went out of existence in 1910, to be resurrected in 1940-1941 as the Society of Vertebrate Paleontology.

The original constitution spelled out four classes of membership: fellows, persons who had published paleontological works and been elected fellows of the GSA; members, persons with an interest in paleontology; correspondents, distinguished foreign paleontologists elected to membership; patrons, persons making grants, gifts, and so on to the Paleontological Society. Originally only fellows could hold society office; in 1949 this restriction was removed, and fellows were merged with members. Numerical growth has been slow and society membership presently numbers about 1,350 persons.

From 1909 to 1935 the Paleontological Society utilized the GSA *Bulletin* as a publication medium. In 1926, meanwhile, because of the growth of the oil industry and the realization of the value of the application of paleontology to oil discovery, the Society of Economic Paleontologists and Mineralogists was organized and began to publish its annual *Journal of Paleontology*. Subsequently, in 1935, an arrangement was worked out between these two societies whereby the short papers, records, and news of the Paleontological Society were to be published in the *Journal,* and the proceedings, monographs, and other lengthier material were to be published by the GSA. At the same time, with financial support provided it by the GSA and the American Association of Petroleum Geologists, the *Journal* was changed to a bimonthly publication. In the 1960s, however, both the GSA and the association withdrew this support, and the *Journal of Paleontology* is now the sole financial and editorial responsibility of the Society of Economic Paleontologists and Mineralogists and the Paleontological Society, each paying half of the publication costs. Some fifty paleontological monographs have been published in addition to numerous articles and notes under these arrangements. In 1974, the Paleontological Society established its own quarterly, *Paleobiology,* which is edited at the University of Chicago. The material in the three volumes published thus far deals with subjects at the interface between paleontology and modern biology.

This close cooperation in publication similarly prevails in regard to annual meetings. The Paleontological Society has always held its meetings with the GSA, and kindred organizations have also been included. Members cross societal lines at these meetings and, for example, attend sessions that most interest them, regardless of societal sponsorship. The places and dates of meetings are arranged jointly, usually during the first week in November in one of the larger cities of the United States, Canada, or Mexico.

The Paleontological Society and its members have contributed much to the study of fossils in particular and to geological and zoological advancement in general. One outstanding achievement was the development of improved techniques for the preparation of fossils, including the use of various acids to free silicified fossils from rock, and better methods of illustrating them for publication. The society was a joint sponsor with the GSA, the Paleontographical Society of London, and the Society of Economic Paleontologists and Mineralogists of the project, under the direction of Dr. Raymond C. Moore, that resulted in the classic *Treatise on Invertebrate Paleontology.* The Paleontological Society also lent support in 1941 to the revival of the International Commission on Zoological Nomenclature and, in 1948, to the founding of the American Geological Institute* (AGI).

The society elects the customary institutional officers; it conducts its business from an office, headed by a secretary, located in Columbus, Ohio.

For further information, see the following articles from a Symposium on Fifty Years of Paleontology, all appearing in the *Journal of Paleontology:*

Norman D. Newell, "Adequacy of the Fossil Record" (May, 1959); Theodor Just, "Progress in Paleobotany" (May, 1959); Henry V. Howe, "Fifty Years of Micropaleontology" (May, 1959); Carl O. Dunbar, "A Half Century of Paleontology" (September, 1959); Alfred Sherwood Romer, "Vertebrate Paleontology, 1908-1958" (September, 1959); and Preston E. Cloud, Jr., "Paleoecology—Retrospect and Prospect" (September, 1959). See also proceedings of the preliminary and first annual meetings of the society appearing in *Bulletin, Geological Society of America* (March, 1910); and H. E. Vokes, "The Paleontological Society," *AAAS Bulletin* (May, 1945).

The archives of the Paleontological Society are deposited in the University of Illinois Archives and are indexed there in record series 15/11/20.

PEABODY MUSEUM OF ARCHAEOLOGY AND ETHNOLOGY. The Peabody Museum was founded in 1866 with a trust of $150,000 from George A. Peabody (1795-1869), a native of Essex County, Massachusetts, who became an international entrepreneur, financier, and philanthropist. The museum was the first in the United States devoted specifically to anthropology. Although the founder took no direct hand in the early affairs of the museum, he did anticipate that it would contribute in a major way to current, hot debates over Darwinian evolution and the origin of the races of man. In the first decades these religio-scientific issues determined the direction of museum activity. Jeffries Wyman (1814-1874), a Harvard comparative anatomist who became the first curator of the museum (1866-1874), concentrated first on buying established European archaeological collections as a comparative basis for New World materials. At the same time he undertook important investigations in the shell heaps of Florida and the New England coast, establishing a tradition of original and meticulous field observation. Wyman also developed a wide network of correspondents in the various growing fields of anthropology, particularly archaeology.

On Wyman's death in 1874, Harvard botanist Asa Gray served briefly as curator, and in 1876 Frederick Ward Putnam, a native of Salem, Massachusetts, and a former student of both Wyman and Louis Agassiz, began a forty-year tenure as curator of the museum. Putnam presided over the transformation of nineteenth-century genteel anthropology into the twentieth-century institutional, academic discipline of anthropology at Harvard—although in some ways Putnam himself remained a stranger in the world of formal accreditation and professionalization that he helped to create. As corresponding secretary of the American Association for the Advancement of Science* (AAAS) for twenty-five years, Putnam was able to raise the museum's visibility and greatly expand the circle of correspondents and contributors. His own fieldwork focused first on Tennessee and Kentucky, and for a quarter of a century he supported Charles Abbott's search for glacial man in the Delaware River valley; but during the 1880s Putnam's interests, and those of the museum, shifted to Ohio. It was under Putnam's direction in 1891-1892 that Warren King Moorehead first excavated the Hopewell sites in southern Ohio—a milestone in North American archaeology.

Putnam's great contribution to archaeology was methodological rather than theoretical: he insisted on attention to stratigraphy, scrupulous sifting and preservation of even mundane materials, and preventing dispersal of collections. Moreover, under his leadership the Peabody Museum fought for protection of archaeological sites, through purchase (Serpent Mound Park in Ohio, 1887), or federal or state government action (Antiquities Act of 1906), a museum tradition that continues strongly today.

During the 1890s the museum undertook its first Central American work, the ten-year exploration of the ruins of Copan, Honduras, under the patronage of Boston financier Charles P. Bowditch. The unflagging enthusiasm of Bowditch from this time until his death in 1921 was the major influence in directing Peabody attention to Mexico and Central America. He was instrumental in the early careers of Herbert J. Spinden, Sylvanus G. Morley, and particularly Alfred M. Tozzer. As a consequence the Peabody Museum took the early lead in Central American ethnology, archaeology, and epigraphy, publishing such seminal studies as Spinden's *Study of Maya Art* (Peabody Museum Memoirs, vol. 6, 1913). Theoretically and methodologically the critical insight of these early years in Central America was the recognition at the Peabody that study of language (written or spoken), living peoples, and archaeological remains must proceed in tandem—that the widening gulfs between the subdisciplines of anthropology posed a great threat to progress in understanding.

In 1897, thirty years after its founding, the Peabody Museum finally merged with Harvard University. From this point the museum began actively to train students in archaeology, physical anthropology, and cultural anthropology. In the same years the board of trustees was replaced by the faculty of the Peabody Museum (not teaching faculty) as the governing body of the museum, and the Peabody began to receive its visiting committee, which has since acted to represent museum interests to the Board of Overseers of Harvard Corporation. By Putnam's death in 1915, the museum had outstripped his fondest aspirations of 1876. From a single room in Boylston Hall the Peabody had acquired a building of its own and became an integral part of Harvard's University Museum. Beginning with a single curator and unpaid assistants, it now boasted a formidable teaching and curatorial staff that included Tozzer (Middle American Ethnology and Archaeology), Roland B. Dixon (Ethnology), Alfred V. Kidder (North American Archaeology and Ethnology), and Earnest A. Hooton (Somatology).

In the post-World War I decade the museum renewed and deepened involvement in Central America while expanding to virtually global scope. Oric Bates's early (1913-1916) work in North Africa paved the way for George Schwab's ethnological work (1918-1950) and the subsequent work of Carleton S. Coon, L. Cabot Briggs, and others. The American School of Prehistoric Research, founded by Charles Peabody and Mr. and Mrs. George Grant MacCurdy in 1921, shifted archaeological attention in a major way back to Old World prehistory, and over two decades the ASPR sponsored field schools throughout Europe. Upon Mr. MacCurdy's death the ASPR became the Department of Old World Archaeology in the Peabody Museum, under the leadership of Hugh Hencken (curator of European Archaeology).

Partly as a result of government support, North American archaeology enjoyed a resurgence during the depression years of the 1930s. At the Peabody the revival of interest was marked by the gradual formation of the Lower Mississippi Survey, an archaeological program begun in the mid-1930s by Philip Phillips and continued to the present time under Stephen Williams. During the interwar period Peabody work in the southwestern United States took major strides, notably through the innovative work of Alfred Kidder and his students in northern Arizona, and, in the late 1930s, with the excavation of Awatovi pueblo by J. O. Brew, Watson Smith, and others. Between 1936 and 1960, Clyde Kluckhohn's New Mexican Navaho studies, along with his Comparative Study of Values in Five Cultures (1946-1954), established new directions and models for social anthropology.

Finally, the Peabody Museum took a major part in the renewed debate, after the Folsom finds in 1928, over the antiquity of man in the New World. The museum's efforts in this field culminated in the Hell Gap (Wyoming) Project (1960-1966, under the direction of Cynthia Irwin-Williams and Henry Irwin), which dated New World man back beyond 8000 B.C. Hell Gap was, in a sense, the lineal descendant of the original concerns of George Peabody and Jeffries Wyman.

Amidst the proliferation of departments, activities, and interests for most of this century, Central America remained the dominant focus of Peabody effort. The firm base provided by Bowditch and Tozzer was strengthened by close proximity to and association (through Kidder and Morley) with the Carnegie Institution of Washington,* whose anthropological records are now housed in the museum. The list of Peabody expeditions to Central and South America runs several pages. In addition to the Carnegie's thirty-year program in Yucatan under Morley, the researches of the following individuals have been of major significance: Spinden, R. E. Merwin, Samuel Lothrop, Doris Stone, John Longyear III, Ledyard Smith, William Bullard, Jr., John Ladd, and Tatiana Proskouriakoff. Gordon R. Willey (Bowditch

Professor of Central American and Mexican Archaeology and Ethnology) has presided over the further growth and development of archeology, and Evon Z. Vogt, Jr. (curator of Social Anthropology) has inspired and invigorated Mexican ethnology through his teaching and fieldwork in Chiapas.

Museum anthropology in the United States has always been divided, and enriched, by the multiple functions of preservation, display, and teaching. In the first forty years of the Peabody Museum curatorial tasks dominated, leaving little energy for teaching. In the early twentieth century, however, training of anthropologists took on primary importance, and the curatorial staff of the museum has usually served as well on the Arts and Sciences Faculty of Harvard. Museum collections have thus come to serve as a critical teaching tool of Harvard anthropology. Like all museums of anthropology the Peabody has severe shortages of space for both storage and display. In a recent innovative move, the museum and the National Endowment for the Humanities entered upon a program in which the museum will circulate exhibits of Peabody collections to smaller museums around the country, thereby spreading its educational role beyond the Boston region.

On October 15, 1980, the Peabody Museum celebrated the opening of its new Center for Archaeological Research and Development for the analysis of organic and inorganic archaeological materials, marking the museum's most recent step in scientific archeology. Consistent with its roots, Peabody Museum anthropology today insists on the critical balance of humanism and science. Equipped with the latest analytical tools, the museum also houses the Institute for Conservation Archaeology, as well as Cultural Survival, Inc., an organization dedicated to help small, threatened societies around the world. In these and other ways the Peabody Museum today, under its current director, Dr. C. C. Lamberg-Karlovsky, champions a broad concept of anthropology as a humanistic science.

The Tozzer Library, opened in 1974 adjacent to the museum, is one of the world's foremost anthropological libraries. In 1979 the library began publishing *Anthropological Literature: An Index to Periodical Articles and Essays*, a valuable current guide to all fields of anthropology. The library houses 135,000 volumes and maintains 1,000 serial publications.

Since 1868 the museum has published its *Annual Reports*, which until 1887 included scientific papers. In 1888 the *Papers of the Peabody Museum* began, and in 1896 the first volume of the larger *Memoirs of the Peabody Museum* appeared. *Bulletins* of the American School of Prehistoric Research began in 1926; Monographs of the Peabody Museum in 1974; *Peabody Museum Bulletins* in 1976. All these series continue currently. In addition, between 1917 and 1932 the ten volumes of *Harvard African Studies* were published. Outside the serial publications, the Peabody Museum Press publishes in all fields of anthropology.

For further information, see the publications discussed above, particularly the *Annual Reports*, 1868 to present. See also J. O. Brew, *People and Projects of the Peabody Museum, 1866-1966* (1966) and *Early Days of the Peabody Museum at Harvard University* (1966). Professor Curtis M. Hinsley, Jr., Colgate University, is currently preparing a cultural history centering on the museum and based on the Peabody Museum and Harvard University Archives.

CURTIS M. HINSLEY, JR.

PIERPONT MORGAN LIBRARY. America's most notable rare book libraries have been created by a few men of great wealth: the Folger in Washington, D.C., Houghton at Harvard, Huntington in California, Lilly in Indiana, Morgan in New York, and Newberry in Chicago. Most catholic in his concerns was J. Pierpont Morgan (1837-1913). His acquisitions of books and manuscripts covered an unusually wide range, from specimens of the earliest written records to first editions of contemporary authors. Morgan also assembled outstanding collections in a dozen departments of fine arts.

The Pierpont Morgan Library is the leading American example of a highly specialized institution devoted to rare books. It constitutes a monument to a father and son, whose efforts extended over nearly a century: the elder Morgan, an international banker, and John Pierpont Morgan (1867-1943).

The first Morgan, the founder, began to gather books and manuscripts as a youth, in the 1850s. At first, his collecting interests appear to have been confined to autographs, such as those for U.S. presidents and signers of the Declaration of Independence. Over the first forty years, the collection developed slowly. A catalog of the books and manuscripts by the American bibliographer Joseph F. Sabin in 1883 revealed few rarities. By the 1890s, however, Morgan was beginning to buy on a spectacular scale.

Before the turn of the century, the Morgan collection had added a Gutenberg Bible on vellum, the 1459 Mainz Psalter, the ninth-century Lindau Gospels, the 4 Shakespeare folios, and original manuscripts of Keats, Scott, Dickens, Byron, and other noted nineteenth-century authors. Further, entire private libraries were acquired en bloc when justified by their quality and suitability. Soon thereafter there were received 270 Rembrandt etchings; William Morris's library, rich in Medieval manuscripts; some 700 incunabula, including 40 from the press of William Caxton, first English printer. During his last few years, Morgan added a major collection of bookbindings, another group of Caxtons, a large group of ninth-century Coptic manuscripts, numerous illuminated manuscripts, more incunabula, and a noteworthy collection of American nineteenth-century literary manuscripts, especially rich in Poe, Hawthorne, and Thoreau.

By the beginning of the twentieth century, the Morgan collection had become so extensive as to require a special building. The architectural firm of McKim, Mead and White was commissioned in 1902 to design the building, to be constructed adjoining the Morgan home on Thirty-Sixth Street in New York City. Charles F. McKim undertook the project in person, planning from the outset to create a Renaissance palazzo, built of fitted marble blocks in the classical Greek manner. Undeterred by cost, the grandiose building, of pinkish Tennessee marble, was finally completed in 1906, furnished sumptuously from the huge Morgan art collection, and decorated with paintings by H. Siddon Mowbray, head of the American Academy in Rome. It has since been designated as a National Historic Landmark by the secretary of the interior. An annex, doubling the size, was completed in 1928, a second addition was occupied in 1962, and a third in 1977.

In his will, published after his death in 1913, the elder Morgan stated, "It has been my desire and intention to make some suitable disposition of my collections . . . which would render them permanently available for the instruction and pleasure of the American people." His wish was realized in 1924, when his son came to the conclusion that the library should go public. Accordingly, it was transferred to a board of trustees, with an endowment for its maintenance.

In a letter to the board, on February 15, 1924, Morgan wrote,

My father's interest and satisfaction in the Library makes it a particularly fitting memorial to him. It is a memorial that keeps alive the memory of his love of rare books and his belief in the educational value of the collection which he has gathered. Since his death, I have constantly endeavored to see that the Library and its contents should be made available in every way possible for the advancement of knowledge and for the use of learned men of all countries, as he delighted to do.

By a special act of the New York Legislature in 1924, the Pierpont Morgan Library was incorporated as a public reference library. Aside from tax exemption, it receives no governmental financial aid.

As the use of the library grew and its collections expanded, new services were begun, including a series of graduate study courses, lectures by leading scholars, a regular series of exhibitions in the library itself and on loan to other institutions, and numerous publications to make the library's resources more widely known and available. The library has been fortunate in its directors, starting with the brilliant librarian Belle Da Costa Greene, who remained in the position until 1948, a total of forty-three years. She was succeeded by Frederick B. Adams, Jr., director from 1948 to 1969, whose achievements included formation of the "Fellows of the Pierpont Morgan Library," with some six hundred members, for the purpose of providing funds for exceptional acquisitions and encouraging the use of the collections. Since 1969, the library has been directed by Charles Ryskamp.

Reflecting the original donors' own interests and collecting proclivities, the Morgan Library's principal collections fall into several distinct categories, which may be briefly summarized as follows:

Medieval and Renaissance Manuscripts. This is a field in which the Morgan Library is unquestionably preeminent. In his *Census of Medieval and Renaissance Manuscripts in the United States and Canada*, Seymour de Ricci cited the Morgan collections as "the most extensive and the most beautifully selected series of manuscripts existing on the American Continent, and it may truthfully claim to be superior in general quality to all but three or four of the greatest national libraries of the Old World." A few among many notable examples are: the Gospels of Countess Matilda of Tuscany, written and decorated in Italy in about 1100; four manuscripts from a Benedictine monastery in southern Germany, including two richly illuminated Gospel books made in England before the Norman Conquest, and another a Missal of Abbot Berthold, one of the finest surviving thirteenth-century German manuscripts; a ninth-century Reims Gospel in perfect condition with the entire text written in gold; a twelfth-century "Life, Miracles and Passion of St. Edmund," one of the two earliest known cycles of pictures illustrating the life of an English saint; two ninth-century illuminated Gospels from Tours and Saint Amand; an Anglo-Saxon Gospel of about the year 1000; a Spanish Apocalypse dated 926; a sumptuous Greek Gospel Lectionary of the eleventh century; a tenth-century Greek illuminated manuscript of Dioscorides's *De Materia Medica*; the earliest manuscript of Aesop's *Life and Fables* in Greek; a monumental Bohemian Bible, dated 1391; a ninth-century Pliny *Natural History*; the oldest and most complete copy known of the *Fables* of Phaedrus; and a number of fifteenth-century Books of Hours. Since 1963, the library has had on deposit the Glazier collection of medieval and Renaissance manuscripts, described as "the finest private collection in this field in the United States."

Many of the early manuscripts acquired by the Morgan Library were important for their text rather than for their miniatures. The Pliny is an example. Among others are volumes of French medieval romances; the early English texts of Chaucer, Gower, and Lydgate; the Saint Augustine written in Merovingian script of the seventh century; the eleventh-century Hinemar; the *Chronicles* of the Scottish writer Hector Boece; and the Tegrimi *Computus*, a North Italian scientific compilation of about 1020.

From the point of view of research use, the library's manuscript collection is one of the most active. The five-year reviews of publications based on Morgan Library materials show that a large proportion of books and articles are concerned with paleography and illumination.

Early Printed Books. The Morgan Library holds about two thousand incunabula, "cradle books," produced during the first fifty years after Gutenberg's invention of printing—not the largest collection in America, but believed to surpass that of any other American library in the number of important early books and the remarkable condition of most of the volumes.

Here, again, there are many extraordinary individual works. To the Gutenberg Bible on vellum was added a perfect copy on paper; the so-called Missale Speciale, which may have been printed by Gutenberg about 1450, predating his Latin Bible; an indulgence printed at Mainz by Gutenberg and dated 1455; the only surviving complete copy of the first edition of Malory's *Morte d'Arthur*, printed by Caxton; the two earliest editions (Rome, 1493) of Columbus's account of his New World discoveries; the first printing of Saint Augustine's *De Civitate Dei* (Subiaco, 1467); Nicolas Jensen's first book, Cicero's *Rhetorica ad Herrennium* (Venice, 1470); the first Bible printed in Italy (Rome, 1471), by Italy's first printers, Sweynheym and Pannartz; works by England's second printer, Wynkyn de Worde, including *The Abbey of the Holy Ghost* (Westminster, c. 1496); the earliest printing of Boccaccio's *Decameron* (Ulm, 1473); first and early editions of Greek and Latin classics; and illustrated books of legends and romances. In building the collection of early printing, the Morgan Library has emphasized the first printing of classical, Biblical, and other texts and woodcut and metal engravings. Particular attention has been paid to the productions of the first presses, which played a part in the early spread of the art of printing. In accordance with this policy, the library possesses a high proportion of the books issued by the first presses of Germany, Italy, France, and the Low Countries.

Chronologically, a consideration of blockbooks should precede those produced by typography. Of these earliest illustrated printed books, all of which are extremely rare, the Morgan Library has a score or more examples.

Autographs, Manuscripts, Letters, and Documents. The Morgan Library holds tens of thousands of letters and hundreds of volumes of authors' original manuscripts. Special fields of concentration are in the Renaissance in Italy, the Reformation in Germany, the Tudor and Stuart periods in England, and the American Revolution and early years of the Republic. In literature there are especially noteworthy collections of manuscript material of La Fontaine, Bossuet, Voltaire, Dumas, Lamartine, Sir Philip Sidney, Milton, Swift, Pope, Sterne, Gray, Horace Walpole, Cowper, Burns, Blake, Scott, Coleridge, Shelley, Keats, Byron, Southey, Jane Austen, the Brontës, the Brownings, Dickens, Thackeray, Wilkie Collins, Meredith, Morris, Ruskin, Kipling, Poe, Emerson, Hawthorne, Thoreau, Holmes, Longfellow, Mark Twain, Bret Harte, and John Steinbeck.

In the Americana section are the first Bible printed in North America, the Eliot Indian Bible (Cambridge, 1663); a six-page George Washington letter of 1788, expressing his hopes for the new nation; 173 autograph letters from Thomas Jefferson to his daughter Matilda; and the original manuscript of Hawthorne's *Tanglewood Tales*. Other individual pieces that stand out are the original autograph manuscript of Keats's *Endymion* and Dickens's *A Christmas Carol*; manuscripts of 10 of Scott's Waverly novels, beginning with the acquisition of *Guy Mannering*; the manuscripts of Thackeray's *Vanity Fair* and *The Rose and the Ring*; several hundred Voltaire letters; the manuscript of Balzac's *Eugénie Grandet*; a long letter from Robert Burns incorporating the text of three poems; the most extensive collection of Dickens manuscripts outside the Victoria and Albert Museum; the largest single collection of Coleridge letters; and thousands of Ruskin letters.

Later Printed Books. Later printed books in the Morgan collection, approximately seventy thousand in number, were selected for their importance in literature and other arts, history, and printing. The collection is particularly notable for first editions, association and presentation copies of major English and Continental authors.

Early Children's Books. The Morgan assemblage of early children's books, described as "probably the most important collection in the United States," begins with the unique copy of the earliest known children's book, dating from about 1487, and concentrates on seventeenth- and eighteenth-century English and Continental children's literature. In addition, there is an outstanding collection of manuscripts, ranging from the original text of Perrault's *Mother Goose* to modern authors.

Music Manuscripts. The collection of musical manuscripts in the Morgan Library is rated second in America only to that of the Library of Congress. The acquisition of several private collections brought autograph scores and letters of composers and musicians, manuscripts of the leading French composers of the nineteenth century, and the most extensive existing collection of Gilbert and Sullivan.

Bookbindings. The Morgan Library is reputed to hold the most comprehensive collection of bookbindings in America, ranging from the ninth century to the twentieth, including all styles and materials and representing most of the leading binders and patrons. For the medieval and Renaissance periods, many of the books retain their earlier monastic and book-trade bindings. After the invention of printing, gilt-tooled leather bindings came into vogue. The golden age was the sixteenth century, when the Grolier and other binders flourished. The library has a number of Parisian bindings belonging to that era. Other specimens of early bindings made in Italy, Sicily, Spain, Bohemia, Holland, Denmark, Hungary, England, Scotland, and Ireland add to the collection's broad scope.

Old Master Drawings. The Morgan Library collection of old master drawings concentrates on artists born before 1800. It consists of about five thousand drawings of outstanding quality for the period covered. Associated with the drawings is the most distinguished collection of Rembrandt prints in America. There are more than one hundred drawings by the Italian architect Piranesi and other important groups of architectural and botanical drawings. Twelve watercolor designs by William Blake for works by Milton are noteworthy, and there are hundreds of drawings, sketchbooks, and albums by Italian, French, Spanish, German, Dutch, Flemish, and British artists.

Ancient Written Records. One gets a sense of universal history from the Morgan Library's major collection of Assyrian and Babylonian seals (cylinder and stamp), cuneiform tablets, and Egyptian, Greek, and other papyri. The papyri fall into three groups: Egyptian, Greek, and Coptic; each group consists of literary works and documents of historical interest. An example of the Greek is a codex of the *Iliad.*

In establishing policies for the Pierpont Morgan Library, its trustees have been guided by two principal considerations: first, to preserve and increase literary, historical, and artistic records of the past, in the best condition possible; and, second, to make them available to scholars, students, and others to the fullest extent consistent with their preservation.

For further information, see *The First Quarter Century of the Pierpont Morgan Library* (1949); Francis Henry Taylor, *Pierpont Morgan as Collector and Patron, 1837-1913* (1957); and Frederick B. Adams, Jr.," *An Introduction to the Pierpont Morgan Library* (1974). See also George K. Boyce, "The Pierpont Morgan Library," *Library Quarterly* (January, 1952); and Israel Shenker, "J. Pierpont Morgan and the Princely Library He Founded," *Smithsonian* (September, 1979).

ROBERT B. DOWNS

POPULATION COUNCIL. The Population Council is an independent, international, nonprofit organization devoted to the search for better understanding of problems related to population. It is a multidisciplinary organization, working and supporting the work of others in the social, health, and human reproductive sciences and engaging in development of contraceptive technology, the study of population policy, and institutional capacity-building and technical assistance in the developing world. The council provides grants and fellowships to developing world students and professionals for study of virtually all aspects of the broad field of population. And a publications program communicates to professionals in the social sciences involved in population issues through scholarly journals, monographs, and bulletins.

The Population Council was established in 1952 by John D. Rockefeller III. As an organization unique at that time in its focus on population, the council spent its first years as a pioneer. In an uneasy climate of opinion, in which birth control could scarcely be discussed publicly, the council placed primary emphasis on research projects and training fellowships in demography and reproductive physiology, granting research support to others when little, if any, was available from other sources. To help developing countries build indigenous capacities to address population issues, the council undertook two major lines of action that have continued to this day: provision of fellowships, and support for regional and national population research and training centers.

The impact of the council's fellowship program on the population field is generally acknowledged to have been considerable. Begun in the 1950s, the fellowship program made investments in human resources that would yield critical returns for the field in the years ahead. When world attention focused on population problems in the 1960s and 1970s, population specialists were already deployed around the world, largely because of the council's efforts. By the end of 1979 the council had awarded fellowships to over 1,000 men and women for advanced training in the fields of demography, the physiology of reproduction, and medical and administrative aspects of family planning. Of these fellows, 750 were from the developing world.

In seeking to strengthen the institutional capacities of developing areas of the world, the council played a central role in the establishment and development of the United Nations' first regional centers for demographic training and research in Bombay (1957), Santiago (1958), and Cairo (1963). The council also contributed to research and training programs in population studies at university centers in the United States at which council fellows studied.

Although extramural grants remained the council's predominant activity until the mid-1960s, already in the late 1950s changes were under way that foreshadowed a new role for the organization in the years to come. The council began to develop an in-house capacity to carry out demographic analysis. And in 1957 the council established a biomedical research laboratory at the Rockefeller Institute, now Rockefeller University, to serve as a focal point for scientific research related to fertility control, providing facilities where young people could be trained and collaborative work carried out with established investigators. Many of the council's early biomedical research grants, as well as work in its own laboratory, dealt with the effects of sex hormones on reproductive functions in the human male and female.

In the 1960s, when individual countries and later world opinion began to focus on the population growth problem, developing countries turned to the council for help in organizing family planning programs and research efforts. The provision of technical assistance, upon request, to governments and private organizations seeking to establish effective programs for provision of family planning information and sources was a new dimension in the council's work. A precedent for such activities had already been established in 1955, when the government of India asked for council advisors to make recommendations on their initiation of a national family planning program. Subsequent calls for assistance came from Pakistan (1959), which sought and received long-term assistance for its family planning program, from Taiwan (1961), South Korea (1962), Turkey (1963), Kenya (1965), Honduras (1965), and elsewhere.

As part of the effort to make family planning services and assistance more readily available around the world, the council initiated during the 1960s the International Postpartum Program to provide family planning services in the context of obstetrical care provided by hospitals in different regions of the world: by the end of 1966 this program included 26 hospitals in 14 countries. Funding from the U.S. Agency for International Development beginning in 1968 permitted expansion to additional hospitals in other countries. By 1974, 138 institutes in 21 countries had participated in the program; over 1.14 million women received family planning services through its efforts.

Recognizing that few women in the developing world give birth in hospitals, the council in 1971 embarked on a maternal and child health-family planning program with the goal of determining the international applicability of a model for providing these services to rural women. Projects were eventually developed in four countries, but implementation required radical modifications in the original concept, not only because of logistical problems but also because the applicability of a single model to a variety of settings was found to be limited.

The growing momentum of government interest in family planning was spurred by the emergence during the 1960s of effective new methods of contraception. Here, too, the council played a major role in the development, clinical testing, statistical evaluation, establishment of local manufacture, and distribution of modern forms of the intrauterine device, or IUD. A Cooperative Statistical Program undertaken by the National Committee on Maternal Health with council funding monitored use of the method by over thirty thousand women. A significant advance was council development (1967-1968) of the Copper T IUD, which provided improved contraceptive action that was to be reconfirmed in extensive clinical trials in the years ahead.

Also in the 1960s, the council developed a systematic and intensive in-house program of demographic research and evaluation to help meet the pressing need for better baseline demographic data and projections, as well as better methods for measuring the impact of family planning programs.

Sponsorship of international conferences was undertaken to stimulate exchange among specialists. Notably the council cosponsored with the Ford Foundation the first International Conference on Family Planning Programs in Geneva, August, 1965, with nearly two hundred participants from thirty-six countries representing a broad range of professional disciplines. In similar fashion, in 1981 the council, the United Nations Fund for Population Activities, and the International Planned Parenthood Federation are cosponsoring the International Conference on Family Planning in the 1980s.

A further broadening of the council's mission in the 1960s was in the area of publications and information. *Studies in Family Planning* was introduced in 1963 as a means to inform professionals in the field of recent and current scientific studies of efforts to implement family planning. In the late 1960s the council formalized its publications and information program, issuing *Studies in Family Planning* on a regular basis and creating other specialized periodicals, along with books and occasional papers. In 1975, the *Population and Development Review* was introduced as a quarterly journal seeking to advance knowledge of the interrelationships between population and socioeconomic development and related issues of public policy.

In the early 1970s, the council broadened the focus of its activities in the social sciences, with particular attention to policy issues in such fields as economics, population education, ethics, law, political science, psychology, and sociology. In addition to staff research, the council provided grant assistance for work related to population policy. The focus of fieldwork began to shift away from the provision and development of demographic training at universities toward collaborative work in applied research, policy analysis, and development planning.

An increased emphasis on applied research was also occurring in the council's biomedical work, with a focus on development and testing of new contraceptives including subdermal contraceptive implants and vaginal rings and continued studies of IUDs. Basic research in biochemistry, electron microscopy, uterine physiology, and reproductive endocrinology was also undertaken. In late 1970 and early 1971, the council formed the International Committee for Contraception Research (ICCR) to provide a noncommercial, international mechanism for identifying, developing, and testing new contraceptive leads. As of 1980, under ICCR, consultant-investigators in seven countries—Austria, Brazil, Chile, Finland, India, Sweden, and the United States—were engaged in design and investigations conducted within the council's own laboratories.

A parallel committee in the social sciences was developed in 1972: the International Committee on Applied Research in Population, composed of program planners, administrators, and researchers from national family planning programs in developing countries was intended to provide a mechanism for identification and study of promising new leads for improved operation of family planning programs and rapid dissemination of research findings. As of 1980, ICARP-Asia and ICARP-Latin America functioned as autonomous organizations with logistical support from the council.

The year 1974 brought a major turning point for the field of population as a whole and for the Population Council as an organization. For the field, the politicization of population issues in the forum of the World Population Conference at Bucharest—in particular, the charge of some country delegates that family planning was being proffered to the exclusion of the more needed broader development assistance—coupled with the growing recognition of professionals in the field of the complexity of interrelationships between population and development and the limitations of family planning programs, triggered a broad-based reappraisal.

In this context, the Population Council found itself without a president and embarked on a search for a new president, rendered the more difficult because of uncertainties over what kind of leadership was needed at this juncture in the organization's life. Long a pioneer in the population field, the council now found itself in the position of being a relatively small organization in a field coming to be dominated by some of the very institutions the council had contributed to strengthening. Increasingly governments and international agencies were establishing their own population programs. Biomedical research into contraceptive technology was being undertaken by a number of groups in the United States and abroad. And funding problems, exacerbated by inflation, were constraining the council's capacity for fellowship and grant making.

The council's major achievements—among them, the Lippes loop, the Copper T, and the formation of ICCR in the biomedical field; assistance to family planning programs in the developing world, the postpartum program, and institutional capacity-building in the area of technical assistance; and policy-oriented research and refinements of techniques for demographic analysis; as well as the fellowship program and the publications program—were undisputed. Yet, even in some of these areas, the scope of council involvement was questioned in some quarters. In the postpartum program, the council role had perhaps been extended beyond that of catalyst and continued longer than necessary. In its reluctance to become involved in the issue of abortion and its heavy focus on the IUD as the principal contraceptive, the council appeared overly conservative. Likewise, the council promotion of KAP—knowledge, attitude, and practice of family planning—surveys was felt to have continued in the face of acknowledgment of their limited scientific validity.

On a broader level, there was questioning whether any organization in a field as complex as that of population should seek to cover such a broad range of activities, from biomedical research to policy research to technical assistance to grant making. Ultimately the question arose whether the council had completed its mission of establishing the legitimacy of the field and should now go out of existence.

After intensive consideration of these issues, the trustees of the council decided that the continuing saliency of population issues and the council's capacity for leadership more than justified continuation of the organization.

In 1976, under a new president, the council began the task of building on its past strengths and redefining its role in such a way as to maintain its historical position in the vanguard of the field. A new organizational structure was adopted, characterized principally by the creation of regional offices for Latin America and the Caribbean; South and East Asia; Sub-Saharan Africa; and West Asia and North Africa, with a high degree of autonomy in pursuit of programs of specific regional relevance. The composition of the board of trustees, wholly American for nineteen years and entirely male for thirteen years, was altered significantly: as of fall 1980, the eighteen board members included five individuals from developing countries and seven women. And sustained efforts were begun to internationalize and diversify sources of council funding.

In substantive areas, the broader focus initiated in the early 1970s was continued, with an even greater emphasis on policy issues. Greater attention was given in several areas to issues at the micro and intermediate levels rather than aggregative analyses: assessment of the roles and status of women in particular settings as factors in development and population change; attention to the user perspective on contraceptive methods and related safety issues; and analysis of fertility behavior in the context of the family and the local institutional setting took precedence over cross-cultural and cross-national surveys.

Council activities can be grouped in three broad areas: biomedical research; policy research; and region-specific programs. Grants, fellowships, and publications play a role in all three areas.

Biomedical research is undertaken in contraceptive development, reproductive physiology of the human male, and the safety and health effects of contraceptives. ICCR is the principal vehicle for the first category of research, and current research focuses on Norplant, a subdermal implant containing progestin, which prevents conception for one to seven years; an estrogen-containing vaginal contraceptive ring; a progestin-releasing IUD; several models of copper-releasing IUDs; and a pregnancy vaccine. Research into the physiology of the human male involves basic research to identify the mechanisms by which sperm develop, mature, and achieve fertilizing capacity. In the area of safety, work has been carried out on the effects of hormones from contraceptive pills and rings on hypertension and blood-clotting factors.

Policy studies involve multidisciplinary research in the social sciences, combining policy analysis and investigation of underlying empirical relationships in population-related policies. In the area of policy analysis, attention is centered on country-level analysis; population-related aspects of development planning; and fertility-modernization relationships. Among the underlying relationships that are the focus of investigation are the proximate determinants of fertility; fertility decision making; and migration and urbanization. The *Population and Development Review* and a working paper series are also elements in the policy studies program.

The regional autonomy that characterizes the council's field program represents an effort to reflect and be responsive to regional and individual country needs and priorities within the two broad areas of council activity: social science research on population; and birth planning research.

The regional program for Latin America and the Caribbean has two main emphases: first, social science research on population is concentrated on development policy issues and on the study of the household, especially family demography; within this perspective particular attention is given also to studies of women's roles and status. In the area of health and birth planning research, focus is on the evaluation of user-oriented programs; within this perspective health and safety issues, including acceptability and continuity in the use of modern contraceptives, receive special attention. Also, breastfeeding and the relationship between lactation and contraception is being studied through pilot projects in several countries of the region. Seminars and publications relating to these program objectives are regular activities in which the regional staff is engaged.

A major theme of the council's program in South and East Asia is the study of demographic impacts of development programs and projects and their implications for women and the identification of ways to incorporate these impacts into development planning. Activities include a regional program of research grants, workshops, and seminars and technical collaboration with planning agencies. Another major component consists of technical assistance to government agencies and research institutions responsible for design, management, and evaluation of birth planning programs.

The major focus of the council's program in Sub-Saharan Africa is strengthening African efforts to develop an adequate knowledge base and a cadre of trained people sensitive to population and development issues, who will in turn be able to propose relevant policies and implement them effectively. The council is involved in the development of the Population Studies and Research Center at the University of Nairobi, a socioeconomic and demographic unit at the Sahel Institute, and a program of short-term training for African women holding decision-making positions, for planners, and for others concerned about women's roles in African development. Another focus of the council's program is the study of infant and child mortality in Africa.

The council's program in the West Asia-North Africa region is focused on capacity-building to solve locally important issues in the areas of international worker migration, urbanization and population distribution, women's economic roles, and effective utilization of population information in national development planning. The program includes training and technical assistance to planning and statistical units, problem-focused study groups in cooperation with local institutions, and a series of regional working papers. Perhaps the most ambitious program is the Middle East Research Awards in Population and Development and an allied fellowship program, which the council administers on behalf of its three sponsors: the Ford Foundation, the International Development Research Center, and the council itself.

Council publications include two professional journals; *Studies in Family Planning*, issued ten times a year, and the *Population and Development Review*, issued quarterly; Fact Books on *Population and Family Planning Programs* and *Induced Abortion*; Public Issues Papers; and a variety of other materials related to individual projects. The council library contains over fifteen thousand volumes on population and development issues.

The headquarters of the council and its centers for biomedical research and the policy studies are located in New York City. A multidisciplinary staff in New York provides core support for international programs. Regional offices in Mexico City, Bangkok, and Cairo respond with a high degree of autonomy to local needs for population-related research and assistance. The council is international in the composition of its staff, which numbers 188, of whom 107 are professionals in the biomedical and social sciences, and in its governing board of trustees. The present chairperson of the board is Robert H. Ebert, and the chief executive officer, president, of the council is George Zeidenstein.

The council's budget approximates fifteen million dollars annually. The council relies for operating monies on a variety of donor organizations, among which are the Rockefeller Foundation, the Ford Foundation, the United Nations Fund for Population Activities, the U.S. Agency for International Development, the World Bank, the Canadian government, and private sources.

For further information, see *The Population Council; A Chronicle of the First Twenty-Five Years* (1978). See also Population Council *Annual Reports* (1977,1978, and 1979). Past papers of the Population Council, including outside evaluation, are on file at the Rockefeller Archive Center, Hillcrest, Pocantico Hills, North Tarrytown, New York 10591.

SUSAN ROBBINS

RAND CORPORATION (RAND). The nonprofit advisory corporation is one of the most striking phenomena of America's defense organization in the post-World War II era. The Rand Corporation is the best known of this family of novel organizations, few in number but influential, which have advised the Department of Defense and other government clients. In 1981 Rand enjoyed its thirty-fifth anniversary as an entity that performs, as stated in the letter contract of March 2, 1946, establishing Rand, "a program of study and research on the broad subject of intercontinental warfare other than surface with the object of recommending to the Army Air Force preferred techniques and instrumentalities for this purpose."

Over the years since its inception (first as a part of the Douglas Aircraft Company and then, in 1948, as an independent nonprofit corporation), Rand has evolved a research program on domestic policy issues as well as national security concerns and has advised state and local governments as well as nondefense clients within the federal government. Once the predominant focus of Rand's work, national security issues now constitute about half (51 percent) of Rand's research activities. Domestic issues, including health, transportation, housing, energy, the civilian space program, and others, comprise the remainder (49 percent). Rand's budget in 1979 amounted to $38.2 million (88 percent from the U.S. government, 2 percent from state and local governments, and 10 percent from foundations and other sources), and it employed eleven hundred scientists, engineers, and support personnel in its Santa Monica, California, and Washington, D.C., offices.

Rand pioneered in the immediate post-World War II period in the development of operations research techniques applied to military decisions and gained worldwide attention for its methodologies and analytical techniques. Rand's work was transformed in the 1950s from operations research—primarily a quantitative technique for assisting in decision making on "suboptimal" or precisely defined issues—into the broader techniques of systems analysis. Systems analysis reflects the application of numerous professional skills, including economists, social scientists, and engineers, as well as natural scientists and mathematicians, to broad strategic policies. This development of a strategic sense by Rand in the 1950s led to its prominent role in the debate over national security issues among the attentive public and within the inner councils of government policy making.

One of Rand's most notable studies during this period was the strategic basing study undertaken for the U.S. Air Force. In this study a team of Rand scientists led by Albert Wohlstetter analyzed the four major options for basing SAC bombers in the coming decade. The prevailing assumptions emphasized the basing of bombers overseas to permit rapid deployment in the event of sharpening tensions. The Rand team showed that SAC bombers, under the concept of forward basing, were vulnerable to enemy attack and proposed instead a less vulnerable system involving the use of U.S. bases, air refueling, and airborne alert. The concept of an invulnerable deterrent grew out of this and similar studies and exerted a strong influence on U.S. strategic doctrine for many years.

Among Rand's other accomplishments were background studies that led to the planning-programing-budgeting system (PPBS) that Secretary Mac-Namara introduced into the Department of Defense in 1961. Rand also conducted studies of military logistics, procurement policies, telecommunications, broad characteristics and feasibility of alternative weapons design, NATO integration, space contingency planning, and other important issues. Rand became the premier "think tank" and the exemplar of a whole new family of organizations: the nonprofit, private corporation, working full time in an advisory capacity through the device of an administrative contract from the sponsoring agency. Other organizations of this kind include the Institute for Defense Analyses (IDA), Center for Naval Analysis, Human Resources Research Organization, the Hudson Institute,* Aerospace, MITRE, and a number of other organizations working for national security agencies. Similar nonprofit organizations also sprang up later in the nondefense areas, but none achieved the success and esteem that Rand has enjoyed.

Rand achieved its peak of influence in the 1960s when many Rand alumni became prominent members of the Kennedy and Johnson administrations. The MacNamara "whiz kids" who managed the Pentagon included Charles Hitch (who became the defense comptroller), Alain Enthoven (who headed the defense systems analysis function), and Henry Rowen (who served in defense and later became a high Budget Bureau official). A 1961 Rand book by Charles Hitch and Roland McKean became the influential statement of Rand's analytic approach to defense issues and one of its most successful books.

Paradoxically, the rise of Rand alumni to influential positions in the government helped contribute to emerging problems that began to afflict the organization. Strains developed in Rand's traditionally good relationship with its major client, the U.S. Air Force, as Rand began to undertake assignments for and had easy access to higher policy levels within the Defense Department. The Air Force feared that its confidential advisory relationship with Rand was now greatly complicated and potentially compromised.

Administrative problems also mounted for Rand as it began to undertake work for more clients, including government agencies in the domestic policy field. A great strength of Rand in the first decade of its existence was its informality and the flexibility of its internal procedures. Rand had been greatly assisted by its ability to attract highly talented researchers who had been involved in the war effort. As the organization aged, and as it began to function in a more complicated external environment, internal administration became more difficult and consumed more energies. The central administrative staff grew in size; the coordination of activities and the management of a large number of individual projects were no longer simple or informal.

Rand has continued to rely on a combination of departmental organization along the lines of major professional skills—for example, physicists, economists, and systems engineers—grouped together in academic-style departments along with a task-oriented project management system superimposed upon the departments. Responsibility for individual projects thus cuts across departmental lines, and the project group becomes an important administrative unit in the management of large-scale studies.

Rand's internal organization and style of operation reflects in brief a combination of industrial, governmental, and academic patterns. Indeed, the function of linking the worlds of industry, government, and academe on issues of broad national importance is one of the historic roles that Rand and its sister organizations have played. It is important for the government to have a source of advice on the costs and capacities of advanced systems apart from the market sector, where firms have a direct stake in weapons procurement decision. Yet it is important for an analytic organization to tap the best thinking in the industrial sector on a broad range of options facing policy makers, and this can only be achieved through nonprofit status. Rand and organizations like it have also performed an important function in helping to create a wider attentive public on defense issues among the intellectual community. More enlightened debate has resulted on issues that were once the exclusive province of the professional military.

Rand encountered perhaps its most difficult period toward the end of the 1960s and in the early 1970s, when the Vietnam War stirred political passions. Rand became involved in the Pentagon Papers controversy when Daniel Ellsberg, while employed by Rand, used Rand facilities to make copies of classified documents for distribution to the news media. Security regulations at Rand were tightened in consequence. But a more serious result was that the military began to return to a more inward-looking style of decision making and relied less on civilian analysts and advisors working outside the framework of government. The analytic style of decision making was partly discredited as a result of its association in the public mind with the war, with body counts, and with oversimplified approaches generally to complex political problems.

For a time, the corporation created an offshoot institute in New York City for the study of urban problems, but this entity never became established on a solid footing and was quietly disbanded after achieving limited success in applying analytic techniques to the problems of fire fighting, solid waste disposal, and law enforcement.

Today, Rand remains a novel and highly successful organization, a source of valuable expertise on a wide range of important national problems. The functions that Rand performs, however, differ somewhat from its earlier role, and its style of operation has changed over the years. It has become less unique as a large number of organizations, both profit-making and nonprofit, have grown up in imitation of Rand to perform analytic services for the government via the administrative contract. The original Project Rand contract, which provided one umbrella agreement under which a great many individual projects could be carried out largely at Rand's own choosing, is now a much smaller part of the total range of Rand activities. Rand has become increasingly oriented to the competition for contracts from numerous government agencies, along with a host of management consulting firms, systems analytic organizations, and other firms.

The Rand Physics Department resigned in block at the end of the 1960s to form an independent consulting organization. As a result, Rand no longer performs work relating to the technical aspects of weapons systems design. Civilian sector issues, as noted previously, now constitute nearly half of Rand's entire research, with large research programs in the areas of energy and of health policy and smaller programs scattered across a number of other agencies. Rand has also become a degree-granting institution in the 1970s with the founding of a small graduate program in public policy analysis.

As Rand approaches its thirty-fifth anniversary, its role as an elite advisory organization for government clients seems assured, even though it has had to function in a more competitive environment and to expand its area of competence beyond the realm of national security. Rand is no longer unique in the functions it performs—as friendly outside critic, source of new ideas, policy analyst—but, as the pioneering organization of its kind, the Rand Corporation has made a lasting contribution to the nation.

For further information, see Bruce L. R. Smith, *The Rand Corporation* (1966), "The Future of the Not-For-Profit Corporation," *Public Interest* (Summer, 1967), and "The Non-Governmental Policy Analysis Organization," *Public Administration Review* (May-June, 1977). See also Paul Dickson, *Think Tanks* (1971); and Daniel Guttman and Barry Winter, *The Shadow Government* (1976).

BRUCE L. R. SMITH

RENAISSANCE SOCIETY OF AMERICA. Following World War I, study materials on the Renaissance flowed into American libraries. It was not until the 1930s, however, that the need developed for increased and broader studies of the period, which the mediaevalists had felt ten or twenty years earlier. Discussion as to such need at meetings of other learned societies, particularly the Modern Language Association of America* (MLA), led to a conference of interested scholars from varied disciplines, which was sponsored and financed by the American Council of Learned Societies* (ACLS). A resultant conference report submitted to the ACLS recommended the creation, within the ACLS, of a Committee on Renaissance Studies, which was subsequently organized in 1938. This committee engaged in various Renaissance studies and surveys of research, but its major accomplishment was the establishment of a number of regional conferences, which have been active to the present day.

Following a period of inactivity during World War II, the ACLS committee resumed its activities, and, in 1948, it was instrumental in establishing the quarterly publication *Renaissance News*. A change in ACLS policy, however, saw the committee terminated in 1952. Prior to its demise, however, the committee voted to set up a new, unaffiliated American Committee on Renaissance Studies (ACRS) to consider the future.

The subsequent meetings and conferences of this group ultimately led to the founding of the Renaissance Society of America in January, 1954, at Columbia University for the purpose, as stated in its constitution, of

the advancement of learning in the field of Renaissance studies, and especially the promotion of interchanges among the various fields of specialization, such as art, architecture, bibliography and the book arts, the classical and modern literature, history, music, medicine, law, philosophy, religion and theology, the sciences and any other field of learning which can deepen or broaden understanding of the Renaissance period.

The constitution also called special attention to the establishment of local and regional groups and to cooperation and affiliation with foreign and international bodies with mutual interests. In addition to adopting the constitution and electing officers, the Renaissance Society also voted to assume publication of *Renaissance News*, changed in 1967 to *Renaissance Quarterly*, a journal that has provided a medium for publication of articles, book reviews and notices, news and reports of the annual meeting of the council of the society and the meetings of its twenty-eight local and regional groups. Long articles were initially published by the society in its *Annual Studies in the Renaissance*; now, however, they are incorporated in the four issues of the *Quarterly*.

The council of the Renaissance Society holds an annual meeting at which representatives of the local and regional groups, elected representatives of various disciplines, other members, and interested individuals meet to discuss programs and policies for furthering scholarship in the Renaissance and to transact society business. The meeting is held in late winter and, in recent years, has been convened in various parts of the country and in conjunction with the annual conference of local or regional groups.

Membership in the Renaissance Society is open to all persons interested in Renaissance study. There are nine categories of membership, including institutional, and the present total membership is about three thousand.

The society elects the customary institutional officers; it conducts its business from an office, headed by an executive director, located in New York City.

For further information, see the following articles appearing in *Renaissance News:* Leicester Bradner, "Renaissance Scholarship in America" (Spring, 1954); and "Renaissance Society of America, an Account of the Executive Board" (Spring, 1954). See also information leaflets published intermittently by the Renaissance Society of America.

RESEARCH FOUNDATION OF ARMOUR INSTITUTE OF TECH-NOLOGY. See IIT Research Institute.

RESEARCH TRIANGLE INSTITUTE (RTI). RTI was created as a separately operated, not-for-profit, corporate entity by joint action of the University of North Carolina at Chapel Hill, Duke University in Durham, and North Carolina State University in Raleigh. Articles of incorporation were filed by the three schools on the last working day of December, 1958. Their action capped more than three years of planning and preparation that would, it was hoped, lead to the nurturing of a new level of economic activity in North Carolina. Impetus for the idea originated in the unlikely circumstance of three major universities being clustered in a geographic configuration that gives the Research Triangle its distinctive name.

The educators, scientists, and businessmen who sparked the Research Triangle's formative years foresaw the possibility that the three schools, with education and research as their products, could offer a key basic resource to attract the technology-based enterprises that were bypassing North Carolina. The state's nonfarm employment was concentrated in traditional industries such as furniture, textiles, and tobacco products. Income, investment, taxes, and the services they pay for lagged. The state was being denied a future of economic opportunity, stability, and growth. Most serious of all, perhaps, too many young men and women, especially those with college degrees, were leaving their native state to find careers elsewhere.

Once the universities were seen not as isolated institutions and athletic rivals but as a single community of shared educational and scientific purposes, characterized as much by unity as by separateness, they could also be seen as the initial link in an education-research-industry chain of economic growth similar to those so successfully demonstrated in the Boston area, Los Angeles, and the San Francisco peninsula. After a second resource had been identified, this one an all but empty fifty-five hundred-acre tract of real estate that was useful mostly for holding two counties together, the science center became a possibility.

The idea that industrial advance is often linked with centers of learning did not, of course, originate in North Carolina, but the state has capitalized on it with singular success. Unlike the situation in some other regions, development of the Research Triangle Park, centered near the three university cities, happened, and was made to happen, on purpose. In 1981 the thirty-five research-based enterprises in the Research Triangle Park employed 17,500 individuals, occupied brick-and-mortar facilities valued at $500 million and had a combined annual payroll of $375 million. In addition, several large manufacturing firms have located just outside the park's boundaries.

Luther B. Hodges, who was governor of North Carolina during the years in which Research Triangle Institute and the Research Triangle Park were established, enthusiastically lent them the full prestige of his office, although neither is a state-supported or state-related activity. After four years as U.S. Secretary of Commerce from 1961 to 1965, Hodges served until his death in 1974 as chairman of the Research Triangle Foundation. The foundation is a separate, nonprofit trusteeship, which promotes and develops the resources of the Research Triangle Park.

RTI is quite distinct from the foundation, performing research under contract with industry and government clients in disciplines ranging across the physical and social sciences. Its research approach and operations are generally similar to those of the older Stanford Research Institute, now SRI International,* and the Battelle Memorial Institute.* RTI is unique, however, in the circumstances of its creation, its purposes, and its corporate organization.

For RTI, its three founding universities are everything: initiators, incorporators, owners, governors, colleagues, partners, friends—the works. Without them the Research Triangle idea, including RTI, could not have been conceived, nor could it have become a reality. Without their close and spirited involvement, RTI and the Research Triangle Park that has grown up around it would not be the thriving enterprises they are. Without the university campuses located at the corners of a three-sided polygon, North Carolina's now famed Research Triangle Park would not even have a name.

According to Dr. George L. Simpson, RTI was the initial force and the unifying mechanism for all that was to follow. Simpson, who later became chancellor of the State University System of Georgia, was a University of North Carolina sociologist who took a three-year assignment from 1956 through 1958 as full-time director of the committee that was charged with the planning and persuasion that started RTI and the Research Triangle

Park along the path from a dream to the glittering realities they are today. When planning and persuasion had taken the committee as far as they could, the time came for another kind of action. This took the form of a whirlwind fund-raising effort during the fall of 1958. It brought $1.5 million (later $2 million) in contributions from corporate and private citizens in North Carolina to back up the committee's faith in its projections for the ultimate success of the Research Triangle idea. With pledges in hand, the committee was reconstituted as the Research Triangle Foundation, and RTI was brought into being as a wholly owned, self-supporting affiliate of the three universities. George R. Herbert, former executive associate director at Stanford Research Institute*, was named RTI president, a position he still holds, and a board of governors was selected.

RTI governance rests with a twenty-seven-member board, thirteen members appointed as representatives of the three campuses, thirteen elected from the business and professional communities, and the institute president.

A grant of $500,000 was provided from the funds contributed to the foundation to finance initial operating deficits until such time as RTI reached the break-even point, a goal Herbert estimated as requiring three years. The foundation subsequently donated 180 acres for RTI's campus. Local enthusiasm and commitment were self-evident as RTI opened for business. But if the institute was to fulfill its roles as namesake and symbol of the Research Triangle idea, and as focal point and trigger for economic development, it had first to demonstrate its viability as a participant in America's dynamic research industry.

During RTI's earliest years, the major concerns engaging the nation's research community included defense and weapons, nuclear physics, electronic communications, information systems, industrial processes, materials and the all-out space effort. The fledgling RTI lacked any recognition or established track record in these fields. The decision had already been made, however, that RTI, benefiting from its regional origins and its clear regional identity, should strive to serve national purposes by building programs and staff that reflected a broad spectrum of the sciences and by attracting a widely diversified sponsorship. Under these policies, RTI research managers initially concentrated on building strength in statistical research studies, natural products chemistry, solid state electronics, civil defense preparedness, and polymer science. Within three years, as Herbert had predicted, these programs achieved operating break-even on a 1962 contract volume of $1.3 million. RTI has been self-supporting ever since.

A brief list of highlight events from those early years would include

Hiring the first handful of professional staff members to carry out some small projects in statistics. RTI today has one of the world's foremost scientific groups for statistical methodology, sampling, and survey research.

A plant-screening contract with the National Cancer Institute was the first step in building RTI's national reputation in medicinal and environmental chemistry, drug metabolism, pharmacology, and the life sciences.

A $300,000 state legislature appropriation for laboratory equipment that was crucial to RTI growth.

An award from the Camille and Henry Dreyfus Foundation for a ten-year program of basic research in polymer physics and chemistry that provided many strengths now evident in RTI's large programs in the physical and analytical sciences.

The small beginnings of solid state engineering activity that has led to RTI's current emphases on environmental sensors, process engineering, and semiconductor research.

Civil defense preparedness research that formed the basis for what are now RTI's extensive capabilities in economics, computer applications, operations analysis, and the structure of social organizations.

Throughout the 1970s, a distinguishing mark of RTI operations was the degree of involvement in programs aimed at improvements in the quality of life. By the end of the decade, three-quarters of RTI research effort (thirty-three million dollars in annual revenue for 1979, a staff of 1,050) was directly concerned with medical care costs, health systems, and health resources; educational evaluation and the assessment of educational outcomes; crime, delinquency, and justice; alcohol and drug abuse; biochemistry and the synthesis of new drugs; antifertility compounds and drug delivery systems; environmental monitoring and measurement, pollution control strategies, and economic impacts; air navigation; biomedical engineering; and solar cells.

Shifting national priorities in the 1980s are not diminishing RTI's attention to societal concerns, but an increased emphasis, building on the skills and experience of more than twenty years, is being given to issues such as civil and military productivity, industrial innovation, technology applications, oceanography, energy conversion and distribution systems, teratology, toxicology, and microelectronics.

In the mid-1970s, the election of four research vice-presidents brought a new management structure into place, centralizing the planning, budgeting, program development, and research responsibilities that previously resided in separate, discipline-oriented units variously designated as laboratories and divisions. The research vice-presidents (for social sciences, statistics, chemistry, engineering) join the president and business vice-presidents in a management council, which sets policy and oversees corporate planning, capital allocations, and other issues of institute-wide concern.

The university relationships remain and will continue to be pervasive. They extend from board governance to consulting arrangements with faculty members, joint staff appointments, frequent seminars and lectures, patent management, and access to computation and library resources.

Nowhere are these mutual efforts more apparent than in collaborative research programs, which call for a portion of the work to be done within RTI and a portion at one or more of the universities. Examples abound in such varied endeavors as built-in-test techniques for complex electronic systems, marijuana dosage formulation, public health, controlled release of contraceptive drugs, epidemiology, mass spectrometry, sample surveys and biostatistics, nutrition, solar cell design and fabrication, radioimmunoassay and the very large Microelectronics Center of North Carolina, an enterprise announced in 1981.

RTI's basic mission, for which there is no end in sight, is to provide scientific research services of the highest quality to clients in industry and government. A key companion mission during the early years was for RTI to be the focal point of the Research Triangle idea, giving visible evidence of growth and activity in the Research Triangle Park by the addition of new staff, new buildings, and new programs and by its record of research accomplishment.

This growth and achievement, it was hoped, would supplement the universities and the area's other attractions as magnets to lengthen the roster of park occupants. It worked out that way to a greater degree than even the most optimistic could have foreseen.

For further information, see the now outdated history of RTI by Louis R. Wilson, *The Research Triangle of North Carolina* (1967); and the more recent thesis by Mary Virginia Currie Jones, "A Golden Triangle of Research" (1978). See also the autobiography, Luther H. Hodges, *Businessman in the Statehouse* (1962); and A. G. Ivey, *Luther H. Hodges, Practical Idealist* (1968).

The best and most recent periodical literature about the RTI, which also provides much historical information about it, includes "A Research Center Flourishes in North Carolina," New York *Times* (February 4, 1977); "RTI Is Giant After 18 Years," Raleigh *News and Observer* (February 6, 1977); "A Park That Reversed a Brain Drain," *Fortune* (July, 1977); and "Research Triangle Park Succeeds," *Science* (June 30, 1978).

C. X. LARRABEE

RESOURCES FOR THE FUTURE, INC. (RFF). Literally, of course, resources for the future is a national and worldwide social and political objective, and one of increasing public and personal attention. But for more than a quarter of a century it also has been a private nonprofit organization located in Washington, D.C. Established in October, 1952, with the cooperation of the Ford Foundation, its institutional purpose is to advance research and education in the development, conservation, and wise use of natural resources and in the improvement of the quality of the environment. Most of the organization's work is in the social sciences—primarily economics—and is broadly concerned with the relationships of people and the natural environment.

RFF traces a good deal of its institutional and intellectual heritage to the (U.S.) President's Materials Policy Commission of the early 1950s, established to evaluate the availability of natural resources for national needs. Its chairman was William S. Paley, chairman of the board of CBS and later chairman of RFF's board as well. The Paley Commission demonstrated that for the twenty-five-year scope of its study the absolute depletion of resources was highly unlikely and that in any case the elasticity of supply guarantees no sudden shift from plenty to exhaustion as long as additional costs are paid. This conclusion was reached at a time of serious doubts to the contrary occasioned by the resource demands of the Korean War, among other factors. Both in its scope and in the kind of thinking it represented, the Paley Commission was a new and important venture for the United States.

Indeed, it was so significant a departure from the ad hoc approaches that characterized resource planning and analysis at the time that several people, including a group of prominent conservationists, thought it a good idea to institutionalize on a continuing basis the kind of analysis represented by the commission's work. Largely because some of these people were from the Ford Foundation and therefore had money as well as foresight, a new organization, RFF, was created.

Over the years, RFF has adopted a steady, balanced, systematic view of the various resource and environmental crises that have paraded across the American scene. The staff has tried, through disciplined research, to understand the factors involved and the interrelationships among them, and they have valued objectivity, for most organizations concerned with these matters have been advocates of one position or another. RFF does not take institutional positions, although individual researchers are free to do so, as in a university.

This does not mean that RFF has been uninterested in policy and action; rather, it means that it has sought to make its primary contribution by defining issues, analyzing the factors involved, appraising alternative policies in terms of the objectives and standards they seek to achieve, examining the feasibility of other objectives altogether, and reporting its conclusions in a straightforward and timely way. There is a place for advocacy study, but RFF has not conceived that as a basic role.

RFF's strategy in choosing research projects has been along two lines. First is the broad and systematic examination of resource and environmental trends and problems. Thus, the staff tries to keep under more or less continuous surveillance such subjects as energy supplies, environmental pollution, land use and management, and water resources. Second, particular problems are selected for study that are thought to be critical, in the sense that, without solution, progress of a more general kind would be held up. The first, more comprehensive research has embraced theoretical, statistical, historical, and methodological work. The second has included applied analysis, case studies, policy background reports, and collections of professional papers on particular subjects. Here are a few past and present examples of what RFF does and why.

Early in its existence, RFF decided to mount a major effort designed to throw light on resource adequacy for future economic growth in the United States, in part because the federal government at that time did not engage in this kind of work. It was felt that such "forward-looking" studies ought to be performed outside of government to avoid any impression that the projections might have a governmental "intent of implementation" behind them. Times have changed, and now, of course, such projects are highly respectable undertakings. In any event, the book that resulted, *Resources in America's Future* (1963), has been among RFF's best sellers. It is now looked upon as the first comprehensive attempt to "model" the U.S. economy, even though that term had not yet come into vogue at the time.

In RFF's early years, data collection and interpretation played a large part. One such compilation, *Trends in Natural Resource Commodities,* came up with findings that were sufficiently intriguing to suggest that a major theoretical research project be mounted to review the past impact of resource depletion and try to draw some conclusions regarding the future. Again, this was a project that was undertaken not only because of staff expertise and interest but also because it was unlikely that anyone else would do it. The book that resulted, Barnett's and Morse's *Scarcity and Growth* (1963), has been a milestone in the theory of scarcity. It has had its share of detractors as well as admirers, but its surest tribute has been that it is impossible to ignore. The point most often raised is that, until the terminal point of its statistics, the central finding—that resource depletion has not been a factor slowing down growth but has been successfully offset by technology—stands up well, but that beginning in the early 1960s things began to change. That is certainly possible, but it is too soon to render a clear verdict.

RFF also had much to do with shaping economic theory in the area of environmental quality. Traditional economic theory slighted the problems of external costs, or externalities, relating to use of environmental resources. Externalities such as air and water pollution were considered to be aberrations of economic systems rather than normal situations in complex, urban-industrial societies (and even in basically agricultural societies under the impetus of rapidly expanding populations). Once the universality of the pollution problem became clear, it was necessary to modify traditional theory accordingly, and this work was undertaken in RFF's environmental quality program. The various outputs from this area of research have had a major impact on economic thinking and writing and have stimulated substantial efforts throughout the United States and abroad.

A major recent project had as its objective the provision of usable analyses through interdisciplinary research on all feasible energy systems, including solar and geothermal as well as fossil and nuclear, giving full consideration to technological, economic, and environmental factors, including the impact on human health and safety. A distinguishing aspect of the project was its explicit recognition that the future probably will not resemble the past. Accordingly, it evaluated realistic conservation possibilities and examined the implications of differing rates and patterns of future energy consumption, as well as the supply options. And its final report—a 555-page book, *Energy in America's Future: The Choices Before Us* (1979)—emphasized techniques and institutional arrangements for achieving preferred strategies. RFF has no certain answers, but it is hoped that this book will narrow the chances for error in the energy area.

Pointed questions about conservation started almost from the moment that OPEC rang down the curtain on the era of cheap energy: Why do Americans use so much energy? Why do they apparently "waste" so much? Why is per capita energy consumption in several advanced industrial economies, whose per capita real incomes approximate U.S. levels, so much lower than in the United States? Accordingly, an RFF study was begun to mobilize data and information that illuminate this issue; to analyze both economic (e.g., relative prices) and noneconomic (e.g., population density) factors that contribute to energy/output variability; and to conjecture about applicability of the findings to the U.S. scene. The result was *How Industrial Societies Use Energy* (1977). The authors identified areas in which the United States could emulate other nations, but they also found that many of the differences in energy use were due to things such as geography, housing stock, and industrial structure.

RFF is taking an objective look at environmental policies, to assess their performance in light of the social and human resources that have been and will be expanded in their behalf. The focus is on the entire policy-making process, from the initial perception of the problems, through the associated legislative, administrative, and legal phases, to the final impact on the environment.

Other projects under way or planned include research on forest economics and policy; an examination of resource and environmental issues in U.S. agriculture; a cooperative agreement with the U.S. Agency for International Development to study energy supply and demand problems in developing countries; and a program to examine how society might strike a balance between the production of goods and services and the environmental and health risks often associated with the processes of production.

As has been stated, original funding for RFF was provided by the Ford Foundation and, through the years, it appropriated some $48 million in support of RFF; ranging from $3.4 million in 1954 to $12 million in 1975. By that year, however, Ford Foundation officials were urging RFF to seek a broader base of support. Although RFF already had been receiving support from the Rockefeller Foundation and the Andrew W. Mellon Foundation, among other grants and contracts arranged with private and public agencies, the need to establish a capital reserve not dependent upon outside sources, was underscored. In 1979, therefore, RFF completed its first fund-raising drive, which, based on a challenge grant from the Ford Foundation, succeeded in establishing such a $22 million reserve fund. The income from the fund will cover about a third of the RFF annual budget.

Administratively, the RFF research staff of about sixty persons operates under the aegis of a twenty-one member board of directors. The first president, the chief executive officer, was Reuben G. Gustavson. He was succeeded by Joseph L. Fisher (1959-1974), Charles J. Hitch (1975-1979), and Emery N. Castle (1979 to the present).

Housed initially in a Nineteenth Street office building in Washington, D.C., RFF moved to quarters in the Brookings Institution* building on Massachusetts Avenue in 1960, and thence to the Brookings annex next door in 1963, where it is presently located.

For further information, see RFF *Annual Reports* (1954 to date). For a history of RFF, see *Resources for the Future—The First Twenty-Five Years 1952-1977* (1977), which includes an analysis of its research programs.

KENT A. PRICE

ROBERT BROOKINGS GRADUATE SCHOOL OF ECONOMICS AND GOVERNMENT. See Brookings Institution.

ROBERT MAYNARD HUTCHINS CENTER FOR THE STUDY OF DEMOCRATIC INSTITUTIONS. Now affiliated with the Santa Barbara campus of the University of California, the Hutchins Center is an independent intellectual center dedicated to clarifying basic issues confronting democratic society.

The center has roots in the Fund for the Republic, established by the Ford Foundation in 1957, to "advance understanding of civil liberties and civil rights." In 1959, the directors of the fund created the Center for the Study of Democratic Institutions to "clarify the basic issues confronting democratic society." From the beginning, the center was the product of the vision of Robert Maynard Hutchins, former dean of the Yale Law School and president of the University of Chicago, who presided over the center until his death in 1977.

In 1959, the center was moved from New York City to Santa Barbara, California. There Robert Hutchins assembled many of the most influential leaders of the age to examine the nature and future of democratic institutions in a period of profound social adjustment and cultural change.

The focus of the undertaking was broadened in the 1960s. The center began to study not only labor unions but the quality of working life; not only churches but the inner spiritual quest; not only schools but the learning process itself. At the same time, the work agenda was expanded to include not only the concerns of this nation but urgent international issues as well. The center initiated conferences and convocations in New York, Washington, D.C., and Los Angeles, Malta, and Geneva on such topics as law of the sea and illegal immigration, exercising an ability to anticipate problems as well as opportunities facing humankind.

In June, 1979, the center became affiliated with the University of California and was renamed to honor its founder. The new Hutchins Center is now located on the Santa Barbara campus of the university, where, remaining politically and financially independent, it reestablished its program with access to the vast resources of the University of California system.

The various segments of the center's work have been guided by one fundamental purpose; to clarify the basic issues confronting democratic society. That task, like the simple exercise of voting, entails continuous responsibility. For although society changes faster than ideas are constructed to comprehend change, the threats to society's democratic foundations persist. The work of clarifying the basic issues will never be superseded or accomplished once and for all.

Interdisciplinary dialogue, the heart of the center's program, stimulates searching criticism that refines the content and expression of the various positions that can be taken on important public issues. The purpose of the dialogue as observed, is to "show what the positions are and what the consequences of taking one or another are likely to be." The dialogue "tries to bring the issues into focus so that they may be clearly seen and intelligently debated." Participants include academics, representatives of the professions, writers, teachers, government officials, public policy makers, business-persons, members of the clergy, and private citizens—a veritable cross section of American intellectual life. Participants are urged not to seek shelter or safe harbor within their own special areas of expertise but to work instead to find a common language of communication, linking the sciences and the humanities together with public issues.

The center also sponsors conferences and convocations, convenes working groups, stimulates research projects, maintains an audiotape program, and offers a range of publications. The *Center Magazine* is sent to more than twenty-five thousand members in the United States and overseas. The tapes are utilized by radio stations, in classroom seminars, for discussion groups, and for individual listening. The intention throughout is to widen the circles of intelligent thought and discussion.

Reorganization in 1979-1980 provided the occasion for extensive rejuvenation of the center's program and purpose. It is planned that the dialogue session remain the core of center work. The conferences will continue and national convocations are being planned. The *Center Magazine* will serve as the primary and most regular means of disseminating information. Occasional papers on selected topics, together with additional regular publications, are presently being prepared. Involvement in public policy and humanistic concerns will be revitalized and balanced by fresh interest in the sciences and the impact of contemporary scientific advances. Also, a new fellowship program is planned for the immediate future. Finally, a series of research projects involving the center will be undertaken. Among subjects to be studied and addressed are energy systems and the energy crisis; ethnic polarities and national unity; the scientific community and social responsibility; the vitality of urban life; and the continuing quest for world peace.

The governing board of directors of the center, together with its officers and present director, Walter H. Capps, have summarized their views of the purpose and the future of the center in the following statement in a 1980 center information pamphlet:

While the Center expands its activities to meet the challenges of the future, the fundamental purposes established in 1957 and rededicated in 1959 and 1969 remain firm. We are committed to an examination of *Democracy* within a framework that is intellectually resilient and free of outside influence and coercion. In an age of fragmentation, one-issue politics, and increasingly narrow fields of expertise, the Center fights to maintain a common language and a broad perspective in the public dialogue. With respect for its tradition, and the daring to strike out into the untouched and the controversial, the work of the Center will continue to stand as a prime safeguard against diminishment of individual liberty, human rights, and personal freedoms.

There is no detailed history of the center, although a great deal has been written, pro and con, about it and its founder, Robert Maynard Hutchins. The foregoing account is primarily based upon an information pamphlet published by the center in 1980.

For further information, see a recent history of the Fund for the Republic and the center by Frank K. Kelly, *Court of Reason* (1981) and an information pamphlet published by the center in 1980. See also a recent account, much of it devoted to the history of the center, appearing in the Santa Barbara *News and Review* (September 20-27, 1979) and a prescriptive commentary on the center by Robert M. Hutchins, "The Mind Is Its Own Place," *Center Magazine* (May-June, 1968).

_S_

SALK INSTITUTE FOR BIOLOGICAL STUDIES. Flushed with the success of their 1955 introduction of poliomyelitis vaccine, Jonas E. Salk, Basil O'Connor, and the March of Dimes turned to another collaboration between science and philanthropy, the establishment in 1961 of the Salk Institute for Biological Studies.

With Salk as founding director, institute scientists began doing research in temporary buildings at 10010 North Torrey Pines Road in La Jolla, California, in 1963. At that site, in the same year, workmen started building the principal structure, which was put into service in 1965. Expenditures by the National Foundation/March of Dimes for construction and furnishing amounted to $20 million. San Diego donated the twenty-seven-acre site, as approved by the people of the city in a referendum. The institute's annual budget, $5 million by 1972, had grown to $18.5 million in 1980. About two-thirds of that amount consisted of core funding and grants to individual scientists at the institute from federal agencies, the remainder coming from corporations, foundations, voluntary health agencies, and individual donors.

In the three-year period 1978-1980, some of the principal grantors were the National Institute of Neurological and Communicative Disorders, National Cancer Institute, National Institute of Child Health, National Institute of General Medical Sciences, and National Institute of Arthritis, Metabolism, and Digestive Diseases. Others have included the National Science Foundation, American Cancer Society, National Multiple Sclerosis Society, National Institute on Alcohol Abuse and Alcoholism, National Institute of Allergy and Infectious Diseases, Environmental Protection Agency, National Aeronautics and Space Administration, and Epilepsy Foundation.

Although funding from the original benefactor, now renamed the March of Dimes Birth Defect Foundation, is not dominant as a percentage of the total budget, the March of Dimes remains parental in that it provides core funding annually for the institute's general operating expenses as well as making individual grants.

The Salk Institute is an independent institution, governed by its board of trustees and advised and assisted by its national council, international council, and a small group of nonresident fellows. The chief executive officer executive officer and president of the institute is Frederic de Hoffmann. Samuel B. Stuart serves as chairman of the board of trustees. Salk is no longer concerned with administration of the institute and is director of one of its eighteen laboratories, where he pursues his current research interests in the field of autoimmunity.

In a word, the focus of the institute's work is the cell. In broader terms, its chief research area is cellular and molecular biology, with neurobiology and cancer being prominent. Alcoholism, human behavioral disorders, and heart disease loom large as potential targets of applications that are developed.

Neurobiology has come to be the predominant area of research at the institute because of a confluence of three developments. First, institute researchers set out to study the brain because of their interest in behavior. Second, the designation of the institute as a Federal Alcohol Research Center brought still another reason for emphasis on the brain. Finally, and perhaps of most importance, discoveries at the institute and elsewhere have lately led to the recognition that the brain is far more responsible than previously realized for hormonal and nervous regulation of other organs, thus holding a key to the development of therapy for diseases seated in virtually all organs and systems within the body.

This emphasis on neurobiology is evident in the accomplishments that most distinguish the institute's work thus far. Its scientists have discovered and synthesized the brain hormones somatostatin and beta-endorphin as well as others. They have demonstrated that antidepressant drugs change the way nerve cells respond to the norepinephrine system. They have shown myasthenia gravis to be an autoimmune disease. In other fields, Salk scientists have identified the specific target of the Rous sarcoma virus (RSV). They have achieved notable progress in their work on lipid molecules in breast cancer research. These are among the most vivid successes of the Salk Institute's first twenty years.

In the field of neurobiology and behavior, some of the specific objects of research at the Salk Institute are the brain's role in regulating fertility, metabolic processes involved in diabetes, and the body's reaction to stress; how the nervous system grows and develops and how mental retardation and some behavioral disorders result from maldevelopment; the specialization of the brain's two halves; the nature of language; the chemical basis of behavior; and brain cell changes wrought by toxic chemicals.

Cellular and molecular biology research includes investigations of cellular communication; the microbe's ability to control its genes; immunity and autoimmunity; and how life began.

Alcohol research seeks knowledge of alcohol's effects on the unborn; alcohol-caused liver damage; hormonal changes resulting from alcohol abuse; and chemical brain receptors for the breakdown products of alcohol.

How cancer starts, the cellular basis of breast cancer, and the control of cell growth are three of the focal points of cancer research at the institute.

Of approximately four hundred publications in 1979, over one-fourth appeared in *Society for Neuroscience Abstracts* (twenty), *Proceedings, National Academy of Sciences USA* (nineteen), *Brain Research* (fourteen), *Journal of Virology* (fourteen), *Nature* (thirteen), *Journal of Molecular Evolution* (nine), *Journal of Biological Chemistry* (eight), and *Endocrinology* (eight), the eight journals in which institute scientists most frequently published. Ten articles were published in *Cell, Cellular Immunology*, and *Journal of Cellular Physiology*.

As its research results gradually unfold and are slowly recognized and evaluated, the institute's reputation in society at large, and even in the scientific community, is more readily assayed by the presence on its staff of highly regarded scientists, including four Nobel laureates, an impressive number by any measure.

Francis Crick won a Nobel Prize in 1962 for his discovery, with James Watson, of the double helix structure of deoxyribonucleic acid (DNA). He was among the first nonresident fellows of the institute, and he began working in residence there in 1976. Long known for his work in advancing the frontiers of the field of molecular biology, Crick has recently turned his attention to how the brain comes to fulfill its ultimate development on the basis of seemingly scant original molecular information. His research into the functional organization of the human brain has the potential of becoming dominant among Crick's fields of inquiry.

A founding fellow of the Salk Institute, Robert Holley won a Nobel Prize in 1968 for his research results with transfer ribose nucleic acid (t-RNA), a molecule which figures in the synthesis of protein from the blueprint of the DNA molecule. Holley's work in the institute's Molecular Biology Laboratory is concerned with discovering the precise chemical nature of the change of a normal cell into a malignant cell. The ultimate, yet distant target of the work of Holley and his colleagues is to identify drugs that can reverse the process and restore normal growth control in the cancer cell.

Renato Dulbecco, a founding fellow, shared the 1975 Nobel Prize in Physiology or Medicine with David Baltimore and Howard M. Temin, for discoveries concerning the interaction between tumor viruses and the genetic material of the cell, that is, that certain viruses can cause varieties of cancer. Much of the work was done while Dulbecco was in residence at the institute during the period 1963-1972. He returned to a professorship at the institute in 1977, and currently the cellular and chemical aspects of breast cancer are subjects of his research.

In 1977 Roger Guillemin was awarded a Nobel Prize for his twenty years of work on brain hormones. He had been a resident fellow at the institute since 1970. Prior to 1970, Guillemin and his team had isolated, purified, and synthesized thyrotropin releasing factor (TRF). Institute researchers have subsequently achieved synthesis of additional brain hormones. Guillemin's work at present is concerned with future elaboration of the role of such brain hormones in the regulation of the chemistry of the brain itself and of other organs.

These Nobel laureates are among the 150 scientists (Ph.D.s and M.D.s) on the staff of 450 persons at the institute. Virtually all its research is done in the laboratories on Torrey Pines Road by resident scientists, postdoctoral fellows, and graduate students from area universities.

The eighteen semiautonomous laboratories at the institute can be grouped under four rubrics:

Neurosciences. Arthur Vining Davis Center for Behavioral Neurobiology, Language and Cognitive Studies Laboratory, Neurobiology Laboratory, Neuroendocrinology Laboratory, Neuropsychology Laboratory, Peptide Biology Laboratory, Receptor Biology Laboratory, and Weingart Laboratory for Developmental Neurobiology.

Growth Control and Cancer. Cancer Biology Laboratory, Cell Biology Laboratory, Mammary Differentiation and Breast Cancer Laboratory, Molecular Biology Laboratory, and Tumor Virology Laboratory.

Immunology Regulation and Development. Autoimmune and Neoplastic Diseases Laboratory, Developmental Biology Laboratory, and Regulatory Biology Laboratory.

Structure and Function of Biological Systems. Chemical Evolution Laboratory and Kieckhefer Center for Molecular Biology.

It is no more than a coincidence that there is one laboratory for each of the eighteen years that have elapsed since research commenced at the institute in 1963. Eighteen years is only a short span in the life of an entity such as the Salk Institute. Although notable results have already been achieved, this "cloistered garden" of Salk's phrase essentially evinces the characteristics of youth. Even physically, there is yet undeveloped space within the "place of encounter" designed by Louis Kahn. The scientific staff is growing in caliber and size, funding is increasing, and, with its emphasis on basic research, the institute is laying groundwork for medical developments in future years.

There is no detailed, general history of the Salk Institute. For further information, see the following articles: Esther McCoy, "Dr. Salk Talks About His Institute," *Architectural Forum* (December, 1967); "The Salk Institute," *Journal of Practical Nursing* (October, 1968); "The Mind of Louis Kahn," *Architectural Forum* (July-August, 1972); Gene Bylinsky, "The Intrepid Scientists of the Salk Institute," *Fortune* (October, 1972); and Nicholas Wade, "Salk Institute: Elitist Pursuit of Biology with a Conscience," *Science* (November, 1972). See also the *Salk Institute Newsletter* (1971 to date).

LESLIE CAINE CAMPBELL

SLOAN-KETTERING INSTITUTE FOR CANCER RESEARCH. See Memorial Sloan-Kettering Cancer Center.

SMITHSONIAN INSTITUTION. The Smithsonian Institution is an independent federal establishment, supported by both federal appropriations and private trust funds and bequests. Under its organic act it is controlled by a body actually called the "establishment," composed of the president, vice-president, and cabinet. In practice, however, oversight has always been instructed to the institution's board of regents, a body composed of the vice-president, chief justice (its chancellor), three members each from the House of Representatives and the Senate, and nine citizen members—two residents of the District of Columbia and seven residents of states— all chosen by joint resolution of Congress. A secretary, elected by the regents and serving at their pleasure, directs the institution's operations and carries out its policies.

In the popular mind the Smithsonian is identified with museums. The institution's umbrella covers eleven of them: the National Museum of Natural History; the National Museum of American History; the National Air and Space Museum; the Hirshhorn Museum and Sculpture Garden; the Freer Gallery of Oriental Art; the Museum of African Art; the National Museum of American Art; the National Portrait Gallery; the Anacostia Neighborhood Museum; the Renwick Gallery; and the Cooper-Hewitt Museum. These galleries combine public exhibits and research by their staffs in appropriate subject areas. In addition the Smithsonian includes other bureaus that are largely or solely dedicated to research. They include the Chesapeake Bay Center for Environmental Studies; the National Zoological Park; the Radiation Biology Laboratory; the Smithsonian Astrophysical Observatory; the Smithsonian Tropical Research Institute, and the Archives of American Art. Finally, there are numerous other offices that support aspects of the institution's life. These include a bureau-level office overseeing museum programs, an office for membership and development (producer of the highly regarded *Smithsonian* magazine), and other offices too numerous to list. Moreover, the Smithsonian is affiliated with the National Gallery of Art, the John F. Kennedy Center for the Performing Arts, and the Woodrow Wilson International Center for Scholars, all operating under independent boards of trustees. Most of the bureaus are located in the vicinity of Washington, D.C., but a number are to be found elsewhere. The Cooper-Hewitt Museum is in New York City; the Astrophysical Observatory, in Cambridge, Massachusetts; the Smithsonian Tropical Research Institute, in Panama. At present the Smithsonian's collections, spread among all its bureaus, number more than seventy-five million items, of which scarcely 5 percent are on exhibit at one time.

Thus, it appears that the Smithsonian is a shelter to widely divergent interests. But how did it become what it is today? To understand its growth and development we must turn to an obscure Englishman, James Smithson, who died in Genoa, Italy, in 1829. Smithson was a natural son of Hugh Percy, Duke of Northumberland. A graduate of Pembroke College, Oxford, he spent most of his life traveling in Europe. He was regarded as an amateur of the sciences, particularly mineralogy and chemistry. Smithson's will made the United States his reversionary legatee for the purpose of "found[ing] at Washington an institution for the increase and diffusion of knowledge among men" from the proceeds of his bequest, amounting to $515,169.

Andrew Jackson announced the legacy to Congress, which promptly began sixteen years of arguing over the gift. The initial dispute lay between those who regarded the gift as an example of British condescension too demeaning for a sovereign state to receive and those who, happy to accept the gift, differed over its proper use. Advocates of a spartan and republican renunciation soon lost; but the contest over how best to use the gift continued for many years. The testator had left no clear guidance about use of his gift, and the issue soon became whether to support pure or practical learning. Supporters of the former proposed creating a library or university. Partisans of the latter view supported schemes for teacher training, practical agronomy, and other interests typical of the day-to-day needs of a young nation.

Finally, in 1846, Congress approved an organic act that sought to balance the competing claims by creating an institution committed to rather general goals. This shifted the controversy to the Smithsonian's board of regents, its supervising body, when it came to select a secretary to direct the institution's operations. The board chose Joseph Henry as the Smithsonian's first secretary.

Joseph Henry was a distinguished theoretical scientist and one of the most noted American physicists of the nineteenth century. He came to the Smithsonian from the presidency of the College of New Jersey (now Princeton), and he had devoted much thought to just how one might actually increase human knowledge. Henry was not blind to the importance of diffusing knowledge and supported a program of publications and exchanges to that end, as the institution still does. However, he gave first attention to fostering original research. Henry appreciated the value of libraries and museums; but he was anxious that the Smithsonian's resources not be diverted from the search for "new" knowledge. It seemed to him that few organizations sponsored research, whereas comparatively many were inclined to support libraries and museums. Even at its founding the Smithsonian's resources were not great, and they were to shrink steadily in comparison with other bodies once nineteenth-century philanthropy was well established. Ironic as it now seems, Joseph Henry opposed the accumulation of museum collections throughout his tenure.

Spencer F. Baird, who served as secretary from 1878 to 1887, had a different vision. A student of natural history rather than the physical sciences,

Baird was anxious to create a national museum. Himself an indefatigable collector, Baird supported others' efforts as well. This he did circumspectly during his years as assistant to Joseph Henry. Even after he succeeded Henry, the resources available to him were never very great. However, Baird was a man of vast energy and personal charm. Mixing these talents with such resources as he could assemble, Baird cultivated amateur and professional collectors throughout the nation. He used contacts with military officers to tap the resources of the expanding West. At other times he might give or loan a few instruments; might perform a small patronage favor through his highly placed Washington friends; or might simply arrange for use of government rations on the frontier. By all these means Baird built up a very great natural history collection—the real basis for our present national collections. It is important to realize that Baird was not merely a collector. His vision was of a great national museum that would hold and care for specimens from which scholars could work to produce new knowledge. The museum as a teaching entity was Baird's goal. In his lifetime and for long afterward there were not the means to do all that he hoped for. Staff, funds, and space were woefully inadequate. Yet his was a beginning on which later generations could build.

The Smithsonian took quite a different turn when Samuel P. Langley succeeded Baird, serving from 1887 to 1906. Langley was an astronomer, pioneering astrophysicist, and investigator of solar radiation. He began programs in those fields which the Smithsonian continues today. Langley was also a student of heavier-than-air flight. In all these fields he and the institution made substantial contributions. In addition, the Smithsonian began its zoo, the National Zoological Park, still one of only a few zoos devoted to research, although it is designed for public instruction as well.

Strange as it seems today, when the Smithsonian is so deeply committed to the arts, the institution long neglected the field almost entirely. The organic act of 1846 expressly authorized an art gallery, but for many years the institution contented itself with copies of a few masterpieces of sculpture and art. Finally, in 1906, the Smithsonian accepted two gifts that established its role in the arts. One, by Harriet Lane Johnston, formed the nucleus of the present National Museum of American Art. The second, from Charles Lang Freer, created the Freer Gallery of Oriental Art, a leading American center for the study of that discipline.

Charles Doolittle Walcott, director of the U.S. Geological Survey, succeeded Langley in 1907, and served until his death in 1927. Walcott was a distinguished authority on Cambrian geology and paleontology. Fittingly enough, it was during his tenure that the present building of the National Museum of Natural History was occupied—chiefly as the new home of the institution's burgeoning natural history collections. Although the Smithsonian remained committed to its scientific pursuits, it was much drawn into the affairs of the larger governmental and scientific community then emerging in Washington. Walcott served on the National Advisory Committee on Aeronautics (now NASA) and on the board of the Carnegie Institution of Washington,* as well as other government and private bodies. He also began efforts to improve the institution's finances. From Smithson's day to Walcott's the Smithsonian had received only a few bequests, mostly small ones. Walcott saw that more private support was needed and began a campaign to raise funds, hoping to strengthen and expand institutional programs. Unhappily his death, followed closely by the Depression, cut short these efforts.

Charles G. Abbot, an astronomer, succeeded Walcott in 1928 and served until 1944. To him fell the difficult task of guiding the Smithsonian through the Depression and most of World War II. These were largely years of retrenchment, and the hopes of the 1920s were necessarily deferred. Still, the institution helped to found the Institute for Research in Tropical America, which was later to become one of its bureaus as the Smithsonian Tropical Research Institute. During this period, too, the Smithsonian began its affiliation with the great new National Gallery of Art, a gift to the nation from Andrew Mellon.

From 1944 to 1953 an ornithologist, Alexander Wetmore, led the institution. Despite the difficulties posed by World War II and, later, the Korean War, the institution began to recover its momentum. The National Air Museum (now the National Air and Space Museum) was created; and the institution's exhibits program began to undergo revision. Plans were laid for an addition to the Museum of Natural History and, more tentatively, for a new museum to house historical and technological collections.

Leonard Carmichael served as secretary from 1953 to 1964. During his administration the Smithsonian was able to secure funding for a substantial program of renovation and expansion. Staff levels were increased and exhibits modernized. In 1957 construction began on a new museum for history and technology (now the National Museum of American History), which gave collections in those fields a much needed separate home for the first time.

S. Dillon Ripley, the present secretary, took office in 1964. During his tenure the following bureau-level organizations have been added to the Smithsonian family: the National Portrait Gallery (1964); Renwick Gallery (1965); Anacostia Neighborhood Museum (1967); Cooper-Hewitt Museum of Decorative Arts and Design (1968); Joseph H. Hirshhorn Museum and Sculpture Garden (1968); Archives of American Art (1970); National Air and Space Museum (1976); and Museum of African Art (1980). The Woodrow Wilson International Center for Scholars (1968) has joined the National Gallery of Art (1936) and John F. Kennedy Center for the Performing Arts (1958) as an affiliated organization controlled by independent trustees.

It is a cliché of our age that information is now growing at a rate too great for mastery. Perhaps so. The Smithsonian, like all organizations devoted to learning, certainly finds itself taxed in many ways as it endeavors to keep abreast of expanding knowledge. That may be the institution's central problem. Nevertheless, the Smithsonian has chosen to keep to its founding purpose—the increase and diffusion of knowledge among men. Research continues across a wide spectrum of endeavor, from coral reefs to human social organization, from tropical ecosystems to the stars. The institution lives daily in intimate association with the past—the stability and perspective that history gives to human thought—and the future—the uncertain and perhaps unknowable edge at which human values and institutions are always tested. How does one increase and diffuse knowledge? That question points to an unending and never quite successful pursuit. Yet, to pursue is the Smithsonian choice.

For further information, see the *Annual Reports of the Smithsonian Institution,* 1847 to date. William J. Rhees produced a useful compilation of documents related to Smithsonian history, drawing on Smithsonian and non-Smithsonian sources, in *The Smithsonian Institution, Documents Relative to Its Origin and History, Volume I (1835-1887),* and *Volume II (1887-1889)* (1901). The first and most detailed history of the institution is George Brown Goode, ed., *The Smithsonian Institution, 1848-1896, The History of Its First Half Century* (1897). More recent works include a particularly appealing volume by Geoffrey T. Hellman, *The Smithsonian: Octopus on the Mall* (1966). Hellman's is perhaps the best introduction to the Smithsonian.

Because each man *was* the Smithsonian to a great degree during his tenure as secretary, readers may wish to consult biographies of Joseph Henry and Spencer Baird. The Henry biography is Thomas Coulson, *Joseph Henry, His Life and Work* (1950). Baird's, which is anecdotal and uncritical, is William Healey Dall, *Spencer Fullerton Baird, a Biography* (1915). Joseph Henry's career is in the process of exhaustive documentation in a multi-volume edition of his papers, edited by Nathan Reingold and published by the Smithsonian Institution Press.

Apart from these works, which introduce the institution and two of its most significant personalities, there is a great deal of periodical and other material devoted to particular aspects of the Smithsonian's activities.

JAMES A. STEED

SOCIAL SCIENCE RESEARCH COUNCIL (SSRC). The initial recommendation for setting up a Social Science Research Council came from the American Political Science Association* (APSA) in 1922. The stated purpose of the proposed organization included the development of research in the social sciences and encouragement of the establishment of centers for social science study. The subsequent deliberations of the incorporating group that ultimately organized the SSRC in 1923-1924, however, led to its incorporation with a broader statement of purpose, and the selection of appropriate means for advancing research in the social sciences was left flexible to meet future needs. This flexibility has been a major factor in the SSRC's successful operation, which has altered over the years as the interests of social scientists have changed.

The influences of World War I upon the individuals who founded it were the underlying reasons for the creation of the SSRC. Their awareness of the social problems that would arise from advances in the natural sciences and technology accompanying that war and of the consequent need for understanding human behavior in the light of such advances led them to provide a mechanism for interdisciplinary effort and cooperation.

The SSRC was incorporated in the State of Illinois on December 27, 1924, by the APSA, the American Economic Association* (AEA), the American Sociological Association* (ASA), and the American Statistical Association* (ASA); they were joined during 1925 by representatives from three other learned societies, the American Historical Association* (AHA), the American Anthropological Association* (AAA), and the American Psychological Association* (APA). The membership of the corporation consists of all former and all current members of its governing board of directors. Thus, the SSRC was created by social science scholars and has since been governed by them.

As an introductory statement in the SSRC *Annual Report* (1978-1979) states:

The Council seeks to advance research in the social sciences in a wide variety of ways: the appointment of committees of scholars to set priorities and make plans for critical areas of social science research; the improvement of research training through training institutes and fellowship programs; the support of individual research through postdoctoral grants; the sponsorship of research conferences, often interdisciplinary and international; and the sponsorship of books and other research publications that may result from these activities.

As an autonomous organization the SSRC has not had to concern itself with the special interests of particular groups or to respond to government policies or pressures. Nor has it been limited by the boundaries of a particular social science. As a result, it has been able to follow an eclectic program divided in varying proportion between basic and applied science, between the development and improvement of basic concepts and methods and the application of social science principles to the pressing social problems of the day.

In realizing its goals the SSRC has always divided its resources between aid to individuals and organized attacks on selected specific problems. Aid to individuals, in the form of research training fellowships at both the predoctoral and postdoctoral levels, has been directed toward promoting the development of research workers rather than supporting research itself.

Grant programs have frequently demonstrated the value and feasibility of departures from traditional educational policies, and many SSRC-sponsored summer research training institutes have provided instruction in fields not yet systematically covered in regular university curricula. Since the 1960s both fellowships and summer institutes have been geared toward encouraging cross-disciplinary study and study in fields of scientific inquiry for which no specialized institutional support was available.

Organized attacks on specific problems have usually been through the work of special committees. These committees analyze problems, develop preliminary plans of research, sponsor conferences in which experts can exchange findings and opinions, and publish reports of those conferences. Often the committees have provided recommendations for solutions or for more intensive study on a particular problem, sponsored the preparation and publication of relevant materials, and conducted seminars and summer institutes for further investigation into the area. Sometimes innovative studies and activities initiated by the SSRC have been taken over on a more permanent basis by other organizations, either private or governmental.

The multifarious activities in diverse fields of inquiry that the SSRC has undertaken have yielded both methodological and substantive accomplishments during its more than fifty-year history. These accomplishments can be divided into several major fields of endeavor: opinion measurement, population studies, agriculture, the professions, politics, national economics, the status of social science, psychological aspects of behavior, linguistics, social indicators, and foreign area studies.

Through its efforts in opinion and attitude measurement the SSRC has contributed much to the improvement of the methods used in basic research and in gathering data for government and commercial purposes. Work undertaken in the 1940s yielded findings that helped to lay a firmer foundation for the practice of survey research. Prompted by the election of 1948, when Harry Truman stunned the pollsters and shook the nation's faith in survey methods in general, the SSRC appointed a committee to analyze, evaluate, and explain the incorrect prediction of Truman's defeat. SSRC work has since contributed substantially to the technique, accuracy, and interpretation of sample surveys in measuring opinions and attitudes of the public.

Early work in the area of population studies concentrated on the economic, psychological, and cultural factors involved in the migration and the redistribution of population stimulated by the economic emergency of the 1930s. More recently the SSRC has worked with the U.S. Bureau of the Census in gathering and disseminating information, collaborating in analyzing and interpreting the social and economic aspects of decennial census data, particularly that information which reflects regional differences, and in planning measures to make official data more accessible for legitimate research.

The SSRC began its work in the field of agriculture by concentrating on the social and economic problems related to disadvantaged rural families and to the transition from the family farm to large-scale agriculture that occurred in the first half of the twentieth century. In later years its work emphasized worldwide problems of agriculture in relation to general economic development and contributed, often indirectly and inconspicuously, toward coping with the obstacles presented by the economic and sociological institutions of peasant societies. There appears to be a definite causal link between SSRC fellowship grants and the work that the recipients of those grants have done to disseminate improved agricultural practices in underdeveloped countries in recent years. Although the SSRC does not currently sponsor a committee or program in the field of agriculture, its past efforts have laid the foundations for ameliorative work that now continues under other auspices.

In an effort to work toward more effective utilization of knowledge, the SSRC has attempted to bring together social scientists and representatives of the professions, especially medicine, law, and education. In the 1950s committees were formed on Psychiatry and Social Science and on Preventive Medicine and Social Science. The Committee on Political Behavior, later supplanted by the Committee on Governmental and Legal Processes, for almost two decades conducted a program of grants for research on these processes; and the SSRC has provided fellowships for social scientists to study law and has conducted summer training institutes on law for social scientists.

The behavioral study of politics conducted by the SSRC has provided useful research on political behavior and the functioning of political institutions. In the 1960s it began exploring the possibilities of studying substantive policy questions, such as civil rights laws and civil disturbance in American cities. In 1972 a new committee on the Comparative Study of Public Policy was formed to continue and broaden this urgently needed study of the substance of public policies. Moreover, the SSRC has continued to offer, through its fellowship program and its sponsorship of summer training institutes, opportunities for political scientists to expand their horizons.

Research on national economies began in the wake of World War II and continued for many years under the leadership of Simon Kuznets, chairman of the SSRC's Committees on Economic Growth from 1949 to 1968. Emphasizing the effect that the whole pattern of social organization and culture has upon the economy of a nation, the committee sponsored conferences to explore the possibilities for interdisciplinary approaches to many of the problems that needed to be solved. In 1959 a Committee on Economic Stability was established and began the task of designing an econometric model of the U.S. economy. Four years later the responsibility for periodic updating of the parameters of that model was assumed by the Brookings Institution.* In 1969 the committee launched an effort to forge links among the international sectors of the econometric models of several national economies. Known as Project LINK, it conducts annual conferences at which representatives of the participating nations discuss developments and innovations along these lines.

In 1966, in order to assess the status and future needs of the social science disciplines, the SSRC appointed a joint committee with the National Academy of Sciences* (NAS) to conduct a survey of the behavioral and social sciences. Using various data-gathering procedures, the committee published the findings of its survey in a 1969 report entitled *The Behavioral and Social Sciences: Outlook and Needs.* In addition to making six major recommendations, the report provided a useful and revealing picture of the social sciences in the United States.

A number of SSRC committees and conferences have been designed to explore the various psychological aspects of social behavior. The recurrent heredity-environment controversy, which has been particularly acute since massive public school desegregation took place in the 1960s, has occasioned committee research work and summer institutes. The SSRC has sought to synthesize and direct research on the interrelations of personality, culture, and social structure through the work of such committees as Personality Development in Youth (1957-1963), Socialization and Social Structure (1960-1967), Comparative Developmental Behavior (1961-1966), Work and Personality in the Middle Years (1972-1979), and Life Course Perspectives on Middle and Old Age (1977 to date). Research on the intellective processes has been done by Committees on Simulation of Cognitive Processes (1957-1966), Intellective Processes Research (1959-1964), and Cognitive Research (1972 to date). The Committee on Learning and the Educational Processes (1962-1971) was designed to bridge the gap between psychologists and professional educators. A new interdisciplinary Committee on Television and Social Behavior was formed in 1973, to promote research on the social and institutional effects of television. The Committee on Transnational Social Psychology, organized in 1964, was concerned with the introduction to European psychologists of ideas and methods that have been developed in the United States.

Over the past quarter-century the SSRC has promoted extensive research in the interrelations of linguistics and the social sciences and their impact on society. Its Committee on Linguistics and Psychology and its offspring, the Committee on Sociolinguistics, formed in 1963, have conducted cross-cultural, comparative research into the language of social groups, the relationship of language to political integration, the development of language in children, and the ethnography of communication.

Two undertakings of the SSRC stand out as major contributions during the past two decades. The first is the establishment of the Center for Coordination of Research on Social Indicators in Washington, D.C., in 1972. Under the guidance of an advisory and planning committee the center coordinates research on the measurement and analysis of social trends. To accomplish this end the center maintains a library and reference service, publishes a newsletter, and initiates contacts among researchers in the United States as well as abroad. Supported largely by grants from the National Science Foundation, the center, in keeping with the SSRC's long history in the social indicators movement, is expected to provide the systematic and objective means of monitoring social change.

The other major contribution has been the SSRC's support of foreign area training and research through which scholars have been able to make contact with unfamiliar, non-Western societies and cultures and their historical, political, economic, social, psychological, and linguistic particularities. Because the program was initially designed to correct a language and culture deficit made painfully obvious during World War II, existing academic sources were utilized at first. Although spread thin, these existing sources served to fill the initial need for the whole-culture, interdisciplinary approach to foreign area study. In 1973, a comprehensive review of foreign area studies in American academic institutions by the SSRC found over twenty times more qualifying area study programs in 1970 than there had been in 1946. This whole-culture approach, which characterizes the area and language movement in the United States, emphasizes understanding all aspects of an alien society. Therefore, most of the SSRC's work in foreign area studies has been undertaken by joint research planning committees appointed by the SSRC and the American Council of Learned Societies* (ACLS). Fiscal and administrative responsibility for the committees is usually shared by the two councils. Most of the funding for joint projects until recent years was provided by the Ford Foundation; the National Endowment for the Humanities is now an important source of support. These joint committees have concentrated their efforts on Latin America, the Near and Middle East, China, Africa, Japan, and Korea.

In addition to the work of these joint committees, the SSRC has played a crucial role in the expansion of knowledge about non-Western societies during the past two decades through its Foreign Area Fellowship Program. Initially conducted with funds from the Carnegie Corporation, the program was terminated in 1953, when the Ford Foundation launched a much larger Foreign Area Fellowship Program. Responsibility for the administration of that program was transferred to a joint committee of the SSRC and the ACLS in 1963, and in 1973 the program was merged with other area research programs of the two councils.

The SSRC has participated with the Department of State and Board of Foreign Scholarships in selecting scholars for grants under the Fulbright-Hays Act. In conjunction with the ACLS it arranges exchange programs between scholars in the United States, the Soviet Union, and the countries of Eastern Europe through the International Research and Exchanges Board, established in 1968.

The SSRC, although operating in a cooperative relationship with its member societies, receives no financial support from them. Its chief sources of revenue in its early years were grants from philanthropic foundations and income from endowment provided it by some of these foundations. During the last few decades the federal government has provided a growing portion of SSRC support through various of its agencies, and today this accounts for over fifty percent of its annual budget.

The relationship between the SSRC and its member societies has been one of cooperation on matters of mutual interest but with complete independence on both sides. The only formal relationship is that the societies select, from slates proposed by the board of directors of the SSRC, one member each every three years. The seventeen-member board is composed of the president, the seven members selected by the societies, and nine at-large directors selected by the board. Although some critics maintain that this is a nondemocratic procedure, the reason for this development was the necessity for getting scholars on the governing board who are not only respected by their fellow academicians but who are also known to be willing to engage in the time-consuming work entailed in election to membership. Significantly, the ACLS after some thirty years of representation based on direct nomination by its societal members in 1946-1947 adopted several features of this procedure.

Originally the chairman of the board of directors served as the executive officer of the SSRC, but since 1929 a separate executive officer has been named. Incumbents from that date until 1948 were: E. B. Wilson, R. S. Woodworth, Robert T. Crane, and Donald R. Young. Pendleton Herring served as president from 1948 until 1968. He was succeeded by Henry W. Riecken (1969-1971), who was followed by Eleanor B. Sheldon (1972-1979). The current president is Kenneth Prewitt.

The SSRC, which maintains its headquarters at 605 Third Avenue, New York, New York 10016, does not hold inclusive annual meetings, its policies and operations being formed and carried through by meetings of the board of directors, plus recommendations of committees and the professional staff. The board elects the principal officers: chairman, vice-chairman, secretary, and treasurer. It appoints the president, the chief executive officer of the SSRC.

For further information, see the *Annual Report* and *Items*, published by the SSRC. For a recent "authorized," albeit succinct and objective, history by a former SSRC staff member, see Elbridge Sibley, *Social Science Research Council: The First Fifty Years* (1974).

SOCIETY FOR ETHNOMUSICOLOGY (SEM). A significant factor in the origin of the SEM was the pioneering work of a small number of Germans, centering in Berlin at the turn of the twentieth century, who became interested in the study of nontraditional, non-European music. In 1930 they formed a society, which shortly thereafter established a quarterly journal. A kind of offshoot of this German society was the organization in 1933 of an American Society for Comparative Musicology (ASCM), whose members automatically received the journal of the German society upon joining. The rise to power of Hitler in Germany and the onset of World War II saw the demise of both organizations.

In 1952 a small group, led by Willard Rhodes, Mieczyslaw Kolinski, David P. McAllester, Alan P. Merriam, and Charles Seeger, began to study ways and means of forming a new society in the United States whereby ethnomusicologists might again be brought into closer contact with others of similar interests. The initial result of their deliberation was the December, 1953, issuance of a *Newsletter*. The overwhelming response to the first five issues —the mailing list grew from seventy-five to about six hundred—was the immediate cause in the formation of the SEM at the annual meeting of the American Anthropological Association* (AAA) in Boston on December 18, 1955. By this time, it should be noted that the term *ethnomusicology* more accurately reflected the objectives and methods of ethnomusicologists than did the earlier *comparative musicology*. Thus they increasingly perceived that what they were doing was the study of music to find out more about culture, and vice versa. Consequently, what they had was a union or melding of music and other disciplines, particularly anthropology and sociology. For a recent discussion of this change, see Alan P. Merriam's "Definitions of 'Comparative Musicology' and 'Ethnomusicology': An Historical-Theoretical Perspective," *Ethnomusicology* (1977).

The publications of the SEM have been a continuing source of information and stimulation to its members. Early issues of the *Newsletter* had been restricted primarily to notes and news; however, this was superseded in 1958 by the SEM's official journal, *Ethnomusicology*, which thrice yearly publishes original articles, book, record, and film reviews, bibliographies, and other material on ethnomusicology. Since 1967 the SEM has also published an *SEM Newsletter* six times a year, which now contains the news and notices formerly carried in the *Newsletter*. Annual awards made by the SEM since 1967 include the Seeger Prize and Jaap Kunst Prize.

The SEM, according to its first president, Willard Rhodes, represents a discipline that claims interest in the music of preliterate cultures, Oriental art music, and the folk music of the world, together with popular music and dance. He also maintained in *Ethnomusicology* (1963) that the ethnomusicologist considers

music not merely as an esthetic object, but as a product and symbol of human behavior, inextricably associated and interrelated with the other elements of culture. This approach stresses the anthropological aspects of the discipline and demands of the researcher an acquaintance with the economy, religion, politics, and social life of the society in which the music plays its role.

The SEM, which maintains its offices under an office director in Ann Arbor, Michigan, has held annual meetings since its founding, often in conjunction with those of the AAA, American Musicological Society* (AMS), or American Folklore Society* (AFS). Membership in the SEM has increased from the initial 472 to about 2,200 in 1979. The governing board of the SEM consists of a president, president-elect, two vice-presidents, secretary, treasurer, and two members-at-large. In addition there is an elected advisory council of about forty-five and an appointed editorial board.

For further information, see "Notes and News," *Ethno-Musicology Newsletter*, no. 6 (1956). See also the articles published in the tenth anniversary issue of *Ethnomusicology* (1963), particularly Willard Rhodes, "A Decade of Progress"; and David P. McAllester, "Ethnomusicology, the Field and the Society."

SOCIETY FOR THE HISTORY OF TECHNOLOGY (SHOT). This society grew out of a study of "general education" for engineers in the early 1950s by the Humanistic-Social Division of the American Society for Engineering Education. Following issuance in 1956 of a report favoring and encouraging the history of technology as a means to interest engineering students in liberal subjects, a special committee headed by Dr. Melvin Kranzberg was appointed to carry through on it. This committee discovered that, although there was a tremendous interest in the history of technology in engineering, industry, and all academic disciplines, the subject was being taught only sporadically, and no organization or publication was specifically devoted to the subject in the United States. With widespread demand that the situation be remedied, Dr. Kranzberg led in the formation of an Advisory Committee for Technology and Society composed of academicians, engineers, and industrialists. The Case Institute of Technology, where Dr. Kranzberg was then a professor of history, sponsored a meeting of this committee in January, 1958, and it was there decided to establish SHOT.

Projected as an interdisciplinary, international organization, SHOT was to encourage the study of the development of technology and its relations with society and culture. To criticisms of "fragmentation" at the time of its formation, Dr. Kranzberg replied that the nature of the subject was interdisciplinary and the new society and its publication must also be so. He added that this would be the first time that engineers, scientists, industrialists, social scientists, and humanists would be getting together to promote studies that were of mutual interest and concern to them.

The first annual meeting of SHOT in December, 1958, fulfilling this mandate, saw it conducting joint programs with the American Historical Association* (AHA) and Section L (History and Philosophy of Science) of the American Association for the Advancement of Science* (AAAS) and also holding annual meetings. Subsequent meetings of SHOT have been held in December of each year, usually with the AHA, AAAS, and other learned societies, such as the History of Science Society.*

Publications of SHOT include the international quarterly, *Technology and Culture*, which first appeared in 1960, and has been edited by Dr. Melvin Kranzberg since its beginning. Also, a series of monographs have been published in conjunction with the MIT Press.

Largely as the result of SHOT publishing articles and arranging sessions at the annual meeting devoted to them, two relatively new and unexplored areas of interest to SHOT have recently emerged. One is industrial archaeology, concerned with the preservation and recording of historical industrial artifacts; the other is the philosophy of technology, dealing with the philosophy and thought on technology and technological change.

SHOT has established three awards: the Abbott Payson Usher Prize, awarded annually to the author of the best article or other work published by SHOT; the Dexter Prize, donated by the Dexter Chemical Corporation and awarded annually to the author of an outstanding book in the history of technology; and the Leonardo da Vinci Medal, awarded annually for outstanding contributions to the history of technology through research, teaching, publication, or other activity. The initial membership of the society consisted of two hundred persons. Today it has grown to over twenty-five hundred.

SHOT elects the customary institutional officers; it conducts its business from an office, headed by a secretary, located in Santa Barbara, California.

For further information, see Melvin Kranzberg, "At the Start," *Technology and Culture* (Winter, 1960); and, in the same issue, "The Society for the History of Technology: A Brief History." See also "Society for the History of Technology," *ACLS Newsletter* (Winter, 1973); and *SHOT Information Pamphlet* (1977).

SOCIETY OF AMERICAN BACTERIOLOGISTS. See American Society for Microbiology.

SOCIETY OF AMERICAN VERTEBRATE PALEONTOLOGISTS. See Paleontological Society.

SOCIETY OF AMERICAN ZOOLOGISTS. See American Society of Zoologists.

SOCIETY OF ARCHITECTURAL HISTORIANS (SAH). In the late 1930s a group of teachers, primarily of architectural history from schools of architecture, were attracted to the summer sessions of Harvard University by the classes in architectural history conducted by Professor Kenneth John Conant. This was the only location at that time where such instruction could be obtained during the summer. Dr. Conant's lectures and these summer sessions gradually led to the idea that a formal organization should be established to promote the study of architectural history.

Previous to this time institutional affiliation for those concerned with architectural history had been confined to the American Institute of Architects or to the College Art Association of America* (CAA). The former was dominated by practicing architects; the latter was controlled by art historians and artists, who viewed architecture as a peripheral field. Also, the journals of architecture were reluctant to accept historical articles, and the *Art Bulletin*, published by the CAA, seldom accepted such articles. The need for a society devoted to architectural history coincided, too, with an increase in academic course offerings in the subject and the increasing recognition that the field formed a unique area of intellectual and cultural import. Finally, in August, 1940, the group centered at Harvard decided to organize as a formal organization, and the American Society of Architectural Historians was founded there at that time, the name being changed to the present "Society of Architectural Historians" in 1947. In January, 1941, the first issue of the triannual, mimeographed *Journal of the American Society of Architectural Historians*, containing articles and other features, appeared and was distributed gratis to approximately 125 members. In 1947, the *Journal* became a quarterly, renamed the *Journal of the Society of Architectural Historians*, which attained printed format in 1950. Also, since 1957, the SAH has issued a *Newsletter* six times a year.

Since 1949, the SAH has made an annual award for the most distinguished work in the history of architecture published by a North American scholar, and, since 1956, this award has included the presentation of the Alice Davis Hitchcock Award. Also since the 1950s, the society has organized field trips to regions containing significant architectural monuments, both in the United States and abroad. A trip to Dublin, Ireland, was very successful as was one to see Palladio's work in and around Vicenza, Italy. Members of the SAH have played an important role, too, in studying the architectural history of their own regions and communities. These studies have served as an important means of bringing many little-known but significant works to the attention of scholars. Also, many SAH members have been active in projects to preserve significant local, regional, and national monuments.

From its founding the SAH has welcomed as members not only architects and professional scholars but also interested laymen. It has become evident that the SAH association propels many of the latter into the ranks of the professionals. In addition to the normal active and student categories of membership, the SAH also includes life, patron, contributing, institutional, and sustaining institutional. Corporate memberships with proportionately larger dues are also offered. At the present time there are some forty-two hundred members in all categories.

The SAH elects the customary institutional officers; it conducts its business from an office, headed by an executive secretary, located in Philadelphia, Pennsylvania.

For further information, see Walter L. Creese, "The Society of Architectural Historians," *Journal of the Society of Architectural Historians* (November, 1950). Historical notes were also supplied by Dean Emeritus Turpin C. Bannister, University of Florida, and Professor Emeritus Alan K. Laing, University of Illinois.

SOCIETY OF BIBLICAL LITERATURE (SBL). A group of about thirty-five Biblical scholars from the New England, New Jersey, New York, and Pennsylvania areas, led by the renowned Frederic Gardner and Philip Schaf, were instrumental in the 1880 founding of the Society of Biblical Literature and Exegesis, shortened in 1962 to the Society of Biblical Literature, to "stimulate the critical study of the Scriptures by presenting, discussing, and publishing original papers on Biblical subjects."

Since the SBL has never taken a doctrinal position, its publications and meetings have provided a forum for Jewish, Roman Catholic, and Protestant scholars. Its quarterly *Journal of Biblical Literature,* published by the SBL for almost a century, carries articles by those of all faiths and is one of the primary mediums for American Biblical scholarship. The SBL also conducts an extensive scholarly publication program through the Scholars Press, Chico, California. Annual meetings of the SBL, devoted primarily to the reading and discussion of scholarly papers, and similar ones sponsored by twelve SBL regions, set up in various parts of this country and Canada, also provide a sounding board for differing interpretations. These regions include, for example, the Midwest (established 1936), Pacific Coast (1941), Southern (1948), New England (1950), and Southwestern (1957).

Other SBL activities include the encouragement its members have given to special projects in the area of Biblical study. These include, for example, various revisions of the Bible, such as the *American Standard Version* and the *Revised Standard Version;* the twelve-volume *Interpreter's Bible;* the several volumes of *The Beginnings of Christianity;* and the International Greek New Testament Project. Although the major interest of SBL is thus the study and interpretation of the Bible, philology and archaeology, where pertinent, have also received attention. From its origin, The American School of Oriental Research in Jerusalem has been affiliated with the SBL.

The original founders of the SBL were Protestant, but many Roman Catholic and Jewish scholars have actively participated in its affairs. Consequently, its present-day active membership of about five thousand includes rabbis, priests, and ministers as well as teachers, students, and other interested persons. In addition, there are honorary members, limited to distinguished foreign scholars.

The SBL elects the customary institutional officers; it conducts its business from an office, headed by an executive secretary, located in Richmond, Virginia.

For further information, see a two-page, mimeographed article on the SBL by Charles F. Kraft, former SBL secretary, based on an address by Henry J. Cadbury at the Diamond Jubilee Dinner at the Union Theological Seminary in New York City, December, 1955. See also "Transactions and Memorabilia of the Fiftieth Anniversary Meeting of the Society," *Journal of Biblical Literature* (January, 1931); and Erwin R. Goodenough, "The Society of Biblical Literature and Exegesis," *World of the Mind* (1958). Also, in 1973 and again in 1977, the SBL published an information pamphlet about its history and activities.

SOCIETY OF BIBLICAL LITERATURE AND EXEGESIS. See Society of Biblical Literature.

SOUTHERN RESEARCH INSTITUTE. Three of the major fields of Southern Research Institute in the 1980s were far removed from the thoughts of the Alabama businessmen who founded the organization in the early 1940s. If asked specifically about these subjects at that time, they likely would have responded that cancer cannot be cured with drugs; air pollution is something of an eyesore, but unavoidable; and *biomaterials* is an unfamiliar term. The concern of these men centered on the paucity of scientific research being conducted in the South and the effect of this shortage on the development of the South's industry, agriculture, and natural resources.

This concern had been expressed by others, but it was amplified and stated more convincingly by two University of Alabama chemistry professors, who proposed a solution to the problem. Drs. Stewart J. Lloyd and George D. Palmer, Jr., urged that a scientific research organization be established to benefit the entire region. Dr. Lloyd made the recommendation in a 1932 report, and he was to repeat it again. Dr. Palmer, concluding a year as president of the Alabama Academy of Science, addressed that body in March, 1940, on "Scientific Research, the Hope of the South," a talk that stressed the need for a research organization. He was invited to repeat his message before the Alabama State Chamber of Commerce meeting in October, 1940. Thomas W. Martin, president of Alabama Power Company and a man committed to the development of his state and region, was in the audience and responded immediately to Palmer's suggestion. He proposed that the state chamber undertake a fund-raising campaign to underwrite a research organization, and a committee was appointed to pursue the idea. Benjamin Russell of Russell Mills, Alexander City, Alabama, was chairman of the committee that met in February, 1941, and unanimously voted that the state chamber should set up a nonprofit organization to be known as Alabama Research Institute. Mr. Martin and W.A. Steadman, president of the chamber, were appointed to draw up papers of incorporation. The sum of twenty-five thousand dollars was set up as a minimum capital budget for the first year, and financial support was to be sought from all possible sources.

The committee worked on the idea for six months, all the while seeking advice from scientists and putting together a charter. According to the law, only ten signatures were required as incorporators, but Tom Martin went to every part of the state and obtained seventy-eight signatures to indicate formally the broad approval for the organization. A constitution and bylaws were prepared, prescribing a not-for-profit organization with its property and business managed by a thirty-nine person board of trustees, and its activities directed by a staff of officers.

In October of 1941, there was a meeting of the incorporators, and five temporary trustees were elected along with the first officers: Erskine Ramsey, honorary chairman; Benjamin Russell, chairman; Milton Fies, treasurer; and W.F. McCown, secretary.

The certificate of incorporation, the constitution, and the bylaws of Alabama Research Institute were filed in the probate office in Montgomery two days later—October 11, 1941. Article 2, object and purpose of the constitution, contains the essence of the thoughts that were going through the minds of these founders:

Alabama Research Institute is formed to promote the general welfare of the State of Alabama and its citizens and for the promotion of other public purposes; to aid through scientific research in the utilization of the natural resources of the State of Alabama and in the development of agriculture, industry, and commerce in the state, and elsewhere.

Alabama Research Institute was destined to be only a paper organization for about three years. Eight weeks after the incorporation came Pearl Harbor, and it seemed to the trustees an impractical, if not impossible, task to launch the new enterprise in the face of great uncertainty over personnel, availability of facilities and equipment, and, certainly, grave questions over the timeliness of a capital funds campaign.

Nine days after Pearl Harbor came another blow to the institute: the death of Benjamin Russell, the first chairman of the organization. Mr. Martin became chairman soon thereafter and served throughout the crucial initial years of operation until his death in 1964.

Mr. Martin made speeches all over the South to stir up interest in research in general and the Alabama Research Institute in particular. Dr. Palmer, as secretary of the newly created Southern Association of Science and Industry, was sending out thousands of letters and printed materials with the same messages. In December of 1943, Mr. Martin convened a meeting of seventy-three of the leading industrialists and businessmen of the South. The time had come for action, he told that audience. Before the meeting was over, he had thirty-five separate pledges, totaling three hundred thousand dollars, including seventy-five thousand dollars from the power company. A search committee began looking for a director.

The tempo of speeches—by Mr. Martin, and many others—picked up. One of the appeals for capital funds was to a group of railroads that covered the South. From three railroad presidents came the suggestion that, because the organization's interests were not limited strictly to the State of Alabama, the name be changed to Southern Research Institute. In June, 1944, the charter and bylaws were changed, and the organization adopted the new name. In August, 1944, a director was appointed: Dr. Wilbur A. Lazier, coming to Birmingham after nineteen years in chemical research with E.I. du Pont de Nemours Co. In the same month, two acres of land, including a two-story white-columned house built in 1896, were purchased for $57,500, and the new institute had an operating location. As carpenters began converting the old home's parlors and bedrooms into laboratories and offices, the new director was busy recruiting scientists and buying equipment. Mr. Martin reported in November, 1944, that $386,000 had been contributed, but that $1 million was needed—for facilities, working capital, and unsponsored research on Southern products.

In April, 1945, the Southern Research Institute began operations with a project for the National Peanut Council: a comprehensive survey of the exact status of research information on peanuts and peanut products and processes, and a defining of lines of investigation, both near-term and long-range, that were regarded as the most likely to benefit the peanut industry. There was also some exploratory research to be done on promising avenues of development. Project no. 2 was for a local mattress company and included, among other tasks, the design of a folding sofa bed.

During the first year the Southern Research Institute billed its clients a total of sixty-six thousand dollars. At the end of the year there were about thirty-three employees, twenty-three of them on the technical staff. The subjects they worked on reflect a variety of Southern resources and products: peanut foods, tobacco, essential oils, citrus byproducts, cotton textiles, paper products, sleep equipment, marine gear, oil exploration, iron castings, cement, domestic heating and air conditioning, wood preserving, synthetic drugs, oleomargarine, dairy products. The capital fund doubled during 1945, from about four hundred thousand to about eight hundred thousand, but the trustees had raised their sights to $2.5 million, instead of $1 million.

In the second year the volume of research tripled—from less than $70,000 to more than $210,000. The staff almost doubled—to fifty-eight, including forty on the technical staff. There was another building, another old house, which was converted into the first biochemistry laboratory. And construction was under way on the first permanent building, an engineering lab, which was dedicated in November, 1947.

Dr. Lazier resigned in March, 1948, to become director of chemical research at Charles Pfizer & Co. in New York. Dr. William M. Murray, Jr., who since joining the institute in 1945 had been an analytical chemist, a division head, and an assistant director, succeeded him. Dr. Murray held that position (the title was changed to president in 1963) for twenty-six years, retiring in 1974.

Dr. Howard E. Skipper, who succeeded Dr. Murray as president, had come to the institute in April, 1946, as director of the Biochemistry Division. He led the biological sciences work from its inception and continues to do so. Individually, and as the leader of a large and diverse research group, Dr. Skipper has made significant contributions to the increasing store of knowledge on the treatment of cancer. He has been honored with numerous prestigious awards, including the 1974 Albert Lasker Basic Medical Research Award and the 1980 Bristol-Myers Award for Distinguished Achievement in Cancer Research. Rollin D. Osgood, Jr., joined the institute in 1946 as business manager, later became treasurer and vice-president, and since 1974 has been executive vice-president, in charge of the administration of the institute's activities.

Founded because of the perceived needs of Southern industry, Southern Research Institute has indeed served its region, not only in its early years but throughout its history, in a continuous stream of research projects sponsored by companies in Alabama and nearby states. But its growth and greatest influence has been in scientific fields that transcend regional boundaries.

Cancer research, for example, has been the largest single research program at Southern Research Institute accounting for more than 50 percent of the effort during several years. It is made up of separate but closely coordinated programs in biochemistry, organic chemistry, biology, pharmacology, pathology, and microbiology. The major areas of research within this program have been the design and synthesis of new drugs, evaluation of the effects of drug treatment, and basic studies on normal and cancer cells. Two classes of anticancer drugs, the nitrosoureas and the imidazole triazenes, have been developed at the Southern Research Institute, and three of these compounds are being used worldwide for treatment of several forms of cancer. Another major contribution has been the development of new concepts of drug treatment, particularly in regimens based on understanding of the kinetics of cell population growth and on the use of combinations of drugs.

The institute has been a pioneer in research in biomaterials and bioengineering—the marriage of modern chemical and engineering technology with biological needs. The institute group has developed a number of systems utilizing microcapsules, fibers, and other polymer shapes to deliver drugs and other biologically active compounds. Other products from this research group have included several materials and devices to meet specific needs for detection or treatment of disease.

In the field of air pollution control, the institute has earned an international reputation as a center for research on electrostatic precipitation and fine-particle technology. This research program ranges from studies in fundamental physics to troubleshooting of specific problems at operating power plants and industrial facilities.

Other subjects of research include characterization of materials of use in extreme conditions, development of electro-optical devices, development of analytical techniques and instruments, synthesis of polymers, and spinning of synthetic fibers.

Research projects are conducted for individual clients or sponsors, who pay the direct costs of the project plus a proportionate share of other operating costs. These revenues are separate from contributed capital funds, which are used only for construction of new facilities and purchase of additional equipment. In 1979 total revenues from research were $15.5 million. The physical facilities included more than a dozen buildings, containing 304,000 square feet of floor space, spread over more than ten acres of property. The staff total reached six hundred in 1980, including seventy-five research professionals with doctorates.

For further information, see W.A. Lazier, "The Southern Research Institute," *Science* (March, 1945); and John Temple Graves, *History of Southern Research Institute* (1955). See also Harold Vagtborg, *Research and American Industrial Development* (1976); William M. Murray, Jr., *Thomas W. Martin—A Biography* (1978); and SRI *Annual Reports* (1945 to date).

JAMES H. STRICKLAND

SOUTHWEST RESEARCH INSTITUTE (SwRI). This not-for-profit applied research organization was founded in September, 1947. The articles were signed in a restored ranch house which, together with a small brick structure, comprised the total original plant.

The founder, colorful oilman-rancher-philanthropist Tom Slick, envisioned the organization as a means of repaying the area that had brought so much wealth to him and his family. Slick had graduated from Yale University with honors in science and had always seen science and technology as a means of ensuring national prosperity and security.

He had already created Southwest Foundation for Research and Education, which had branches in the biomedical and agricultural sciences. He also created the Institute of Inventive Research, whose function was to encourage inventions and to finance the foundation from royalties on those inventions. After screening one hundred thousand inventions with only one hundred deemed worthy of development, and finding only ten brought in royalties of any kind, this organization was liquidated. The agricultural branch of the foundation was effective in brush control and cattle nutrition research but was discontinued because the service duplicated the program of Texas A&M University. The foundation continues, however, as a growing center of biomedical research with an annual budget of over five million dollars and a staff of three hundred. The foundation maintains the world's largest baboon colony, whose two thousand inhabitants provide excellent models for humans in biomedical studies on atherosclerosis, cancer, and fertility.

The Southwest Research Institute was first headed by Dr. Harold Vagtborg. Slick induced him to leave his position as founding president of Midwest Research Institute* (MRI) at Kansas City, Missouri, which had made an excellent beginning under his leadership. Vagtborg had come to MRI after he, Dr. Jesse E. Hobson (later of Stanford Research Institute, now SRI International* [SRI]) and Dr. Henry T. Heald (later of the Ford Foundation) founded Armour (now IIT Research Institute* [IITRI]) Research Institute of Chicago.

The job was not an easy one, but Slick and Vagtborg welcomed the challenge. And a challenge it was. Other research institutes, such as Battelle Memorial Institute* (BMI), had large endowments; were associated with universities, for example, Stanford Research Institute; or existed in already industrialized areas.

San Antonio presented none of these advantages. The only industries were clothing manufacturers, two local breweries, and the military installations. Local colleges and universities offered no advanced degrees in science or engineering, and there was no adequate library closer than Austin seventy miles away.

Slick, who continued his father's tradition as King of the Wildcatters, was seen by his fellow oilmen as heading for an expensive and time-consuming dry hole. Vagtborg's industrial and academic friends shook their heads and predicted that even his Danish determination could not surmount the obstacles.

For a while, it seemed they might be right. Research income during the first year did not even reach one hundred thousand dollars, but there was no stopping Slick and Vagtborg. Slick still believed in his new creation, although most of the financial support was going to the earlier established Institute of Inventive Research. Vagtborg wore a series of hats. He was the salesman for science and technology throughout the area. He was the salesman for the capabilities of the Southwest Research Institute, which benefitted from area understanding of the promise of science, and he was the salesman of services to those national clients he had known from his previous associations.

Under his direction, the Southwest Research Institute developed a reputation for service to the automotive and aviation industries in problems of fuels and lubricants. One of the first uses of bacteria for industrial waste treatment and a study of smog in Los Angeles marked the institute's beginnings in the environmental field.

Vagtborg continued to meet the payrolls (although sometimes barely), and the program began to expand. However, the technical program needed tightening into an effective instrument. For this, he persuaded Martin Goland to leave Midwest Research Institute in 1955 and come to SwRI. Vagtborg had watched the rising career of the young aeronautical engineer from the time Goland had worked for Dr. Clifford Furnas at the Cornell Aeronautical Laboratory. It was Vagtborg who had induced Goland to go to MRI to head the Applied Mechanics Department. Now, Goland was Vagtborg's choice to tighten up SwRI.

Goland, a Brooklyn native, at first saw the Texas job as only an interlude in his career; he never thought of staying on a fifteen hundred-acre spread of marginal cattle land eight miles west of San Antonio, which Slick had deeded out of one of his ranches, Essar, (S-R, "scientific research"). For what he viewed as a brief stay, he did make one request: he wanted his office air-conditioned. He set the pace, and other air conditioning soon followed throughout the other offices and laboratories.

The institute prospered and expanded under the new team. In 1959, Vagtborg stepped down as its executive head to reorganize the foundation and to set up a cancer treatment center at the San Antonio Medical Center, which numbered him among its founders. His successor and the incumbent was Martin Goland.

The institute evolved into eleven divisions, each headed by a technical vice-president. Lieutenant General Austin Betts (Retired) and W. Lyle Donaldson were named senior vice-presidents. Andrew Khourie was recruited from SRI to shore up the financial operations.

The 1980 annual report shows gross revenues of $82,180,000, with a payroll of $34 million to the staff of 1,845 (585 of them with professional degrees). Laboratory and supporting space measures 750,000 square feet, with a total net worth of $47,607,000. Headquarters are located in San Antonio, and there are offices in Houston and Washington, D.C.

The institute is the location of the U.S. Army Fuels and Lubricants Research Laboratory, staffed and managed by institute personnel. Despite the fact that the institute is located 150 miles from the ocean on a cactus-lined hill, SwRI is where the world's first deep-diving submarine, the *Aluminaut*, was conceived, designed, and model-tested. SwRI is the world's largest independent automotive research laboratory. Sulphlex, a new paving material made of sulfur and nonpetroleum-based additives, is now being tested on highways in six states. Its SwRI inventors say that using Sulphlex instead of asphalt could save 133 million barrels of imported oil per year.

The institute conducts some seven hundred projects annually. One-third of these projects are sponsored by government agencies, with the balance sponsored by individuals and corporations.

For further information, see Harold Vagtborg, *Southwest Research Center* (1973) and *Research and American Industrial Development* (1976). See also Robert Lubar, "The Adventures of Tom Slick," *Fortune* (July, 1960).

JACK HARMON

SRI INTERNATIONAL (SRI). Originally created as Stanford Research Institute, SRI International has long been known by its acronym, SRI, but the three names are used interchangeably. The international name was adopted in 1970, following a legal separation from Stanford University. However, neither of these moves involved any change in SRI's charter purpose or operating principles as a nonprofit research institute.

The idea of creating a scientific research institute at Stanford University first arose in the 1920s. The late Dr. Robert E. Swain, who was professor of chemistry, then head of the department, later vice-president and acting president of the university, and finally professor emeritus, began thinking about the concept in 1925.

Swain was a friend of Herbert Hoover, Stanford's most distinguished alumnus, who was then secretary of commerce in the Coolidge administration. Hoover had played a leading role in founding Stanford's Graduate School of Business and, together with the Carnegie Corporation of New York, had helped the university create a Food Research Institute for work on problems of production, distribution, and consumption of foodstuffs. Also, he had given Stanford some money to house his growing collection of documents associated with World War I and its aftermath. The Hoover Library, later to be known as the Hoover Institution on War, Revolution and Peace,* was on its way to becoming a world-renowned organization.

Being greatly concerned about stimulating the growth of American industry and its productivity, Hoover was much interested in Swain's proposal for an institute at Stanford. Throughout his stay in Washington, D.C., Hoover kept in touch with Swain and encouraged the university to follow through on the idea. His interest continued unabated after returning to private life at the university in the early 1930s, and later in the decade he urged the Stanford trustees to action.

Planning had been delayed because of the Great Depression, but in 1939 it appeared that the time was right to bring Swain's vision into reality. Meanwhile, Swain and his university colleagues, with Hoover's strong encouragement, had articulated the concept and role for a Stanford-affiliated center with an industrial orientation and an emphasis on applied research. They kept advancing the theme that the application of science for useful purposes was and would continue to be a noble cause in improving the lot of mankind.

This idea had emerged four centuries earlier during the age of commerce and discovery. Francis Bacon believed that the world's attention should be turned from a medieval emphasis on deductive reasoning to the kingdom of man, to human society and its many problems. He had contended, as Swain was to emphasize, that this could best be done through the applied sciences and that the chief task for mankind was to make the world a better place for human habitation.

The scientists of the sixteenth century were indeed greatly concerned about a discouraging tone in the idea that "an increase in knowledge is an increase in sorrow." William Harvey, Johann Kepler, Galileo, René

Descartes, Robert Boyle, Sir Isaac Newton, John Locke, Spinoza, and others argued for a more robust confidence in what science might achieve in the betterment of man's life. Bacon maintained that one of the main objectives of research should be to create a "rich storehouse for the glory of the Creator and the relief of man's estate." This dedication led him to create Salomon's House, a foundation devoted to "enlarging the bounds of human empire." Thus, we find the conceptual forerunner of present-day institutes and research foundations partly if not wholly in the pattern Swain and Hoover visualized for Stanford. As Swain emphasized on several occasions during the 1930s, even Albert Einstein in his quest for new knowledge often spoke about the great unsolved problems of human endeavor. He maintained that they must be the final focus of all technical pursuits.

There was by no means widespread agreement during the 1930s that the rise of American applied research organizations was a beneficial movement. Many social scientists in particular were concerned that resources would be drawn away from educational and basic research pursuits in the nation's universities. Earlier in the 1930s, however, Hoover and Swain had interested Stanford's president, Dr. Ray Lyman Wilbur, in the research institute concept. Wilbur was then serving as Hoover's secretary of interior. Upon returning to Stanford following Franklin Roosevelt's election as president, he began working with Swain and Hoover in an attempt to move matters along. Together, they gradually generated some enthusiasm within a small circle of California industrialists. Unfortunately, the advent of World War II brought the initiative to an end. The time was simply not right to generate financial support for a new Stanford institute, whatever its aims.

In 1945, again at Hoover's urging, a new step was taken. It involved three men, Swain, H. Dudley Swim (a Stanford alumnus and businessman), and Dr. Philip Leighton, new head of the university's Chemistry Department. Wilbur appointed the trio as a committee to take up the cudgel. Calling themselves the "Three Musketeers," they lost no time in studying the need, purposes, and organizational concepts. Their thoughts were on the western part of the United States and its great challenges in economic and industrial development following World War II. They looked at similar institutions elsewhere in the nation and soon decided that needs and opportunities in the West were more than ample. They urged Stanford and its trustees to move quickly in creating a nonprofit institute within the university structure aimed at speeding up industrialization of the American West. The Musketeers felt that the situation called for speedy action, particularly with rapidly rising research interests within both government and business. They thought the "golden time" was at hand.

Meanwhile, an independent initiative along the same lines arose in Southern California. With encouragement from both business and the state, and with Stanford's quiet accord, a Pacific Research Foundation had been created. Its purposes and the motivation of its leaders were centered on stimulating basic and applied research in universities throughout the western part of the United States. The basic idea was to move along in some way in conjunction with Stanford University.

While all this was going on, another step was under way in Northern California. Stanford's new president, Dr. Donald B. Tresidder, and its vice president, Dr. Alvin C. Eurich, had gained strong support from a group of Western businessmen headed by Atholl McBean, a prominent industrialist and director of several large corporations. They soon became known as the "Northern Troika" in the initiatives that led to SRI's creation. They asked Dr. Henry T. Heald, president of the Illinois Institute of Technology and later head of the Ford Foundation, for counsel on the need, concept, and organization of a Western research institute. Heald urged that a nonprofit entity within Stanford be created without delay. The basic idea was to provide a public service to industry and government in developing the Western economy. No one was thinking at the time about an institute with national, let alone international, interests. Stanford lost no time in making a move. Within a few months a charter was prepared. Much of the conceptual effort was provided by Eurich; McBean promised financial support by business; Tresidder convinced the university trustees that the right time had arrived. Thus, SRI was created in October, 1946, only a little more than a year after the post-World War II initiative had been launched. The speed and clarity of action were remarkable by any standards—then and now—that one may apply.

The most astonishing feature is that the original charter, drafted some thirty-five years ago, has stood the test of time in a rapidly changing world without even a single word being altered. SRI's basic purposes from the outset have been crystal clear: to assist Stanford University in its broad mission; generate new scientific information; apply science for useful purposes in solving problems for business and government; and contribute to the peace and prosperity of mankind. It is clear that the founders had in mind that SRI would devote its attentions first to the American West. But, in due course, they broadened its scope to a national and then an international scale. Perhaps, more importantly, they insisted from the beginning that the new institute should include both the "hard" and "soft" sciences—and particularly industrial economics and the management sciences—in its scope. This was a new approach for research institutes in the United States and elsewhere. Still more important in many respects is an insistence during the 1950s that SRI strive to become "a significant international institution" in all its fields of interest. Indeed, it is in the "soft" sciences and its worldwide operations that SRI has over the years made some of its most important contributions.

Although sound in concept and organization from the very beginning, SRI was not exactly an instant success following its formation in 1946. Financial problems mounted month by month; the first chief executive departed within a year; the second launched a growth program that strained the organization in diverse ways. Even so, his name—Dr. J. E. Hobson—will forever be linked with bringing SRI to world renown by the mid-1950s. In some respects SRI's founding years ran from 1945 through 1955. Even so, an acting president in 1947 observed, "The Institute has been founded but is not yet established." In 1956, E. Finley Carter, then chief executive of Stanford Research Institute, recognized that SRI had entered its "ever-widening orbit." In retrospect, the "upward surge" to orbit began in 1950, and continues in full force today with a staff of some thirty-three hundred people spread around the world and an annual budget approaching two hundred million dollars. Trials and tribulations occur in all organizations, but one must ask about contributions within their basic purposes. SRI has had its share of problems, and it has made some major contributions to business and government as well as the public at large. Much of the electronic technology in modern worldwide banking originated in SRI's laboratories; its international pursuits have certainly strengthened the world business system; its economic planning assistance has sped up economic development in many countries including the United States, Mexico, Saudi Arabia, and India, to name only a few.

In perspective, three features in SRI's development are highly significant. It was founded at the right time, in the right place, under the right auspices, and with the right concept. Furthermore, it has adapted to changing times, thus becoming worldwide in scope and size far beyond the founders' early visions yet within their public service concept of "applying science for useful purposes." Finally, SRI was founded on the concept of direct university leadership in strengthening business, industry, and government and in stimulating economic and social progress. This was a new approach—indeed an experiment—as SRI emerged on the scene in 1946. The initiative was immensely successful, so much so that by mutual agreement the two institutions concurred twenty-five years later that each could best pursue its goals independently in a legal sense. Even so, they remain committed to each other in substance and in operations. In many respects the nation as well as the world at large are beneficiaries of an early vision within Stanford and among a few far-sighted business executives in the university's larger family.

For further information, see Maurice Caullery, *Universities and Scientific Life in the United States* (1939); Myron J. Rand, et al., *Industrial Research Laboratories of the United States* (1950); and Weldon B. Gibson, *SRI: The Founding Years* (1980).

WELDON B. GIBSON

STANFORD RESEARCH INSTITUTE. See SRI International.

_T_

TILDEN TRUST. See New York Public Library, Astor, Lenox and Tilden Foundations, The.

TRAINING SCHOOL FOR PUBLIC SERVICE. See Institute of Public Administration.

_U_

UNIVERSITIES RESEARCH ASSOCIATION, INC. (URA). This association is a nonprofit membership corporation of universities, incorporated in the District of Columbia. Its membership consists of fifty-three universities, fifty-two of them broadly distributed throughout the United States, and one, the University of Toronto, in Canada. All of the member institutions have graduate study programs in science. Each is active in particle physics. Over two-thirds have departments of astronomy or their equivalent.

URA was formed in direct response to a national need. The 1950s had been a period of intense activity in the field of particle accelerator design. With the recognition of the alternate gradient focusing principle in 1952, and the success of the accelerators based on that principle, including the 28 and 33 GeV accelerators at the European Organization for Research and the Brookhaven National Laboratory, it became apparent that an accelerator of much higher energy was technically feasible and scientifically desirable. Studies at Brookhaven, the University of California's Lawrence Berkeley Laboratory, and the California Institute of Technology led to proposals to the U.S. Atomic Energy Commission (AEC) for support of design studies for accelerators in the 100 GeV to 1000 GeV range at both Brookhaven and the Lawrence Berkeley Laboratory. By 1962 more than a dozen accelerator proposals, costing much more than the anticipated level of national funding, had been made.

To consider the array of proposed accelerators, a committee under the joint sponsorship of the President's Science Advisory Committee and the General Advisory Committee of the AEC was appointed with Professor Norman F. Ramsey of Harvard University as chairman. In 1963 the Ramsey Committee issued a report recommending an ordered program of concentrated effort toward high energy. Among the principal recommendations was the construction of a 200 GeV synchrotron, to be initiated in fiscal year 1967 and completed in fiscal year 1972. Following review of these recommendations by panels of the National Academy of Sciences* (NAS) and the

President's Science Advisory Committee, in 1965 the AEC submitted to the president and the Congress a program incorporating the 200 GeV machine. In recognition of the national nature of the facility, the AEC invited proposals from all of the states. A total of 125 proposals were received.

In the belief that a truly national organization was needed to construct and operate the accelerator at whatever site was finally selected, the president of the NAS, Frederick Seitz, called together a group of university presidents. Representatives of the twenty-five universities who attended readily agreed to form a consortium of universities for that purpose. In June of 1965, the Universities Research Association was incorporated; in September the council of presidents had its first meeting to adopt the bylaws; and in November they elected the twenty-one trustees of the organization. In December of 1965, the URA trustees held their first meeting.

In December of 1966, the AEC selected the community of Weston, Illinois, approximately thirty miles southwest of the Chicago O'Hare Airport, as the site of the accelerator facility. In January of 1967, URA entered into a contract with the AEC for the design of a 200 GeV proton synchrotron, an accelerator significantly more powerful than any in existence at the time. Within two months Professor Robert R. Wilson of Cornell University had been selected to direct the effort. In advance of congressional appropriations, URA committed funds provided by member universities to the accelerator design project.

The beginning of construction was authorized in April of 1968. Operation of the accelerator at design energy was achieved in March of 1972, ahead of schedule and under the $250 million construction budget. A contract for the operation of the National Accelerator Laboratory (Fermilab) was signed on April 6, 1972. URA has continued to operate the laboratory since that time for the AEC, the Energy Research and Development Agency, and the Department of Energy. Under URA direction the operating energy of the accelerator was steadily increased until reaching 500 GeV in 1976. Through the use of superconducting magnets, the accelerator is now being modified to produce 1,000 GeV in the fixed target mode and 2,000 GeV in the center-of-mass system when operating as a colliding beam device.

Since 1972 Fermilab, under the management of URA, has provided a primary source of data for more than fifteen hundred experimental particle physicists. During the past year scientists from seventy U.S. and sixty foreign institutions have participated in research at the laboratory. The past decade has been particularly rich with respect to the number of fundamental discoveries and new insights obtained in the field of elementary particle physics. Among the contributions at Fermilab was the discovery of a meson, the upsilon, indicating the existence of a fifth type of quark, the b-quark. This, together with the discovery of the tau lepton at the Stanford

Linear Accelerator in 1975, has verified the existence of a third family of quark/lepton elementary particles.

Although the creation of URA was clearly inspired by the special considerations of the 200 GeV accelerator, its organization was specifically designed for response on a national basis to the needs of science over a broad area. The articles of incorporation of June 21, 1965, provide for the construction and operation of facilities in "the physical and biological sciences."

In June of 1975, in response to a URA proposal, the National Cancer Institute of the U.S. Department of Health, Education, and Welfare awarded a \$279,000 first-year grant for a Cancer Therapy Facility at Fermilab. Construction of the facility was completed in 1976, with donated funds received primarily through the American Cancer Society and the Illinois Cancer Council. The purpose of the facility is to explore the effectiveness of fast neutrons versus that of X-rays in the management of certain types of cancer. Neutrons are produced utilizing protons extracted from the Fermilab accelerator. Operation of the facility under a \$1 million annual grant is continuing.

Because of the close relationship between the understanding of fundamental particles and their interactions, and the determination of cosmological observables, the common ground shared by high energy physics and astronomy has been of continuing interest to the URA members and trustees. Pursuant to that interest, in 1975 URA enthusiastically responded to a request from American X-ray astronomers to cooperate in a proposal to establish and manage a national institute for X-ray observatories. A URA Committee on X-ray Astronomy was organized to prepare a proposal for the X-ray observatory institute. The proposal was submitted by URA to the National Aeronautics and Space Administration (NASA) in September, 1976. Subsequently Dr. Noel Hinners, associate administrator of NASA for Space Science, in a meeting with URA President Ramsey, expressed a favorable reaction to the proposal but stated that NASA's first priority for such an organization was the Space Telescope Science Institute. Three years later, in the fall of 1979, NASA issued a request for proposals to manage the Space Telescope Science Institute. URA submitted such a proposal but was not selected to manage the institute.

The council of presidents of URA meets once each year to review association operations, elect new trustees, and address policy issues, new activities, and bylaw amendments as necessary. Active management of the association is delegated to a board of trustees. The board is composed of twenty-five members, one each from the fifteen groups of neighboring institutions known as regional trustees, and ten trustees-at-large. An appropriate balance of scientific and administrative trustees is maintained. The present membership includes eight physicists, six astronomers, and eleven science administrators. The trustees meet quarterly. Their principal responsibilities include election of the corporate officers and selection of activity directors, definition of management policy, guidance to activity directors, review of activity budgets and contract performance, and technical and administrative program evaluation. The business of the board is conducted with the assistance of standing committees on Particle Physics, Astronomy, and Administration. The president of URA is the chief executive officer of the corporation. He is responsible to the board of trustees for the implementation of policies established by it and for informing the members of the board on all important matters affecting the quality and the financial integrity of the corporation and the institutions it manages. He is assisted in the execution of these responsibilities by a vice-president, a treasurer-controller, and a secretary of the corporation.

The first chairman of the council of presidents was President Gaylord Harnwell of the University of Pennsylvania. The present chairman is President William G. Bowen of Princeton University. Presidents of the following universities have also served as chairman of the council: Rice, Indiana, Carnegie-Mellon, Rochester, Tulane, Rockefeller, Massachusetts Institute of Technology, State University of New York at Stony Brook, Cornell, Colorado, and the University of California at San Diego.

The first chairman of the board of trustees was Professor Harry D. Smyth of Princeton University. He was succeeded in 1970 by Professor Robert F. Bacher of the California Institute of Technology, who served in the position until 1973, when he was succeeded by Professor A. Geoffrey Norman of the University of Michigan. In 1975 Professor Norman was succeeded by Professor Milton G. White of Princeton University. Professor White was succeeded in 1979 by Dr. Harry Woolf, director, Institute for Advanced Study* (IAS).

The first president of URA was President J. C. Warner of the Carnegie Institute of Technology, who in 1965, prior to the election of the first board of trustees, served temporarily in that position until succeeded in 1966 by Professor N. F. Ramsey. Professor Ramsey has occupied the position since 1966 with two interruptions. His service was broken by a year in Europe, during which time Professor Robert Bacher served as the URA president. Professor Ramsey was succeeded in 1979 by Professor Milton White, but was recalled to the presidency six months later by the untimely death of Professor White in October of 1979.

Each member university has agreed to contribute up to one hundred thousand dollars to URA on the call of the URA trustees. Although only ten thousand dollars per university has thus far been assessed, the availability of these funds has been a great source of assistance to the corporation. The initial construction of buildings at Fermilab, later repurchased by the AEC, contributed to saving approximately one year in accelerator construction time. The URA funds have been almost exclusively used for expenditures that for one reason or another, could not be made with funds derived from the government.

The offices of Universities Research Association are located in Suite 550 at 1100 Connecticut Avenue, Washington, D.C. 20037.

For further information, see Daniel S. Greenberg, *The Politics of Pure Science* (1967); M. Stanley Livingston, *Particle Accelerators: A Brief History* (1969); Leonard Greenbaum, *A Special Interest* (1971); and Anton G. Jackim, *Science Policy Making in the United States and the Batavia Accelerator* (1975). See also R. R. Wilson, "The Batavia Accelerator," *Scientific American* (February, 1974); and J. R. Sanford, "The Fermi National Accelerator Laboratory," *Annual Review of Nuclear Science* (1976).

The following hearings before the Joint Committee on Atomic Energy also provide information about URA: *High Energy Physics Research Before the Subcommittee on Research, Development, and Radiation*, 89th Cong. 2d sess., 2, 3, 4, 5 March 1965; and *AEC Authorizing Legislation FY 1969*, 90th Cong. 2d sess., 30, 31 January, 5, 6 February (Part 1), and 7, 21 February (Part 2), 1968.

NORMAN F. RAMSEY
JAMES C. MATHESON

UNIVERSITIES SPACE RESEARCH ASSOCIATION (USRA). This association was created on March 12, 1969, but the history of its origins extends back to the summer of 1966, when the National Aeronautics and Space Administration (NASA) administrator requested the help of the National Academy of Sciences* (NAS) in forming a national consortium to take over the management of the Lunar Receiving Laboratory. The president of the NAS, Dr. Frederick Seitz, first turned to the Universities Research Association* (URA), which had recently been created to operate the National Accelerator Laboratory. Dr. Seitz raised the issue of NASA's involvement at a URA meeting in the fall of 1966. However, because of budgetary concerns with the National Accelerator Laboratory, URA did not wish to assume any additional responsibilities.

To satisfy its immediate needs, NASA took the management of the Lunar Receiving Laboratory on its own but left open the possibility of wider participation of the academic community through an institute. At this time the idea of a Lunar Science Institute (LSI) took form. To develop further the concept of the LSI, the NAS created a committee under the chairmanship of Dr. Kenneth Pitzer to study NASA-university relations. In the fall of 1967, the Pitzer Committee recommended the establishment of the LSI, initially to be operated by Rice University under a subcontract with the NAS, but eventually to be operated by a university consortium. The Pitzer Committee concluded that the pattern established at LSI could form the basis for the development of a much broader link between NASA and the academic community.

NASA and NAS planning for LSI continued through the winter of 1967-1968, and on March 1, 1968, President Lyndon B. Johnson announced the creation of LSI. The NAS and the NASA continued to hope that URA would broaden its activities to include space and would agree to manage the LSI. However, on July 16, 1968, the URA board of trustees voted unanimously that it should not become involved in the Lunar Science Institute. Faced with the decision of the URA board, and with time for the receipt of the first lunar samples drawing closer, President Seitz of the academy invited the presidents of all URA universities, and additionally a few other universities involved in space science research, to join a new university consortium. On October 13, 1968, representatives of these forty-five invited universities met to discuss conditions under which a consortium would take responsibility for the Lunar Science Institute. Following this meeting, President Seitz wrote the presidents of each university represented, requesting formal notification of their willingness to become members of an institution to be named Universities Space Research Association (USRA) and incorporated in the District of Columbia. A meeting of thirty-three interested universities was subsequently held on December 15, 1968. Provisional articles of incorporation were adopted, and an interim managing committee, the Universities Organizing Committee for Space Science, was formed.

There followed continued negotiations with URA, however, but finally in February, 1969, the Council of the National Academy of Sciences met to discuss the issue of consortium management of LSI. President Seitz subsequently wrote the acting administrator, Dr. Thomas Paine, that the NAS felt that it would not be wise to spend further time negotiating with URA. He recommended moving ahead with the establishment of an independent consortium of universities that would be specifically oriented toward the problems of the National Aeronautics and Space Administration. In a meeting with Dr. Seitz and others on February 18, Dr. Paine concurred. The Universities Space Research Association was then incorporated in the District of Columbia on March 12, 1969.

Interim management of the Lunar Science Institute by the National Academy of Sciences continued through 1969. During this time NASA funded the refurbishment of the West Mansion, located on Rice University property adjacent to the Manned Spacecraft Center in Houston, which was to house the LSI, and a contract between NASA and USRA was developed for the operation of the institute by the newly formed consortium. Work on the West Mansion was begun in February, 1969. The building was occupied in October, 1969, and formally dedicated on January 4, 1970. USRA's contract for the operation of the LSI began in December, 1969.

The first president of USRA was Dr. A. R. Kuhlthau, a professor at the University of Virginia. He served on an acting basis from December 9, 1969, until April 24, 1970, when he was formally named president. The USRA headquarters was moved to Charlottesville, Virginia, so that Dr. Kuhlthau could devote half his time to the organization and operation of USRA.

USRA initially concentrated on the management of LSI (renamed the

Lunar and Planetary Institute in 1978), but even at that time the consortium began to explore other possible projects involving NASA. The first of these, a study project in conjunction with the Marshall Space Flight Center (MSFC) in the area of materials processing in space, began in 1970. This initial grant was followed by a contract with MSFC in 1971, and the USRA sponsorship by NASA of research dealing with materials processing in space has continued to the present. The next major involvement with NASA was the setting up in 1972 of another institute, the Institute for Computer Applications in Science and Engineering (ICASE), which was located at the Langley Research Center in Virginia. ICASE operation has also continued to the present. In 1976 USRA expanded its activities at MSFC into the area of cloud microphysics. Recently this subject area studied has shifted somewhat toward atmospheric processes as they might be observed from space.

Also in 1976, Dr. Alexander J. Dessler, then and now chairman of the Department of Space Physics and Astronomy at Rice University, became the second and current president of USRA. Consequently, the headquarters of the association were then moved to Rice University. In 1978, however, a decision was reached that USRA had arrived at the point in its operations that a permanent headquarters was needed. Thereupon, managerial offices, under the direction of a secretary, were set up at Columbia, Maryland, approximately forty-five miles from Washington, D.C.

USRA's birth coincided with the beginning of a post-Apollo retrenchment at NASA. That fact, coupled with the mission orientation of NASA, has caused USRA to grow relatively slowly. More than once USRA has had to cut back its activities in response to budget cuts imposed on NASA. Despite this slow growth, the original objectives of the founders of USRA are being realized. The consortium has grown to fifty-two members and has established, with NASA's involvement, a management structure that is responsive both to NASA and to the university community. The consortium is oriented toward the problems of the space agency and now facilitates the interaction between NASA and the university community at six of NASA's seven centers.

For further information, see USRA booklets, *Organizational Information 1980-1981*, and *Articles of Incorporation and Bylaws*, undated. See also Luther J. Carter, "Lunar Science Institute: Link between NASA and Academe," *Science* (March, 1969).

W. D. CUMMINGS

UNIVERSITY CORPORATION FOR ATMOSPHERIC RESEARCH (UCAR). Following World War II and on into the 1950s, the atmospheric scientists of the United States were faced with a number of interrelated challenges that they were not very well prepared to meet. These included the ever increasing importance and need for better weather forecasting associated with the growth of civil and military aviation; the promises held out by computers for development of new weather prediction techniques; the unknowns in weather modification; and the need for fundamental knowledge related to increasing air pollution. Funding for research at that time to meet these challenges, however, was primarily confined to individual atmospheric science research projects in universities, usually through the normal types of grants or contracts. On the whole, funding for both basic and applied research was far below the level needed for a vigorous national research effort.

It is against this background that, in 1956, the National Academy of Sciences* (NAS) set up a Committee on Meteorology to consider and recommend means by which to increase the understanding and control of the atmosphere. In a 1958 report this committee made the following major recommendations: increase federal funding for basic atmospheric research 50 to 100 percent; and establish a national atmospheric institute, operated by a corporation or universities under contract with the National Science Foundation. With foundation encouragement, a group from departments of meteorology in fourteen universities organized a University Committee on Atmospheric Research, which considered and endorsed these recommendations. The outcome, initially with support funds supplied by the NAS and later the foundation, was the chartering in 1959 of a University Corporation for Atmospheric Research (UCAR) and the establishment in 1960 of a National Center for Atmospheric Research (NCAR) under its auspices and control.

Dr. Walter Orr Roberts was named the first director of NCAR, and Boulder, Colorado, was chosen as the site for the center. By early 1961, as an interim measure, space for the new center had been leased from the University of Colorado, and Roberts began assembling a scientific staff. From its beginnings, NCAR was set up to provide a center where first-rate scientists could pursue their research interests using facilities too large and expensive for any one institution to maintain for its own use. Also, NCAR was designed to provide unified planning for atmospheric research programs that could respond to national and international needs.

A major development within UCAR during its early years was the effecting of a merger with the High Altitude Observatory, an institution which had existed under Roberts's direction since 1946, whereby it became a division of NCAR. During this early period, too, research programs in atmospheric dynamics, chemistry, and physics were established; computer facilities for NCAR research were installed; the National Scientific Balloon Facility began operations in 1963 at Palestine, Texas; visitor programs to foster nationwide scientific interchange were established; and the Research Aviation Facility was formed and began operations with one aircraft in 1964. Also in that year construction of the main NCAR laboratory, just south of Boulder, was begun, and it was completed late in 1966.

In the 1960s and 1970s, NCAR scientists and engineers developed strong, ongoing basic research programs that, from time to time, produced not only fundamental contributions to knowledge but also information of value in dealing with national issues. For example, in the mid-1960s, NCAR began observational and theoretical studies of the chemistry of the atmosphere. When national policy decisions had to be made in the 1970s about stratospheric pollution, NCAR was positioned to supply useful information about such questions as the effect of methanes on the stratospheric ozone layer. As early as 1967, NCAR began participating in and managing field research programs on the role of tropical atmosphere in the global-scale atmospheric circulation. In the early 1970s it conducted the National Hail Research Experiment aimed, in part, at testing the feasibility of using cloud seeding to reduce hail damage to crops and understanding why various seeding approaches would or would not be effective.

The university community had and continues to have a strong advisory and participatory role in these and subsequent NCAR programs. UCAR and NCAR officials believe that the importance of this collaboration cannot be overstated, in that it makes possible research efforts that would have been difficult to undertake given other institutional arrangements.

Before NCAR came into existence and again in the early 1970s, however, there were complaints from some university scientists that NCAR might be a competitor for federal research funds, particularly from the NSF, and then some allegations in the 1970s that NCAR was unresponsive to university needs. New mechanisms were eventually developed in the university-NCAR-NSF relationship to ensure more effective participation by the university community in the planning, operation, and review of NCAR programs.

Thus the initial support and almost all of NCAR's funding for its first two decades of existence came from the National Science Foundation and largely for basic research. Beginning with the late 1970s and as the 1980s begin, however, it is becoming increasingly obvious that atmospheric problems are falling within the range of interest of mission-oriented governmental agencies such as the Environmental Protection Agency, the Departments of Transportation, Energy, and Interior, and the National Oceanic and Atmospheric Administration (NOAA). In response to this interest, UCAR is actively exploring new projects that utilize the talents of the universities, in addition to its operations of NCAR. For example, UCAR recently concluded a contract with NOAA under which UCAR has advised NOAA on the design of a system for monitoring the ocean processes and ocean-atmospheric interaction that affect climatic variation. Also, Dr. Robert M. White, president of UCAR and former head of NOAA, suggested at a recent congressional hearing that UCAR be assigned a national program of weather modification research. Actual and potential programs of this type will probably work changes in UCAR-NCAR methods of operation. In the past, for example, NCAR's facilities have been fully funded by the National Science Foundation, and there was no direct charge to user scientists. Under a policy initiated during the current fiscal year with the concurrence of the National Science Foundation, user charges have been imposed on scientists from NCAR and from universities whose work requires NCAR facilities and is funded by agencies other than the National Science Foundation.

The responsibility for charting the UCAR-NCAR course in these uncharted waters rests with a seventeen-member governing board of trustees elected by the representatives of UCAR member universities, which presently numbers forty-nine. The president of UCAR is Dr. White, who is chief executive officer. Dr. Wilmot N. Hess is director of NCAR.

For further information, see "UCAR and NCAR: A History," *NCAR Quarterly* (November, 1972); Elizabeth Lynn Hallgren, *The University Corporation for Atmospheric Research and the National Center for Atmospheric Research, 1960-1970* (1974); and Henry Lansford, "The Center for Atmospheric Research," *Mosaic* (March-April, 1980). See also various informational pamphlets published intermittently by UCAR-NCAR as well as UCAR and NCAR *Annual Reports*.

V

VIRGINIA HISTORICAL AND PHILOSOPHICAL SOCIETY. See Virginia Historical Society, The.

VIRGINIA HISTORICAL SOCIETY, THE. For 150 years—longer than half the states of the Union have been in existence—the Virginia Historical Society has sought to preserve the treasures of the past. The Virginia historical agency is the fourth oldest among state societies. In unbroken fashion through two centuries, Virginians have supported the organization with what former Senator J. William Fulbright once called "a mystic sense of a continuing contract between generations."

Few depositories in America can boast of holdings as varied and valuable as those found inside the Richmond-based organization. Much of the society's wealth is directly attributable to its growth—a saga of persistence and devotion worthy of high praise.

Motivated by a desire "to collect and preserve materials for the civil and physical history of Virginia," twenty-eight gentlemen met in the House of Delegates chamber of the State Capitol on December 29, 1831, and established the Virginia Historical and Philosophical Society. Its birth came closely behind the formation of similar groups in Massachusetts, New York, and Pennsylvania, yet it ranked first in the illustriousness of its leader. Chief Justice of the U.S. Supreme Court John Marshall headed the Old Dominion society during its initial four years. Former President James Madison was the first person elected to honorary membership in the association.

The society's early growth was slow but steady. Monthly meetings were held in the homes of executive committee members. During the period 1848-1853 it published the only historical journal in the South. The *Virginia History Register and Literary Companion* stressed colonial history and was eclectic in nature. Its circulation was never the equal of its quality.

Gifts to the Richmond group came in a trickle. Some donations were of questionable value. An altar cloth from a defunct Episcopal Church in central Virginia was accepted with enthusiasm, for it was elaborately adorned with figures depicting the battle of Jericho. The embroidery was truly impressive until one noticed Israelites storming Jericho with cannon and mortars—one thousand years before such weapons were developed.

Four years of civil war all but destroyed the Virginia Historical Society. The April, 1865, fire that swept through downtown Richmond commensurate with the Confederate evacuation of the capital incinerated most of the society's records; the endowment, which had been patriotically invested in Confederate bonds, by war's end was gone with the wind; and during the "Reconstruction" years a fourth of its five thousand books simply disappeared.

Stability did not begin in earnest until 1893, when the John Stewart family donated to the Virginia Historical Society (as it was by then called) the Lee mansion on East Franklin Street. That same year also witnessed the establishment of a quarterly journal, the *Virginia Magazine of History and Biography*. It remains the oldest such state publication still in print.

Lee House, where General Robert E. Lee spent the immediate postwar months, served as society headquarters for sixty years. By the early 1950s, thanks to the generosity of a legion of donors, the building was literally bulging at the seams. Providentially, the society received its largest bequest shortly thereafter. From the estate of Mr. and Mrs. Alexander Weddell, a prominent Richmond couple, it inherited Virginia House (a reconstructed English manor), a magnificent collection of printed Virginiana, plus an endowment that became the base for a greatly increased operating budget. The generosity of the Weddells, the society's 1948 annual report stated, placed the agency in a position in which it could perform in the future a greater service to the people of Virginia than it had been able to do theretofore.

Eleven years of planning and construction followed, which resulted in the shift of the society's facilities to Richmond's west side and an enlarged Battle Abbey. This merger with the famous Confederate memorial hall, where massed battle flags and Charles Hoffbauer's murals continue to flank the entryway, makes the building one of Richmond's most popular and impressive attractions.

Artifacts, memorabilia, portraiture, and a wide variety of cultural exhibits draw large numbers of people annually to Battle Abbey. However, the society is better known as one of the principal research centers in the United States. Students and scholars alike flock to the library with such regularity as to give the staff scant relaxation during working hours.

The society's holdings are especially strong in Revolutionary and Civil War history, local histories, genealogy, British history and heraldry, early travels, architecture, agriculture, cookery, and works by and about Virginians. Included in the 3.5 million manuscripts are the major portion of William Byrd's papers. Equally valuable are the papers of the Lee and

Custis families. This huge collection spans many generations of two of the state's most influential clans. The Preston collection numbers thirty thousand pieces and is so extensive that a recently prepared typescript-genealogy of the family runs to three bound volumes.

The society is especially rich in Civil War manuscripts. General J. E. B. Stuart's letterbook and Mrs. Robert E. Lee's personal cookbook are items of inestimable worth. In the Virginia agency's vaults are the original draft of General Jubal A. Early's memoirs along with that Virginian's major papers. Wartime letters, diaries, and reminiscences from scores of Old Dominion Confederates are also preserved.

A few of the highly revealing but almost forgotten holdings are beginning to gain public notice. For example, a master's thesis is currently being prepared on Colonel Thomas T. Munford's recollections of the Appomattox Campaign; another thesis under way revolves around the wartime diary of Colonel Osmun Latrobe, who was General James Longstreet's chief of staff.

Over one hundred thousand books rest on the society's shelves. Among the priceless titles are Richard Hakluyt's volumes on English navigation. Published between 1589 and 1600, this series sparked the settlement of Virginia a decade later. Other printed holdings are a first edition (London, 1624) of John Smith's *Generall Historie of Virginia*; a 1733 Williamsburg edition of the acts of the colonial assembly; Edmund Pendleton's only printed monograph, *An Address . . . to the American Citizens on the Present State of Our Country* (1799); James Monroe's copy of the George Wythe compilation, *Reports of Cases Decided in the Virginia High Court of Chancery* (1796); twenty different printings of Thomas Jefferson's incomparable *Notes on the State of Virginia*; and Robert E. Lee's much-used wartime copy of the Episcopal *Book of Common Prayer*.

Newspapers are extremely difficult to preserve. They generally end up as floor mats, fire starters, and garbage bags; when left alone, they self-destruct. However, in the society's newspaper collection there are 42,500 separate issues. They begin with the 1736-1740 numbers of the Williamsburg *Virginia Gazette*, which were the first issues of the colony's oldest newspaper.

The society owns six thousand maps, including John White's 1590 *Americae Pars*, the first separate map ever drawn of the Virginia area. Heavily used in the cartographic collection are seventy county maps prepared during the Civil War by Confederate engineers.

Dominating one hundred thousand photographic negatives are the A. Aubrey Bodine collection of Civil War battlefield and historic sites (five hundred items) and the well-known Michael Miley collection (eight hundred items).

Portraiture is the foundation for much of the beauty on regular display at Battle Abbey. The society owns more than six hundred portraits of Virginian and American notables. Yet because of space limitations, no more than sixty works can be shown at one time. In addition to magnificent likenesses of William Byrd II, Washington, Jefferson, and others, the society has many paintings of outdoor scenes. Lewis Miller's watercolor drawings of southwest Virginia have long held national attention.

The 1,180 pieces of Confederate currency that the society owns gives it the largest collection of Civil War money known to exist in one place. The Maryland Steuart collection of Confederate weapons and accoutrements could more than fill several rooms.

Equally impressive is the annual increase in the society's research materials. Acquisitions for 1979 alone included 44,230 manuscripts and 2,170 books. In recent years the Virginia organization has been fortunate indeed where endowment is concerned. In 1948 the society was struggling on a three hundred thousand-dollar base. Today the endowment approaches the four-million-dollar mark.

One of the Old Dominion agency's greatest assets is the traditional courtesy of its staff. This is a remarkable compliment when one remembers that daily requests for information range from the search for a great-great-uncle named John Jones to "please send me everything you have on George Washington." A major weakness at the moment is a shortage of space. If book and manuscript acquisitions continue at their present rate—and they must if the depository is to maintain its reputation for excellence—a major expansion of the physical plant will be mandatory before this decade ends.

The future, however, looks bright because strong leadership has always characterized the society. Its presidents have included Henry St. George Tucker, William Cabell Rives, Hugh Blair Grigsby, William Gordon McCabe, Virginius Dabney, and D. Tennant Bryan. Four Pulitzer prize recipients (Dabney, Douglas S. Freeman, Lenoir Chambers, and David J. Mays) have served on its board of trustees, as have judges, physicians, attorneys, historians, bankers, and businessmen of proven talents.

After a century and a half, the basic goal of the Virginia Historical Society remains the same: to preserve wisdom and beauty from the past so that the future can be faced with knowledge and confidence.

For further information, see the following articles appearing in the *Virginia Magazine of History and Biography:* William G. Stanard, "History of the Virginia Historical Society" (October, 1931); Richard Beale Davis, "A Fitting Representation: Seventy-Five Years of the *Virginia Magazine of History and Biography*" (July, 1967); and James I. Robertson, Jr., "Virginia Historical Society: The Energies of Some for the Enrichment of All" (April, 1978). See also William M. E. Rachal, "The formation of the Virginia Historical Society," in Darrett B. Rutman, ed., *The Old Dominion: Essays for Thomas Perkins Abernethy* (1964).

JAMES I. ROBERTSON, JR.

_W_

WINTERTHUR MUSEUM. See Henry Francis du Pont Winterthur Museum.

WISTAR INSTITUTE OF ANATOMY AND BIOLOGY, THE. Caspar Wistar was born in Philadelphia in 1761, and on graduation from the William Penn Charter School was so proficient in Latin that he was able to use it for conversational purposes. He earned a medical degree from the University of Edinburgh in 1786, and returned to Philadelphia, where he commenced practice the following year, rapidly taking high rank in the profession. He was elected professor of chemistry in the College of Philadelphia in 1789, became a physician of the Philadelphia Dispensary in 1787 and, in 1793, of the Pennsylvania Hospital. From 1808 until his death, he occupied the anatomy chair at the University of Pennsylvania. Teaching anatomy to medical students in the nineteenth century, without visual aids, was quite a challenge. Dr. Wistar began to collect anatomical specimens in 1808 in order to instruct his students more thoroughly. This was the origin of what was to become the Wistar Institute of Anatomy and Biology.

Caspar Wistar numbered among his friends Thomas Jefferson, whom he succeeded as president of the American Philosophical Society* (APS), and Benjamin Rush, the physician with whom he worked to quell the disastrous yellow fever epidemic of 1793.

It was the custom of Dr. Wistar to entertain members of the American Philosophical Society weekly, bringing together doctors and scientists in other fields. After his death in 1818, his friends organized the Wistar Association, which has continued to this day, except for a brief interruption during the Civil War, to host dinners several times a year for prominent Philadelphians and their guests.

Dr. Wistar was assisted in the work of collecting anatomical specimens by his colleague and successor, Dr. William Edmonds Horner. The rights to this Wistar-Horner collection resided with the University of Pennsylvania until the late nineteenth century. The collection included natural and synthetic specimens of dried, embalmed, and formalin-preserved human material as well as models fabricated from wax or sculptured in wood. Rare texts of the era were also included as well as a set of surgical instruments, circa 1850-1863. Today this collection is the nucleus of the Wistar Museum.

In the final quarter of the nineteenth century, interest in the Wistar-Horner collection waned. When the dean of the medical school decided on a campaign to raise funds to rejuvenate the collection, he appealed to the great-nephew of Dr. Caspar Wistar, Brigadier General Isaac J. Wistar. General Wistar, at the time president of two venerable Philadelphia institutions, the Academy of Natural Sciences of Philadelphia* and the American Philosophical Society, responded immediately with a donation. But the idea of a separate institute began to intrigue him. In 1892 he founded, under an indenture of agreement with the trustees of the University of Pennsylvania, the Wistar Institute of Anatomy and Biology.

Isaac J. Wistar (1827-1905) was the oldest child of Caspar Wistar, M.D. (1801-1867), who was the second of three sons of Thomas Wistar (1765-1851), the younger brother of Dr. Caspar Wistar (1761-1818). Educated at local Quaker schools, he tried his hand at accounting and farming, and then, following news of the discovery of gold in California, Isaac Wistar set out in April, 1849, to make his fortune. Following travels that took him from California through the Northwest Territories, he accumulated some capital by supplying outlying miners and trappers with provisions. Wistar returned to San Francisco and for a modest sum purchased 160 acres of land. Here he built a small frame house and set about sowing 100 acres of wheat and the remainder in barley. But the life of a rancher-farmer was not sufficiently exciting for this adventurer. He soon joined a group aboard the barque, *New World*, for a voyage to Puget Sound to trade for local fir timber, whale oil, and salmon from the Indians. A second expedition aboard the half-rigged brig, *Kate Heath*, searched for and found a harbor on the uncharted Oregon coast.

Neither trading nor farming, however, were providing the fortune that Wistar had come to seek. He turned to law, served an apprenticeship with an established San Francisco law firm, successfully passed the bar examination in 1854, and became junior partner in the law firm of Baker and Wistar. Wistar returned to Philadelphia for a visit in the fall of 1857, was welcomed back into his family circle, and was eventually persuaded to practice his new profession in his native city. He was admitted to practice before the Supreme Court of Pennsylvania in 1858, and before the Supreme Court of the United States in 1860.

Wistar's former law partner, Colonel Edward D. Baker, was elected U.S. Senator from Oregon in 1861, and warned him to abandon law for the study of military tactics. The bombardment of Fort Sumter and the ensuing Civil War proved the wisdom of his advice. Accepting President Lincoln's call for volunteers for the Union Army, Wistar was commissioned a lieutenant colonel, later colonel of volunteers, and aided in the recruitment of men for the California Regiment, and later the seventy-first Pennsylvania Regiment. Participating in a number of Civil War engagements, Wistar was wounded at the battles of Ball's Bluff and Antietam. Following an attack of typhoid fever, Colonel Wistar was sent home in 1862, married in that year, and then returned to active service. He was promoted to brigadier general before recurrence of the fever forced him to resign his commission in 1864. Following the Civil War, Wistar became a successful businessman. He headed a number of corporations, including the Union Canal Company and Pennsylvania Canal Company, and, in partnership with the Pennsylvania Railroad, the Susquehanna Coal Company.

This was the man who founded the Wistar Institute and, after the University of Pennsylvania presented a plot of ground on Thirty-Sixth Street between Woodland Avenue and Spruce Street, erected thereon a museum and laboratory building at a cost of $125,000. Eventually, in a deed of trust dated October 1, 1898, General Wistar turned over the sum of $340,000 to be used as an endowment for the institute.

The institute was to be governed by a board of managers to include the oldest lineal male descendant of the father of the donor, two representatives of the Academy of Natural Sciences of Philadelphia, and such others as might be needed to fulfill its purpose.

Dr. Harrison Allen, an active medical practitioner who for many years had been an enthusiastic investigator in comparative anatomy, was appointed the first director. The defined purpose of the institute was to house the collection of anatomical specimens and preparations amassed, in part, over the years by General Wistar's great-uncle, Professor Caspar Wistar. In addition to its museum, the institute was equipped with laboratories and facilities to enable investigators to study comparative anatomy and experimental biology and engage in ancillary scientific research.

Dr. Horace Jayne succeeded Dr. Allen as director of the institute and, during his ten-year administration, not only expanded the anatomical collection and the growing anatomical library but supervised the installation of a machine shop for the production of metal-glass museum cases, formerly only found in foreign museums.

In January, 1905, Dr. Milton J. Greenman, who had acted as associate director from the time of the opening of the institute, was elected director. With the concurrence of General Wistar, the Wistar Institute hosted a national conference in April, 1905, to discuss the scientific policy of the institute. As a result, an advisory board was organized and arrangements made to hold annual meetings in Philadelphia.

Professor Henry H. Donaldson, professor of neurology at the Ogden School of Science at the University of Chicago, joined the Wistar staff in 1906, and led a group of young Wistar scientists in intensive study of the brain. He was assisted by Dr. S. Hatai. Their work was expanded by Drs. Helen Dean King and Edward B. Meigs. Because much of the research was performed on laboratory animals, extensive data were collected on the animal of choice, the albino rat. The Wistar Institute maintained a large animal colony for the use of its investigators; requests from other research laboratories for these animals were also honored, and what came to be known as the Wistar rat helped to spread the reputation of the institute. Eventually, the Wistar rat was turned over to a commercial breeding house in order to permit Wistar scientists to devote more time to their research interests.

In 1923 a complete printing press organization was established on the premises so that the institute could exert more efficient control over the well-known journals and publications bearing its imprint, some dating from 1908. Wistar journals were continuously published at the institute through December, 1979, and included: *American Journal of Anatomy*, *American Journal of Physical Anthropology*, *Anatomical Record*, *Journal of Cellular Physiology*, *Journal of Comparative Neurology*, *Journal of Experimental Zoology*, *Journal of Morphology*, and *Teratology*. They were turned over to a commercial publisher as a result of a thorough review of the institute's priorities.

On the death of Dr. Greenman in April, 1937, Dr. Edmond J. Farris was appointed executive director of the institute, and he and his associates pursued studies in human fertility. Partly because of the changing emphasis in biological and medical research, the institute's facilities were no longer adequate to attract those investigators who wished to work in the forefront of biological science, and the significance of its scientific contributions declined.

Hilary Koprowski, M.D., was appointed director of the Wistar Institute on May 1, 1957. Through grants from the federal government, private enterprise, and personal donations, the laboratories were completely modernized, and a new team of scientific investigators was attracted to the institute.

In the 1960s and 1970s, as a result of Wistar research, vaccines were developed against poliomyelitis, rabies, and rubella. Wistar scientists made important contributions in the study of atherosclerosis and, more recently, in the field of nutrition. In 1961, Wistar scientists reported that they had isolated and developed a standard method for growing human diploid, or normal, cell strains; WI-38 became a universally used laboratory tool to study human viruses and for the development of more efficient and safe human vaccines. The study of aging, from birth through death, at the cellular level was pioneered in Wistar laboratories in the 1960s. In the early 1970s, Wistar scientists undertook the study of multiple sclerosis, the tragic debilitating disease of young adults, and in 1973 the institute was designated a Multiple Sclerosis Research Center by the National Institutes of Health and the National Multiple Sclerosis Society.

Early work in cancer research was hampered by limited laboratory space. In 1971, Wistar received one of the first matching-fund construction grants under President Nixon's Conquest of Cancer Plan. Foundation, corporate, and private donations were raised to permit the first major expansion since Wistar's incorporation. In June, 1975, fifty-one new laboratories were dedicated to cancer research, and on June 12, a dedication symposium on "Perspectives in Cancer Biology" featured Dr. Raymond Latarjet of Paris and Dr. Salvador Luria of MIT as cochairmen; speakers included Drs. Henry Kaplan, James Holland, Wallace P. Rowe, Walter Bodmer, David Baltimore, Neils K. Jerne, and Michael Stoker.

Since the opening of the new cancer research facility, over half of the research activities at the institute have been designed to advance the understanding of the genetic and environmental causes of cancer, including the study of the conversion of normal cells into malignant or abnormal cells, immune response to tumor viruses, and the effects of chemical carcinogens on cells in culture. Recent advances in medical technology have led to Wistar's first human hybridoma, a cell-line producing human monoclonal antibodies, as well as many extensively characterized mouse-human hybridomas. The new work on monoclonal antibodies is revolutionizing the field of biomedical research, and scientists at the Wistar Institute are in the forefront of these pioneering studies.

Presently, Dr. Koprowski leads a multinational group of over one hundred scientists and their technical support staff. Eighty percent of the current annual budget is received via the competitive peer review process of the National Institutes of Health and the National Science Foundation. Nonfederal sources of income include the American Cancer Society, the National Multiple Sclerosis Society, and the Commonwealth of Pennsylvania. Investment of its endowment, plus royalty income from its licensing agreements on Wistar-developed inventions, are supplemented by annual foundation, corporate, and private donations, including contributions by the volunteer organization established in 1965 as the Friends of the Wistar Institute.

Wistar's board of managers, chaired by Mr. John W. Eckman, is composed of twenty-five businessmen, scientists, and private individuals, including a Wistar family representative and two representatives of the Academy of Natural Sciences of Philadelphia.

Visitors continue to be intrigued by the Wistar-Horner collection exhibited in the Wistar Museum; Wistar offices continue to be located on the site of the original building at Thirty-Sixth and Spruce streets, Philadelphia.

For further information, see *Autobiography of Isaac Jones Wistar* (1937). See also R.E. Billingham and H. Koprowski, "The Wistar Institute of Anatomy and Biology," *Nature* (September, 1959); and David Kritchevsky and William Purcell, "The Wistar Institute," *Karger Gazette* (April, 1974).

MARGARET P. O'NEILL DAVIS

WOODS HOLE OCEANOGRAPHIC INSTITUTION. Although officially incorporated in January of 1930, the original concept of the Woods Hole

Oceanographic Institution goes back at least to 1924 and the first of a series of discussions between Frank R. Lillie, then director of the Marine Biological Laboratory* (MBL) in Woods Hole, Massachusetts, and Wickliffe Rose, the new president of the Rockefeller funded General Education Board. Their discussions with each other and with other interested individuals ranged over the interests of biology in general, then began to focus on oceanography, and eventually resulted in the appointment of a Committee on Oceanography by the National Academy of Sciences* (NAS) "to consider the share of the United States of America in a worldwide program of Oceanographic Research."

Chaired by Lillie, the distinguished committee—William Bowie of the U.S. Coast and Geodetic Survey, E.G. Conklin of Princeton University, B.M. Duggar of the University of Wisconsin, John C. Merriam of the Carnegie Institution of Washington,* T. Wayland Vaughan of the Scripps Institution of Oceanography, and Frank R. Lillie were the initial appointees, with Henry B. Bigelow of Harvard University and Arthur L. Day of the Carnegie Institution of Washington added a bit later—began its serious work in 1928 with summer meetings at the MBL. Their purpose was to examine the status and problems of oceanographic research in Europe and America and to lay the ground for a study of the best ways to supplement American agencies. Committee member Henry Bryant Bigelow of the Harvard University Museum of Comparative Zoology was asked to devote full time for a year to the business of the committee. The preliminary report he compiled during the year recommended, among other items, the establishment of a well-equipped oceanographic institution on the Atlantic coast, where there was no center devoted to the study of the oceans.

The recommendation was accepted, and the Committee on Oceanography formed the nucleus of a board of trustees for the new institution. Lillie was elected president of the corporation and Bigelow director of the laboratory. Because of geographic advantages, including a deep-water port and the assured scientific cooperation and good will of the MBL and the U.S. fisheries laboratory already established there, Woods Hole was chosen as the site. In January of 1930, the Woods Hole Oceanographic Institution was incorporated "to prosecute the study of oceanography in all its branches, to maintain a laboratory or laboratories, together with boats and equipment and a school for instruction in oceanography and allied subjects."

The Rockefeller Foundation allowed the new institution one million dollars for construction, boats, equipment, and upkeep, one million for endowment, and half a million for ten years of operating expenses. In 1935, the annual grant of fifty thousand dollars was replaced by the addition of one million dollars in endowment funds. The initial grant allowed construction of a four-story laboratory, a 40-foot coastal-dragger type boat for nearshore work, and a 142-foot steel-hulled ketch for open ocean research.

The latter, named *Atlantis*, was perhaps the most important, as little work had been done in the Atlantic for nearly fifty years. The hydrographic, light-intensity, and meteorological studies, along with the biographical collections undertaken on her maiden voyage in the summer of 1931, marked the beginning of an important new round of Atlantic investigations. For another six years, R/V *Atlantis* was the only American research ship large enough to undertake extensive work in the open ocean, and for fifteen more she was one of only a few.

In their inquiry into the state of American oceanography the NAS committee had turned up only a handful of oceanographers; so Bigelow was faced with "bringing up" a staff for the new institution. The early staff was made up of various university professors who spent their summer in Woods Hole. These included a physiologist, a paleontologist, several chemists, a meteorologist, and various biologists. Within several years, those who returned each summer to Woods Hole and participated in the weekly *Atlantis* cruises could certainly be considered oceanographers.

The turn of the decade brought profound change to oceanography. Columbus Iselin, who succeeded Bigelow as director in 1940, and the institution's trustees offered its facilities to the government for war work. The summertime staff of sixty expanded to a year-round complement of more than three hundred, and the operating budget skyrocketed from $135,000 to over $1 million.

Although the war work was largely applied in character (including the prevention of marine fouling on ships and studies of underwater acoustics and underwater explosions), a great deal of basic research was conducted as well because it was recognized that the state of the understanding of the oceans was not sufficient for generalizations to be drawn. Two aspects of Navy-sponsored war work have had lasting effects on oceanography. First, it attracted to the field many scientists who had had no previous experience with marine work but who were intrigued by the problems the field offered. Second, it afforded the Navy an understanding of the importance of oceanography in its general operations and left with many naval officers the appreciation of the contributions the science of oceanography could make to the operations of the fleet.

Following the war, there was a period of uncertainty about the future of oceanography. Costs of research at sea had been considerably inflated by the wartime economy, and the interests of oceanographers had broadened considerably, essentially from an interest in the description of the steady state or average conditions to a desire to follow the ocean's dynamic processes, a process that required year-round rather than summer-only attention. It was clear that government subsidy would be needed to continue off-shore observations. So it was that the conjunction of private oceanography and public need that had developed during the war was on the way to becoming the standard for peacetime as well.

Through the late 1940s the institution continued to settle into its expanded postwar state. Oceanographers who had been sent elsewhere returned, and many of those who had come to Woods Hole during the war returned to prewar positions or found new ones elsewhere. By 1950, when Admiral Edward H. Smith, with long experience in oceanography through the Coast Guard's Ice Patrol, took over the directorship from Columbus Iselin, personnel numbered 257 and the operating budget was about $516,000 for the year. Forty-six papers were published.

The institution's first support from the National Science Foundation, which had been established in 1950, came in 1952 for work on summer plankton blooms in Long Island Bays and for eight training fellowships. Since then, the foundation's share of institution operating funds has grown slowly and steadily until it surpassed the Navy support for basic research. In 1979, the National Science Foundation provided 52 percent of the $31 million total. Twenty-two percent came from Navy contracts in 1979, 8 percent from other governmental agencies, and 18 percent from private sources.

Admiral Smith retired in 1956, and Columbus Iselin again took the helm for two years until Dr. Paul M. Fye, who had been in charge of the wartime work on underwater explosives, returned to Woods Hole to become the fourth director of the Woods Hole Oceanographic Institution. Also in 1958, conversion of R/V *Chain* from a Navy deep-sea salvage tug to a research vessel marked the beginning of big-ship oceanography. The period following the first satellites sparked interest in and support for oceanography along with other sciences, and the future looked bright. Committees were appointed to consider new research vessels, land acquisition, a building program, and educational policy. As the 1950s closed, the institution's annual operating budget stood at $3.8 million, the fleet included five off-shore vessels ranging from 93 to 213 feet in length, a coastal vessel, and two aircraft, and $3 million had been awarded for construction of *Atlantis II*, one of today's academic fleet workhorses.

Oceanography continued to boom as the new decade began. The operating budget had doubled in three years, from $2.4 million in 1957, to $5 million in 1960. What had been an amorphous "scientific staff" was organized into six departments in 1962. Some reorganization in 1967 brought the departments to their present arrangement of departments of Biology, Chemistry, Geology and Geophysics, Ocean Engineering, and Physical Oceanography. In 1970, a Marine Policy and Ocean Management Program was initiated to bring social scientists, economists, lawyers, and those from other disciplines to Woods Hole to apply their skills to problems of ocean policy.

Students have always been involved in work at Woods Hole, and during the first forty years many had pursued thesis research at the institution while enrolled in various universities. This educational function was formalized in 1968, with a charter change and the signing of an agreement with the Massachusetts Institute of Technology for a joint degree-granting program. To date 113 graduate degrees have been awarded (including three solely by the institution), and about ninety students are presently enrolled in the joint program.

Today the Woods Hole Oceanographic Institution continues as a private, nonprofit corporation dedicated to the prosecution of "the study of oceanography in all its branches." Although a great deal more is known about the current systems, animal populations, and chemistry of the water column as well as the configuration of the sea floor and the layers beneath it, there are as many new questions today in oceanography as there were fifty years ago.

In a paper written for the Third International Congress on the History of Oceanography in 1980, Roger Revelle, former director of the Scripps Institution of Oceanography, commented that "the scientific output of the Oceanographic [Woods Hole] has been enormous," mentioning the total output of scientific papers which now approaches five thousand. Revelle also presented a short list of "impressive research results" that emphasize the diversity of work done at Woods Hole. These included the description and theoretical understanding of the Gulf Stream, invention of the bathythermograph (a continuous temperature-depth recording device), the discovery of mesoscale eddies (the oceanographic counterpart of cyclonic storms in the atmosphere at mid-latitudes), pioneering work in the recording of marine mammal sounds, contributions to the proof of sea-floor spreading, and extensive work in the spreading centers at the boundaries of the earth's great crustal plates. The discovery in 1977 of hot water vents erupting into the ambient near-freezing waters twenty-five hundred meters deep in the Galapagos Rift has set off several new areas of inquiry and promises answers to some of the historic conundrums of ocean science.

The scientific staff of the Woods Hole Oceanographic Institution now numbers about one hundred, and there are one hundred on the technical staff. Another six hundred people provide support services, ranging from ships' crew members and secretarial positions to carpentry, laboratory assistant, and administrative positions. Scottish mathematician and oceanographer John H. Steele became the fifth director in 1977.

The initial one-acre, single-story laboratory institution has expanded over its fifty years of life to encompass holdings of some two hundred acres and four large laboratories along with a variety of smaller facilities. In 1980, the three large research vessels operated by the institution averaged more than two hundred days at sea per year, the research submersible *Alvin* makes about one hundred deep dives annually, and the original coastal research vessel *Asterias* has just been replaced by a somewhat larger namesake.

The one hundred members of the corporation of the Woods Hole Oceanographic Institution are drawn from academe, business, and industry, and there are twenty-four members of the governing board of trustees.

For further information, see Frank R. Lillie, *The Woods Hole Marine Biological Laboratory* (1944); Susan Schlee, *The Edge of an Unfamiliar World: A History of Oceanography* (1973) and *On Almost Any Wind: The Saga of the Oceanographic Research Vessel "Atlantis"* (1978); Roger Revelle, "The Oceanographic and How It Grew," *Oceanography: The Past. Proceedings of the Third International Congress on the History of Oceanography*, (1980).

VICKY CULLEN

WORCESTER FOUNDATION FOR EXPERIMENTAL BIOLOGY. This nonprofit research institute in the biomedical sciences was founded in 1944 under the codirection of Drs. Hudson Hoagland and Gregory Pincus and was based on their scientific interests. These men both received their doctorates at Harvard in 1927 and became friends. Both became instructors in the then Department of General Physiology after a postdoctoral year as National Research Council (NRC) Fellows at Harvard and a period of study abroad on postdoctoral fellowships.

In 1931, Hoagland, at age thirty-one, after a year at Cambridge University doing research in neurophysiology in the laboratory of E. D. Adrian, went to Clark University in Worcester, Massachusetts, as professor of physiology and chairman of the Department of Biology. Pincus remained at Harvard as an assistant professor in general physiology, where his research in mammalian reproduction became widely recognized. After two three-year terms as assistant professor, the Pincus appointment was not renewed for reasons that to many were both obscure and unjustified. When Pincus learned of this he was at Cambridge University for a period of work in reproduction physiology at the Strangeways Laboratories, and at about this time he had published an important book, *The Eggs of Mammals*.

During the 1930s the Great Depression made jobs hard to come by, and Hoagland, believing in the outstanding scientific ability of his friend, in 1938 raised a modest sum to bring him to his department at Clark University as visiting professor. Clark had no money to pay Pincus for salary or budget, but the two scientists had been successful in the past in obtaining research grants from several private foundations, and this success continued and grew for the next six years before they left Clark and founded the foundation in 1944. Hoagland gave up his tenured professorship, and on a Guggenheim Fellowship joined with Pincus in establishing the new institution. At that time there were some twelve people, including two other Ph.D.s, sharing about one hundred thousand dollars in grant funds raised by Hoagland and Pincus at Clark. The new institution had no endowment, no fees from patients, no students, and no income from patents. It existed and still does exist on grants and gifts. Its current annual income is over seven million dollars. Some 83 percent of this is from the National Institutes of Health and the National Science Foundation. Private funds have made it possible to purchase 120 acres of residential land just east of Worcester in the town of Shrewsbury, and both private and federal funds have built a campus of a dozen buildings housing laboratories, library, cafeteria, assembly halls, classrooms, and offices. A modest endowment has also resulted from gifts and legacies. The foundation's board of trustees varies between thirty and thirty-five persons, primarily distinguished scientists, businessmen, and members of the medical and legal professions.

The work of the foundation is now divided among four major fields: Endocrinology and Reproduction, Neuroscience and Behavior, Molecular Biology, and Cancer Research. The first two of these were the fields of the original founders, and cancer research in relation to endocrinology was also in the early category. With the death of Pincus in 1967, and the retirement of Hoagland in 1969, a new scientific director was brought in by the trustees. He is Mahlon Hoagland, Harvard M.D., the son of Hudson Hoagland. After a tenured post as associate professor at the Harvard Medical School, Mahlon Hoagland went to Dartmouth Medical School in 1967 as professor and head of the Department of Biochemistry. He left Dartmouth to become president and research director of the foundation in 1970.

While at Harvard he made important contributions to molecular biology. Thus he and Paul Zamecnik discovered transfer RNA, one of the essential steps in cellular protein synthesis. He identified the amino acid-activating enzymes involved in combining with transfer RNA, and for this he was awarded the Franklin Medal. Under his direction, the cancer program has shifted from studies of steroids in relation to cancer, an active field at the foundation in the 1950s and 1960s, to basic studies of cell growth, for example, the role of genetic factors and possible viruses in cancer as well as refined studies of cellular biochemistry and enzymology. An outstanding group of young molecular biologists was recruited, together with Dr. Paul Zamecnik, now professor emeritus of oncology at Harvard, one of the most brilliant workers in the field and Mahlon's former chief, and Dr. Federico Welsch, M.D., Ph.D., as vice-president and executive director of the foundation.

The foundation over the years has had an active teaching program. In years past, when they were available, it has had several postdoctoral programs financed by the National Institutes of Health and the Ford Foundation. The first and largest of these was the NIH program in steroid chemistry and physiology. Another was a Ford Foundation program in human reproduction. This involved a grant for an addition to a building and salaries for the postdoctoral students and course staff. It was for students from underdeveloped countries planning to return home and work to reduce population growth. NIH made funds available for a similar program for training American postdoctoral students. A fourth training program was financed by the National Institute of Mental Health to train psychiatrists and other postdoctoral students in research in behavioral science and mental illness. These programs, each lasting one or two years, resulted in forty to fifty M.D.s or Ph.D.s in residence from various fields that were stimulating to the foundation staff.

The Commonwealth of Massachusetts Department of Education empowered the foundation to give Sc.D. degrees, both honorary and earned, the latter to people with Ph.D. or M.D. degrees. Honorary Sc.Ds have been conferred but no earned ones because routine lab facility for courses taught for credit are not available. Some of the foundation staff have held courtesy faculty appointments at various universities, and some Ph.D.s have thus been granted to students by their universities for thesis work done at the foundation.

The best-known contribution of the foundation was the development and extensive testing of the first and still perhaps most widely used fertility-controlling oral contraceptive. This was due to the work of Pincus, M. C. Chang, who is still on the staff at age seventy, and John Rock, professor emeritus of gynecology and obstetrics at Harvard. During the 1950s no major foundation or government agency would fund such a project because of sexual taboos and legal and religious pressures. This situation has changed drastically in recent years with the National Institutes of Health and large foundations joining in the support of contraceptive research. This has resulted from recognition of the magnitude of the unprecedented population explosion resulting primarily from rapidly falling death rates, especially in the developing countries. As early as the 1940s, however, foundation directors were convinced of the great importance of birth control.

The late Mrs. Stanley McCormick, a friend of Margaret Sanger, heard of the work of Pincus and visited him and others at the foundation and subsequently volunteered to finance the work on oral contraceptives. Pincus accordingly obtained from a number of pharmaceutical companies a wide range of natural and synthetic steroid substances to try on animals (rats and rabbits). The syntheses of these several hundred steroids had been patented by the companies—for use in problems having nothing to do with contraception or in hopes a use might one day be found for them.

With M. C. Chang conducting the animal studies, he and Pincus found about a dozen steroids that inhibited ovulation in animals. Pincus selected the most promising compounds with maximum inhibition of ovulation and minimum side effects. The most promising of these was a product of G. D. Searle Company with the trade name of Enovid. It was in use as a prescription drug to ease menstrual pain and regularize the rhythms.

Pincus and Chang wished to test it on women, and Dr. John Rock, although a Catholic, also thought the reduction of birth rates highly desirable and essential for civilization, and he agreed to assemble from his wide practice a group of women willing to cooperate. The first clinical tests were carried out by him on a small group of volunteers. Gynecological tests were used to determine whether or not ovulation was inhibited. The success of this pilot study led Pincus to organize a test of some ten thousand women in Puerto Rico and Haiti through Planned Parenthood Clinics. Extensive tests of side effects were also carried out. These clinical tests were under the immediate supervision of Dr. Ramon Celso-Garcia, a colleague of Dr. Rock.

The success of the tests ushered in the effective use of the "Pill," the first effective and safe oral contraceptive.

Although these results were of much social value, other basic work of the foundation has been of great importance. Thus, much has been learned over the years about stress and the role of the adrenocortical steroid hormones in controlling some of its effects, and new steroids of value have also been synthesized. Pioneering work in electrophysiology of the brain and its metabolism as well as studies of sensory nerve impulses have been conducted, and the present research in molecular biology has much promise, especially in relation to cancer research.

When the foundation was set up it was thought by many to have small chance of survival because it had little money and no direct university connection. It not only survived but prospered for thirty-six years. This may have been because in 1946 federal funds became increasingly available for basic research. Also Pincus and Hoagland in their early forties had established themselves as scientists with many publications and had the ability to attract first-rate scientists, particularly from abroad, to come to the foundation. But without federal support success would probably have been very limited.

For further information, see the Worcester Foundation *Annual Reports*, 1945 to date. See also Hudson Hoagland, *The Road to Yesterday* (1974). This autobiography, by the founder of the foundation, contains a history of the organization.

HUDSON HOAGLAND

LEARNED SOCIETIES— COUNCILS— RESEARCH INSTITUTIONS

This appendix provides, in alphabetical order in each case, an organizational listing divided into three categories: learned society, council, and research institution. In arriving at this division, although in a few cases the decision as to which category an organization fell into was a fine one, and although other elements such as scope of operations were considered, the two major determining factors were membership and source of funds for operation.

Learned societies are organizations that include individuals and, in a few cases, other organizations as members. Generally, a significant portion of their income needed for operations is provided by members.

Councils are organizations that include other organizations, particularly learned societies, as members or are very closely associated with them. A few include both organizations and individuals as members. A few derive a considerable portion of their operating income from members; however, most depend upon governmental, foundation, or business support for a major portion of their operating expenses.

Although some research institutions have individuals and other organizations as members and all have much in common with the learned societies and councils, individual or organizational membership is not a major characteristic of the research institutions. Generally, they have individual endowments that play a much more significant role in their operating expenses than in the case of the learned societies or councils.

LEARNED SOCIETIES

American Academy and Institute of Arts and Letters
American Academy of Arts and Sciences
American Academy of Religion
American Anthropological Association
American Antiquarian Society
American Association for the Advancement of Slavic Studies
American Association of Anatomists
American Association of Immunologists
American Association of Pathologists, Inc.
American Astronomical Society

American Chemical Society
American Comparative Literature Association
American Dialect Society
American Economic Association
American Folklore Society
American Geophysical Union
American Historical Association
American Institute of Nutrition
American Mathematical Society
American Meteorological Society
American Musicological Society
American Numismatic Society
American Oriental Society
American Philological Association
American Philosophical Association
American Philosophical Society, Held at Philadelphia, for Promoting Useful Knowledge
American Physical Society
American Physiological Society
American Political Science Association
American Psychological Association
American Society for Aesthetics
American Society for Eighteenth-Century Studies
American Society for Legal History
American Society for Microbiology
American Society for Pharmacology and Experimental Therapeutics
American Society for Theatre Research
American Society of Biological Chemists
American Society of International Law
American Society of Parasitologists
American Society of Zoologists
American Sociological Association
American Statistical Association
American Studies Association
Archaeological Institute of America
Association for Asian Studies
Association for Symbolic Logic
Association of American Geographers
Association of American Law Schools
Bibliographical Society of America
Botanical Society of America
College Art Association of America
Ecological Society of America
Econometric Society
Economic History Association
Electrochemical Society, Inc.
Entomological Society of America
Genetics Society of America
Geochemical Society
Geological Society of America
Hispanic Society of America
Historical Society of Pennsylvania, The
History of Science Society
Institute of Mathematical Statistics
Linguistic Society of America

Massachusetts Historical Society
Mathematical Association of America
Medieval Academy of America
Metaphysical Society of America
Modern Language Association of America
New-York Historical Society
Organization of American Historians
Paleontological Society
Renaissance Society of America
Society for Ethnomusicology
Society for the History of Technology
Society of Architectural Historians
Society of Biblical Literature
Virginia Historical Society, The

COUNCILS

American Association for State and Local History
American Association for the Advancement of Science
American Association for the Advancement of the Humanities
American Council of Learned Societies
American Council on Education
American Geological Institute
American Institute of Biological Sciences
American Institute of Physics
American Social Science Association
Federation of American Societies for Experimental Biology
Independent Research Libraries Association
International Council for Philosophy and Humanistic Studies
International Council of Scientific Unions
International Social Science Council
National Academy of Sciences
Social Science Research Council

RESEARCH INSTITUTIONS

Academy of Natural Sciences of Philadelphia
American Enterprise Institute for Public Policy Research
American Geographical Society
American Museum of Natural History
Argonne Universities Association
Aspen Institute for Humanistic Studies
Associated Universities, Inc.
Association of Universities for Research in Astronomy, Inc.
Battelle Memorial Institute
Bernice P. Bishop Museum
Brookings Institution
Carnegie Endowment for International Peace
Carnegie Institution of Washington
Center for Advanced Study in the Behavioral Sciences
Center for Applied Linguistics
Charles F. Kettering Foundation
Council on Foreign Relations, Inc.

Dumbarton Oaks Research Library and Collection
East-West Center
Eleutherian Mills-Hagley Foundation
Field Museum of Natural History
Folger Shakespeare Library
Foreign Policy Association
Foreign Policy Research Institute
Fox Chase Cancer Center
Franklin Institute, The
Hastings Center, Institute of Society, Ethics and the Life Sciences
Henry Francis du Pont Winterthur Museum
Hoover Institution on War, Revolution and Peace
Hudson Institute
Huntington Library, Art Gallery, Botanical Gardens
IIT Research Institute
Institute for Advanced Study
Institute for Sex Research
Institute of Early American History and Culture
Institute of Public Administration
John Crerar Library, The
Library Company of Philadelphia, The
Linda Hall Library
Lowell Observatory
Marine Biological Laboratory
Memorial Sloan-Kettering Cancer Center
Midwest Research Institute
National Geographic Society
Newberry Library, The
New York Academy of Medicine, The
New York Public Library, Astor, Lenox and Tilden Foundations, The
Oak Ridge Associated Universities
Peabody Museum of Archaeology and Ethnology
Pierpont Morgan Library
Population Council
Rand Corporation
Research Triangle Institute
Resources for the Future, Inc.
Robert Maynard Hutchins Center for the Study of Democratic Institutions
Salk Institute for Biological Studies
Smithsonian Institution
Southern Research Institute
Southwest Research Institute
SRI International
Universities Research Association, Inc.
Universities Space Research Association
University Corporation for Atmospheric Research
Wistar Institute of Anatomy and Biology, The
Woods Hole Oceanographic Institution
Worcester Foundation for Experimental Biology

CHRONOLOGY

This appendix provides a chronological listing of organizations discussed in this volume. It should be noted that the names of these organizations are those in use at the present time. Some are, of course, different from what they were at the founding of the organization (see Appendix 3, Genealogy).

As the reader will note, 4 of the organizations listed in this appendix were founded in the eighteenth century; in the nineteenth century, 9 organizations were founded in the decades prior to 1850, and 35 in the remaining decades of that century. The remaining 112 organizations were founded in the twentieth century.

1731

Library Company of Philadelphia, The

1743

American Philosophical Society, Held at Philadelphia, for Promoting Useful Knowledge

1780

American Academy of Arts and Sciences

1791

Massachusetts Historical Society

1804

New-York Historical Society

1812

Academy of Natural Sciences of Philadelphia
American Antiquarian Society

1824

Franklin Institute, The
Historical Society of Pennsylvania, The

1831

Virginia Historical Society, The

1839

American Statistical Association

1842

American Oriental Society

1846

Smithsonian Institution

1847

New York Academy of Medicine, The

1848

American Association for the Advancement of Science
New York Public Library, Astor, Lenox and Tilden Foundations, The

1851

American Geographical Society

1858

American Numismatic Society

1863

National Academy of Sciences

1865

American Social Science Association

1866

Peabody Museum of Archaeology and Ethnology

1869

American Museum of Natural History
American Philological Association

1876

American Chemical Society

1879

Archaeological Institute of America

1880

Society of Biblical Literature

1883

Modern Language Association of America

1884

American Historical Association
Memorial Sloan-Kettering Cancer Center

1885

American Economic Association

1887

American Physiological Society
Newberry Library, The

1888

American Association of Anatomists
American Folklore Society
American Mathematical Society
Geological Society of America
Marine Biological Laboratory
National Geographic Society

1889

American Dialect Society
Bernice P. Bishop Museum

1890

American Society of Zoologists

1892

American Psychological Association

1893

Botanical Society of America
Field Museum of Natural History

1894

John Crerar Library, The
Lowell Observatory
Wistar Institute of Anatomy and Biology, The

1898

American Academy and Institute of Arts and Letters

1899

American Astronomical Society
American Physical Society
American Society for Microbiology

1900

Association of American Law Schools

1901

American Association of Pathologists, Inc.
American Philosophical Association

1902

American Anthropological Association

Carnegie Institution of Washington
Electrochemical Society, Inc.

1903

American Political Science Association

1904

Association of American Geographers
Bibliographical Society of America
Hispanic Society of America

1905

American Sociological Association

1906

American Society of Biological Chemists
American Society of International Law
Entomological Society of America
Institute of Public Administration

1907

Organization of American Historians

1908

American Society for Pharmacology and Experimental Therapeutics
Paleontological Society

1909

American Academy of Religion

1910

Carnegie Endowment for International Peace

1912

College Art Association of America
Federation of American Societies for Experimental Biology

1913

American Association of Immunologists

1915

Ecological Society of America
Mathematical Association of America

1916

Brookings Institution

1918

American Council on Education
Council on Foreign Relations, Inc,
Foreign Policy Association

1919

American Council of Learned Societies
American Geophysical Union
American Meteorological Society
Hoover Institution on War, Revolution and Peace
Huntington Library, Art Gallery, Botanical Gardens
International Council of Scientific Unions

1924

American Society of Parasitologists
History of Science Society
Linguistic Society of America
Pierpont Morgan Library
Social Science Research Council

1925

Battelle Memorial Institute
Medieval Academy of America

1927

Charles F. Kettering Foundation
Fox Chase Cancer Center

1928

American Institute of Nutrition

1930

Econometric Society
Henry Francis du Pont Winterthur Museum
Institute for Advanced Study
Woods Hole Oceanographic Institution

1931

American Institute of Physics
Genetics Society of America

1932

Folger Shakespeare Library

1934

American Musicological Society

1935

Association for Symbolic Logic
Institute of Mathematical Statistics

1936

IIT Research Institute

1940

American Association for State and Local History

Dumbarton Oaks Research Library and Collection
Economic History Association
Society of Architectural Historians

1941

Association for Asian Studies
Southern Research Institute

1942

American Society for Aesthetics

1943

American Enterprise Institute for Public Policy Research
Institute of Early American History and Culture

1944

Midwest Research Institute
Worcester Foundation for Experimental Biology

1946

Associated Universities, Inc.
Linda Hall Library
Oak Ridge Associated Universities
SRI International

1947

Institute for Sex Research
Southwest Research Institute

1948

American Geological Institute
American Institute of Biological Sciences
Rand Corporation

1949

Aspen Institute for Humanistic Studies
International Council for Philosophy and Humanistic Studies

1950

Metaphysical Society of America

1951

American Studies Association

1952

Eleutherian Mills-Hagley Foundation
International Social Science Council
Population Council
Resources for the Future, Inc.

1954

    Center for Advanced Study in the Behavioral Sciences
    Renaissance Society of America

1955

    Foreign Policy Research Institute
    Geochemical Society
    Society for Ethnomusicology

1956

    American Society for Legal History
    American Society for Theatre Research

1957

    Association of Universities for Research in Astronomy, Inc.

1958

    Research Triangle Institute
    Society for the History of Technology

1959

    Center for Applied Linguistics
    Robert Maynard Hutchins Center for the Study of Democratic Institutions
    University Corporation for Atmospheric Research

1960

    American Association for the Advancement of Slavic Studies
    American Comparative Literature Association
    East-West Center

1961

    Hudson Institute
    Salk Institute for Biological Studies

1965

    Argonne Universities Association
    Universities Research Association, Inc.

1969

    American Society for Eighteenth-Century Studies
    Hastings Center, Institute of Society, Ethics and the Life Sciences
    Universities Space Research Association

1972

    Independent Research Libraries Association

1977

    American Association for the Advancement of the Humanities

GENEALOGY

This appendix provides an alphabetical listing of the organizations included in this volume and includes any changes in their titles that have occurred since their founding.

The organizations in this appendix are titled as major entries by the name they bear at the present time. The year when that usage began follows the name.

In cases where the present-day name is different from that used earlier, the earlier name or names are provided immediately below the present-day name as subentries, and the inclusive dates of the use of the name or names is provided. Subentries preceded by a ")" have merged or affiliated to create the major entry organization listed immediately above.

Academy of Natural Sciences of Philadelphia, 1812-

American Academy and Institute of Arts and Letters, 1976-
)American Academy of Arts and Letters, 1904-1976
)National Institute of Arts and Letters, 1898-1976

American Academy of Arts and Sciences, 1780-

American Academy of Religion, 1963-
National Association of Biblical Instructors, 1922-1963
Association of Biblical Instructors in American Colleges and Secondary Schools, 1909-1922

American Anthropological Association, 1902-

American Antiquarian Society, 1812-

American Association for State and Local History, 1940-

American Association for the Advancement of Science, 1848-

American Association for the Advancement of Slavic Studies, 1960-

American Association for the Advancement of the Humanities, 1977-

American Association of Anatomists, 1908-
Association of American Anatomists, 1888-1908

American Association of Immunologists, 1913-

American Association of Pathologists, Inc., 1976-
)American Society for Experimental Pathology, 1913-1976
)American Association of Pathologists and Bacteriologists, 1901-1976

American Astronomical Society, 1914-
Astronomical and Astrophysical Society of America, 1899-1914

American Chemical Society, 1876-

American Comparative Literature Association, 1960-

American Council of Learned Societies, 1919-

American Council on Education, 1918-

American Dialect Society, 1889-

American Economic Association, 1885-

American Enterprise Institute for Public Policy Research, 1954-
American Enterprise Association, 1943-1954

American Folklore Society, 1888-

American Geographical Society, 1871-
American Geographical and Statistical Society, 1851-1871

American Geological Institute, 1948-

American Geophysical Union, 1919-

American Historical Association, 1884-

American Institute of Biological Sciences, 1948-

American Institute of Nutrition, 1928-

American Institute of Physics, 1931-

American Mathematical Society, 1894-
New York Mathematical Society, 1888-1894

American Meteorological Society, 1919-

American Museum of Natural History, 1869-

American Musicological Society, 1934-

American Numismatic Society, 1907-
American Numismatic and Archaeological Society, 1865-1907
American Numismatic Society, 1858-1865

American Oriental Society, 1842-

American Philological Association, 1869-

American Philosophical Association, 1901-

American Philosophical Society, Held at Philadelphia, for Promoting Useful Knowledge, 1769-
)The American Society for Promoting and Propagating Useful Knowledge, Held at Philadelphia, 1766-1769
)American Philosophical Society, 1743-1769

American Physical Society, 1899-

American Physiological Society, 1887-

American Political Science Association, 1903-

American Psychological Association, 1892-

American Social Science Association, 1865-1912

American Society for Aesthetics, 1942-

American Society for Eighteenth-Century Studies, 1969-

American Society for Legal History, 1956-

American Society for Microbiology, 1960-
Society of American Bacteriologists, 1899-1960

American Society for Pharmacology and Experimental Therapeutics, 1908-

American Society for Theatre Research, 1956-

American Society of Biological Chemists, 1906-

American Society of International Law, 1906-

American Society of Parasitologists, 1924-

American Society of Zoologists, 1914-
Society of American Zoologists, 1902-1914
American Morphological Society, 1890-1902

American Sociological Association, 1959-
American Sociological Society, 1905-1959

American Statistical Association, 1839-

American Studies Association, 1951-

Archaeological Institute of America, 1879-

Argonne Universities Association, 1965-

Aspen Institute for Humanistic Studies, 1949-

Associated Universities, Inc., 1946-

Association for Asian Studies, 1956-
  Far Eastern Association, 1941-1956

Association for Symbolic Logic, 1935-

Association of American Geographers, 1904-
)American Society for Professional Geographers, 1943-1948

Association of American Law Schools, 1900-

Association of Universities for Research in Astronomy, Inc., 1957-

Battelle Memorial Institute, 1925-

Bernice P. Bishop Museum, 1889-

Bibliographical Society of America, 1904-

Botanical Society of America, 1893-

Brookings Institution, 1927-
)Robert Brookings Graduate School of Economics and Government, 1924-1927
)Institute of Economics, 1922-1927
)Institute for Government Research, 1916-1927

Carnegie Endowment for International Peace, 1910-

Carnegie Institution of Washington, 1902-

Center for Advanced Study in the Behavioral Sciences, 1954-

Center for Applied Linguistics, 1959-

Charles F. Kettering Foundation, 1927-

College Art Association of America, 1912-

Council on Foreign Relations, Inc., 1918-

Dumbarton Oaks Research Library and Collection, 1940-

East-West Center, 1960-

Ecological Society of America, 1915-

Econometric Society, 1930-

Economic History Association, 1940-

Electrochemical Society, Inc., 1930-
    American Electrochemical Society, 1902-1930

Eleutherian Mills-Hagley Foundation, 1952-

Entomological Society of America, 1906-
)American Association of Economic Entomologists, 1889-1953

Federation of American Societies for Experimental Biology, 1912-

Field Museum of Natural History, 1905-
    Field Columbian Museum, 1894-1905
    Columbian Museum of Chicago, 1893-1894

Folger Shakespeare Library, 1932-

Foreign Policy Association, 1921-
    League of Free Nations Association, 1918-1921

Foreign Policy Research Institute, 1955-

Fox Chase Cancer Center, 1974-
)Institute for Cancer Research, 1945-1974
)Lankenau Hospital Research Institute, 1927-1963
)American Oncologic Hospital, 1905-1974

Franklin Institute, The, 1971-
    The Franklin Institute of the State of Pennsylvania for the Promotion of the
    Mechanic Arts, 1824-1971

Genetics Society of America, 1931-

Geochemical Society, 1955-

Geological Society of America, 1889-
    American Geological Society, 1888-1889

Hastings Center, Institute of Society, Ethics and the Life Sciences, 1969-

Henry Francis du Pont Winterthur Museum, 1930-

Hispanic Society of America, 1904-

Historical Society of Pennsylvania, The, 1824-

History of Science Society, 1924-

Hoover Institution on War, Revolution and Peace, 1919-

Hudson Institute, 1961-

Huntington Library, Art Gallery, Botanical Gardens, 1919-

IIT Research Institute, 1963-
    Armour Research Foundation, 1943-1963
    Research Foundation of Armour Institute of Technology, 1936-1943

Independent Research Libraries Association, 1972-

Institute for Advanced Study, 1930-

Institute for Sex Research, 1947-

Institute of Early American History and Culture, 1943-

Institute of Mathematical Statistics, 1935-

Institute of Public Administration, 1932
    National Institute of Public Administration, 1921-1932
)Training School for Public Service, 1911-1921
)Bureau of Municipal Research, 1906-1921

International Council for Philosophy and Humanistic Studies, 1949-

International Council of Scientific Unions, 1931-
    International Research Council 1919-1931

International Social Science Council, 1952-

John Crerar Library, The, 1894-

Library Company of Philadelphia, The, 1731-

Linda Hall Library, 1946-

Linguistic Society of America, 1924-

Lowell Observatory, 1894-

Marine Biological Laboratory, 1888-

Massachusetts Historical Society, 1791-

Mathematical Association of America, 1915-

Medieval Academy of America, 1925-

Memorial Sloan-Kettering Cancer Center, 1960-
)Sloan-Kettering Institute for Cancer Research, 1945-1960
)Memorial Hospital for the Treatment of Cancer and Allied Diseases, 1916-1960
    General Memorial Hospital for the Treatment of Cancer and Allied Diseases,
      1899-1916
    New York Cancer Hospital, 1884-1899

Metaphysical Society of America, 1950-

Midwest Research Institute, 1944-

Modern Language Association of America, 1883-

National Academy of Sciences, 1863-

National Geographic Society, 1888-

Newberry Library, The, 1887-

New York Academy of Medicine, The, 1847-

New-York Historical Society, 1804-

New York Public Library, Astor, Lenox and Tilden Foundations, The, 1895-
)Tilden Trust, 1886-1895
)Lenox Library, 1870-1895
)Astor Library, 1848-1895

Oak Ridge Associated Universities, 1946-

Organization of American Historians, 1965-
    Mississippi Valley Historical Association, 1907-1965

Paleontological Society, 1908-
)Society of American Vertebrate Paleontologists, [1900]-1910

Peabody Museum of Archaeology and Ethnology, 1866-

Pierpont Morgan Library, 1924-

Population Council, 1952-

Rand Corporation, 1948-

Renaissance Society of America, 1954-

Research Triangle Institute, 1958-

Resources for the Future, Inc., 1952-

Robert Maynard Hutchins Center for the Study of Democratic Institutions, 1979-
    Center for the Study of Democratic Institutions, 1959-1979

Salk Institute for Biological Studies, 1961-

Smithsonian Institution, 1846-

Social Science Research Council, 1924

Society for Ethnomusicology, 1955-

Society for the History of Technology, 1958-

Society of Architectural Historians, 1947-
   American Society of Architectural Historians, 1940-1947

Society of Biblical Literature, 1962-
   Society of Biblical Literature and Exegesis, 1880-1962

Southern Research Institute, 1944-
   Alabama Research Institute, 1941-1944

Southwest Research Institute, 1947-

SRI International, 1970-
   Stanford Research Institute, 1946-1970

Universities Research Association, Inc., 1965-

Universities Space Research Association, 1969-

University Corporation for Atmospheric Research, 1959
)High Altitude Observatory, 1946-1960

Virginia Historical Society, The, 1870-
   Virginia Historical and Philosophical Society, 1831-1870

Wistar Institute of Anatomy and Biology, The, 1894-

Woods Hole Oceanographic Institution, 1930-

Worcester Foundation for Experimental Biology, 1944-

AREAS OF DISCIPLINARY-GENERAL INTEREST

In the listing that follows some twenty disciplinary-general areas of interest or interests are provided, followed by the organizations that operate in the area. A large number of organizations are grouped under one of the three headings into which knowledge is currently categorized: humanities, natural and biological sciences, and social sciences and social studies. Where two or more organizations can be listed, either in a separate or overlapping disciplinary or general area of interest, a further disciplinary or general area of interest breakdown has been provided.

Some organizations, for example, the Smithsonian Institution and the American Philosophical Society, which are interested in and operate in more than one disciplinary or general area of interest, have been so listed.

Applied and Industrial Research

Battelle Memorial Institute
IIT Research Institute
Midwest Research Institute
Rand Corporation
Research Triangle Institute
Southern Research Institute
Southwest Research Institute
SRI International

Archaeology

Archaeological Institute of America
Peabody Museum of Archaeology and Ethnology

Astronomy

American Astronomical Society
Association of Universities for Research in Astronomy, Inc.
Lowell Observatory
Smithsonian Institution

Atmospheric and Oceanographic Studies

American Meteorological Society
Marine Biological Laboratory
Universities Space Research Association
University Corporation for Atmospheric Research
Woods Hole Oceanographic Institution

Biological and Health Sciences

American Association of Anatomists
American Association of Immunologists
American Association of Pathologists, Inc.
American Institute of Biological Sciences
American Institute of Nutrition
American Physiological Society
American Psychological Association
American Society for Microbiology
American Society of Biological Chemists
American Society of Parasitologists
American Society of Pharmacology and Experimental Therapeutics
American Society of Zoologists
Botanical Society of America
Entomological Society of America
Federation of American Societies for Experimental Biology
Genetics Society of America
Hastings Center, Institute of Society, Ethics and the Life Sciences
Marine Biological Laboratory
New York Academy of Medicine, The
Population Council
Salk Institute for Biological Studies
Wistar Institute of Anatomy and Biology, the
Worcester Foundation for Experimental Biology

Cancer

Fox Chase Cancer Center
IIT Research Institute
Memorial Sloan-Kettering Cancer Center
Midwest Research Institute
Oak Ridge Associated Universities
Research Triangle Institute
Southern Research Institute
Universities Research Association, Inc.
Wistar Institute of Anatomy and Biology, The
Worcester Foundation for Experimental Biology

Chemistry, Geology, and Physics

American Chemical Society
American Geological Institute
American Geophysical Union

American Institute of Physics
American Physical Society
Electrochemical Society, Inc.
Geochemical Society
Geological Society of America
Paleontological Society

Ecology and Geography

American Geographical Society
Association of American Geographers
Ecological Society of America
National Geographic Society
Resources for the Future, Inc.

Economics, Mathematics, and Statistics

American Economic Association
American Mathematical Society
American Statistical Association
Association for Symbolic Logic
Econometric Society
Economic History Association
Institute for Advanced Study
Institute of Mathematical Statistics
Mathematical Association of America

Fine Arts, Music, and Theater

American Academy and Institute of Arts and Letters
American Musicological Society
American Numismatic Society
American Society for Aesthetics
American Society for Theatre Research
College Art Association of America
Smithsonian Institution
Society for Ethnomusicology

Government and Public Policy

American Council on Education
American Enterprise Institute for Public Policy Research
American Political Science Association
Brookings Institution
Hoover Institution on War, Revolution and Peace
Hudson Institute
Institute of Public Administration
Robert Maynard Hutchins Center for the Study of Democratic Institutions

History

American Antiquarian Society

American Association for State and Local History
American Historical Association
American Society for Legal History
Economic History Association
Historical Society of Pennsylvania, The
History of Science Society
Institute of Early American History and Culture
Massachusetts Historical Society
New-York Historical Society
Organization of American Historians
Smithsonian Institution
Society for the History of Technology
Society of Architectural Historians
Virginia Historical Society, The

Humanities

American Academy of Arts and Sciences
American Association for the Advancement of the Humanities
American Council of Learned Societies
American Philosophical Association
American Philosophical Society, Held at Philadelphia, for Promoting Useful Knowledge
American Society for Aesthetics
Aspen Institute for Humanistic Studies
Hastings Center, Institute of Society, Ethics and the Life Sciences
Institute for Advanced Study
International Council for Philosophy and Humanistic Studies
Metaphysical Society of America

International Relations

American Society of International Law
Carnegie Endowment for International Peace
Council on Foreign Relations, Inc.
Foreign Policy Association
Foreign Policy Research Institute
Hoover Institution on War, Revolution and Peace
Hudson Institute

Language and Linguistics

American Dialect Society
American Philological Association
Center for Applied Linguistics
Linguistic Society of America
Modern Language Association of America

Law

American Society of International Law
Association of American Law Schools

Libraries

American Antiquarian Society
Dumbarton Oaks Research Library and Collection
Folger Shakespeare Library
Hoover Institution on War, Revolution and Peace
Huntington Library, Art Gallery, Botanical Gardens
Independent Research Libraries Association
John Crerar Library, The
Library Company of Philadelphia, The
Linda Hall Library
Massachusetts Historical Society
Newberry Library, The
New York Academy of Medicine, The
New-York Historical Society
New York Public Library, Astor, Lenox and Tilden Foundations, The
Pierpont Morgan Library
Virginia Historical Society, The

Literature

American Academy and Institute of Arts and Letters
American Comparative Literature Association
Bibliographical Society of America
Modern Language Association of America
Society of Biblical Literature

Museums

American Museum of Natural History
Bernice P. Bishop Museum
Eleutherian Mills-Hagley Foundation
Field Museum of Natural History
Henry Francis du Pont Winterthur Museum
Smithsonian Institution

Natural and Biological Sciences

Academy of Natural Sciences of Philadelphia
American Academy of Arts and Sciences
American Association for the Advancement of Science
American Philosophical Society, Held at Philadelphia, for Promoting Useful Knowledge
Argonne Universities Association
Associated Universities, Inc.
Carnegie Institution of Washington
Charles F. Kettering Foundation
Franklin Institute, The
Institute for Advanced Study
International Council of Scientific Unions
National Academy of Sciences
Oak Ridge Associated Universities
Smithsonian Institution
Universities Research Association, Inc.

Regional and Period Studies

American Association for State and Local History
American Association for the Advancement of Slavic Studies
American Oriental Society
American Society for Eighteenth-Century Studies
American Studies Association
Association for Asian Studies
East-West Center
Eleutherian Mills-Hagley Foundation
Hispanic Society of America
Historical Society of Pennsylvania, The
Institute of Early American History and Culture
Massachusetts Historical Society
Medieval Academy of America
New-York Historical Society
Renaissance Society of America
Virginia Historical Society, The

Religion

American Academy of Religion
Society of Biblical Literature

Social Sciences and Studies

American Academy of Arts and Sciences
American Anthropological Association
American Association for the Advancement of Science
American Folklore Society
American Philosophical Society, Held at Philadelphia, for Promoting Useful Knowledge
American Political Science Association
American Psychological Association
American Social Science Association
American Sociological Association
Center for Advanced Study in the Behavioral Sciences
Charles F. Kettering Foundation
Hoover Institution on War, Revolution and Peace
Hudson Institute
Institute for Advanced Study
Institute for Sex Research
International Social Science Council
National Academy of Sciences
Population Council
Resources for the Future, Inc.
Smithsonian Institution
Social Science Research Council

SOCIETAL AND INSTITUTIONAL MEMBERSHIP

This appendix lists those institutions included in this volume which are affiliated in some manner with other institutions also included.

It will be noted that the International Council for Philosophy and Humanistic Studies, International Council of Scientific Unions, International Social Science Council, and the unions that are members of each are also listed in this appendix. Although histories of the unions are not provided in this volume, their affiliation and association with each international council is touched on in the history of the individual council.

American Association for the Advancement of Science

American Academy of Arts and Sciences
American Anthropological Association
American Association of Anatomists
American Association of Immunologists
American Astronomical Society
American Chemical Society
American Economic Association
American Folklore Society
American Geographical Society
American Geological Institute
American Geophysical Union
American Institute of Biological Sciences
American Institute of Physics
American Mathematical Society
American Meteorological Society
American Philosophical Association
American Physical Society
American Physiological Society
American Political Science Association
American Psychological Association
American Society for Aesthetics
American Society for Experimental Pathology
American Society for Microbiology
American Society for Pharmacology and Experimental Therapeutics

American Society of Biological Chemists
American Society of Parasitologists
American Society of Zoologists
American Sociological Association
American Statistical Association
Archaeological Institute of America
Association for Symbolic Logic
Association of American Geographers
Botanical Society of America
Ecological Society of America
Electrochemical Society, Inc.
Entomological Society of America
Genetics Society of America
Geochemical Society
Geological Society of America
History of Science Society
Institute of Mathematical Statistics
Linguistic Society of America
Mathematical Association of America
Oak Ridge Associated Universities
Paleontological Society
Society for the History of Technology

American Council of Learned Societies

American Academy of Arts and Sciences
American Academy of Religion
American Anthropological Association
American Antiquarian Society
American Comparative Literature Association
American Dialect Society
American Economic Association
American Folklore Society
American Historical Association
American Musicological Society
American Numismatic Society
American Oriental Society
American Philological Association
American Philosophical Association
American Philosophical Society, Held at Philadelphia, for Promoting Useful Knowledge
American Political Science Association
American Psychological Association
American Society for Aesthetics
American Society for Eighteenth-Century Studies
American Society for Legal History
American Society for Theatre Research
American Society of International Law
American Sociological Association
American Studies Association
Archaeological Institute of America
Association for Asian Studies
Association of American Geographers
Association of American Law Schools

Bibliographical Society of America
College Art Association of America
Economic History Association
Hispanic Society of America
History of Science Society
Linguistic Society of America
Medieval Academy of America
Metaphysical Society of America
Modern Language Association of America
Organization of American Historians
Renaissance Society of America
Society for Ethnomusicology
Society for the History of Technology
Society of Architectural Historians
Society of Biblical Literature

American Council on Education

American Chemical Society
American Council of Learned Societies
American Historical Association
American Political Science Association
American Psychological Association
Association of American Law Schools
Brookings Institution
Modern Language Association of America
Salk Institute for Biological Studies
Smithsonian Institution

American Geological Institute

American Geophysical Union
Geochemical Society
Geological Society of America
Paleontological Society

American Institute of Biological Sciences

American Association of Anatomists
American Museum of Natural History
American Physiological Society
American Society for Microbiology
American Society of Parasitologists
American Society of Zoologists
Botanical Society of America
Ecological Society of America
Entomological Society of America
Genetics Society of America
National Museum of Natural History (Smithsonian Institution)

American Institute of Physics

American Astronomical Society

American Geophysical Union
American Physical Society
Geological Society of America

Federation of American Societies for Experimental Biology

American Association of Immunologists
American Institute of Nutrition
American Physiological Society
American Society for Experimental Pathology
American Society for Pharmacology and Experimental Therapeutics
American Society of Biological Chemists

Independent Research Libraries Association

American Antiquarian Society
American Philosophical Society, Held at Philadelphia, for Promoting Useful Knowledge
Folger Shakespeare Library
Historical Society of Pennsylvania, The
Huntington Library, Art Gallery, Botanical Gardens
John Crerar Library, The
Library Company of Philadelphia, The
Linda Hall Library
Massachusetts Historical Society
Newberry Library, The
New York Academy of Medicine, The
New-York Historical Society
New York Public Library, Astor, Lenox and Tilden Foundations, The
Pierpont Morgan Library
Virginia Historical Society, The

International Council for Philosophy and Humanistic Studies

International Association for the History of Religions
International Committee for the History of Art
International Committee of Historical Sciences
International Congress of African Studies
International Federation for Modern Languages and Literature
International Federation of Societies for Philosophy
International Federation of the Societies of Classical Studies
International Musicological Society
International Union for Oriental and Asian Studies
International Union of Academics
International Union of Anthropological and Ethnological Sciences
International Union of Prehistoric and Protohistoric Sciences
Permanent International Committee of Linguists

International Council of Scientific Unions

International Astronomical Union
International Geographical Union
International Mathematical Union
International Union of Biochemistry

International Union of Biological Sciences
International Union of Crystallography
International Union of Geodesy and Geophysics
International Union of Geological Sciences
International Union of Immunological Societies
International Union of Nutritional Sciences
International Union of Pharmacology
International Union of Physiological Sciences
International Union of Pure and Applied Biophysics
International Union of Pure and Applied Chemistry
International Union of Pure and Applied Physics
International Union of Radio Science
International Union of the History and Philosophy of Science
International Union of Theoretical and Applied Mechanics

International Social Science Council

International Association of Legal Science
International Economic Association
International Geographical Union
International Law Association
International Peace Research Association
International Political Science Association
International Sociological Association
International Union for the Scientific Study of Population
International Union of Anthropological and Ethnological Sciences
International Union of Psychological Science
World Association for Public Opinion Research
World Federation for Mental Health

Social Science Research Council

American Anthropological Association
American Economic Association
American Historical Association
American Political Science Association
American Psychological Association
American Sociological Association
American Statistical Association

INDEX

Page numbers in **boldface** indicate the location of the main entry.

American Physical Society, 24, 77-78, 82, **99-101**

American Physiological Society, **101-4**, 117, 221

American Political Science Association, 45, 71-72, **104-5**, 126, 443-44

American Psychological Association, **106-8**, 109, 444

American Public Health Association, 108

American Registry of Professional Entomologists, 220

American Research Center, 131

American Research Institute, 131

American School of Classical Studies, 131, 199

American School of Oriental Research, 131, 454

American School of Prehistoric Research, 131, 404-5

American Social Science Association, 7, 53, 69, 104, **108-9**, 124, 126

American Society for Aesthetics, **109-10**

American Society for Clinical Nutrition, 76

American Society for Comparative Musicology, 450

American Society for Eighteenth-Century Studies, **110-11**

American Society for Engineering Education, 451

American Society for Experimental Pathology, 36-38, 221

American Society for Legal History, 72, **111-12**

American Society for Microbiology, **112-15**

American Society for Pharmacology and Experimental Therapeutics, 101, **115-16**, 221

American Society for Professional Geographers, 151

American Society for Promoting and Propagating Useful Knowledge, Held at Philadelphia, 97

American Society for Theatre Research, **117**

American Society of Architectural Historians, 453

American Society of Biological Chemists, 75, 101, **117-20**, 221

American Society of International Law, **120-22**

American Society of Naturalists, 112, 124

American Society of Parasitologists, **122-23**

American Society of Tropical Medicine and Hygiene, 123

American Society of Zoologists, **124-25**, 251

American Sociological Association, 45, **125-27**, 444

American Sociological Society. See American Sociological Association

American Statistical Association, **127-30**, 209, 300-301, 444

American Studies Association, **130-31**

American Type Culture Collection, 113

American Vacuum Society, 78

American Youth Commission, 50

Amory, Francis, 10

Anatomical Journal Trust, 33

Anderson, Edwin H., 390-91

Anderson, Martin, 272-73

Anderson, Robert O., 138

Anderson, Thomas F., 244

Anderson School for Natural History, 332

Andrews, Charles M., 297

Andrews, Clement W., 315-16

Andrews, Edward Deming, Shaker collection of, 263

Andrews, Roy Chapman, 87

Angell, Norman, 172

Anthropological Society of Washington, 14-15

Antiquities Act (1906), 403

Archaeological Institute of America, 45, 94, **131-33**, 189

Argonne National Laboratory, 133-37

Argonne Universities Association, **133-37**

Ariyoshi, George R., 203

Armbruster, Frank, 276

Armory Show (1913), 263

Armour Institute of Technology, 282-83

Armour Research Foundation, 283, 350

Armstrong, Hamilton Fish, 191, 194

Aspen Institute for Humanistic Studies, **137-42**

Associated Colleges of the Midwest, 376

Associated Midwest Universities, 134

Associated Universities, Inc., **142-46**

Association for Asian Studies, **146-48**

Association for Sociology of Religion, 127

Association for Symbolic Logic, **148-49**

Association of American Anatomists, 32

Association of American Geographers, **149-52**

Association of American Geologists and Naturalists, 22-23, 254

ABOUT THE EDITOR

JOSEPH C. KIGER is Professor of History at the University of Mississippi. His earlier works in this area include *Operating Principles of the Larger Foundations* and *American Learned Societies*.